Money and Monetary Policy
in Interdependent Nations

RALPH C. BRYANT

Money and Monetary Policy in Interdependent Nations

THE BROOKINGS INSTITUTION
WASHINGTON, D.C.

Copyright © 1980 by
THE BROOKINGS INSTITUTION
1775 Massachusetts Avenue, N.W., Washington, D.C. 20036

Library of Congress Cataloging in Publication Data:

Bryant, Ralph C   1938–
  Money and monetary policy in interdependent nations.
  Bibliography: p.
  Includes index.
  1. Money.   2. Monetary policy.   I. Title.
HG221.B7219   332.4   80-19225
ISBN 0-8157-1130-1
ISBN 0-8157-1129-8 (pbk.)

9 8 7 6 5 4 3 2 1

THE BROOKINGS INSTITUTION is an independent organization devoted to nonpartisan research, education, and publication in economics, government, foreign policy, and the social sciences generally. Its principal purposes are to aid in the development of sound public policies and to promote public understanding of issues of national importance.

The Institution was founded on December 8, 1927, to merge the activities of the Institute for Government Research, founded in 1916, the Institute of Economics, founded in 1922, and the Robert Brookings Graduate School of Economics and Government, founded in 1924.

The Board of Trustees is responsible for the general administration of the Institution, while the immediate direction of the policies, program, and staff is vested in the President, assisted by an advisory committee of the officers and staff. The by-laws of the Institution state: "It is the function of the Trustees to make possible the conduct of scientific research, and publication, under the most favorable conditions, and to safeguard the independence of the research staff in the pursuit of their studies and in the publication of the results of such studies. It is not a part of their function to determine, control, or influence the conduct of particular investigations or the conclusions reached."

The President bears final responsibility for the decision to publish a manuscript as a Brookings book. In reaching his judgment on the competence, accuracy, and objectivity of each study, the President is advised by the director of the appropriate research program and weighs the views of a panel of expert outside readers who report to him in confidence on the quality of the work. Publication of a work signifies that it is deemed a competent treatment worthy of public consideration but does not imply endorsement of conclusions or recommendations.

The Institution maintains its position of neutrality on issues of public policy in order to safeguard the intellectual freedom of the staff. Hence interpretations or conclusions in Brookings publications should be understood to be solely those of the authors and should not be attributed to the Institution, to its trustees, officers, or other staff members, or to the organizations that support its research.

Foreword

FOR INDIVIDUAL nations and for the world as a whole, much of the twentieth century has been characterized by economic turbulence. Two world wars and many smaller conflicts have caused severe economic dislocations. Aggregate economic activity has been plagued by large cyclical oscillations, including a global depression and several deep recessions. Inflation has at times become virulent; in the last decade inflation has been rapid even when economic activity has been sluggish and unemployment high. The relative prices of energy and other natural resources have changed dramatically, necessitating major changes in production and consumption and causing large redistributions of income and wealth. International financial arrangements have periodically been in turmoil, most recently with the abandonment of the Bretton Woods adjustable-peg system and the ensuing large variations, even over short runs, in the exchange rates of major currencies.

The causes and consequences of these turbulent changes in economic conditions in many cases have been poorly understood. Not only the world itself, therefore, but economists' conceptualizations of the world have undergone important transformations. In particular, monetary and macroeconomic theory have been in continuing ferment since the early 1930s.

Along with the economic turbulence and the ferment in economic theory, two secular trends have been manifest during the last three decades. On the one hand, nation states have become increasingly interdependent as economic units: cross-border trade in goods and services has grown faster than domestic economic activity, and cross-border financial links have increased more rapidly than domestic financial intermediation. On the other hand, the political cohesion that characterized the postwar period when a small number of nations dominated international decisionmaking is rapidly disappearing. The greater diffusion of political power is partly attributable to the dissolution of colonial empires and the consequent creation of many new nation states. The outcomes of wars have been another contributing factor. To an even greater extent, however, the broader diffusion of political power has followed from and merely reflected a broader diffusion of economic wealth.

Policymakers must somehow cope with these developments as they try to formulate and implement national economic policy. When new turbulence occurs, it demands—or at the least seems to demand—a policy response. Increasing economic interdependence and political pluralism heighten the difficulties in determining appropriate responses. Policy decisions are made no easier by the basic disagreements among economists about the theoretical framework within which decisions should be analyzed and formulated.

Ralph C. Bryant takes these fundamental problems confronting a nation's policymakers as his starting point. In effect, his book is a treatise on the theory of national economic policy, with special emphasis on the decisions of central banks about national monetary policy. It seeks to provide an analytical framework and operating guidelines that will enable policymakers to carry out their responsibilities as well as possible given the manifold constraints to which they are subject.

As noted in the author's preface, the book is not concerned primarily with economic policy in the United States and is not directed exclusively at an American audience. The analytical framework developed here, if appropriately adapted to specific circumstances and institutions, has relevance for central banks and national governments more generally. The Brookings Institution shares the author's hope that the book will find its way into the hands of many non-American readers.

Because of its focus on policy decisions, this book is in the tradition of Brookings research. It is not a typical Brookings book, however, because of its substantial theoretical content and its technical complexity. Its closest Brookings precursors are the book by John G. Gurley and Edward S. Shaw, *Money in a Theory of Finance* (1960), and the essay, "Analytical Foundations of Fiscal Policy," by Alan S. Blinder and Robert M. Solow, in *The Economics of Public Finance* (1974). This book, in both purpose and style, bears many resemblances to those two earlier works.

Ralph C. Bryant is a senior fellow in the Brookings Economic Studies program. Before joining Brookings in 1976, he served on the staff of the Board of Governors of the Federal Reserve System as director of the Division of International Finance and associate economist of the Federal Open Market Committee.

An account of how the book came to be written and acknowledgments to the institutions and individuals who helped the author during its writing are contained in the author's preface. Brookings is especially grateful to the Rockefeller Foundation for a grant that has helped support the author's work at Brookings.

The views expressed here are those of the author and should not be ascribed to the Rockefeller Foundation or to the officers, trustees, or other staff members of the Brookings Institution.

BRUCE K. MACLAURY
President

July 1980
Washington, D.C.

Contents

Author's Preface   *xvii*

INTRODUCTION

1. Main Themes   **3**
Economic Openness and National Economic Policy *3*
Money as the Key Variable in the Conduct of Monetary Policy *5*
Alternative Strategies for Monetary Policy under Conditions of
    Interdependence *7*
Exchange-Rate Variability and National Monetary Policy *8*
The Plan of the Book *9*

2. Basic Concepts of the Theory of Economic Policy   **11**
National Governments, Policy Agencies, and Central Banks *11*
Targets, Instruments, and Intermediate Variables *12*
Economic Structure and Structural Models *14*
Theoretical Characterizations of Policy Decisions *15*

3. What Is the Money Stock in an Open Economy?   **18**
Illustrative Riddles *18*
Elements of a Definition of Money *19*
Current Statistical Practices *21*
Does It Matter? *21*

PART ONE: MONETARY AGGREGATES IN A CLOSED ECONOMY

4. Why Do We Need a Concept and Definition of Money?   **41**
Descriptive Concepts and Definitions *42*
Money: Not a Policy Instrument *44*
A Prescriptive Motive *47*
Interrelationships of Descriptive and Prescriptive Rationales *48*

5. Aggregate Demand and Supply Functions for Money   **50**
A Schematic Representation of Sector Balance Sheets *50*
The Aggregate Demand for Money *53*
The Money Supply Process *57*
Alternative Models of Macroeconomic Behavior for the Economy as a
    Whole *63*

6. Money as an Intermediate Target of Monetary Policy   **69**
Basic Characteristics of a Money Strategy *69*
Issues Raised by a Money Strategy *72*
Three Levels of Issues *80*

PART TWO: NATIONAL MONETARY AGGREGATES IN AN OPEN ECONOMY

7. **Rudiments of Monetary Theory for an Open Economy**   83
   The Demand for Means of Payment in a Two-Currency World *83*
   Portfolio Behavior of Nonbanks in an Open Economy *88*
   Financial Intermediaries in an Open Economy *92*
   Asset Demands and Liability Supplies of Macroeconomic Sectors *94*

8. **Alternative Definitions of the National Money Stock**   97
   Schematic Debtor-Creditor Relationships in an Eight-Sector World
      Economy *97*
   Eurocurrency Assets and Liabilities *99*
   Asset Substitutability and Exchange-Rate Variability *102*
   Illustrative Definitions of the National Money Stock *103*
   Descriptive Uses of Money Concepts *107*
   The National Money Stock as an Intermediate Target: An Illustrative
      Case *108*
   A Second Example *113*
   Exclude International Debtor-Creditor Relationships? *114*
   Successfully Offset Interdependence Effects? *116*
   Purge Home Money of International Interdependencies? *118*

9. **The "Correct" Definition of National Money**   123
   Two Impossibility Theorems *123*
   Bank Credit and Other Financial Aggregates *124*
   Illustrations of the Blind Spot in the Existing Literature *125*
   An Intermediate-Target Strategy under Conditions of Interdependence *131*

PART THREE: INTERDEPENDENCE AND THE THEORY OF ECONOMIC POLICY

10. **Interdependence and National Economic Policy: Alternative
    Paradigms**   135
    Interdependence and Economic Policy: Basic Hypotheses *135*
    The Nearly Closed Paradigm *137*
    The Small and Open Paradigm *138*
    The Supranational Paradigm *140*
    The Intermediate Interdependence Paradigm *142*
    Choosing among Alternative Paradigms *142*
    Essential Characteristics of the Intermediate Interdependence
       Paradigm *145*
    Economic Structure versus Political Structure *148*
    De Jure Sovereignty versus De Facto Control *149*

11. **National Economic Policy under Conditions of Intermediate
    Interdependence**   151
    Concepts, Definitions, and Representation of Economic Structure *152*
    What is *Interdependence?* *156*
    Determinants of Economic Structure and the Degree of
       Interdependence *159*
    Reduced-Form Representation of Economic Structure *161*
    Simple Analytics of the National Policy Problem *163*
    Optimizing Determination of Target Values *164*
    Multiperiod Dynamic Generalization *165*
    Uncertainty and Game-Theoretic Aspects *167*

12. **Interdependence and National Economic Policy: The Degree of
Autonomy**   **171**
The Effectiveness of Policy Instruments *171*
National Policy Multipliers and Autonomy *174*
Interdependence and the Degree of Autonomy *177*
Interdependence and Disturbance Multipliers *187*

13. **Interdependence and National Economic Policy: Controllability and
National Welfare**   **191**
Interdependence and the Degree of Controllability *191*
National Economic Welfare *199*
The Performance of National Policymakers *200*
Interdependence and Welfare *203*

PART FOUR: THE CONDUCT OF MONETARY POLICY IN A CLOSED ECONOMY

14. **Macroeconomic Policy Actions in a Closed Economy**   **209**
Monetary-Policy Actions and Operating Regimes *209*
Fiscal-Policy Actions and Budgetary Operating Regimes *220*
Institutional Procedures for the Financing of a Budget Surplus or
    Deficit *225*
The Consolidated Government Budget Constraint *228*
Policy Actions, Policy Regimens, and the Symbiosis between Fiscal and
    Monetary Policies *231*

15. **Alternative Strategies for Conducting Monetary Policy**   **238**
The Policy Problem prior to Strategy Choice *238*
What Differentiates Alternative Strategies? *240*
Comparing Alternative Strategies *241*
Periodicity of Decisionmaking in Single-Stage and Two-Stage Strategies *243*
Use of New Information in Revising Decisions *246*
"Rules" and "Discretion" *249*
Strategies That Use Money as an Intermediate Target *250*
Evaluation of Alternative Strategies *252*
Possible Justifications for a Money Strategy *253*
Money Strategies versus Intermediate-Target Strategies in General *257*

16. **Model Choice and Strategy Choice**   **259**
Model Choice: Still an Unsettled and Controversial Subject *259*
Model Choice and Fiscal Policy *261*
The Significance of the Reliability and Controllability Propositions *263*
Resource Costs of Alternative Strategies *265*
Recursive and Nonrecursive Models of Macroeconomic Behavior *266*
Are the Recursiveness Conditions Required for a Two-Stage Decision
    Process Likely to Be Present? *276*

17. **The Economics of Strategy Choice**   **278**
Making the Best Use of New Data When the Policymaking Model Is
    Recursive *278*
Making the Best Use of New Data When the Policymaking Model Is Not
    Recursive *291*
Conclusions about the Information-Flow Justification for a Money
    Strategy *293*
The Controversy of Rules versus Discretion *294*

Uncertainty and Model Choice *295*
The Uncertainty Justification for a Money Strategy *297*
Summary of the Economic Case against Intermediate-Target Strategies *303*

18. **Money Strategies and the Politics of Monetary Policy**   **306**
Interrelationships between Policy Actions and Private-Sector
    Decisionmaking *306*
Self-Imposed Limits on Discretion by Means of Announcements of Policy
    Intentions *309*
If a Rule, Why a Money Rule? *313*
The Politics of Monetary Policy within the National Government *315*
Political Independence of the Central Bank *318*
Arguments For and Against Central Bank Independence *319*
Monetary-Policy Rules and Central Bank Independence *321*
"Insulation" Justifications for a Money Strategy *325*
Monetary Policy's Role in Macroeconomic Stabilization Policy as a
    Whole *326*
Coordination with Fiscal Policy under Alternative Strategies *327*
Surrogate Targets and Policy Myopia *330*

19. **Instrument Choice and Instrument Variation**   **334**
Stabilizing Interest Rates *334*
Stabilizing a Financial Aggregate versus Stabilizing an Interest Rate *336*
Instrument Choice in a Comparative-Statics Context *337*
Instrument Choice and Instrument Variation in a Dynamic Context *342*
Pegging Rules versus Discretionary Adaptation *344*
Discretionary Adaptation versus Fine Tuning *348*
Activism versus Lack of Action *350*

PART FIVE: THE CONDUCT OF NATIONAL MONETARY POLICY IN AN OPEN
ECONOMY

20. **Monetary-Policy Actions in an Open Economy**   **355**
Official Intervention in Foreign-Exchange Markets *356*
Alternative Operating Regimes for External Monetary Policy *365*
"Domestic" and "External" Monetary Policy *373*

21. **The Unity of National Macroeconomic Policies**   **379**
Fiscal-Policy Actions and Budgetary Financing in an Open Economy *379*
The Consolidated Government Budget Constraint in an Open Economy *381*
The Holistic Unity of National Macroeconomic Policy *385*

22. **Fixed versus Flexible Exchange Rates**   **387**
Greater Variability in Exchange Rates *387*
Instrument Options for Monetary Policy in a Comparative-Statics
    Framework *391*
Pegging External Reserves versus Pegging the Exchange Rate *393*
Dynamic Evolution of an Open Economy *404*
Alternative External Pegging Regimes over a Longer Run *406*
Choosing between Fixed and Flexible Exchange Rates in a Comparative-
    Statics Context *410*
Instrument Choice and Instrument Variation in a Dynamic Context *411*
Pegging Rules versus Discretionary Adaptation for External Monetary
    Policy *412*
Managed Fixing or Floating *415*

xiii

23. **Exchange-Rate Variability, Autonomy, and Controllability**   417
Supranational Constraints and National Independence *417*
National Autonomy and Controllability in the Absence of Supranational
    Constraints: Five Issues *419*
Viability of Alternative National Policy Regimens *420*
Exchange-Rate Variability and Influence over Ultimate Targets:
    Comparative-Statics Analysis *423*
Policy Impacts and Controllability in a Dynamic Context *428*
Does Variability in Exchange Rates Insulate the National Economy? *432*
Does Variability in Exchange Rates Free Macroeconomic Policy to Focus
    on the Domestic Economy? *436*
Are Nations Dis-integrated When Exchange Rates Are More Variable? *438*

24. **Strategies for Domestic Monetary Policy under Conditions of
Interdependence**   442
Information-Flow and Uncertainty Justifications for a Money Strategy *442*
Do Open Economies Have the Recursive Structure Required by a Money
    Strategy? *444*
Integrating the Domestic and External Aspects of Policy Decisions *445*
Purist and Inward-Looking Variants of a Money Strategy *446*
The Role of Monetary Aggregates in a Strategy of Discretionary Instrument
    Adaptation *449*
Game-Theoretic Interactions between the Nation's Central Bank and the
    World Private Sector *451*

25. **International Cooperation**   453
The Non-Independence of Policy Actions of National Governments *453*
The Governmental Budget Constraint for the World as a Whole *459*
Policy Flexibility: The Individual Nation versus the World as a Whole *463*
Game-Theoretic Analysis of National Policy Decisions *464*
Explanations for Noncooperative Behavior *468*
Supranational Traffic Regulations *470*
A "World" Instrument of Macroeconomic Policy: Changes in Outside
    Reserves *475*
International Coordination of National Policy Decisions *477*
A Catalytic Role for Supranational Institutions *480*

CONCLUDING SUMMARY

26. **Guidelines for the Conduct of National Monetary Policy**   485
Basic Guidelines for National Monetary Policy *485*
Interdependence and National Policy Decisions *487*
Ultimate Objectives and the Unity of National Policy *488*
The Money Stock as an Intermediate Target of Monetary Policy *488*
Instrument Choice and Instrument Variation in a Single-Stage Strategy *493*
Discretionary Adaptation for External Monetary Policy *495*
Fine Tuning, Rules, and Discretion *496*
Strategy Choice: False and Genuine Issues *497*
The Nation and the Global Economy *499*
Theory and Common Sense *501*

APPENDIXES

A. Further Notes to Chapter 11: The Mathematical Representation of a
Two-Nation World Economy   505

B. Further Notes to Chapter 17: Comparison of Two-Stage and Single-
Stage Strategies with Coefficient Uncertainty   518
C. Supplement to Chapter 22: An Illustrative Framework for
Analyzing Monetary Policy in a Small and Open Economy   522

Selected Bibliography   **543**

Name Index   **570**

Subject Index   **574**

Tables

3-1. Definitions of the National Money Stock in Canada   23
3-2. Definitions of the National Money Stock in France   24
3-3. Definitions of the National Money Stock in the Federal Republic of
Germany   26
3-4. Definitions of the National Money Stock in Japan   28
3-5. Definitions of the National Money Stock in Italy   30
3-6. Definitions of the National Money Stock in the United Kingdom   32
3-7. Definitions of the National Money Stock in the United States, 1979 and
Earlier Years   34
3-8. Definitions of the National Money Stock in the United States, 1980 36
5-1. Schematic Balance Sheet of the Central Bank, Closed Economy   51
5-2. Schematic Balance Sheet of the Fiscal Authority, Closed Economy   51
5-3. Schematic Consolidated Balance Sheet for Financial Intermediaries
(Banks), Closed Economy   52
5-4. Schematic Consolidated Balance Sheet for All Private-Sector Nonbanks,
Closed Economy   52
5-5. Simplified Quasi-Systemic Macroeconomic Model   67
7-1. Schematic Balance Sheet for an Individual Nonbank Resident in the Home
Country   89
7-2. Schematic Balance Sheet for an Individual Financial Intermediary (Bank) in
the Home Country   94
8-1. The Home National Money Stock: Definitions Emphasizing Home
Residency of the Holders of Money   104
8-2. The Home National Money Stock: Definitions Emphasizing Home
Residency of the Issuers of Money   105
8-3. The Home National Money Stock: Definitions Emphasizing Denomination
of Assets in the Home-Currency Unit   106
14-1. Schematic Budget Statement and Balance Sheet of the Central Bank, Closed
Economy   211
14-2. Schematic Budget Statement and Balance Sheet of the Fiscal Authority,
Closed Economy   222
15-1. Alternative Types of Strategies for Conducting Monetary Policy   244
20-1. Schematic Budget Statement and Balance Sheet of the Home-Country
Central Bank   357
20-2. Schematic Budget Statement and Balance Sheet of the Home-Country
Fiscal Authority   358
20-3. Initial Asset Exchanges Involved in a Sale of Foreign Exchange by the
Home Central Bank before Any Offsetting "Domestic" Transactions   361
20-4. Combined "External" and "Domestic" Asset Exchanges Involved in a Sale
of Foreign Exchange When the Home Central Bank Uses a Domestic
Reserve-Aggregate Regime   363

20-5. Combined "External" and "Domestic" Asset Exchanges Involved in a Sale
of Foreign Exchange When the Home Central Bank Uses a Domestic
Interest-Rate Regime   364
22-1. Short-Run Comparative-Statics Effects of Illustrative Nonpolicy
Disturbances under Alternative Regimens for Home Monetary Policy   403

Figures

7-1. The Cash-Management Problem of an Economic Unit Having Receipts and
Payments in Two Currencies   86
8-1. Schematic Network of Liability-Asset Relationships in a Two-Nation World
Economy   98
8-2. Simplified Liability-Asset Relationships to Be Considered When Defining
the National Money Stock   100
10-1. The Nearly Closed Paradigm   138
10-2. The Small and Open Paradigm   139
10-3. The Supranational Paradigm   141
10-4. The Intermediate Interdependence Paradigm   143
11-1. Structural Representation of a Two-Nation World Economy   158
11-2. Reduced-Form Representation of a Two-Nation World Economy   162
13-1. Factors Influencing the Controllability of the Home Economy   198
13-2. Factors Influencing the Overall Successfulness of Home Economic Policy   204
14-1. An Illustrative Classification of Alternative Policy Regimens, Closed
Economy   232
16-1. Causal Interrelationships in the Simplest Money-Income Model   268
16-2. Causal Interrelationships in the Extended *IS-LM* Model   270
16-3. Causal Interrelationships in a Variant of the Extended *IS-LM* Model Where
Money Supply Does Not Depend on Interest Rates   271
16-4. Causal Interrelationships in a Dynamic Variant of the Extended *IS-LM*
Model Where Money Supply Does Not Depend on Interest Rates   272
16-5. Causal Interrelationships in a Dynamic Variant of the Extended *IS-LM*
Model with Money Supply Dependent on Interest Rates   274
16-6. Causal Interrelationships in a Dynamic Variant of the Extended *IS-LM*
Model That Is Recursive within a Single Time Period but Not Recursive
over a Succession of Time Periods   275
17-1. Causal Interrelationships in the Illustrative Model 17-1   280
17-2. Causal Interrelationships in the Illustrative Model 17-4   293
18-1. Typology of Normative Positions on the Two Issues of Rules versus
Discretion and Political Independence for the Central Bank   323
22-1. Time Paths of the Exchange Rate and External Reserve Assets for Four
Different Evolutions of a Nation's Economy   389
22-2. Alternative Regimens for National Monetary Policy in the Absence of
Supranational Constraints   413

Author's Preface

MY GUIDING AIM in writing this book has been practical: to help policymakers in national governments improve their conduct of economic policy, in particular monetary policy.

Substantial scope for improving policy exists. A sound conceptual and analytical framework is a prerequisite for good decisionmaking. Yet policy decisions are often made without the benefit of such a framework. Few individuals can already articulate a sound framework when they first assume high-level policy responsibilities. And the demands of day-to-day policymaking leave little time for reflection to develop one through on-the-job training.

If my efforts have been successful, this book can significantly help policymakers and their advisers in formulating a dependable framework for their own circumstances. The analysis and guidelines developed in the book grow out of today's best-practice economic theory. In that sense, they represent as sound a framework as is currently available to policymakers. The guidelines are not a detailed manual that can be straightforwardly applied to specific policy issues for specific nations; I doubt that a manual of that sort can be written. But the guidelines do constitute a solid foundation on which to anchor the analysis of specific policy decisions.

To assert that this book summarizes the implications of today's best-practice economic theory for the conduct of national monetary policy is, I readily acknowledge, a sweeping and possibly presumptuous claim. Even to identify what constitutes that theory is a tall order, especially if international aspects are taken into account adequately.

Some notable developments in monetary and macroeconomic theory during the middle third of this century are now well understood and generally accepted. The writings of John Maynard Keynes and of those elaborating on his insights, together with the refinement of national income accounting, brought substantial progress in understanding the aggregate flows of income, expenditure, and saving in the economy, including the role of government taxes and expenditures. Monetary economists significantly improved their theoretical understanding of microeconomic financial behavior and the functioning of financial markets. Some economists—for example, James Tobin, Don Patinkin, and John Gurley and Edward Shaw—made progress toward integrating monetary theory into a coherent overall macroeconomic theory. And economists such as Milton Friedman, Karl Brunner, and Allan Meltzer successfully led a campaign to rescue monetary policy from the relative eclipse into which it had been cast by the preoccupation with fiscal policy of most Keynesian economists.

For the most part, however, these improvements in theory and policy analysis ignored international transactions and international creditor-debtor relationships. The economists revising the theory ruthlessly simplified their analytical difficulties by restricting attention to the hypothetical case of an economy closed to the rest of the world. It was left to specialists in international trade and finance to extend the new theoretical insights to such complexities as exchange rates, international trade in goods, and cross-border flows of financial capital. In the United States, where many of the improvements in theory originated, the relative neglect of international complications was especially pronounced.

For their part, specialists in international trade and finance remained preoccupied with their special problems. Hence the advances in monetary and macroeconomic theory for the closed-economy case percolated only slowly into international economics. It was only after the middle of the 1960s, for example, that a majority of economists in international finance began to apply the concepts of portfolio-balance theory to cross-border capital flows.

Eventually, most of the new insights of closed-economy theory were transferred. By the end of the 1970s, spurred also by events themselves (such as the demise of the Bretton Woods adjustable-peg system for exchange rates), the analytical framework applied to international economic problems had undergone a substantial transformation. In part, this book is a product of that transformation and a road map of its main features.

Macroeconomic theory—the bulk of it, unfortunately, still preoccupied with the closed-economy case—continues in a state of ferment as this is written. Three manifestations of the ferment are particularly noteworthy. First, macroeconomic theorists are trying to improve their understanding of stock-flow interactions through time. (Examples are the dynamic processes by which net real investment adds to the outstanding stock of the economy's physical capital and by which imbalances in the government budget change the outstanding stock of financial claims on the government and central bank.) These interactions and their consequences are critical determinants of the short- and long-run impacts on the economy of policy actions and nonpolicy exogenous events. Second, interest continues to grow in so-called disequilibrium macroeconomics, a reformulation of macroeconomic theory without the assumption that prices adjust to clear markets instantaneously. Third, theorists are now intensively exploring ways of dealing more adequately with expectations. One aspect of this effort is the recent spate of work on a "rational-expectations" characterization of the interactions between government and the private sector.

Because of the continuing ferment in closed-economy macroeconomics, the task of incorporating new theoretical developments into the analysis of open economies is not complete. And economists focusing on open economies may themselves generate new theoretical insights, including some important enough to force closed-economy theorists to abandon their habitual neglect of international complications.

This book could be said to be premature because of these possibilities for further evolution in economic theory. Without doubt, some of what is written here will require revision as the result of future research. Nevertheless, ample reason exists to make the book available now. Government officials can scarcely call a halt to policy decisions until economic theorists resolve the controversial issues that divide current opinion. And policymakers will always confront a world where concepts and theories can change; good policy will always require decisions based on the least inadequate knowledge available at the time. Even if the evolution of macro-economic theory should continue as rapidly as in recent years, therefore, this interim report can be useful.

At least one salient feature of the analytical perspective stressed here is likely to become more, not less, appropriate as time passes. That feature is the integration of domestic and international considerations in a single decisionmaking procedure. The tendency to separate the domestic and external aspects of national policy, like the separation of closed-economy theory and international economics from which it is derived, is a serious impediment to good policymaking. As national economies become increasingly interdependent, the need for an integrated policy approach will become even more compelling.

Policymakers acquire one type of knowledge and experience. They know at first hand what questions are deemed to require answers. They must often deal with all of those questions simultaneously. They have a keen sense of the political and institutional constraints that must condition policy decisions. They speak a relatively nontechnical language.

Most academics in the social sciences acquire a very different type of knowledge and experience. They are less practical than policymakers; in particular, their sense of which questions to ask is likely to be less well grounded in reality. But they have more time to reflect carefully on the answers. They are free to deal with one question at a time. And, increasingly, academics in the social sciences conduct their research using technical languages and tools that can be understood only with great effort, if at all, by policymakers and laymen.

If the policy and the academic communities are to perform their functions well, each must communicate the key features of their knowledge and insights to the other. Never easy, this communication has become even more difficult in recent decades because of the increasingly specialized nature of the social sciences. Authors thus have powerful incentives to select one community or the other as their audience, giving up on the effort to communicate with both simultaneously.

Although my ultimate objective is to reach policymakers and their advisers, that audience is unlikely to be persuaded unless the policy guidelines here can command broad support among academic economists. Because some of the book's conclusions are certain to be controversial in the academic community, moreover, the only hope of enlisting academic support for those conclusions is to provide the analysis that underpins them.

This book is therefore a stubborn attempt to write for both the policy and the academic communities—indeed, to build a bridge between them. I say *stubborn* because most of the colleagues with whom I discussed the dilemma advised me to abandon the attempt. Approximately half of them urged me to make the book less technical so that it would be more easily accessible to my ultimate audience. The other half argued precisely the opposite, that the analysis should be directed only at fellow economists and presented in the austere, professional style of the academic journal. The one point on which virtually all agreed is that the bridge-building attempt is likely to collapse into the gap between the two communities, making excessive demands on the policymaker and yet failing to satisfy the academic.

No doubt the book will be judged an unhappy compromise by some members of each community. But I have been encouraged in my stubbornness by the reactions to publication of Francis Bacon's *Novum Organum* in 1620. A copy of Bacon's book was given to King James; how diligently he tried to read it is unclear, but he was overheard to remark to a courtier that the book "like the peace of God, passeth all understanding." The verdict of the Oxford scholars was that "a fool could not have written the book, and a wise man would not." Those verdicts from the policymaking and the academic communities in Bacon's day, however, proved to be inaccurate forecasts of his book's influence. For many reasons, of course, my book cannot be compared to Bacon's. But I hope that, in an analogous way, my pessimistic colleagues may turn out to be wrong about my attempt to build a bridge between the two communities. At the least, I trust that I will not be too severely reproached for trying. The goal of bridging the gap between the policymaker and the academic is surely a worthy objective.

A major reason for the length of the book is its frequent inclusion of bibliographical references and of footnote elaborations or qualifications of points made in the text. That material has been included as part of the bridge-building effort. I regret that some readers will find it an encumbrance. Yet it will assist fellow economists to evaluate the controversial parts of my analysis, and it will help strongly interested readers to digest the argument and to locate supplementary references. The needs of those latter readers have been uppermost in my mind in deciding what to include and exclude.

Most of my professional experience has been with American institutions. I have tried here, however, to abstract from the institutional differences among particular nations, thereby to focus on analytical fundamentals relevant for all central banks and national governments. Except inadvertently, the analysis is not tailored to the problems of macroeconomic policy in the United States. Because of the greater economic openness of most other nations, the book should attract at least as much interest in other countries as in the United States.

The reader deserves one final word of explanation about what follows. Just as I may be criticized for my bridge-building ambitions, I may also be chastised for untrammeled eclecticism. For I have refused to take one or the other side in the polarized and often artificial debates that persist in the literature on macroeconomic policy. To give some prominent examples: this book is neither Keynesian nor monetarist; it favors neither money nor interest rates as the centerpiece of monetary policy; it rejects both rigidly fixed exchange rates and freely flexible exchange rates; it eschews not only rules but also fine tuning; it argues neither that market failures are rife nor that markets always work efficiently. Some well-meaning friends have tried to nudge me out of the middle of the road, in part to make the book more controversial and thereby more likely to attract attention. For better or worse, I have stubbornly ignored this counsel as well. It is true that extreme positions usually command greater public attention than moderate views. But my purpose here is to discuss sound policy, not to stimulate controversy. Given that purpose, one can do worse than be an untrammeled eclectic. Indeed, if asked to recommend an epigraph for the facade of a central bank, I might well suggest the advice given by Phoebus to the impetuous Phaethon: *medio tutissimus ibis* (you will go most safely by the middle way). That dictum is not an infallible guide to sound policy. But it will very often keep those holding the reins from making egregious errors.

Readers able to take the time to read the entire book will want to follow the advice that the King of Hearts gave to the White Rabbit: "begin at the beginning and go on till you come to the end: then stop." The identification of main themes in chapter 1 and the concluding summary in chapter 26 provide an overview of the book; those who are too busy to explore the book more extensively can learn its principal conclusions by reading those two chapters. Readers interested primarily in one or another specialized topic can readily locate the relevant chapters by consulting the table of contents, chapter 1, and the index.

I have accumulated a long list of debts in the writing of this book. The first ideas for parts of the analysis, and the initial effort to put them down on paper, go back to the academic year 1969–70 in London when I was the recipient of an International Affairs Fellowship of the Council on Foreign Relations. In addition to the Council's help that year, I enjoyed the hospitality of the Department of Political Economy of University College London and of the Bank of England. In countless ways the book bears the stamp of my years of work with the Board of Governors of the Federal Reserve System. Much of any practical merit in the book can be traced to what I learned during that challenging and congenial association. I am especially grateful for the Board's willingness to finance my first year at the Brookings Institution as a Federal Executive Fellow on leave of absence from my duties at the Board, and for the Board's understanding when I made the difficult decision to stay at Brookings to complete the task rather than return to the Board's staff. The debt I owe to the Brookings Institution for supporting my work, and to the Rockefeller Foundation for financial support, is correspondingly great. Most Brookings projects have a less strong emphasis on theory and a shorter gestation period than this book; I admire the flexibility and courage of Brookings in being willing to gamble on my effort.

My intellectual debts to the insights of earlier authors are far too numerous to mention here. (Readers of the footnotes will encounter my explicit acknowledgments of those debts.) Virtually all the substantive points I make have been made by someone else at some previous time. Such originality as my book may have consists in the way it integrates existing ideas and applies them rightly.

Several colleagues and friends—Dale W. Henderson, John H. Kalchbrenner, Arthur M. Okun, Walter S. Salant, and Peter A. Tinsley—have been unusually helpful in discussing the ideas in the book or in advising me on the drafting of the manuscript. Because their suggestions and criticisms have greatly improved the final product, not only the author but also the reader is in their debt. The untimely death of Art Okun occurred as the book was being prepared for publication. For me, as for so many others, Art provided intellectual stimulation of the highest order and set an inspiring example in all of life's other dimensions. Nothing about this book could gratify me more than to be able to believe that some small part of Art's wisdom and humane caring about policy issues has rubbed off into these pages.

During the long period when the book was in preparation, many other colleagues and friends helped me by commenting on drafts of parts of the manuscript, corresponding about specific points, or reacting to my ideas in conversations. For this help I am grateful to, among still others, Masanao Aoki, Charles A. Atkins, Richard Berner, Russell S. Boyer, Coralie Bryant, Peter B. Clark, Ben W. Crain, David Dod, William Fellner, Charles Freedman, Benjamin M. Friedman, Milton Friedman, Lance W. Girton, Gottfried Haberler, Patric H. Hendershott, George B. Henry, Arthur B. Hersey, James C. Ingram, Peter Isard, John H. Kareken, Peter B. Kenen, Robert O. Keohane, Lawrence B. Krause, Robert Z. Lawrence, Leon N. Lindberg, Ronald I. McKinnon, Bruce K. MacLaury, Charles S. Maier, Ronald Müller, Joseph A. Pechman, Larry J. Promisel, Don E. Roper, Stephen W. Salant, Robert L. Sammons, Jeffrey R. Shafer, Robert Solomon, Gilbert Y. Steiner, Guy V. G. Stevens, P. A. V. B. Swamy, Edwin M. Truman, Paul A. Volcker, Raymond Vernon, Douglas Waldo, Mason Willrich, Paul Wonnacott, and John T. Woolley. Several of these persons gave especially generously of their time and thereby enabled me to make important improvements.

At Brookings, I have benefited from the able research assistance of Leo K. Simon, Cynthia Nethercutt, Jesse Abraham, David S. Bates, and Stephen L. Smith. I am grateful to Charlotte Kaiser for skillful typing of the numerous drafts of the manuscript, to Penelope Harpold and Judith Cameron for verification of the bibliographical references, and to Florence Robinson for assistance in the preparation of the index.

The nurture and needling provided by my wife and daughters have been indispensable encouragements from beginning to end.

All of those mentioned—institutions, economists, policymakers, friends, co-workers, family—are sufficiently entangled with my writing of the book to be, in some degree, accessories before the fact. But none can fairly be indicted for any sins of commission or omission that still remain.

R.C.B.

Introduction

CHAPTER ONE

Main Themes

THIS BOOK focuses on two themes and their interrelationships: the role of money in monetary policy and the interdependence of nations' economies. Its main purposes are to advance the understanding of monetary macroeconomics under conditions of economic openness and to recommend sound guidelines for the conduct of national monetary policy in a single, open economy.

Economic Openness and National Economic Policy

The world is organized politically into nation states. The geographical boundaries of a nation are typically assumed to define the domain within which its national government has constitutional and political authority to adjust the instruments of economic policy. Governments are confronted with strong demands to formulate economic policy so as to achieve essentially national objectives—for example, the maintenance of high employment within the geographical boundaries of the political unit.

Yet the economic organization of the world has evolved in ways that have progressively reduced the economic significance of national boundaries. This increasing economic openness has, in turn, exacerbated the mismatch between the political domains within which decisions are made about the use of economic policy instruments and the effective economic domains within which those instruments have significant impacts.

For the time being an *open economy* may be defined as an economy associated with a nation state in which a significant proportion of economic and financial activity involves *international transactions*—that is, transactions for which one of the two parties is a resident, the other a nonresident. The stock counterparts to international transactions are *international creditor-debtor relationships*—assets or liabilities of residents of an open national economy vis-à-vis nonresidents. International transactions and international creditor-debtor relationships are absent altogether in a (hypothetical) *closed economy*. *Openness* and *interdependence* are used here as rough synonyms.[1]

The benefits and tensions associated with the coexistence of national political autonomy and world economic interdependence are scarcely new phenomena. Politicians and economists in the eighteenth and nineteenth centuries were often

---

1. More precise analytical concepts are presented in part 3.

preoccupied with them.[2] Philip II of Spain, the sultans of the sixteenth-century Ottoman Empire, and the rulers of Genoa and Venice knew them well.[3] Indeed, they are as old as the growth of "national" political consciousness and hence "international" trade.

The implications of economic openness for national autonomy have once more become a topical issue. This is in part because the degree of economic interdependence has been increasing in recent decades. This trend resumes a pattern that had characterized the period from the early nineteenth century to 1913 but was interrupted by two world wars and the depression years of the 1930s.[4]

An equally important explanation for the renewed topicality of the issue is a heightened awareness of interdependence. Many national leaders now perceive the phenomenon more keenly and devote more attention to it than, say, fifteen years ago. But the enhanced perception extends to mass opinion as well. References to interdependence in the public discussion of nations' foreign policies are by now commonplace. Indeed, the phenomenon has been so often discussed, and the discussion has elicited such complex responses in domestic politics, that interdependence imagery has even come to rival national security symbolism in the rhetoric used to articulate national goals.[5]

One would surmise that so topical an issue would have received careful analytical treatment in each of the several social science disciplines. By now, surely, should we not have in hand analytical definitions for the various dimensions of interdependence and be able to identify—conceptually and empirically—the main determinants of the degree of openness? I cannot speak with confidence about other disciplines. In economics, however, those foundations have not yet been laid adequately. Far too many discussions of economic interdependence rely on rhetoric and intuition instead of analysis. One of my aspirations in what follows, therefore, is to contribute to a more analytical approach to economic interdependence.

It seems reasonable to take for granted, at least as a working assumption, that a nation's government will want to use the policy instruments at its disposal to achieve unabashedly national objectives. But to what degree is it able to do so in an open economy? Political authority to act independently does not guarantee a nation's government the ability to attain its goals.

The fundamental distinction between political sovereignty over a nation's policy actions and effective control over the evolution of its economy immediately raises

2. See, for example, Adam Smith, *Of Systems of Political Economy*, vols. 1 and 2: *An Inquiry into the Nature and Causes of the Wealth of Nations* (London: Oxford University Press, 1976), pp. 426–688; Jacob Viner, *Studies in the Theory of International Trade* (Harper, 1937; Kelley, 1965); J. H. Clapham, *Machines and National Rivalries (1887–1914)*, vol. 3: *An Economic History of Modern Britain* (New York: Macmillan, 1938; England: Cambridge University Press, 1938), pp. 1–507; Albert Imlah, *Economic Elements in the Pax Britannica: Studies in British Foreign Trade in the 19th Century* (Harvard University Press, 1958).

3. Fernand Braudel, *The Mediterranean and the Mediterranean World in the Age of Philip II*, trans. Siân Reynolds (Harper and Row, 1972), pt. 2.

4. Simon Kuznets, *Modern Economic Growth: Rate Structure and Spread*, Studies in Comparative Economies, 7 (Yale University Press, 1966), chap. 6; Robert Solomon with Anne Gault, "The Economic Interdependence of Nations: An Agenda for Research" (Washington, D.C., 1977); Walter S. Salant, "International Transmission of Inflation," in Lawrence B. Krause and Walter S. Salant, eds., *Worldwide Inflation: Theory and Recent Experience* (Brookings Institution, 1977), pp. 175–80.

5. Robert O. Keohane and Joseph S. Nye, *Power and Interdependence: World Politics in Transition* (Little, Brown, 1977), chap. 1.

many issues; all concern, in one way or another, the consequences of interdependence for national economic policy and national welfare. Six questions identify the most important of those issues. First, which aspects of economic openness are the most critical determinants of a national government's ability to achieve national macroeconomic objectives? Second, how do changes in the degree of interdependence alter the effective autonomy of a nation's economic policy? Is it possible that some types of increases in interdependence augment rather than undermine national autonomy? Third, are increases in the degree of interdependence beneficial or harmful for the achievement of national objectives? Fourth, should national governments deliberately try to encourage or discourage increases in interdependence? Fifth, should nations try to "coordinate" their macroeconomic policy actions and, if so, on what basis? Finally, does a smoothly functioning world political and economic order require supranational traffic regulations and, if so, of what sort?

Each of the preceding questions is taken up in the chapters that follow. Note that the questions have been couched in terms of macroeconomic stabilization policy as a whole, not monetary policy in particular. But more specific versions of the same questions are equally important for the formulation and implementation of national monetary policy.

Money as the Key Variable in the Conduct of Monetary Policy

For many decades monetary theorists and other economists have studied the channels through which the actions of central banks influence the economy and have debated the strength of those influences. Much attention has also been devoted to the operating strategies that are or could be followed by central banks as they pursue ultimate policy objectives. "Money" figures prominently in this literature, especially so in the areas where there is controversy. Debate has been most intense over the theoretical and empirical definition of the stock of money, the appropriate specification of the demand for and supply of money, and the role those macroeconomic relationships should play in the conduct of monetary policy.

Although controversy continues, one type of approach to monetary policy has gained broad acceptance in the last ten to fifteen years. It is increasingly widely believed that money, somehow defined, should play a central role in the conduct of monetary policy. In particular, there has been growing support for the recommendation that the central bank specify a target time path for the stock of money and then direct its energies at the objective of making the actual stock follow this target path closely.

Money, as generally defined, is not an actual instrument of central bank policy. The central bank does not have a lever marked M that it can set hour by hour or day by day, thereby exactly controlling the stock of money. Rather, the outstanding amount of money—say, currency in circulation plus one or more types of deposit claims on financial intermediaries—is determined at any given time not only by the behavior of the central bank but also by the behavior of the financial intermediaries and the nonfinancial private sector. Nor is the stock of money an ultimate objective of monetary policy. The ultimate goals of policy are such variables as output, employment, and the price level.

Thus the stock of money, like the great majority of macroeconomic magnitudes, is an intermediate variable from the perspective of policymakers. The central bank cannot control it perfectly. And it is not sought in its own right as a final goal of policy.[6]

The recommendation that policymakers set a target time path for the money stock and then seek to keep the stock on that path may be characterized as advocacy of an intermediate-target strategy for conducting monetary policy, with money acting as the key intermediate variable. The essence of the strategy is to use money as a surrogate—a temporary stand-in—for the ultimate objectives of policy. Monetary-policy decisions made in this way are thus formulated and executed in two separate stages. First, at periodic intervals an "upper-stage" calculation fixes the target time path for money judged to be most consistent with the true, ultimate objectives. Second, more or less continuously in a series of "lower-stage" decisions, the instruments proper are manipulated to try to keep the money stock close to its target path.

There is ample evidence from newspapers and academic journals that this approach to monetary policy has become increasingly influential. Perhaps the most notable evidence, however, has come from the policymakers themselves. Many of the central banks of the major industrial countries have significantly altered their operating objectives and procedures in the direction of setting monetary-aggregate targets, announcing the targets publicly, and then using the instruments of policy to adhere to those targets. A process of gradual change began in the United States in 1970.[7] The Deutsche Bundesbank began to emphasize a monetary-aggregate target in 1974.[8] Canadian monetary policy shifted its general orientation and operating procedures in 1975.[9] The Bank of England joined the trend in 1976.[10] A complete list of countries shifting toward the use of a monetary aggregate as an intermediate target of monetary policy in the 1970s would be considerably longer.[11]

6. Instruments, ultimate-target variables, and intermediate variables are defined precisely in chapter 2.

7. See *Open-Market Policies and Operating Procedures—Staff Studies* (Board of Governors of the Federal Reserve System, 1971); *Monetary Aggregates and Monetary Policy* (Federal Reserve Bank of New York, 1974), particularly Alan R. Holmes, Paul Meek, and Rudolf Thunberg, "Open Market Operations in the Early 1970's: Excerpts from Reports Prepared in 1971, 1972, and 1973," pp. 114–34; "The Strategy of Monetary Control," *Federal Reserve Bulletin*, vol. 62 (May 1976), pp. 411–21; and "The Implementation of Monetary Policy in 1976," *Federal Reserve Bulletin*, vol. 63 (April 1977), pp. 323–36.

8. See *Monthly Report of the Deutsche Bundesbank*, vol. 26 (July 1974 and December 1974), vol. 27 (January 1975), vol. 28 (January 1976), vol. 29 (January 1977); and *Report of the Deutsche Bundesbank, 1974*, and ibid., *1975*, and *1976*.

9. See Bank of Canada, *Annual Report, 1975* and ibid., *1976;* George Freeman, "Recent Innovations in the Bank of Canada's Approach to Monetary Policy," paper prepared for December 1976 conference on international financial relations, Graduate Institute of International Studies, Geneva.

10. See "Speeches by the Governor of the Bank of England," *Bank of England Quarterly Bulletin*, vol. 17 (March 1977), p. 48; "Economic Commentary," ibid. (June 1977), pp. 147–55, ibid., March 1978, pp. 31–37; Bank of England, *Report and Accounts for the Year ended 28th February 1978*, pp. 6–10.

11. See, for example, Bank for International Settlements, *Forty-Sixth Annual Report* (Basle: Bank for International Settlements, June 1976), pp. 24–39, 133–35, and *Forty-Eighth Annual Report* (June 1978), pp. 39–60; and Warren D. McClam, "Targets and Techniques of Monetary Policy in Western Europe," *Banca Nazionale del Lavoro Quarterly Review*, no. 124 (March 1978), pp. 3–27. As this book was being published, I learned of two sources that survey this trend in central bank policies: Organization for Economic Cooperation and Development, *Monetary Targets and Inflation Control* (OECD, 1979); and M.

Many policymakers and monetary economists advertise these changes in operating objectives and procedures as an unqualified improvement in the conduct of monetary policy. But are they?

In one respect, I believe, the changes are an improvement. Central banks have been making more information available about what they aim at and how they try to implement their goals. As a result, the private sector has more to go on when assessing current and prospective monetary policy. That, in turn, it can plausibly be argued, facilitates sound decisions in the private sector and thereby helps to promote the ultimate objectives of macroeconomic policy.

In more important respects, however, the increasing emphasis on money as a surrogate target is *not* an advance in the conduct of monetary policy. At the very least, the trend toward money as an operating target deserves a more searching examination than it typically receives. A major purpose of this book is to fill that need.

Alternative Strategies for Monetary Policy under Conditions of Interdependence

The consequences of economic openness for a nation's economic policy could be examined without paying special attention to money and monetary policy. And the relative merits of using money as an intermediate target of monetary policy would warrant evaluation even if an economy's relationships with the rest of the world were ignored. But central banks cannot separate the two subjects when making policy decisions. Directly or indirectly, therefore, much of this book is conditioned by a single question that combines the two: How does economic openness affect the case in favor of using the money stock as an intermediate target of monetary policy?

To cope with the question adequately, one must go back to basic concepts in macroeconomic theory and policy for open economies. Most notably, one is driven to ask: What is money? That conundrum has already generated an extensive discussion in the theoretical literature concerned exclusively with a closed economy. The definitional and conceptual difficulties become much more acute, however, once international creditor-debtor relationships get their nose into the tent.

For many purposes and for some approaches to conducting monetary policy, the definition of money is an unimportant matter. If national central banks in significantly open economies are to be urged to use the money stock as an intermediate target, however, it becomes important to select the "best" definition of money. Central banks can scarcely aim at a target without knowing what the target is![12]

T. Sumner, "The Operation of Monetary Targets," in Karl Brunner and Allan H. Meltzer, eds., *Monetary Institutions and the Policy Process,* Carnegie-Rochester Conferences on Public Policy, vol. 7 (North-Holland, forthcoming).

12. Kenneth Boulding put the dilemma nicely:

> We must have a good definition of Money,
> For if we do not, then what have we got,
> But a Quantity Theory of no-one-knows-what,
> And this would be almost too true to be funny.

(See *Journal of Money, Credit, and Banking,* vol. 1 [August 1969], p. 555. Participants at the monetary

The underlying rationale for the strategy of using the money stock as an intermediate target and the conditions required for its validity are not adequately explained elsewhere in the literature, even for a closed economy. Hence the analysis that follows goes back to first principles on this subject, too. It is necessary to set forth and clarify the case in favor of a money strategy before appraising and, eventually, rejecting it.

Because money strategies are widely advocated, this book concentrates on them. Much of the analysis calls attention to their drawbacks. But the analysis would be seriously incomplete if it merely criticized money strategies. A perfect strategy does not exist. And monetary-policy decisions have to be guided by some strategy. The relevant appraisal must therefore be comparative: How well or how poorly do money strategies perform vis-à-vis something else—something else at least equally feasible in practice?

The book therefore contains considerable discussion of alternative strategies. The main alternatives are first identified and then compared with intermediate-target strategies that focus on money. That comparison is initially made without bringing in international considerations but is subsequently extended to the open-economy case in part 5.

Exchange-Rate Variability and National Monetary Policy

From the mid-1960s to mid-1970s the world of international finance was in fairly continuous turmoil. One of the most notable consequences of the turmoil was a progressive crumbling, and finally a formal dismantling, of the Bretton Woods adjustable-peg system governing currency exchange rates.

Before 1973, in accordance with obligations stated in the then-current language of Article IV of the Articles of Agreement of the International Monetary Fund, virtually all major countries maintained their exchange rates within narrow margins around an infrequently changed par value. Subsequently, however, with the abandonment of most supranational constraints on exchange-rate movements, individual nations have been free to allow as much or as little variability in exchange rates for their currencies as they wish.[13]

The new scope for national discretion and the resulting changes in the manner and degree of exchange-rate variability have understandably triggered a renewed interest in issues associated with alternative exchange-rate arrangements (so-called exchange-rate regimes). Central banks, in particular, have to be concerned with many of those issues: exchange-rate variability and variations in the nation's external reserve assets are the very stuff of national monetary policy in an open economy. Several chapters in this book will therefore analyze official exchange-market intervention and alternative exchange-rate arrangements in some detail.

One of the important issues is a special case of the general questions about interdependence and autonomy: whether, and if so, how, the capacity of a central

---

conference that inspired this poesy were concerned almost exclusively with the definitional issues in a closed economy.)

13. The abandonment of the constraints occurred de facto in 1973 and de jure in the version of Article IV drafted in 1975–76 and formally adopted in 1978.

bank to use the instruments of national monetary policy to exert control over the evolution of the national economy is importantly affected by the manner and degree of exchange-rate variability.

It is conventionally argued in international economics that flexible exchange rates "insulate" nations' economies from one another and allow central banks to pursue "independent" monetary policies. A closely related proposition asserts that greater flexibility in exchange rates itself represents a reduction in economic interdependence—as it were, a "dis-integration" of national economies from each other. The analysis here evaluates those generalizations, explaining why the first is incorrect, and why the second is, at the least, misleading.

The most difficult exchange-rate issues are those bearing directly on the choice of a strategy for implementing monetary policy. These, too, are aired in the chapters to follow. For example, it is necessary to ask how—if at all—differing exchange-rate arrangements alter the arguments for and against the use of money as the key variable in the conduct of monetary policy. Because the analysis eventually rejects a money strategy as inferior, moreover, there is finally a need to outline how exchange-rate variability and variations in external reserves should be integrated into a preferred strategy for the conduct of monetary policy in an open economy.

The analysis of exchange-rate issues is postponed until part 5. Some readers may regard the omission of those issues in earlier parts of the book as unjustified. A strong case can be made, however, for an exposition that highlights more basic considerations before bringing in alternative assumptions about exchange-rate arrangements. Far more than is commonly supposed, it is those more basic considerations rather than the manner and degree of exchange-rate variability that chiefly determine what can, and cannot, be accomplished with national monetary policy in an open economy.

The Plan of the Book

The two following chapters complete this introduction to the themes that recur throughout the book. Chapter 2 identifies the basic concepts of the theory of economic policy. Chapter 3 calls attention to the ambiguities of the concept of money in a world of many national currencies and extensive international creditor-debtor relationships.

Part 1 begins the analysis with first principles, using the more familiar theoretical context of a closed economy. The analysis examines the purposes for which a concept and definition of money may be required and reviews the traditional formulations of the aggregate demand and supply functions for money. It concludes with an exposition and an initial examination of the strategy of using the money stock, somehow defined, as the intermediate target of monetary policy.

Part 2 considers monetary aggregates in the context of an open economy. After outlining some rudiments of the theory required for analyzing financial behavior under conditions of openness, it identifies alternative definitions of the national money stock and appraises the significance of the differences between the closed economy and the open economy for the workability of a strategy using some definition of national money as an intermediate target.

Part 3 turns to the general implications of interdependence for national economic policy. It develops an appropriate analytical framework within which to study the conditions of intermediate interdependence and then directs attention to the consequences of interdependence for the ability of a nation's policymakers to exert control over the national economy.

Part 3 provides a theory of national macroeconomic policy at a high level of abstraction. Part 4 refocuses the discussion on monetary policy, on the ability of the central bank to use monetary instruments to achieve ultimate objectives, and on alternative strategies for conducting monetary policy. Part 4 suppresses international considerations to highlight the major issues about alternative strategies in an economical way and asks the hypothetical question: Which is the preferred strategy for conducting monetary policy in a closed economy?

Part 5 pulls the major themes of the book together by considering the ability of a nation's central bank to use its monetary instruments to achieve national ultimate objectives of macroeconomic policy. Building on the closed-economy analysis in part 4, part 5 provides a sound conceptual framework within which to formulate decisions about "external" monetary policy, including the traditionally discussed choice between fixed and flexible exchange rates. Unlike the existing literature in monetary theory and international economics, part 5 also integrates the analysis of "domestic" monetary policy and external monetary policy, showing that the principles and procedures applied to one are equally relevant for the other.

The analysis in this book presumes a myopic national perspective; it asks how a nation should conduct its monetary policy to serve national objectives. Chapter 25 emphasizes several critical problems that are ignored by this national myopia: the inevitable non-independence of nations' policy actions, the resulting pressure for supranational traffic regulations, and the problems and potentialities of other forms of international cooperation.

The final chapter sets out broad guidelines for the conduct of monetary policy that follow from the main conclusions of the analysis.

CHAPTER TWO

Basic Concepts of the Theory of Economic Policy

THE ANALYSIS that follows is a treatise on the theory of economic policy. It uses several concepts as building blocks. Some of these, such as the targets and instruments of policymakers, will be familiar to many readers. Others require explanation—for example, the distinction between ultimate and intermediate targets, and between potential and actual instruments. As a foundation and point of reference for subsequent chapters, all the basic concepts are defined in this chapter. The chapter also comments briefly on theoretical characterizations of policy decisions and indicates how this book relates to the existing literature on the theory of economic policy.

National Governments, Policy Agencies, and Central Banks

The principal unit of political and economic interest in the book is the individual *nation*. Although many aspects of the argument are general enough to apply to nations at all stages of economic development, the analysis applies chiefly to those with so-called mixed economies and fairly advanced financial institutions.

Most transactions in mixed economies are planned and carried out by *private* (nongovernmental) *decisionmaking units*—collectively, the *private sector*—which include *households, firms* (nonfinancial corporations), and *financial intermediaries* (banks and other types of private financial institutions). The *national government*, however, also plays a key role in shaping the *economic system* of the nation (alternatively, the *national economy*). Not only does the government engage in economic transactions itself, it may largely determine the legal, regulatory, and institutional regime within which all private economic transactions take place.

The national government is the locus of *policy agencies,* which are each charged with responsibility for the formulation and implementation of a part of the nation's economic policy. The number of policy agencies and their institutional characteristics vary greatly from nation to nation. They usually include a *fiscal authority*—for example, the Treasury or Ministry of Finance—and a *monetary authority.* In most nations the monetary authority is the *central bank;* sometimes, however, the functional responsibilities of the monetary authority are shared by the central bank and the fiscal authority.

National economic policy is a protean term. In principle, it can refer to a coherent set of decisions worked out in concert by the various policy agencies. At the other extreme, it can serve merely as a label—indeed, a misleading label—for the composite outcome of uncoordinated agency decisions.

11

Few subjects are as controversial in the study of politics as the conceptualization of "the state" (national government) and the interrelations of the components of the state (the various policy agencies). In the political history of monetary policy, moreover, no topic is more important and sensitive than the degree of political independence of the monetary authority from the rest of the national government.[1]

The political and sociological interactions of the policy agencies, important though they are, fall largely outside the scope of this book. In the theoretical analysis here, therefore, such complications are usually suppressed by positing that the fiscal authority and the central bank coordinate their decisionmaking—in other words, that a single centralized policy authority is responsible for the entirety of national economic policy.

When no danger of confusion exists, subsequent chapters often use the simple term *policymakers* for those who make policy decisions. *Policy authority* is used when giving emphasis to the assumption of centralized, coordinated decisionmaking. If the context requires the distinction, *central bank* and *fiscal authority* are used to denote, respectively, the policymakers responsible for decisions about the two main branches of economic management: *monetary policy* and *fiscal policy*.[2]

The concept of a centralized policy authority within the national government is a fictional construct greatly at variance with political reality. In the real world, policy agencies and their associated bureaucracies have some measure of autonomy, so that their decisions are, at best, imperfectly coordinated. To what degree does the disparity between political reality and the construct of a centralized policy authority vitiate the conclusions drawn from a theoretical analysis that suppresses this disparity? This important question is best put aside for the time being; in chapter 18 I return to the problem.

Targets, Instruments, and Intermediate Variables

Further concepts needed for the theory of national economic policy derive from the existence and duties of the policy authority. In particular, the policy authority is conceptualized as having objectives, or *ultimate targets*. Greater analytical precision can be given to the concept of objectives or targets if one postulates that the policy authority has preferences defined over the time paths of *ultimate-target variables*. Ultimate-target variables are macroeconomic magnitudes assumed to affect the well-being of individuals or the social well-being of the nation directly or else, for the purposes of policy decisions, are believed to be satisfactory proxies for still more remote and fundamental goals. The volume of output, the average price level, and the number of persons employed are examples of variables often regarded as ultimate targets.

One can think of the preferences of the policymakers as embodied in a *policy loss function* (or, alternatively, a *social welfare function*) that ranks alternative outcomes for the evolution of the national economy. Such a function specifies,

1. References to both sets of literature are given in chapter 18.
2. Although the analytical framework of the theory of policy may also be applied to allocative and regulatory (microeconomic) decisions made by policy agencies, the focus of this book is on so-called macroeconomic, or stabilization, policy.

among other things, how conflicting objectives are to be traded off against each other and how intertemporal comparisons of well-being are to be made. The loss or social welfare function relevant for the policy authority is of the so-called nonindividualistic type. It might or might not be paternalistic. But at the very least it will presume interpersonal and intertemporal comparisons of individual welfares (the traditional allergy of most of welfare economics notwithstanding).[3]

The concepts of preferences, ultimate-target variables, and a policy loss function do not presuppose a pluralist, democratic conceptualization of the nation's political system. The preferences and loss function might be those, for example, of a ruling elite or a dictator in control of the policy authority. But these concepts do assume the national government has a unified set of preferences that can serve as an unambiguous yardstick for judging alternative outcomes.[4]

The policy authority has command over a collection of *policy instruments*. As a convenient shorthand, I speak of the policy authority making decisions about, and taking actions to adjust, the "settings" on its various instruments. A *policy action* is an alteration of the setting on an instrument. A package policy action is one in which the settings on several instruments are adjusted simultaneously. To illustrate, if commercial banks must maintain required reserves at the central bank equivalent to some fraction of the outstanding amount of their demand-deposit liabilities, the reserve–requirement ratio is an instrument of monetary policy. The instrument setting is the numerical value of the ratio—for example, 13 percent. An increase in the ratio from 13 to 14 percent is a policy action using this instrument. An increase in the reserve–requirement ratio combined with an increase in the central bank's discount rate and a reduction of $5 billion in a discretionary category of government expenditure constitutes a package action employing instruments of both monetary policy and fiscal policy.

In subsequent chapters it is necessary to stress the distinction between potential instrument variables and actual instruments. An economic variable is not only a potential but also an *actual instrument* (1) if it is possible for the policy authority to control that variable precisely and (2) if in fact the authority chooses to control it precisely. A variable is a *potential instrument* if the policy authority could control it precisely but does not do so. Not all potential instruments can be actual instruments. To illustrate, a short-term market interest rate (such as the rate at which commercial banks lend immediately available funds to each other) and the quantity of a central-bank liability (such as the aggregate deposits of commercial banks at the central bank) are both potential instrument variables. Moreover, each is a

3. A more detailed discussion appears in part 3. For a review of the concept of group (or social) welfare functions as used in welfare economics and the distinctions between individualistic, nonindividualistic, and paternalistic functions, see Amartya Sen, *On Economic Inequality* (London: Oxford University Press, 1973), and J. de V. Graaff, *Theoretical Welfare Economics* (London and New York: Cambridge University Press, 1957). *Policy loss* connotes negative welfare. Policymakers may be construed as minimizing the value of a policy loss function or maximizing the value of a social welfare function; no substantive issue is affected by which of these two concepts is used in formulating a theory of policy decisions.

4. As soon as one abandons the simplifying assumption of a single policy authority, it becomes necessary to specify separate preferences for the various policy agencies and to analyze the process of conflict over objectives *within* the national government. In that more complex institutional environment, an unambiguous yardstick for evaluating alternative evolutions of the national economy no longer exists. Economists have so far largely ignored the game-theoretic issues that pervade intragovernmental politics (see chapter 18).

leading candidate for the primary actual instrument of monetary policy. Once one of the two is chosen as an actual instrument, however, the other cannot be controlled precisely and must remain merely a potential instrument variable.

The notion of precise controllability is the essential aspect of the concept of policy instruments. A potential instrument variable must be such that its value can be set day by day, or even hour by hour, if the policy authority deems it desirable. For an actual instrument, there can be no slippage between the intended setting and the achieved setting. From the perspective of the policy authority, policy instruments are "exogenous" variables.

Ultimate-target variables are only a subset of the "endogenous" variables that constitute the economic system of the nation.[5] Most endogenous economic magnitudes are *intermediate variables*. These variables are not pursued in their own right as final goals of policy; more precisely, policymakers do not have preferences with respect to them directly, and they do not appear as arguments in the policy loss function. Neither can the policy authority control them precisely. Intermediate variables are removed from actual instrument variables by one or more links in a chain of behavioral causation.

Economic Structure and Structural Models

Consider now a further set of concepts: the relationships that link the economic behavior of all the decisionmaking units—private and governmental—in the national economic system. These *behavioral relationships* are manifold, and their interactions highly complex. Among other things, this nexus determines the pattern of causal links between policy instruments, intermediate variables, and ultimate-target variables. For shorthand reference, it is convenient to use the term *economic structure* to designate this nexus of behavioral relationships and their interactions. The term *structural model* refers to an effort by economists or others to capture the most important features of the "true" economic structure in a theoretical or empirical model.

The true economic structure cannot be known, fully or reliably, by any of the decisionmaking units in the economic system. An analysis of macroeconomic developments, whatever the economic system, does not need to assume (indeed, should not assume) that the economic structure is known by any of the participants in the system (including the national policy authority). It does need, on the other hand, to postulate the existence of the economic structure and attempt to model it.

Many different efforts can be made to model the same economic structure. Models can be carelessly devised, even implicitly presumed (for example, a back-of-envelope sketch); at the other extreme, models can be explicit and systematic (for example, an econometric model designed in accordance with best-practice economic theory).[6] Modeling attempts can be more or less successful. A model

5. The classification of variables as endogenous or exogenous is a matter of theoretical perspective and analysis, not a question of the inherent characteristics of actual macroeconomic variables. In later chapters I discuss the distinction between endogenous and exogenous variables in some detail.

6. Some models may bypass the stage of representing economic structure, working only with the "reduced form," or "final form," of a structural model that itself is only implicit. See part 3.

may be formulated primarily for conducting descriptive analysis or for making prescriptive recommendations, or for doing both.

A model of some sort is a logical prerequisite for decisions by the policy authority on what to do with its instruments—and for prescriptive recommendations about those decisions by nongovernmental observers. Were a policymaker to insist that he makes decisions without using a model, he would be either quibbling over semantics, lying, or fooling himself.

A final set of concepts can, for the time being, be grouped together and referred to as *nonpolicy disturbances*. Defined loosely, nonpolicy disturbances are factors other than governmental policy instruments that determine the evolution of the national economy. Some nonpolicy disturbances are best thought of as changes in magnitudes that are represented in a structural model as exogenous variables. Weather conditions and demographic trends are two examples. Other types of disturbances are best conceptualized as exogenous "shocks" to the values of variables that are otherwise endogenously determined in a structural model.[7]

One can imagine a third type of nonpolicy shock or disturbance: unpredictable alterations in the parameters or other features of the hypothesized economic structure itself (for example, changes in consumer preferences). Phenomena of this type are characterized as *changes in economic structure*.

Theoretical Characterizations of Policy Decisions

The concepts discussed above enable economists to construct a prescriptive theory of economic policy. The outlines of this theory are by now familiar, even to many policymakers. The analytical insights in the existing literature are attributable in large part to Jan Tinbergen and Henri Theil.[8] In recent years their themes and insights have been extended by the application of "optimal control" techniques to problems of macroeconomic policy.[9]

In this traditional approach, the task of the policy authority is to select settings

7. An example of such a shock is an unexpected, "autonomous" increase in investment activity. It can be represented in a structural model by a sizable positive value for the stochastic error term in the equations for investment expenditures (because fluctuations in the explanatory variables in the equations cannot account for the increase). For further discussion, see part 3.

8. Tinbergen's seminal work is *On the Theory of Economic Policy*, 2d ed. (Amsterdam: North-Holland, 1963). See also *Economic Policy: Principles and Design* (Amsterdam: North-Holland, 1956), in which he extends and applies the concepts and techniques of the 1952 essay. Theil's work includes *Economic Forecasts and Policy*, 2d rev. ed. (Amsterdam: North-Holland, 1961); Theil and P. J. M. van den Bogaard, *Optimal Decision Rules for Government and Industry* (Amsterdam: North-Holland, 1964); and Theil, "Linear Decision Rules for Macrodynamic Policy Problems," in Bert G. Hickman, ed., *Quantitative Planning of Economic Policy* (Brookings Institution, 1965), pp. 18–42. The last reference summarizes the approach of the first two works. Additional references on the theory of economic policy include Karl A. Fox, Jati K. Sengupta, and Erik Thorbecke, *The Theory of Quantitative Economic Policy with Applications to Economic Growth, Stabilization and Planning*, 2d ed. (Amsterdam: North-Holland, 1973); William Brainard, "Uncertainty and the Effectiveness of Policy," *American Economic Review*, vol. 57 (May 1967, *Papers and Proceedings, 1966*), pp. 411–25; and Benjamin M. Friedman, *Economic Stabilization Policy: Methods in Optimization* (Amsterdam: North-Holland, 1975; New York: American Elsevier, 1975).

9. A good general reference on optimal control theory is Gregory C. Chow, *Analysis and Control of Dynamic Economic Systems* (Wiley, 1975). See also Chow, "Problems of Economic Policy from the Viewpoint of Optimal Control," *American Economic Review*, vol. 63 (December 1973), pp. 825–37; and J. H. Kalchbrenner and P. A. Tinsley, "On the Use of Optimal Control in the Design of Monetary Policy," Special Studies Paper 76 (Board of Governors of the Federal Reserve System, July 1975).

for its instruments that will bring about desirable values for its ultimate objectives. (Alternative outcomes are more or less desirable according to how they rank in terms of the underlying preferences embodied in the policy loss function.) Given the available knowledge of the economic structure and information about the current position of the economy, the policy authority chooses to use the structural model deemed the least inadequate. The policy authority is not so foolish as to aim at an outcome that it judges cannot be attained within the constraints of its preferred model. A more precise statement of the task of policy, then, is the selection of instrument settings judged most likely to bring about the best feasible combination of values of ultimate-target variables.

The traditional approach is thus a theory of decisions—a recommended procedure for choosing a best course of action under conditions of uncertainty. Stated more formally in terms of its analytical logic, the theory recommends that the policy authority minimize the expected value of its policy loss function subject to the constraints of its uncertain structural model.

A distinction is often drawn between positive economics and normative economics. Positive economics analyzes things as they are and allegedly eschews value judgments. Normative economics is concerned with making recommendations about how things ought to be and requires value judgments. Self-evidently, the traditional theory of economic policy is highly normative. The job of policymakers is prescriptive: they have to decide, somehow, where to fix the settings on the government's policy instruments (even if only to "do nothing" by leaving the settings unchanged). The theory of economic policy adopts this operational perspective of the policymakers.[10]

Two important objections have been voiced against the traditional theory of economic policy. First, as in almost all economic theory (positive and normative), the mainstream analysis postulates that decisionmakers *can* behave as rational actors who canvass all feasible options and then systematically choose a best course of action in accordance with given preferences. A few economists and a large group of psychologists and other social scientists, however, argue that this assumption conforms poorly with empirical observation of decisionmaking, particularly that done by large organizations such as government agencies. In their view, a "cybernetic" or "cognitive" model better describes real-life decision processes than the rational-actor paradigm. Seen from a cybernetic perspective, recommending that policymakers follow the analytic precepts of the traditional theory is like urging a fish to ride a bicycle.[11]

A more recent challenge to the traditional theory of economic policy comes from

---

10. For the distinction between positive and normative economics see, for example, Milton Friedman, "The Methodology of Positive Economics," *Essays in Positive Economics* (Chicago and London: University of Chicago Press, 1953). This distinction, if pressed too zealously, can justifiably be challenged on philosophical grounds. "Pure" positive economics, devoid of any value judgments, is an illusion; the mere selection of topics about which to formulate theories and make analytical statements presupposes normative choices. See, for example, Thomas S. Kuhn, *The Structure of Scientific Revolutions*, 2d ed. (University of Chicago Press, 1970). It remains true that the normative content of theories can vary greatly. The theory of policy, by adopting the policymakers' perspective, unabashedly emphasizes normative considerations.

11. The alternative approach is often associated with Herbert Simon; see, for example, James G. March and Herbert A. Simon, *Organizations* (New York: Wiley, 1958; London: Chapman and Hall, 1958). Other references and a summary of the main argument are given in John D. Steinbruner, *The Cybernetic Theory of Decision: New Dimensions of Political Analysis* (Princeton University Press, 1974).

economists focusing on game-theoretic interactions between policymakers and the private sector. This criticism, sometimes dubbed the rational expectations view, faults the traditional approach for ignoring or paying insufficient attention to the implications for policymakers' decisions of expectations in the private sector about those decisions.[12]

Both these objections are discussed in later chapters. The reader is warned at the outset, however, that neither receives central attention. The analysis here is squarely in the tradition of the prescriptive theory of policy. Its chief difference from the mainstream of the existing literature is its greater emphasis on the openness of the national economy.

12. This recent challenge is typified by Robert E. Lucas, Jr., "Econometric Policy Evaluation: A Critique," in Karl Brunner and Allan H. Meltzer, eds., *The Phillips Curve and Labor Markets*, vol. 1: *Carnegie-Rochester Conferences on Public Policy* (North-Holland, 1976), pp. 19–46. See also Thomas Muench and Neil Wallace, "On Stabilization Policy: Goals and Models," *American Economic Review*, vol. 64 (May 1974, *Papers and Proceedings, 1973*), pp. 330–37; and Thomas J. Sargent and Neil Wallace, "Rational Expectations and the Theory of Economic Policy," *Journal of Monetary Economics*, vol. 2 (April 1976), pp. 169–83.

CHAPTER THREE

What Is the Money Stock
in an Open Economy?

THIS CHAPTER identifies the conceptual and definitional issues concerning money analyzed in parts 1 and 2.

Illustrative Riddles

Imagine a firm in West Germany that imports and wholesales beef products, purchasing the bulk of its imports in Argentina. Suppose the firm has a sizable call deposit denominated in U.S. dollars in a London bank (a "Eurodollar" deposit).[1] In which nation's money supply, if any, does that Eurodollar deposit belong? Does it belong in the German money supply, since the holder of the deposit is a resident of Germany? Does it belong in the U.K. money supply, since the deposit is a liability issued by a bank located in the United Kingdom? Should the deposit be counted in the money supply of the United States, since the deposit is denominated in U.S. dollars? Perhaps the deposit, or some of it, should be considered part of the Argentine money supply, since the holder of the deposit purchases goods and services produced by the Argentine economy? Should the deposit be ignored altogether in statistics of national money supplies? To what extent should the answers to these questions differ if the owner of the deposit is a commercial bank rather than a nonbank?

Consider a second example that omits the complexity of the Eurocurrency markets. Suppose a Mexican commercial bank is extensively involved in financing Mexico's trade with Europe, Japan, and Latin America, as well as with the United States. Suppose it has a large correspondent balance (demand deposit) with a New York commercial bank. This demand deposit is not considered part of Mexico's money stock. Although an interbank liability, until 1980 it was counted as part of the money stock of the United States. Are the statistical practices in Mexico and the United States appropriate? If transactions between Mexican and European economic units are usually cleared through this correspondent balance in New York, should the statisticians and policymakers in European central banks be taking notice?

Finally, consider an example that abstracts from nation states and different national currency units. Imagine that comprehensive information on the balance sheets and the income-account statements for each economic unit resident in the

---

1. Definitions of Eurodollar and Eurocurrency banking and references to the literature are given in chapter 8.

state of West Virginia is made available to an unemployed economist. Imagine further that the economist has access to a small army of statistical clerks and a large computer, and that he is asked to construct the income and product accounts, the flow-of-funds accounts, and the balance-of-payments accounts for West Virginia. If the economist is competent, all the requested calculations are reasonably straightforward and noncontroversial. Perfect information and the requisite resources of manpower and data processing are available. No conceptual ambiguity is involved. But if the economist is asked to construct the West Virginia money stock, regardless of how sophisticated his knowledge of monetary economics may be, he will not be able to give a noncontroversial response. He will encounter the well-known difficulties of deciding which types of monetary assets to include and exclude (for example, whether to include time deposits at banks and passbook accounts at savings and loan associations) and how to treat the assets and liabilities that financial intermediaries in West Virginia have vis-à-vis each other. But most troublesome of all will be questions stemming from the openness of the West Virginia economy; here the economist's calculations will founder. Should the deposits of West Virginia residents with financial intermediaries in Ohio and Kentucky be included or excluded? How should the economist treat the deposits that residents of Ohio and Kentucky have made with financial intermediaries in West Virginia? What should be done with the claims of West Virginia banks on banks in New York and Pittsburgh, and with deposits that banks outside the state hold in West Virginia banks?

Elements of a Definition of Money

As one ponders the issues raised by the preceding examples, it becomes clear that there are, in principle, at least six sets of decisions that have to be made in defining a nation's or an area's money stock.

First, decisions must be made about the *categories of institutions* whose liabilities are to be included. Certain government agencies, commercial banks, and the many different types of nonbank financial intermediaries are candidates.

Second, decisions are necessary about the *geographical locations of the liability-issuing institutions*. One possible choice is to include only those institutions located within the geographical boundaries of the nation or area whose money stock is being constructed. Or the choice could be less restrictive. For example, the money stock of the "home" nation (the country for which the money stock is being defined) could include not only the deposit liabilities of home banks but also the deposit liabilities of foreign banks to residents of the home nation.

Third, once the categories of institutions and their geographical locations have been delimited, decisions must be made about the *types of liabilities* to be included. For example, coins and currency issued by central banks might be included but not other types of liabilities of central banks and other government agencies. Demand or sight deposits in banks might be included but not time deposits or bank liabilities in the form of debentures or equity claims.

Fourth, decisions need to be made about the *currency denomination* of liabilities to be included. Some types of liabilities denominated in the currency unit of the home nation will always be included. But it may or may not be thought appropriate to include liabilities denominated in the currency units of foreign nations.

A fifth set of decisions must be made about the *types of economic unit to whom the relevant liabilities are owed*. Here, too, it may be thought appropriate to exclude certain types. For example, if the desired definition of money includes only assets held by the nonbank private sector, then liabilities of the selected institutions to commercial banks and possibly also to nonbank financial intermediaries must be excluded. And, to take another illustration, decisions must be made about whether to exclude the holdings of liquid assets of federal government agencies, local and municipal governments, and nationalized industries or public corporations.

Finally, decisions have to be made about the *geographical locations of the economic units to whom the relevant liabilities are owed*. Attention could be restricted to economic units resident within the geographical boundaries of the nation or area whose money stock is being constructed. But again, the choice could be less restrictive. For example, the money stock of the home nation could include the deposit liabilities of home banks to foreign as well as home economic units.

The number of possible combinations of these six elements is large indeed. Of course they are interdependent: the decisions made about one tend to bear on the decisions about the others. Only three of the elements—the first, the third, and the fifth—need to be considered in a closed economy.

The conventional approach to definition of the money stock turns on a concept of "the public" that excludes the central bank and the commercial banks. Certain other government agencies, for example the fiscal authority, and certain nonbank financial intermediaries may be excluded as well. All other economic units are considered part of the public. Money is then defined as a subset of the financial assets owned by the public. In principle, the definition of money proceeds from the asset side—that is, from the perspective of the public. In practice, data tend to be available only from the liability side. Thus the requisite information is obtained from the institutions, predominantly financial intermediaries, that are deemed to have money liabilities to the public.

The notion that money is only a subset of the public's financial assets has always generated controversy, even when international considerations are ignored. Certain assets must be designated as having the characteristics of money; the remaining assets must be regarded as not having those characteristics, or as not having them in sufficient degree. One part of the literature stresses the *medium-of-exchange*, or means-of-payment, attribute of assets. Another part emphasizes the attributes of assets as a *store of value* (for example, certainty about capital value, degree of ready marketability, and hence "liquidity").

Once attention is focused on the openness of a nation's economy, these familiar difficulties are compounded. With assets and liabilities denominated not only in the home currency but also in one or more foreign currencies, exchange rates and exchange-rate expectations enter the picture. The assets and liabilities denominated in foreign currencies are additional candidates for selection as money and further complicate the debate about the means-of-payment and the store-of-value attributes—the "moneyness"—of money. In defining the public, it now becomes necessary to decide whether some foreign residents should be included (for example, if foreign firms hold liquid assets denominated in the home currency or if they have liquid-asset claims on home financial intermediaries). For the domestic public, there are the questions of how to treat their assets denominated in foreign currencies and their claims on financial intermediaries located abroad. Possible differences between *intraeconomy* and *international* behavioral relationships may suggest a reconsideration of the treatment of the assets and liabilities of financial intermediaries vis-à-vis each other; for example, it could be decided *not* to exclude interbank claims if one of the banks is a foreign bank. Finally, and not least important, it is more difficult to collect data; for example, some of the liability-issuing institutions from which data need to be obtained may be located outside the nation's political jurisdiction.

Current Statistical Practices

What do national governments do about these difficulties when compiling statistics of national money stocks? As can be seen from tables 3-1 through 3-8 at the end of the chapter, countries do not generally agree on what constitutes preferred concepts or appropriate practices. Some countries (for example, France, Italy, and West Germany) include liabilities denominated in foreign currencies; others (for example, Canada) do not. Home-currency liabilities of domestic banks to foreign residents are included in the money stocks of some countries (for example, the United States, Japan, and France) but are excluded in the statistics of other countries (for example, Italy and West Germany). Considerable diversity exists in the treatment of government agencies as holders of money. In one important respect the practices of all major nations are uniform: None of the national money stocks includes liquid-asset claims of domestic residents on financial intermediaries located outside the country. But even this uniformity cannot be attributed to a consensus on the preferred conceptual treatment; it merely reflects the difficulty of obtaining the relevant data.

Differences in institutional environments, in degrees of financial openness, and in amounts of resources devoted to data collection can partly explain the diversity in national statistical practices evident in tables 3-1 through 3-8.[2] But that diversity also reflects a fundamental lack of clarity in monetary theory itself. If monetary economists, responding at the level of concepts and definitions, cannot satisfactorily answer the questions posed at the beginning of the chapter, it is not surprising that government statisticians have still greater difficulties in coping with the same problems at the practical level.

Does It Matter?

The discussion above points out some conceptual ambiguities that have to be resolved when defining the money stock for an open economy. But in the process too much is taken for granted.

2. I have not looked closely into the statistical practices of nations other than the seven shown in the tables, nor am I aware of a secondary source that carefully summarizes the statistical practices of other nations. But an examination of the statistics of other countries would undoubtedly show them to be as diverse as those in the tables. The information in tables 3-1 through 3-6 is partly based on investigations and an unpublished paper by Larry J. Promisel of the Division of International Finance of the Board of Governors of the Federal Reserve System, whose assistance I gratefully acknowledge.

Consider again the case of the German nonbank that maintains a call Eurodollar deposit in a London bank. All but one of the questions asked about that example presumed that the Eurodollar deposit ought to be assigned to the money stock of *some* country—if not to the German then to the U.K. or the U.S. money stock, or perhaps even to the Argentine money stock. But why? And why to just one of the countries? Does an analytical basis exist for assigning an international debtor-creditor relationship to one of the nations involved and *not* to the other?

More important, one should not take for granted even the significance of the questions about the money stock. What difference can it make, for example—to what purposes or ends—whether the call Eurodollar deposit in the illustrative riddle appears in any of the money stocks of Germany, the United Kingdom, the United States, or Argentina? More broadly, is the definition of the money stock in an open economy an issue that ought to matter greatly to monetary economists? If so, why?

One cannot satisfactorily address these last issues until one has answered the logical prior question: Why is it useful, even for a hypothetical closed economy, to distinguish between money and nonmoney financial assets?

Table 3-1. *Definitions of the National Money Stock in Canada*

Selected characteristics of the definition		Type of definition[a]			
		Narrow (M1)	Expanded narrow (M1-B)	Broader (M2)	Broadest (M3)
Home issuers of money and types of liabilities included in money definition	Central bank and government agencies	Currency in circulation outside banks and the Bank of Canada	Same as for M1	Same as for M1	Same as for M1
	Commercial banks (private banking sector)[b]	Demand deposits (net of estimated private sector float)	Deposits included in M1 plus all other chequable deposits	Deposits included in M1-B plus personal nonchequable and fixed term deposits plus nonpersonal nonchequable notice deposits	Deposits included in M2 plus nonpersonal fixed term deposits and bearer term notes plus deposits denominated in foreign currencies
	Other financial intermediaries[c]	Liabilities of intermediaries outside the banking system are not regarded as money	Same as for M1	Same as for M1	Same as for M1
Currency denomination of the money liabilities of home issuers		Canadian dollars only	Canadian dollars only	Canadian dollars only	Canadian dollars and foreign currencies
Home nonbank holders of liquid assets and treatment of their holdings of money-like assets	Individuals, partnerships, and nonfinancial corporations	Included	Included	Included	Included
	Government agencies other than the central bank	Holdings of local and provincial governments are included (holdings of Government of Canada are not included)	Same as for M1	Same as for M1	Same as for M1
	Other financial intermediaries[c]	Included	Included	Included	Included

(continued on next page)

Table 3-1 (continued)

Selected characteristics of the definition	Type of definition[a]				
	Narrow (M1)	Expanded narrow (M1-B)	Broader (M2)	Broadest (M3)	
Treatment of liabilities of home financial intermediaries to foreign economic units	Included if denominated in Canadian dollars (not included if denominated in foreign currencies)	Same as for M1	Same as for M1	Same as for M1	
Treatment of liabilities of foreign financial intermediaries to home economic units	Not included (regardless of type or currency denomination)	Same as for M1	Same as for M1	Same as for M1	

a. Definitions in use in the autumn of 1979. For statistical data, see for example *Bank of Canada Review* (December 1979), pp. S2, S46.
b. The commercial banking system in Canada comprises privately owned banks chartered by Parliament under the Bank Act ("chartered banks").
c. Other financial intermediaries include local credit unions and caisses populaires, trust and mortgage loan companies, investment funds, insurance companies, sales finance and consumer loan companies, and Canadian financial institutions affiliated with foreign banks.

Table 3-2. *Definitions of the National Money Stock in France*

Selected characteristics of the definition	Type of definition[a]		
	Narrow (disponibilités monétaires M_1)	Broader (masse monétaire M_2)	Broadest (ensemble des liquidités M_3)
Home issuers of money and types of liabilities included in money definition — Central bank and government agencies	Coins and notes in circulation outside the banking sector (Banque de France); current accounts at the Banque de France, the Post Office, and the Treasury	Liabilities included in narrow definition plus time deposits at the Treasury	Liabilities included in broader definition plus other liquid liabilities of the Treasury, the Post Office, and other government agencies
Commercial banks (private banking sector)[b]	Sight deposits	Deposits included in narrow definition plus time deposits, certificates of deposit, and savings deposits	Deposits included in broader definition

Other financial intermediaries[c]	Sight deposits and other current accounts	Liabilities included in narrow definition	Liabilities included in narrow definition plus other liquid and short-term liabilities (for example, savings deposits)
Currency denomination of the money liabilities of home issuers	French francs and foreign currencies	French francs and foreign currencies	French francs and foreign currencies
Home nonbank holders of liquid assets and treatment of their holdings of money-like assets			
Individuals, partnerships, and nonfinancial corporations	Included	Included	Included
Government agencies other than the central bank	Included	Same as for narrow definition	Same as for narrow definition
Other financial intermediaries[c]	Some may be included	Same as for narrow definition	Same as for narrow definition
Treatment of liabilities of home financial intermediaries to foreign economic units	Liabilities to foreign nonbanks are included (liabilities to foreign banks are not included)	Same as for narrow definition	Same as for narrow definition
Treatment of liabilities of foreign financial intermediaries to home economic units	Not included (regardless of type and currency denomination)	Same as for narrow definition	Same as for narrow definition

a. Definitions in use in autumn of 1979. For statistical data, see for example Banque de France, *Bulletin Trimestriel*, no. 33 (December 1979), tableau statistiques I: 1–4; Institut National de la Statistique et des Etudes Economiques, *Bulletin Mensuel de Statistique* (January 1980), p. 54.

b. The banking sector includes banks "inscribed" by the Conseil National du Credit (deposit banks, merchant banks [banques d'affaires], and long- and medium-term credit banks) plus banking institutions with "special legal status" whose activities are concentrated in particular sectors (for example, popular banks [extending loans to small and medium-sized firms], agricultural credit institutions [caisses de crédit agricole], and the Banque Française du Commerce Exterieur).

c. Financial intermediaries other than banks proper include savings banks (caisses d'épargne) and finance companies and other financial enterprises (établissements financiers).

Table 3-3. *Definitions of the National Money Stock in the Federal Republic of Germany*

Selected characteristics of the definition		*Type of definition* [a]		
		Narrow (money stock M1)	*Broader* (money stock M2)	*Broadest* (money stock M3)
Home issuers of money and types of liabilities included in money definition	Central bank and government agencies	Currency in circulation (excluding commercial banks' cash balances but including DM notes and coins held abroad); sight deposits at the Bundesbank	Same as for M1	Same as for M1
	Commercial banks (private banking sector) [b]	Sight deposits	Deposits included in M1 plus time deposits and funds borrowed for less than 4 years	Deposits included in M2 plus savings deposits at statutory notice
	Other financial intermediaries [c]	Liabilities of financial institutions outside the banking sector are not regarded as money	Same as for M1	Same as for M1
Currency denomination of the money liabilities of home issuers		Deutschemark and foreign currencies	Deutschemark and foreign currencies	Deutschemark and foreign currencies

Home nonbank holders of liquid assets and treatment of their holdings of money-like assets			
Individuals, partnerships, and nonfinancial corporations	Included	Included	Included
Government agencies other than the central bank	Included[d]	Same as for M1	Same as for M1
Other financial intermediaries[c]	Included	Included	Included
Treatment of liabilities of home financial intermediaries to foreign economic units	Not included (regardless of type and currency denomination)	Same as for M1	Same as for M1
Treatment of liabilities of foreign financial intermediaries to home economic units	Not included (regardless of type and currency denomination)	Same as for M1	Same as for M1

a. Definitions in use in the autumn of 1979. For statistical data, see for example *Monthly Report of the Deutsche Bundesbank*, vol. 31 (December 1979), statistical section, pp. 2–5.

b. The definition of the banking system includes most financial intermediaries doing business in the Federal Republic of Germany. The predominant type of bank is the "all-purpose" commercial bank (Universalbank), which engages in all types of banking business. In addition to commercial banks (including German branches of foreign banks), the banking system includes central giro institutions, savings banks, credit cooperatives, mortgage banks, installment sales financing institutions, banks with special functions, and postal giro and postal savings bank offices. In nations other than Germany, many of these latter types of institutions are regarded as nonbank financial intermediaries outside the banking system.

c. Financial intermediaries outside the banking system include building and loan associations, insurance companies, and social security funds.

d. Holdings of government-sector institutions at the Bundesbank are not included.

Table 3-4. Definitions of the National Money Stock in Japan

Selected characteristics of the definition		Type of definition[a]		
		Narrow (money M1)	Broader (money and quasimoney M2)	Broadest (M3)
Home issuers of money and types of liabilities included in money definition	Central bank and government agencies	Coins and notes in circulation outside the banking sector (Bank of Japan)	Same as for narrow definition	Liabilities included in narrow definition plus postal savings accounts
	Commercial banks (private banking sector)[b]	"Deposit money"[c]	Deposits included in narrow definition plus other types of deposits ("quasimoney")[d,e]	Deposits included in M2 plus trust accounts
	Other financial intermediaries[f]	"Deposit money" liabilities of mutual loan and savings banks, credit associations, the Norinchukin Bank, and the Shoko Chukin Bank[c]	Liabilities included in narrow definition plus other types of deposits ("quasimoney") at mutual loan and savings banks, credit associations, the Norinchukin Bank, and the Shoko Chukin Bank[d,e]	Liabilities included in M2 plus deposits at agricultural cooperatives, fishery cooperatives, credit cooperatives, and labor credit associations
Currency denomination of the money liabilities of home issuers		Japanese yen only	Japanese yen and foreign currencies	Japanese yen and foreign currencies

Home nonbank holders of liquid assets and treatment of their holdings of money-like assets			
Individuals, partnerships, and nonfinancial corporations	Included	Included	Included
Government agencies other than the central bank	Holdings of local governments are included	Same as for narrow definition	Same as for narrow definition
Other financial intermediaries[f]	Some may be included	Same as for narrow definition	Same as for narrow definition
Treatment of liabilities of home financial intermediaries to foreign economic units	Not included	Liabilities to foreign nonbanks are included (liabilities to foreign banks and foreign official institutions are not included)	Same as for M2
Treatment of liabilities of foreign financial intermediaries to home economic units	Not included (regardless of type and currency denomination)	Same as for narrow definition	Same as for narrow definition

a. Definitions in use in autumn of 1979. For statistical data, see for example Bank of Japan, *Economic Statistics Monthly*, vol. 54 (December 1979), pp. 15–24.

b. The banking sector includes city banks, regional banks, trust banks, and long-term credit banks.

c. "Deposit money" is defined as the total of demand deposits (current deposits, ordinary deposits, deposits at notice, special deposits, and deposits for tax payments) in private and public deposits minus checks and bills held by financial institutions whose liabilities are included in the money definitions. Trust accounts at banks are excluded.

d. "Quasimoney" is defined as the total of private and public deposits other than demand deposits. In the case of mutual loan and savings banks, it also includes installments.

e. Financial intermediaries were authorized to issue certificates of deposit in May 1979. The Bank of Japan thus began in 1979 to publish a series for "M2 plus certificates of deposit."

f. Other financial intermediaries include mutual loan and savings banks, credit associations, other financial institutions specialized in dealing with small business (for example, credit cooperatives and the Shoko Chukin Bank), financial institutions specialized in dealing with agriculture, forestry, and fishery (for example, agricultural cooperatives and the Norinchukin Bank), insurance companies, and securities finance companies.

Table 3-5. *Definitions of the National Money Stock in Italy*

Selected characteristics of the definition		Type of definition[a]		
		Narrow (liquidita' primaria M1)	*Broader* (attività liquide del pubblico M2)	*Broadest* (M3)
Home issuers of money and types of liabilities included in money definition	Central bank and government agencies	Coins and notes in circulation (Banca d'Italia); current accounts held at the Banca d'Italia and the Treasury; current accounts held at Post Office Savings Fund[b]	Liabilities included in narrow definition plus savings accounts and postal certificates at Post Office Savings Fund[b]	Liabilities included in M2 plus short-term Treasury securities
	Commercial banks (private banking sector)[c]	Current accounts	Liabilities included in narrow definition plus savings and time deposits	Same as for M2
	Other financial intermediaries[d]	Liabilities of intermediaries outside the banking system are not regarded as money	Same as for narrow definition	Same as for narrow definition
Currency denomination of the money liabilities of home issuers		Italian lire and foreign currencies	Italian lire and foreign currencies	Italian lire and foreign currencies

Home nonbank holders of liquid assets and treatment of their holdings of money-like assets		
Individuals, partnerships, and nonfinancial corporations	Included	Included
Government agencies other than the central bank	Included except for national government deposits at the Post Office	Same as for narrow definition
Other financial intermediaries[d]	Some may be included	Same as for narrow definition
Treatment of liabilities of home financial intermediaries to foreign economic units	Not included (regardless of type and currency denomination)	Same as for narrow definition
Treatment of liabilities of foreign financial intermediaries to home economic units	Not included (regardless of type and currency denomination)	Same as for narrow definition

a. Definitions in use in the autumn of 1979. For statistical data, see for example Banca d'Italia, *Bollettino*, vol. 34 (September 1979), pp. 158–61.

b. The Cassa Depositi e Prestiti (Central Post Office Savings Fund) is operated as a special department of the Treasury. It collects savings through savings accounts and postal savings certificates but also accepts current accounts (primarily from enterprises and public organizations).

c. The banking system consists of public law banks, banks of national interest, ordinary credit banks, popular cooperative banks, savings and pledge banks, rural and handicraft banks, and the central institutions that serve the smaller and specialized banks (for example, the Credit Institute for Savings Banks, the Central Institute for Popular Banks, and the Credit Institute for Rural and Handicraft Banks).

d. Other financial intermediaries include special credit institutions that specialize in medium- and long-term lending (Istituti di Credito Speciale), insurance companies, and social insurance institutes.

Table 3-6. *Definitions of the National Money Stock in the United Kingdom*

Selected characteristics of the definition		Type of definition[a]		
		Narrow (money stock M1)	Broader (money stock sterling M3)	Broadest (money stock M3)
Home issuers of money and types of liabilities included in money definition	Central bank and government agencies	Notes and coin in circulation with the public (liability of the Issue Department of the Bank of England)	Same as for M1	Same as for M1
	Commercial banks (private banking sector)[b]	Sight deposits and liabilities[c]	Deposits included in M1 plus other sterling deposits[c]	Deposits included in sterling M3 plus deposits denominated in foreign currencies[c]
	Other financial intermediaries[d]	Liabilities of financial institutions outside the banking sector are not regarded as money	Same as for M1	Same as for M1
Currency denomination of the money liabilities of home issuers		Pounds sterling only	Pounds sterling only	Pounds sterling and foreign currencies
	Individuals, partnerships, and nonfinancial corporations	Included	Included	Included

Home nonbank holders of liquid assets and treatment of their holdings of money-like assets			
Government agencies other than the central bank	Not included	Sight and other deposits of central government, local authorities, and public corporations are included	Same as for sterling M3
Other financial intermediaries[d]	Included	Included	Included
Treatment of liabilities of home financial intermediaries to foreign economic units	Not included (regardless of type and currency denomination)	Same as for M1	Same as for M1
Treatment of liabilities of foreign financial intermediaries to home economic units	Not included (regardless of type and currency denomination)	Same as for M1	Same as for M1

a. Definitions in use in the autumn of 1979. For statistical data, see for example *Bank of England Quarterly Bulletin*, vol. 19 (December 1979), statistical annex, tables 11.1–11.3; Central Statistical Office, *Financial Statistics*, no. 212 (December 1979), section 7.

b. The banking sector in the United Kingdom includes British banks (London clearing banks, Scottish clearing banks, Northern Ireland banks, accepting houses, other British banks), overseas banks, consortium banks, specialized banking institutions that make up the discount market, and the National Girobank.

c. The banks' gross figures for deposits and advances are adjusted to allow for sterling transit items. It is assumed that 60 percent of the total value of transit debit items less transit credit items affects deposits and hence this amount is deducted from gross deposits.

d. "Other financial institutions" in the United Kingdom—not considered part of the banking sector—include building societies, trustee savings banks, finance houses, insurance companies, superannuation funds, unit trusts, investment trusts, and property unit trusts.

Table 3-7. Definitions of the National Money Stock in the United States, 1979 and Earlier Years

Selected characteristics of the definition		Type of definition[a]			
		Narrow (M1)	Broad, banks only (old M2)	Broad (old M3)	Very broad (M5)
Home issuers of money and types of liabilities included in money definition	Central bank and government agencies	Currency in circulation outside the Treasury, Federal Reserve, and vaults of commercial banks	Same as for M1	Same as for M1	Same as for M1
	Commercial banks (private banking sector)[b]	Demand deposits (adjusted to exclude interbank demand deposits, cash items in process of collection, and Federal Reserve float)	Deposits included in M1 plus savings deposits plus time deposits other than large negotiable certificates of deposit	Same deposits included in old M2	Deposits included in old M3 plus large negotiable time certificates of deposit
	Other financial intermediaries[c]	None included	None included	Savings and time deposits at nonbank thrift institutions (savings and loan associations, mutual savings banks, and credit unions)	Same deposits included in old M3

	U.S. dollars[d]	U.S. dollars[d]	U.S. dollars[d]	U.S. dollars[d]	U.S. dollars[d]
Currency denomination of the money liabilities of home issuers					
Home nonbank holders of liquid assets and treatment of their holdings of money-like assets — Individuals, partnerships, and nonfinancial corporations	Included	Included	Included	Included	Included
Government agencies other than the central bank	Holdings of state and local governments are included (holdings of federal government agencies are excluded)	Same as for M1	Same as for M1	Same as for M1	Same as for M1
Other financial intermediaries[c]	Included	Included	Included	Included[e]	Included[e]
Treatment of liabilities of home financial intermediaries to foreign economic units	Included[d]	Included[d]	Included[d]	Included[d]	Included[d]
Treatment of liabilities of foreign financial intermediaries to home economic units	Not included (regardless of type or currency denomination)	Same as for M1	Same as for M1	Same as for M1	Same as for M1

a. For statistical data, see for example, *Federal Reserve Bulletin*, vol. 65 (December 1979), p. A14.

b. Commercial banks include both member banks of the Federal Reserve System and nonmember banks.

c. Other financial intermediaries include savings and loan associations, mutual savings banks, credit unions, money market mutual funds, other mutual funds, finance companies, insurance companies, and brokerage and securities firms.

d. Banks and nonbank financial intermediaries in the United States generally have not issued liabilities denominated in foreign currencies. Thus the monetary authorities in the United States have so far not been confronted with the decision whether or not to include liabilities denominated in foreign currencies in definitions of the U.S. money stock.

e. For this definition, nonbank thrift institutions both hold money (their liquid-asset claims on commercial banks) and issue money (their deposit liabilities to individuals, partnerships, nonfinancial corporations, and state and local governments).

Table 3-8. Definitions of the National Money Stock in the United States, 1980[a]

Selected characteristics of the definition		Narrow (M1-A)	Expanded narrow (M1-B)	Broad (new M2)	Very broad (new M3)	Liquid assets (L)
				Type of definition: 1980[b]		
Home issuers of money and types of liabilities included in money definition	Central bank and government agencies	Currency in circulation outside the Treasury, Federal Reserve, and vaults of commercial banks	Same as for M1-A	Same as for M1-A	Same as for M1-A	Liabilities included in M1-A plus U.S. Treasury savings bonds and liquid marketable debt of the U.S. Treasury
	Commercial banks (private banking sector)[c]	Demand deposits (adjusted to exclude interbank demand deposits, cash items in process of collection, and Federal Reserve float)	Deposits included in M1-A plus other checkable deposits[d]	Deposits included in M1-B plus savings deposits, small time deposits, and overnight security repurchase agreements[e]	Liabilities included in new M2 plus large time deposits and term security repurchase agreements	Liabilities included in new M3 plus bankers acceptances
	Other financial intermediaries[f]	None included	Demand deposits and other types of checkable deposits[d]	Deposits included in M1-B plus savings deposits, small time deposits, and money market mutual fund shares[e]	Liabilities included in new M2 plus large time deposits and term security repurchase agreements issued by savings and loan associations	Liabilities included in new M3 plus commercial paper[g]
Currency denomination of the money liabilities of home issuers		U.S. dollars[h]	U.S. dollars[h]	U.S. dollars[h]	U.S. dollars[h]	U.S. dollars[h]
Home nonbank holders of liquid	Individuals, partnerships, and nonfinancial corporations	Included	Included	Included	Included	Included

assets and treatment of their holdings of money-like assets					
Government agencies other than the central bank	Holdings of state and local governments are included (holdings of federal government agencies are not included)	Same as for M1-A	Same as for M1-A	Same as for M1-A	Same as for M1-A
Other financial intermediaries[f]	Included	Partially included[i]	Not included[j]	Same as for new M2	Same as for new M2
Treatment of liabilities of home financial intermediaries to foreign economic units	Liabilities to foreign nonbanks are included (liabilities to foreign official institutions and foreign commercial banks are not included)	Same as for M1-A	Same as for M1-A	Same as for M1-A	Same as for M1-A
Treatment of liabilities of foreign financial intermediaries to home economic units	Not included (regardless of type or currency denomination)	Same as for M1-A	Includes overnight Eurodollar deposit liabilities of Caribbean branches of U.S. banks to U.S. nonbank residents	Same as for new M2	Includes all maturities of Eurodollar deposit liabilities of foreign banks (including branches of U.S. banks) to U.S. nonbank residents[k]

a. In February 1980 the Board of Governors of the Federal Reserve System announced major changes in the official definitions of U.S. monetary aggregates. For background discussion and further details about the changes, see *Improving the Monetary Aggregates* (Board of Governors of the Federal Reserve System, 1976); "A Proposal for Redefining the Monetary Aggregates," *Federal Reserve Bulletin*, vol. 65 (January 1979), pp. 13–42; and "The Redefined Monetary Aggregates," ibid., vol. 66 (February 1980), pp. 97–114.

b. For statistical data, see for example, *Federal Reserve Bulletin*, vol. 66 (March 1980), p. A-14.

c. Commercial banks include both member banks of the Federal Reserve System and nonmember banks.

d. "Checkable" deposits other than demand deposits include NOW accounts (negotiated orders of withdrawal), ATS accounts (authorizing automatic transfers from savings to demand accounts), and credit union share draft balances.

e. "Small" time deposits are those issued in denominations of less than $100,000.

f. Other financial intermediaries include savings and loan associations, mutual savings banks, credit unions, money market mutual funds, other mutual funds, finance companies, insurance companies, and brokerage and securities firms.

g. Commercial paper is issued not only by finance companies acting as intermediaries but also directly by nonfinancial corporations.

h. Banks and nonbank financial intermediaries in the United States generally have not issued liabilities denominated in foreign currencies. Thus the monetary authorities in the United States have so far not been confronted with the decision whether or not to include liabilities denominated in foreign currencies in definitions of the U.S. money stock.

i. M1-B excludes an estimate of the amount of demand deposits held at commercial banks by thrift institutions and other nonbank financial intermediaries that is used in servicing the checkable deposits issued by the nonbank intermediaries themselves. The estimated amount of this adjustment was negligible as of December 1979, owing to the still small size of checkable deposits issued by the nonbank intermediaries.

j. New M2 excludes all demand deposits held at commercial banks by thrift institutions and other nonbank financial intermediaries. This "consolidation adjustment" assumes that the nonbank intermediaries hold demand deposits at commercial banks only for the purpose of servicing their own liabilities (checkable, savings, and time deposits).

k. In practice, timely data are available only for the liabilities to U.S. nonbank residents of foreign banks located in the United Kingdom and in Canada.

PART ONE

Monetary Aggregates in a Closed Economy

CHAPTER FOUR

Why Do We Need a Concept and Definition of Money?

IT IS COMMONLY assumed that there are one or more purposes for which a concept and definition of money are needed. But that assumption deserves scrutiny. This chapter therefore examines possible reasons for singling out a particular collection of financial assets and designating that collection as money.

Because economic theories prominently feature something called money, it is tempting to argue that an empirical counterpart is needed for that reason alone. Taken by itself, however, such an argument has little merit. It must be demonstrated that these theories use a concept of money for a convincing purpose and that they contain, implicitly if not explicitly, information on how the empirical counterparts should be constructed.[1]

It is helpful at the outset to distinguish between two categories of reasons for wanting a concept and definition of money. First, suppose it is necessary to gather various financial assets into a bundle to analyze accurately some aspect of the behavior of economic units. In that case specifying the relevant bundle theoretically and defining an empirical counterpart serves a *descriptive* purpose. Various aspects of behavior might command analytical attention. Accordingly, several different descriptive bundles might need to be specified. Each could be labeled *money*, though at the risk of semantic confusion. Second, suppose it is asserted that some aggregate bundle of financial assets can—and should—play a central role in the conduct of monetary policy. Then a *prescriptive* purpose is served by specifying and empirically defining that bundle. It, too, might be labeled *money*, but again at the risk of semantic confusion.

The difference between descriptive and prescriptive concepts of money corresponds roughly to the distinction between positive and normative economics. The motive for using a descriptive concept is to analyze how people actually behave;

---

1. The literature bearing on this subject is immense. A basic source is Milton Friedman and Anna Jacobson Schwartz, *Monetary Statistics of the United States: Estimates, Sources, Methods*, Studies in Business Cycles 20 (New York: National Bureau of Economic Research, 1970), particularly pt. 1, pp. 89–198, "The Definition of Money." An interesting discussion of historical usage is presented in J. C. Gilbert, "The Demand for Money: The Development of an Economic Concept," *Journal of Political Economy*, vol. 61 (April 1953), pp. 144–59. A. P. Andrew, "What Ought to Be Called Money?," *Quarterly Journal of Economics*, vol. 13 (January 1899), pp. 219–27, is a vivid reminder that the definition of money has interested economists for a long time.

Two of the most helpful articles on the basic analytical issues are J. R. Hicks, "A Suggestion for Simplifying the Theory of Money," *Economica*, New Series, vol. 2 (February 1935), pp. 1–19, reprinted in American Economic Association, *Readings in Monetary Theory* (Blakiston, 1951), pp. 13–32; and James Tobin, "Money, Capital, and Other Stores of Value," *American Economic Review*, vol. 51 (May 1961, *Papers and Proceedings, 1960*), pp. 26–37. For a concise summary of the standard view of the functions of money, see Tibor Scitovsky, *Money and the Balance of Payments* (Rand McNally, 1969), pp. 1–11.

normative value judgments, if not absent, at least play a secondary role in the analysis. When a prescriptive concept is articulated, however, the purpose is ineluctably associated with recommendations for how people—for example, policymakers—*should* behave. The distinction between descriptive and prescriptive concepts, like the distinction between positive and normative economics, can be challenged by philosophers. It can nonetheless prove helpful when, as in the present case, a single word has multiple connotations and the subject area is controversial.

The discussion that follows identifies some descriptive reasons for wanting a concept and definition of money and then emphasizes that the assets typically labeled *money* for descriptive purposes cannot serve as an instrument of the central bank's monetary policy. A possible policy-oriented motive for defining money is identified. The chapter then concludes by pointing out the interrelationships of such a prescriptive concept and the concepts used for descriptive analysis.

Descriptive Concepts and Definitions

One potential justification for a descriptive concept emphasizes the attributes of various financial assets as mediums of exchange, or means of payment. Economists sympathetic to this emphasis give analytical prominence to such phenomena as the costs of carrying out transactions and the lack of synchronization of payments and receipts. The following proposition, which can be labeled the *means-of-payment behavioral hypothesis,* provides a succinct statement of this line of thinking:

(4-A) **Microeconomic units differentiate in their asset-holding behavior between those assets that are and those that are not widely accepted as a means of payment by other economic units.**

Suppose proposition 4-A is believed to be an accurate generalization about microeconomic behavior. It is then a short step further to argue that it is important when studying macroeconomic behavior to construct an aggregate composed of financial assets having a high degree of acceptability as a means of payment. Such an aggregate will then play a significant role in macrotheoretical explanations of asset holding. It might be identified as a separate asset in the financial sectors of econometric models of the economy. In other words, such a means-of-payment aggregate will be a regular, and possibly important, feature of analytical descriptions of macroeconomic financial behavior.

A second potential justification for a descriptive concept of money may be labeled the *liquid-assets behavioral hypothesis.* It focuses on the "liquidity" of assets—in particular, attributes such as ready marketability and certainty of nominal value. Economists sympathetic to this emphasis advance the following proposition:

(4-B) **Microeconomic units differentiate in their asset-holding behavior between those assets that have a high degree of liquidity and those that do not.**

For present purposes there is no need to try to provide a precise definition of liquidity; suppose merely that some definition is offered. Suppose further that proposition 4-B is judged to be an accurate characterization of the behavior of microeconomic units. In that event, the hypothesis, self-evidently, has important implications for economists' analyses of macroeconomic behavior. In particular, economists' theories and empirical research will give prominent attention to one or more collections of those financial assets deemed to have a high degree of liquidity.

The means-of-payment attributes of various financial assets and their attributes as stores of value are the two major topics discussed in the literature on the definition of money. A third is concerned with the role of money as a numeraire, or unit of account. In modern economies with highly developed financial sectors, however, there is no unit-of-account justification—no reason separable from the means-of-payment and the liquid-assets behavioral hypotheses—for specifying a descriptive concept of money. This third topic in the literature is therefore ignored in what follows.[2]

Unlike propositions 4-A and 4-B, which have been called a priori approaches to defining money, a third possible justification for specifying a descriptive concept eschews deductive theorizing. This approach may be labeled the *hypothesis of observed empirical regularity* and summarized as follows:

(4-C) **The collective behavior of microeconomic units in an economy exhibits a strong empirical regularity between an aggregate bundle of particular financial assets and certain other macroeconomic magnitudes (for example, the price level). The theoretical explanation for this observed behavior need not be specified; but the existence of the regularity may be inductively inferred from ex post economic data.**

Ignore for the moment the issue of whether available empirical evidence supports this third hypothesis. The point to note here is that if proposition 4-C is supported by evidence, it can justify empirical delineation of the particular financial macroaggregate and its use in analytical descriptions of macroeconomic behavior.[3]

In sum, three different descriptive hypotheses can be identified. Each embodies a strong assertion about economic behavior, and thus each can stand on its own as a potential justification for the construction and use of a specified financial macroaggregate.[4]

From the standpoint of semantic clarity, it would be preferable to avoid attaching the protean label *money* to any of the three aggregates. An aggregate of assets with high degrees of acceptability as a means of payment could more accurately be described by a word like *media*. *Liquid assets* would be a clearer term for an

2. A modern exchange economy is unimaginable without prices quoted in terms of some common unit of account and without at least one asset that serves as a widely accepted medium of exchange and generalized store of value. If one is concerned with theoretically rationalizing the transition from a barter economy to an exchange economy in which a single asset serves as both medium of exchange and unit of account, it is necessary to say more about the unit-of-account attributes of that asset. However, once the subject of interest is an economy having a wide variety of financial assets fixed in nominal magnitude (several of which have a high degree of acceptability as a means of payment and all of which serve as a generalized store of value), there is no separate unit-of-account function that distinguishes any one of these assets from the others. Note also that it is not even logically necessary for the economy's unit of account to be identified with one of these financial assets; see, for example, the discussion in Don Patinkin, *Money, Interest, and Prices: An Integration of Money and Value Theory*, 2d ed. (Harper and Row, 1965), pp. 13–17. For analysis of the pros and cons of using the same asset as both a medium of exchange and the unit of account, see Jürg Niehans, *The Theory of Money* (Johns Hopkins University Press, 1978).

3. For criticism of the a priori approaches and advocacy of this third approach, see Friedman and Schwartz, *Monetary Statistics of the United States*, especially pp. 137–98.

4. The three are not necessarily mutually exclusive.

aggregate derived from the hypothesis emphasizing the liquidity attributes of assets. The third type of aggregate might be designated *NAP* ("not a priori") *money* to distinguish it from the other two.

But habits of associating the word *money* with each of the three types of aggregates are deeply entrenched. A recommendation to abandon *money* for alternative terms would justifiably be dismissed as quixotic. The best that can be hoped for is that all who use the three concepts are aware of the problem and avoid confusion in their analyses.

Although each of the three hypotheses identified above leads to a conclusion that descriptive analysis requires a concept and definition of money, empirical evidence could in principle show that all three hypotheses are false. For completeness, therefore, consider an agnostic position:

(4-D)   **No financial asset or bundle of assets has qualitatively greater significance than any other at either the microeconomic or macroeconomic level; adequate descriptive analysis must consider economic agents' demands for and supplies of all major types of assets (and liabilities) and should not be preoccupied with any one particular aggregation scheme.**

The reader can better appreciate the force of the agnostic view by trying to supply an answer to the following hypothetical problem. Imagine that the word *money* is abolished by legislative fiat and that all members of society cooperate by refraining from using the word. More precisely, suppose that the language used in ordinary discourse refers only to particular assets (for example, "You will have to pay me either in currency or with a certified check"; or "How large is your time deposit account at your bank?"). Suppose further that, when it is necessary to refer to aggregations of particular assets, the only terms used are ones such as *wealth, financial assets, funds, liquid assets,* and *media.* Suppose finally that the name of a currency unit is used whenever occasions arise to refer to nominal values or when a unit-of-account word is required (for example, "How many dollars do I need to buy that automobile?" or "The dollar value of GNP is $1.3 trillion"). In such a world, is there any reason for ordinary people or economists to invent a new concept and a new word to replace the term *money?*

Money: Not a Policy Instrument

Before proceeding to a possible prescriptive rationale for a concept and definition of money, it is essential to understand that money in any of its three descriptive incarnations is an intermediate economic variable from the perspective of policymakers.

To make explicit a chain of reasoning that is usually only implicit in discussions of the conduct of monetary policy, consider the logic of the following propositions:

(4-E)   **The national government, having legal jurisdiction over various types of policy instruments, should take policy actions (and, when appropriate, refrain from taking policy actions) to influence ultimate-target variables deemed by the nation's citizens to be important to their well-being.**

(4-F)   The ultimate-target variables should include (for example) the price level, the volume of output, and the level of employment. Other things being equal, policy actions should be conducted so as to keep the price level stable, the rate of economic growth rapid, and the level of employment high; to the extent that these goals are incompatible, the policymakers should have explicit preferences as to how to trade them off against one another.

(4-G)   The central bank, having proximate jurisdiction over the instruments of monetary policy, should be governed by the two preceding injunctions no less so than the fiscal authority and any other agencies with responsibilities for national economic policy; the use of the instruments of monetary policy and fiscal policy should be integrated in a coherent macroeconomic policy.

(4-H)   The variables that are potential instruments of monetary policy include (for example) the interest rate charged to borrowers at the discount window of the central bank, reserve-requirement ratios imposed by the central bank on deposit liabilities of financial intermediaries, central-bank holdings of various marketable securities, and various liabilities of the central bank such as the quantity of commercial-bank reserves.

(4-I)   Policy actions, including changes in the instrument settings for monetary policy, may have powerful effects on the ultimate-target variables.

(4-J)   It is, and should be, a matter of great interest to appraise the nature and strength of the effects of monetary-policy actions and to understand the channels through which they occur.

Of the six propositions in this sequence, two—4-H and 4-I—are merely descriptive. The other four propositions are manifestly prescriptive. The prescriptive content notwithstanding, a majority of policymakers and economists probably subscribe to all these propositions. Some controversy can be generated by 4-G, but even that proposition is sufficiently mildly worded to warrant the support of many proponents of a politically independent central bank.

For the purposes of this chapter, the significant point about the chain of reasoning summarized in 4-E through 4-J is that there is nowhere any mention of money. Subscribing to the argument that *monetary policy* is important does not require having a view one way or another about *money*.

Proposition 4-H emphasizes that the instruments of monetary policy are such things as discount rates, reserve-requirement ratios, and asset and liability items on the central bank's own balance sheet. A deeply embedded tradition in conventional macroeconomic theory, however, is to simplify greatly the representation of the economy's financial sectors. Thus that theory typically specifies an aggregative variable M, refers to it as money, and assumes that M can be and is exogenously determined by the policymakers. In the theory, money plays the role of an instrument; that is, the central bank can precisely fix the stock of M from one moment to the next.

To take the most prominent illustration, the standard textbook *IS-LM* models include the variable *money* as if M itself is the actual instrument by which the central bank influences the economy. This conceptual simplification goes at least as far back in the literature as Keynes's *General Theory* and Hicks's expositional synthesis.[5] Philip Cagan's essay on the use of money in open-market operations and William Poole's paper on optimal choice of monetary policy instruments follow the same tradition.[6]

Suppose proposition 4-H could be legitimately reworded so as to make money an instrument of monetary policy. Then the six propositions, 4-E through 4-J, would constitute a sufficient prescriptive justification for having a concept money and for defining an empirical counterpart. Changes in the money stock would, unambiguously, constitute policy actions. The empirical counterpart of M would be constructed so as to include only those financial assets the supplies of which were directly and precisely manipulated by the central bank.

But proposition 4-H *cannot* be validly reworded to include money. In all its current conventional definitions, the outstanding stock of money at any given time is strongly affected by the behavior of private economic units—both financial intermediaries and the nonfinancial public—as well as by the policy actions of the central bank. If the central bank chooses to do so, it can undoubtedly have a powerful influence on the stock of money by diligently adjusting its actual instruments. The greater the number of short-run periods over which the value of the money stock is averaged, the greater the degree of control that the central bank can exert over that average value. But the central bank's control can never be precise. It cannot fix the stock of money exactly from one short-run period to the next. From the perspective of policymakers in the central bank, money is inevitably an *endogenous intermediate variable;* it cannot be an instrument.

Whatever merits it may have as a simplification, the convention of using the variable M as a policy instrument in macroeconomic theories permits a crucial ambiguity to exist about the role of money in those theories. One cannot tell if M is included solely as a simplified representation of the instruments of monetary policy, or whether, in addition, M is included because it has other roles to play—for example, as a variable important in its own right in explaining the economic behavior of asset holders.

For the purposes of this book and, in my view, for the purposes of monetary economics generally, it is necessary to have a theoretical framework that more faithfully represents the instruments of monetary policy actually used by central banks in the real world. Such a framework forces analysts to treat money as an intermediate endogenous variable and strips M of its raison d'être in the theory as a policy instrument. If an aggregate called money is to be incorporated in a theory at all, a separate theoretical purpose is required.[7]

5. J. R. Hicks, "Mr. Keynes and the 'Classics': A Suggested Interpretation," *Economica,* New Series, vol. 5 (April 1937), pp. 147–59, reprinted in Richard S. Thorn, ed., *Monetary Theory and Policy: Major Contributions to Contemporary Thought* (Praeger, 1976), pp. 297–309.

6. Philip Cagan, "Why Do We Use Money in Open Market Operations?" *Journal of Political Economy,* vol. 66 (February 1958), pp. 34–46; William Poole, "Optimal Choice of Monetary Policy Instruments in a Simple Stochastic Macro Model," *Quarterly Journal of Economics,* vol. 84 (May 1970), pp. 197–216.

7. Many years ago James Tobin noted the disadvantages of treating money in macroeconomic theories as though it is an exogenously determined instrument of monetary policy; see "Money, Capital, and Other Stores of Value." Others who have stressed the point include Roger N. Waud, "Proximate Targets and Monetary Policy," *Economic Journal,* vol. 83 (March 1973), pp. 1–20; and Benjamin M. Friedman, "Targets, Instruments, and Indicators of Monetary Policy," *Journal of Monetary Economics,* vol. 1 (October 1975), pp. 443–73.

A Prescriptive Motive

Suppose an analyst's overriding interest is to study the impacts of the instruments of monetary policy on ultimate-target variables. Suppose further that the analyst wants to avoid the ambiguity inherent in treating money as an instrument of monetary policy. Will the analyst still have a definite need—a prescriptive justification—for a concept and definition of money?

Consider two additional propositions:

(4-K)   **There exists for the economy as a whole a particular aggregate bundle of financial assets reliably linked through one or more behavioral relationships to the ultimate-target variables of national economic policy; knowledge about these relationships is markedly less uncertain than knowledge about the other macroeconomic behavioral relationships constituting the structure of the economy.**

(4-L)   **Policymakers are able to adjust the actual instruments of monetary policy so as closely to control that same aggregate of financial assets.**

By themselves, 4-K and 4-L are primarily descriptive assertions about the economic system.[8] Suppose analysts believe these two propositions are supported by empirical evidence and also subscribe to propositions 4-E through 4-J. They might then jump to yet another proposition as a seemingly natural next step:

(4-M)   **Policymakers should conduct monetary policy by (1) setting a target time path for that same aggregate of financial assets, and then (2) seeking to keep the actual stock of the aggregate as close as possible to the target path through diligent adjustment of the instruments of monetary policy.**

Clearly, 4-M is a prescriptive recommendation. Whether it is a conclusion that follows logically from the premises in 4-K and 4-L is an issue that requires analysis in later chapters.

The approach to conducting monetary policy recommended in this last proposition can be characterized as an *intermediate-target strategy*, because the financial aggregate that serves as the proximate focus of policy actions is an intermediate variable.

The three propositions 4-K through 4-M, together with 4-E through 4-J, provide a potentially defensible response to the question: Why is a definition of money needed? If analysts believe proposition 4-K is true, they have a clear motive for trying to locate that bundle of financial assets for which the proposition holds. If they also believe 4-L is true, they might think that the central bank should, so to speak, operate through the aggregate bundle in its efforts to influence ultimate-target variables. In turn, such reasoning could lead analysts to jump to the conclusion that the aggregate bundle should be used as the key intermediate variable in an intermediate-target approach to the conduct of monetary policy.

It would be possible to carry out whatever research is required to identify the collection of financial assets referred to in propositions 4-K through 4-M without ever using the term *money*. Moreover, the central bank could try to control the

8. The mere designation of certain magnitudes as ultimate-target variables, however, presupposes normative choices (in other words, preferences and a loss function).

financial aggregate as a means of influencing the ultimate-target variables without any need of the word *money*. Given the assumptions made, however, the analyst and the central bank would have a valid reason for specifying the particular aggregate. And, apart from considerations of semantic clarity, there would be no reason to object if *money* is the label given to the intermediate-target variable.

Propositions 4-K through 4-M contain the essential elements of the answer that many monetary economists will give if asked why they believe it useful to employ a concept and definition of money in the conduct of monetary policy. Such a response is especially likely to come from economists who consider themselves "monetarist" in persuasion. Yet advocacy of an intermediate-target rationale for money is by no means restricted to monetarists.[9]

Interrelationships of Descriptive and Prescriptive Rationales

Thus, as seen above, four possible rationales for defining money can be identified. Each is potentially defensible in the sense that it provides a logically consistent motive for constructing a specific bundle of assets. Each could be supported—or undermined—by evidence bearing on the empirical accuracy of its underlying propositions.

Of the four rationales, however, only the intermediate-target justification is manifestly prescriptive and thus directly relevant to the conduct of monetary policy.

Consider, for example, the means-of-payment and the liquid-assets behavioral hypotheses (propositions 4-A and 4-B). These hypotheses by themselves do not have any implications for the formulation of economic policy. Empirical magnitudes intended to measure means-of-payment balances or holdings of liquid assets derive from propositions about microeconomic behavior. But such aggregates might have no more significance for monetary policy than any other aggregative variable in macroeconomic theories or models. More specifically, suppose that a central bank has an array of accurately measured financial aggregates that includes a means-of-payment aggregate but also aggregative variables for the private sector's holdings of other assets at banks, other assets at nonbank financial intermediaries, government securities, corporate securities, equities, life insurance reserves, and claims on pension funds. Of what use will these various financial aggregates be in policymaking? Each might capture some important characteristics of the behavior of private economic units and thus embody potentially useful information. But the descriptive perspective of the means-of-payment and the liquid-assets behavioral hypotheses provides no obvious rationale for paying greater attention to one of the aggregates than to the others. The existence of any one aggregate, or all, might not have any special bearing on the problem facing the central bank; namely, how to

9. Monetarists can be distinguished from other economists by the greater emphasis they place on the stock of money in their descriptive analyses of the economy and in their prescriptive recommendations for the conduct of monetary policy. For efforts to provide a more precise definition of monetarism, see the introduction in Jerome L. Stein, ed., *Monetarism* (Amsterdam: North-Holland, 1976); and Thomas Mayer, "The Structure of Monetarism," *Kredit und Kapital* (2:1975) and ibid. (3:1975). For an influential monetarist statement of the intermediate-target rationale (though not labeled as such), see Friedman and Schwartz, *Monetary Statistics of the United States*, especially pp. 89–92 and 139; note that propositions 4-E through 4-M above are consistent with Friedman and Schwartz both in avoiding a definition of money based on a priori theoretical reasoning and in insisting that *some* definition of money is required for prescriptive recommendations about monetary policy.

choose those settings for its policy instruments that will most favorably influence its ultimate targets.

Even the hypothesis of observed empirical regularity has no direct bearing on the conduct of monetary policy. It may be possible ex post to observe many empirical regularities in the macroeconomic behavior of the economy. Therefore, even if proposition 4-C were shown to be supported by empirical evidence, the conclusion would not follow that that particular regularity had unique significance for economic policy.

The intermediate-target rationale for defining money, on the other hand, relates directly to the formulation and implementation of monetary policy. The basic purpose of identifying and empirically measuring the financial aggregate is to facilitate the decisions that have to be made by the central bank. Logically, then, the intermediate-target justification is in an entirely different class from the three descriptive motives for defining money.

That is not to say there are no connections between the descriptive concepts and the prescriptive justification. It is, in fact, quite likely that opinions about the usefulness of a descriptive concept will strongly affect opinions about the existence and nature of the aggregate defined prescriptively in propositions 4-K through 4-M. For example, if analysts subscribe to the means-of-payment behavioral hypothesis, that view can be a basis for their belief in proposition 4-K and hence a major consideration in their support for using the money stock as an intermediate target of monetary policy.

Two further points deserve emphasis. First, the three descriptive rationales for formulating concepts of money are certain to lead to *different* empirical magnitudes when an effort is made to identify and measure empirical counterparts to the concepts. Thus, though the various advocates of using money as an intermediate target may regard the financial aggregate of propositions 4-K through 4-M as coterminous with one of the descriptive concepts of money, the various advocates cannot all be right.[10]

Second, though advocates of a money-as-intermediate-target strategy may well appeal to one of the descriptive hypotheses as a partial rationalization for their advocacy, there is no necessary connection between analysts' views about the usefulness of a descriptive concept and their prescriptive views about monetary policy. For example, some analysts may subscribe to either the means-of-payment hypothesis or the liquid-assets behavioral hypothesis and yet reject all three of the propositions 4-K through 4-M. More generally, knowledge of the views of policymakers or economists about the various descriptive hypotheses does not imply knowledge of their views about money in a policy context.

The chapters that follow are primarily concerned with monetary policy rather than descriptive monetary theory and therefore emphasize the intermediate-target justification for defining and employing a financial aggregate called money. There often is no need to ask whether an advocate of using money as an intermediate-target variable buttresses that advocacy with a belief in proposition 4-A or, alternatively, with a belief in either 4-B or 4-C. The critical assertions for the subsequent analysis are propositions 4-K through 4-M.

10. For example, those analysts who associate the intermediate-target variable of proposition 4-K with a liquid-asset definition of money hold views that are incompatible with those who appeal to the means-of-payment behavioral hypothesis as an explanation for their belief in 4-K.

CHAPTER FIVE

Aggregate Demand and Supply
Functions for Money

ADDITIONAL background is required before it is possible to analyze the rationale for a policy strategy of using the money stock as an intermediate target. This chapter therefore provides schematic balance sheets showing the assets and liabilities of various sectors of the national economy; it reviews the conventional formulations in macroeconomic theory of the aggregate demand and supply functions for money; and it outlines alternative ways of modeling the links between money demand and supply and the other macroeconomic behavioral relationships characterizing the economy.

A Schematic Representation of Sector Balance Sheets

To facilitate the discussion here and in later chapters, tables 5-1 and 5-2 present schematic balance sheets for the central bank and the fiscal authority. Tables 5-3 and 5-4 present consolidated balance sheets for financial intermediaries and all other economic units in the economy.

Two simplifications embodied in tables 5-1 through 5-4 are especially noteworthy. First, it is assumed that only one class of financial intermediary—henceforth referred to as banks—operates in the economy. The schematization thereby suppresses all distinctions among the various types of commercial banks (for example, clearing banks and merchant banks) and nonbank financial intermediaries (such as savings and loan associations, mutual savings banks, credit unions, issuers of commercial paper, and mutual funds) found in industrial countries with highly developed financial markets. Second, no distinction is made among types of nonbank economic units. For example, households and nonfinancial corporations are consolidated rather than shown separately.

How might *money* be defined in the institutional context depicted in these tables? First consider various combinations of items on the balance sheet of the central bank. In what follows, these aggregates are collectively referred to as *central bank money* or *reserve money*. The possibilities are traditionally labeled and defined as indicated in equations 5-1 through 5-6:

(5-1) Net free reserves: $\qquad$ $RF = RX - RB.$

(5-2) Unborrowed reserves: $\qquad$ $RU = RT - RB = RR + RF.$

(5-3) Total reserves: $\qquad$ $RT = RR + RX = RU + RB.$

Table 5-1. *Schematic Balance Sheet of the Central Bank, Closed Economy*[a]

Assets	
RB	Borrowings by financial intermediaries from the central bank (borrowed reserves)[b]
S^{CB}	Holdings of government debt securities[c]
OA^{CB}	Other assets (for example, buildings and real estate and other tangible assets)

Liabilities and capital accounts	
RT	Liquid claims of financial intermediaries on the central bank (total reserves), subdivided into:
RR	Required reserves
RX	Excess reserves
CUR	Currency in circulation[d]
Dep^G	Deposit balance of the government (fiscal authority) with the central bank
NW^{CB}	Surplus and capital accounts (net worth)

a. A superscript on a symbol indicates the sector for which an item is an asset or net worth; CB indicates the central bank, G, the fiscal authority.

b. This item takes the form of so-called discounts or advances in many countries; the term *borrowed reserves* is used primarily in the United States.

c. For simplicity, it is assumed that the central bank does not hold securities issued by economic units in the private sector and that security holdings of the central bank are marketable liabilities of the fiscal authority.

d. Currency is assumed to be held only by nonbanks. In actual practice, financial intermediaries maintain a modest inventory of currency (so-called vault cash).

Table 5-2. *Schematic Balance Sheet of the Fiscal Authority, Closed Economy*[a]

Assets	
Dep^G	Deposit balance of the fiscal authority with the central bank
OA^G	Other assets of the government (for example, tangible assets)

Liabilities and balancing item	
S	Debt securities issued by the government,[b,c] subdivided into:
S^{CB}	Holdings of the central bank
S^B	Holdings of the financial intermediaries
S^N	Holdings of the nonbank private sector
NW^G	Balancing item[d]

a. A superscript indicates the sector for which an item is an asset or net worth; G indicates the fiscal authority; CB, the central bank; B, the bank sector; N, the nonbank sector.

b. In most countries government-owned enterprises engage in the production of goods as well as conventional government services. For simplicity, the capital assets and financial liabilities associated with these goods-producing activities are suppressed in this schematization.

c. All debt securities issued by the government are assumed to be marketable; distinctions are not made among securities as to date of maturity.

d. This is usually a negative item corresponding to the net claims on the government of the private sector.

(5-4) Monetary base: $$MB = RT + CUR.$$

(5-5) Unborrowed monetary base: $$MBU = RT + CUR - RB$$
$$= RU + CUR.$$

(5-6) Monetary base plus government
deposit balance: $$MBG = MB + Dep^G.$$

Conventional definitions of money rule out financial intermediaries as *holders* of money.[1] Therefore, none of the reserve-money aggregates in equations 5-1

1. This statement applies to the definitions in conventional use in recent decades but not to definitions in earlier centuries.

Table 5-3. *Schematic Consolidated Balance Sheet for Financial Intermediaries (Banks), Closed Economy*[a]

	Assets
RR	Required reserves held against deposit liabilities
RX	Excess reserves[b]
S^B	Holdings of government debt securities
L	Loans made to nonbanks[c]
TA^B	Tangible assets (for example, buildings)
	Liabilities and capital accounts
RB	Borrowings from the central bank (borrowed reserves)[d]
D	Deposit claims of nonbanks, subdivided into:
Dmp	Deposits widely accepted as means of payment
Dot	Other deposits
NW^B	Surplus and capital accounts (net worth)[e]

a. A superscript indicates the sector for which an item is an asset or net worth; B indicates the bank sector.

b. It is assumed that financial intermediaries do not hold currency.

c. All loans of financial intermediaries are assumed to be made to nonbanks.

d. This item takes the form of so-called discounts or advances in many countries; the term *borrowed reserves* is used primarily in the United States.

e. The net worth of financial intermediaries is an asset from the perspective of the nonbank sector (in other words, it is included in TA^N in table 5-4).

Table 5-4. *Schematic Consolidated Balance Sheet for All Private-Sector Nonbanks, Closed Economy*[a]

	Assets
CUR	Holdings of currency
D	Deposit claims on financial intermediaries, subdivided into:
Dmp	Deposits widely accepted as means of payment
Dot	Other deposits
S^N	Holdings of marketable government debt securities
TA^N	Tangible assets and other claims[b]
	Liabilities and net worth
L	Loans from financial intermediaries
W^N	Net worth of the nonbank sector

a. Because all nonbank economic units have been combined in this schematic representation, the claims and liabilities that link households and firms have been consolidated. The superscript N indicates that the nonbank sector holds the item as an asset or net worth.

b. Includes equity claims on financial intermediaries (the item NW^B on the consolidated balance sheet for banks).

through 5-6 is typically associated with the money discussed in chapter 4. To identify money proper in the context assumed here, some combination of items must be selected from the asset side of the balance sheet for nonbanks (table 5-4).

Given the schematic assumptions, there are only three likely candidates. The broadest definition includes currency and all deposit liabilities of the banks ($CUR + D$); this variant corresponds roughly to the so-called M_2 type of definition of money. The second definition presumes that the deposit liabilities of the banks can be divided into two groups, with the deposits in one group having much greater acceptability as a means of payment than the deposits in the other. Money is then taken to be the sum of currency and the deposits that are widely accepted as a means of payment $(CUR + Dmp)$; this aggregate corresponds roughly to the conventional M_1 type of definition. (The conceptual difference between Dmp and Dot is typically associated with the distinction between demand or sight deposits and time or term deposits. The means-of-payment attributes of various types of deposits differ across countries and time, however, and the correctness and sharpness of that distinction thus varies from one institutional context to another.) The third possible definition identifies money solely with the currency holdings of nonbanks (CUR).[2]

The Aggregate Demand for Money

The most frequently encountered formulation of an aggregate demand function for money is

(5-7)
$$\frac{M^d}{P} = f\left(r, \frac{Y}{P}\right),$$

where M^d is the aggregate demand for money balances expressed in nominal terms; P is the general level of prices for goods and services; Y is aggregate nominal income; and r is a vector of expected interest rates or rate-of-return variables. All variables in equation 5-7 pertain to the holders of money collectively, here assumed to be all nonbanks; for example, Y represents the nonbanks' aggregate income, and the vector r includes representative measures of the returns expected by nonbanks on the various assets held in their wealth portfolios. This conventional formulation of money demand appears, often as a component of the elementary IS-LM macroeconomic model, in any number of textbooks.[3] Empirical articles also frequently take some version of 5-7 as a starting point for regression specifications.[4]

Efforts to put empirical flesh and blood on the bones of this conventional theory often identify the nominal value of the gross national product (GNP) with Y and the implicit price deflator for GNP with P. The vector of return variables, r, differs in detail from one study to the next, as of course the particular definition of money itself does.[5] Other important differences occur in the empirical research because

2. The suggestion is sometimes made that the money stock should include the government's holdings of cash balances. Given the simplified context of tables 5-1 through 5-4 (which assumes, among other things, that the government holds a cash balance with the central bank but not any deposit balances with commercial banks), that suggestion would give rise to definitions $CUR + D + Dep^G$ or $CUR + Dmp + Dep^G$.

3. For examples, see David E. W. Laidler, *The Demand for Money: Theories and Evidence* (International Textbook, 1969), chap. 1, app. A, and chaps. 5 and 8; William H. Branson, *Macroeconomic Theory and Policy* (Harper and Row, 1972), pp. 60–71, 227–51; and Rudiger Dornbusch and Stanley Fischer, *Macroeconomics* (McGraw-Hill, 1978), chaps. 4 and 7.

4. See, for example, Stephen M. Goldfeld, "The Demand for Money Revisited," *Brookings Papers on Economic Activity, 3:1973,* pp. 577–646 (hereafter *BPEA*). See also his "The Case of the Missing Money," *BPEA, 3:1976,* pp. 683–730, and the literature cited there.

5. In principle, the vector of expected return variables (r) includes an "own" rate of return on money and the rates of return or borrowing costs on all other assets and liabilities in the portfolios of nonbanks. Money demand is positively related to its own return and negatively related to the returns on alternative

of different functional specifications and alternative treatments of lags in the relationship.[6]

Despite the apparent widespread agreement that equation 5-7 adequately represents the aggregate demand for money, there are several notable differences in interpretation, the most important of which concerns the variable Y/P. The differences tend to correspond to the alternative descriptive concepts of money identified in chapter 4.

The Transactions School

One view, which may be labeled the transactions school and is associated with the means-of-payment behavioral hypothesis summarized in proposition 4-A, stresses the attributes of money as a medium of exchange. According to this school, GNP belongs as a variable in the aggregate demand function for money because it serves as a proxy for the volume of transactions or expenditures requiring the use of money. The implicit assumption is that GNP and the volume of money-financed transactions move so closely together that the former is a good surrogate for the latter. Within the schematic context of tables 5-1 through 5-4, the transactions school would define money as $CUR + Dmp$, currency plus means-of-payment deposits in financial intermediaries.[7]

---

assets. In theory, the return variables should be *real* rates of return. Conventional analysis and empirical research tend to ignore the distinctions between real versus nominal and expected versus actual rates of return and simply employ actual nominal rates as arguments in asset-demand functions (including an implicit return of zero for the own rate on money). It can be shown that it is a matter of indifference whether real or nominal expected rates are used if an additional hypothesis can be shown to be true, namely that asset demands do not depend on the level of expected real interest rates but only on the absolute differences among the expected real rates.

6. Good sources for reviewing these differences and their possible implications in the context of the demand for money in the United States are Goldfeld, "The Demand for Money Revisited"; and Edgar L. Feige and Douglas K. Pearce, "The Substitutability of Money and Near-Monies: A Survey of the Time-Series Evidence," *Journal of Economic Literature*, vol. 15 (June 1977), pp. 439–69. For an article giving a tabular survey of empirical studies for other industrial countries, see M. M. G. Fase and J. B. Kune, "The Demand for Money in Thirteen European and Non-European Countries," *Kredit und Kapital* (3: 1975). James M. Boughton's "Demand for Money in Major OECD Countries," *Occasional Studies* (OECD, January 1979), pp. 35–57, is a recent comparative survey.

7. The theoretical basis for a transactions demand for money is discussed in well-known articles by William J. Baumol, "The Transactions Demand for Cash: An Inventory Theoretic Approach," *Quarterly Journal of Economics*, vol. 66 (November 1952), pp. 545–56; and by James Tobin, "The Interest Elasticity of Transactions Demand for Cash," *Review of Economics and Statistics*, vol. 38 (August 1956), pp. 241–47. One important extension of the Baumol-Tobin results is to make payments and receipts stochastic rather than deterministic; see, for example, Merton H. Miller and Daniel Orr, "A Model of the Demand for Money by Firms," *Quarterly Journal of Economics*, vol. 80 (August 1966), pp. 413–35; and Miller and Orr, "The Demand for Money by Firms: Extensions of Analytic Results," *Journal of Finance*, vol. 23 (December 1968), pp. 735–59. Recent contributions to the transactions theory of money demand include Robert E. Anderson, "The Individual's Transactions Demand for Money: A Utility Maximization Approach," *Journal of Monetary Economics*, vol. 2 (April 1976), pp. 237–56; Robert W. Clower and Peter W. Howitt, "The Transactions Theory of the Demand for Money: A Reconsideration," *Journal of Political Economy*, vol. 86 (June 1978), pp. 449–66; George A. Akerlof and Ross D. Milbourne, "The Sensitivity of Monetarist Conclusions to Monetarist Assumptions: Constant Lag versus Constant Target-Threshold Monitoring," Special Studies Paper 117 (Board of Governors of the Federal Reserve System, June 1978); and Peter A. Tinsley and Bonnie Garrett, "The Measurement of Money Demand" (Board of Governors of the Federal Reserve System, 1978). For a survey of the theory of money demand with an emphasis on transactions costs, see Robert J. Barro and Stanley Fischer, "Recent Developments in Monetary Theory," *Journal of Monetary Economics*, vol. 2 (April 1976), pp. 133–67. More generally, there has been a renewed interest in recent years in transactions costs and their incorporation in macroeconomic theory; see the discussion in Jürg Niehans, *The Theory of Money* (Johns Hopkins University Press, 1978), chaps. 1–6; and in Arthur M. Okun, *Prices and Quantities: A Macroeconomic Analysis* (Brookings Institution, forthcoming).

The Utility School

An alternative view, the utility school, eschews explanations of why people hold money and assumes that money can be treated as yielding utility directly, like all other goods demanded by economic units.[8] In this interpretation, the inclusion of GNP in equation 5-7 may be loosely rationalized on the grounds that it serves as a constraint, or "scale" variable; this variable then plays a role in the demand for money similar to the role of current income in conventional formulations of the consumption function.[9] Many proponents of the utility school define money more broadly than proponents of the transactions school. In the context of tables 5-1 through 5-4, for example, they would select the $CUR + D$ concept, currency plus all deposits in financial intermediaries.

The Yale Portfolio-Balance Tradition

Another formulation of the aggregate demand for money builds on the approach of the transactions school but also embeds the demand for money in a system of asset-demand equations for the entire portfolio. This tradition is most closely associated with James Tobin and other economists at Yale University; it may be expressed as

$$(5\text{-}8) \qquad \frac{M^d}{W^N} = f\left(r, \frac{Y}{W^N}\right),$$

where W^N is the nominal wealth of the nonbank holders of money.[10] Income or GNP still appears in equation 5-8 as a proxy for transactions, but money demand (as well as all other asset demands and liability supplies) is expressed as a proportion of wealth. This specification helps to emphasize the balance-sheet constraints that must hold at all times—for the individual economic unit and for the economy as a whole.[11]

The Chicago Tradition

A final alternative formulation derives largely from Milton Friedman and other economists at the University of Chicago. It somewhat resembles the approach of

8. See, for example, the comparison of the demand for money with the demand for refrigerators in Laidler, *The Demand for Money*, pp. 40–43. Laidler argues, "It has never proved necessary to investigate the nature of the psychological satisfaction that arises from the consumption of other goods in order to analyze the demand for them. . . . It becomes sufficient to postulate that money yields services to its owner, and then to analyze the determinants of the demand for money in the same way as one might for any other good" (p. 42).

9. On theoretical grounds, however, wealth is a more logical scale variable than current income; see equation 5-8 or equation 5-9.

10. See, for example, James Tobin, "A General Equilibrium Approach to Monetary Theory," *Journal of Money, Credit and Banking*, vol. 1 (February 1969), pp. 15–29; William C. Brainard and James Tobin, "Pitfalls in Financial Model Building," *American Economic Review*, vol. 58 (May 1968, *Papers and Proceedings, 1967*), pp. 99–149. The specification of equation 5-8 imposes the additional assumption that money demand (and other asset demands and liability supplies) is homogeneous of degree one in wealth.

11. The theory argues that, given W^N and all the return variables included in r, M^d is positively related and other asset demands are negatively related to the volume of transactions (proxied by Y). Albert Ando, Karl Shell, and Franco Modigliani argue that the demand for money in a general portfolio model need *not* be dependent on wealth if an asset exists that dominates money in all respects except in its acceptability as a means of payment. See Ando and Modigliani, "Some Reflections on Describing Structures of Financial Sectors," in Gary Fromm and Lawrence R. Klein, eds., *The Brookings Model: Perspective and Recent Developments* (Amsterdam: North Holland, 1975; New York: American Elsevier, 1975), pp. 525–63. See, however, James Tobin's comments, ibid., pp. 565–67.

the utility school. It differs from equation 5-7 primarily in the variety of income or wealth arguments it entertains as constraints on demand. One version utilizes "permanent income" rather than current income. Another, as in equation 5-9, substitutes wealth for an income variable:

$$(5\text{-}9) \qquad \frac{M^d}{P} = f\left(r, \frac{W^N}{P}, \ldots\right).$$

Still another variant includes both wealth and current income. Further refinements of this view introduce a distinction between human and nonhuman wealth and include an explicit consideration of price expectations.[12]

Disaggregated Approaches

The demand functions described thus far are aggregative at the outset: whatever money is, its components are lumped together, and a single demand function like equation 5-7, 5-8, or 5-9 is specified for the aggregate. The usual rationale for an aggregative approach is that the individual components of money are much closer substitutes for one another than for other assets. An alternative approach that permits this assumption to be tested explicitly involves the breaking down of broader money aggregates into their components and the specification of separate demand functions for each component. In the context of tables 5-1 through 5-4 and with the broader, M_2 type of money definition, such a disaggregated approach might specify

$$(5\text{-}10a) \qquad \frac{CUR^d}{W^N} = CUR^d\left(r, \frac{Y}{W^N}\right),$$

$$(5\text{-}10b) \qquad \frac{Dmp^d}{W^N} = Dmp^d\left(r, \frac{Y}{W^N}\right),$$

$$(5\text{-}10c) \qquad \frac{Dot^d}{W^N} = Dot^d\left(r, \frac{Y}{W^N}\right).$$

The vector of rate-of-return variables in 5-10 includes, in principle, the own returns for all three of the components of money as well as the returns on other balance-sheet items in the portfolios of nonbanks.[13] Given 5-10, the aggregate demand function for money is the sum of the demands for the individual components:

$$(5\text{-}11) \qquad M^d = CUR^d\left(r, \frac{Y}{W^N}\right)W^N + Dmp^d\left(r, \frac{Y}{W^N}\right)W^N + Dot^d\left(r, \frac{Y}{W^N}\right)W^N.$$

Further Issues

Summaries of the demand for money at the macroeconomic level typically fail to differentiate between various types of nonbank economic units. The implicit assumption is that the behavior of all nonbank demanders can be reasonably well

---

12. See, for example, Milton Friedman, *The Optimum Quantity of Money and Other Essays* (Aldine, 1969), pp. 51–67; Milton Friedman, "A Theoretical Framework for Monetary Analysis," *Journal of Political Economy*, vol. 78 (March-April 1970), pp. 193–238; and Laidler, *The Demand for Money*, chap. 8.

13. The specification in 5-10 is analogous to 5-8 since a disaggregated approach is often espoused by those working in the portfolio-balance tradition. But disaggregated functions along the lines of 5-7 or 5-9 can be specified.

approximated by one of the preceding aggregate functions. But in fact, empirical evidence suggests that this assumption is not warranted, at least for the United States. It would be rather surprising if, for example, the demand for money by firms could be correctly represented by the same theoretical model as that used to describe the demand for money by households.[14]

Another important set of complexities is suppressed in the preceding summary. The asset-demanding and liability-supplying behavior of nonbanks may differ considerably in the short run from their behavior in the intermediate run and the long run. For one thing, economic units facing significant transaction and information costs will themselves want to adjust their behavior with lags.[15] Moreover, various externally imposed constraints may mean that some variables cannot immediately be adjusted to new "equilibrium" values in the short run, whereas adjustments can occur over an intermediate or long run. Hence a "disequilibrium" analysis of the short run may be required that takes account of rationing phenomena and that does not impose the assumption that prices adjust flexibly and promptly to clear all markets.[16] Yet such an analysis for the short run should be consistent with—and, through explicit dynamics, linked to—an equilibrium treatment of the more traditional, market-clearing type for the intermediate or long run. Because of balance-sheet constraints, if one financial asset or liability is out of adjustment in the short run, at least one other balance-sheet item must also be out of adjustment.[17] Adequate analysis of these phenomena would be complicated even if the study of asset demands and liability supplies could be compartmentalized from other aspects of macroeconomic behavior. But such compartmentalization is not legitimate.[18] Macroeconomic theory, even for the case of a completely closed economy, is still in a state of ferment about these issues.

The Money Supply Process

Summarizing the conventional wisdom about the money supply process is more difficult than describing the conventional formulations of the aggregate demand for money.[19] The difficulties stem partly from the lack of consensus among economists

14. For some relevant evidence, see Goldfeld, "The Demand for Money Revisited," pp. 626–32, and "The Case of the Missing Money," pp. 708–20; Barry J. Wilbratte, "Some Essential Differences in the Demand for Money by Households and by Firms," *Journal of Finance*, vol. 30 (September 1975), pp. 1091–99; Helen T. Farr, Richard D. Porter, and Eleanor M. Pruitt, "The Demand Deposit Ownership Survey," in *Improving the Monetary Aggregates: Staff Papers* (Board of Governors of the Federal Reserve System, 1978); and Tinsley and Garrett, "The Measurement of Money Demand." The implication of this evidence is that a schematic institutional framework for studying macroeconomic financial behavior ought to postulate (in contrast to table 5-4) separate balance sheets and, hence, separate behavioral functions for the household and nonfinancial corporate sectors.

15. See, for example, Benjamin M. Friedman, "Financial Flow Variables and the Short-Run Determination of Long-Term Interest Rates," *Journal of Political Economy*, vol. 85 (August 1977), pp. 661–89.

16. See, for example, Donald P. Tucker, "Macroeconomic Models and the Demand for Money under Market Disequilibrium," *Journal of Money, Credit and Banking*, vol. 3 (February 1971), pp. 57–83.

17. Brainard and Tobin, "Pitfalls in Financial Model Building."

18. See Tucker, "Macroeconomic Models," Barro and Fischer, "Recent Developments in Monetary Theory," pp. 146–49, and John Muellbauer and Richard Portes, "Macroeconomic Models with Quantity Rationing," *Economic Journal*, vol. 88 (December 1978), pp. 788–821.

19. For a more detailed survey of the literature on the demand for money than that given in the preceding section, see C. A. E. Goodhart, *Money, Information and Uncertainty* (London and Basingstoke: Macmillan, 1975), chaps. 2–3; Laidler, *The Demand for Money;* and Niehans, *The Theory of Money*, chaps. 1–6.

on the subject and partly from the complexity of the money supply process in economies with highly developed financial sectors.

Basic Elements

The fundamental point about the supply of money is summarized in chapter 4: money is an endogenous intermediate variable whose supply as well as demand is strongly influenced by the behavior of private economic units. This point is prominently illustrated even in the schematic balance sheets in tables 5-1 through 5-4. The deposit components of money, Dmp and Dot, are not liabilities of the central bank or the fiscal authority but rather liabilities of privately operated financial intermediaries. Although the central bank can influence the deposit-supplying behavior of commercial banks by taking policy actions, it cannot precisely fix the volume of the deposits from one short-run period to the next.

The aggregate function for the supply of money must therefore take into account not only policy actions of the central bank and fiscal authority but also the profit-motivated actions of banks. The basic elements of such a function, at the highest level of abstraction, may be expressed as

(5-12) $$M^s = g[X; h^B(i, \ldots)],$$

where M^s denotes the supply of money, X represents a vector of policy instruments, and $h^B(i, \ldots)$ is a complicated function characterizing the behavior of the banks supplying the money liabilities included in M^s. The instruments in the vector X will differ among nations and may differ according to the analytical purpose for which a representation of the money supply process is required. In principle, the bank function $h^B(i, \ldots)$ includes intermediate variables relevant to all aspects of asset-demanding and liability-supplying behavior. At a minimum, it includes a long list of expected return and cost variables, symbolized by the vector i. Even if money is defined as only currency and means-of-payment deposits, i must include not only the interest rate paid on (or service costs associated with) the banks' means-of-payment liabilities but also the return earned by the banks on their loans, the return earned on securities holdings, the interest rate earned on reserves held at the central bank, the interest cost of borrowing from the central bank, and the interest rate paid on other deposit liabilities. The ellipsis in $h^B(i, \ldots)$ serves as a reminder that a complete function is likely to contain other arguments as well. At least for some types of banking systems (for example, where some interest rates are constrained by regulatory controls) or under some types of disequilibrium assumptions about short-run banking behavior, the function will include such nominal magnitudes as the outstanding amounts of the banks' deposit liabilities.

Efforts to model the money supply process have varied greatly among authors and among nations. The following discussion summarizes only those differences of view that are relevant to the subsequent analysis.[20]

Multiplier Approaches

The most parsimonious approach to the analysis of the money supply process was developed by Milton Friedman and Anna Schwartz and by Philip Cagan.[21]

20. For more comprehensive and detailed discussions, see for example Niehans, *The Theory of Money*, chaps. 9 and 12; and Goodhart, *Money, Information and Uncertainty*, chaps. 6–8.

21. See Milton Friedman and Anna Jacobson Schwartz, *A Monetary History of the United States, 1867–1960*, Studies in Business Cycles 12 (Princeton University Press for the National Bureau of Economic

They identify three "proximate determinants" of the money stock associated with three different types of behavioral units: the amount of "high-powered money," determined by the central bank;[22] the ratio of deposits in banks to the banks' holdings of high-powered money, viewed as being determined by the behavior of the banking system (given whatever reserve requirements and other regulations may be imposed by the central bank); and the ratio of nonbanks' money holdings in the form of deposits to their holdings of high-powered money (currency), viewed as being determined by the behavior of the nonbank sector.[23] To illustrate within the schematic context above, if money is defined as nonbanks' holdings of currency and all deposits ($M \equiv CUR + D$) and high-powered money is defined as the monetary base ($H \equiv RT + CUR$), then algebraic manipulation of these two identities enables one to write

$$(5\text{-}13) \qquad M \equiv H \left[\frac{\dfrac{D}{RT}\left(1 + \dfrac{D}{CUR}\right)}{\dfrac{D}{RT} + \dfrac{D}{CUR}} \right]$$

Alternatively, if b is defined as the ratio D/RT, if n is defined as the deposit-currency ratio D/CUR, and if m is defined as $b(1 + n)/(b + n)$, then 5-13 may be written as

$$(5\text{-}14) \qquad M \equiv mH.$$

The variable m is commonly referred to as the multiplier—the factor that, when multiplied by H, yields the money stock.

As usually presented, the multiplier approach acknowledges that m is an intermediate variable determined in a complex way by the behavior of financial intermediaries and the nonbank sector. But it fails to specify the relevant behavioral relationships and the manner in which they interact. The behavioral relationships are only implicit in the ratios around which the discussion is organized.

Strictly speaking, 5-14 is not a money supply function but merely an ex post identity that is true by definition.[24] Yet the identity can be converted into an aggregate supply function if some additional assumptions are made. Suppose it is assumed that the central bank chooses to use H as a policy instrument. Then one might write, for example,

$$(5\text{-}15) \qquad M^s = m(b, n)H,$$

and also

$$(5\text{-}16) \qquad b = b(i, \ldots ; X'),$$

Research, 1963), app. B; and Philip Cagan, *Determinants and Effects of Changes in the Stock of Money, 1875–1960*, Studies in Business Cycles 13 (New York: National Bureau of Economic Research, 1965). See also Albert E. Burger, *The Money Supply Process* (Belmont, California: Wadsworth, 1971).

22. High-powered money is any one of the concepts of central-bank money given in equations 5-1 through 5-6 above; most authors associate it with the monetary base (currency held by nonbanks plus the liabilities of the central bank to the private banking system). "High-powered" refers to the fact that each unit of central-bank money can serve as a reserve base for several units of "ordinary" money (deposit liabilities of the banks).

23. In typical empirical applications, "banks" are only commercial banks. Nonbank financial intermediaries are therefore lumped together with households and firms as part of the nonbank sector (a procedure with problematic analytical consequences).

24. Moreover, multipliers analogous to m in 5-14 could be defined for any other definitions of M and H, or indeed for any other economic variables. See, for example, Goodhart, *Money, Information and Uncertainty*, pp. 129–36.

(5-17) $$n = n\left(r, \frac{Y}{W^N}, \dots\right),$$

where i, r, Y, and W^N have the same definitions as before and X' is a vector of policy instruments other than the monetary base (for example, the discount rate and reserve-requirement ratios).

The specification summarized in 5-15 through 5-17 has the merit of emphasizing the behavioral elements in the determination of the multiplier. Suppose, however, that an analyst ignores these behavioral relationships, viewing the multiplier not as a complex intermediate variable but merely as a parameter. That conceptual view leads to the simple expression

(5-18) $$M^s = \overline{m}H,$$

where $\overline{m}$ is the parameter value of the multiplier.[25]

Disaggregated Structural Approaches

In recent years, many researchers have attempted to develop more explicit models of the behavioral relationships underlying the money supply process. Karl Brunner and Allan Meltzer have published a number of relevant papers.[26] Theoretical analyses of the behavior of financial intermediaries have been published by, among many others, Richard Porter, William Brainard, and John Kareken.[27] Empirical research on the money supply process and more generally on models of the financial sector in the United States includes the work of Frank de Leeuw, Franco Modigliani and others, Patric Hendershott, Thomas Thomson and others, and Donald Hester and James Pierce.[28] Less analytical work seems to have been done on the money supply process for industrial countries other than the United States.[29]

25. In practice, m is not a relatively constant parameter. Instead, as predicted by equations 5-16 and 5-17, it changes in response to changes in private economic behavior. For recent references on the multiplier approach and problems that arise in implementing it in the United States, see Peter A. Frost, "Short-Run Fluctuations in the Money Multiplier and Monetary Control," *Journal of Money, Credit and Banking*, vol. 9, pt. 2, *Essays in Honor of Karl Brunner* (February 1977), pp. 165–81; and Albert E. Burger and Robert H. Rasche, "Revision of the Monetary Base," *Federal Reserve Bank of St. Louis Review*, vol. 59 (July 1977), pp. 13–28.

26. See, for example, Karl Brunner, "A Schema for the Supply Theory of Money," *International Economic Review*, vol. 2 (January 1961), pp. 79–109; and Brunner and Allan H. Meltzer, "Money, Debt, and Economic Activity," *Journal of Political Economy*, vol. 80 (September-October 1972), pp. 951–77. See also Benjamin M. Friedman and Kenneth C. Froewiss, "Bank Behavior in the Brunner-Meltzer Model," *Journal of Monetary Economics*, vol. 3 (April 1977), pp. 163–78.

27. Richard C. Porter, "A Model of Bank Portfolio Selection," *Yale Economic Essays* (Fall 1961), reprinted in D. Hester and J. Tobin, eds., *Financial Markets and Economic Activity*, Cowles Foundation for Research in Economics, Monograph 21 (John Wiley, 1967); William C. Brainard, "Financial Intermediaries and a Theory of Monetary Control," *Yale Economic Essays* (Fall 1964), reprinted in Hester and Tobin, eds., *Financial Markets and Economic Activity; and John H. Kareken, "Commercial Banks and the Supply of Money: A Market-Determined Demand Deposit Rate," *Federal Reserve Bulletin*, vol. 53 (October 1967), pp. 1699–712.

28. See Frank de Leeuw, "A Model of Financial Behavior," in James S. Duesenberry and others, eds., *The Brookings Quarterly Econometric Model of the United States* (Chicago: Rand McNally, 1965; Amsterdam: North Holland, 1965), pp. 465–530; and "A Condensed Model of Financial Behavior," in Duesenberry and others, eds., *The Brookings Model: Some Further Results* (Rand McNally, 1969); Franco Modigliani, Robert Rasche, and J. Philip Cooper, "Central Bank Policy, the Money Supply, and the Short-Term Rate of Interest," *Journal of Money, Credit and Banking*, vol. 2 (May 1970), pp. 166–218; Patric H. Hendershott, *A Flow-of-Funds Financial Model: Estimation and Application to Financial Policies and Reform* (Lexington Books, 1977); Thomas Thomson, James L. Pierce, and Robert T. Parry, "A Monthly Money Market Model," *Journal of Money, Credit and Banking*, vol. 7 (November 1975), pp. 411–31; and Donald D. Hester and James L. Pierce, *Bank Management and Portfolio Behavior*, Cowles Foundation for Economic Research, Monograph 25 (Yale University Press, 1975).

29. For descriptions of the national institutions and references to the existing literature, see Organisation for Economic Co-operation and Development, Department of Economics and Statistics, *The Role of*

It is impractical and unnecessary to summarize the literature here. For the purposes of the discussion in later chapters it is sufficient to outline the main features of a disaggregated structural approach. That outline can then serve as an illustrative alternative to the simple aggregative approach of multiplier analysis. As before, the exposition is in terms of the institutional context assumed in tables 5-1 through 5-4.

The customary point of departure is the reserve-aggregate identities in equations 5-1 through 5-6, which in turn are closely related to the central bank's balance-sheet identity. Consider, for example, the identity 5-5 for the unborrowed monetary base—$MBU \equiv RR + RF + CUR$—and the demands for its three components. Banks engaged in deposit-supplying activity in the short run are often modeled as rate setters (setting the interest rate they pay on their deposits) and quantity takers (accepting whatever quantity of deposits nonbanks wish to hold at that rate). With that assumption, the supply of bank deposits in the short run can be expressed as

$$(5\text{-}19a) \qquad Dmp^s = Dmp^d,$$

$$(5\text{-}19b) \qquad Dot^s = Dot^d,$$

where the nonbanks' demands Dmp^d and Dot^d might be given by, for example, equations 5-10b and 5-10c. If ρ_1 and ρ_2 are the reserve-requirement ratios imposed on the two types of deposit, the banks' derived demand for required reserves is thus

$$(5\text{-}20a) \qquad RR^d = \rho_1 Dmp^d + \rho_2 Dot^d.$$

The banks' demand for free reserves (excess reserves, RX, less borrowed reserves, RB) will, in principle, depend on all the returns and costs associated with their portfolios:[30]

$$(5\text{-}20b) \qquad RF^d = RF^d(i, \ldots).$$

The demand for the currency component of the unborrowed monetary base is a demand by nonbanks (see, for example, equation 5-10a). If the demands for the three components are added together, then

$$(5\text{-}21) \qquad MBU^d = \rho_1 Dmp^d + \rho_2 Dot^d + RF^d + CUR^d.$$

Finally, suppose that the central bank chooses to use the unborrowed monetary base as a policy instrument, and that all the various interest rates and other intermediate variables in the financial sector adjust until the demands for the unborrowed base are in equilibrium with the supply determined by the central bank. Those further assumptions then justify the writing of a short-run equilibrium condition:

$$(5\text{-}22) \qquad \overline{MBU}^s = \overline{MBU} = MBU^d.$$

Monetary Policy in Demand Management: The Experience of Six Major Countries, Monetary Studies Series (OECD, 1975); see also the separate studies for Japan (1972), Italy (1973), Germany (1974), and France (1974); Donald R. Hodgman, *National Monetary Policies and International Monetary Cooperation* (Little, Brown, 1974); Karel Holbik, ed., *Monetary Policy in Twelve Industrial Countries* (Federal Reserve Bank of Boston, 1973).

30. The ellipsis in the function again serves as a reminder that arguments other than return and cost variables are likely to be present in a complete specification; see the discussion of 5-12 above.

Substitution of 5-21 into 5-22 and rearrangement of the terms then results in

$$(5\text{-}23) \quad \overline{MBU}^s - RF^d + (1 - \rho_1)Dmp^d + (1 - \rho_2)Dot^d = CUR^d + Dmp^d + Dot^d.$$

The right-hand side of 5-23 represents the aggregate demand for money, M^d, expressed as the sum of disaggregated demands as in 5-11. The left-hand side can be interpreted as an aggregate supply function for money, M^s. As in 5-12 or 5-15 through 5-17, money supply in 5-23 depends on the policy instruments of the central bank ($\overline{MBU}^s$, ρ_1, and ρ_2) and all the determinants of the behavior of the banking system.[31]

A treatment of the money supply process such as that embedded in 5-23 cannot be divorced from the particular financial-sector model of which it is a part. The complete model will have numerous other behavioral equations and a number of other equilibrium conditions, all interacting simultaneously.

Further Issues

The preceding overview of the money supply process suppresses many complexities. The institutional environment of tables 5-1 through 5-4, for example, presumes only one class of financial intermediary. As other types of financial intermediaries and hence additional types of money and near money are incorporated in the conceptual model of the financial sector, the complications grow exponentially. One must amend the function that defines the aggregate demand for money and the modeling of the other asset-demanding aspects of nonbanks' behavior. But the complications arise particularly in the modeling of the money supply process and the interactions among the various types of intermediaries.[32]

It was noted above that the asset-demanding and liability-supplying behavior of nonbanks may differ significantly in the short run, the intermediate run, and the long run. This is equally true of bank behavior. Banks adjust their asset demands and liability supplies with lags because of transaction and information costs. And the need for a disequilibrium analysis of the short run is probably even greater for banks than for nonbanks. Consider, for example, the interest rates paid by banks. If, as suggested earlier, banks are in the short run rate setters and quantity takers with respect to their deposit liabilities, the modeling effort must specify how the banks adjust the rates over time in response to their exogenous (from the banks' perspective) deposit flows. In the short run, the rates (and hence other bank-determined variables) may be "effective" but disequilibrium values; as rates are

31. In this illustration, the determinants of bank behavior influence the supply of money through the banks' demand for net free reserves (see equation 5-20b). Because the banks' demand for excess reserves is positively related to the interest that can be earned on them (the federal funds rate in the United States) while their desire to borrow from the central bank is negatively related to the central bank's discount rate, the supply of money is a positive function of short-term interest rates.

32. See, for example, John G. Gurley and Edward S. Shaw, *Money in a Theory of Finance* (Brookings Institution, 1960). See also the work on flow-of-funds models by Patric Hendershott, *A Flow-of-Funds Financial Model;* Barry Bosworth and James S. Duesenberry, "A Flow of Funds Model and Its Implications," Conference Series 10, *Issues in Federal Debt Management* (Federal Reserve Bank of Boston, 1973), pp. 39–149 (Brookings Reprint T-005); and William L. Silber, *Portfolio Behavior of Financial Institutions: An Empirical Study with Implications for Monetary Policy, Interest-Rate Determination and Financial Model-Building* (Holt, Rinehart, and Winston, 1970). In the United States, where banks are divided into two groups (members and nonmembers of the Federal Reserve System), modeling must also take into account differences in the behavior of the various banks attributable to different regulatory environments.

adjusted to new desired values with the passage of more time, however, they (and hence other bank-determined variables) may better be regarded as "notional" and equilibrium values in the more traditional sense of economic modeling. As noted earlier, these issues of disequilibrium macroeconomics are complex, and the theory and research techniques for dealing with them are still evolving.[33]

Finally, the preceding summary fails to emphasize that policymakers can manipulate their instruments in a number of ways and that, indeed, it is not a trivial matter to determine what variables are the actual policy instruments. The elements of the vector X in any particular specification of the function 5-12 should be those variables that the policymakers do in fact use as instruments in their operations from one short-run period to the next. Part 4 takes up this problem in detail. The general point to note here is that alternative operating procedures used by the central bank and fiscal authority require alternative specifications of the money supply process and have quite different implications for the analysis of monetary-policy actions.[34]

Alternative Models of Macroeconomic Behavior for the Economy as a Whole

Subsequent chapters refer to alternative analytical representations of the links between the nexus of money demand and supply and the other macroeconomic behavioral relationships characterizing the economy. This section presents sketches of such models. Detailed descriptions are not provided. No mention is made, for example, of lagged effects or other complications that arise in multiperiod, dynamic models. The discussion deliberately avoids assessment of the relative merits of alternative modeling approaches.

The Simplest Money-Income Model

The simplest conceivable model linking money and national income contains only two macroeconomic aggregates as endogenous variables, money and income.

Suppose, for example, that an analyst is content to model the money supply process with a simple multiplier approach. And suppose that, instead of using one of the formulations of money demand above, the analyst adopts a similar approach for the relationship between the money stock and income:

$$(5\text{-}24) \qquad\qquad M^d = \bar{k}Y,$$

33. Several important references are given in the survey article by Barro and Fischer, "Recent Developments in Monetary Theory." See also Muellbauer and Portes, "Macroeconomic Models with Quantity Rationing"; Ray C. Fair and Dwight M. Jaffee, "Methods of Estimation for Markets in Disequilibrium," *Econometrica*, vol. 40 (May 1972), pp. 497–514; and Gary Smith and William Brainard, "Estimation of the Savings Sector in a Disequilibrium Model" (December 1974). Closely related issues are discussed in Okun, *Prices and Quantities*.

34. As an interim illustration, the central bank can potentially control either some market interest rate (such as the interbank short-term lending rate) or some financial quantity on its own balance sheet (such as one of the reserve-money aggregates) but cannot simultaneously control both the rate and the quantity. Cogent analysis requires clarity about how the central bank chooses to behave. If the central bank selects an interest rate as its main operating instrument, for example, it would be a serious analytical error to specify 5-15 as though high-powered money (H) is an exogenous instrument of policy or to specify 5-23 as though the unborrowed monetary base (MBU) is fixed by the central bank.

where $\bar{k}$ is interpreted not as a complicated function of other endogenous variables but as an exogenous parameter (a velocity multiplier).[35] Suppose further that money demand and supply are assumed to interact through an equilibrium condition to produce the actually observed money stock. Given these assumptions, the analyst might write:

$$M^s = \bar{m}H$$

(5-25) $$M^d = \bar{k}Y$$

$$M^s = M = M^d.$$

From a purely formal modeling perspective, 5-25 is logically capable of generating equilibrium values of the variables M and Y, given exogenous values for the monetary base H and the two parameters $\bar{m}$ and $\bar{k}$.

Extended IS-LM Models

The model outlined in 5-25 is extremely simplified. Two of its simplifications might be considered especially problematical. First, it contains no explicit representation—even at the highest level of abstraction—of the nonfinancial aspects of macroeconomic activity and of the instruments of economic policy other than those of monetary policy. The approach identifies money demand and supply as the only aspects of macroeconomic behavior worth including in the model. Second, because it treats the money multiplier m and the reciprocal of income velocity k merely as exogenous parameters, 5-25 is inconsistent with key points of the generally accepted theory of money demand and supply summarized earlier. In particular, it ignores the dependence of both money demand and supply on interest rates.

Suppose that an analyst wishes to avoid these two simplifications yet still model the behavior of the economy at a very high level of abstraction. As before, let Y represent nominal national income and M the nominal value of the money stock. Let r denote "the" interest rate, an abstract concept associated with the general level of interest rates in the economy. To avoid restricting attention to the monetary base as an instrument of monetary policy, define X^M as a vector of all the central bank's policy instruments; for example, X^M could include reserve-requirement ratios and the central bank's discount rate as well as a reserve-money aggregate such as the monetary base. Similarly, define X^F as a vector of all the government's other policy instruments, including especially its fiscal-policy instruments. Finally, let Z represent a vector of nonpolicy exogenous variables (for example, some "autonomous" determinants of private-sector investment).

Given these definitions, suppose the analyst expresses the money demand function as[36]

(5-26) $$M^d = f(r, Y).$$

---

35. The income velocity of money is defined as the ratio of nominal national income to the money stock, that is, $V_y \equiv Y/M$. If k is defined as the reciprocal of velocity, the identity can be rewritten as

$$M \equiv \left(\frac{1}{V_y}\right) Y \equiv kyP,$$

where $y \equiv Y/P$ is national income in real terms and P is the price level (GNP deflator). This ex post identity is not, of course, a money demand function. But it can be converted into 5-24 if one is willing to make restrictive assumptions about the behavior of money demanders and if one is content to assume that k can be approximated by the exogenous parameter $\bar{k}$.

36. This specification is a particular variant of the function 5-7, which can be written as $M^d = k(r)Y$, or more generally as 5-26, if the demand for real money balances is assumed to be homogeneous of degree one in real income.

A counterpart money supply function might be written as

(5-27) $$M^s = m(r, X^M).$$

Although still highly abstract, 5-27 acknowledges the dependence of money supply not only on policy instruments but also on endogenous variables partially determined by the private sector. Suppose further that the analyst postulates the following equation as a summary representation of the nonfinancial aspects of economic activity:

(5-28) $$Y = g(r, Z, X^F),$$

in which income is assumed to depend on interest rates and on both policy and nonpolicy exogenous variables.[37]

With the preceding assumptions and an equilibrium condition for money demand and supply, the analyst will then have specified a simplified IS-LM-MS representation of macroeconomic behavior:

(5-29)
$$Y = g(r, Z, X^F)$$
$$M^d = f(r, Y)$$
$$M^s = m(r, X^M)$$
$$M^s = M = M^d.$$

This model differs from the elementary IS-LM model, used in many macroeconomic textbooks, in its explicit representation of a money supply function and its allowance for a larger number of exogenous variables, but it is otherwise identical. After taking the equilibrium condition into account, 5-29 is, in concept, a three-equation model capable of determining the three endogenous variables Y, M, and r once exogenous values for X^M, X^F, and Z have been specified.[38]

Because Y is *nominal* income and the price level does not appear in 5-29 explicitly, IS-LM-MS models do not address the question of how changes in the nominal value of income (and output) are allocated between changes in real income and changes in the price level.[39]

The omission of the price level, P, from the IS-LM-MS type of model is unsatisfying in many ways. Even analysts with a strong preference for small models may thus prefer to go one step further to postulate a model in which real output and

37. Conceivably the model could assume that economic activity also depends directly on the money stock, directly on the instruments of monetary policy, or directly on both: $Y = g'(r, M, Z, X^F, X^M)$.

38. As described in the text, the model specified in 5-29 assumes that a reserve-money aggregate rather than a short-term interest rate is used (in addition to reserve-requirement ratios and the discount rate) as an actual instrument of monetary policy. An alternative formulation of 5-29 can postulate that the central bank uses the interest rate, r, as an actual policy instrument. In that case, any reserve-money aggregate appearing in the model (such as the monetary base H) has to be regarded as endogenous; for example, the money supply function might be specified as

$$M^s = m(H, r, X^M),$$

with X^M now interpreted as a vector of all policy instruments except the exogenous interest rate. In this alternative formulation of the IS-LM-MS framework, the model would therefore become a three-equation system determining the three endogenous variables Y, M, and H.

39. The variable Y in the model could be interpreted as real income if the price level were assumed to be fixed. Although this interpretation of the model was once common in textbook expositions, it is now less often encountered—for obvious reasons. When Y is interpreted as nominal income, however, the model is theoretically deficient insofar as it fails to make a distinction between real and nominal interest rates.

the price level are endogenously determined together. For example, these analysts might write:

$$\frac{M^d}{P} = f(r, y)$$

$$M^s = m(r, X^M)$$

(5-30) $$M^s = M = M^d$$

$$y = g(r, Z, X^F)$$

$$P = h(y, Z)$$

$$Y = Py.$$

In this further extension of the *IS-LM* model, the vector of variables Z might include, for example, a concept of potential ("high-employment") output. For the purposes of this simple model, potential output is assumed to be exogenously given; the price-level equation presumably specifies that P rises faster the smaller the gap between potential and actual output.[40] Note that, since the price level appears in the model explicitly, the money demand function is now identical with 5-7. In principle, the equation system of 5-30 is capable of jointly determining values for y, P, Y, M, and r once exogenous values for the variables in X^M, X^F, and Z have been specified.[41]

Simplified Quasi-Systemic Models

The extended *IS-LM* models of macroeconomic activity just described link the money demand-supply nexus to the rest of the economy in a rudimentary way and therefore cannot be described as oriented exclusively to the "money market." Nonetheless, it can be argued, those models give disproportionate emphasis to money supply and demand. And in any case, they are not broadly systemic, that is, they do not try to represent all of the most salient aspects of macroeconomic behavior.

Consider the model summarized in table 5-5. Unlike the preceding models, this one introduces an explicit distinction between the supply of and demand for output. It begins to differentiate among the various demands for output by specifying separate behavioral relationships for consumption, investment, and government expenditures. It provides for a rudimentary treatment of employment, wages, and the labor market. And it specifies somewhat more detail about the macroeconomic role of the government (the fiscal authority).

The model presented in table 5-5 might be termed quasi-systemic. Its treatment of the nonfinancial aspects of the national economy goes considerably beyond the extreme simplifications of, say, the model shown in 5-30. Nonetheless, it still relies solely on aggregative money demand and supply functions to represent the financial aspects of macroeconomic behavior.

40. In addition to this link between prices and output, the real-income function in the model conceivably can postulate that output depends on the price level.
41. An alternative formulation of 5-30 can specify r as an exogenous policy instrument and thereby substitute a reserve-money aggregate such as H in place of r as the fifth endogenous variable.

Table 5-5. *Simplified Quasi-Systemic Macroeconomic Model*

VARIABLES

Endogenous		*Exogenous*	
M	Money stock	X^M	Vector of instruments of monetary policy (for example, borrowed reserves, discount rate, reserve-requirement ratios)
r	Interest rate		
y	Real income/output		
P	Price level		
C	Consumption		
I	Investment	X^F	Vector of instruments of fiscal policy (for example, tax rates, discretionary government expenditures)
G	Government expenditures		
L	Labor force		
W	Nominal wage rate		
Y	Nominal income		
Y_d	Disposable income	Z	Vector of nonpolicy exogenous variables (for example, population, existing capital stock, household net worth)
T	Government tax receipts		
B	Government budget position		

BEHAVIORAL RELATIONSHIPS AND IDENTITIES

Model sector	*Equation*
Money market:	
Money demand	$\dfrac{M^d}{P} = f(r, y, Z)$
Money supply	$M^s = m(r, X^M)$
Equilibrium condition for money market	$M^s = M = M^d$
Demands for output (product market):	
Equilibrium condition for product market[a]	$y = \dfrac{C}{P} + \dfrac{I}{P} + \dfrac{G}{P}$
Consumption function	$\dfrac{C}{P} = C\left(\dfrac{Y_d}{P}, P, r, Z, X^F\right)$
Private investment demand[b]	$\dfrac{I}{P} = I(y, P, r, Z, X^F)$
Total government expenditure	$\dfrac{G}{P} = G(y, P, X^F)$
Supply of output (labor market):	
Production function[b]	$y = g(L, Z)$
Wage-setting process	$\dfrac{W}{P} = h(L, Z)$
Supply of labor	$L = L(W, P, Z)$
Nominal income and product	$Y = yP$
Disposable income	$Y^d = Y - T$
Real government tax receipts	$\dfrac{T}{P} = T(y, P, X^F)$
Government budget surplus or deficit[b]	$B = T - G$

a. National income and product identity in real terms.
b. The model is applicable only to the short run (because the existing capital stock is assumed to be fixed exogenously, the consequences of investment for the capital stock are ignored, and the consequences of imbalances in the government's budget for household net worth are ignored). For discussion of the dynamic interrelationships of balance-sheet stocks and income-statement flows, see parts 4 and 5.

Systemic Models with Financial Sectors

Finally, suppose analysts adopt a more systemic approach when modeling not only the real but also the financial sectors of the economy. The resulting models will incorporate a wide range of assets and liabilities rather than focus on money alone. And they will specify behavioral demand and supply functions for the various assets and liabilities. Endogenous financial variables in such models might include, for example, the outstanding amounts of securities, deposits, and currency held by nonbanks; the amounts of securities, loans, free reserves, and required reserves held by banks; and the interest rates on deposits, securities, loans, and interbank lending. The disaggregated structural approach to the money-supply process outlined in equations 5-19 through 5-23 can be part of a financial sector of this more systemic type.

When a systemic approach to financial behavior is combined with detailed modeling of the real side of the economy, the resulting overall models tend to be large and complex. Even a model combining the simplified nonfinancial relationships of table 5-5 and the schematic financial environment of tables 5-1 through 5-4 can entail some thirty to forty endogenous variables.[42] Macroeconomic models that attempt to incorporate a large amount of institutional detail may contain several hundred endogenous variables.[43] As an offset to their complexity, systemic models can, of course, embody more of the existing knowledge of macroeconomic behavior and allow for a wider variety of links between financial and nonfinancial variables than smaller models.

The term *systemic* is used here as a loose synonym for *comprehensive*. But any model, even the simplest money-income model 5-25, can be interpreted as a system if it purports to relate ultimate-target variables to policy instruments in a logically consistent manner. Larger or more comprehensive models, moreover, are not necessarily better.[44]

42. For a description and discussion of a small systemic model of this type, see for example Albert Ando, "Some Aspects of Stabilization Policies, the Monetarist Controversy, and the MPS Model," *International Economic Review,* vol. 15 (October 1974), pp. 514–71.

43. See, for example, Lawrence R. Klein and Edwin Burmeister, eds., *Econometric Model Performance: Comparative Simulation Studies of the U.S. Economy* (University of Pennsylvania Press, 1976).

44. Model-choice issues are considered further in part 4.

CHAPTER SIX

Money as an Intermediate Target
of Monetary Policy

THE VIEW that money should be used as an intermediate target in the conduct of monetary policy is not a necessary consequence of conventional formulations of the aggregate demand for and supply of money. But many economists make extensive use of those aggregate functions when rationalizing such a strategy.

Basic Characteristics of a Money Strategy

Consider again the two key propositions on which advocacy of a money strategy typically rests:[1]

(6-A) **There exists for the economy as a whole a particular bundle of financial assets—the money stock—reliably linked through one or more behavioral relationships to the ultimate-target variables of national economic policy; knowledge about these relationships is markedly less uncertain than knowledge about the other macroeconomic behavioral relationships constituting the structure of the economy.**

(6-B) **Policymakers are able to adjust the actual instruments of monetary policy so as closely to control the money stock.**

The words *one or more behavioral relationships* appear in proposition 6-A because proponents of a money strategy can choose to model the links between money and ultimate-target variables in terms of numerous behavioral relationships (a systemic approach) or, alternatively, only a few or even one. Advocacy of a money strategy is most often encountered in conjunction with a simplified money-market model that concentrates on a single relationship: the aggregate demand for money.

The Links between Money and Ultimate-Target Variables

Proponents of a money strategy who rely on the prevalent money-market model believe that, by itself, the aggregate demand function for money satisfies the criterion in 6-A of a reliable (strictly speaking, least unreliable) link between a key intermediate variable and ultimate-target variables.

In support of this belief, it can be pointed out that each alternative demand function in chapter 5 contains the price level as an argument. Moreover, aggregate

---

1. The discussion in chapter 4 leaves moot whether the financial aggregate referred to in propositions 4-K and 4-L can be identified as the stock of money. Propositions 6-A and 6-B assert that the relevant magnitude is in fact the money stock.

income—GNP—appears directly as a variable in equations 5-7 and 5-8. In formulations such as equation 5-9, even though the current value of GNP may not be present directly, such aggregative variables as "permanent GNP" or national wealth are assumed to be arguments of the function; it can thus be claimed that these latter variables are closely related to current GNP. Incontrovertibly, policymakers commonly take the price level and real GNP as ultimate-target variables.

The contention that aggregate demand functions for money provide a direct link between the money stock and ultimate-target variables is not airtight. If one believes that the volume of transactions is the theoretically appropriate argument in the money-demand function, one must acknowledge that GNP has slipped into the function as a poor cousin on the strength of an undocumented assertion that the volume of transactions and GNP are proportional to one another.[2] Those who favor the utility-school approach to money demand ought to acknowledge that it is not a trivial transformation to go from wealth or permanent income to the current value of GNP.[3] Nonetheless, these caveats are probably not so serious as to invalidate the generalization that there exists a financial aggregate—money, somehow defined—the macroeconomic demand for which is related reasonably directly to several of the variables that policymakers take as their ultimate targets.[4]

Direct linkage of the money stock to ultimate-target variables is not necessarily "reliable" linkage. And the demand for money can be somewhat reliable without being "markedly less uncertain" than other macroeconomic behavioral relationships. But proponents of a money strategy applied in conjunction with a money-market model commonly assert that knowledge about the aggregate demand for money is in fact significantly greater than knowledge about other aspects of macroeconomic behavior. To state their assertion in another way: the demand for money is "more stable" than other aggregative relationships.

The Links between Policy Instruments and Money

A money strategy presupposes the correctness not only of proposition 6-A but also of 6-B: policymakers must be able to adjust their policy instruments so as "closely" to control the money stock. Proposition 6-B can be rephrased in terms of the money-supply function in equation 5-12. Policymakers must know how to alter the settings on the various policy instruments in the vector X and must act on that knowledge to make the observed money stock closely track a particular target path. In practice, this means that policymakers must constantly—and dexterously—manipulate their instruments to offset the effects of changes in private-sector endogenous variables—changes in the arguments of $h^B(i, \ldots)$—that also determine

2. Gross national product (GNP) is intended to be a measure of *final* output and thus, in principle, excludes all intermediate and financial transactions associated with producing that output. GNP may thus be a less inadequate proxy for national economic welfare than for the (gross) total of transactions giving rise to a transactions demand for money. GNP also includes some imputed transactions that do not require actual cash settlement and therefore do not give rise to the holdings of transactions balances. On these points, see Charles Lieberman, "The Transactions Demand for Money and Technological Change," *Review of Economics and Statistics*, vol. 59 (August 1977), pp. 307–17, and the references cited there.

3. Permanent income is often approximated by a weighted average of current and past incomes, and current income can be loosely interpreted as the current-period return on wealth. Yet it is no straightforward matter to pin down these relationships more precisely, especially when dealing with macroaggregates.

4. Remember, however, that part 1 assumes a hypothetical economy that is completely closed to the rest of the world!

the amount of money supplied. If not appropriately offset, private-sector behavior will cause the money stock to deviate from the path desired by the policymakers.

Proponents of a strategy using money as an intermediate target acknowledge that the behavior of the private sector generates endogenous variations in the money stock. But they believe that policymakers can, and should, overcome these endogenous variations by adjusting their policy instruments. In their view, if the central bank exercises its powers and knowledge appropriately, the actual path of the money stock can be made to coincide quite closely over time with a policy-determined target path.

Like the links between money and ultimate-target variables, the links between policy instruments and the money stock can be modeled in terms of many or only a few behavioral relationships. The most common approach models the links in a fairly simple way—for example, as in the money-supply function in equation 5-15 or, even more simply, as in equation 5-18. More systemic modeling of the links between instruments and money involves the specification of a more detailed nexus of financial-sector interrelationships—for example the hypothesized model from which the money supply function in equation 5-23 is derived.

The Intermediate-Target Recommendation

If propositions 6-A and 6-B could both be shown to be correct, a prima facie case might seem to exist for a prescriptive recommendation, namely,

(6-C) **Policymakers should conduct monetary policy by (1) setting a target time path for the money stock, and then (2) seeking to keep the money stock as close as possible to that target path through diligent adjustment of the instruments of monetary policy.**[5]

Some characteristics of a money strategy, as the subsequent analysis shows, are not adequately captured in propositions 6-A through 6-C. Even so, they summarize in a broadly faithful way the views of those who contend that money should play a unique and important role in the conduct of monetary policy. The three propositions are certainly the core of the monetarist approach to monetary policy. But they are also implicit in the monetary-policy recommendations of many who would be uncomfortable with the monetarist label.[6]

---

5. Proposition 6-C bears the same relationship to 4-M that 6-A and 6-B bear to 4-K and 4-L.

6. To be sure, those holding views about the special significance of money may not always refer to money as an intermediate target. In practical policymaking situations, the recommendation in proposition 6-C is offered with varying degrees of enthusiasm; virtually every proponent inserts a caveat or a qualification. But the essentials are correct. Were they not, it would be difficult to account for the enormous amount of ink spilled on the subject of monetary aggregates and their role in monetary policy. The following excerpts from Milton Friedman's 1967 presidential address to the American Economic Association provide a key illustration. "How should monetary policy be conducted to make the contribution to our goals that it is capable of making? . . . The first requirement is that the monetary authority should guide itself by magnitudes that it can control, not by ones that it cannot control. . . . I believe that a monetary total is the best currently available immediate guide or criterion for monetary policy—and I believe that it matters much less which particular total is chosen than that one be chosen. A second requirement for monetary policy is that the monetary authority avoid sharp swings in policy. . . . My own prescription is still that the monetary authority go all the way in avoiding such swings by adopting publicly the policy of achieving a steady rate of growth in a specified monetary total." "The Role of Monetary Policy," *American Economic Review,* vol. 58 (March 1968), pp. 14–15, reprinted in Friedman, *The Optimum Quantity of Money and Other Essays* (Aldine, 1969), pp. 108–09.

A Two-Stage Decision Process

The complete decision problem facing policymakers is to select the time sequences of instrument settings that are judged most likely to bring about the best feasible time paths for ultimate-target variables. Any strategy for implementing monetary policy must provide a solution to this problem.

Intermediate-target strategies decompose this problem into two subordinate problems, with decisions at the two stages made separately and sequentially. The *upper-level decision* involves reasoning backward from desired time paths for the ultimate targets to a target path for the money stock, a process that makes use of the behavioral relationships thought to link the ultimate targets and the money stock. Then, in the second stage, the upper-level calculation of the target path for money is taken as given. Utilizing the behavioral relationships thought to link the money stock to the policy instruments themselves, this *lower-level decision* involves calculation of time paths for the instrument settings designed to keep the actual money stock tracking its target path as closely as possible. Together the lower-level and upper-level decisions provide a solution to the larger problem.

Intermediate-target strategies not only dichotomize the larger decision problem. They also presuppose different periodicities of decisionmaking: upper-level calculations of the target path for money are revised only occasionally (in an extreme variant, never); but lower-level decisions are revised more or less continuously. Policymakers scrutinize closely deviations of the actual money stock from its target time path (some of which are inevitable because of the endogenous elements in the determination of money); with each observation of new data for the actual value of money, they may adjust the instruments to minimize future deviations. Money thus becomes the proximate focus of policy actions. A given upper-level specification of the target time path for the money stock is the day-by-day operating objective of lower-level decisions.

The decomposition of policy decisions into two stages and the differing periodicity of decisionmaking for each stage are the key characteristics that differentiate an intermediate-target strategy from other strategies.

Intermediate-target strategies can vary considerably among themselves because the periodicities for upper-level decisions about the target path for money can vary. Furthermore, proponents of money strategies may differ among themselves in the degree of detail they use in attempting to model the behavioral relationships relevant to the two decision levels.[7]

Issues Raised by a Money Strategy

The preceding description identifies the basic features of a money strategy. The remainder of this chapter begins to subject these features to critical scrutiny.

Reliability of the Links between Money and Ultimate Targets

Because proponents of a money strategy applied in conjunction with a money-market model regard 6-A as a proposition about the aggregate demand for money, they give particular attention to the relative "stability" of that demand function.

---

7. Discussion of these and other differences is deferred until part 4.

What is meant when it is asserted that the demand for money is more stable than other macroeconomic relationships? Unfortunately, both the supporters and the critics of this assertion are often imprecise. Used loosely, greater *stability* connotes greater regularity and predictability. Statements made in conjunction with empirical research commonly associate more stability with smaller unexplained variance in estimated money-demand equations and with greater success in forecasting accuracy in and out of the sample period. The concept of stability—or, in the language of proposition 6-A, markedly less uncertain knowledge—includes the degree to which the money-demand behavioral relationship is knowable by policymakers and can be used by them in predicting the consequences of policy actions.[8]

The question of the stability of the demand for money has generated a flood of journal articles in recent decades. After intense research and debate in the United States in the 1950s and 1960s, in the early 1970s professional opinions about the demand for money and its significance appeared to converge.[9] Developments during the 1974–79 period, however, undermined that emerging consensus and brought the issue back into prominence.[10]

Some argue that the stability of a macroeconomic relationship depends on the number of variables appearing as arguments in the behavioral function. Milton Friedman and Anna Schwartz, for example, state:

> The notion of a "stable" demand function, which has played so large a role in our examination of the empirical magnitude that it is best to term "money," is meaningless unless something is specified about the variables included in the function. The "instability" of a particular function can always be interpreted as the result of omitting some relevant variables. The existence of a stable function for anything can never be contradicted if the number of variables included is permitted to be indefinitely large. Implicitly, therefore, the term "stability" used in empirical discussions always means "relative" stability of a function of a "small number of variables." And the terms in quotation marks are not capable of specification on a strictly abstract level.[11]

Don Roper suggests generalizing this argument into a definition of stability: "the greater the number of variables needed to explain a given percent of the variance of the dependent variable in question, the less stable the relationship."[12]

8. For a discussion of possible interpretations of stability in the demand function, see Don Roper, "The Role of the Demand for Money versus Neutrality in Monetarist Thought" (September 1975); and an earlier, published version of the paper, "Two Ingredients of Monetarism in an International Setting," *Intermountain Economic Review*, vol. 6 (Spring 1975).

9. See, for example, David E. W. Laidler, *The Demand for Money: Theories and Evidence* (International Textbook, 1970), chap. 9; Alan S. Blinder and Robert M. Solow, "Analytical Foundations of Fiscal Policy," in Blinder and Solow and others, *The Economics of Public Finance* (Brookings Institution, 1974), pp. 57–78; and Stephen M. Goldfeld, "The Demand for Money Revisited," *Brookings Papers on Economic Activity*, 3:1973, pp. 577–646.

10. On the recent period in the United States, see Jared Enzler, Lewis Johnson, and John Paulus, "Some Problems of Money Demand," *BPEA*, 1:1976, pp. 261–80; Stephen M. Goldfeld, "The Case of the Missing Money," *BPEA*, 3:1976, pp. 683–730; Michael J. Hamburger, "Behavior of the Money Stock: Is There a Puzzle?" *Journal of Monetary Economics*, vol. 3 (July 1977), pp. 265–88; Peter A. Tinsley and Bonnie Garrett, "The Measurement of Money Demand" (Board of Governors of the Federal Reserve System, 1978); and Richard D. Porter, Thomas D. Simpson, and Eileen Mauskopf, "Financial Innovation and the Monetary Aggregates," *BPEA*, 1:1979, pp. 213–29.

11. Milton Friedman and Anna Jacobson Schwartz, *Monetary Statistics of the United States: Estimates, Sources, Methods*, Studies in Business Cycles 20 (New York: National Bureau of Economic Research, 1970), p. 197. The same argument appears in Friedman, *The Optimum Quantity of Money and Other Essays*, p. 62.

12. "The Role of the Demand for Money versus Neutrality in Monetarist Thought," p. 8. In private correspondence with the author, Milton Friedman argued that "there is no unambiguous metric for counting variables" and that therefore a precise definition of stability cannot be obtained in this direction.

Whatever the best connotation of stability may be, *relative* stability is the important issue for proposition 6-A. Knowledge about all aspects of macroeconomic behavior is uncertain and therefore unreliable to some degree. Proponents of a money strategy need not, and usually do not, argue that the demand for money is highly stable in some absolute sense. They merely assert that it is more reliable than other macroeconomic behavioral relationships, which assertion in turn leads them to believe that it should receive preeminent attention in the formulation of monetary policy.

For example, in 1956 Milton Friedman wrote:

> There is perhaps no other empirical relation in economics that has been observed to recur so uniformly under so wide a variety of circumstances as the relation between substantial changes over short periods in the stock of money and in prices; the one is invariably linked with the other and is in the same direction; this uniformity is, I suspect, of the same order as many of the uniformities that form the basis of the physical sciences. And the uniformity is in more than direction. There is an extraordinary empirical stability and regularity to such magnitudes as income velocity that cannot help impressing anyone who works extensively with monetary data.[13]

This may be a stronger argument than most monetary, and even monetarist, economists would make today (and possibly stronger than even Friedman himself would make). But it nicely illustrates proposition 6-A and the special significance attributed to the demand for money by proponents of the strategy of using the money stock as an intermediate target.

When an analyst uses a very simple model that emphasizes the money market, such as the equations of 5-25, there is no difference (in the context of the model) between asking about the stability of the demand for money and asking about the reliability of the links between the money stock and ultimate-target variables. When more systemic models are used, however, the links between money and ultimate targets are much more complex. Then the correctness of proposition 6-A cannot be checked by examining the properties of the model's money-demand function alone. The larger the model and the greater the degree of simultaneous interaction among its endogenous variables, the greater the probability that analysis of the links between money and ultimate targets will require analysis of all the relationships in the model.[14]

Control of the Money Stock

The numerous economists who advocate the use of a money strategy in conjunction with a money-market model think of the links between policy instruments and the money stock in terms of a simple aggregate function describing the money supply process. From their point of view, therefore, the issue of the correctness of proposition 6-B is a straightforward question of the stability of this supply function.

13. *The Optimum Quantity of Money and Other Essays,* p. 67. See also the similar passages on pp. 62–63.

14. Advocates of a money strategy who favor the use of more systemic models tend nonetheless to be supporters of proposition 6-A. They still believe that the money stock is a variable of special significance and that the links connecting ultimate-target variables to money are somehow more reliable or more important than the links between ultimate targets and the many other intermediate variables in the economy. They may not arrive at this belief, however, as a result of preoccupation with the demand for money.

Like the stability of money demand, the stability of money-supply functions is much discussed in the literature. Unfortunately, a similar fuzziness prevails. There is no consensus on a precise concept of stability appropriate for the study of money supply behavior. The scope for conflicting views is even greater than with the demand for money, owing to the greater variety of approaches for conceptualizing the money supply process. One broad theme—an association between the concept of stability and the ability of the central bank to control the supply of money closely—is always encountered. Yet the term *closely* is seldom given an unambiguous definition.

The notion of the central bank's control of the money stock presupposes the existence of target values for money toward which the actual money stock will be guided and of policy actions intended to achieve that guidance. Close control accordingly implies that deviations of the money stock from the given target values will be minor. But neither the target nor the actual money stock is a single-value magnitude; rather, each is a time series of values. Close control thus cannot be defined without explicitly bringing in the temporal element.

What reference period should the analyst use in focusing on discrepancies between the target path and the actual path of the money stock? One possibility is to take a long period, say an entire year. The analyst then pays almost no attention to discrepancies occurring at particular points during the year and focuses on the difference between the annual average value of the target and that of the actual money stock. Alternatively, if a reference period of a quarter or a month is chosen, attention is focused on quarterly average or monthly average discrepancies. If weekly or daily data are available, the reference period may be still shorter; to appraise the closeness of control, the analyst may then take into account the discrepancy between the target value and actual value during each week.

The issue of what reference period is appropriate relates to the question of how small a discrepancy must be to be considered minor. For example, if the reference period is weekly, a temporary (say, one-week) departure of the actual path from the target path by as much as x percent might be thought consistent with close control of the money stock. With a one-year reference period, however, a difference of x percent between the annual averages might be considered much too large to be regarded as minor.

If analysts adopt a long reference period, like one year, they in effect give almost exclusive attention to the *average* position of the actual money path vis-à-vis the target path. Temporary shortfalls are judged to cancel out temporary overshoots; virtually no weight is given to the variance of the actual path around the target path. As the reference period is shortened, however, progressively more weight is implicitly assigned to the variance.

Suppose the central bank's ability to control the money stock is appraised only in terms of the mean difference between the actual time path and the target path. On that basis, the central bank's ability to exert control can be said to be greater the longer the reference period. The central bank will have much less difficulty generating an annual average money stock that deviates from the annual average target value by x percent than it will have keeping each weekly average stock within plus or minus x percent of the weekly target path.

What is the appropriate definition of close control? Much of the literature emphasizes only the mean difference between the actual path and the target path and thereby stresses the point that the central bank can control the money stock quite closely when a sufficiently long reference period is chosen. But a priori selection of a long reference period merely begs the question of whether short-run variance in the money stock should be deemed relevant.[15]

The more exclusively an analyst's model emphasizes the money market, the simpler it is—or at least seems to be—to analyze the ability of the central bank to control the money stock closely. When more systemic models are used, however, the links between policy instruments and money are much more complex. Controllability of the money stock can then no longer be studied merely in terms of a simplified money-supply function. Analysis of most, or conceivably all, of the behavioral relationships in the model may be required to establish the correctness— or incorrectness—of proposition 6-B.[16]

Choice of a Definition of Money

How should policymakers select the "correct" or "best" definition of the money stock to use as their intermediate target?[17]

It is clear from propositions 6-A and 6-B that at least two criteria are relevant to the choice of a definition. The first argues for selecting the definition with the least uncertain causal links between money and ultimate-target variables. The second suggests choosing the financial aggregate that can be controlled most closely and easily.

Unfortunately, the two criteria are not compatible. As the analyst or policymaker searches for the financial aggregate most reliably linked by behavioral relationships to ultimate-target variables, he tends to move along the chains of causal relationships in behavioral functions in the direction of ultimate targets. The more reliable an aggregate is in its links to ultimate targets, the less easily and closely it can be controlled by manipulation of the instruments of monetary policy. Conversely, the more closely an aggregate is tied to policy instruments, the more complex and

---

15. Part 4 places the controllability issue in its proper perspective with other issues raised by intermediate-target strategies. References dealing with the stability of money-supply behavior and the capacity of the central bank to control the money stock include David I. Fand, "Some Issues in Monetary Economics," in *Federal Reserve Bank of Saint Louis Review*, vol. 52 (January 1970), pp. 10–15; William Poole and Charles Lieberman, "Improving Monetary Control," *BPEA*, 2:1972, pp. 293–335; Richard G. Davis, "Implementing Open Market Policy with Monetary Aggregate Objectives," in *Monetary Aggregates and Monetary Policy* (Federal Reserve Bank of New York, 1974), pp. 7–19; John H. Ciccolo, "Is Short-run Monetary Control Feasible?" in ibid., pp. 82–91; James L. Pierce and Thomas D. Thomson, "Some Issues in Controlling the Stock of Money," in *Controlling Monetary Aggregates II: The Implementation*, Conference Series 9 (Federal Reserve Bank of Boston, 1973); Steven M. Roberts and Marvin S. Margolis, "Control of the Money Stock with a Reserve Aggregate," *Journal of Money, Credit and Banking*, vol. 8 (November 1976), pp. 457–76; Paul DeRosa and Gary H. Stern, "Monetary Control and the Federal Funds Rate," *Journal of Monetary Economics*, vol. 3 (April 1977), pp. 217–30.

16. Even a systemic-model proponent of a money strategy will probably classify himself as a supporter of proposition 6-B. It makes no difference whether the policymaking model contains a highly disaggregated representation of the money-supply process or merely a simplified aggregate function like 5-25 or 5-27. If the money stock is to be used as an intermediate-target variable and lower-level decisions are to be continuously directed toward minimizing deviations of the actual stock from a target time path, policymakers must be able to control the money stock fairly closely (again, with some acceptable operational connotation being given to the term *closely*).

17. The context of the discussion here is explicitly *prescriptive*. The issue of which definition of money may be preferable for *descriptive* purposes is not discussed.

numerous the behavioral relationships between it and the ultimate-target variables. Thus the price for selecting an aggregate that can be more closely controlled is increasing uncertainty about the links between that aggregate and the ultimate targets.

As an illustration, consider again the alternative money aggregates of the schematic context of tables 5-1 through 5-4. If policymakers choose nonbanks' currency holdings (CUR) as their intermediate-target variable, they could probably control that aggregate better than any other conventional money candidate.[18] Yet nonbanks regard CUR and means-of-payments deposits (Dmp), and perhaps also other deposits (Dot), as close substitutes. Hence a monetary total of the M_1 type ($CUR + Dmp$) or M_2 type ($CUR + D$) probably exhibits a more reliable causal connection to such ultimate-target variables as real income and the price level than CUR does. The cost to policymakers of improving the reliability of the money-income or money-prices links by selection of the M_1 or M_2 definition as the intermediate target, however, is a reduction in their ability closely to control the intermediate target.

Now imagine that policymakers do not restrict their search to conventionally defined money aggregates. Suppose they add up all the financial assets owned by nonbanks—credit-market claims as well as money.[19] All substitutions that nonbanks make among various financial assets (for example, in response to changes in expected returns) are then suppressed within this broad aggregate. Hence this total-assets aggregate may prove to be more reliably linked to real income and the price level than the narrow money aggregates are.[20] However, the authorities could control such a broad aggregate, if at all, much less closely than the money aggregates. In short, the ranking of various financial aggregates in terms of their potential controllability is probably the reverse of their ranking in terms of reliable links to ultimate-target variables.[21]

Policymakers do not have a simple, clear basis for trading off controllability and reliability when selecting an intermediate-target variable. Accordingly, they have no self-evident basis for choosing the "correct" prescriptive definition of the money stock.

Validity of a Two-Stage Decision Process

The essence of an intermediate-target strategy is to make upper-level decisions about the target path for the key intermediate variable independently of, and much less frequently than, lower-level decisions about the settings for the policy instru-

18. This statement is correct in principle (CUR is, after all, the only asset of the nonbanks that is a liability item on the central bank's own balance sheet); but it could be made true in practice only if the authorities forced an institutional change in their own payments practices on the rest of the economy. As discussed in part 4, policymakers may be better able to control the monetary base than CUR (because the monetary base is a potential instrument even without any change in the government's own payments practices).

19. In the symbols of table 5-4, this aggregate is $CUR + D + S^N$.

20. As a suggestive indication that this may be true for the United States, see *An Introduction to Flow of Funds* (Board of Governors of the Federal Reserve System, 1975), chart 10, p. 22.

21. This line of reasoning can be carried even further: if the authorities selected an aggregate composed of the total of all real and financial assets owned by nonbanks (in the symbols of table 5-4, $CUR + D + S^N + TA^N$), they might have a magnitude still more reliably linked to income and the price level but still less amenable to control. As far as I am aware, the empirical research already conducted by others for the case of the United States is broadly consistent with my assertions. Nonetheless, this reasoning requires more theoretical analysis and further empirical research before it can be advanced with confidence.

ments. One basic question to ask about a money strategy, therefore, is whether the causal behavioral relationships characterizing the structure of the economy permit the larger decision problem facing policymakers to be decomposed into two separate, subordinate problems. It is necessary to ask, in other words, whether the links between policy instruments and money can validly be broken off from the links between money and ultimate-target variables and operated on independently of them. In technical terms, the issue is whether the structure of the economy is sufficiently *recursive,* in an appropriate way, to justify a two-stage decision process centered on the money stock.

The underlying question is whether the "true" structure of the economy exhibits the appropriate recursiveness. Policymakers confront the issue when they specify their model of how the economy works.

Part 4 grapples with this difficult issue, explaining in greater detail why it is important and analyzing its implications for strategy choice. For the time being, it must suffice to warn the reader by introducing another proposition:

(6-D)   The causal links between the instruments of monetary policy and the money stock, and between the money stock and ultimate-target variables, are appropriately recursive so that monetary-policy decisions may be justifiably decomposed into two separate sets of decisions.

This assertion deserves to be ranked with propositions 6-A and 6-B as logical prerequisites for a recommendation that the money stock somehow defined be used as the intermediate target in a two-stage approach to monetary policy.

Other Questions, of Even Greater Importance

The preceding subsections identify some—but not all—of the questions that arise in connection with money strategies. The implications of the questions that remain to be asked, moreover, are even more critical.

First, although part 1 is preoccupied with the money stock, no convincing rationalization for that preoccupation has yet been advanced. There are many intermediate variables in the economy. Many of them are financial. Perhaps, then, attention ought to be given to the possibility of using an intermediate variable other than money as a proximate operating target for monetary policy.

The reader should ask himself, for example, why part 1 fails to include a chapter entitled "Why Do We Need a Concept and Definition of the Long-Term Interest Rate?" Or why does part 1 not focus on aggregate demand and supply functions for bank credit and suggest bank credit as an intermediate-target variable? Indeed, consider the following, more general, versions of the propositions discussed earlier:

(6-A')   There exists for the economy as a whole a particular . . . reliably linked through one or more behavioral relationships to the ultimate-target variables of national economic policy; knowledge about these relationships is markedly less uncertain than knowledge about the other macroeconomic behavioral relationships constituting the structure of the economy.

(6-B')   Policymakers are able to adjust the actual instruments of monetary policy so as closely to control that . . . .

(6-D') **The causal links between the instruments of monetary policy and . . . and between that intermediate variable and ultimate-target variables are appropriately recursive so that monetary-policy decisions may be justifiably decomposed into two separate sets of decisions.**

The pertinent question is why some definition of the money stock rather than of any other intermediate variable is the appropriate magnitude to replace the ellipses in 6-A', 6-B', and 6-D'.

A conceivable answer is that evidence already in hand indicates the correctness of choosing the money stock as the best intermediate-target variable. That answer wrongly presumes, however, that the issue is already widely recognized and that careful research has shown that money outperforms all other intermediate variables as the focal point for a two-stage decision process. To stop here and evaluate the existing research that bears, or might be alleged to bear, on this question would sidetrack the analysis. Suffice it to note that many researchers have simply taken money for granted as an intermediate target without examining any evidence.

The next questions that need to be asked are even more antithetical to the line of reasoning followed here in part 1. Why is it desirable to place so much emphasis on one intermediate-target variable, *whatever that variable may be?* Why, indeed, decompose the overall decision problem into two stages at all? What justifies the difference between the upper-level and the lower-level periodicities of decision-making? Why not derive preferred time paths for policy instruments from the best feasible time paths of the ultimate-target variables in a single, integrated decision rather than interpose a two-stage process that pivots on some intermediate target?

Imagine that new evidence comes to light proving to everyone's satisfaction that other candidates for the role of intermediate-target variable are inferior to the money stock and that propositions 6-A, 6-B, and 6-D are all correct. Would it then follow that the recommendation in 6-C ought to be adopted forthwith? Not at all. For reasons discussed in part 4, such issues as the relative stability of the demand for money and the controllability of the money stock are much less important than typically supposed, *no matter how they are resolved.* The fundamental issue is whether to use a two-level, two-periodicity decision process in the first place.

Finally, what about other goals of macroeconomic policy besides the price level and real GNP? And what about instruments of macroeconomic policy other than those of monetary policy? In principle, the instruments of monetary policy may have significant impacts on all of the ultimate-target variables of the government, not merely on those that conveniently happen to be proxied by arguments in the aggregate demand function for money. Similarly, the instruments of fiscal policy may have significant impacts on most or all of the ultimate-target variables. Can it be valid, then, to formulate and implement monetary-policy decisions in isolation rather than as part of an integrated approach to macroeconomic policy as a whole? If monetary policy does aim at the same ultimate targets as fiscal policy, does the implementation of monetary policy through a money strategy facilitate or impede a coordinated implementation of overall economic policy? Alternatively, perhaps it is politically undesirable or politically infeasible to strive for a coordinated approach to macroeconomic policy decisions. If one believes that central banks should be politically independent and have independently formulated targets, how then should one assess the relative merits of alternative strategies for implementing monetary policy?

Three Levels of Issues

The issues concerning money and monetary policy raised in this chapter are on three levels. Most of the issues on the first level relate narrowly to strategies making use of the money stock as an intermediate target—to the theoretical plausibility of the strategies and the empirical accuracy of the propositions on which advocacy of them must rest. At this level, analysis must largely accept the conceptual frame of reference promulgated by those who favor money strategies. At the second level, the frame of reference is broader; the subject becomes alternative strategies for conducting monetary policy. Intermediate-target strategies—and money strategies in particular—must be compared with other approaches to the conduct of monetary policy. Finally, at the third level, the frame of reference becomes broader still. The analysis must then cope with the problem of how the conduct of monetary policy fits into the larger picture where not only monetary policy but also fiscal policy and many other governmental actions influence the evolution of economic activity. A much wider range of economic issues has to be addressed, and it becomes hopelessly artificial to ignore the politics of monetary policy.

The three levels of issues parallel three indisputable facts: the money stock is not the only intermediate variable that might be chosen as a proximate operating target for monetary policy; an intermediate-target strategy is only one possible approach to the formulation and implementation of monetary policy; and monetary policy is only a part of national macroeconomic policy as a whole.

If the analysis that follows took up all three levels of questions about the conduct of monetary policy while maintaining an artificial institutional context that suppresses the economic interdependence of national economies, it would reinforce the prevalent, but quite wrong, tendency to compartmentalize monetary policy into "domestic" and "external" aspects. Thus the next step in the analysis is to shift the context to an open economy having extensive financial links with the rest of the world.

Part 2 continues to focus on money. It addresses only the first level of issues identified above. It thus presumes—though only as a working hypothesis—the existence of a monetary aggregate, defined somehow, that policymakers decide to use as an intermediate-target variable in the execution of monetary policy.

National Monetary Aggregates in an Open Economy

Rudiments of Monetary Theory
for an Open Economy

THIS CHAPTER identifies some rudiments of monetary theory for the behavior of economic units in an open economy. The institutional framework is international, but in the simplest possible form. The world is assumed to consist of only two nations, home and foreign. Each has a separate currency. Each national economy is assumed to be significantly open; that is, residents of the home nation engage in extensive transactions in goods and services with and have sizable amounts of assets and liabilities vis-à-vis residents of the foreign nation.[1]

The Demand for Means of Payment in a Two-Currency World

As a starting point, consider the narrow question of holding and using means of payment in an open economy.

Each income-account transaction between a home and a foreign economic unit and each international relationship between a debtor in one nation and a creditor in the other is denominated in either the home or the foreign currency. Residents of each nation may thus have transactions denominated not only in their own currency but in the currency unit of the other country. This must be true for residents of at least one of the nations.[2]

The selection of currency to be used as the means of payment in international transactions can conceivably be determined by some conventional rule of thumb. For example, all payments made to a nonresident could be denominated in the currency of the nonresident's country; analogously, home economic units could

---

1. The balance of payments of the home economy is defined as a double-entry bookkeeping record of the flows of payments and receipts, over a specified period of time, between residents of the home and the foreign nations. The transactions in goods and services with foreign residents are *current-account* transactions in the balance of payments. Changes in the assets and liabilities vis-à-vis foreign residents are *capital-account* transactions. *Resident* has a precise definition tied to the geographical territory of the nation; see, for example, International Monetary Fund, *Balance of Payments Manual,* 4th ed. (Washington, D.C.: IMF, 1977).

2. An exchange of goods or services between a home and a foreign resident involves a contractual obligation in which the transaction is valued (invoiced) in one of the currency units, and the means of payment is specified (the currency of settlement). Although the currency of invoicing can, in principle, differ from the currency of settlement, the two are almost always the same. Similarly, while asset and liability contracts can stipulate valuation in terms of one currency unit and require settlement in another, the common practice is for valuation and settlement to be in the same currency. (The so-called unit-of-account or basket-valued bonds are the main instance in which a distinction is made in practice between valuation and settlement.) Currency *denomination* as used in the text refers to the currency of settlement; the broader term is used since it is unnecessary here to make the distinction between valuation and settlement.

have all their receipts denominated in the home currency. In practice, however, the choice of currency is likely to depend both on other aspects of the bargain between buyer and seller and on the transaction costs associated with the alternative possibilities for currency denomination. A dependence of currency denomination on these economic considerations is consistent with a strong influence of traditional customs and institutional arrangements.[3]

At first glance, the currency denomination of the means of payment used in international transactions might seem irrelevant. For example, a simple flow analysis might seem to indicate that the choice of means of payment does not affect balance-of-payments and exchange-market developments. The assertion in such an analysis is that whether a home importer of foreign goods pays for his merchandise in home currency, which is then sold spot (or was previously sold forward) by the foreign exporter for foreign currency, or whether the home importer pays in foreign currency that was previously purchased (spot or forward), there will in either case be the same net flow supply of home currency (demand for foreign currency) in the exchange market.

The difficulty with this superficial flow conclusion is its lack of grounding in an analysis of the portfolio behavior of economic agents—of *stock* demands for and supplies of assets and liabilities. Before the settlement date of an international transaction, the payer must have in his possession—even if only momentarily—a stock of the requisite means of payment at least as large as the size of the transaction. At any moment of time, therefore, an aggregation over all home economic units about to make international payments or anticipating their future means-of-payments needs would reveal an inventory of internationally usable means of payment. The currency composition of this "snapshot" inventory would reflect the denomination of the various international payments that are about to be made or are being anticipated. Similarly, if one were to aggregate over home economic units that have recently received payment for international transactions, the currency composition of that snapshot inventory would reflect the denomination of the recent international receipts. Many economic units might appear in both aggregations, as payers and payees.

To be sure, an economic unit in the home country can obtain foreign-currency means of payment merely by purchasing the required amounts from the foreign exchange market just when they are needed.[4] If the stream of required payments can be adequately foreseen, the amounts required for future dates can be purchased by buying appropriately timed forward-exchange contracts. Analogous exchange-market alternatives are open to home economic units receiving payment in the foreign currency and to foreign economic units making or receiving payments in the home currency.

---

3. These customs and arrangements evolve partially in response to cost considerations. Until recently, empirical information on the currency denomination of international transactions was virtually nonexistent. The facts we do have are primarily the result of Sven Grassman's work. See his *Exchange Reserves and the Financial Structure of Foreign Trade* (Lexington Books, 1973); "A Fundamental Symmetry in International Payment Patterns," *Journal of International Economics*, vol. 3 (May 1973), pp. 105–16; and "Currency Distribution and Forward Cover in Foreign Trade: Sweden Revisited 1973," ibid., vol. 6 (May 1976), pp. 215–21.

4. For a nonbank economic unit, going to the foreign exchange market typically means buying or selling foreign currency at a commercial bank with which the unit does other business.

If exchange-market facilities exist and are well developed, why do home economic units choose to hold average balances of foreign-currency means of payment greater than zero? The explanation lies in two facts: payments and receipts cannot be perfectly synchronized (either in general or in terms of currency denomination), and an exchange between assets denominated in home currency and those denominated in foreign currency involves nonzero transaction costs.[5]

Consider home economic units having frequent payments to make in the foreign currency. Rather than going to the foreign exchange market and instantaneously acquiring the requisite amounts of means of payment for each separate transaction, the units may reduce transaction costs by accumulating foreign-currency balances in times when receipts exceed payments and by making less frequent, lump-sum conversions out of assets denominated in the home currency. Similarly, home units having frequent foreign-currency receipts may be able to reduce transaction costs by accumulating individual receipts and making less frequent, larger-sized conversions rather than instantaneously converting each receipt into assets denominated in the home currency.

In the extreme case in which every international transaction of the home economy were denominated in the home currency, a snapshot inventory of internationally usable means of payment held by home residents would reveal no balances of foreign-currency means of payment. That inventory would be indistinguishable, except conceptually, from an inventory of the means of payment used to settle purely domestic transactions. In that extreme case, however, home residents would have a significant amount of means-of-payment liabilities to foreigners denominated in the home currency. In the opposite polar case, all international transactions would involve payment in or receipt of the foreign currency; home residents would not then have means-of-payment liabilities to foreigners denominated in the home currency but would hold sizable transactions balances denominated in the foreign currency. In the general case, between these two extremes, the demands of each nation's residents for means of payment are not coterminous with their demands for means of payment *denominated in their national currency.*

The theoretical problem is shown schematically in figure 7-1. An economic unit is assumed to have payments and receipts denominated in both the home and the foreign currencies. Its total liquid assets are divided into four categories: means of payment ("cash") denominated in the home currency, means of payment denominated in the foreign currency, liquid assets ("bills") denominated in the home currency that do not serve as a means of payment (either in the domestic economy or in international transactions), and liquid assets denominated in the foreign currency that are not used as a means of payment. Receipts and payments in the home currency are not synchronized; in the first instance they add to or subtract

5. The bid–ask spread in foreign exchange trading (the difference between simultaneous selling and buying prices quoted by dealers) makes it impossible to convert without cost a home-currency asset into a foreign-currency asset, and vice versa. The size of this spread is small relative to the value of transactions, and it may diminish as the size of individual transactions increases. It is doubtful, however, that the transaction costs are sufficiently small to be negligible for any category of transaction. Nonpecuniary transaction costs (for example, the time taken to plan and execute a transaction) are also not likely to be negligible. Empirical evidence on the size of transaction costs in the foreign exchange markets is scant; see, however, Jacob A. Frenkel and Richard M. Levich, "Covered Interest Arbitrage: Unexploited Profits?" *Journal of Political Economy*, vol. 83 (April 1975), pp. 325–38; and Roger M. Kubarych, *Foreign Exchange Markets in the United States* (Federal Reserve Bank of New York, 1978).

Figure 7-1. *The Cash-Management Problem of an Economic Unit Having Receipts and Payments in Two Currencies*

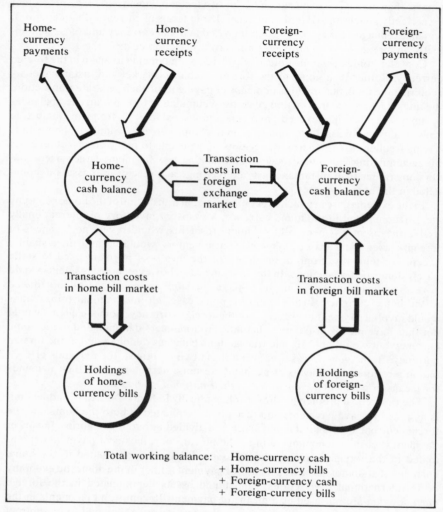

from holdings of home-currency cash. Foreign-currency receipts and payments proximately affect the size of the foreign-currency cash balance. Each category of assets has its "own" rate of return.[6] The rates of return on the noncash liquid assets in the two currencies are assumed to be greater than the corresponding yields on the cash balances. Three types of transaction costs have to be considered: the costs of exchanging home-currency cash for home-currency bills (and vice versa), the costs of exchanging foreign cash for foreign bills (and vice versa), and the costs in the foreign exchange market of converting means of payment in one currency into means of payment in the other currency.[7]

Not every home economic unit will have positive amounts of funds in each of the four categories of liquid assets shown in figure 7-1. For units with a small volume of transactions or for those without payments and receipts denominated in the foreign currency, one or two or even three of these categories may be zero. But the more open the economy, the greater the number of transactors with nonzero demands for foreign-currency means of payment and, perhaps, for foreign-currency bills. At a minimum, this conceptual framework is applicable to economic units— for example, commercial banks—that are the major participants in the foreign exchange market. These major participants in turn provide the retail market in foreign exchange for those economic units having small or less-frequent transactions denominated in foreign currency.

This characterization of the demand for foreign-currency means of payment is merely a further generalization of the theoretical literature on the transactions demand for money. That literature, which deals only with the hypothetical case of a closed economy, shows that the share of cash in a broader total of liquid assets varies directly with the volume of transactions and the size of transaction costs and varies inversely with the difference in yield between cash and noncash substitutes. A satisfactory analysis of the multicurrency counterpart to those single-currency models does not yet exist. On the basis of the work done thus far, however, the outlines of the open-economy generalization are reasonably clear. Two conclusions in particular can be conjectured to hold across a broad range of models.[8] First, the profit-maximizing size of the foreign-currency cash balance is a function of the currency composition as well as of other characteristics of the economic unit's flows of payments and receipts. Other things being equal, the larger the volume of foreign-currency transactions, the larger the demand for means of payment de-

6. The nominal yields on cash denominated in the home currency, in the foreign currency, or in both, can be zero (because, for example, they are fixed at zero by the regulatory authorities). But such yields can also be positive.

7. These transaction costs typically have both a fixed and a variable element—for example, a small fixed cost per transaction and a charge varying with the amount of the transaction. The variable charge can be either proportional to the size of the transaction or (with decreasing costs) decline as a proportion of transaction size.

8. Using figure 7-1 as a framework, I have done some preliminary analysis bearing out these conclusions in the context of models analogous to those used by William J. Baumol, "The Transactions Demand for Cash: An Inventory Theoretic Approach," *Quarterly Journal of Economics*, vol. 66 (November 1952), pp. 545–56 and James Tobin, "The Interest-Elasticity of Transactions Demand for Cash," *Review of Economics and Statistics*, vol. 38 (August 1956), pp. 241–47. The main published work discussing these issues is by Alexander K. Swoboda, *The Euro-dollar Market: An Interpretation*, Princeton Essays in International Finance, 64 (Princeton University Press, 1968) and K. Alec Chrystal, "Demand for International Media of Exchange," *American Economic Review*, vol. 67 (December 1977), pp. 840–50. See also Ronald I. McKinnon, *Private and Official International Money: The Case for the Dollar*, Princeton Essays in International Finance, 74 (Princeton University Press, 1969).

nominated in foreign currency. Second, the size of the foreign-currency cash balance depends on all types of transaction costs, particularly the costs in the foreign exchange market of converting one currency into the other.

Portfolio Behavior of Nonbanks in an Open Economy

An economic unit's transactions demand for means of payment has thus far been considered in isolation. In principle, that demand needs to be analyzed as part of a comprehensive theory of the unit's behavior. At a minimum, a broader microtheory should encompass the entire balance sheet of the behavioral unit, treating jointly each asset demand and liability supply. Preferably, the theory should analyze balance-sheet and income-account decisions together, thus providing an integrated analysis of the unit's portfolio and income-account behavior through time. An appropriate theory for an open economy should also differentiate among types of economic unit. In principle, no less than three theories need to be specified: one each for households, nonfinancial firms, and financial intermediaries. These microeconomic theories, together with a representation of the behavior of the fiscal authority and the central bank, can then serve as the building blocks for an appropriate macroeconomic theory.

The required microeconomic theories, and a fortiori the general-equilibrium macroeconomics, do not yet exist in satisfactory form.[9] Even if they did, it would be impractical to provide a detailed exposition here. Fortunately, for the purposes of the chapters that follow it is sufficient to identify some salient characteristics that such theories must incorporate. This chapter outlines those characteristics.

The schematic balance sheet shown in table 7-1 identifies categories of assets and liabilities that may be found on the balance sheet of an individual economic unit in the private nonbank sector of the home economy. As in chapter 5, no distinction is made between nonbank households (the ultimate consumers and asset holders) and nonbank firms (the nonfinancial producer sector). In keeping with the assumption that the home and foreign economies are significantly open, the home nonbank is assumed to have assets and liabilities denominated in both currencies vis-à-vis economic units resident in both the home and the foreign economies.

Table 7-1 is more complex than the nonbank balance sheet in table 5-4 but only because of the incorporation of currency denomination and international relationships among creditors and debtors. Note especially that it presumes a classification of economic units in the world economy into eight sectors: home nonbanks, home

9. It may be debated how far theory has advanced in analyzing the behavior of microeconomic agents even for a *closed* economy. Probably a majority of economists will acknowledge that the closed-economy theory is still plagued with important unresolved issues. For an *open* economy in a world of many currency units, there is no ambiguity; the relevant microtheories for households, firms, and financial intermediaries exist in, at best, very rudimentary form. For surveys of the state of microeconomic monetary theory for a closed economy, see Jürg Niehans, *The Theory of Money* (Baltimore and London: Johns Hopkins University Press, 1978), chaps. 2–4 and Robert Barro and Stanley Fischer, "Recent Developments in Monetary Theory," *Journal of Monetary Economics*, vol. 2 (April 1976), pp. 133–67. For a general-equilibrium, macroeconomic treatment of balance-sheet (but not consumption and production) decisions in a closed economy, see the accounting and analytical framework in James Tobin, "A General Equilibrium Approach to Monetary Theory," *Journal of Money, Credit and Banking*, vol. 1 (February 1969), pp. 15–29.

Table 7-1. *Schematic Balance Sheet for an Individual Nonbank Resident in the Home Country*[a]

Home-currency units

	Assets
CUR	Holdings of currency, subdivided into:
$CURh_{CB}$	Home currency
$\pi CURf_{FCB}$	Foreign currency
Dmp	Deposit claims on financial intermediaries, widely accepted as a means of payment, subdivided into claims on:
$Dmph_B$	Home banks, denominated in home currency
$\pi Dmpf_B$	Home banks, in foreign currency
$Dmph_{FB}$	Foreign banks, in home currency
$\pi Dmpf_{FB}$	Foreign banks, in foreign currency
Dot	Other deposit claims on financial intermediaries, subdivided into claims on:
$Doth_B$	Home banks, denominated in home currency
$\pi Dotf_B$	Home banks, in foreign currency
$Doth_{FB}$	Foreign banks, in home currency
$\pi Dotf_{FB}$	Foreign banks, in foreign currency
S	Security claims on governments, liquid and long-term, subdivided into:
Sh_G	Securities issued by the home government, denominated in home currency
πSf_{FG}	Securities issued by the foreign government, in foreign currency
A	All other financial claims, liquid and illiquid, subdivided into claims on:
Ah_N	Other home nonbanks, denominated in home currency
πAf_N	Other home nonbanks, in foreign currency
Ah_{FN}	Foreign nonbanks, in home currency
πAf_{FN}	Foreign nonbanks, in foreign currency
Ah_B	Nondeposit claims on home banks (including equity interest)
πAf_{FB}	Nondeposit claims on foreign banks (including equity interest)
TA	Value of tangible assets owned (land, structures, capital equipment), subdivided into:
TA_{home}	Assets located in the home economy
$\pi TA_{foreign}$	Assets located in the foreign economy

	Liabilities and net worth
L	Loans from financial intermediaries, subdivided into loans from:
Lh^B	Home banks, denominated in home currency
πLf^B	Home banks, in foreign currency
Lh^{FB}	Foreign banks, in home currency
πLf^{FB}	Foreign banks, in foreign currency
BOR	Borrowings from other nonbanks, subdivided into borrowings from:
$BORh^N$	Other home nonbanks, denominated in home currency
$\pi BORf^N$	Other home nonbanks, in foreign currency
$BORh^{FN}$	Foreign nonbanks, in home currency
$\pi BORf^{FN}$	Foreign nonbanks, in foreign currency
W	Net worth

a. The following assumptions are made: currency is issued only by central banks; governments issue debt securities only in their own currency unit; and nonbanks do not borrow from central banks or fiscal authorities. These assumptions, especially the latter two, are schematic simplifications at variance with actual circumstances in many countries.

A subscript on a symbol indicates the sector for which the item is a liability; a superscript indicates the sector for which the item is an asset: N = home nonbanks; B = home banks; CB = home central bank; G = home fiscal authority; FN = foreign nonbanks; FB = foreign banks; FCB = foreign central bank; FG = foreign fiscal authority. The currency in which an item is denominated is indicated by h (home) or f (foreign). To express entries in units of home currency, an asset or liability denominated in foreign currency is multiplied by the exchange rate (the price of a unit of foreign currency in terms of home currency), denoted by π.

banks, the home central bank, the home fiscal authority, foreign nonbanks, foreign banks, the foreign central bank, and the foreign fiscal authority.[10]

Table 7-1 illustrates the earlier point that the demands of many economic units for means of payment in a highly open economy are not coterminous with their demands for means of payment denominated in the home currency. Thus, a home nonbank might hold as many as six separate types of means of payment: currency, means-of-payment deposits in home banks, and means-of-payment deposits in foreign banks, each denominated in the foreign as well as the home currency unit. An analogous point applies a fortiori to the demand for liquid assets as a whole. The total demand for liquid assets need not be coterminous with either the demands for liquid assets denominated in the home currency or the demands for liquid-asset claims on economic units resident in the home economy. As many as sixteen separate items on the asset side of the nonbank's balance sheet might warrant inclusion in the aggregate of demands for liquid assets.

A fully developed microeconomic theory for the portfolio behavior of the nonbank whose balance sheet is shown in table 7-1 must specify joint-decision rules for each of the categories of asset demands and liability supplies. Moreover, the system of behavioral equations summarizing those rules must be consistent with the balance-sheet identity that total assets equal total liabilities plus net worth at every point in time.

Portfolio decisions are made on the basis of expectations formed under conditions of uncertainty. The most important variables in the theory determining the nonbank's portfolio decisions are the expected rates of return on each asset and the expected borrowing costs associated with each liability. Measures of the dispersion of each expected return or cost around its mean are also relevant (unless, improbably, the nonbank is entirely averse to risk). The expected real returns associated with holding an asset depend on the asset's nominal yield, expected gains or losses resulting from changes in its capital value, and the expected change in the prices of goods relevant to the economic unit's consumption.[11] Even for an economic environment with a single currency unit, appropriate specification of the expected return and dispersion variables is complex. The existence of two currency units and an exchange rate linking them introduces still more complexity. Economic units in a two-currency world must form expectations of changes in the exchange rate (or, equivalently, expectations of future values of the exchange rate) because such changes generate alterations in capital values and income receipts and hence affect the real value of net worth.

The differences among monetary theorists that lead to differing views about the appropriate scalar arguments in money-demand equations (and more generally in asset-demand and liability-supply equations) for a closed economy generate still further differences in approach for the open-economy case. Theories stemming from the transactions school hypothesize that a nonbank's portfolio decisions are significantly influenced not only by its net worth but also by additional scalar variables such as the volumes of its transactions in both the home and the foreign

10. The principle of the notation used in table 7-1 and in the subsequent discussion is to denote four aspects of balance-sheet items: the type of asset or liability (main part of the symbol), its currency denomination (final letter), the sector for which the item is an asset (superscript), and the sector for which the item is a liability (subscript). When sufficiently obvious from the context, a superscript or a subscript is omitted.

11. Analogous considerations apply to expected real borrowing costs associated with owing a liability.

currencies.[12] The utility school, however, rejects an emphasis on transactions and might employ only the nonbank's net worth as a scalar variable. That approach is simpler and somewhat less affected by the complications of an open economy than the theories emphasizing transaction costs and the degree of synchronization of payments and receipts.

One possible representation of a system of behavioral equations for the nonbank may take the following general form:

$$(7\text{-}1) \quad \left\{ \begin{array}{l} \cdots \\ Z_{ij}^N = f_{ij}\left(\hat{r}_j^h, \hat{r}_j^f, \dfrac{T_j^h}{W_j}, \dfrac{\pi T_j^f}{W_j}, \ldots\right) W_j \\ \cdots \\ \pi Z_{ij}^N = f_{ij}\left(\hat{r}_j^h, \hat{r}_j^f, \dfrac{T_j^h}{W_j}, \dfrac{\pi T_j^f}{W_j}, \ldots\right) W_j \\ \cdots \end{array} \right\} \quad i = 1, \ldots, 28.$$

The Z_{ij}^N are the twenty-eight balance-sheet items in table 7-1; the subscript i refers to the particular asset or liability, while j is the individual nonbank to which the system of equations pertains. Liabilities are treated as negative assets. The net worth of the nonbank is W_j. The large number of variables summarizing the expected returns and costs and the measures of their dispersion is partitioned into two subvectors. The symbol $\hat{r}_j^h$ stands for the subvector of return, cost, and dispersion variables associated with assets and liabilities denominated in the home currency; the circumflex and the subscript j indicate that the variables are expectations formed by the individual nonbank. Similarly, $\hat{r}_j^f$ represents all the expected returns, costs, and dispersions associated with assets and liabilities denominated in the foreign currency (expressed in home-currency units); the nonbank's expectation of changes in the exchange rate is a component of each individual expected return and cost contained in this subvector.[13] The variables T_j^h and T_j^f denote the volumes of the nonbank's transactions in, respectively, the home and the foreign currencies; this illustrative system of behavioral equations is thus in the spirit of the transactions-school approach to portfolio decisions.

If a variable influences the nonbank's decisions about one of the asset demands or liability supplies, the same variable must also affect at least one other demand or supply. In the general case, suggested in 7-1, the complete list of determining variables may appear in each of the behavioral equations in the system.[14]

12. The theory of the demand for means of payment in the preceding section, if appropriately embedded in a system of behavioral relationships for the entire balance sheet, is in accordance with this school.

13. There are sixteen balance-sheet items in table 7-1 denominated in foreign currency. The subvector $\hat{r}_j^f$ thus contains at least thirty-two elements (an expected value and a dispersion measure for each of the returns or costs). The expected return expressed in home-currency units for an individual foreign-currency asset Z_{sj}^N might be written as $(\hat{r}_{sj} + \hat{\pi}_j)$, where $\hat{r}_{sj}$ represents the nonbank's expectation of the return on asset s in foreign-currency units and $\hat{\pi}_j$ represents its expectation of the change in the exchange rate. In principle, portfolio decisions depend not only on the expected values and dispersions of returns and costs but also on their covariation.

14. For example, if an increase takes place in the volume of foreign-currency transactions with wealth, expected returns, and other determining variables remaining unchanged, the nonbank can only increase its holdings of foreign-currency means of payment by reducing its holdings of some other assets or increasing one or more of its liabilities. For discussion of this and other points that arise in specifying a logically consistent representation of portfolio behavior, see William Brainard and James Tobin, "Pitfalls in Financial Model Building," *American Economic Review*, vol. 58 (May 1968, *Papers and Proceedings, 1967*), pp. 99–149.

An important fact is evident even from this sketchy outline: the exchange rate and various foreign and foreign-currency variables are pervasive elements in the portfolio decision rules of the home nonbank.[15]

The system of decision rules in the equations 7-1 is sufficiently general to apply to the behavior of any nonbank. For most applications of practical interest, one would have to distinguish between, at a minimum, households and nonfinancial corporations. Microeconomic theory for a large firm operating in an open economy poses especially difficult problems. Full allowance must be made both for extensive international transactions and for the integration of operations in the home country with the production, investment, and financial decisions that are carried out in the foreign country through subsidiaries or other affiliates.[16]

Financial Intermediaries in an Open Economy

Table 7-2 provides an analogous balance sheet for an individual financial intermediary (bank) in the home economy. Because the home and foreign economies are assumed to be significantly open, the bank issues liabilities and holds assets in both of the currency units vis-à-vis foreign as well as home economic units.

As in the case of a nonbank, a fully developed microeconomic theory for the bank's behavior must specify a system of behavioral equations summarizing the decision rules used to allocate all its assets and liabilities. The general structure of such a system, for example, might be of the following form:

$$(7\text{-}2) \quad \left\{ \begin{array}{l} \cdots \\ Z^B_{ik} = f_{ik}\left(\hat{r}^h_k, \hat{r}^f_k, D^h_k, \pi D^f_k, T^h_k, \pi T^f_k, NW_k, \ldots \right) \\ \cdots \\ \pi Z^B_{ik} = f_{ik}\left(\hat{r}^h_k, \hat{r}^f_k, D^h_k, \pi D^f_k, T^h_k, \pi T^f_k, NW_k, \ldots \right) \\ \cdots \end{array} \right\} \quad i = 1, \ldots, 35.$$

The Z^B_{ik} are the thirty-five balance-sheet items in table 7-2, excluding the bank's surplus and capital accounts, NW; the subscript k denotes the individual bank k. Liabilities are treated as negative assets. The expected return, cost, and dispersion variables relevant to the bank are partitioned into two subvectors, $\hat{r}^h_k$ and $\hat{r}^f_k$; the former pertains to assets and liabilities denominated in home currency, the latter to those denominated in foreign currency. The expected change in the exchange rate in this case, as in the nonbank case, is an important constituent of each of the returns and costs contained in the subvector $\hat{r}^f_k$.

15. For example, the exchange rate π appears directly in the left-hand side of all asset-demand and liability-supply equations where the asset or liability is denominated in foreign currency. It is an element of the argument πT^f_j, the volume of the nonbank's transactions denominated in foreign currency expressed in home-currency units. The expected change in the exchange rate is a constituent of every return or cost variable in the subvector $\hat{r}^f_j$.

16. For discussions of the current state of the art, see John H. Dunning, ed., *Economic Analysis and the Multinational Enterprise* (London: Allen and Unwin, 1974), especially chapters by Guy V. G. Stevens, Thomas O. Horst, Raymond Vernon, and W. M. Corden; and Michael Adler and Bernard Dumas, "The Microeconomics of the Firm in an Open Economy," *American Economic Review*, vol. 67 (February 1977, Papers and Proceedings, 1976), pp. 180–89.

Financial intermediaries behave in the short run as quantity takers when supplying some types of deposit liabilities; that is, they set the interest yield and other terms on the deposits and accept whatever quantity of the deposits their customers choose to hold on those terms. Their behavior as quantity takers is even more pronounced if government regulatory controls, such as interest-rate ceilings, constrain their ability to set the terms on deposit liabilities. Thus the variables D_k^h and D_k^f are included in equations 7-2 to represent vectors of home-currency and foreign-currency nominal magnitudes—for example, quantities of certain types of the bank's deposits—relevant to the bank's portfolio allocation decisions.[17]

The variables T_k^h and T_k^f denote the bank's transactions denominated in the home and foreign currencies. A commercial bank making a retail market in foreign exchange for its customers may be considered to have a derived transactions demand for means of payment denominated in foreign currency. Other things being equal, an increase in the bank's foreign-currency transactions, which in turn partly depends on increases in the foreign-currency transactions of its customers, induces the bank to hold larger balances of foreign-currency means of payment.

Even less effort has been devoted to formulating microeconomic theories for financial intermediaries in an open economy than for nonbanks.[18]

Asset Demands and Liability Supplies of Macroeconomic Sectors

The two preceding sections postulate balance sheets and decision rules for a representative nonbank and a representative bank in the home country. Analogous balance sheets and systems of equations can be specified for nonbanks and banks in the foreign country. Just as the behavioral equations for Z_{ij}^N for a home nonbank j and for Z_{ik}^B for a home bank k are given in 7-1 and 7-2, comparable sets of behavioral relationships might be specified for a foreign nonbank $m—Z_{im}^{FN}$ ($i = 1, \ldots, 28$)—and for a foreign bank $n—Z_{in}^{FB}$ ($i = 1, \ldots, 35$). The rudiments of the microtheories outlined here are sufficiently nonspecific and noninstitutional to make the differences between schematic balance sheets and decision rules for home and foreign economic units merely presentational.[19]

Suppose detailed information were available for the balance sheets of each economic unit in the two-nation, two-currency world economy considered here. Suppose all the balance sheets for microeconomic units were aggregated to obtain macroeconomic sector balance sheets for each of the eight sectors distinguished

17. The discussion in chapter 5 of the money supply process deals with complexities of this sort briefly and notes that even closed-economy theory is in ferment about how to handle them. The equation system in 7-2 is intended only as an illustration. In a detailed microeconomic model for a bank, some of the equations would specify an interest rate rather than the associated balance-sheet quantity as the decision variable.

18. Charles Freedman, "Micro Theory of International Financial Intermediation," *American Economic Review*, vol. 67 (February 1977, *Papers and Proceedings, 1976*), pp. 172–79, surveys the scant literature and notes some relevant references.

19. The balance sheets for foreign economic units would be expressed in units of foreign currency. Assets and liabilities denominated in home currency (*foreign* currency from the perspective of the foreign economic unit) would be multiplied by $1/\pi$, where π is the home-currency value of a unit of foreign currency.

Table 7-2. *Schematic Balance Sheet for an Individual Financial Intermediary (Bank) in the Home Country*[a]

Home-currency units

	Assets
RRh_{CB}	Reserves required against deposit liabilities, held at the home central bank
RXh_{CB}	Excess reserves held at the home central bank
Dmp	Means-of-payment transactions balances held with other banks, subdivided into balances with:
$Dmph_B$	Other home banks, denominated in home currency
$\pi Dmpf_B$	Other home banks, in foreign currency
$Dmph_{FB}$	Foreign banks, in home currency
$\pi Dmpf_{FB}$	Foreign banks, in foreign currency
Dot	Claims on other banks that are not means-of-payment balances,[b] subdivided into claims on:
$Doth_B$	Other home banks, denominated in home currency
$\pi Dotf_B$	Other home banks, in foreign currency
$Doth_{FB}$	Foreign banks, in home currency
$\pi Dotf_{FB}$	Foreign banks, in foreign currency
S	Security claims on governments, liquid and long-term, subdivided into:
Sh_G	Securities issued by the home government, denominated in home currency
πSf_{FG}	Securities issued by the foreign government, in foreign currency
L	Loans to nonbanks, subdivided into loans to:
Lh_N	Home nonbanks, denominated in home currency
πLf_N	Home nonbanks, in foreign currency
Lh_{FN}	Foreign nonbanks, in home currency
πLf_{FN}	Foreign nonbanks, in foreign currency
TA	Value of tangible assets owned, subdivided into:
TA_{home}	Assets located in the home economy
$\pi TA_{foreign}$	Assets located in the foreign economy

	Liabilities and net worth
RBh^{CB}	Discounts and other borrowing from the home central bank (borrowed reserves)
Dmp	Means-of-payment deposit liabilities, subdivided into liabilities to:
$Dmph^N$	Home nonbanks, denominated in home currency
$\pi Dmpf^N$	Home nonbanks, in foreign currency
$Dmph^{FN}$	Foreign nonbanks, in home currency
$\pi Dmpf^{FN}$	Foreign nonbanks, in foreign currency
$Dmph^B$	Other home banks, in home currency
$\pi Dmpf^B$	Other home banks, in foreign currency
$Dmph^{FB}$	Foreign banks, in home currency
$\pi Dmpf^{FB}$	Foreign banks, in foreign currency
Dot	Other deposit liabilities, subdivided into liabilities to:
$Doth^N$	Home nonbanks, denominated in home currency
$\pi Dotf^N$	Home nonbanks, in foreign currency
$Doth^{FN}$	Foreign nonbanks, in home currency
$\pi Dotf^{FN}$	Foreign nonbanks, in foreign currency
$Doth^B$	Other home banks, in home currency[c]
$\pi Dotf^B$	Other home banks, in foreign currency[c]
$Doth^{FB}$	Foreign banks, in home currency[c]
$\pi Dotf^{FB}$	Foreign banks, in foreign currency[c]
NW	Surplus and capital accounts (net worth)

earlier (banks, nonbanks, the central bank, and the fiscal authority in both the home and the foreign economies). Suppose further that each bank and nonbank, in both economies, employed portfolio decision rules of the general sort described above. Finally, suppose that a careful, if not perfect, aggregation of the microeconomic decision rules were carried out to produce four systems of macroeconomic behavioral relationships, one each for the aggregate of home banks, home nonbanks, foreign banks, and foreign nonbanks.[20]

The resulting sector balance sheets for home nonbanks and foreign nonbanks, and for home banks and foreign banks, would closely resemble the balance sheets shown in tables 7-1 and 7-2. Differences would exist only because intrasector assets and liabilities would have been consolidated. For example, borrowing by one home nonbank from another would disappear from both sides of the consolidated balance sheet for the home nonbank sector as a whole.[21] Thus, with appropriate consolidation adjustments, tables 7-1 and 7-2 can also serve as macroeconomic balance sheets for all four private sectors.

Analogously, the equation systems in 7-1 and 7-2 can serve, if suitably adjusted, as schematic representations of aggregate behavioral relationships for the same four sectors. In the macroeconomic versions of the systems, the subscripts indicating the individual microeconomic units are eliminated and all the variables in the equations become aggregates for the macroeconomic sectors.[22]

The macroeconomic sector behavioral relationships hypothesized above play a role in the discussion of aggregate demand and supply functions for money in the next chapter and in the analysis in part 5.

---

20. It would of course be extremely difficult to perform such an aggregation; see Henri Theil, *Linear Aggregation of Economic Relations* (Amsterdam: North-Holland, 1954). An aggregation comparable in spirit underpins the monetary macroeconomics in Tobin, "A General Equilibrium Approach to Monetary Theory."

21. After consolidation of intrasector assets and liabilities, the sector balance sheet for each nation's nonbanks contains twenty-four categories of assets and liabilities plus aggregate net worth. The sector balance sheet for each nation's banks has twenty-seven items plus an aggregate of the banks' surplus and capital accounts.

22. For all the instances in which economic units in one sector have balance-sheet relations vis-à-vis economic units in a different sector, the aggregation assumed here does not aggregate over types of assets and liabilities but only over the individual economic units within each sector. Thus the hypothesized sector balance sheets and equation systems still contain the detail by type of financial asset and liability. The resulting sets of sector equations may be designated as Z_i^N ($i = 1, \ldots, 24$) for home nonbanks, Z_i^{FN} ($i = 1, \ldots, 24$) for foreign nonbanks, Z_i^B ($i = 1, \ldots, 27$) for home banks, and Z_i^{FB} ($i = 1, \ldots, 27$) for foreign banks.

---

a. This schematization identifies categories of assets and liabilities analogous to those in the closed-economy balance sheet for the consolidated banking sector shown in table 5-3. The following assumptions are made: banks do not hold currency; banks have claims on nonbanks only in the form of loans; home banks do not hold any claims on the foreign central bank; the fiscal authorities and central banks do not hold deposits in private banks; the requirements of the central bank and fiscal authority in one country for means-of-payment balances denominated in the currency unit of the other country are met by holding a transactions balance at the other country's central bank; the needs of a fiscal authority for a transactions balance in its own currency unit are met by a deposit in its own central bank.

See table 7-1, note a, for explanation of subscript and superscript notation. To avoid introducing new symbols here, the individual bank's assets and liabilities vis-à-vis other banks are shown either as *Dmp* or *Dot* even though the majority of these assets and liabilities might not be deposits in the usual sense of the term.

b. These claims of the bank on other banks could be deposits or, alternatively, loans arranged primarily at the initiative of the borrowing banks.

c. These liabilities of the bank to other banks could be deposits or, alternatively, borrowings arranged primarily at the initiative of the bank under consideration.

Fortunately, the subsequent analysis does not require a theoretical foundation any more rigorous than that summarized here. Were it necessary to expand the exposition in this chapter, it would be impossible to avoid taking a position on some difficult issues that monetary theorists have not yet satisfactorily resolved.[23] Monetary theory for an open economy has illustrious parents and aunts and uncles. So far, however, comparative neglect has kept the offspring in the stage of infancy.

23. Three examples may be mentioned. First, the exposition here has concentrated on portfolio decisions. Difficult dynamic stock-flow problems arise as soon as one tries to integrate consumption-saving behavior with portfolio decisions (for households) or production-investment behavior with financial management (for firms). Second, equation systems of the sort in 7-1 and 7-2 commonly assume that home economic units think of their balance sheets exclusively in terms of home currency (the home currency is their preferred "financial habitat"), and vice versa for foreign economic units. Yet if an economic unit purchases both home and foreign goods and hence should use the prices of both home and foreign goods in the price index used to calculate the real value of net worth, such assumptions are theoretically unsatisfactory. Third, the appropriate specification of expectations of inflation and exchange-rate changes is problematic and controversial.

CHAPTER EIGHT

Alternative Definitions of the National Money Stock

MOST ADVOCATES of money as an intermediate target focus their attention on the aggregate demand for and supply of money. They regard the money-demand function as a direct, reliable link between the money stock and ultimate policy objectives such as the price level and aggregate output. And they view the money-supply function as a channel through which, by variation of its policy instruments, the central bank can closely control the money stock.

To advocate that an individual nation's central bank follow a money strategy is to recommend that some definition of *that nation's* money be used as an intermediate target in the effort to achieve *that nation's* ultimate policy objectives. Yet debate about the merits of a money strategy is typically conducted with all international considerations suppressed and hence without attention to the appropriate definition of national (or home) money. This chapter corrects that omission by exploring alternative ways of defining the money stock as an intermediate-target variable in an open economy.

Schematic Debtor-Creditor Relationships in an Eight-Sector World Economy

Chapter 7 uses schematic balance sheets of individual microeconomic units to generate hypothetical balance sheets and behavioral relationships for the nonbank and bank sectors in the home and foreign economies. The matrix in figure 8-1 summarizes the debtor-creditor relationships that may exist among the eight sectors of this two-nation "world" economy. Within this context, a particular financial aggregate can be readily defined by indicating which of the categories of assets or liabilities—which cells in the matrix—it includes.

Although there are in principle over 100 cells to be considered, many of them are ignored in what follows. The diagonal cells are blocked out because intrasector items (for example, the liabilities of one home bank to another home bank) were consolidated at the time the sector balance sheets were constructed. Several rows are shaded in accordance with the simplifying assumption introduced in chapter 7 that neither the home nor foreign governmental sectors issue liabilities denominated in a currency other than their own national currency. Other simplifying assumptions used in chapter 7 result in the suppression of still other cells (for example, the liabilities of a nation's banks to their fiscal authority and the liabilities of one nation's central bank to the other nation's private banks).

Figure 8-1. *Schematic Network of Liability-Asset Relationships in a Two-Nation World Economy*[a]

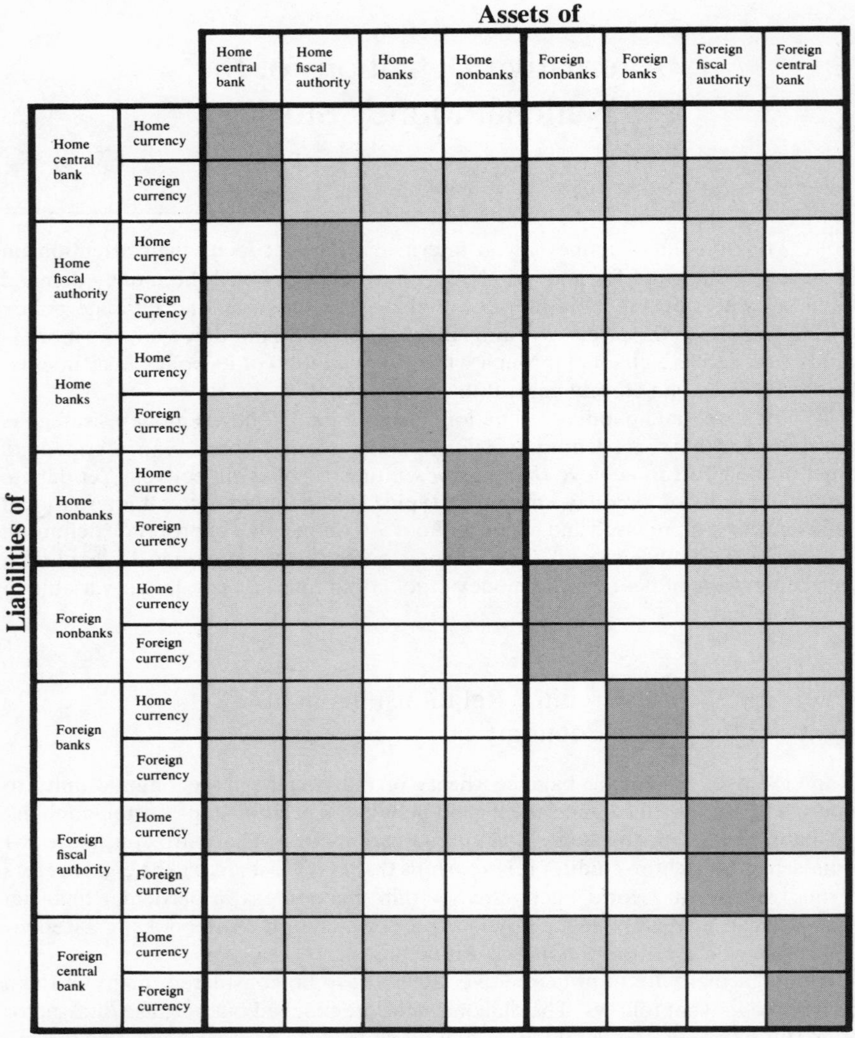

Assets of

Liabilities of		Home central bank	Home fiscal authority	Home banks	Home nonbanks	Foreign nonbanks	Foreign banks	Foreign fiscal authority	Foreign central bank
Home central bank	Home currency								
	Foreign currency								
Home fiscal authority	Home currency								
	Foreign currency								
Home banks	Home currency								
	Foreign currency								
Home nonbanks	Home currency								
	Foreign currency								
Foreign nonbanks	Home currency								
	Foreign currency								
Foreign banks	Home currency								
	Foreign currency								
Foreign fiscal authority	Home currency								
	Foreign currency								
Foreign central bank	Home currency								
	Foreign currency								

a. See text for explanation.

Even without the shaded cells, figure 8-1 includes too many debtor-creditor relationships to permit a simplified analysis of alternative definitions of national monetary aggregates. The subsequent discussion therefore also ignores all the liabilities of a nation's nonbank sector to banks in its own nation and to both banks and nonbanks in the other nation (whether denominated in the home or the foreign currency). For many analytical purposes, and even if the focus is exclusively on assets with a high degree of liquidity, it is probably inappropriate to neglect those nonbank liabilities. In real life, nonbanks have large amounts of accounts payable and accounts receivable; they borrow by issuing liquid liabilities such as commercial paper. In a significantly open economy, many home nonbanks may have nonnegligible amounts of liabilities to foreign nonbanks and banks, and nonnegligible amounts of assets, including liquid assets, that are claims on foreign nonbanks. The exclusion of nonbank liabilities from the subsequent analysis is thus justified solely on the grounds of expositional simplicity.

A simplified version of figure 8-1 is shown in figure 8-2. Greater detail is provided for the liabilities of the two bank sectors and of the two central banks and fiscal authorities. The assets of the central banks and the liabilities of the nonbank sectors are omitted, as are the cells that are shaded in figure 8-1. Each of the forty-two cells remaining for consideration in figure 8-2 is given a number to facilitate the subsequent discussion.[1]

The analysis here assumes that the home and foreign economies are significantly open and hence that nonnegligible amounts of assets are associated with each of the unshaded cells in figures 8-1 and 8-2. In reality, individual nations have widely varying degrees of financial interpenetration with foreign economies. At one extreme are some nations for whom the magnitudes in many of the cells are as yet trivial relative to the size of the economy. For a few of the industrialized nations with highly developed financial markets, on the other hand, appreciable amounts exist of virtually all the asset categories in the matrixes.[2] The practical relevance for a nation's monetary policy of the points stressed below depend, of course, on the actual empirical magnitudes involved.

Eurocurrency Assets and Liabilities

The preceding schematic representation of world financial interrelationships does not refer explicitly to "Eurobanks" or the "Eurocurrency" markets. Yet it none-theless subsumes all the debtor-creditor relationships commonly referred to as Eurocurrency assets and liabilities.

An unwary reader of the literature on Eurocurrency markets could form an impression that Eurocurrency banking is altogether different from the regular banking characteristic of "domestic" financial activity within nations. But that impression is an impediment to clear analysis. Eurocurrency markets are not a

1. As before, it is assumed that banks do not hold currency. Figure 8-2 also assumes that fiscal authorities neither hold nor issue currency.
2. More precisely, they exist in all the cells in the three quadrants of the matrixes other than the southeast. The southeast quadrant represents the relations between pairs of nonresident sectors—that is, "domestic" finance in the rest of the world.

Figure 8-2. *Simplified Liability-Asset Relationships to Be Considered When Defining the National Money Stock*[a]

Liabilities of			Assets of					
			Home fiscal authority	Home banks	Home nonbanks	Foreign nonbanks	Foreign banks	Foreign fiscal authority
Home central bank	Home currency	Currency			1	22		
		Deposit liabilities	3	2				33
Home fiscal authority	Home currency	Short- and long-term securities		4	5	23	28	
Home banks	Home currency	Means-of-payment liabilities			6	24	29	
		Other deposit liabilities			7	25	30	
	Foreign currency	Means-of-payment liabilities			8	26	31	
		Other deposit liabilities			9	27	32	
Foreign banks	Home currency	Means-of-payment liabilities		16	10	34		
		Other deposit liabilities		17	11	35		
	Foreign currency	Means-of-payment liabilities		18	12	36		
		Other deposit liabilities		19	13	37		
Foreign fiscal authority	Foreign currency	Short- and long-term securities		20	14	38	39	
Foreign central bank	Foreign currency	Deposit liabilities	21				41	40
		Currency			15	42		

a. See text for explanation.

phenomenon sui generis but merely part of a general nexus of financial interrelationships among open economies.

Eurocurrency banking is the denomination of bank assets and liabilities in a currency other than the currency unit of the nation where the bank is located.[3] To be sure, in their regulatory and supervisory treatment of banks, governmental authorities in most nations differentiate between domestic-currency and external-currency assets and liabilities, and between relations vis-à-vis resident customers and nonresident customers. These differences create differential incentives for the growth of the various categories of assets and liabilities. Less stringent regulation of the external-currency portions of banks' balance sheets is a major—probably the most important—explanation of the rapid growth of Eurocurrency banking.[4] Once regulatory differences are acknowledged, however, the only reason to differentiate between Eurocurrency and regular banking is because the latter involves denomination of assets and liabilities in the domestic currency whereas the former does not.

Whether obligations are denominated in domestic or external currency is of critical importance for many issues. Since the denomination of transactions and obligations in external currencies as well as in the domestic currency is a pervasive feature of economic life in open economies, however, there is no compelling reason for singling out external-currency banking and analyzing it in a class by itself.

In the 1960s and 1970s, the typical Eurocurrency deposit was akin to a time certificate of deposit. Unlike a bank's demand or sight liabilities denominated in the currency of the nation where the bank is located, Eurocurrency deposits were not widely usable as a means of payment.[5] Furthermore, most Eurocurrency deposits were *interbank* assets and liabilities. Even after estimates of interbank redepositing are subtracted from estimates of the gross size of Eurocurrency assets, only about one-third of net Eurocurrency deposits in the mid-1970s were owned by nonbanks.[6]

3. When banks located in Europe began issuing deposits and making loans denominated in U.S. dollars in the years following the 1958 return to greater convertibility of European currencies, the resulting activity became known as the Eurodollar market. Somewhat later, banks in Europe came to issue deposits and make loans denominated in external currencies other than the U.S. dollar; the broader term Eurocurrency markets then came into widespread use. By the end of the 1970s, so-called Eurocurrency or offshore banking had spread to many non-European financial centers and had grown to very large magnitudes. For descriptions of Eurocurrency banking, see for example Paul Einzig and Brian S. Quinn, *The Euro-Dollar System: Practice and Theory of International Interest Rates*, 6th ed. (St. Martin's Press, 1977). Data and commentary on recent trends appear in the annual reports of the Bank for International Settlements. Important analytic references include Alexander K. Swoboda, *The Euro-dollar Market: An Interpretation*, Princeton Essays in International Finance, 64 (Princeton University Press, 1968); John Hewson and Eisuke Sakakibara, *The Eurocurrency Markets and Their Implications* (Lexington Books, 1975); Jürg Niehans and John Hewson, "The Eurodollar Market and Monetary Theory," *Journal of Money, Credit and Banking*, vol. 8 (February 1976), pp. 1–27; Charles Freedman, "A Model of the Eurodollar Market," *Journal of Monetary Economics*, vol. 3 (April 1977), pp. 139–61; Ronald I. McKinnon, *The Eurocurrency Market*, Princeton Essays in International Finance, 125 (Princeton University Press, 1977); and Helmut W. Mayer, *Credit and Liquidity Creation in the International Banking Sector*, BIS Economic Papers, 1 (Bank for International Settlements, November 1979).

4. See the statements by Ralph C. Bryant and Henry C. Wallich, in *The Eurocurrency Market Control Act of 1979*, Hearings before the subcommittees on Domestic Monetary Policy and on International Trade, Investment and Monetary Policy of the House Committee on Banking, Finance and Urban Affairs, 96 Cong. 1 sess. (Government Printing Office, 1979), pp. 104–24, 183–205.

5. This statement applies even to the bulk of call Eurocurrency deposits (those without a fixed maturity and redeemable immediately at the request of the depositor).

6. For detailed discussion of the facts in this paragraph and the distinction between the gross and net sizes of the Eurocurrency market, see Helmut W. Mayer, "The BIS Concept of the Eurocurrency Market,"

As presently constituted, therefore, Eurocurrency markets play a more prominent role in channeling funds to financial institutions than in providing intermediation and maturity transformation between ultimate nonbank lenders and nonbank borrowers. This critical point is often overlooked in superficial analyses that lump Eurocurrency deposits with other types of deposits, casually labeling the total as money.

Figures 8-1 and 8-2 have the pedagogical virtue of embedding what are commonly called Eurocurrency assets and liabilities in a comprehensive structure of world financial interdependence. Not only are foreign banks assumed to have loans and deposits denominated in home currency, home banks are assumed to have loans and deposits denominated in foreign currency.[7]

The reader should not be misled because no separate mention is made of Eurocurrency assets and liabilities in what follows. The analysis deals directly with the implications of Eurocurrency banking for national monetary policies but in a way that avoids the nomenclature and compartmentalized perspective common in the existing literature.

Asset Substitutability and Exchange-Rate Variability

If virtually all economic units perceive the attributes of both assets in a pair as identical and if all units incur identical transaction costs in selling or purchasing the assets, the returns on the two assets will be driven to equality. By definition such assets are *perfect substitutes*.

The analysis here assumes that the assets identified in figures 8-1 and 8-2 have differing combinations of attributes and differing transaction costs. Furthermore, it is assumed that preferences for owning the assets or issuing the liabilities (based in part on perceptions of the attributes and transaction costs) differ among microeconomic units within each private sector of the world economy and, to an even greater degree, when the sectors are compared with one another. By assumption, an increase in the expected return on any one asset induces some economic units to want to hold somewhat more of that asset and to diminish or leave unchanged their demands for the others.[8] Yet the degree of substitutability is finite: all the assets are assumed to be *imperfect substitutes*.

Consider two assets, one denominated in the home currency and the other in the foreign currency. In an imaginary world where the exchange rate between the two currencies is rigidly fixed and is (credibly) expected to remain fixed permanently, each individual economic unit will compare its expectations of the returns on the two assets without regard for the exchange rate (because the expected change in

Euromoney (May 1976), pp. 60–66; and Mayer, "The BIS Statistics of International Banking: Coverage, Netting-out Methods, Problems of Interpretation," paper prepared for Sixteenth General Conference of the International Association for Research in Income and Wealth (August 1979).

7. From the perspective of the United States, external-currency banking has so far developed asymmetrically. Foreign banks, including foreign branches and affiliates of American banks, make dollar loans and issue dollar deposits on a very large scale ("Eurodollars"). But banks in the United States have very small amounts of assets and liabilities denominated in foreign currencies (there are as yet no significant amounts of "AmeroDM," "Amerosterling," or "Ameroyen" deposits).

8. In technical terms, each economic unit regards the assets as strict gross substitutes.

the exchange rate is always identically zero). An economic unit will regard the assets as more or less imperfect substitutes but principally because of attributes other than currency denomination; currency denomination will be a secondary if not irrelevant matter.[9] In the real world where the exchange rate can fluctuate, on the other hand, economic units must form and act upon uncertain expectations of changes in the exchange rate. Because of exchange-rate variability (actual or potential), economic units must regard the different currency denominations of the two assets as critically important attributes and an additional reason for treating them as imperfect substitutes.

The degrees to which a microeconomic unit regards the various assets and liabilities on its balance sheet as substitutes—so to speak, the response coefficients in its behavioral equations—are central elements in the description and analysis of the unit's portfolio allocation decisions. Similarly, the degrees of substitutability among assets and the form and degree of exchange-rate variability are important features of macroeconomic analysis of interdependent national economies.

For the immediate purposes of this and the following chapter, no more need be said about asset substitutability. Nor is it necessary to be precise about the form and degree of variability in the exchange rate. The points to be made are sufficiently general to be applicable regardless of whether the exchange rate is fixed for the time being or continuously flexible.

Illustrative Definitions of the National Money Stock

The following discussion refers in a shorthand manner to alternative definitions of the national money stock for the home country. A catalogue of these alternatives is presented in tables 8-1, 8-2, and 8-3. Each alternative is given a letter designation (for example, M_r). The tables identify the sector holding that money as an asset, the sector issuing the counterpart liabilities, the types of assets or liabilities deemed to be money, and the currency denomination of the assets or liabilities. The tables also indicate the cells in figure 8-2 that, added together, generate a particular definition.

The five alternatives shown in table 8-1 proceed from the asset side; that is, they emphasize the home residence of asset holders. The presumption underlying the definitions is that assets held by nonresidents of the home economy, whatever their "moneyness" attributes in other respects, are not eligible to be part of the *home* national money stock. Two of the alternatives, M_a and M_d, follow the tradition dominant in recent monetary history of regarding nonbanks as the only holders of money. The other three presume that the home money stock includes not only nonbank assets but also certain claims on foreigners of home banks and the home

9. Apart from the continued denomination of transactions in one or the other currency, which in turn can give rise to differentiated demands for home-currency and foreign-currency means of payment (see chapter 7), economic units would have no reason to care about the currency denomination of their assets and liabilities. With the exchange rate permanently fixed, moreover, the denomination of transactions in one currency or the other—indeed, the very existence of two currency units—would presumably be a vestigial remnant of an earlier period when the exchange rate had been variable and economic interdependence between the two nations had been much less extensive.

Table 8-1. *The Home National Money Stock: Definitions Emphasizing Home Residency of the Holders of Money*

Symbol	Description	Sector(s) holding money[a]	Sectors issuing counterpart liabilities[a]	Types of assets included	Currency denomination of assets included	Counterpart cells in figure 8-2
M_a	Assets of home nonbanks widely usable as a means of payment	N	CB, B, FB, FCB	Currency plus means-of-payment deposits	Home and foreign	1, 6, 8, 10, 12, 15
M_b	Assets of home nonbanks and the home fiscal authority widely usable as a means of payment	N, G	CB, B, FB, FCB	Currency plus means-of-payment deposits	Home and foreign	1, 6, 8, 10, 12, 15, 3, 21
M_c	Assets of home nonbanks widely usable as a means of payment plus means-of-payment balances in foreign currency held by other home sectors	N, B, G	CB, B, FB, FCB	Currency plus means-of-payment deposits	Home and foreign	1, 6, 8, 10, 12, 15, 16, 18, 21
M_d	Total liquid assets of home nonbanks	N	CB, B, G, FB, FG, FCB	Assets deemed to have a high degree of liquidity	Home and foreign	1, 6, 8, 10, 12, 15; parts or all of 5, 7, 9, 11, 13, 14
M_e	Liquid assets of home nonbanks plus liquid assets held abroad of other home sectors	N, B, G	CB, B, G, FB, FG, FCB	Assets deemed to have a high degree of liquidity	Home and foreign	1, 6, 8, 10, 12, 15, 16, 18, 3, 21; parts or all of 5, 7, 9, 11, 13, 14, 17, 19, 20

a. Sector designations: N = home nonbank; B = home bank; G = home fiscal authority; CB = home central bank; FN = foreign nonbank; FB = foreign bank; FG = foreign fiscal authority; FCB = foreign central bank.

Table 8-2. *The Home National Money Stock: Definitions Emphasizing Home Residency of the Issuers of Money*

Symbol	Description	Sector(s) holding money[a]	Sectors issuing counterpart liabilities[a]	Types of liabilities included	Currency denomination of liabilities included	Counterpart cells in figure 8-2
M_j	Means-of-payment liabilities of home banks and home central bank to home nonbanks and all foreign economic units	N, FN, FB, FG	CB, B	Currency plus means-of-payment deposits	Home and foreign	1, 6, 8, 22, 24, 26, 29, 31, 33
M_k	Means-of-payment liabilities of home banks and home central bank to home nonbanks and foreign nonbanks	N, FN	CB, B	Currency plus means-of-payment deposits	Home and foreign	1, 6, 8, 22, 24, 26
M_m	Means-of-payment liabilities of home banks and home central bank to home nonbanks	N	CB, B	Currency plus means-of-payment deposits	Home and foreign	1, 6, 8
M_n	Liquid-asset liabilities of home financial institutions to home nonbanks and all foreign economic units	N, FN, FB, FG	CB, B, G	Assets deemed to have a high degree of liquidity	Home and foreign	1, 6, 8, 22, 24, 26, 29, 31, 33; parts or all of 5, 7, 9, 23, 25, 27, 28, 30, 32
M_p	Liquid-asset liabilities of home financial institutions to home nonbanks	N	CB, B, G	Assets deemed to have a high degree of liquidity	Home and foreign	1, 6, 8; parts or all of 5, 7, 9

a. See table 8-1, note a, for sector designations.

Table 8-3. *The Home National Money Stock: Definitions Emphasizing Denomination of Assets in the Home-Currency Unit*

Symbol	Description	Sector(s) holding money[a]	Sectors issuing counterpart liabilities[a]	Types of assets included	Currency denomination of assets included	Counterpart cells in figure 8-2
M_q	Means-of-payment claims of all nonbanks denominated in home currency	N, FN	CB, B, FB	Currency plus means-of-payment deposits	Home	1, 6, 10, 22, 24, 34
M_r	Means-of-payment claims on home financial institutions denominated in home currency of home nonbanks and all foreigners	N, FN, FG, FB	CB, B	Currency plus means-of-payment deposits	Home	1, 6, 22, 24, 33, 29
M_s	Means-of-payment claims of home nonbanks denominated in home currency	N	CB, B, FB	Currency plus means-of-payment deposits	Home	1, 6, 10
M_t	Means-of-payment claims of home nonbanks on home financial institutions denominated in home currency	N	CB, B	Currency plus means-of-payment deposits	Home	1, 6
M_u	Liquid-asset claims of all nonbanks denominated in home currency	N, FN	CB, B, G, FB	Assets deemed to have a high degree of liquidity	Home	1, 6, 10, 22, 24, 34; parts or all of 5, 7, 11, 23, 25, 35
M_v	Liquid-asset claims on home financial institutions denominated in home currency of home nonbanks and all foreigners	N, FN, FB, FG	CB, B, G	Assets deemed to have a high degree of liquidity	Home	1, 6, 22, 24, 33, 29; parts or all of 5, 7, 23, 25, 30
M_w	Liquid-asset claims of home nonbanks on home financial institutions denominated in home currency	N	CB, B, G	Assets deemed to have a high degree of liquidity	Home	1, 6, parts or all of 5, 7

a. See table 8-1, note a, for sector designations.

fiscal authority. The alternatives M_b and M_e include even the home fiscal authority's cash balance held with the home central bank.[10]

The alternatives illustrated in table 8-2 retain an emphasis on home residency but are constructed by proceeding from the liability side. The presumption in table 8-2 is that national money includes only liabilities of economic units resident in the home nation. Three of those alternatives, however, allow nonresidents to be counted among the *holders* of home money thus defined; one, M_k, restricts the foreign holders to the foreign nonbank sector. The narrowest alternatives shown in table 8-2, M_m and M_p, require both the issuers and the holders to be residents of the home economy.

A third set of definitions, in table 8-3, emphasizes currency denomination as the main feature of the definition. In contrast with the earlier alternatives, the seven definitions in that table presume that the home national money stock excludes any asset or liability denominated in the foreign currency.

Descriptive Uses of Money Concepts

Before turning to different definitions of national money as alternative possibilities for an intermediate-target variable in the conduct of monetary policy, it is instructive to note some concepts that might be used if an analyst's purpose is merely the descriptive study of the economic behavior of the nation's residents.

The first step in selecting a descriptive concept and definition is a demarcation of the particular group or groups of home residents whose behavior is of interest. The second step is the specification of a hypothesis about the manner in which the portfolio and the income and spending decisions of those home residents require a differentiation between money and other assets.

As an example, suppose an analyst is interested in studying the behavior of the home nonbank sector and believes that nonbanks make a sharp distinction—with respect to international as well as domestic transactions—between assets that are widely usable as a means of payment and those that are not.[11] He might then focus on the subset of assets included in M_a as defined in table 8-1.

An analyst with that descriptive purpose will encounter empirical difficulties deciding which assets are widely usable as a means of payment. He might not be able to identify a sharp dividing line between assets that have and those that do not have a sufficiently high degree of that attribute. But the principle of selection will be clear. Assets widely usable as a means of payment will be included regardless of whether they are claims on home or foreign institutions and regardless of whether they are denominated in the home or the foreign currency.[12]

10. As shown in the tables in chapter 3, several nations (but not the United States) include the liquid-asset balances of the fiscal authority in their definitions of the national money stock. Since the question of how to treat the cash balances of government agencies is of secondary concern here in part 2, the alternatives shown in tables 8-1, 8-2, and 8-3 do not give prominence to this issue.

11. Such an analyst would subscribe to an open-economy variant of proposition 4-A in chapter 4.

12. Descriptive macroeconomic analysis, if carefully done, often requires judicious disaggregation of highly aggregative data. As noted in chapter 7, analysis of the behavior of the nonbank sector often requires distinguishing between households and firms. Because behavior depends on the currency denomination of transactions and on expected changes in the exchange rate, analysis often must distinguish between means-of-payment balances denominated in the home currency and those in the foreign currency rather

Consider a second example of a descriptive use of a money definition. Imagine an analyst who wishes to focus on the behavior of home nonbanks but doubts the empirical relevance of an emphasis on the means-of-payment attributes of assets. If such an analyst believes instead that the relevant behavioral distinction is between assets that have a high degree of liquidity and those that do not, he might focus on the fourth alternative shown in table 8-1, M_d.

Several empirical difficulties can be encountered in constructing M_d in practice. The analyst will need to give operational significance to the concept of liquidity (for example, by providing empirical content for such asset attributes as ready marketability and certainty of nominal value). Since liquidity refers to an amorphous collection of asset attributes, operational criteria will be problematic. Again, however, the principle of selection will be unambiguous given some sort of operational criteria. The entire range of liquid assets owned by home nonbanks will be included in such a definition of money, not merely those liquid assets denominated in home currency or those involving claims on home financial institutions.

Descriptive uses of alternative concepts of the national money stock pose no logical or theoretical problems that need detain us here. The distinguishing characteristic of a descriptive use is its analysis of some aspect of the behavior of home economic units in the light of a hypothesis specifying why and how some concept of money is significant for that behavior. Descriptive analysis of financial behavior in an open economy of course requires consideration of currency denomination, exchange rates, and international debtor-creditor relationships. But there is no conceptual ambiguity about the domain of the analysis or the criteria for selecting the assets or liabilities to be studied.

The National Money Stock as an Intermediate Target: An Illustrative Case

Ambiguities abound, however, if it is argued that a definition of money is needed for a prescriptive purpose in the conduct of monetary policy.

Should it wish to follow a money strategy, a nation's central bank has a plethora of alternative definitions of national money from which to choose its intermediate-target variable. In effect, it must search among the numerous candidates—for example, those shown in tables 8-1, 8-2, and 8-3—and select the one that promises to be "correct" or "best."[13]

At least two criteria, derived from the reliability and controllability propositions of a money strategy, are relevant for such a search.[14] The central bank seeks a definition for which the causal links between home money and home ultimate targets are subject to the least uncertainty. Yet it also seeks a definition permitting home money to be easily and closely controlled with the instruments of home monetary policy.

---

than lump the two together. Even so, the aggregation of assets included in M_a conceivably can play a role in the descriptive analysis of the financial behavior of the home nonbank sector.

13. Because the discussion that follows focuses on theoretical criteria, it implicitly assumes that empirical data are available permitting the construction of all alternatives. Since in practice some of the requisite data are not available, the choice of a definition is even more problematic than indicated here.

14. For brevity in what follows, propositions 6-A and 6-B are referred to, respectively, as the reliability and controllability propositions.

An instructive way to appraise alternative definitions as candidates for the central bank's intermediate target is to analyze the underlying demand and supply functions.[15]

To illustrate, suppose the central bank considers selecting M_d, the total liquid assets of home nonbanks, as its proximate policy target. Definition M_d has twelve components. Seen from the liability side, six different sectors issue the obligations: home banks, foreign banks, and the central banks and fiscal authorities of both nations. Seen from the asset side, all the components are claims of a single sector. The definition includes components denominated in foreign as well as home currency.[16]

Because the only holders of M_d are home nonbanks, the aggregate demand function closely resembles the behavioral equations for an individual home nonbank:

$$(8\text{-}1) \qquad M_d^{demand} = f^N\left[\hat{r}_N^h, \hat{r}_N^f, \frac{T_N^h}{W_N}, \frac{\pi T_N^f}{W_N}, \ldots\right]W_N,$$

where as before $\hat{r}_N^h$ and $\hat{r}_N^f$ represent the subvectors of return, cost, and dispersion variables associated with balance-sheet items denominated in the home and the foreign currency, T_N^h and T_N^f are the volumes of transactions denominated in the two currencies, and W_N is net worth. The superscript and subscript N serve as reminders that the function $f^N[\ldots]W_N$ and each of its arguments refer to the aggregation of all individual units within the home nonbank sector.[17]

The aggregate supply function for M_d must be built up from the behavior of both the home and foreign banking systems and the policy behavior of both home and foreign governmental units. At the most abstract level, by analogy with the notation used in chapter 5, it may be written:

$$(8\text{-}2a) \qquad M_d^{supply} = g\left[X^{CB}; X^G; X^{FCB}; X^{FG}; f^B(\ldots); \pi f^{FB}(\ldots)\right].$$

The symbols X^{CB} and X^{FCB} represent vectors containing the policy instruments of the home and the foreign central banks. The vectors of instruments of the home and the foreign fiscal authorities are denoted X^G and X^{FG}.[18] The notation $f^B(\ldots)$ represents the complicated function characterizing the deposit-supplying behavior of home banks, while $\pi f^{FB}(\ldots)$ is a corresponding function, expressed in home-currency units, for the supply behavior of foreign banks. The general character of

---

15. Proceeding in this manner is especially appropriate from the perspective of those advocates of a money strategy who favor a money market rather than a systemic approach to the modeling of the national economy.

16. In the notation of chapter 7, M_d measured in home-currency units can be written as

$$M_d \equiv CURh_{CB} + Dmph_B + Doth_B + Dmph_{FB} + Doth_{FB} + Sh_G$$
$$+ \pi(CURf_{FCB} + Dmpf_B + Dotf_B + Dmpf_{FB} + Dotf_{FB} + Sf_{FG}),$$

where the N superscript on each of the twelve components is understood rather than shown explicitly.

17. In terms of the sector-wide systems of portfolio equations hypothesized at the end of chapter 7, the right-hand side of 8-1 is the summation of twelve of the individual equations in the system Z_i^N ($i = 1, \ldots, 24$).

18. Two of the components of M_d are direct obligations of fiscal authorities (the liquid-asset portions of Sh_G and πSf_{FG}). Even when the money stock does not include liabilities of the fiscal authority, the settings on fiscal as well as monetary instruments have an important bearing on the quantity of money actually supplied. The interrelationships between monetary and fiscal policies are analyzed in chapters 14 and 21.

these latter two functions may be specified further, using the notation of chapter 7, as:

(8-2b) $$f^B\left(\hat{r}_B^h, \hat{r}_B^f, D_B^h, \pi D_B^f, T_B^h, \pi T_B^f, NW_B, \ldots \right)$$

and

(8-2c) $$\pi f^{FB}\left(\hat{r}_{FB}^f, \hat{r}_{FB}^h, D_{FB}^f, \frac{1}{\pi}D_{FB}^h, T_{FB}^f, \frac{1}{\pi}T_{FB}^h, NW_{FB}, \ldots \right),$$

where B and FB again refer to the aggregation of all banks in the home and foreign nations.[19]

Specification of the demand and supply functions highlights a fact with wide ramifications: the behavior underlying the determination of home money, defined as M_d, is riddled with *foreign* and *foreign-currency* complications. Three manifestations of this interaction of home and foreign variables warrant special emphasis.

First, the exchange rate and expectations of changes in the exchange rate are ubiquitous elements in both the demand for and supply of M_d. The same is true for interest rates paid on the liabilities of foreign residents and for expectations of changes in those rates. These international complications pervade the demand and supply nexus not only because M_d includes components that are claims on foreigners and claims denominated in foreign currency, but fundamentally because expectations of changes in the exchange rate and foreign interest rates appear throughout the systems of asset-demand and liability-supply equations characterizing the behavior of home nonbanks, home banks, and foreign banks.

The presence of the exchange rate and numerous foreign and foreign-currency variables in the demand and supply functions facilitates the transmission to the home economy of policy actions and nonpolicy disturbances originating abroad. Similarly, it facilitates the dissipation abroad of policy actions and nonpolicy disturbances originating at home. Compared with the hypothetical case of a closed economy, therefore, the chain of causal links leading from home policy instruments through home money to home ultimate targets becomes significantly weakened and more uncertain. The international interdependencies undermine the links at the lower (instruments-to-M_d) and upper (M_d-to-ultimate targets) stages of the causal chain and thus call into question both the reliability and the controllability propositions upon which advocacy of M_d as an intermediate target has to rest.

The second point deserving emphasis concerns the "scale" variables in the demand function for M_d. Recall that in the closed-economy case it seemed plausible to accept the contention that those scalar arguments provide direct links between the money stock and the ultimate objectives of policymakers. But the scalar arguments in equation 8-1, particularly the two measures of transactions volumes, are not the ultimate objectives of the home policymakers. Nor can it be plausibly argued that they are closely correlated with those ultimate-target variables.

19. The function $f^B(\ldots)$ is in effect the summation of four of the sector-wide equations in the system Z_i^B ($i = 1, \ldots, 27$) hypothesized at the end of chapter 7. Analogously, since M_d contains four components that are liabilities of foreign banks, $\pi f^{FB}(\ldots)$ is the home-currency equivalent of the summation of four of the sector-wide equations in the system Z_i^{FB} ($i = 1, \ldots, 27$). In deriving both the aggregate demand for and aggregate supply of M_d, the assumed procedure is to specify separately the demands and supplies for each individual component of the money stock and then to build up the aggregate demand and supply functions from those disaggregated relationships.

In a world with two currency units and two significantly interdependent national economies, the demands of home nonbanks for means of payment (and therefore also for liquid assets) denominated in the two currencies depend on the volumes of their transactions in the two currencies. The relationships of the two transactions volumes to home GNP, however, need not be simple relationships of direct proportionality. Nor is it clear that stable correlations necessarily exist.

The accounting identity for gross national product defines home GNP as total expenditures by home residents (where consumption, investment, and government expenditures include spending on home-produced output and on imports) *plus* exports (home-produced output sold to foreigners) *minus* imports (foreign-produced output purchased by home residents). Suppose import transactions are denominated exclusively in foreign-currency means of payment whereas export transactions are denominated only in home currency.[20] Imagine a situation in which home consumers decide to switch a sizable amount of their spending away from home-produced output to imported goods (with no change in their saving rate). Imports—and hence the volume of foreign-currency transactions by home residents—will initially rise. The initial reduction in spending on home goods will generate a contractionary movement in home output and incomes (and after a time will also have secondary effects in reducing import spending). Other things being equal, foreigners' spending on home exports will rise somewhat because of the stimulus imparted to foreign output and incomes by the initial switch in consumption spending. The relationships among the volume of home-currency transactions, the volume of foreign-currency transactions, and the nominal value of GNP will thus change significantly. Conceivably, the volume of foreign-currency transactions and the demand for foreign-currency means of payment could rise while the value of GNP declines.[21]

More is said below about the complex relationship between transactions volumes and national GNP in a significantly open economy. For now it is sufficient to stress the less direct and much looser nature of the links between the scalar arguments in the demand function for M_d and the ultimate targets of home policymakers. If M_d is selected as the central bank's intermediate-target variable, these looser links will raise doubts about the reliability proposition underlying a money strategy.[22]

Consider now a third characteristic of the behavior underlying the determination

20. This assumption is used here to illustrate the point in the text; the argument is equally valid, mutatis mutandis, for more realistic assumptions.

21. The outcomes for home-currency transactions, foreign-currency transactions, and home nominal GNP depend on, among other things, what is assumed about the flexibility of prices and wages and whether the exchange rate is assumed to be fixed, managed, or left to float freely (on the latter point see part 5).

22. The discussion here and elsewhere in the text gives prominence to the volume and currency denomination of transactions. Economists with preferences for the utility-school approach will object to this emphasis and argue that the proper (and perhaps the only) scalar argument in the demand function for M_d should be the net worth of home nonbanks (W_N). Such economists may also contend that W_N is more directly and reliably correlated with home GNP than transactions volumes. Thus, economists of the utility school may choose to give little weight to the point stressed in the text. Even economists of the utility school, however, should have some doubts about the scalar arguments in their version of the demand function for M_d. As pointed out in chapter 6, the transformation from national wealth or the aggregate net worth of nonbanks to national output and income is far from trivial even in a closed economy. In an open economy, home residents purchase both home and foreign output and hold their wealth in both home-currency and foreign-currency assets; the real value of current home output is not identical with the real command over goods and services resulting from production of that current home output. More important still, the relationships among home GNP and the saving and wealth of home residents are likely to be less direct and less certain because home residents will value their savings and wealth in terms of a price index including not only home but also foreign prices.

of M_d. The policy instruments of the *foreign* government and the deposit-supplying behavior of *foreign* banks enter directly into the supply function for the *home* money stock. These facts will place home policymakers following an intermediate-target strategy in a qualitatively different position from the situation that would prevail in a closed economy. In a closed economy, only the home central bank and home fiscal authority would act to adjust exogenous policy instruments; as they tried to keep the money stock close to an intermediate-target path by adjusting their instruments, moreover, policymakers would have to cope only with the effects of the endogenous behavior of home banks. In an open economy with money defined as M_d, however, home policymakers must try to offset the endogenous influences on home money of the behavior of the foreign as well as the home banking system. To use M_d as their proximate operating target, therefore, home policymakers must model the behavior not only of home but also of foreign banks, and the influence of foreign policy actions on both foreign and home banks. Plainly, the resulting characterization of the money supply process will be considerably more complex and uncertain than in a closed economy.[23]

The fact that the policy instruments of the central bank and fiscal authority of the foreign nation are integral features of the supply process for M_d can be an especially troublesome complication for home policymakers. The foreign policymakers have ultimate objectives of their own and presumably care little, if at all, about achievement of the ultimate targets of home policymakers. The foreign and the home objectives may not be attainable simultaneously. Even if both sets of objectives are compatible, moreover, adjustments of the foreign instruments by the foreign policymakers may be just as likely to undermine as to facilitate the achievement of home objectives.[24] In particular, unanticipated actions of the foreign policymakers and the resulting responses of the foreign and home banking systems alter the relationships between home instruments and the home money stock that home policymakers expect to prevail. Because the potential is greater for surprises in the instruments-to-money links, the ability of the home policymakers to control M_d is adversely affected.[25]

The combined consequences of the problems identified with M_d undermine any presumption in favor of using it as an intermediate target.

---

23. It may be asked, Why is it necessary for home policymakers to model foreign behavior explicitly? Why can't they merely estimate the amount of liquid-asset claims on foreigners that home nonbanks wish to hold and then seek to have domestic institutions supply the appropriate amount of the remaining components of home money so that the combined target for M_d itself is achieved? The problem is that the demand of home nonbanks for liquid-asset claims on foreigners cannot be sensibly projected without making projections of (among other things) the exchange rate and foreign interest rates, which in turn cannot be estimated without specifying foreign policy actions and without modeling the resulting behavior of the foreign and home banking systems.

24. While adjustments of the foreign instruments are exogenous policy actions for the foreign authorities, they are of course noncontrollable disturbances from the perspective of home economic policy. Part 3 discusses this point in greater detail.

25. The most direct effects occur in the lower stage of the two-stage decision process. Unanticipated foreign policy actions and the responses of the two banking systems also adversely affect the upper-stage relationships underpinning a strategy using M_d as an intermediate target. The links between money and ultimate targets expected by the home policymakers are altered and made more uncertain (for example, through unanticipated effects on foreign interest rates and the exchange rate and on expectations of those rates). Even with unchanged upper-stage links, moreover, an unexpected deviation of the actual stock of M_d from its target path causes the ultimate targets of the home policymakers to turn out differently from what had been desired and expected.

A Second Example

Suppose the central bank selects the M_r concept of home money (see table 8-3) as its pivot for a two-stage money strategy. That definition excludes all balance-sheet items denominated in foreign currency and includes only the liabilities of home financial institutions. Does M_r avoid the difficulties encountered with M_d?[26]

Because only the home central bank and home banks issue the liabilities included in M_r, the aggregate supply function is somewhat less complex than that for M_d:

$$(8\text{-}3) \qquad M_r^{supply} = g\left[X^{CB}; f^B\left(\hat{r}_B^h, \hat{r}_B^f, D_B^h, \pi D_B^f, T_B^h, \pi T_B^f, NW_B, \ldots \right) \right].$$

As before X^{CB} represents the policy instruments of the home central bank and $f^B(\ldots)$ is a deposit-supply function of home banks for the means-of-payment liabilities included in M_r.

Although an exclusive focus on the liabilities of home financial institutions purchases some simplification in the supply function, the cost of that simplification is an increased complexity in the demand function. Seen from the asset side, M_r is held by four sectors: home nonbanks, foreign nonbanks, foreign banks, and the foreign fiscal authority. Hence the demand function is of the general form:

$$(8\text{-}4a) \qquad M_r^{demand} = g\left[f^N(\ldots); \pi f^{FN}(\ldots); \pi f^{FB}(\ldots); \pi f^{FG}(\ldots) \right].$$

The underlying behavior of the three private sectors, using the notation of chapter 7 and expressing all demands in terms of home-currency units, may be represented as:[27]

$$(8\text{-}4b) \qquad f^N\left(\hat{r}_N^h, \hat{r}_N^f, \frac{T_N^h}{W_N}, \frac{\pi T_N^f}{W_N}, \ldots \right) W_N.$$

$$(8\text{-}4c) \qquad \pi f^{FN}\left(\hat{r}_{FN}^f, \hat{r}_{FN}^h, \frac{T_{FN}^f}{W_{FN}}, \left(\frac{1}{\pi}\right) \frac{T_{FN}^h}{W_{FN}}, \ldots \right) W_{FN}.$$

$$(8\text{-}4d) \qquad \pi f^{FB}\left(\hat{r}_{FB}^f, \hat{r}_{FB}^h, D_{FB}^f, \frac{1}{\pi} D_{FB}^h, T_{FB}^f, \frac{1}{\pi} T_{FB}^h, NW_{FB}, \ldots \right).$$

The aggregate demand and supply functions for M_r are very different from the functions for M_d. Yet the behavior underlying the determination of M_r is likewise riddled with foreign and foreign-currency complications.

Although M_r includes components denominated only in home currency and the liabilities of only home financial institutions, the behavior of the demanders and

26. The M_r definition corresponds to the narrowest and most frequently discussed concept of money in use in the United States before 1980. See tables 3-7 and 3-8 for U.S. definitions. For M_r to correspond exactly to the pre-1980 narrow definition in the United States (so-called M_1), savings and loan associations and mutual savings banks must be treated as nonbanks, while currency and demand deposits must be regarded as the only assets widely usable as a means of payment.

27. In terms of the sector-wide systems of portfolio equations hypothesized at the end of chapter 7, the function $f^N(\ldots)$ is a summation of the equations for $CURh_{CB}^N$ and $Dmph_B^N$ in the system Z_i^N ($i = 1, \ldots, 24$); $\pi f^{FN}(\ldots)$ is the home-currency equivalent of a summation of the two analogous equations in the system Z_i^{FN} ($i = 1, \ldots, 24$); and $\pi f^{FB}(\ldots)$ is the home-currency equivalent of the equation for $Dmph_B^{FB}$ in the system Z_i^{FB} ($i = 1, \ldots, 27$).

suppliers depends in numerous ways on the exchange rate, on foreign interest rates, and on expectations of those rates. International interdependencies thus raise questions about the use of M_r as an intermediate target analogous to those that arise with respect to M_d. Again the problems occur both at the lower stage (can M_r be closely controlled in the light of the influence of international variables on supply behavior?) and at the upper stage (will interdependence with the rest of the world weaken and render more uncertain the linkages of M_r to home ultimate targets?).

Moreover, even more than for M_d, the various scalar arguments in the demand function for M_r are poorly correlated with the ultimate targets of home policymakers. Even the transactions volumes and the net worth of *home* nonbanks (see 8-4b) may not have a direct, dependable relationship to national objectives (for example, home GNP). More troublesome still, the scalar variables in the remaining components of the aggregate function (see 8-4c and 8-4d) are the transactions volumes and net worth of *foreign* nonbanks, *foreign* banks, and the *foreign* fiscal authority. Those arguments are likely to be more highly correlated with the ultimate targets of the *foreign* government (for example, foreign GNP) than with home ultimate objectives. From the point of view of the suitability of M_r as an intermediate target for home monetary policy, stronger correlations with foreign than with home ultimate targets are plainly perverse.[28]

Exclude International Debtor-Creditor Relationships?

Some of the complications that undermine use of M_d and M_r as intermediate-target variables occur because the behavior of foreign economic units contributes directly to the determination of the home money stock. Thus, imagine a third illustrative case in which the home central bank retreats to an extremely limited definition in its search for the best intermediate-target variable.

The definition identified in table 8-3 as M_t restricts attention to home characteristics in every respect. It excludes any asset not owned by a home resident, any liability not issued by a home financial institution, and any item not denominated in the home currency. Viewed from the asset side, the definition restricts attention to nonbanks. It excludes any liquid asset not widely usable as a means of payment. Hence M_t has only two components: home nonbanks' holdings of currency issued by the home central bank and holdings of means-of-payments deposits in home banks.

Aggregate demand and supply functions for M_t are somewhat less complex than those for any of the alternative definitions in tables 8-1, 8-2, and 8-3. The behavior of home nonbanks alone underlies the demand function:[29]

$$(8-5) \qquad M_t^{demand} = f^N \left[\hat{r}_N^h, \hat{r}_N^f, \frac{T_N^h}{W_N}, \frac{\pi T_N^f}{W_N}, \ldots \right] W_N.$$

28. The details of derivation of the aggregate demand function for M_r differ if one specifies asset-demand equations according to the utility-school approach rather than the transactions-school approach. The point stressed is pertinent, however, no matter which approach is used.

29. The demand function for M_t is similar in general form to that for M_d shown in equation 8-1; however, the function for M_t represents a summation over only two of the individual equations in the system Z_i^N ($i = 1, \ldots, 24$) whereas the function for M_d requires an aggregation over twelve of those equations.

The supply function includes only the instruments of the home central bank and models only the behavior of home banks:

$$(8\text{-}6) \qquad M_t^{supply} = g\left[X^{CB}; f^B\left(\hat{r}_B^h, \hat{r}_B^f, D_B^h, \pi D_B^f, T_B^h, \pi T_B^f, NW_B, \ldots \right) \right].$$

However, the exclusion of all international debtor-creditor relationships from the definition of home money does not keep international interdependencies from intruding in the nexus of money demand and supply. Inspection of equations 8-5 and 8-6 is sufficient to show that an irreducible minimum of foreign and foreign-currency complications contaminates the relationships between home instruments and home money, and between home money and home ultimate targets, no matter how narrow the definition of home money.

On behalf of M_t as an intermediate target, it can justifiably be pointed out that the interdependencies are more circuitous. Rather than influencing components of the home money stock directly, for example, policy actions of the foreign central bank and fiscal authority affect home money only indirectly by generating changes in variables such as the exchange rate and foreign interest rates that are arguments in the behavioral functions of home banks and home nonbanks. The behavior of foreign banks influences the supply process for M_t in a similarly roundabout way. Because they are indirect, furthermore, the interdependencies tend to have less powerful effects on the determination of M_t itself.[30] Therefore, the home central bank will undoubtedly experience fewer difficulties in keeping M_t close to a policy-determined target path than with more comprehensive definitions of home money.

Other things being equal, better controllability is a reason for preferring one definition of money over another as an intermediate target. In the case of M_t, however, other things are not equal: the cost of achieving better control over home money by defining it so narrowly is the introduction of still greater uncertainty into the upper-stage links between home money and home ultimate targets. The exclusion from M_t of all international debtor-creditor relationships does not mean the home central bank can afford to ignore the effects of those relationships on home *ultimate* targets. The narrow definition merely forces the central bank to deal with all those effects at the time the target path for the money stock is selected.[31] Choosing M_t as the intermediate target thus sacrifices reliability in the upper-stage decision process to maximize controllability at the lower stage.

Similarly, M_t might seem to have an advantage compared to M_r because the aggregate demand function for M_t contains no scalar variables correlated more closely with foreign rather than home ultimate targets. But that advantage is illusory; it derives merely from narrowing the scope of the intermediate-target variable so

30. When all balance-sheet items for which foreign residents are demanders or suppliers are excluded from the home money stock, most of the international interdependencies remaining in the demand and supply functions take the form of "cross-price" substitution effects (for example, reductions in home nonbanks' demands for home-currency deposits in home banks in response to greater expected returns on assets denominated in foreign currency). To the extent that foreign residents are demanders and suppliers of components included in the definition of home money, on the other hand, more of the interdependencies are direct "own-price" effects (for example, increases in home nonbanks' demand for foreign-currency deposits in foreign banks in response to greater expected returns on those deposits). Own-price effects are typically assumed to be larger in absolute magnitude than cross-price effects (in both consumer-demand and asset-demand theory).

31. Pretending that international debtor-creditor relationships do not have consequences for home ultimate targets would make decisions about the money target path easier but would also be a fundamental analytical error.

that, by definition, foreign residents do not hold home money. Variations in the deposits of foreign residents in home banks—regardless of whether the home central bank includes those deposits in its definition of the money stock—will influence home *ultimate* targets and must therefore be taken into account in either the upper or lower stage of the money strategy.

Successfully Offset Interdependence Effects?

Some readers may argue that international interdependencies need not prove troublesome for a money strategy because the central bank can take them into account and offset their consequences. Cannot the central bank, they may ask, derive a target path for home money that appropriately allows for the international variables affecting the links between money and home ultimate targets? And cannot the central bank keep money itself reasonably close to that target path by adjusting its instruments so as correctly to offset any undesired international influences?

In a hypothetical paradise for policy activists the interdependencies would not be troublesome. Home policymakers would possess an accurate model summarizing the behavioral relationships characterizing the home economy, the foreign economy, and their interactions. The world economic structure would remain conveniently fixed, or would at least change only in ways that policymakers could predict ex ante. Home policymakers could thus accurately project the impacts of their policy actions on the home and foreign economies (including the indirect feedbacks on the home economy of the initial impacts abroad). They could also correctly project both the policy actions of the foreign policymakers and the nonpolicy disturbances originating in the private sectors of the world economy. Finally, home policy instruments would not be subject to boundary constraints on their use, would be costless to adjust, and would be powerful enough to offset any deviations of home target variables from their desired paths.[32]

Policymaking in reality, however, is entirely different from the activist's paradise. None of the ideal conditions of that paradise is met or even approximated. The central problem of strategy choice is to select the least inadequate way of making decisions in the face of severe uncertainty.

Even in a closed economy, skilled policymakers could not acquire enough knowledge and information to offset all disturbances causing their target variables to veer off course. The openness of a national economy exacerbates the difficulties, by compounding the uncertainty about economic structure and by adding foreign policy actions and nonpolicy disturbances originating abroad to the list of exogenous shocks that home policymakers try to offset.[33]

Advocates of using the money stock as an intermediate target, especially those

32. For a closed-economy description of the activist's paradise and a discussion of the consequences of relaxing its key assumptions, see Arthur M. Okun, "Fiscal-Monetary Activism: Some Analytical Issues," *Brookings Papers on Economic Activity, 1:1972*, pp. 123–63.

33. If the real world did correspond to the activist's paradise, all strategies would yield identical recommendations for instrument settings! No controversy could exist about the appropriate definition of home money for use as an intermediate target. Indeed, the very notion of an intermediate-target strategy would be silly; no reason, good or bad, would exist for decomposing policy decisions into two stages with different periodicities for the two sets of decisions.

that favor the simpler money-market models, believe that the aggregate demand and supply functions for money are more stable than other macroeconomic relationships. One view of stability, it will be recalled, turns on the smallness of the number of variables appearing as arguments in the functions. The preceding analysis of M_d, M_r, and M_t can be expressed in similar terms. For each of those definitions of home money, an open economy confronts national policymakers with demand and supply functions containing more variables in greater variety than in an otherwise comparable closed economy. Thus more behavioral parameters must be known or estimated. Practically speaking, however, they are not known and can be estimated only imperfectly. Worse still, the openness of the economy increases the likelihood of changes in economic structure that alter the behavioral relationships summarized in the functions.[34] In short, the aggregate demand and supply functions for M_d, M_r, and M_t are less stable—less knowable and the estimates of them less reliable—than the functions through which the central bank would operate in a hypothetical but otherwise comparable closed economy.

The ideal definition of home money as an intermediate target, it may seem natural to argue, should abstract from open-economy complications. The home central bank should be able to look to its ultimate targets, operating on home money as a pivot, without getting thrown off course by interactions between the home and the foreign economies. Since M_d, M_r, and M_t fail to pass muster, perhaps the central bank can find some other definition corresponding to that ideal among the remaining alternatives in tables 8-1, 8-2, and 8-3.

Unfortunately for anyone holding such hopes, analogous problems arise with *any* of those other definitions. No matter which alternative the home central bank selects as its intermediate-target variable, the openness of the economy will impair the strength and dependability of the links through which the central bank must operate in conducting a money strategy.

Foreign and foreign-currency variables pervade the demand and supply functions for each of the other definitions of home money. Those international variables are channels through which policy actions and nonpolicy disturbances originating outside the nation are transmitted to the home economy and through which home policy actions are dissipated abroad. All definitions are subject in one way or another to the basic problem. From the perspective of the home central bank, furthermore, the demand and supply functions for each definition are less stable than they would be without the presence of the international variables.

An examination of each definition in tables 8-1, 8-2, and 8-3 likewise fails to uncover an alternative for which the scalar arguments in the demand function are highly and dependably correlated with home ultimate targets. Nor can the central bank be confident of closely controlling any definition of home money. The fewer the difficulties in controlling a variant, the more undependable the links between the scalar arguments in the demand function and the home ultimate targets—and, more generally, the less reliable the behavioral relationships underlying the upper-stage specification of a target path for the money stock.

---

34. When deviations first occur from the expected evolution of the economy, home policymakers do not know what disturbances caused them, whether they are transitory and hence will be reversed, or whether they are permanent and represent changes in the underlying economic structure. Changes in the structure are especially difficult to predict ex ante and are therefore especially problematic for policy decisions.

Purge Home Money of International Interdependencies?

Some readers may be tempted to turn over one last stone in a search for a definition of home money purged of international interdependencies. The definitions in tables 8-1, 8-2, and 8-3 include or exclude in their entirety the individual cells in the matrix of figure 8-2. But now imagine a very different procedure, one that purports to isolate the appropriate balances that ought to be included in the home money stock *without regard for the criteria of geographical residency and currency denomination*. In particular, suppose an analyst suggests that the central bank try to select from among the liquid assets of each economic unit in the world only those balances "used to finance transactions with the home nation." The intent of this suggestion is to isolate those liquid assets "used for spending on home goods, services, and securities" or those "associated with transactions on home goods and securities markets." For purposes of discussion let this collection of liquid assets be designated M_y.

One idea underlying the suggestion of M_y as applied to a two-nation world economy seems to be the separation of all transactions (on both income and capital account) into four groups. The first group includes each transaction for which the two economic units involved are both home residents ("domestic" or home–home transactions). The second group contains each transaction between two foreign residents (foreign–foreign transactions). The third and fourth groups together contain all remaining transactions involving a home economic unit on one side and a foreign economic unit on the other ("international" transactions).

The second idea implicit in the suggestion of M_y is that economic units unambiguously associate particular liquid-asset holdings with particular types of transactions. Thus, it is assumed to be possible to identify balances associated with home–home transactions (call them type 1 balances); these are to be included in the home money stock. Balances associated with foreign–foreign transactions (type 4 balances) are to be excluded from the home money stock. Next, the idea seems to require that each international transaction be assigned either to the home or the foreign country, with a counterpart assignment of the remaining balances of liquid assets. Type 2 and type 3 balances are associated with international transactions assigned to, respectively, the home economy and the foreign economy. If this further segregation and assignment can be achieved, so the argument goes, an unambiguous basis will exist for determining whether each liquid-asset holding in the world should be included in (types 1 and 2) or excluded from (types 3 and 4) the home money stock.

The suggestion for construction of M_y is thus prompted by a desire to isolate those liquid-asset balances associated with home–home transactions and a certain subset of home–foreign transactions. That desire in turn stems from the attempt to find a definition of home money the demand function for which contains scalar arguments appropriately correlated with the ultimate targets of home policymakers. If the scalar arguments in the demand function depend exclusively on "home transactions," the argument runs, such target variables as home GNP will then be linked directly to the home money stock. The ultimate targets of the foreign policymakers (for example, foreign GNP), on the other hand, will be purged from the demand for home money. A judicious definition of home money will thereby maximize the directness, and hence also the reliability, of the links between home money and home ultimate targets.

Attractive though it might seem, this last suggestion for choosing a money definition for use as an intermediate target is even more problematic than alternatives already considered. First, M_y would not be a suitable intermediate-target variable even if a meaningful definition along these lines could be constructed. Second, the theory implicit in the suggestion is defective and therefore no good reason exists for trying to construct such a definition in the first place.

Consider the suitability of M_y as an intermediate target. By construction, its aggregate demand function would allegedly have scalar arguments closely correlated with the level of economic activity of the home economy, regardless of whether foreign nonbanks, foreign banks, and the foreign fiscal authority hold money-like claims on home financial institutions. But the supply of M_y would depend on the behavior of the foreign banking system and on the instrument settings chosen by the foreign policymakers, with troublesome implications analogous to those pointed out in the case of M_d. Worse still, the money *supply* process would depend on the multitude of parameters determining the allocation of *demanders'* holdings among balances of types 1, 2, 3, and 4. By trying to sketch its main features, the reader can verify for himself that the aggregate supply function for M_y, even at the most abstract theoretical level, is an analytical nightmare.

The problem with the M_y concept is not merely that empirical data disaggregating individuals' transactions and liquid-asset holdings are unavailable in practice. If data availability were the sole problem, protagonists of this theoretical concept could reasonably fall back on a recommendation to define home money in such a way—call it M_z—as to *approximate* M_y, given the practical constraints of available data.[35] But even the most feasible approximation would be problematic as an intermediate-target variable. For the contortions required to produce a demand function maximizing the directness and reliability of the money-to-ultimate-targets links would hopelessly complicate the links on the supply side between the central bank's instruments and the money stock. Whatever desirable properties M_y (or its approximation, M_z) might have on the demand side would be obtained at the expense of controllability.[36]

The impossibility of the home central bank controlling M_y or M_z is a sufficient reason for the central bank to reject those definitions as intermediate targets. Once the theoretical premises underlying this concept of home money are subjected to scrutiny, however, even its putative rationale crumbles away.

Consider the premise that an individual economic unit associates specific types of transactions with specific holdings of liquid assets. No doubt there is a weak

35. For example, protagonists of the M_y concept might propose that home statisticians analyze the aggregate assets represented by the individual cells in figure 8-2 and then decide to include the assets in a cell *in their entirety* as a component of M_z if the assets in that cell are judged to be "preponderantly" of types 1 and 2.

36. Definitions M_y and M_z may thus be thought to occupy the opposite end of a spectrum from M_t. Whereas use of M_t as the intermediate target would sacrifice the reliability of upper-stage links to maximize the controllability of the money stock, use of M_y or M_z would imply giving no weight to controllability in the lower-stage links in order to maximize reliability in the upper stage.

sense in which this association exists. Chapter 7 draws attention to a frequently neglected example: the need for a home economic unit to hold means-of-payment balances denominated in foreign as well as home currency. Moreover, the institutional considerations and transaction costs that give rise to such associations do not normally change rapidly over time. It is wrong to presume, however, that the general association between transactions and methods of payment is so strong and so extensive that it permits an unambiguous identification of particular liquid-asset balances with particular transactions *where the transactions are disaggregated by location of the counterpart transacting party.*

An example without the complications of two currency units helps make the point. Imagine a wholesaler in Virginia who buys and sells tobacco with economic agents located in the states of North Carolina and Pennsylvania ("imports" and "exports") as well as with agents in Virginia ("domestic" transactions). Suppose 55, 18, and 27 percent of the merchant's payments and receipts in the most recent period are transactions with, respectively, residents of Virginia, North Carolina, and Pennsylvania. In these circumstances it is doubtful that the merchant could unambiguously associate 55 percent of his means-of-payment balances with his payments and receipts vis-à-vis residents of Virginia. Nor would he necessarily hold 18 and 27 percent of his means-of-payment balances with banks in North Carolina and Pennsylvania. If the merchant routes all his payments and receipts through a single account in a Virginia bank, no association will exist between the geographical pattern of transactions and the geographical allocation of liquid-asset holdings. Note, moreover, that the proportions of the merchant's transactions with each state vary in response to economic events. If the tobacco crop fails in North Carolina and the price of Carolina tobacco rises sharply, for example, the merchant will purchase less tobacco from North Carolina and more from Virginia. But the merchant probably does not view the proportions of his transactions carried out with individual states as decision parameters per se.

Analogous problems are involved even when nations issue separate currency units. Imagine again the example in chapter 3 in which a German merchant imports and wholesales beef and holds a variety of liquid assets denominated in several currencies—including a call Eurodollar deposit in a London bank. The currency composition of the merchant's liquid assets is dependent upon the currency pattern of his transactions. The currency pattern, while related to the geographical pattern of the transactions, is not perfectly correlated with it. Transactions with Argentine residents might be denominated in U.S. dollars and give rise to fluctuations in the Eurodollar account, for example. Moreover, the German merchant probably does not regard the geographical proportions of his payments and receipts (beef imports from Argentina and sales of beef to German home residents as proportions of total transactions, and so on) as decision parameters per se. Despite a behavioral link between the *currency denomination* of transactions and the *currency denomination* of asset demands, therefore, the merchant cannot partition his liquid-asset holdings unambiguously into the *geographical categories* presupposed in the concept of M_y.

Since no convincing microeconomic rationale exists for closely associating the geographical allocation of liquid assets with the geographical pattern of transactions, a macroeconomic rationale is equally suspect. Even if perfect data were available, liquid assets could not be divided into home components (types 1 and 2) and foreign components (types 3 and 4).

Finally, consider the premise that all transactions in a two-nation world economy can be divided into four groups: home–home, foreign–foreign, home–foreign assigned to the home country, and home–foreign assigned to the foreign country. The definitions of the first two categories are conceptually clear. But what of the last two? Is there a theoretical basis for assigning each international transaction either to the home or the foreign nation?

A moment's reflection is sufficient to see that no plausible basis exists. Take the example of an import of beef from Argentina by the German merchant. This transaction represents a purchase of goods—an export—from Argentina. An Argentine resident delivers beef in exchange for a financial claim transferred to him by a German resident. Since the occurrence (or nonoccurrence) of the transaction affects economic activity and prices in Argentina, the transaction "belongs to" the Argentine economy. Yet the transaction is a purchase of goods—an import—by Germany. It simultaneously influences economic activity and prices in Germany. Thus the transaction "belongs to" the German economy just as much as to Argentina.

The difficulty here lies with the mistaken presumption that an international transaction can be "assigned" either to one nation or the other. The essence of an open-economy situation is that the home and the foreign economies are joined together by international transactions. An international transaction affects *both* economies simultaneously. This basic fact of interdependence makes it uninteresting to try to associate the transaction exclusively with one economy.

Indeed, given a home economy with significant openness, it is not valid to regard even a transaction in which *both parties* are foreign residents as exclusively assignable to the foreign economy. Foreign–foreign transactions can significantly affect home economic activity, and vice versa for home–home transactions. While it may seem natural to associate "domestic" transactions solely with the economy whose residents carry them out, a more thoughtful analysis must reject this superficial association.

Economists commonly acknowledge the interdependence of flow variables in open economies (for example, exports, imports, activity levels). The basic concepts of national income accounting provide for this interdependence. Econometric models of open economies at a minimum include an equation that endogenously explains aggregate imports; exports, even if taken as exogenous to the model, are acknowledged as a potentially important determinant of activity levels and prices. On reflection, therefore, it is puzzling how economists could advocate an M_y concept of the home money stock and the assignment of transactions by country that such a concept presupposes.

One possible explanation for the puzzle is that, at a superficial level of analysis, the M_y concept seems to require not an assignment of *flow* variables such as transactions but merely an assignment of *stocks* of financial assets and liabilities. It may seem less unnatural to speak of a liquid asset as "belonging to" the home economy than, say, an export transaction.

But that difference is only superficial. Why should one seek to assign financial stock relationships uniquely to one economy or the other simply because the creditor and debtor happen to live in different nations? And why assume that financial relationships among foreign residents have no implications for the home economy? The same conditions of interdependence that make it impossible to assign transactions should also lead one to reject an assignment of assets and liabilities by country.

This last point not only demolishes any theoretical presumption in favor of an M_y or M_z definition of home money. It suggests the futility of trying to purge any national macroeconomic variable of international interdependencies.

CHAPTER NINE

The "Correct" Definition
of National Money

THIS CHAPTER states the conclusions that result from the preceding analysis and provides some illustrations of how the conclusions have been overlooked in monetary theory.

Two Impossibility Theorems

The rationale for using the money stock as an intermediate target of monetary policy rests on the alleged predictability and dependability of two relationships: the links between the policy instruments of the central bank and money, and the links between money and the ultimate targets of policy. For an open economy the rationale must postulate predictable and dependable relationships between *home* policy instruments and *home* money, and between *home* money and *home* ultimate targets.

As shown in chapter 8, however, both parts of this rationale are significantly less plausible than when applied to a closed economy. When each conceivable possibility for defining home money is evaluated, the conclusion is that a strategy using money as the central bank's intermediate-target variable encounters serious difficulties over and above those present in a closed economy. The common source of the difficulties for all concepts of home money is the interdependence of the home economy with the rest of the world.

What, then, is the appropriate definition of the national money stock in an open economy? Alas, this question, while it seems to demand one, does not have a straightforward answer. A search for the "correct" definition of home money is especially problematic if the intent is to locate a variant uncontaminated by international interdependencies that can suitably serve as an intermediate target of monetary policy. Such a definition is a will-o'-the-wisp.

A central conclusion that emerges from chapter 8 can be summarized as an impossibility theorem:

(9-A)   **In a significantly open economy, the national money stock cannot be defined in such a way that it will be impervious to interactions between the home and the foreign economies.**

Regardless of how the central bank in an open economy chooses to conduct its monetary policy and define home money, the money stock has the characteristics of an endogenous variable. Compared with a hypothetical closed economy, moreover, the elements of endogeneity in the process determining the money stock are more numerous and likely to exert a more powerful influence.

This first conclusion implies a second theorem about the ability of the central bank to conduct monetary policy with an intermediate-target strategy:

(9-B)   **In a significantly open economy, there is no national monetary aggregate that the central bank can control closely *and* that has a direct, reliable relationship with the ultimate targets of national economic policy.**

Because no monetary aggregate is impervious to interactions between the home and foreign economies, none exists that can serve as a trustworthy pivot for a national monetary policy free of troublesome international interdependencies. Interdependence compromises the ability of home policymakers to use home money as a proximate operating target regardless of how money is defined.[1]

Conventional wisdom in international economics asserts that freely flexible exchange rates insulate national economies from each other. While theorems 9-A and 9-B may seem intuitively acceptable for a world of fixed exchange rates, some readers may thus be inclined to deny their general applicability. In fact, however, the theorems apply whatever the nature of the exchange regime governing transactions between assets denominated in home currency and foreign currency.[2]

Bank Credit and Other Financial Aggregates

Chapter 8 and the preceding conclusions focus only on the national money stock. But the underlying analysis can readily be extended. In fact, theorems 9-A and 9-B apply to *all* monetary or financial aggregates, however constructed. In particular they apply not only to aggregates built up from the liability side of the balance sheets of financial intermediaries, but also to financial aggregates constructed from the liability side of the balance sheets of nonbanks (the asset side of financial intermediaries' balance sheets).

This general applicability of the theorems has considerable practical relevance. Not all central banks choose the money stock as an intermediate target of monetary policy. Some, for example, tend to favor bank credit.[3]

Suppose chapter 8 were focused on bank credit instead of money. Analogous conundrums about a national definition of bank credit would then be encountered.[4]

---

1. A corollary of the two theorems applies to money demand and supply: in a significantly open economy it is not possible to specify aggregate demand and supply functions for money in a way that will both accurately describe actual behavior and enable the central bank to operate through those functions to influence national ultimate targets abstracting from the interdependent determination of the home and foreign economies. The force of this corollary does not depend on considerations of data availability or empirical feasibility.

2. Issues raised by variability in exchange rates, and in particular the assertion that a national economy can be insulated from the rest of the world by perfectly flexible exchange rates, are analyzed in detail in part 5.

3. Organisation for Economic Co-operation and Development, *The Role of Monetary Policy in Demand Management: The Experience of Six Major Countries,* Monetary Studies Series of the Department of Economics and Statistics (OECD, 1975); Donald R. Hodgman, *National Monetary Policies and International Monetary Cooperation* (Little, Brown, 1974).

4. For example, it would not be clear whether "credit" should be defined exclusively as funds borrowed by home economic units from home banks, or whether in addition it should include funds borrowed from banks located abroad. It would be necessary to make a decision about including or excluding loans

Moreover, a search for a definition of home bank credit uncontaminated by economic interdependence with the rest of the world and suitable for use as an intermediate-target variable would be equally frustrated. In a significantly open economy no bank-credit aggregate is impervious to interactions between the home and the foreign economies. There is no definition of national bank credit that the home central bank can control closely and that has a direct, reliable relationship with the ultimate targets of home economic policy. A quest for a "correct" definition of bank credit for use as an intermediate target would be a search for a will-o'-the-wisp no less than the effort to select a definition of home money free of troublesome international interdependencies.

Two points need to be remembered if these conclusions are to be kept in perspective. First, the theoretical analysis applies to economies that are significantly open. Nothing has yet been said, one way or the other, about the quantitative implications of the conclusions for any actual nation. Second, the conclusions pertain to the prescriptive use of monetary aggregates in the process of formulating and implementing monetary policy. The issues that arise in choosing an appropriate definition of national money for one or another descriptive purpose are logically separable and outside the scope of the present discussion.

Illustrations of the Blind Spot in the Existing Literature

The consequences of international interdependence for the definition of the national money stock, and more generally for the role of money in national monetary policy, are typically overlooked or inadequately characterized in the literature on monetary economics. Several illustrations, two of them drawn from discussions of the money stock in the United States, can help to clarify the implications of the preceding analysis.

Friedman-Schwartz Ideal Definition of U.S. Money

Consider first the following quotation from Milton Friedman and Anna Schwartz, the leading academic authorities on the monetary statistics of the United States and two of the strongest proponents of the view that money should play a central role in the conduct of monetary policy:

> The "public" of the United States, ideally defined, excludes the monetary authorities and all banks, whether operated by private individuals, partnerships, corporations, or governments, and includes all other individuals, partnerships, and government agencies resident in the United States and its possessions. For the public so defined, we would have liked to determine the total holdings of U.S. currency, the four classes of U.S. dollar deposits listed, and savings and loan shares. In practice we have had to depart from this ideal. The departures are explained by a single circumstance: the basic data we use are reported by the issuers of currency and by the banking institutions whose liabilities are so misleadingly termed "deposits," rather than by the holders of the currency and the deposits. As a consequence, it is often necessary to make the coverage of the data correspond to the geographic location or other char-

---

denominated in foreign currency. And it would be conceivable to base the definition on the funds loaned by home lenders (regardless of whether the loan recipient were a home or a foreign resident), rather than on funds received by home borrowers.

acteristics of the issuers of currency or of the banking institutions or correspond to the character of their liabilities, rather than, as we should prefer, to the characteristics of the holders and of their monetary assets.[5]

Friedman and Schwartz thus have an "ideal" notion of the public (the private sector) and a corresponding "ideal" definition of money, contingent on the criterion of home residency of the holders of money (in this case, residency within the geographical boundaries of the United States and its possessions). In terms of the alternatives discussed in chapter 8, Friedman and Schwartz are advocates of M_d as the appropriate definition of the U.S. money stock.

Friedman and Schwartz use their definition of money to analyze national macroeconomic developments, including especially the impacts of monetary-policy actions. The opening passages of their book emphasize that the purpose for which they develop a definition of the U.S. money stock is to be able to predict changes in prices and nominal income in the United States.[6] In other writings Friedman urges the Federal Reserve System to specify a target path for the U.S. money stock so defined and to use its instruments to keep the stock growing along that path.[7]

Although Friedman and Schwartz overlook the fact, a fundamental difficulty arises when their ideal definition of the money stock is juxtaposed with the purpose for which they wish to use it. Their implicit assumption is that the aggregate of liquid assets held by the private sector resident *in the United States* is the relevant financial magnitude for predicting prices and income *in the United States*. If Friedman and Schwartz had incorporated the interdependence of the U.S. economy and the rest of the world into their analysis and confronted that assumption explicitly, they would have had to reject it as theoretically incorrect.

The basic point can be highlighted by thinking, as in chapter 3, about the money stock of West Virginia. Suppose it were possible to construct the M_d definition of money for that state. This "ideal definition" (a la Friedman and Schwartz) would comprise the total holdings of liquid assets owned by nonbank economic units resident within the state of West Virginia. Now ask how sanguine one could be about using M_d for West Virginia to predict the price level in West Virginia and the aggregate income of West Virginia residents. Self-evidently, using the demand for West Virginia M_d to predict West Virginia prices and West Virginia income would be unsuccessful unless at the same time one took into account the interstate transactions carried out by West Virginia residents and hence the simultaneous

5. Milton Friedman and Anna Jacobson Schwartz, *Monetary Statistics of the United States: Estimates, Sources, Methods,* Studies in Business Cycles, 20 (New York: National Bureau of Economic Research, 1970), pp. 58–60; see also pp. 73–74. These passages and the related footnotes are the only places in their book where Friedman and Schwartz discuss the open-economy, conceptual aspects of U.S. monetary statistics. There is more discussion of the open-economy aspects of U.S. monetary developments in their earlier book, *A Monetary History of the United States, 1867–1960,* Studies in Business Cycles, 12 (Princeton University Press for National Bureau of Economic Research, 1963); see for example pp. 25–29, 51–52, and 89–90. Even in this earlier volume, however, the open-economy aspects receive little attention in the formulation of the theoretical framework (see ibid., app. B).

6. *Monetary Statistics of the United States,* p. 1; compare also pp. 18, 43–44, 89–91, and 139.

7. See, for example, "The Role of Monetary Policy," *American Economic Review,* vol. 58 (March 1968), pp. 1–17, reprinted in Friedman, *The Optimum Quantity of Money and Other Essays* (Aldine, 1969). Friedman's writings tend not to use such terms as *intermediate target* and *ultimate target;* but his views about the proper conduct of monetary policy clearly constitute advocacy of the strategy of using money as an intermediate target.

determination of prices and income in West Virginia with prices and income in neighboring states. By themselves, variations in the holdings of liquid assets by the private sector resident *in West Virginia* would not be the only, and perhaps not even the main, financial magnitude relevant for predicting variations in prices and income *in West Virginia*.

Next, suppose a Federal Reserve official were to go to Charleston, West Virginia and once a week purchase or sell securities, potentially in large volume, at a public auction. Suppose buyers and sellers participating in the auction must be economic units resident in West Virginia. Self-evidently, again, the Federal Reserve could not closely control the *West Virginia* money stock through these regional open-market operations, let alone exert a special regional influence on *West Virginia* prices and incomes.

The situation of the United States vis-à-vis the rest of the world, or even Belgium's situation vis-à-vis the remainder of Europe, is different in many critical respects from West Virginia's situation vis-à-vis the rest of the United States. The dissimilarities—separate currency units, exchange rates, economic barriers at national boundaries, heterogeneity of social and political institutions—require that the West Virginia analogy be used with caution. But there are also important similarities. The issue here is whether these similarities can be neglected when defining and using monetary aggregates at the level of the nation state.

Friedman and Schwartz completely ignore the similarities. Moreover, they do not make a case for ignoring the interdependence of the U.S. economy and the rest of the world on the ground that its consequences are small enough to be ignored for practical purposes. Rather, they speak of an *ideal* definition of the U.S. money stock and departures from that alleged ideal.

Federal Reserve Advisory Committee on Monetary Statistics

A second illustration of how American economists fail to perceive the implications for monetary aggregates of the interdependence of national economies is provided by the 1976 report of the Federal Reserve's Advisory Committee on Monetary Statistics.[8] The report is mentioned here for what it illustrates about the concepts and theory prevalent in the literature, not because of its practical recommendations for U.S. monetary statistics.

The summary recommendations of the report contain the following passage:

> At present, all deposits of foreign individuals and businesses, foreign commercial banks, and foreign central banks and other official institutions at banks in the United States are included in the U.S. money stock, and no U.S. dollar deposits abroad (for example, Eurodollars) are included, no matter who owns them. We recommend including foreigners' deposits in the United States where these are likely to be used primarily for purchases of U.S. goods, services, and securities and excluding all U.S. dollar deposits abroad—mainly because there is no practical way of incorporating

8. The Federal Reserve Board appointed this committee of academic experts in January 1974 to "review the basic monetary statistics (especially the so-called monetary aggregates) used by the Federal Reserve in formulating and conducting monetary policy, to evaluate the adequacy of those statistics, and to present suggestions for their improvement where this seems desirable." The committee was chaired by G. L. Bach; other members were Phillip D. Cagan, Milton Friedman, Clifford G. Hildreth, Franco Modigliani, and Arthur M. Okun. Its report is *Improving the Monetary Aggregates* (Board of Governors of the Federal Reserve System, 1976).

these data into current U.S. money stock series even though some such balances may be held primarily with a view to purchases in the United States.[9]

Later, in a section that provides a more detailed discussion of the international aspects of the monetary statistics, the report argues:

> If the demand for dollar deposits by any group of holders is controlled primarily by forces other than those that control the demand for money by the U.S. public (basically the volume of domestic transactions, wealth, and interest rates), there is a prima facie case for the exclusion of that group of holders and holdings.[10]

At still another point, when discussing dollar-denominated deposits at banks outside the United States, the Committee comments: "It is likely that [dollar deposits of foreign businesses and investors at foreign banks] are not significantly related to transactions in the United States. Thus, we recommend that they not be included in the U.S. monetary aggregates."[11]

As these and other passages in the report indicate, the Advisory Committee was attracted to the line of reasoning suggesting the M_y concept of money. In principle, the committee argues, the various categories of deposits and other liquid assets in the world, by whomever held, should be included in or excluded from the U.S. money stock depending on whether they are or are not associated with "U.S. transactions" or "spending on U.S. goods, services, and securities." In practice, the committee concedes, this theoretical definition is difficult to implement because of lack of data and the costs of acquiring additional data. Hence they fall back on the best feasible approximation to that concept—an M_z definition. They reason, for example, that the liabilities of banks in the United States to foreign commercial banks should be excluded because they are held "primarily" for purposes such as clearing Eurodollar transactions rather than "primarily" for making payments in U.S. goods and securities markets.[12]

For reasons given in chapter 8, the implicit theory underlying the Advisory Committee's attraction to a "domestic" definition of the U.S. money stock is defective. Transactions in an open economy cannot logically be segregated into those that are and those that are not determinants of *national* income and prices. Nor can liquid assets in the world be meaningfully divided into those primarily held to carry out domestic and nondomestic transactions. Thus, even in theory, the committee's notion of purging foreign influences from money and income, thereby producing an uncontaminated relationship between domestic money and domestic transactions, does not stand up to analysis.

The passages from the Advisory Committee's report quoted above illustrate the least adequate elements in the committee's reasoning. Since the committee's

---

9. The summary goes on to conclude: "Applying these criteria, we recommend that deposits of foreign commercial banks and foreign central banks and other official institutions in the United States be excluded from the U.S. money stock, since these are apparently held primarily for clearing Eurodollar transactions, for financing foreign exchange transactions, and as international monetary reserves; but that deposits of foreign individuals and businesses continue to be included." *Improving the Monetary Aggregates,* p. 4.

10. Ibid., p. 16.

11. Ibid., p. 20.

12. The Advisory Committee's views about the liabilities of U.S. banks to foreigners and the behavior associated with them are based in part on an informative research paper prepared by the Federal Reserve staff; see Helen T. Farr, Lance Girton, Henry S. Terrell, and Thomas H. Turner, "Foreign Demand Deposits at Commercial Banks in the United States," in *Improving the Monetary Aggregates: Staff Papers* (Board of Governors of the Federal Reserve System, 1978), pp. 35–54.

operational recommendations are based on that reasoning, their report warrants the criticism leveled against it here. It would be unfair to the committee's report, however, not to acknowledge several passages that pay lip service to the difficulties associated with a domestic concept of the money stock. In particular, the summary includes the following statement:

> In an open economy like that of the United States, interactions between domestic and international transactions on trade and capital accounts make it impossible for the monetary authorities to consider only domestic consequences of their actions—and by the same token make any purely domestic measure of the money stock to a degree unsatisfactory as an intermediate target variable. As there is no one ideal concept of money for domestic monetary control purposes, so there is no one ideal concept for an open economy or for the world economy.[13]

This disclaimer did not have much influence on the committee's reasoning. Just as the committee failed to address the underlying rationales for and fundamental difficulties associated with the use of money as an intermediate target of monetary policy, it did little to integrate its perceptions of the openness of the U.S. economy into its analysis of U.S. monetary statistics.[14]

Money in the Monetary Approach to the Balance of Payments

Unlike that large part of monetary theory developed only for the case of a closed economy, the monetary approach to the balance of payments does not ignore the joint determination of the national money stock and economic developments outside the home nation. The monetary approach fails to deal adequately, however, with the difficulties of defining national money and of specifying the role of national money in an internally consistent macroeconomic theory for an open economy.[15]

The typical exposition of the monetary approach highlights the demand for and the supply of money. For example, Jacob Frenkel and Harry Johnson stress that "the essential assumption of the monetary approach . . . is that there exists an aggregate demand function for money that is a [stable] function of a relatively small number of aggregate economic variables."[16] Yet little attention is paid to what

13. *Improving the Monetary Aggregates*, p. 4. This passage and analogous caveats (see, for example, p. 16) were added to the report partly in response to my comments on an earlier draft.

14. The Advisory Committee's failure to address the basic issues can be partially, but not wholly, explained by its restrictive mandate from the Federal Reserve Board. The committee was asked to "study and make recommendations only on the statistics in question—not to evaluate monetary policy or to investigate the significance of the aggregates relative to interest rates or credit market indicators" (see introduction to the report). I share the view of other critics that the committee accepted its mandate too meekly and thereby failed to make as useful a contribution to understanding of the issues as would otherwise have been possible.

15. The recent literature on the monetary approach to the balance of payments revives an eighteenth and nineteenth century emphasis on international aspects of monetary theory that had become somewhat dormant in the first few decades following the worldwide depression of the 1930s. The approach is described and further references are given in Jacob A. Frenkel and Harry G. Johnson, eds., *The Monetary Approach to the Balance of Payments* (University of Toronto Press, 1976); International Monetary Fund, *The Monetary Approach to the Balance of Payments* (IMF, 1977); Michael Mussa, "A Monetary Approach to Balance-of-Payments Analysis," *Journal of Money, Credit and Banking*, vol. 6 (August 1974), pp. 333–51; and Marina v. N. Whitman, "Global Monetarism and the Monetary Approach to the Balance of Payments," *Brookings Papers on Economic Activity, 3:1975*, pp. 491–536. Although the blind spot pointed out in the text is a serious weakness, the monetary approach to the balance of payments has nonetheless made valuable contributions to analysis of the financial consequences of interdependence (see part 5 below).

16. "The Monetary Approach to the Balance of Payments: Essential Concepts and Historical Origins," in Frenkel and Johnson, eds., *The Monetary Approach to the Balance of Payments*, pp. 24–25.

money is, who holds it, and who issues it. No distinctions are made, for example, among the domestic demand for domestic money, the total demand for domestic money (by foreign as well as home economic units), and the domestic demand for money-like assets (regardless of currency denomination or location of the issuing financial institutions). Some contributors to the approach merely ignore the distinctions. Others resort to the simplifying *assumptions* that nonbanks resident in the home country are the only holders of money-like assets denominated in the home currency, that home financial institutions are the only issuers of such assets, and that nonbanks and banks in the home country do not hold money-like assets denominated in foreign currency.[17]

The restrictive assumptions of the approach lull its advocates into specifying an aggregate demand function of the form:

$$(9\text{-}1) \qquad\qquad \frac{M^d}{P} = f\left(r, \frac{Y}{P}\right),$$

where M^d is the demand for home money, Y is the nominal GNP of the home country, P is the general price level in the home country, and r is a vector of interest rates on assets denominated in the home currency issued by home financial institutions. Despite the fact that the approach is intended to address the problems of an open economy, the analysis is centered on an aggregate demand function for money identical to the function appropriate for a completely closed economy![18]

As this peculiarity suggests, the monetary approach to the balance of payments is problematic in two ways. First, it ignores or assumes away many of the categories of money-like assets and liabilities that can link an open economy to the rest of the world (see figure 8-2). In real life, many national economies have significant amounts of such assets or liabilities. Thus, until the approach is modified to take such complications into account, its conclusions are of uncertain applicability.[19]

Second, the approach's theoretical specification of the demand for money is clearly defective. The function 9-1 asserts that the demand for the national money of the home country is unaffected by expected changes in the exchange rate or in foreign interest rates. An analogous function for the rest of the world asserts that the demand for foreign money is unaffected by expected changes in the exchange rate and in home interest rates. But demand functions of this sort cannot easily be reconciled with the rudiments of open-economy monetary theory outlined in chapter 7 (regardless of what simplifying assumptions may be used in defining national money). A money-demand function such as 9-1 is all the more implausible when assessed in the light of the monetary approach's assumptions about nonmoney assets. Users of the approach commonly assume that nonmoney assets denominated in the home currency (for example, bonds) are very close substitutes for nonmoney assets denominated in foreign currency. Yet, simultaneously, the demand function

17. The typical exposition of the approach also fails to indicate whether the author regards liquidity, usability as a means of payment, or still some other attribute as the distinguishing characteristic of the assets deemed to be money.
18. See chapter 5, equation 5-7.
19. The simplifying assumptions of the monetary approach cannot all be correct simultaneously. In an open economy, some home residents must have nonzero demands for foreign-currency means of payment or some foreign residents must have nonzero demands for home-currency means of payment (see chapter 7).

9-1 assumes zero substitutability between home and foreign monies. The combination of these contrasting substitutability assumptions is anomalous: why should financial interdependence work vigorously through one aspect of private portfolio decisions but be absent altogether from another, closely related aspect?

These considerations cast substantial doubt on the contention that the aggregate demand for national money is a well defined, stable function of only a few *domestic* macroeconomic variables.[20]

An Intermediate-Target Strategy under Conditions of Interdependence

The preceding illustrations of inadequate analysis of the concept of a nation's money stock are not isolated instances. With few exceptions, the literature of monetary economics either ignores economic interdependence or else fails to characterize its implications accurately for the role played in monetary theory by the nation's money stock.

A rigorous analysis of the role of national money in the conduct of national monetary policy requires as background a better understanding of the phenomenon of interdependence and its consequences for macroeconomic policy in general. Hence part 3, which follows.

It may help the reader to take stock briefly of the argument thus far, as a prelude to part 3 and the subsequent analysis of money strategies in part 4.

The analysis in part 2 gives the benefit of the doubt to the view that a single financial aggregate—money, somehow defined—should be assigned a pivotal role in monetary policy. The discussion focuses on the differences between a closed economy and an open economy for the plausibility of using money as an intermediate target.

Probing into the interdependencies of a nation's economy and the rest of the world plainly adds a new section to the catalogue of thorny issues identified in chapter 6. Whatever doubts one might already have about the tractability of a money strategy for the hypothetical context of a closed economy can only be magnified when the openness of a nation's economy is taken into account.

Imagine that the policymakers in the home central bank, unlike the existing literature, pay substantial attention to the interdependence of the nation's economy and the rest of the world. As shown in chapters 7 and 8, the policymakers cannot then avoid the conclusion that there is no correct definition of home money for all purposes, and certainly no "domestic" definition uncontaminated by interdependence. But suppose they nonetheless happen to be wedded to a two-stage money strategy for national monetary policy. In that event, they must still regard the issue of the definition of money as urgent; they must choose which of the definitions will be least troublesome as their intermediate-target variable.

The criteria of reliability and controllability will both be relevant for the choice, but neither can dominate to the exclusion of the other. To make matters worse, the more the policymakers gravitate toward a definition of money that they believe

---

20. No empirical research of which I am aware, for any nation, has carefully tested this contention and provided convincing evidence in support of it.

reduces uncertainty in the causal interrelationships between money and their ultimate-target variables, the less closely that aggregate will be controllable with the instruments of national monetary policy. Conversely, the greater the weight given to close controllability, the larger the uncertainty that must be accepted about the links between money and the ultimate objectives.

Even in a completely closed economy, the choice of the definition of money to use as an intermediate-target variable would encounter these difficulties to some degree. But the trade-off between upper-stage reliability and lower-stage controllability is more acute when the national economy is significantly open.

The openness of a nation's economy also heightens other difficulties associated with a money strategy. The most striking feature of an intermediate-target approach is its different periodicities of decisionmaking for the upper and lower stages. Because the upper-stage decision is revised only infrequently, the strategy limits the ability of the central bank to take into account international influences on the home economy. During the interval between revisions of the upper-stage decision, for example, the central bank tries to keep the money stock on a previously determined target path even though unexpected events occurring abroad may render that previous upper-stage decision obsolete.

Why might it be helpful to decompose the overall policy problem into two stages, using the money stock as a pivot between the two? Why employ different periodicities for the two levels of decisions? As foreshadowed in chapter 6, these aspects of an intermediate-target strategy require justification regardless of the degree to which a nation's economy is open to the rest of the world. The need for a justification of a two-stage, two-periodicity procedure is all the more pressing, however, when national policy must be conducted under conditions of extensive interdependence.

PART THREE

Interdependence
and the Theory of Economic Policy

Interdependence and National Economic Policy: Alternative Paradigms

PART 2 is narrowly concerned with the consequences of economic openness for money and monetary policy. But economic openness has implications that extend far beyond the financial sectors of a nation's economy. And national monetary policy is only a part of national macroeconomic policy. Before continuing the analysis of monetary policy, therefore, there is a need to digress from monetary issues and, on a map covering a larger territory, to locate what has already been said. Inevitably, a more comprehensive map must have a smaller scale and suppress many details. The map sketched here in part 3, however, has two offsetting advantages. It places money and monetary policy into perspective in the broader context of national economic policy as a whole. And it enables later chapters to deal more systematically with the consequences of interdependence for the autonomy of national economic policy and the controllability of the national economy.

Interdependence and Economic Policy: Basic Hypotheses

Part 2 concludes that, no matter how the money stock for a nation may be defined, economic interdependencies with the rest of the world weaken the links between the instruments of national monetary policy and the money stock, and between the money stock and national ultimate targets, and thereby undermine the ability of policymakers to use the money stock as an intermediate operating target for national monetary policy.

If placed in proper perspective, that conclusion is a special case of a more general and pervasive phenomenon:

(10-A′) **In a significantly open economy, interdependence with the rest of the world typically loosens the relationships between national policy instruments and national ultimate targets.**

The comparison implicit in 10-A′ is between a significantly open economy and a (hypothetical) closed economy. But this fundamental theoretical proposition can also be expressed as a comparison of some particular open economy at two different points in time:

(10-A) **If an open economy experiences an increase (decrease) in economic interdependence with the rest of the world, the relationships between national policy instruments and national ultimate targets will typically be loosened (strengthened).**

This alternative formulation is, of course, the one relevant for empirical research on actual economies.

In principle, it will be argued, proposition 10-A applies to all national policy instruments, all national ultimate targets, and all the complex relationships that link them together. Specifically, it applies not just to policy actions that can be taken by a nation's monetary authority but also to the instruments of fiscal policy and to other governmental policy instruments (for example, regulatory policies). It applies no matter what operating strategies are employed to manipulate the policy instruments. In the case of monetary policy, it is applicable whatever intermediate variable (for example, money, or credit, or an interest rate) might be selected as a proximate target of policy. Equally important, it is relevant for alternative strategies for implementing policy that reject a concentration on intermediate-target variables. It is apposite whatever the nature of the exchange regime governing transactions between assets denominated in home currency and foreign currency.[1]

When national economic policy is examined as a whole, therefore, the impossibility theorems of chapter 9 need to be generalized. For example, theorem 9-A becomes, after generalization, a theoretical statement about all variables associated with a nation's economy:

(10-B) It is impossible in a significantly open economy to define macroeconomic variables in such a way that they will be impervious to interactions between the home and the foreign economies.

Theorem 10-B applies to both intermediate variables and variables deemed to be ultimate targets of national policy—at a minimum, in other words, to all "endogenous" variables.[2]

The second impossibility theorem in chapter 9 deals with the conduct of monetary policy, in particular the use of money as a proximate operating target. In its more comprehensive version that theorem becomes a proposition about intermediate-target strategies in general:

(10-C) In a significantly open economy, there is no national intermediate variable that the nation's policymakers can control closely _and_ that has a direct, reliable relationship with the ultimate targets of national economic policy.

Theorems 10-B and 10-C, like their more specific counterparts in part 2, are not counterintuitive—at least not for a world economy characterized by fixed exchange rates. They merely emphasize the often forgotten fact that there is no theoretically correct way of isolating for analysis, independently of its interactions with the rest of the world, any aspect of macroeconomic behavior in a significantly open economy.

Grant for the moment that these impossibility theorems are valid.[3] And consider

---

1. To repeat the essential caveat once again: nothing has yet been said, one way or the other, about the quantitative significance of these matters for actual economies. The assertion that proposition 10-A is germane not only for a world of fixed exchange rates but also for one in which exchange rates are flexible is discussed in part 5.

2. The appropriate categorization of variables in a particular analysis as endogenous or exogenous depends critically, of course, on the purpose and scope of that analysis. This point is given further attention below.

3. The analysis in chapters 12 and 13 returns to propositions 10-A through 10-C and the issue of their validity, while much of part 5 is devoted to analyzing interdependence under conditions of exchange-rate variability.

now the question of how the analysis of national economic developments and policy might cope with their implications. Four alternative approaches can be taken. The remainder of this chapter articulates the paradigms, or conceptual frames of reference, with which each approach is associated.[4]

The Nearly Closed Paradigm

Consider first the approach that results from looking at the world through the conceptual lenses of the nearly closed paradigm. The main features of this paradigm are portrayed schematically in figure 10-1. Arrows in the diagram indicate the channels of causation or interaction considered to be important; the widths of the arrows suggest the relative importance attributed to the various channels.[5]

As suggested in figure 10-1 by the smaller space and symbols associated with the foreign economy, the fact that a particular national economy being studied is part of a larger world economy warrants, at best, secondary analytical attention. Moreover, interactions of the home economy with the rest of the world tend to be treated in an ad hoc, piecemeal fashion rather than as an integral part of the conceptual framework. Those channels of international interaction that are explicitly considered are few in number. Foreign influences on the home economy (indicated in the diagram by the broken arrow) are taken as exogenous. No effort is made to account for influences of the home economy on foreign economic developments; hence all subsequent repercussions on the home economy are also neglected.

An approach based on this national, nearly closed paradigm is thus severely myopic about everything except the "domestic" economy. In both theoretical and practical discussions, the implications of propositions 10-A through 10-C are virtually ignored. If, to take a pertinent illustration, there is an interest in implementing national economic policy by operating through a certain home intermediate variable as an operating target, application of this paradigm presupposes that the policymakers can ignore international interdependencies, at least as a first approximation, and concentrate solely on the relationships between the intermediate target and the home ultimate-target variables.

The nearly closed paradigm may well be the characterization of national macroeconomic activity most frequently employed by economists and government policymakers in the larger and least open industrial countries. Such is certainly the

---

4. The discussion that follows uses the word *paradigm* less precisely than Thomas S. Kuhn, in his second thoughts, recommends; see *The Structure of Scientific Revolutions,* 2d ed. (University of Chicago Press, 1970), esp. pp. 174–91. For our purposes, however, there is no need for the more subtle nuances of Kuhn's revised terminology (for example, "disciplinary matrix," "symbolic generalization," "exemplar"). Kuhn's seminal book forces readers to be more conscious of the conceptual lenses through which they are accustomed to viewing the subject matter of their disciplines. The purpose of the discussion here is to promote a similar awareness for the more limited area of international economics.

5. Figure 10-1 is drawn, as are the three subsequent diagrams, without showing the possibility that some policy instruments may affect ultimate targets directly (that is, without first affecting one or more intermediate variables). The exclusion or inclusion of this possibility does not influence the comparison of paradigms that is subsequently made in the text. For simplicity, the diagrams also omit the influences of nonpolicy exogenous variables; these variables are explicitly brought into the analysis later in the chapter.

Figure 10-1. *The Nearly Closed Paradigm*

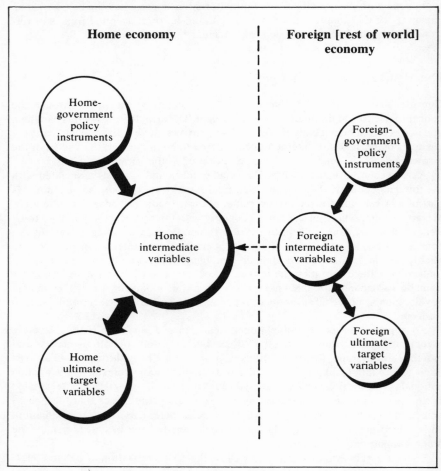

case in the United States. But there are two other paradigms in vogue, both of which pay greater attention to economic openness.

The Small and Open Paradigm

The small and open paradigm, represented schematically in figure 10-2, postulates an economy whose relationships with the rest of the world loom large relative to the size of the economy itself but are small relative to the world as a whole. In contrast to the nearly closed paradigm, foreign exogenous influences play an enormously important part in influencing many macrovariables in the home economy. Users of this paradigm often assume, for example, that the home-currency

Figure 10-2. *The Small and Open Paradigm*

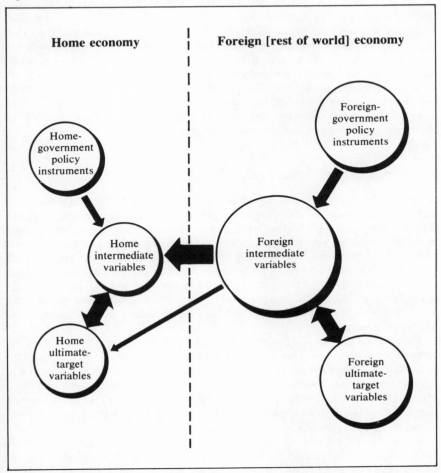

price of individual traded goods produced at home cannot differ from the home-currency price of similar traded goods produced in other nations; because the home economy is conceptualized as small, home production and home consumption of traded goods are assumed not to affect the world price. Analogous assumptions are often made about financial markets. For example, apart from qualifications (depending on the particular analysis) about differing expected rates of inflation or expectations about exchange-rate changes, analysts may postulate that interest rates in the home economy cannot differ from interest rates in the rest of the world, which are exogenously given.[6]

---

6. The links between the foreign exogenous and the home endogenous variables can be specified in several different ways, which in turn can lead to important differences in the resulting analyses.

One cannot fault the small and open paradigm for ignoring or deemphasizing international influences. Indeed, certain of those influences take pride of place over all other aspects of the analysis. Note, on the other hand, that the international influences still run in only one direction. The rest-of-the-world economy plays a large role in driving the national economy; but nothing that happens in the national economy can have any impact on the rest of the world. On closer inspection, therefore, the small and open paradigm is not as dissimilar from the nearly closed paradigm as might appear at first glance. Both paradigms are designed to enable their users to ignore reciprocal international interactions. One postulates virtual independence, while the other assumes a large measure of dependence. Neither allows for or attempts to analyze genuine interdependence.

The Supranational Paradigm

A third approach to the analysis of macroeconomic activity, the supranational paradigm, adopts a global rather than national perspective. As suggested by figure 10-3, the supranational paradigm characterizes economic activity as taking place in a highly integrated world economy. Commodities and financial assets are regarded as very good substitutes everywhere in the world. In fact, the degree of such substitutability and the degree of perfection in the integration of markets is assumed to be sufficiently great to necessitate a world aggregation of macroeconomic variables. At least to a first approximation, therefore, the economic phenomena associated with political boundaries and political decisions—with the nation state itself—are ignored.

Policymakers in national governments do not perceive the world in terms of the supranational paradigm. This frame of reference may, however, be employed by individuals or organizations whose activities require or facilitate a transnational point of view.[7] It has also found favor from time to time among economic theorists, especially those who emphasize monetary influences. In the latter application, it is most often found in conjunction with the assumption of fixed exchange rates among national currencies.

A notable example of the application of the supranational paradigm is an analysis of *world* inflation in terms of the *world* money supply, somehow defined. Such an analysis uses macroeconomic variables that are aggregations of national variables, but the national variables are of little or no interest per se.[8]

As another illustration, consider again the relationship between macroeconomic activity in West Virginia and the West Virginia money stock. Even a monetarist economist would not believe that, by themselves, variations in the holdings of liquid assets by the residents of West Virginia are the only (and perhaps even the dominant) financial magnitude relevant for predicting variations in prices and incomes in West Virginia. The impossibility theorems 10-B and 10-C are especially

---

7. For a discussion of transnational actors and relationships, see Robert O. Keohane and Joseph S. Nye, Jr., *Transnational Relations and World Politics* (Harvard University Press, 1972).

8. See, for example, Michael Parkin, Ian Richards, and George Zis, "The Determination and Control of the World Money Supply under Fixed Exchange Rates, 1961–71," *Manchester School of Economics and Social Studies*, no. 3 (September 1975), pp. 293–316.

Figure 10-3. *The Supranational Paradigm*

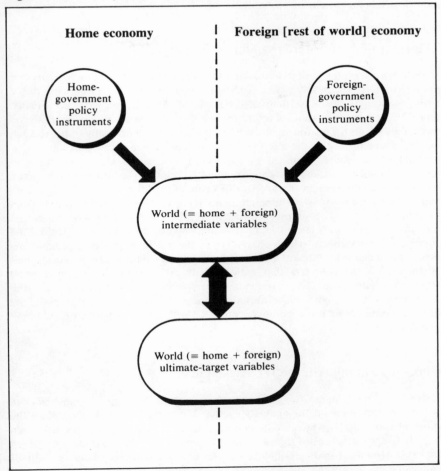

applicable to the West Virginia economy because of the high degree of integration between commodity and asset markets in West Virginia and those in the remainder of the United States. Thus, it not only seems natural, but may even prove analytically preferable, to jettison a concentration on West Virginia macroeconomic variables and to adopt a supranational (in this example, supraregional) approach.

Without doubt, the conceptual lenses of the supranational paradigm correct for the domestic-economy myopia encouraged by the nearly closed paradigm. In fact, they may overcorrect. In a thorough application of the supranational paradigm, it may no longer be possible to identify a national economy at all. The unit of analysis becomes the world. Nation states lose their identities as distinct economic entities and are treated as regions that do not play an analytically separable role in determining macroeconomic activity for the world as a whole. It is necessary to raise questions about, for example, income distribution before a good reason exists to focus analysis on nations individually.

The Intermediate Interdependence Paradigm

In different ways, the supranational and the small and open paradigms represent polar extremes. The nearly closed paradigm, given its superficial treatment of the home economy's openness, may also be said to represent an extreme. Finally, therefore, still another frame of reference needs to be articulated, one that falls on the middle ground. This fourth alternative, presented schematically in figure 10-4, may be characterized as the intermediate interdependence paradigm.

Analyses conducted from the perspective of this paradigm, as the arrows in figure 10-4 indicate, make allowance for numerous channels of interaction between the home and the foreign (rest-of-world) economies. Moreover, this framework emphasizes genuine two-way interaction, not merely unidirectional causation from one part of the world economy to the other. Yet the distinction between home and foreign variables is no less prominent than in figures 10-1 and 10-2. Unlike the supranational approach, which characterizes the world economy as comprising nearly homogeneous, integrated markets, the intermediate interdependence paradigm retains the postulate that national political boundaries may have great *economic* significance. The intermediate perspective not only allows for—but presupposes the existence of—differential impacts of the policy instruments of the home government on home-country, compared with rest-of-world, ultimate-target variables.

Choosing among Alternative Paradigms

Differences among paradigms tend to be fundamental. Yet objective analysts can try to compare them. If the analysts can agree on evaluative criteria and on the range of problems to which a common paradigm is to be applied, they will often be able to agree that one of the alternative frames of reference is preferable (given those constraints at that particular time). But choice among alternative paradigms cannot be made on theoretical grounds alone. And even when empirical considerations are introduced, there is never an absolute, timeless sense in which one particular paradigm can be deemed correct.[9]

These general observations about the role of paradigms in professional disciplines are equally germane for the alternative approaches to studying economic openness identified above. The degree to which each of the four may be appropriate (or inappropriate) depends importantly on the purpose of the analysis. It also depends, a fortiori, on the country or part of the world economy being studied. There are certain purposes or circumstances for which each might be judged preferable. Some national economies, for example, may be judged to conform well with the assumptions of the small and open paradigm. What may be even more important, the

9. Kuhn, *The Structure of Scientific Revolutions*, particularly chaps. 7–11.

Figure 10-4. *The Intermediate Interdependence Paradigm*

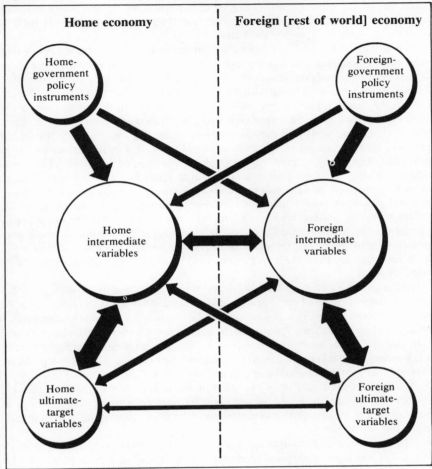

small and open paradigm may be judged theoretically less intractable.[10] Even though the supranational paradigm cannot be defended as empirically well-suited to the entire world economy, at least it may be argued that a global perspective is applicable to the markets for particular commodities. A supranational approach may also be propounded as a safeguard against the potential pitfalls associated with the nearly

10. Many Australian and Scandinavian economists, for example, are strongly influenced by both these considerations in their theoretical and empirical research. For some of the relevant references, see Odd Aukrust, "Inflation in the Open Economy: A Norwegian Model," in Lawrence B. Krause and Walter S. Salant, eds., *Worldwide Inflation: Theory and Recent Experience* (Brookings Institution, 1977), pp. 107–66; and Jorgen Gelting, "National Autonomy of Stabilization Policy," in Albert Ando, Richard Herring, and Richard Marston, eds., *International Aspects of Stabilization Policies,* Conference Series, 12 (Federal Reserve Bank of Boston, June 1974), pp. 55–71.

closed or the small and open perspectives.[11] For some problems and for some countries, on the other hand, the degree of economic integration *within* national boundaries may conceivably be so much greater than *across* those boundaries that analysis is justified in ignoring the latter.

A multiplicity of paradigms can be advantageous for another reason. However different the conceptual lenses through which analysts view the world, it can be argued that there is only one objective state of nature. Hence if alternative conceptual frames of reference are applied with the same objective in mind, and with sufficient care to the same circumstances, each approach should, in principle, lead to the same conclusions. Only if the approaches pay insufficient attention to qualifications and needed refinements will they generate substantively incompatible results. In practice, however, any one approach is bound to neglect qualifications or fail to introduce needed refinements. For example, application of the nearly closed paradigm to a single nation's economy is certain to result in a glossing over of some important channels of international interdependence, whereas use of the supranational paradigm cannot help but suppress some significant respects in which different nations' economies are not fully integrated. Hence, this line of reasoning continues, the surest recipe for obtaining a well-balanced account of some phenomenon is to encourage the clash of alternative points of view. Deficiencies in each approach are then likely to be corrected by the countervailing virtues of its competitors.[12]

Although the existence of a multiplicity of paradigms may be advantageous for the evolution of a field of professional activity toward a more systematic, scientific state, the concern here is with economic policy in *significantly open* economies.[13] That fact alone should preclude use of the nearly closed paradigm. If a careful effort is made to refine the nearly closed approach so that international interdependencies can be adequately taken into account, moreover, the resulting analysis will probably resemble an approach based on the intermediate paradigm.

Nor are the small and open paradigm or the supranational paradigm suitable frames of reference for the discussion here. Because both are characterizations of polar or near-polar cases, their assumptions make them, even at the level of theory, much too restrictive.

The supranational paradigm must be rejected for another reason. The primary interest of this book is *national* economic policy. It may be a moot point, at least in some economists' minds, whether it is appropriate to focus so narrowly on macroeconomic activity and economic policy in single nations. But *if* that is the objective of an analysis, there can be no doubt that the supranational paradigm is

11. For a thoughtful discussion of the potential disadvantages of a national perspective and the potential fruitfulness of a supranational frame of reference, see Walter S. Salant, "A Supranational Approach to the Analysis of Worldwide Inflation," in Krause and Salant, eds., *Worldwide Inflation*, pp. 633–55. Marina v. N. Whitman also discusses this issue in "Global Monetarism and the Monetary Approach to the Balance of Payments," *Brookings Papers on Economic Activity, 3:1975*, pp. 491–536.

12. For a similar expression of this point of view but in the context of a comparison of alternative paradigms for studying political behavior, see John D. Steinbruner, *The Cybernetic Theory of Decision: New Dimensions of Political Analysis* (Princeton University Press, 1974).

13. On the questions of whether a profession or a field of study can be said to exist in the presence of a multiplicity of paradigms, and whether it can be labeled "scientific" (whether, for example, a field is construed as making progress because it is a science or is construed as a science because it makes a particular type of progress), see Kuhn, *The Structure of Scientific Revolutions*, pp. 10–42, 144–73.

inappropriate. Because of its working assumptions, a supranational perspective rules out a focus on national economic policy.

It is an important implication of the analysis in part 2 that the relationship between the money stock in an open economy and macroeconomic activity and prices in that economy cannot be adequately analyzed within the national, nearly closed frame of reference. The relationship between macroeconomic activity in West Virginia and the West Virginia money stock is a still more obvious example of a problem for which the nearly closed paradigm is inapplicable. For the West Virginia case, it was argued, one might even be driven to adopt a supraregional approach. But, at best, that earlier argument is incomplete. Imagine an analyst who has no independent interest in macroeconomic activity and prices in the United States as a whole, but instead wishes to focus exclusively on macroeconomic activity and prices in West Virginia. It would be of no help to such an analyst to recommend a supraregional approach if its adoption requires the jettisoning of West Virginia macroeconomic variables.

Application of a supranational approach is not straightforward even when the object of attention is an aggregation of nations or regions. For example, who would formulate "world" ultimate-target variables? Does it make sense—even conceptually—to aggregate the separately determined targets of different nations' policy authorities and generate world target variables in that manner? Are the separately determined targets of the various nations' authorities compatible with each other— in the sense that it would be possible actually to attain all the targets ex post? Given those difficulties, will a theorist following this approach be compelled to abandon the assumption that each nation's government has separate policy instruments that are adjusted to influence separately determined national objectives? And if the approach requires the supposition of a world social welfare function, is there a political theory that can plausibly justify the requisite, associated assumption of a world policymaking authority?[14]

In sum, despite its lesser familiarity and greater complexity relative to the other three paradigms employed in international economic theory, the intermediate interdependence paradigm is the only one that can advance the analysis here. The final sections of this chapter identify the main features that differentiate this paradigm and stress two of its key implications.

Essential Characteristics of the Intermediate Interdependence Paradigm

Most of the concepts that constitute the elements of the intermediate interdependence paradigm are shared in common with the nearly closed and the small and open paradigms. These familiar building blocks of the theory of economic policy include the national government, the policy authority charged with the responsibility for national economic policy, the collection of policy instruments over which the authority has command, the ultimate-target variables that represent the objectives

---

14. Analogous questions can be asked about a national social welfare function and a national policy authority. While such national concepts are problematic too (see below and chapter 18), they are far less so than their world analogs.

of the authority, the economic structure of the national economy, the structural model summarizing the policy authority's uncertain knowledge of economic structure, and the nonpolicy disturbances taken as exogenous in the authority's model.[15]

The intermediate interdependence paradigm, however, marshalls these building blocks in a distinctive way. Six characteristics set it apart from other approaches to the analysis of international economic developments.

First, with the important exception of economic structure, the intermediate paradigm employs at least two of the above constituent elements. There must be two or more nations, and hence two or more separate national governments.[16] Each government has a policy authority. The "world" thus has at least two separate loci of policy decisionmaking. Each nation's authority has policy instruments and ultimate targets, so again there are two or more sets of these basic elements. Nonpolicy disturbances may originate within each country. Each country has its own currency. The "two-ness" must be explicit. A careful treatment of "the other country" is what chiefly distinguishes the intermediate interdependence paradigm from the nearly closed and the small and open paradigms.

Second, the intermediate paradigm presupposes that the policy authorities of the separate national governments are formally independent of each other, just as the national governments themselves are treated as legally independent, sovereign entities. Each nation's authority is free to exercise the legal sovereignty it enjoys; thus, each authority can adjust its instruments in whatever manner it deems best.

A third characteristic of the intermediate paradigm is its strong national focus. Each nation's policy authority is assumed to have objectives that are identifiably different from the objectives of the authorities of other nations. In the general case, there need be little overlap, or perhaps none at all, between these objectives. For example, the policy authority in Belgium might be concerned exclusively with the welfare of residents of Belgium, and hence give no weight to the welfare of residents of other nations or to the degree to which other nations' authorities are attaining their national objectives. Moreover, one set of national targets may conflict directly with the national targets of other countries. For example, any development that has the effect of increasing the welfare of Belgian residents—even at the expense of the welfare of residents of other countries—might be deemed beneficial by the Belgian policy authority. If so, and if the Belgian authority believes it can encourage such a development by altering the settings on Belgian policy instruments, that development might be actively sought by the Belgian authority.

The three characteristics of the intermediate interdependence paradigm just described pertain to the *political* organization of the world—to governmental decisionmaking units and their activities and ends. How do the political units of nations and policy authorities coexist with the intermediate paradigm's conceptualization of the *economic* organization of the world?

15. Refer to chapter 2 for definitions and discussions of these basic concepts. Any approach to macroeconomic problems that seeks to focus on national economic policy must use the building blocks of national governments and policy authorities, national instruments, and national ultimate objectives. The concepts of economic structure, structural model, and exogenous disturbances are fundamental constituents of any analytical paradigm for studying any problem in macroeconomics.

16. For many purposes, it is important whether a theoretical analysis assumes merely two—or, alternatively, more than two—separate nations. Here, as in part 2, the complications that would be introduced by allowing for a world economy composed of more than two nations are suppressed.

The fourth salient characteristic of the intermediate paradigm is its presumption that the effective domains of economic markets and the geographical borders of governmental jurisdictions are not coterminous. Its treatment of the structure of the world economy therefore eschews the assumption of two-ness. It does not accept the simplification that the world economy can "almost" be decomposed into independent and additive national components (the result of applying the nearly closed paradigm seriatim to each nation's economy). Hence, rather than postulating separate economic structures, one for each nation's economy, the intermediate paradigm predicates a single economic structure for the entire system of national economies and their interrelationships.[17]

The emphasis placed on a single economic structure stems from the need to analyze interactions between the various national economies that constitute the larger world economy. Note, however, that this general formulation leaves open the question of how extensive the interactions may be. More specific information about the structure itself has to be obtained or assumed before anything further can be said about the degree of interdependence.

A fifth characteristic of the intermediate paradigm follows naturally from the postulate of one economic structure: in principle, the policy instruments of each nation may have impacts on *all* economic variables in the world economy. Nothing in the approach requires that each instrument must significantly influence every variable in the entire world system; a model of the economic structure, however, must explicitly allow for the possibility of such worldwide impacts. In a world of two nations with the home and foreign economies composing the world economic system, for example, it must be possible for policy actions taken by the home authority to have an impact on all foreign as well as all home economic variables. The reverse must also be possible: policy actions of the foreign government must be able to influence economic variables throughout the world economy. This general formulation leaves open the matter of the relative intensity of these influences. Nothing in the approach precludes the possibility that home policy instruments may have notably more powerful impacts on home than on foreign variables, and vice versa.

The sixth differentiating characteristic of the intermediate interdependence paradigm is analogous to the preceding one but concerns the impacts of nonpolicy disturbances rather than the results of changes in the settings of policy instruments. In principle, the paradigm presupposes that nonpolicy disturbances, wherever originating, have effects on all economic variables in the world economy. One can imagine classifying disturbances into two groups: those originating at home and those originating in the foreign economy.[18] It is an essential characteristic of the intermediate paradigm that both categories of disturbance be allowed to have worldwide impacts. An analysis of a crop failure in the home economy, for example, should explicitly include the effects on foreign prices and economic activity, not merely on home variables. A change in saving behavior by the residents of the

17. Similarly, each nation's authority predicates a structural model for the entire world system rather than just its own economy. Because knowledge about the common economic structure is uncertain and perceptions of it vary across nations, the structural models of each nation's authority are likely to differ appreciably. (This point is discussed further in chapters 11, 12, 13, and 25.)

18. In cases where a disturbance cannot be exclusively associated with either the home economy or the rest-of-world economy, an arbitrary assignment may be made to one of the two categories.

foreign economy should alter the outcome for some or all aspects of economic activity in the home country. As with the impacts of policy instruments, the relative intensity of the impacts of nonpolicy disturbances on the home and the foreign economies is a matter left open for further investigation or assumption.

This description of the intermediate interdependence paradigm is amplified in the next chapter. The discussion there makes use of a mathematical formalization that facilitates a more precise analysis. Even the preceding summary, however, is sufficient to indicate that this way of thinking about national economic policy draws attention to some important problems that are frequently ignored or underemphasized.

Economic Structure versus Political Structure

An analyst employing the intermediate interdependence paradigm is forced to pay attention to the tension that may exist between the political and the economic structures of the world. The paradigm leaves open the possibility that the effective economic structure may coincide closely with the political division of the world into nations. In practice, however, because it postulates a single economic structure for the entire system of national economies and their interrelationships, the paradigm loads the dice the other way. An analyst is not able to neglect the noncoincidence that may exist between national governmental jurisdictions and the effective domains of economic markets unless he can obtain or assume information about the economic structure that will validate such neglect.[19]

Most analysts of national economic policy have ignored or underemphasized the problem generated by the interplay between political and economic structure.[20] If they acknowledge it at all, their tendency is to genuflect before the problem but to avoid incorporating it in the framework of the analysis. In the nearly closed paradigm, for example, markets are implicitly considered to stop at national political boundaries. Certain infringements of that assumption are then recognized—exports, imports, other international transactions—and ad hoc allowances are made for those exceptions. But in all major respects, the rest of the world remains exogenous to the analysis.

It is an interesting fact that the customary use of language reveals a tendency for the political structure to dominate thought patterns, even in international economics. Businessmen, government officials, and economists commonly identify markets with nations—using phrases such as "penetrating the *German* market," "weakness in the *British* automobile market," or "price increases in the soybean

---

19. For discussions of the role of governments as providers of "public goods" and the possibilities for private economic behavior to conflict with regional or national governmental jurisdictions, see Richard N. Cooper, "Worldwide Regional Integration: Is There an Optimal Size of the Integrated Area?" *Economic Notes*, vol. 3 (Siena: Monte dei Paschi di Siena, 1974); and Mancur Olson, Jr., "The Principle of 'Fiscal Equivalence': The Division of Responsibilities Among Different Levels of Government," *American Economic Review* (May 1969, *Papers and Proceedings, 1968*), pp. 479–87. See also Cooper's *Economic Mobility and National Economic Policy*, 1973 Wiksell Lectures (Stockholm: Almqvist and Wiksell, 1974) and Cooper, *The Economics of Interdependence: Economic Policy in the Atlantic Community* (McGraw-Hill for the Council on Foreign Relations, 1968).

20. A recent exception is Assar Lindbeck, "Endogenous Politicians and the Theory of Economic Policy," Institute for International Economic Studies, seminar paper 35 (Stockholm: IIES, October 1973); and Lindbeck, "Stabilization Policy in Open Economies with Endogenous Politicians," *American Economic Review*, vol. 66 (May 1976, *Papers and Proceedings, 1975*), pp. 1–19.

market *in the United States.*" It is customary usage, moreover, to speak of "the home economy" or "the domestic economy" or "the national economy." Note, however, that as one allows for the possibility of a progressively higher degree of noncoincidence between the borders of national governmental jurisdictions and the effective domains of economic markets, a progressively larger element of ambiguity creeps into this use of language. One way to bring out this point is to recall to mind the conceptual difference between gross national product and gross domestic product. Gross national product is defined as the income accruing to factors of production owned by residents of a particular area or nation, regardless of the geographical location of those factors. Gross domestic product is defined as the income accruing to factors of production physically located within the geographical boundaries of a particular area or nation, regardless of the residency of the owners of those factors of production. Which is the more appropriate concept to use when speaking of "the national economy"? If the national economy is highly open, and in particular if economic markets are sufficiently integrated so that factors of production are highly mobile across the political boundaries that define the nation, then the two concepts may diverge significantly.[21] More important, at some point neither concept can comfortably be associated with the phrase "the national economy." The nation—as a well-defined *political* entity—might still exist. But the national economy—as a clearly defined *economic* entity—will not.

It is an advantage of the intermediate interdependence paradigm that it juxtaposes the politics of nationhood and the economics of integrated markets and thereby encourages an explicit examination of the interplay between them.

De Jure Sovereignty versus De Facto Control

As visualized by analysts employing the intermediate interdependence paradigm, each nation's policy authority adjusts the settings on its own instruments. Each is formally independent. Each has its own objectives, quite different from the goals of other nations' authorities. Yet the policy actions of one nation's authority may have significant impacts on the objectives of the others. It is only in a political sense, therefore, that one can regard each nation's authority as independent.

The intermediate interdependence paradigm thus forces the analyst to distinguish between *de jure sovereignty* of national economic policy and *de facto control* over national economic developments. The former involves the formal command over policy instruments; the latter, the ability to influence specified targets by skillful manipulation of policy instruments.[22]

The distinction between the formal authority to take policy actions and the effective ability to use instruments to influence targets is a distinction that would be crucial even for the case of a completely closed economy. The government of a closed economy might have formal command over a wide range of policy instru-

21. The gross national product of Monaco, for example, is presumably significantly larger than its gross domestic product.
22. This distinction is a basic feature of the approach to economic policy pioneered by Tinbergen, developed by Theil, and continued by those advocating use of the methods of optimal control. For an early recognition of the relevance of the distinction to national economic policy in the context of an interdependent world economy, see J. Tinbergen, *Economic Policy: Principles and Design* (Amsterdam: North-Holland, 1956), pp. 143–46. See also Cooper, *The Economics of Interdependence*, pp. 4–6, 260–64.

ments, but such command would not guarantee close control over economic activity. The government's ability to influence the economy—the degree of its *actual* control—depends on such factors as the accuracy of its knowledge of the economic structure and the potency of its policy instruments.

A fortiori in an open economy, formal independence to initiate policy actions does not ensure that instruments will be effective in achieving targets. Some part of the impact of a national policy authority's actions will fall on foreign economies rather than on the home economy. Policy actions taken by other nations or nonpolicy disturbances originating abroad may buffet the home economy in unexpected and possibly adverse ways. The home nation's authority may be free to adjust its policy instruments in a completely independent manner. But setting its instruments so as actually to achieve desired time paths for ultimate-target variables is an entirely different and altogether more uncertain matter.[23]

A majority of the populace of individual nations may fail to appreciate the distinction between de jure sovereignty and de facto control. But the policy authorities themselves are less likely to overlook the distinction. Each nation's authority, unless it is very short-sighted, recognizes that its own decisions are contingent on the decisionmaking behavior of its foreign counterparts. The authority of the home nation knows that it cannot determine appropriate settings for its own policy instruments without, inter alia, taking into account the settings on the instruments of authorities in the rest of the world. The analogous dilemma faces policy authorities in foreign countries. The interdependence of their individual decisions is a critical characteristic of the situation no matter what the level of abstraction at which the separate national authorities attempt to formulate and implement their policies.

These problems of interdependent decisionmaking bear strong resemblances to the problems studied in duopoly or oligopoly theory. An oligopolistic firm is unable to make pricing and output decisions until it makes some assumptions about the behavior of its competitors. These problems also have marked similarities to issues treated in the literature on game theory. National policy authorities can be likened to game players. The authorities' policy actions can be characterized as strategies. The different objectives of the individual authorities can be embodied in payoff functions. A payoff matrix can be developed arraying the possible outcomes that result from the alternative ways of combining the national policy actions.

Is it fruitful to apply oligopoly theory as an analytical tool in the present context, with national policy authorities substituted for firms as the decisionmaking units? Does recognition of the similarities between game situations and the problems faced by national decisionmakers argue for applying the concepts and tools of game theory? Are oligopoly theory and game theory sufficiently well-developed to make important contributions to the analysis of intermediate interdependence? For the moment, these questions remain moot. It is sufficient at this point in the analysis to recognize the theoretical similarity of the issues and the central role played by oligopoly and game-theoretic elements in policymaking by national authorities in an interdependent world economy.

23. The most explicit effort to focus on these issues in the existing theoretical literature is the study by Ronald I. McKinnon and Wallace E. Oates, *The Implications of International Economic Integration for Monetary, Fiscal, and Exchange-Rate Policy,* Princeton Studies in International Finance, 16 (Princeton University Press, 1966). Further references are given in subsequent chapters.

CHAPTER ELEVEN

National Economic Policy under Conditions of Intermediate Interdependence

CHAPTER 10 identifies the main features of a frame of reference within which to analyze intermediate interdependence. This chapter and appendix A develop a more detailed and precise characterization of that paradigm.

The general purpose of the following discussion is theoretical clarification. Its specific objective is to set forth the basic analytics of macroeconomic policy decisions for a national economy that is significantly open. It does not describe what national policymakers think or do in real life. Nor does it make recommendations for how, in practice, they should formulate and implement policy.

This elaboration of the intermediate interdependence paradigm draws extensively on the existing theory of economic policy. Although that theory has been developed only in terms of a closed economy, or alternatively in terms of a small and open economy for which foreign variables are taken as exogenous, many of the concepts and analytical techniques are readily adaptable to the conditions of intermediate interdependence. Readers familiar with the work of Jan Tinbergen and Henri Theil will recognize what follows as a generalization of their analysis to a two-nation world economy. The discussion of the dynamic, multiperiod aspects draws on the literature on optimal control theory and its application to macroeconomic policy. The analysis of the open-economy aspects builds on the work of Richard Cooper.[1]

The exposition tries to steer between the Scylla of woolly verbiage and the Charybdis of needlessly complex mathematics. Many fear one of these perils more than the other and therefore give one or the other the wider berth. Those who find the ensuing characterization less sophisticated mathematically than they prefer should bear in mind that the purpose of the discussion is to clarify concepts and issues, not to derive new analytical results. Those who find the chapter technical

1. The basic references on the closed-economy theory are given in chapter 2. For Cooper's work and related discussions, see Richard N. Cooper, *The Economics of Interdependence: Economic Policy in the Atlantic Community* (McGraw-Hill for the Council on Foreign Relations, 1968); *Economic Mobility and National Economic Policy*, 1973 Wiksell Lectures (Stockholm: Almqvist and Wiksell, 1974); "Worldwide or Regional Integration: Is There an Optimal Size of the Integrated Area?" *Economic Notes*, vol. 3 (Siena: Monte dei Paschi di Siena, 1974); "Macroeconomic Policy Adjustment in Interdependent Economies," *Quarterly Journal of Economics*, vol. 83 (February 1969), pp. 1–24; Don E. Roper, "Macroeconomic Policies and the Distribution of the World Money Supply," *Quarterly Journal of Economics*, vol. 85 (February 1971), pp. 119–46; Cooper's comments in Robert A. Mundell and Alexander K. Swoboda, eds., *Monetary Problems of the International Economy* (University of Chicago Press, 1969), pp. 235–41; his comments in Emil Claassen and Pascal Salin, eds., *Stabilization Policies in Interdependent Economies* (Amsterdam, London: North-Holland, 1972), pp. 116–22; and his discussion in Albert Ando, Richard Herring, and Richard Marston, eds., *International Aspects of Stabilization Policies*, Conference Series, 12 (Federal Reserve Bank of Boston, 1974), pp. 133–38.

will, I hope, still invest the time to read it. A mathematical representation of the theory strips the logic of choice down to its analytical skeleton.

Concepts, Definitions, and Representation of Economic Structure

The world economic structure can be represented, at least conceptually, by a system of mathematical equations. Many of the equations are behavioral relationships summarizing how particular macrogroupings of economic units make income-account and balance-sheet decisions. As in all structural economic models, other equations represent budget or balance-sheet identities. Still others may characterize the manner in which markets for particular goods or particular assets are assumed to clear. If the structural model is consistently specified, with the various identities and market-clearing equations all taken correctly into account, it will contain exactly as many structural equations as jointly dependent, endogenous variables.

A structural model used in conjunction with the intermediate interdependence paradigm must highlight national political jurisdictions even though it postulates a single-world economic structure. The simplest case that meets this theoretical requirement, used throughout this exposition, is a world of two nations—the home and the foreign countries.

Many variables in a world structural model may be characterized naturally as either home or foreign. For example, the *home* label might naturally be attached to variables representing income-account transactions between two groups of home residents or claims of one group of home residents on another group of home residents. Transactions and debtor–creditor relationships among foreign residents could be labeled *foreign* variables. But many other variables in the world structural model cannot be designated as either home or foreign except on arbitrary grounds. Examples include the exchange rate between the home and the foreign currencies, prices and interest rates that have relevance to both home and foreign transactors, and any variable associated with transactions or asset-liability relationships between a group of home residents and a group of foreign residents. The numbers and types of variables that cannot be naturally labeled home or foreign depend on the degree of noncoincidence between economic markets and political jurisdictions.

Let the symbol y_{it} represent the value in period t assumed by some variable i modeled as an endogenous part of the world economic structure. Suppose the list of all endogenous variables is divided into two parts, with each variable assigned either to a home or a foreign sublist. This arbitrary division of the variables along political lines need not affect any analytical conclusions about the economic structure so long as the structural relationship for each variable is specified correctly (including, of course, any "international" interactions that may be relevant). A superscript h or f indicates whether a variable, or group of variables, is classified as belonging to the home or the foreign set.

Each nation's policy authority is assumed to have a set of ultimate-target variables on which it focuses attention. The home authority is assumed to be concerned only with home variables as ultimate targets, while the foreign authority is concerned exclusively with foreign variables. There is no overlap between each authority's list of ultimate-target variables.[2] The symbol $y_t^{*h} = [y_{1,t}^{*h}, \ldots, y_{n^*,t}^{*h}]'$ is used to indicate the vector of endogenous variables—assumed to be n^* in number—that are the ultimate-target variables for the home policy authority. The m^* ultimate-target variables of the foreign authority are represented as $y_t^{*f} = [y_{1,t}^{*f}, \ldots, y_{m^*,t}^{*f}]'$. All endogenous variables that are not ultimate-target variables (that is, all the intermediate variables) are written as $y_t^h = [y_{n^*+1,t}^h, \ldots, y_{n,t}^h]'$ and $y_t^f = [y_{m^*+1,t}^f, \ldots, y_{m,t}^f]'$. Altogether, there are $n + m$ endogenous variables in the model, n of which are labeled *home* and m of which are labeled *foreign*.

The preceding definitions produce a four-way partitioning of the endogenous variables. Let Y_t stand for the entire set of t-period values, and let them be arranged in an $(n + m) \times 1$ column vector, as follows:

$$
(11\text{-}1) \quad Y_t \equiv
\begin{bmatrix}
y_t^{*h} \\
\hline
y_t^h \\
\hline
y_t^{*f} \\
\hline
y_t^f
\end{bmatrix}
\equiv
\begin{bmatrix}
y_{1,t}^{*h} \\
\vdots \\
y_{n^*,t}^{*h} \\
\hline
y_{n^*+1,t}^h \\
\vdots \\
y_{n,t}^h \\
\hline
y_{1,t}^{*f} \\
\vdots \\
y_{m^*,t}^{*f} \\
\hline
y_{m^*+1,t}^f \\
\vdots \\
y_{m,t}^f
\end{bmatrix}
\begin{array}{l}
n^* \text{ home ultimate-target} \\
\text{variables.} \\
\\
n - n^* \text{ home intermediate} \\
\text{variables.} \\
\\
m^* \text{ foreign ultimate-target} \\
\text{variables.} \\
\\
m - m^* \text{ foreign intermediate} \\
\text{variables.}
\end{array}
$$

Let X_t^h represent the vector of t-period values of the policy instrument variables controlled by the home authority and X_t^f the corresponding vector of foreign

2. The assumption of *no* overlap, adopted here for expositional simplicity, is probably unrealistic. A few endogenous variables may be regarded by both the home and the foreign authorities as ultimate-target variables; furthermore, both authorities taken together may have incompatible objectives with respect to some common target variable. The exchange rate or various balance-of-payments aggregates (for example, changes in international reserves) are examples. These important complications are ignored in the text.

instrument variables. The column vector X_t that includes both the home and foreign policy instruments has altogether $k + l$ elements:

$$(11\text{-}2) \qquad X_t \equiv \begin{bmatrix} X_t^h \\ ---- \\ X_t^f \end{bmatrix} \equiv \begin{bmatrix} x_{1,t}^h \\ \cdot \\ \cdot \\ \cdot \\ x_{k,t}^h \\ ---- \\ x_{1,t}^f \\ \cdot \\ \cdot \\ \cdot \\ x_{l,t}^f \end{bmatrix} \quad \begin{array}{l} k \text{ home instrument variables.} \\ \\ \\ \\ \\ l \text{ foreign instrument variables.} \end{array}$$

In addition to policy instruments, two other types of predetermined variables need to be represented in the structural model. An exogenous variable that is not a policy instrument may be represented by the symbol z_{it}. As in the case of the endogenous variables, let the z_{it} be divided into home and foreign groups, and let arbitrary assignments be made when it does not seem natural to make that division. The column vector Z_t has $r + s$ elements:[3]

$$(11\text{-}3) \qquad Z_t \equiv \begin{bmatrix} z_t^h \\ ---- \\ z_t^f \end{bmatrix} \equiv \begin{bmatrix} z_{1,t}^h \\ \cdot \\ \cdot \\ \cdot \\ z_{r,t}^h \\ ---- \\ z_{1,t}^f \\ \cdot \\ \cdot \\ \cdot \\ z_{s,t}^f \end{bmatrix} \quad \begin{array}{l} r \text{ home nonpolicy exogenous} \\ \text{variables.} \\ \\ \\ \\ s \text{ foreign nonpolicy exogenous} \\ \text{variables.} \end{array}$$

The third type of predetermined variable in the structural model includes past-period values of endogenous variables. The exposition here includes one-period lags only, even though many of the variables in a realistic model would be lagged by more than one period.[4] The notation $y_{i,t-1}^h$ or $y_{j,t-1}^f$ is used for all lagged values of home or foreign variables regardless of whether they are ultimate-target or merely intermediate variables. Hence the lagged values of the endogenous variables relevant for the t-period representation of the model are incorporated into a single $(n + m) \times 1$ column vector Y_{t-1}:

---

3. For expositional simplicity, this mathematical characterization of the structural model does not include lagged values of policy instruments (for example, $x_{i,t-1}^h$) and lagged values of nonpolicy exogenous variables (for example, $z_{j,t-3}^f$). This exclusion (a realistic model would certainly contain such lagged values) does not affect the validity of the generalizations that follow; see appendix A for a further discussion.

4. A more general formulation than the one presented in the text would include j different $(n + m) \times 1$ column vectors $Y_{t-1}, Y_{t-2}, \ldots, Y_{t-j}$ where j is the maximum length of lag. No loss of generality in the conclusions results from the simplifying assumption in the text, however; see appendix A.

$$(11\text{-}4) \quad Y_{t-1} \equiv \begin{bmatrix} y_{t-1}^h \\ \hline y_{t-1}^f \end{bmatrix} \equiv \begin{bmatrix} y_{1,t-1}^h \\ \vdots \\ \vdots \\ y_{n,t-1}^h \\ \hline y_{1,t-1}^f \\ \vdots \\ \vdots \\ y_{m,t-1}^f \end{bmatrix}$$

n lagged values of home endogenous variables.

m lagged values of foreign endogenous variables.

Each structural relationship for an endogenous variable is specified to include a stochastic error term that has a given mean and finite variance.[5] Hence the model includes the following column vector of $n + m$ error terms, where the ordering corresponds to the ordering of variables in Y_t:

$$(11\text{-}5) \quad E_t \equiv \begin{bmatrix} e_t^{*h} \\ \hline e_t^h \\ \hline e_t^{*f} \\ \hline e_t^f \end{bmatrix} \equiv \begin{bmatrix} e_{1,t}^{*h} \\ \vdots \\ \vdots \\ e_{n^*,t}^{*h} \\ \hline e_{n^*+1,t}^h \\ \vdots \\ \vdots \\ e_{n,t}^h \\ \hline e_{1,t}^{*f} \\ \vdots \\ \vdots \\ e_{m^*,t}^{*f} \\ \hline e_{m^*+1,t}^f \\ \vdots \\ e_{m,t}^f \end{bmatrix}$$

error terms for n^* home ultimate-target variables.

error terms for $n - n^*$ home intermediate variables.

error terms for m^* foreign ultimate-target variables.

error terms for $m - m^*$ foreign intermediate variables.

5. These additive error terms represent the minimum possible concession to the problem of uncertainty about the economic structure. Compare the familiar reasons for specifying many economic and all econometric models in stochastic rather than completely deterministic form; see, for example, Carl F. Christ, *Econometric Models and Methods* (Wiley, 1966), pp. 23–31; J. Johnston, *Econometric Methods* (McGraw-Hill, 1963), pp. 3–9. In chapters 2 and 10, the term "nonpolicy disturbances" is used to connote the influences on endogenous variables of both (1) changes in the values of nonpolicy exogenous variables and (2) nonzero values of stochastic error terms. These two categories of "disturbance" can be combined for some analytical purposes, but in the general case it proves helpful to distinguish between them. The problem of uncertainty is discussed later in this chapter and in considerable detail in part 4.

The definitions 11-1 through 11-5 permit a mathematical representation of a structural model of the world economy. The structure for one time period (period t), expressed in matrix form, is:

$$(11\text{-}6) \qquad \Gamma Y_t + \Phi X_t + \Omega Z_t + \Lambda Y_{t-1} + E_t = 0.$$

In this representation, the structural relationships are assumed to be linear in form.[6] The symbols Γ, Φ, Ω, and Λ are matrixes of structural coefficients, assumed for the time being to be deterministic parameters.

The coefficient matrixes in the equation system 11-6 are the central feature of this symbolic representation of the world economic structure. The elements of these matrixes are the behavioral parameters that describe how, and by how much, each variable interacts with the other variables.

What is *Interdependence?*

What features distinguish a *significantly open* economy? What more precisely is meant by *the degree of economic interdependence* between a home economy and the rest of the world?

If they are to be given a precise substantive content, the concepts of economic openness and interdependence are inseparable from the analytical representation of economic structure.[7] To speak analytically about the openness of a *national* economy requires analytical statements about the *world* economic structure of which it is a part—with particular emphasis on those features of the analyst's structural model that bear, directly or indirectly, on the international transactions that link the national economy to the rest of the world. It is not sufficient to speak vaguely of the "sensitivity" or "vulnerability" of economic developments within one nation to developments in other nations. An analytical discussion must highlight the actual behavior—the decisionmaking rules, so to speak—that lies behind such sensitivity or vulnerability.

In the context of the general characterization of a world structural model summarized in the equation system 11-6, the degree of openness or interdependence of the home and the foreign economies depends on, and should be defined in terms of, certain characteristics of the coefficient matrixes Γ, Φ, Ω, and Λ.

The interdependence aspects of the economic structure are more readily apparent if the $n + m$ equations of 11-6 are written in more detailed form, with the vectors Y_t, X_t, Z_t, and Y_{t-1} partitioned as before, and with the matrixes of structural coefficients partitioned into submatrixes to conform with the partitioning of the

---

6. For a discussion of the assumption of linearity in economic models, its advantages, its restrictiveness, and feasible methods for linearizing nonlinear models, see, for example, Benjamin M. Friedman, *Economic Stabilization Policy: Methods in Optimization* (Amsterdam and Oxford: North-Holland, 1975; New York: American Elsevier, 1975), esp. chaps. 2–5; Gregory C. Chow, *Analysis and Control of Dynamic Economic Systems* (Wiley, 1975), esp. chap. 6.

7. Chapter 1 defined an *open economy* as an economy associated with a particular nation state in which a significant proportion of economic and financial activity involves international transactions. The phrase *economic interdependence* has been used loosely to refer to the interactions among open national economies. Those definitions have so far served well enough as a general characterization. Before the problems of an open economy can be analyzed rigorously, however, a more precise characterization is required.

variable vectors. This is done in the top panel of figure 11-1. The shaded submatrixes are of particular interest from the point of view of interdependence. The submatrix Γ_{14}, for example, pertains to the n^* equations for the n^* home ultimate-target variables, but its coefficients summarize the extent to which foreign intermediate variables directly influence the home ultimate-target variables. The submatrix Φ_{41} summarizes the direct influences of the k home instrument variables in the $m - m^*$ structural equations for the foreign intermediate variables. And the submatrix Λ_{22} contains all the structural coefficients associated with the n lagged values of foreign intermediate and ultimate-target variables in the $n - n^*$ equations for home intermediate variables. The shaded submatrixes are subsequently referred to as the *interdependence submatrixes;* the unshaded ones are designated *domestic.*

It is instructive to ask how the equation system would appear if the world economic structure consisted of two completely closed economies. In that situation, characterized by an absence of any international interactions and thus a complete coincidence between the effective domains of economic markets and national political jurisdictions, all the elements of all the interdependence submatrixes of Γ, Φ, Ω, and Λ would be identically equal to zero (see the lower panel of figure 11-1). In such a situation there would be little if any reason for combining the two national models into a "world" system of equations. The world economy would be completely decomposable into two subsystems that could be analyzed independently.[8]

Suppose one of the two economies is modeled in terms of the small and open paradigm. In that case, the interdependence submatrixes in the equations for the other country's variables will have elements identically equal to zero. For example, if the home economy is a very small part of the world economy, foreign variables will strongly influence, in some cases perhaps determine completely, the value of home variables; but the analyst will ignore any influence of home variables on foreign variables and, hence, any second- or third-round feedbacks. The small and open paradigm does not allow for two-way interdependence, only a one-way dependence.[9]

In a situation of intermediate interdependence, while many of the structural coefficients in the interdependence submatrixes will have nonzero values, the interdependence submatrixes will no doubt be much sparser than the submatrixes referring to the domestic impacts of domestic variables. Similarly, one will presumably find smaller absolute values for most interdependence coefficients relative to the values of analogous structural coefficients in the domestic submatrixes of the model.

A *change* in interdependence or in the degree of openness results when one or more of the elements of one or more of the interdependence submatrixes is altered.

8. For a discussion of equation systems that are "decomposable," "completely decomposable," "nearly decomposable," and "nearly completely decomposable," see Franklin M. Fisher and Albert Ando, "Two Theorems on *Ceteris Paribus* in the Analysis of Dynamic Systems," *American Political Science Review,* vol. 56 (March 1962), pp. 108–13; and Fisher, "On the Independent Use of Two or More Sets of Policy Variables," *Journal of Political Economy,* vol. 75 (February 1967), pp. 77–85. See also appendix A.

9. In terms of figure 11-1, the submatrixes Γ_{31}, Γ_{32}, Γ_{41}, and Γ_{42} will have elements all identically equal to zero, whereas Γ_{13}, Γ_{14}, Γ_{23}, and Γ_{24} will generally have nonzero elements. Similar patterns will hold for the submatrixes of Φ, Ω, and Λ. Technically, the matrixes Γ, Φ, Ω, and Λ will be block-triangular and the equation system will be block-recursive.

Figure 11-1. *Structural Representation of a Two-Nation World Economy*

Interdependence between the Home and the Foreign Economies

$$\begin{bmatrix} \Gamma_{11} & \Gamma_{12} & \Gamma_{13} & \Gamma_{14} \\ \Gamma_{21} & \Gamma_{22} & \Gamma_{23} & \Gamma_{24} \\ \Gamma_{31} & \Gamma_{32} & \Gamma_{33} & \Gamma_{34} \\ \Gamma_{41} & \Gamma_{42} & \Gamma_{43} & \Gamma_{44} \end{bmatrix} \begin{bmatrix} y_t^{*h} \\ y_t^h \\ y_t^{*f} \\ y_t^f \end{bmatrix} + \begin{bmatrix} \Phi_{11} & \Phi_{12} \\ \Phi_{21} & \Phi_{22} \\ \Phi_{31} & \Phi_{32} \\ \Phi_{41} & \Phi_{42} \end{bmatrix} \begin{bmatrix} X_t^h \\ X_t^f \end{bmatrix} + \begin{bmatrix} \Omega_{11} & \Omega_{12} \\ \Omega_{21} & \Omega_{22} \\ \Omega_{31} & \Omega_{32} \\ \Omega_{41} & \Omega_{42} \end{bmatrix} \begin{bmatrix} z_t^h \\ z_t^f \end{bmatrix} + \begin{bmatrix} \Lambda_{11} & \Lambda_{12} \\ \Lambda_{21} & \Lambda_{22} \\ \Lambda_{31} & \Lambda_{32} \\ \Lambda_{41} & \Lambda_{42} \end{bmatrix} \begin{bmatrix} y_{t-1}^h \\ y_{t-1}^f \end{bmatrix} + \begin{bmatrix} e_t^{*h} \\ e_t^h \\ e_t^{*f} \\ e_t^f \end{bmatrix} = \begin{bmatrix} 0 \\ 0 \\ 0 \\ 0 \end{bmatrix}$$

Complete Absence of Interdependence between the Home and Foreign Economies

$$\begin{bmatrix} \Gamma_{11} & \Gamma_{12} & 0 & 0 \\ \Gamma_{21} & \Gamma_{22} & 0 & 0 \\ 0 & 0 & \Gamma_{33} & \Gamma_{34} \\ 0 & 0 & \Gamma_{43} & \Gamma_{44} \end{bmatrix} \begin{bmatrix} y_t^{*h} \\ y_t^h \\ y_t^{*f} \\ y_t^f \end{bmatrix} + \begin{bmatrix} \Phi_{11} & 0 \\ \Phi_{21} & 0 \\ 0 & \Phi_{32} \\ 0 & \Phi_{42} \end{bmatrix} \begin{bmatrix} X_t^h \\ X_t^f \end{bmatrix} + \begin{bmatrix} \Omega_{11} & 0 \\ \Omega_{21} & 0 \\ 0 & \Omega_{32} \\ 0 & \Omega_{42} \end{bmatrix} \begin{bmatrix} z_t^h \\ z_t^f \end{bmatrix} + \begin{bmatrix} \Lambda_{11} & 0 \\ \Lambda_{21} & 0 \\ 0 & \Lambda_{32} \\ 0 & \Lambda_{42} \end{bmatrix} \begin{bmatrix} y_{t-1}^h \\ y_{t-1}^f \end{bmatrix} + \begin{bmatrix} e_t^{*h} \\ e_t^h \\ e_t^{*f} \\ e_t^f \end{bmatrix} = \begin{bmatrix} 0 \\ 0 \\ 0 \\ 0 \end{bmatrix}$$

An increase in interdependence or openness may be said to occur whenever there is an increase in the absolute value of one or more of the structural coefficients in the interdependence submatrixes of any of the matrixes Γ, Φ, Ω, or Λ.[10]

The typical discussion in the existing literature, encountered in both economics and international relations, uses the terms *openness* or *interdependence* as though their analytical content were self-evident. The frequent result of that imprecision, however, is a woolly treatment of the issues.[11] Even when an effort is made to define interdependence, there is a tendency to divorce the concept from economic behavior itself and instead to associate it with broad descriptive indexes—for example, the ratio of a nation's exports or imports to its gross national product, or the ratio of financial assets held abroad to total financial assets owned by a nation's residents. These indexes, though they are the resultants of economic behavior, are several stages removed from the actual behavioral relationships themselves.

In contrast, the treatment here insists on a close identification of economic openness and interdependence with particular characteristics of the behavioral relationships themselves. This identification encourages analysis of the considerations that chiefly determine the degree of interdependence and facilitates a rigorous discussion of its consequences. Specifically, one is led to focus on the responses of the world economy, and of each of its national parts, to particular policy actions and to particular nonpolicy disturbances. The fuzzy question "What are the consequences of interdependence?" becomes a much more precise set of questions: "How are the responses to policy actions and to nonpolicy disturbances conditioned by various characteristics of the economic structure?" Similarly, loose questions about the consequences of an *increase* or a *decrease* in interdependence translate into an examination of how the impacts of policy actions and nonpolicy disturbances are altered when there is some well-defined change in the economic structure.

Determinants of Economic Structure and the Degree of Interdependence

The characteristics of the world economic structure that determine the degree of openness of a nation's economy may be grouped under four headings: (1) the behavior of private economic units resident at home and abroad, (2) the governmental regulatory environments, home and foreign, that constrain private behavior, (3) the technological and institutional environments that condition private and governmental behavior, and (4) supranational institutions and treaties that constrain the behavior of national governments.

Of the four categories, the behavior of private economic units is by far the most important. In principle, macroeconomic models specify aggregative relationships consistent with the decision rules of individual microeconomic units—for example, the consumption-saving decisions of households, the investment behavior of firms, the labor supply-and-demand decisions of households and firms, and the portfolio decisions by which households, firms, and financial intermediaries allocate their

10. Increases in interdependence are discussed further in chapter 12.
11. For an exception, and for one of the more analytical contributions, see Robert O. Keohane and Joseph S. Nye, *Power and Interdependence: World Politics in Transition* (Little, Brown, 1977), pt. 1.

net worths. The interactions among the variables of structural model 11-6—the macroeconomic counterparts of the microeconomic decision rules—are summarized in the matrixes of structural coefficients.

Various substitutability parameters that characterize private decisionmaking are the most important determinants of economic openness. These include, for example, the proclivities of home and foreign residents to substitute goods produced abroad for domestic goods in response to price changes, the tendency of labor to migrate across national boundaries in response to changes in relative wages, and the sensitivities of home and foreign portfolio decisions to changes in the expected returns on assets denominated in the home and the foreign currencies.[12]

Regulations and other microeconomic policies of national governments help to shape the environments in which private economic decisions are made. Some are explicit restraints or incentives affecting particular activities (for example, antipollution controls, housing subsidies). Others, such as national tax systems and legal-judicial procedures, are more diffuse in their impacts. Many may be specifically aimed at, or differentially affect, an economy's international transactions—for example, tariffs or quotas on imported goods, special financing credits for exports, barriers to the emigration or immigration of persons, and controls over the international movement of financial capital.

The representation of economic structure in the policymakers' model needs to be consistent with, and capture the most significant influences of, these governmental regulatory environments. If a regulatory feature of the home or foreign environment changes, the structural model can then be altered accordingly. Suppose, for example, the foreign government imposes new, effective capital controls on the flow of funds from abroad. Ideally, the structural representation of many of the financial-sector equations in 11-6 would be respecified, especially some of the coefficients in the interdependence submatrixes.

Viewed from a historical perspective, increases in interdependence among nations occur primarily because of changes in technology and institutional and sociocultural evolution. Innovations in transportation and communications technology, for example, have sharply reduced the relative costs of transporting goods and transmitting information among nations. New institutions, governmental or private, may be viewed either as a response to the evolution of economic and social life or as quasi-independent influences helping to determine that evolution. Whichever way the causation runs, such institutional change may have profound consequences for economic interdependence. The rapid growth of multinational corporations and banks is a prominent example.[13]

Only a model with myriad details could represent this third category of determinants of economic structure directly. But the representation of behavioral relationships in the model should reflect these features of the environment indirectly. A decline in transport costs, for example, should ideally be incorporated into the prices of goods available in one nation and produced in another. To the extent that the transactions of multinational corporations across national borders respond very

---

12. These substitutability parameters appear prominently as nonzero coefficients in the interdependence submatrixes of Γ, Φ, Ω, and Λ.
13. See, for example, Raymond Vernon, *Sovereignty at Bay: The Multinational Spread of U.S. Enterprises* (New York and London: Basic Books, 1971).

differently from the transactions of other private agents to national policy instruments or nonpolicy exogenous disturbances (for example, because transfer prices among the corporations' affiliates differ from the prices for arm's-length transactions),. separate behavioral relationships and substitutability parameters must be specified in the model to capture these differences. In principle, therefore, the structural coefficients in equations 11-6 should embody the interaction among macroeconomic variables as shaped by the technological and institutional environment in the home nation and in the rest of the world.

The influence of supranational institutions and treaties must also be reflected in the structural model to the extent that they significantly affect macroeconomic behavior. The obligations imposed on national authorities by the exchange-rate provisions of the Articles of Agreement of the International Monetary Fund are a prominent example.[14] The provisions of the General Agreement on Tariffs and Trade are another. Such constraints on the behavior of national authorities may not be binding. They are the least important of the four categories of determinants of economic structure and the degree of interdependence. But they could become more important in future decades.

Reduced-Form Representation of Economic Structure

At least conceptually, if not readily in practice, the equations 11-6 that characterize the world economic structure can be "solved" to obtain the t-period reduced form of the system:

$$(11\text{-}7) \qquad Y_t = AX_t + BZ_t + LY_{t-1} + U_t.$$

Each of these $n + m$ reduced-form equations expresses one of the endogenous variables as a function only of the policy-instrument variables, the other predetermined variables, and the stochastic error terms. Figure 11-2 displays the reduced-form equation system of 11-7 in the more extended form comparable to figure 11-1.

The individual reduced-form coefficients—the elements of A, B, and L—are derived in a complicated way from the original structural coefficients. In general, each reduced-form coefficient is a function of all the structural coefficients in Γ and a column of the coefficients in Φ, Ω, or Λ.[15] Each reduced-form error term in the vector U_t is in general a complicated linear function, depending on the elements of Γ, of all the contemporaneous structural error terms (also see appendix A).

Even though many individual elements of the structural coefficient matrixes themselves will undoubtedly be zero, therefore, each reduced-form coefficient will in general have a nonzero value. Particular variables may be immune from *direct* interdependence effects, yet are sure to be exposed to international influences *indirectly* so long as interdependence exists elsewhere in the economic structure.

To illustrate, suppose nonbank financial intermediaries in the home economy (for example, savings and loan associations in the United States or building societies

---

14. See part 5 for a discussion.
15. For example, each coefficient in A is, in general, a function of all the structural coefficients in Γ and a column of the coefficients in Φ.

Figure 11-2. *Reduced-Form Representation of a Two-Nation World Economy*

Interdependence between the Home and Foreign Economies

$$\begin{bmatrix} y_t^{*h} \\ y_t^h \\ \hline y_t^{*f} \\ y_t^f \end{bmatrix} = \begin{bmatrix} A_{11} & A_{12} \\ A_{21} & A_{22} \\ \hline A_{31} & A_{32} \\ A_{41} & A_{42} \end{bmatrix} \begin{bmatrix} X_t^h \\ \hline X_t^f \end{bmatrix} + \begin{bmatrix} B_{11} & B_{12} \\ B_{21} & B_{22} \\ \hline B_{31} & B_{32} \\ B_{41} & B_{42} \end{bmatrix} \begin{bmatrix} z_t^h \\ \hline z_t^f \end{bmatrix} + \begin{bmatrix} L_{11} & L_{12} \\ L_{21} & L_{22} \\ \hline L_{31} & L_{32} \\ L_{41} & L_{42} \end{bmatrix} \begin{bmatrix} y_{t-1}^h \\ \hline y_{t-1}^f \end{bmatrix} + \begin{bmatrix} u_t^{*h} \\ u_t^h \\ \hline u_t^{*f} \\ u_t^f \end{bmatrix}$$

Complete Absence of Interdependence between the Home and Foreign Economies

$$\begin{bmatrix} y_t^{*h} \\ y_t^h \\ \hline y_t^{*f} \\ y_t^f \end{bmatrix} = \begin{bmatrix} A_{11} & 0 \\ A_{21} & 0 \\ \hline 0 & A_{32} \\ 0 & A_{42} \end{bmatrix} \begin{bmatrix} X_t^h \\ \hline X_t^f \end{bmatrix} + \begin{bmatrix} B_{11} & 0 \\ B_{21} & 0 \\ \hline 0 & B_{32} \\ 0 & B_{42} \end{bmatrix} \begin{bmatrix} z_t^h \\ \hline z_t^f \end{bmatrix} + \begin{bmatrix} L_{11} & 0 \\ L_{21} & 0 \\ \hline 0 & L_{32} \\ 0 & L_{42} \end{bmatrix} \begin{bmatrix} y_{t-1}^h \\ \hline y_{t-1}^f \end{bmatrix} + \begin{bmatrix} u_t^{*h} \\ u_t^h \\ \hline u_t^{*f} \\ u_t^f \end{bmatrix}$$

in the United Kingdom) issue deposit liabilities and make mortgage loans only in home currency vis-à-vis only home residents. The *structural* equations describing the aggregative deposit and mortgage activity of these intermediaries will then exclude all foreign variables in the model (the coefficients in the relevant rows of the submatrixes Γ_{23}, Γ_{24}, Φ_{22}, Ω_{22}, and Λ_{22} will all be identically zero). The fact that the intermediaries have no international assets and liabilities, however, certainly does not imply that the *reduced-form* equations for their deposit and mortgage activity will not vary with changes in the foreign variables. Monetary-policy and fiscal-policy actions of the foreign government, for example, can have significant impacts on the intermediaries' mortgage lending, despite the absence of direct interdependence in the structural equations (in general, the coefficients in the relevant rows of the reduced-form submatrixes A_{22}, B_{22}, and L_{22} will all have nonzero values).

Notwithstanding the importance of indirect interdependence effects, a situation of *intermediate* interdependence in the structural coefficient matrixes generates a pattern of coefficient values in the reduced-form matrixes reflecting only moderate rather than strong interdependence. Again it is instructive to examine the polar case in which interdependence is absent altogether. If each individual coefficient in the interdependence submatrixes of the structural model has a value of zero (bottom panel of figure 11-1), then each element of the corresponding interdependence submatrixes in the reduced form of the model is identically equal to zero (bottom panel of figure 11-2). More generally, it can be shown (see appendix A) that if all the elements of each of the interdependence submatrixes in the structural model are very small (approach the limiting case of zero), all the elements in the corresponding submatrixes in the reduced form of the model are also small (approach the value of zero).

The reduced-form equations may also be written as:

(11-8) $$Y_t = A^h X_t^h + A^f X_t^f + BZ_t + LY_{t-1} + U_t.$$

This representation differs from 11-7 only in that the policy instruments (and the associated coefficients) of the home and the foreign nations are shown separately.

Simple Analytics of the National Policy Problem

The basic task to be performed by the home policy authority is to select settings for its policy instruments (X_t^h) that will bring about—or are most likely to bring about—the best, feasible values for the home ultimate-target variables (y_t^{*h}). Analogously, the foreign authority wishes to select settings for the foreign instruments (X_t^f) that will lead to attainment of the best, feasible values for the foreign ultimate-target variables (y_t^{*f}). Each national authority's ranking of alternative outcomes—its choice of "best"—is derived from its underlying preferences. Each authority's judgments about feasibility are derived from its view of the constraints imposed by the world economic structure.

Each country's authority, because of its national preoccupations, approaches the constraints imposed by the world economic structure differently. In principle, both the home and the foreign authority wish to use a reduced form of their structural model; only by working with a reduced-form representation can a policy authority deal with the constraints of the world economic structure in an analytically manageable way. Neither authority, however, is equally interested in all parts of 11-8. The home authority focuses on the subset of n^* reduced-form equations for the home ultimate-target variables, which may be written:

$$(11\text{-}9) \qquad y_t^{*h} = A_1^h X_t^h + S_t^{*h}.$$

The instrument vector X_t^h is controlled by the home authority itself; A_1^h, a submatrix of A, contains the coefficients relating the home instruments to the home ultimate targets. The vector S_t^{*h} lumps together all the other influences on the home target variables that are not controllable by the home authority. The foreign authority, in principle, devotes its main attention to the m^* equations for the foreign target variables:

$$(11\text{-}10) \qquad y_t^{*f} = A_3^f X_t^f + S_t^{*f},$$

where S_t^{*f} is the vector of all influences on the foreign target variables not controllable by the foreign authority.

Assume for the moment that the home authority can specify a set of fixed, best feasible values for its n^* ultimate-target variables in period t, say, $\hat{y}_t^{*h} = \hat{y}_{1,t}^{*h}, \hat{y}_{2,t}^{*h}, \ldots, \hat{y}_{n^*,t}^{*h}$. Similarly, suppose that the foreign authority can specify (for period t) a set of m^* best feasible values, $\hat{y}_t^{*f}$, for the foreign ultimate-target variables.

Given such fixed target values and the other assumptions made, each authority's policy decision for period t might seem straightforward. In principle, the home authority should solve its subset of n^* equations in terms of its own instrument variables, X_t^h. The home authority should then substitute into that solution the desired values $\hat{y}_t^{*h}$ of its target variables. If values for the components of S_t^{*h} are available or can be predicted, the home authority will then be able to calculate the particular settings $\hat{X}_t^h = \hat{x}_{1,t}^h, \hat{x}_{2,t}^h, \ldots, \hat{x}_{k,t}^h$ appropriate for attaining the particular targets $\hat{y}_t^{*h}$. By analogous reasoning, the foreign authority should solve its subset of m^* equations in terms of the foreign instrument variables and then calculate the settings $\hat{X}_t^f$ appropriate for attaining the specified foreign targets $\hat{y}_t^{*f}$. (See appendix A for further details.)

The mathematical characterization outlined above summarizes the logic of choice required of each nation's authority as it tries to employ its controllable means to achieve national ultimate ends while taking account of the constraints that influence the ends and restrict the means.

Even as an analytical abstraction, however, the preceding description is unsatisfactory in four respects. First, the best feasible values for national target variables $\hat{y}_t^{*h}$ and $\hat{y}_t^{*f}$ are specified independently instead of being determined as an integral part of the analysis. Second, the preceding account focuses only on decisions for a single period, period t, when in actual practice a multiperiod dynamic analysis is required. Third, little is said about uncertainty, even though uncertainty and procedures for dealing with it are perhaps the most pervasive aspect of macroeconomic decisionmaking. Fourth, game-theoretic elements—which are also at the core of policymaking by national authorities in a situation of intermediate interdependence—are glossed over altogether.

The first two of these difficulties can be resolved fairly readily by suitable modifications of the conceptual framework. The latter two cannot.

Optimizing Determination of Target Values

Rather than assume that each policy authority specifies (as it were, ex cathedra) a fixed value for the desired levels of its ultimate-target variables, it is preferable to substitute an optimizing procedure that makes explicit the problem of trade-offs among competing national objectives.[16]

The necessary amendments to the theory for the case of a closed economy have been worked out in detail by Henri Theil. In essence, a decisionmaker is characterized as having an explicit policy loss (or social welfare) function that he seeks to minimize (or maximize). That function is then superimposed on the economic structure of the model, and the interaction of the loss function and the structural model determines both target values and instrument settings.[17]

For the case of intermediate interdependence, a loss function is required for each nation's authority. For purposes of exposition, these loss functions may be expressed in quadratic form. A general quadratic form for the loss function of the home authority, for example, is:

$$(11\text{-}11) \qquad W_t^h = w_o^h + c'Y_t + d'X_t^h + \tfrac{1}{2}Y_t'CY_t + \tfrac{1}{2}X_t^{h'}DX_t^h,$$

16. A less common view is that policymakers engage in "satisficing" rather than optimizing behavior. For an example of this latter view, see P. Mosley, "Towards a 'Satisficing' Theory of Economic Policy," *Economic Journal*, vol. 76 (March 1976). Further references are given in chapter 18.

17. See especially Theil, *Economic Forecasts and Policy*, 2d rev. ed. (Amsterdam: North-Holland, 1961), chaps. 7 and 8; and, with coauthor P. J. M. van den Bogaard, *Optimal Decision Rules for Government and Industry* (Amsterdam: North-Holland, 1964), chaps. 1 and 2. On the merits of an optimizing as opposed to a fixed-target approach, see also Jürg Niehans, "Monetary and Fiscal Policies in Open Economies under Fixed Exchange Rates: An Optimizing Approach," *Journal of Political Economy*, vol. 76 (July/August 1968), pt. 2, and J. Marcus Fleming, "Targets and Instruments," *International Monetary Fund Staff Papers*, vol. 15 (November 1968), pp. 387–404.

where W_t^h is the loss to be minimized. The amount of the loss is assumed to depend not only on the values taken by the endogenous variables but also on the settings of the home policy instruments. Inclusion of the instrument settings in the loss function facilitates the representation in the analysis of boundary constraints on the instruments or costs that may be associated with varying their settings. The column vectors c and d and the matrixes C and D include the individual weighting coefficients that embody the preferences of the home policymakers. An analogous loss function for the foreign policy authority might be written:

$$(11\text{-}12) \qquad W_t^f = w_o^f + g'Y_t + p'X_t^f + \tfrac{1}{2}Y_t'GY_t + \tfrac{1}{2}X_t^{f'}PX_t^f.$$

The loss functions 11-11 and 11-12 are very general formulations. They allow for the possibility that each nation's authority might attach nonzero weights to all of the endogenous variables in the world and all of its own policy instruments. And they allow for the possibility of nonzero weighting coefficients for cross-products of two endogenous variables or of two instrument variables (that is, some or all of the off-diagonal elements of the matrixes C, D, G, and P could have values other than zero). But some of these possibilities may reasonably be ignored. All the weighting coefficients for cross-product terms may be equal to zero; that assumption is commonly made in a closed-economy context. Much more critical to the discussion here, the home policy authority may attach little if any welfare value to what happens to foreign variables, while the foreign authority may assign no weight in its loss function to what happens to home variables.[18] Economic interdependence does not imply interdependence of political preferences. (Appendix A discusses plausible specifications of the home and the foreign loss functions in which each authority biases its preferences in a nationalistic way towards its own objectives.)

The home authority, given a loss function such as that specified in equation 11-11, can select the settings for its policy instruments by means of an explicit optimizing procedure. In essence, the reduced-form constraints are substituted into the loss function and the resulting expression is minimized with respect to the vector of home instrument variables. The result is a joint determination of best feasible values for the home ultimate-target variables and home instrument settings designed to bring about the attainment of those targets.

Following an analogous procedure, the foreign authority could employ its loss function 11-12 and its version of the world model to select optimizing values for foreign instrument settings and foreign ultimate-target variables. (For a more detailed discussion, see appendix A.)

Multiperiod Dynamic Generalization

The structural model of the world economy and the decision problem faced by a nation's policy authority have thus far been characterized for a single time period (period t). At least in principle, there is little difficulty in relaxing this restriction. An extension to a multiperiod generalization requires merely that all definitions and equations be specified for time paths for the variables rather than single-period

---

18. Recall, however, the important caveat stated earlier in this chapter about the classification of variables as *home* or *foreign*.

values. The general case can be represented by assuming that the analysis spans T time periods, with period 1 as the current period. Each variable in the model then has both a sequence of values extending into the future as far as the finite horizon (period T) and a history of past values. Since lagged values of the variables appear in the structural equations, the past history of variables—the "initial conditions"— is directly relevant for determining the variables in period 1, period 2, and so on.

In effect, therefore, the structural equations in 11-6 should be interpreted as a snapshot of some particular period t during the interval of time $1 \leq t \leq T$. The moving-picture counterpart of 11-6, a time sequence of snapshots of the structural equations for all T periods, makes use of notation employing stacked vectors and matrixes (see appendix A) and may be written:

(11-13) $$\Gamma Y + \Phi X + \Omega Z + \Lambda Y_{t-1} + E = 0.$$

Analogously, the reduced-form representation of the system for all T periods may be written:

(11-14) $$Y = A^h X^h + A^f X^f + BZ + LY_{t-1} + U.$$

From the point of view of an authority making a multiperiod decision about the settings for its policy instruments, the reduced-form representation, 11-14, has the disadvantage that the lagged influences of the endogenous variables Y_{t-1} are intermingled with the exogenous forces—X^h, X^f, Z, and U—that influence the system. But this disadvantage can be rectified by rewriting 11-14 in a way that eliminates all lagged values of the endogenous variables other than the initial conditions. The result, derived and explained in appendix A, is the entire $T(n + m)$ system of "final-form" equations:

(11-15) $$Y = R^h X^h + R^f X^f + QZ + V.$$

Here R^h, R^f, and Q are the final-form coefficient matrixes; V combines the effects of the stochastic error terms and the initial conditions.[19]

Policymakers' decision problems are inevitably multiperiod in nature. Policy actions taken in period 1 ("today") will still be altering the behavior of the endogenous target variables many periods hence. Thus, even though there will be a new opportunity in period 2 ("tomorrow" or "next month") to reset the values of the policy instruments, an intelligent decision taken today cannot focus solely on period 1 but must also analyze the likely effects of policy for many periods in the future. Because the equations 11-15 display the behavior of the world economic system over time, they are a major improvement over the one-period representation in equations 11-8. What was before only implicit now becomes explicit: the task for a nation's policy authority is to choose *time paths* for the settings on the national instruments that are judged most likely to bring about best feasible *time paths* for the national target variables.

To complete the generalization to all T periods, a multiperiod version of the national loss functions must be specified. These functions are formally similar to their one-period analogs. For example, the home loss function might be written:

(11-16) $$W^h = w_o^h + c'Y + d'X^h + \tfrac{1}{2}Y'CY + \tfrac{1}{2}X^{h'}DX^h.$$

19. For a general reference on the derivation of the final-form equations of a model, see Henri Theil, *Principles of Econometrics* (Wiley, 1971), pp. 463–65.

But the generalized functions are defined over all T periods, and the weighting vectors and matrixes thus must embody intertemporal preferences as well as preferences across variables during any one period of time.

The difficult intertemporal issues that arise in trying to give concrete form to the weighting vectors and submatrixes in multiperiod loss functions can be sidestepped here. Those issues are identified in appendix A. It is sufficient here to reemphasize that each national authority's preferences have a national bias that pervades the subvectors and submatrixes of the multiperiod stacked vectors and matrixes in a manner analogous to that for the one-period case.

It is noted above for the one-period case how a procedure that superimposes a national loss function on the constraint of a model can be used to derive national instrument settings that are "optimal." An analogous procedure can be applied in the multiperiod case, as shown in appendix A.

Uncertainty and Game-Theoretic Aspects

Policy decisions in real life must be made under conditions of great uncertainty. The more open the national economy, the more extreme this uncertainty. A particularly troublesome type of uncertainty is associated with the prospective policy actions of other nations' authorities, who likewise have aspirations as controllers of the economic system. The preceding description and the amplification of it in appendix A fail to give sufficient analytical prominence to these uncertainty and game-theoretic aspects of national decisions; they create an impression of definiteness and controllability that is positively misleading.

If a nation's authority possessed all the knowledge and information presumed by the preceding description, determination of the appropriate settings for policy instruments would require merely clerical calculations. But recall just how much has been presumed! The nation's authority is assumed to have available, first, a structural model appropriate for describing the world economy. Second, the authority is assumed to believe, correctly, that this structure will remain unchanged over the policy horizon (or, alternatively, will change in a predictable way). These assumptions taken together mean that, third, the authority knows how the world economic system will respond to changes in the settings for the nation's policy instruments. Fourth, the authority is assumed to be able to specify its preferences sufficiently precisely to articulate an explicit loss function; and, fifth, the authority is assumed to be able to make reliable projections of the future time paths of the nonpolicy exogenous variables (Z) and the structural stochastic error terms (E). Finally, the home authority is presumed to be able to make reliable projections of the time paths of the policy instruments controlled by the foreign authority (X^f).

In actual policymaking situations, each of these six presumptions is likely to be invalid.

Policymakers do not have reliable structural models of macroeconomic behavior. The coefficients that appear in aggregative behavioral relationships are not known with confidence. The form of those relationships (for example, the presence or absence of nonlinearities) is uncertain. The dynamics of responses over time (for example, the lengths of lags and the shapes of lag distributions) are poorly understood. There may even be uncertainty about which variables appear in which of the behavioral relationships.

Knowledge is particularly uncertain about the structural relationships that link a national economy to the rest of the world. Since economists have not yet specified an adequate model even in theoretical terms, the concept of an integrated, empirical model of *world* economic structure is itself visionary. A presumption that policymakers have reliable knowledge about the coefficients in the interdependence submatrixes of such a model can only be labeled a fantasy.[20]

Indeed, uncertainty is still more deep-rooted. Analysis of policy choices would be impossible if one could not presume that a structure of some sort exists whose features, in principle, can be discovered or estimated. But there is no sound basis for assuming, as in equations 11-6 and 11-13, that this structure is unchanging over time and deterministic except for additive stochastic error terms with given means. A representation that incorporates the possibility of changes in economic structure over time is analytically more difficult, but obviously preferable.[21] And why should policymakers incorporate stochastic elements in their model only by allowing the intercept of an equation to be a random variable (that is, by including only an additive stochastic error term)? A better approach is to treat all the structural coefficients (slopes as well as intercepts) as stochastic. An analytical framework in which the structural coefficients are modeled as stochastic and, in addition, sequentially correlated over time would be better still. After all, policymakers have to deal with an underlying economic structure that is not only uncertain in a static sense but that changes over time in an unknown manner.[22]

Because its knowledge of the structure of the national and the world economy is highly uncertain, the national authority has a limited ability to predict the consequences of changes in the settings of its instruments. This type of uncertainty, for reasons discussed in the next chapter, has especially troublesome implications for policy decisions.

Uncertainty is greater about economic structure than about the preferences of the policymakers themselves. Even so, it is no trivial matter for a nation's authority to articulate preferences as systematically and precisely as implied by the loss function shown in equation 11-16.[23] In this respect, too, the framework in this chapter has the pedagogical disadvantage of diverting attention from the uncertainty aspects that figure so prominently in actual policymaking.

Suppose that the home and the foreign authorities were miraculously presented with reliable estimates of the world structural model (equations 11-13), that they were assured the structure would remain unchanged over the next T periods, and

20. Strictly speaking, an authority needs to know only the final-form equations of its model (11-15) in order to derive the optimizing settings for its instruments (so long as the underlying structure remains unchanged). But it is the ultimate fantasy to presume that a policy authority can obtain reliable knowledge of the final-form equations—in particular the matrixes R^h and R^f, which play such a critical role in calculations of the optimizing instrument settings—without first specifying and estimating the underlying structural model.

21. One method is to make some or all of the structural coefficients a deterministic function of observable variables. But this method still generates deterministic (albeit changing) coefficients and results in a nonlinear model.

22. Parts 4 and 5 return to this problem of "coefficient uncertainty." For references on random coefficient models and analysis of the case in which coefficients are both stochastic and sequentially correlated over time, see P. A. V. B. Swamy and P. A. Tinsley, "Linear Prediction and Estimation Methods for Regression Models with Stationary Stochastic Coefficients," Special Studies Paper 78 (Board of Governors of the Federal Reserve System, 1976), and *Journal of Econometrics*, in press.

23. The difficulties become acute as soon as one ceases to regard a national policy authority as a centralized decisionmaking unit that behaves as a single-minded rational actor. See chapter 18.

that each authority were able to articulate a detailed national loss function. The two authorities would then have the requisite knowledge of R^h, R^f, and Q for the decisionmaking procedure outlined above. But an attempt to implement that procedure would still be plagued by uncertainty.

Each authority has to project or make assumptions about the time paths of the nonpolicy exogenous variables contained in the Z vector. Even projections for the current period are subject to error, and projections for periods further in the future are subject to increasingly greater error. Similarly, each authority has to make necessarily uncertain projections or assumptions about the structural error terms E (from which projections of the final-form disturbance terms V can then be derived).[24]

A final source of uncertainty can be the most troublesome of all to deal with systematically. The home authority can perform its optimizing computations only by making projections or assumptions about the evolution of policy in the foreign country. But meanwhile the foreign authority can determine its preferred instrument settings only after predicting the course of home policy.

The essential indeterminateness of the situation is sharply exposed in equations A-34 through A-37 in appendix A. Home policymakers' calculations for the optimal instrument settings $\hat{X}^h$ are a function of S^h, which depends importantly on X^f. But the settings $\hat{X}^f$ preferred by the foreign authority are a function of S^f, which in turn depends on X^h. There are two would-be controllers, both simultaneously seeking to control an interdependent system. Not even an information-producing miracle that swept away all the other sources of uncertainty could resolve this game-theoretic indeterminateness. It could only be eliminated by a *political* miracle: a consolidation of the two loci of governmental decisionmaking and the application (to the whole world economy) of a single, agreed loss function.[25]

The combined presence of many different sources generates an overall uncertainty greater than the sum of its individual sources. Consider, for example, the dilemma of the home authority at the beginning of period 2. In period 1, instrument settings for $\hat{X}^h$ will somehow have been decided, based on an assumed structural model and on projections of X^f, Z, and E; the home authority will then have implemented that part of $\hat{X}^h$ referring to period 1 ($\hat{X}_1^h$), and will simultaneously have expected to observe a particular outcome for the endogenous variables in period 1, say $\hat{Y}_1$. But at the beginning of period 2, a set of new observations—the actual values of Y_1—will already have invalidated the earlier expectations.[26] To revise the optimizing instrument settings for period 2 and subsequent periods in an intelligent manner, the home authority needs to know why the actual values Y_1 differed from the "targeted" values $\hat{Y}_1$. But any explanation of those discrepancies is itself uncertain. If data for past developments are reported promptly, the authority can check its predictions of Z_1 and X_1^f against the actual facts and thus discern whether errors in those predictions are an important source of the discrepancies between

24. One possible projection, but by no means the best in all circumstances, is to set each element of E equal to zero.

25. Expectational, game-theoretic interactions between a national government and *private* economic units—the focus of the rational-expectations challenge to the theory of economic policy—are discussed in chapter 18.

26. This assumes that ex post data for developments in period 1 are available to be used in computations for period-2 decisions. In practice, not even that much information will be available for many of the variables (see part 4).

$\hat{Y}_1$ and actual Y_1. But the authority is not able to allocate with confidence any remaining discrepancies to the other potential sources of error. In particular, the home authority is unsure whether the remaining discrepancies should be attributed to nonzero realizations for the stochastic error terms E_1 or, alternatively, to a change somewhere in the economic structure itself. If the correct interpretation could be known, the implications for future policy of these alternative possibilities would be quite different.

Even though uncertainty is rife, efforts to make decisions systematically have some hope of success. For one thing, the formal framework outlined above can be amended to give greater analytical prominence to uncertainty. Under some (admittedly quite restrictive) conditions, optimization in the presence of uncertainty involves formulating expected values for all the noncontrolled variables and then proceeding as though the problem is deterministic rather than stochastic.[27] Many analytical techniques for forecasting are available; improvements in the techniques continue to be made; projections of exogenous variables for one period ahead can often be made within tolerable margins of error. (Appropriate analytical procedures require projections of the exogenous variables for all T periods, but the projections for values more than one period into the future can be subsequently revised in the light of later information.) Differences between expected and realized values for variables in the periods just past can—and should—be used to modify instrument settings for the current and future periods. Procedures for making these adjustments can be explicitly appended to the calculations for determining optimal settings.[28] More hopeful still, progress is being made in adapting the techniques of control theory for cases in which structural models are assumed to have stochastic coefficients.[29] Modeling the structural coefficients as stochastic makes it possible to incorporate a priori beliefs or empirical information about the reliability (variances and covariances) of the coefficients directly into the analysis. Indeed, the analytical techniques of optimal control may prove to be most useful to a policy authority when uncertainty is severe, precisely because they provide a systematic procedure for conditioning decisions in accordance with perceptions of the types and relative degrees of uncertainty.

Nonetheless, despite such promising considerations, the initial verdict stands. Uncertainty is a pervasive determinant of macroeconomic decisionmaking—the more so the more open the nation's economy—and the framework outlined here fails to deal with it adequately.

27. For the cases in which structural models are linear, known, and deterministic except for additive stochastic error terms, so-called "first-period certainty equivalence" holds. See Theil and van den Bogaard, *Optimal Decision Rules for Government and Industry,* chap. 4. If an open-loop-with-feedback strategy is adopted in these cases or, equivalently, if feedback control equations are calculated and used, one can speak of "multiperiod certainty equivalence" (for an explanation of these terms, see appendix A). See Chow, *Analysis and Control of Dynamic Economic Systems,* chap. 7, esp. pp. 173–74. These certainty-equivalence results do not apply, however, when there is uncertainty about the impacts of the policy instruments themselves (R^h and R^f in the equation system 11-15). This point is further emphasized in chapter 12.

28. See, for example, John H. Kareken, Thomas Muench, and Neil Wallace, "Optimal Open Market Strategy: The Use of Information Variables," *American Economic Review,* vol. 63 (March 1973), pp. 156–72; Chow, *Analysis and Control of Dynamic Economic Systems,* chap. 8; P. A. Tinsley, "On Proximate Exploitation of Intermediate Information in Macroeconomic Forecasting," Special Studies Paper 59 (Board of Governors of the Federal Reserve System, April 1975); Kenneth D. Garbade, *Discretionary Control of Aggregate Economic Activity* (Lexington Books, 1975). Chapter 17 provides a detailed discussion and additional references.

29. References to the relevant literature are given in chapter 17.

CHAPTER TWELVE

Interdependence and National Economic Policy: The Degree of Autonomy

CHAPTER 11 presents an analytical characterization of the decision process required if a nation's policymakers systematically try to match national controllable means with national ultimate ends. With that foundation, it becomes possible to give analytical content to discussions of the effectiveness of a nation's policy instruments. That clarification about instrument effectiveness in turn facilitates a more precise analysis of the consequences of economic interdependence for the effective autonomy of national economic policy, the controllability of the national economy, and the degree to which policymakers can be successful in attaining national goals.

The Effectiveness of Policy Instruments

Rigorous characterizations of the impacts of policy actions in a closed economy employ the concept of multipliers. This same concept is essential for analysis of the impacts of policy actions under conditions of intermediate interdependence.

A policy multiplier relates two variables to each other: some exogenous policy instrument, say x_i, and some endogenous variable, say y_j. Let there be a specified change in x_i that in turn brings about a change in y_j. The usual definition of the multiplier is the ratio of these two changes: dy_j/dx_i.[1]

Policy multipliers are single-valued coefficients in a comparative statics framework. In a multiperiod model in which all variables are time paths, the relevant multipliers are also dynamic; the notation dy_j/dx_i then refers to an entire time series (a vector of values) that expresses, period by period, the changes in the time path of y_j attributable to a specified pattern of changes in the time path of x_i.

The relevant changes in y_j and x_i are deviations from time paths that would otherwise have prevailed. That is, two time sequences of settings for x_i are postulated, a benchmark path and an alternative. The multiplier time series quantifies the differential impact on y_j of the two paths for x_i. In concept, x_i is the only exogenous feature of the model that differs between the benchmark and alternative cases: dy_j/dx_i refers to the impact of dx_i on y_j when all policy instruments except

1. The multiplier concept is well established in the closed-economy literature on econometric models and the theory of economic policy. Among the most useful references are H. Theil, *Economic Forecasts and Policy*, 2d. rev. ed. (Amsterdam: North-Holland, 1961), chap. 7; Theil in association with P. J. M. van den Bogaard, *Optimal Decision Rules for Government and Industry* (Amsterdam: North-Holland, 1964, chaps. 2 and 4; and Benjamin M. Friedman, *Economic Stabilization Policy: Methods in Optimization* (Amsterdam and Oxford: North-Holland; New York: American Elsevier, 1975), chap. 5.

171

x_i and all other types of disturbances are unchanged from their benchmark paths. The time paths of all endogenous variables, on the other hand, differ between the benchmark and alternative cases.[2]

A *policy action* must be defined for all periods up to the time horizon of the policymakers' analysis.[3] Policy actions can thus take a wide variety of forms—for example, a once-for-all change in the setting of an instrument in period 1 with the new setting maintained thereafter; a change in period 1 reversed in period 2 or some later period; or a change in the rate of growth applicable to all future periods. The associated multipliers are of course different for differing forms of policy action.

Statements about the characteristics of a multiplier dy_j/dx_i are synonymous with statements about the *effectiveness* of the policy action dx_i in influencing y_j. The larger the mean in absolute value and the smaller the variance and covariances of the particular multiplier, the more effective is the instrument x_i in influencing y_j.[4] Comparison of the characteristics of the two multipliers dy_j/dx_i and dy_m/dx_i is equivalent to analyzing the *relative effectiveness* of the policy action dx_i in influencing two different endogenous variables y_j and y_m. The appropriate way to analyze rigorously the *comparative advantage* of two alternative policy actions dx_i and dx_k in influencing a particular endogenous variable y_j is to compare the two multipliers dy_j/dx_i and dy_j/dx_k.[5]

The effectiveness of policy instruments in influencing particular endogenous variables should be sharply distinguished from statements about the *overall effectiveness* of macroeconomic policy. The former, more limited use of the term refers to the potency of an instrument or a set of instruments in influencing the endogenous variables when all other exogenous influences are unchanged. In contrast, overall effectiveness presumably refers to the overall performance of policymakers in attaining specified goals. Concepts of overall performance can have no meaning independent of the specified goals; they are logically dependent on *both* the policymakers' loss function and their model of how the world works. Policy multipliers and the effectiveness of individual policy instruments depend solely on the model.

2. Define $\hat{x}_{i,t}$ and $\mathring{x}_{i,t}$ as, respectively, the alternative and benchmark values in period t of the policy instrument x_t. Similarly, let $\hat{y}_{j,t}$ and $\mathring{y}_{j,t}$ denote the associated alternative and benchmark values for y_j in period t. As used in the text, dy_j/dx_i refers to the time series:

$$\frac{\hat{y}_{j,t} - \mathring{y}_{j,t}}{\hat{x}_{i,t} - \mathring{x}_{i,t}}, \qquad t = 1, 2, \ldots, T.$$

For all policy instruments x_k other than x_i, the definition assumes that $\hat{x}_{k,t} = \mathring{x}_{k,t}$, $t = 1, 2, \ldots, T$.

3. That is, $dx_{i,t} \equiv \hat{x}_{i,t} - \mathring{x}_{i,t}$ for $t = 1, 2, \ldots, T$ where period T is the most distant period to which the policymakers look.

4. This definition of effectiveness does not deal unambiguously with cases in which changes occur in the expected value and the variance of a multiplier in the same direction. Suppose, for example, that the absolute value of the mean of a multiplier dy_j/dx_i is increased, but its variance is also increased proportionately. Has the effectiveness of x_i with respect to y_j remained unchanged, increased, or decreased? One method of dealing with these ambiguous cases is to use the coefficient of variation as a test. This statistic is defined as the ratio of the standard deviation (square root of the variance) to the mean. With that procedure, the effectiveness of x_i in influencing y_j would be judged respectively to have increased, remained unchanged, or declined according to whether the coefficient of variation of dy_j/dx_i were reduced, left unchanged, or increased.

5. An alternative concept of effectiveness that could conceivably be adopted (and was discussed in the early literature) is the change in x_i needed to bring about a specified change in some target variable y_j^* *holding all other target variables unchanged*—in other words, dx_i/dy_j^*. See, for example, J. Tinbergen, *On the Theory of Economic Policy*, 2d ed. (Amsterdam: North-Holland, 1963), pp. 53–55. However, once one abandons the concept of fixed target values or fixed time paths for ultimate-target variables, this alternative approach to defining effectiveness becomes much less useful.

To avoid the confusion that can result from using "effectiveness" in two different senses, the subsequent discussion uses the term to refer only to policy multipliers and will employ other terms—the *successfulness of policy* or *economic welfare*— when referring to more comprehensive concepts concerned with the overall performance of policy.[6]

A distinction should also be made between the effectiveness of policy instruments and the degree of *controllability* that policymakers can exert over target variables. The ability of policymakers to control target variables depends in part on the magnitude and reliability of policy multipliers. But it is influenced by a number of other factors as well.[7]

The most important causes of changes in the effectiveness of instruments are changes in basic behavioral relationships—in economic structure.

When a structural change alters the magnitude of a multiplier, the change is also likely to alter the degree of controllability, the successfulness of policy, and economic welfare. Evaluating the impact of a structural change on any of those broader concepts, however, is a complex matter. The structural change may affect not only certain policy multipliers but also many other aspects of the economic system (for example, *disturbance multipliers*). To reach a judgment whether a structural change reduces or increases the degree of controllability, the successfulness of policy, or economic welfare, one must therefore evaluate all the consequences of the change and their net impact.

Although the conventional definition of a policy multiplier presupposes that all exogenous variables except the individual instrument x_i are maintained on their benchmark paths, it may not be feasible in a realistic policy situation to vary each instrument independently. When such conditions prevail, analysis of exogenous policy actions must be careful to specify a package combination of instrument changes. Similarly, the effectiveness of those instruments has to be judged in the light of package multipliers. This point becomes especially important in a situation of intermediate interdependence.

Can a policymaker, using the multiplier dy_j/dx_i, always obtain any desired impact on a target variable y_j merely by selecting the correct policy "dose" (the amount of the change in x_i)? Even if the absolute value of a multiplier is small, for example, can the desired effect be obtained by sufficiently increasing the size of the policy dose? In realistic policy situations the answer is decisively negative, for two reasons.

First, some sizes of policy doses may not be institutionally or politically feasible. Policy instruments can be subject to boundary conditions. Alternatively, the costs associated with using instruments can vary with the size of the dose.[8]

---

6. The concepts of policy successfulness and economic welfare are defined and discussed in chapter 13.

7. See chapter 13.

8. On the possibility that some instruments may be subject to boundary conditions, see for example Tinbergen's original discussion in *On the Theory of Economic Policy*, chap. 6. In applications of the theory of economic policy using the techniques of dynamic programming, boundary conditions on the instruments can be enforced by means of inequality constraints. The alternative approach to modeling of these phenomena is to incorporate the costs of using instruments directly into the loss function to be minimized. See, for example, the treatment in chapter 11; in Theil in association with van den Bogaard, *Optimal Decision Rules for Government and Industry;* and in Friedman, *Economic Stabilization Policy.*

Second, and even more important, the values of the relevant policy multipliers are uncertain in any practical decisionmaking situation. And uncertainty about policy multipliers is an especially critical type of uncertainty for policy decisions.[9]

In contrast with other forms of uncertainty for which it may often prove sensible to form expectations of the uncertain coefficients or variables and treat those expected values as certainties, policymakers should never ignore uncertainty about policy multipliers. Even if it were feasible to use policy doses of any size, it would be inappropriate to select those instrument settings that would be dictated by focusing only on the expected values of multipliers and ignoring their variances and covariances.[10] Moreover, all available instruments should be fully utilized no matter how few the target variables that are the objective of policy and no matter how plentiful the number of instruments.

As a general presumption, an individual policy instrument x_i should be used less aggressively the more uncertain are its multipliers. More broadly stated, the greater the uncertainty associated with the values of policy multipliers, the less active policymakers should be in adjusting the settings on their instruments. These presumptions apply in normal times and when structural changes occur. In particular, structural changes that reduce the effectiveness of one or more policy instruments should typically lead to less aggressiveness in the use of those instruments.[11]

National Policy Multipliers and Autonomy

How should the effectiveness of a nation's policy instruments be analyzed under conditions of intermediate interdependence? As the preceding section suggests, the most fruitful approach is to identify the effectiveness of a national policy instrument with the expected values, the variances, and the covariances of its multipliers. Statements about the effectiveness of a group of instruments—for example, all national policy instruments—should be generalizations about the characteristics of the multipliers associated with that group of instruments.

Effectiveness of which nation's instruments, and vis-à-vis which nation's variables? With international interdependence, there are four different groups of national policy multipliers that must be distinguished: (1) home own-variable multipliers, which express the impacts of home policy instruments X^h on home endogenous variables; (2) home foreign-impact multipliers, expressing the impacts of home instruments on foreign endogenous variables; (3) foreign home-impact multipliers, where the policy instruments are those of the foreign government (X^f) but the impacts are on home endogenous variables; and (4) foreign own-variable multipliers, where both the impacts and the instruments are foreign.[12]

9. The remainder of this section summarizes some key conclusions generated by theoretical analysis of multiplier uncertainty in closed-economy models. See especially William Brainard, "Uncertainty and the Effectiveness of Policy," *American Economic Review*, vol. 57 (May 1967, *Papers and Proceedings, 1966*), pp. 411–25.

10. If there is reason to believe that the policy multipliers have nonzero covariances with nonpolicy exogenous disturbances, those covariances should also be taken into account.

11. The generalization that taking multiplier uncertainty into account should reduce the aggressiveness of policy action can be shown to be incorrect in certain theoretical cases. Even in terms of simple, closed-economy models, much further research remains to be done on this subject.

12. Throughout part 3 I consider only two loci of national decisionmaking and hence only two sets of instruments and two sets of national target variables. The number of categories of cross-national multipliers

It will be convenient in the subsequent discussion to have a shorthand way of referring to these various groups of multipliers. Accordingly, the notation dY^h/dX^h is used to refer to the home own-variable multipliers as a class. The other three groups of multipliers are denoted by dY^f/dX^h, dY^h/dX^f, and dY^f/dX^f, respectively.[13]

These four groups of national policy multipliers are implicit in the analytical framework developed in chapter 11. The dY^h/dX^h and the dY^f/dX^h multipliers are embedded in R^h, the first of the final-form coefficient matrixes shown in equations 11-15. The matrix R^f in 11-15 contains all the multipliers pertaining to the foreign policy instruments.[14]

Since R^h and R^f are matrixes of coefficients in the final-form equations, they contain all the different dynamic multipliers required to analyze the effects, over as many as T periods in the future, of a policy action initiated today.[15] Given the expositional simplifications employed in chapter 11, moreover, the final-form coefficients are time-invariant and nonstochastic and therefore by themselves summarize whatever analytical story there is to tell about the effectiveness of the policy instruments X^h and X^f.[16]

(the impact of one nation's instruments on the endogenous variables of another) that have to be considered increases exponentially with the number of nations separately identified.

13. This notation belies the complexity of what it represents. In the case of the class of home own-variable multipliers, for example, dY^h/dX^h stands for a total of nk individual dynamic multipliers. Recall also that each individual multiplier is not a single number but rather an entire time series (a vector containing T components).

14. The matrix R^h is block triangular (see appendix A, expression A-26). The coefficients relevant for deducing the home own-variable multipliers are in the first n rows of the various $(n + m) \times k$ submatrixes of R^h; the last m rows of the various submatrixes contain the coefficients relevant to the home foreign-impact multipliers. Analogously, the dY^h/dX^f and the dY^f/dX^f multipliers are contained, respectively, in the first n and last m rows of the various $(n + m) \times l$ submatrixes of the block-triangular matrix R^f defined in appendix A, expression A-27.

15. The one-period, so-called impact multipliers are contained in the (identical) submatrixes along the main diagonals in A-26 and A-27; these are, of course, identical with the reduced-form coefficients in equations A-3 and A-8. To derive the various dynamic multiplier series for T periods into the future (sometimes referred to as the "total multipliers"), the analyst must use coefficients from all of the T submatrixes along the bottom border of R^h and R^f. The matrix of total multipliers in the case of the home policy instruments, for example, is obtained by adding the successive coefficient submatrixes R_1^h, R_2^h, . . ., R_T^h; if M_T^h is used to denote this $(n + m) \times k$ matrix, it can be seen from A-24 and A-26 that

$$M_T^h = A^h + LA^h + L^2A^h + \ . \ . \ . \ + L^{T-1}A^h,$$

which for very large T converges to the expression

$$M_T^h = (I - L)^{-1}A^h,$$

where I is the identity matrix of order $(n + m) \times (n + m)$. For background reference on the computation of impact, interim, and total multipliers, see Henri Theil, *Principles of Econometrics* (Wiley, 1971), pp. 463–65; Arnold Zellner and Franz Palm, "Time Series Analysis and Simultaneous Equation Econometric Models," *Journal of Econometrics*, vol. 2 (1974), pp. 17–54. See Carl F. Christ, "Judging the Performance of Econometric Models of the U.S. Economy," *International Economic Review*, vol. 16 (February 1975), pp. 54–74; and Gary Fromm and Lawrence R. Klein, "The NBER/NSF Model Comparison Seminar: An Analysis of Results," *Annals of Economic and Social Measurement*, vol. 5 (Winter 1976), pp. 1–28, for two recent examples of discussions of multipliers derived from econometric models.

16. The exposition in chapter 11 postulates structural coefficients that are fixed parameters and a linear form for all structural relationships. So long as the structure remains unchanged, the elements of R^h and R^f are therefore also fixed parameters. In particular, the various multiplier time series for an x_i are (1) independent of benchmark time paths for the other exogenous variables and (2) independent of the initial conditions Y_0. Even if the assumption of fixed structural coefficients were retained, nonlinearity in the behavioral relationships would cause policy multipliers to be dependent on the time paths for all the variables (exogenous and endogenous) in the system. Once the structural coefficients are conceptualized as stochastic (having nonzero variances and covariances), the derivation of final-form multipliers and their variance-covariance matrix becomes extremely complex. The basic points to be made in the text are not invalidated by ignoring these complexities.

Consider national macroeconomic policy from the perspective of the home country. All four groups of policy multipliers significantly influence the degree of controllability of the nation's economy and the overall successfulness of this policy, as is stressed below. But one of the four—the home own-variable multipliers—must be of especial concern to home policymakers. The home own-variable multipliers are the gauges of the effectiveness of home instruments vis-à-vis the variables that are the object of policy. They relate what the home authority can actually do to what it hopes to achieve.

Given the framework of chapter 11 and the preceding discussion of multipliers, it is now possible to give analytical content to the notion of *de facto control* (introduced in chapter 10) and to such related concepts as *autonomy*. Consider the following definition:

> **(12-A)** **The autonomy of a nation's economic policy refers to the effectiveness of the nation's policy instruments in influencing national target variables. The larger in absolute value and the less uncertain are national own-variable multipliers, the greater the degree of autonomy.**

This definition of autonomy is theoretically precise and applicable in principle to empirical analysis. It facilitates a systematic investigation of the consequences of international interdependence for national macroeconomic policy.[17]

What factors determine the degree of a nation's autonomy? An answer to this question is extraordinarily complex. In principle, a correct answer must take into account the values of virtually every structural coefficient in the entire world economic system.

Recall that the home own-variable multipliers do not depend exclusively (in some cases, perhaps even predominantly) on "domestic" economic behavior. On the contrary, they embody the indirect consequences of behavior throughout the world economic system.[18] This means, among other things, that a structural change occurring virtually anywhere in the world may alter the home own-variable multipliers. Such an alteration may be significant or negligible, depending on all the empirical circumstances. But the theoretical point should be clear: under conditions of intermediate interdependence, not a sparrow falls abroad but that it may have some impact on the autonomy of home economic policy.

Chapter 11 preserves the distinction between ultimate-target variables and intermediate variables, and the final-form matrixes R^h and R^f contain multipliers with respect to both types of endogenous variables in both nations. The analysis here in part 3 does not, however, focus on the issues of monetary-policy strategy treated in parts 1 and 2 (nor does it prejudice their resolution in one way or the other). Home policymakers have a strong interest in, at a minimum, the home own-variable multipliers referring to their ultimate-target variables. Depending on their views about conducting policy with an intermediate-target strategy, they may or may not have a strong interest in those home own-variable multipliers that express the impact of home instruments on home intermediate variables.

17. This definition differs, however, from the woolly connotation commonly given to "autonomy" in the existing literature. The loose usage encountered in the literature is more akin to the broader concept that I label *controllability*.

18. Each of the home own-variable multipliers embedded in R^h is conditioned by *all* of the elements of the structural matrixes Γ and Λ and by some of the elements of Φ, not merely by the elements in the home "domestic" submatrixes.

Interdependence and the Degree of Autonomy

The Basic Hypothesis

Defined analytically, an increase or decrease in economic interdependence is a change in particular characteristics of the world economic structure (in terms of chapter 11, an alteration in the elements of the interdependence submatrixes in one or more of the matrixes of structural coefficients Γ, Φ, Ω, and Λ). If translated into more precise terms, therefore, the assertion in proposition 10-A that an increase (decrease) in interdependence typically loosens (strengthens) the relationships between a nation's policy instruments and its ultimate targets becomes a proposition about the effects on home own-variable multipliers of the postulated change in interdependence. "Loosening" implies reductions in the absolute values of dY^h/dX^h, increases in their variances and covariances, or both. "Strengthening" implies effects in the opposite direction. Proposition 10-A can thus be restated as a hypothesis about interdependence and autonomy:

(12-B) **A structural change that increases (diminishes) the economic interde-**
pendence of a nation's economy with the rest of the world typically
reduces (augments) the autonomy of its economic policy.

Evaluation of the Hypothesis

The analytical procedures required to examine the correctness of this hypothesis about interdependence and autonomy are complex, but theoretically straightforward.

Consider the question of evaluating 12-B within the context of some particular structural model of the world economy that features, among other things, a separate identification of the ultimate-target variables and the policy instruments of the home nation. In principle, such a model can be solved to obtain its final form and the various groups of policy multipliers—in particular, the home own-variable multipliers. In principle, if not easily in practice, the variances and covariances of the multipliers can be derived as well as their expected values. Now let the original model be modified by various changes in economic structure, each of which involves increasing interdependence. For each modification, let a comparison be made between dY^h/dX^h in the benchmark case ("before") and dY^h/dX^h following the increase in interdependence ("after"). This comparison will reveal, for each individual multiplier in the group, whether the means have been reduced in absolute value and whether the variances and covariances have been increased. Depending on the typical result of the comparison, proposition 12-B can be judged correct or incorrect.

The results of evaluating 12-B in the context of a particular structural model might depend primarily on idiosyncrasies of that model. Evidence supporting the correctness of 12-B in a truly general sense, therefore, would have to show that structural changes identifiable as increasing interdependence typically generate reductions in autonomy across a wide range of alternative models of the world economy.

The required procedures can be described more precisely in terms of the illustrative model of the world economy presented in chapter 11 (see equations 11-6). In principle, the consequences of a change in economic structure for the policy multipliers of such a model can be obtained by repeating the procedures for calculating the multipliers but replacing the original with the altered structural coefficients. Consider the "impact" policy multipliers in the reduced-form coefficient matrix A (equations 11-7). Define $d\Gamma$, $d\Phi$, $d\Omega$, and $d\Lambda$ as matrixes (of the same order as Γ, Φ, Ω, and Λ) that contain the changes in the original structural coefficients. For most structural changes, the majority of the elements of $d\Gamma$, $d\Phi$, $d\Omega$, and $d\Lambda$ will be equal to zero. From these definitions and from the equations for computing A, it is possible to calculate the changes in the impact multipliers dA. An analogous calculation yields the matrix dL, the changes in the reduced-form coefficients of the lagged endogenous variables.[19] In turn, these computations can be combined with the formulas for deriving the final-form coefficient matrixes to obtain the changes in the dynamic multipliers dR^h and dR^f. These procedures apply to any structural changes, not just those associated with changes in the degree of interdependence.[20]

As an example of a change in interdependence, suppose that a group of home residents become more aware, and hence take greater advantage, of opportunities for profitably substituting between home-currency and foreign-currency assets in response to changes in their expected returns. This change might be represented as a change in four submatrixes of the original structural coefficients, as follows:

$$(12\text{-}5) \qquad d\Gamma = \left[\begin{array}{cccc} 0 & 0 & 0 & 0 \\ 0 & d\Gamma_{22} & 0 & d\Gamma_{24} \\ \hline 0 & 0 & 0 & 0 \\ 0 & 0 & 0 & 0 \end{array}\right] \; ;$$

$$(12\text{-}6) \qquad d\Lambda = \left[\begin{array}{cccc} 0 & 0 & 0 & 0 \\ 0 & d\Lambda_{22} & 0 & d\Lambda_{24} \\ \hline 0 & 0 & 0 & 0 \\ 0 & 0 & 0 & 0 \end{array}\right] .$$

19. The equations for the original impact multipliers, A, and the original reduced-form coefficients for the lagged endogenous variables, L, are shown in A-3 and A-5 in appendix A. The altered impact multipliers are given by

$$(12\text{-}1) \qquad (A + dA) = -(\Gamma + d\Gamma)^{-1}(\Phi + d\Phi).$$

The change in the impact multipliers, dA, can be written after rearrangement of terms as

$$(12\text{-}2) \qquad dA = [\Gamma^{-1} - (\Gamma + d\Gamma)^{-1}]\Phi - (\Gamma + d\Gamma)^{-1}(d\Phi).$$

The new reduced-form coefficients for the lagged endogenous variables are

$$(12\text{-}3) \qquad (L + dL) = -(\Gamma + d\Gamma)^{-1}(\Lambda + d\Lambda);$$

the change in the L matrix can be written

$$(12\text{-}4) \qquad dL = [\Gamma^{-1} - (\Gamma + d\Gamma)^{-1}]\Lambda - (\Gamma + d\Gamma)^{-1}(d\Lambda).$$

20. Compare Theil, *Optimal Decision Rules for Government and Industry*, pp. 43–51, and *Economic Forecasts and Policy*, pp. 429–44. In those discussions Theil outlines an analytical procedure to be followed

Suppose also that the structural change leaves unaffected the coefficients directly associated with the policy instruments (so that $d\Phi$ is a null matrix). Observe that in 12-5 and 12-6 the postulated change is shown as affecting not only some of the original interdependence coefficients in Γ_{24} and Λ_{24} but also some of the domestic coefficients relating home variables to each other (some of the elements of Γ_{22} and Λ_{22}). This is suggested by the balance-sheet identities that constrain microeconomic behavior. Home economic units cannot allocate a greater share of their wealth to foreign-currency assets without simultaneously reducing the share of their wealth allocated to home-currency assets—which in turn may involve an increased sensitivity to rates of return on both types of assets.

Given an increase in interdependence such as that implied by 12-5 and 12-6, calculations of the matrix dA will reveal the consequences of the change for impact multipliers. Further calculations, making use of dL and the formulas for final-form coefficient matrixes, will display the consequences for all the dynamic multipliers. These results will then reveal whether the absolute values of the individual home own-variable multipliers have declined or risen. For the case posited in 12-5 and 12-6, suppose the typical outcome is a decline in the absolute value of the multipliers. The interpretation of this result will be that increased substitutability by home residents between home-currency and foreign-currency assets reduces the autonomy of home macroeconomic policy. Opposite results would have to be interpreted as evidence contrary to the generalization in 12-B.

The coefficient matrixes in the discussion of the preceding example are implicitly treated as though their elements are fixed, known parameters. But policy decisions must take into account not only the expected values of policy multipliers but also the degree of uncertainty associated with them. Accordingly, an assessment of dY^h/dX^h before and after an increase in interdependence must compare the variances and covariances of the multipliers as well as their expected values.

The need to incorporate uncertainty into the analysis makes the required calculations extraordinarily complicated. The structural coefficients themselves have to be treated as stochastic rather than deterministic. Thus increases in interdependence must be defined not only in terms of how they affect the expected values of the structural coefficients but also how they influence the structural variances and covariances. In the illustration of an increased substitutability by home residents between home-currency and foreign-currency assets, for example, it becomes necessary to specify not only such matrixes as those for $d\Gamma$ and $d\Lambda$ in 12-5 and 12-6 but entire, new variance-covariance matrixes for Γ and Λ. This first necessary step in the analysis is no trivial matter given the existing state of theoretical and empirical knowledge of structural economic behavior. Moreover, even if all the inputs relating to the structural coefficients can be provided, the calculation of the policy multipliers becomes much more complex. It is necessary to derive the variances and covariances of the home own-variable multipliers from the expected values, variances, and covariances of the underlying structural coefficients. Although this general problem has been addressed in a closed-economy context,[21]

---

by a decisionmaker who is confronted by a change in the coefficients of his equation system and wishes to compute his "optimal reaction" to that change. Theil commences his analysis, however, with the reduced form of the equation system—he assumes that R^h, dR^h, R^f, and dR^f are already known—and does not focus attention on the policy multipliers per se.

21. See, for example, A. S. Goldberger, A. L. Nagar, and H. S. Odeh, "The Covariance Matrixes of Reduced-form Coefficients and of Forecasts for a Structural Econometric Model," *Econometrica*, vol. 29

and although in the context here it may be no more theoretically intractable than other aspects of the analysis, the required computations are nonetheless formidable.[22]

To sum up so far: increasing interdependence and autonomy can be given analytical definitions. A plausible hypothesis can be put forward about the impacts of the one on the other. Procedures can be specified for testing the hypothesis. The *question* is clear.

But what is the answer? For particular structural models, is proposition 12-B true or false? Does the generalization hold up across a wide range of alternative models? Is it possible to conclude that increasing interdependence undermines autonomy for actual open economies?

Unfortunately, given the current state of knowledge, a satisfactory answer cannot be provided. Direct evidence does not exist.

Can presumptive conclusions about the correctness of proposition 12-B be reached by reasoning in purely theoretical terms? Suppose, for example, one attempts to analyze 12-B in terms of the mathematical properties of partitioned matrixes and their inverses without specifying an *explicit* structural model. I have pursued that line of attack and tentatively concluded that it will not bear fruit. The effects of a change in interdependence on dY^h/dX^h depend critically on the specific signs and magnitudes of the various structural coefficients. This dependence can be illustrated for the general case of a system of $n + m$ equations and can be worked out in more detail for simple explicit models where there are only a few endogenous variables and only one or two policy instruments in each country. Neither line of investigation suggests that proposition 12-B is necessarily true or false independently of the signs and magnitudes of the underlying structural coefficients and independently of the origin of the increase in interdependence. The possibility cannot be ruled out that some types of increases in interdependence in some varieties of structural model may enhance rather than reduce the autonomy of national economic policy. Explicit information or assumptions about the structural coefficients and about the type of increase in interdependence thus seems to be a prerequisite for testing the correctness of 12-B.[23]

What research strategy should be pursued in future evaluations of this hypothesis? The most practical approach to take in the near-term future may be to examine

---

(October 1961), pp. 556–73; Arthur S. Goldberger, *Econometric Theory* (Wiley, 1964), pp. 364–80; Gregory C. Chow, *Analysis and Control of Dynamic Economic Systems* (Wiley, 1975), pp. 244 ff.; Phoebus J. Dhrymes, "Restricted and Unrestricted Reduced Forms: Asymptotic Distribution and Relative Efficiency," *Econometrica*, vol. 41 (January 1973), pp. 119–34; and A. L. Nagar and S. N. Sahay, "The Bias and Mean Squared Error of Forecasts from Partially Restricted Reduced Form," *Journal of Econometrics*, vol. 7 (1978), pp. 227–43.

22. Suppose an increase in interdependence results in a reduction in the absolute value of the means of certain home own-variable multipliers but simultaneously reduces the multipliers' variances or covariances. Should the combination of these changes be construed as a reduction in effective autonomy? In making interpretations in these ambiguous cases, an analyst must use some method of weighting changes in variances and covariances against changes in expected values (see note 4 above).

23. I have carried out a few suggestive numerical experiments with a computer program for inverting matrixes in which "multipliers" were calculated making use of arbitrary matrixes of "structural coefficients" partitioned into "home," "foreign," and "interdependence" submatrixes. These calculations, while not empirical evidence per se, amply confirm the fact that some combinations of signs and magnitudes of the initial "structural coefficients" interacting with some types of changes in the elements of the "interdependence submatrixes" can increase rather than reduce the absolute values of "own-variable multipliers."

12-B in the context of small, two-nation theoretical models. These models should be specified to incorporate the best macroeconomic theory currently available. Explicit derivation of the policy multipliers in such models before and after well-defined perturbations representing changes in interdependence would then provide theoretical evidence of the sort not now available.[24] Over the longer run, it should be possible to conduct similar experiments with empirically estimated, multiregion models of the world economy.[25]

Refinements of the Hypothesis

Proposition 12-B can be formulated in a more refined way by developing several further corollaries.

Consider first the expected values of the policy multipliers—the foreign own-variable multipliers and the two classes of cross-national multipliers as well as dY^h/dX^h. The following hypothesis seems a likely corollary of 12-B:

(12-C) **The typical result of increases in interdependence is to reduce the absolute values of the means of both classes of own-variable multipliers dY^h/dX^h and dY^f/dX^f but to increase the absolute values of the means of the cross-national multipliers dY^f/dX^h and dY^h/dX^f.**

Further theoretical or empirical analysis may show that 12-C should be qualified. For example, it is conceivable that the results for the policy multipliers may be systematically dependent on the particular type of increase in interdependence.[26] Pending such future research, however, it seems appropriate to leave 12-C in an unqualified form.

The intuitive notion underlying propositions 12-B and 12-C is that after an increase in interdependence, a given-sized policy action in one nation will typically have greater spillover effects on variables in the rest of the world, whereas less of the impacts will remain in the nation initiating the action. Implicitly, that notion may presuppose that there is a fixed amount of total impact (total effect on "world"— that is, combined home and foreign—variables) built into a given-sized policy action. The assumption of fixed total impact surely cannot be strictly correct. And for some types of increases in interdependence, changes in the country distribution—so to speak, the composition—of policy impacts might well result in significant alteration in the aggregate impacts for the world as a whole.[27] If cases exist in which autonomy is enhanced rather than reduced by increases in interdependence, I conjecture that the greater interdependence in those cases significantly increases the total impact of a given-sized dose of national policy.

24. For an example of the type of small—but large enough—model that may be appropriate, see Jeffrey R. Shafer, "The Macroeconomic Behavior of a Large Open Economy with a Floating Exchange Rate" (Ph.D. dissertation, Yale University, 1976).

25. See, for example, R. Berner and others, "A Multi-Country Model of the International Influences on the U.S. Economy: Preliminary Results," International Finance Discussion Paper 115 (Board of Governors of the Federal Reserve System, December 1977); and H. Howe and others, "Assessing International Interdependence with a Multi-Country Model," International Finance Discussion Paper 138 (Board of Governors of the Federal Reserve System, April 1979).

26. As an illustration: increased substitutability by home residents between home and foreign assets might have different consequences for the various multipliers than increased substitutability by foreign residents between foreign and home assets.

27. Compare Walter S. Salant, "International Transmission of Inflation," in Lawrence B. Krause and Walter S. Salant, eds., Worldwide Inflation: Theory and Recent Experience (Brookings Institution, 1977), pp. 199–200.

These last reflections suggest a further hypothesis based on weaker assumptions than 12-C, and therefore even more likely to be correct:

(12-D) Increases in interdependence will reduce the impacts of national instruments on national variables relative to the impacts of national instruments on variables in other countries.

Define $|dy_j^h/dx_i^h|$ as the absolute value of the mean of the home own-variable multiplier dy_j^h/dx_i^h before the increase in interdependence, and define $|\overline{dy_j^h/dx_i^h}|$ as the absolute value of the mean of the same multiplier following the increase in interdependence. Assume analogous definitions for the absolute values of the means, before and after the increase in interdependence, of members of the other three groups of policy multipliers. Hypothesis 12-D can then be stated more formally in terms of the following inequalities.

(12-E) For home policy instruments:

$$\frac{|\overline{dy_j^h/dx_i^h}|}{|\overline{dy_m^f/dx_i^h}|} < \frac{|dy_j^h/dx_i^h|}{|dy_m^f/dx_i^h|}, \qquad i = 1, \ldots, k.$$

(12-F) For foreign policy instruments:

$$\frac{|\overline{dy_j^f/dx_i^f}|}{|\overline{dy_n^h/dx_i^f}|} < \frac{|dy_j^f/dx_i^f|}{|dy_n^h/dx_i^f|}, \qquad i = 1, \ldots, l.$$

In 12-E, the inequality may not hold for every conceivable pair of home and foreign endogenous variables (each pair of j and m). But I conjecture that it definitely holds when y_j^h and y_m^f are "similar" variables in both countries (for example, home output and foreign output; home prices and foreign prices). Analogously, the inequality in 12-F presumably holds true, if not for each pair of home and foreign endogenous variables, then at least when the comparison of impacts on y_j^f and y_n^h is between functionally similar variables in the two countries.

The hypothesis summarized in 12-D through 12-F deals with the relative effectiveness of particular national policy instruments vis-à-vis home and foreign variables. It asserts that a nation's instruments will be relatively less effective in influencing home variables after an increase in interdependence.

If 12-D through 12-F are correct, corollaries about the comparative advantage of a nation's policy instruments are also likely to hold:

(12-G) Increases in interdependence will reduce the impacts on national target variables of national policy instruments relative to the impacts of foreign policy instruments.

Note that 12-D and 12-G are related, but not identical; 12-D is concerned with the impacts of particular policy instruments on various endogenous variables (including target variables) of the home nation and the rest of the world, whereas 12-G focuses on the impacts of various home and foreign policy instruments on particular national target variables. Hypothesis 12-G may also be stated more formally as a set of inequalities:

(12-H) For home target variables:

$$\frac{|\overline{dy_j^{*h}/dx_i^h}|}{|\overline{dy_j^{*h}/dx_l^f}|} < \frac{|dy_j^{*h}/dx_i^h|}{|dy_j^{*h}/dx_l^f|}, \qquad j = 1, \ldots, n^*.$$

(12-J) For foreign target variables:

$$\frac{|dy_j^{*f}/dx_i^f|}{|dy_j^{*f}/dx_k^h|} < \frac{|dy_j^{*f}/dx_l^f|}{|dy_j^{*f}/dx_k^h|}, \qquad j = 1, \ldots, m^*.$$

These inequalities are supposed to hold for all possible pairs of home and foreign instruments—in other words, 12-H for all combinations of i and l and 12-J for all combinations of i and k.[28]

The degree of autonomy is as much a function of the uncertainty associated with national own-variable multipliers as it is of the expected values themselves. It is thus necessary to supplement 12-C through 12-J with hypotheses concerning the consequences of increasing interdependence for the *variances* of national policy multipliers.

Consider first the prior question of how the variances of the structural coefficients may be altered when a change in interdependence occurs. Since the "true" values of structural coefficients are unknown to a nation's policymakers, both the means and the variances of the coefficients have to be estimated or assumed a priori. (Indeed, from the perspective of the policymakers, a change in interdependence can only mean, by definition, a change in the *estimated or assumed* means of the structural coefficients in the interdependence submatrixes of Γ, Φ, Ω, or Λ.) It seems plausible to suppose that

(12-K) The typical concomitant of an increase in interdependence is an augmentation of uncertainty about economic structure.

More specifically:

(12-K') Following an increase in interdependence, the (estimated or assumed) variances of many structural coefficients will be increased; the remaining structural coefficients will typically have unchanged variances; only in rare instances will any of the structural coefficients have a reduced variance.

This hypothesis applies to all the matrixes of structural coefficients. And it applies not merely to the variances of the coefficients in the interdependence submatrixes but also to the variances of the structural coefficients that relate one domestic variable to another.

---

28. As an illustrative evaluation of the hypotheses, consider the analytics of interdependence and autonomy in the context of the simplest possible two-country version of the Keynesian expenditure model. That model has only four behavioral parameters: a marginal propensity to spend and a marginal propensity to import in each of two countries. The four behavioral parameters are treated as deterministic and known. There are only two exogenous variables, autonomous expenditures in the home country and autonomous expenditures in the foreign country. (It makes no practical difference in the model whether these two exogenous variables are interpreted as policy instruments or as nonpolicy disturbances.) In this simple (and theoretically deficient) model, when the marginal propensities of both countries increase together by a proportional amount, hypotheses 12-C through 12-J are borne out completely. The impact of this type of increasing interdependence on the absolute values of the multipliers in this model has already been reported by Richard N. Cooper, *Economic Mobility and National Economic Policy,* 1973 Wiksell Lectures (Stockholm: Almqvist and Wiksell, 1974), p. 61. When the marginal propensity to import increases in one of the two countries but not in the other, hypotheses 12-C through 12-J are partly true and partly false. For example, when the home marginal propensity to import increases, the changes in the multipliers for home autonomous expenditures (that is dY^h/dA^h and dY^f/dA^h) are consistent with 12-C and 12-E; but the changes in the multipliers for foreign autonomous expenditures (dY^h/dA^f and dY^f/dA^f) are not consistent with 12-C and 12-F. My hunch is that these latter cases of inconsistency are caused not by the falsity of the hypotheses but rather the inadequacy of the simple model.

Why is uncertainty about economic structure likely to be augmented when increases in interdependence occur? The explanation lies primarily in the differential availability and cost of information. National policymakers have only inadequate knowledge about economic structure and current economic developments, and acquisition of additional information is costly. These points are especially germane for the international aspects of a nation's economic policy. National authorities typically possess much less and much poorer information about economic developments abroad than at home. The costs of obtaining more information about developments in the rest of the world typically exceed the costs of acquiring additional information about domestic developments. What little reliable knowledge exists about economic structure pertains mainly to its domestic aspects. To be sure, once increases in interdependence occur, and especially if they occur frequently, a nation's authority will be required to pay greater attention to structural economic behavior outside the nation. Particular attention will need to be devoted to those aspects of the behavior of home and foreign residents—the interdependence coefficients—that link the nation's economy with the remainder of the world economy. If the national economy became extremely open, there might not then be a *relative* lack of information about the nonnational aspects of economic structure.[29] But most national economies fall far short of that advanced degree of openness. For the typical situation confronting most national policy authorities, hypothesis 12-K is highly plausible.

If increasing interdependence typically generates more uncertainty about the underlying structural coefficients, the conclusion follows directly that it also tends to create greater uncertainty about the national policy multipliers. (The variances of the multipliers, as noted above, are a function of the variances of the structural coefficients.) All four groups of policy multipliers are likely to be affected in the same direction. In particular

(12-L) **Increases in interdependence will typically increase the variances of national own-variable multipliers.**

(12-M) **Increases in interdependence will typically increase the variances of cross-national multipliers.**

Proposition 12-C hypothesizes that the absolute values of the means of cross-national multipliers are augmented by increases in interdependence. Proposition 12-M is not inconsistent with 12-C; it merely asserts that the degree of uncertainty associated with dY^f/dX^h and dY^h/dX^f will be heightened even as the expected values of those impacts are augmented.

Why the Hypothesis Matters

Why should a nation's policymakers be concerned about the consequences for autonomy of changes in interdependence? Suppose the expected values of the home own-variable multipliers dY^h/dX^h are reduced by an increase in interdependence. Cannot the home policy authority simply compensate for the reduction in the multipliers by correspondingly enlarging the sizes of its policy doses? Does it matter that the sizes of the policy doses have to be augmented to achieve any given expected impact on the nation's target variables?

29. But at that stage there also might not be a well-defined "national economy" (see the discussion of economic structure and political structure in chapter 10).

Consider first the problems that would arise even if policymakers ignored the presence of uncertainty about their policy multipliers.

Other things being equal, increases in the required sizes of policy doses raise the probabilities that policy will run up against boundary conditions on the use of instruments. And if there are costs incurred when the settings on instruments are changed and those costs vary with the amount of the change, it may not be desirable to administer larger doses. National policymakers thus cannot be better off and probably will be worse off if they are forced to take larger sized policy actions.

Even in a relatively closed economy, the constraints imposed on policy decisions by boundary conditions and the costs attributable to instrument variation can be troublesome.[30] But the trouble will be made more severe as an economy becomes more open, because increases in openness increase the likelihood that constraints will become binding and that additional costs will have to be incurred.

Suppose again that the home country experiences an increase in interdependence because of greater substitutability by home residents between assets denominated in the home and the foreign currencies. Suppose further that the increase in asset substitutability reduces the own-variable multipliers for home fiscal instruments. In the period after the structural change occurs, suppose it takes, for example, a 30 percent larger change in tax rates and a 25 percent larger change in government purchases of goods and services to bring about a given desired impact on national output and employment. In this situation, the home legislature might not approve— or be slow to approve—fiscal actions larger than those that would have been required before the increase in interdependence; this impasse can be characterized as an inability to use instruments as desired because of constraints imposed by boundary conditions. Alternatively, if changes in tax rates or government expenditures larger than those previously required were to be implemented, greater inefficiencies in achieving the nonstabilization objectives of the home government may result. (The additional inefficiencies may arise, for example, because government expenditure categories deviate by larger amounts from levels judged to be socially optimal from an allocative point of view.) In either case the home authority will be far from indifferent about the reduction in its autonomy brought about by the increase in interdependence.

Examples of boundary conditions and instrument-variation costs in the area of monetary policy are less common. Monetary instruments in most countries have variation costs that are relatively low. For example, policy actions may take the form either of frequent, small changes or of more intermittent, larger changes without generating obviously different costs.[31] Even with monetary policy, however, there are limits to the plausible size of policy doses. These limits can be considered a function both of the degree of openness of a nation and of its size in relation to the rest of the world. Imagine an open economy in three hypothetical situations that differ from each other because of, among other things, different degrees of substitutability by home residents between home-currency and foreign-currency assets. Assume that the expected values of the national own-variable multipliers for open-market operations in the three situations are (relative to each other) large,

30. See, for example, the discussion of instrument costs in Arthur M. Okun, "Fiscal-Monetary Activism: Some Analytical Issues," *Brookings Papers on Economic Activity, 1:1972*, pp. 123–63.

31. This statement is less plausible for policy actions such as changes in the central bank's discount rate. Moreover, the assertion deserves more careful analysis than it is possible to give it here.

average, and small. Suppose further that the sizes of open-market operations required to achieve a given impact on national target variables are equivalent to, respectively, 0.01 percent, 1 percent, and 10 percent of the nominal wealth of the nation's residents. Of the three situations, the first would obviously be least uncomfortable for the nation's central bank. There may be substantial doubt, moreover, about whether the central bank in the third situation can carry out open-market operations so large that they are equivalent to one-tenth of the wealth of national residents.[32]

Alterations in the expected values of national own-variable multipliers brought about by increases in interdependence might have still further implications for policy decisions. The prospective costs and benefits of "coordination" between the home and foreign policy authorities will be altered by changes in the relative effectiveness and the comparative advantage of national instruments. In turn, the changes in prospective costs and benefits might (perhaps even should) affect the willingness of the national authorities to consider more cooperative behavior. Even in the absence of cooperative behavior, the home authority will have to contend in the new situation with larger disturbances to home target variables caused by given-sized policy actions of the foreign authority.

The last few paragraphs ignore the consequences of increased interdependence for the variances of national policy multipliers. Now consider the same question again when uncertainty about the policy multipliers is introduced: Does it matter that the sizes of policy doses may have to be augmented to achieve any given expected impact on the nation's target variables?

The general presumption that policy actions should be less aggressive the more uncertain are the magnitudes of policy multipliers applies in particular to actions taken after a structural change increases the variances of multipliers. In such cases the risks of going wrong are enhanced for any given-sized doses of policy action. Other things being equal, so long as policymakers are averse to risk, the prudent course is to become more cautious and decrease the size of the policy dose (relative to the dose computed solely on the basis of the mean of the multiplier).

This general presumption has been established by economists working with theoretical models of a closed economy. But it is applicable a fortiori to an open economy: increases in interdependence will result in greater uncertainty about the national own-variable multipliers, which in turn implies the home policy authority should be more cautious. Focusing attention on the variances of dY^h/dX^h thus reinforces the conclusion that results from reasoning solely in terms of the expected values. When increases in interdependence occur, the home authority cannot fully compensate for reductions in the expected values of its policy multipliers simply by augmenting the sizes of policy doses.[33]

---

32. Lance Girton and Dale Henderson make use of the notion of a "plausible sized open-market operation" in their discussion of the effectiveness of monetary policy and relative economic size in "Critical Determinants of the Effectiveness of Monetary Policy in the Open Economy," in M. Fratianni and K. Tavernier, eds., *Bank Credit, Money, and Inflation in Open Economies,* a supplement to *Kredit und Kapital* (3:1977).

33. If interpreted literally, equations A-12, A-17, and A-37 in appendix A imply that policymakers should compensate for any changes in (the expected values of) the dY^h/dX^h multipliers by making proportional alterations in the size of the policy doses. Plainly, such an interpretation, by ignoring the degree of uncertainty associated with the multipliers, is wrong.

The result of this analysis of interdependence and autonomy can be stated succinctly in a summary proposition:

(12-N) **Policy multipliers for national instruments with respect to national economic targets will typically be reduced and made more unreliable by increasing economic interdependence.**

Strictly speaking, 12-N is a hypothesis yet to be verified. Nonetheless, it is frequently treated in what follows as an established proposition.

Interdependence and Disturbance Multipliers

The concept of a multiplier assumes that none of the exogenous variables in a structural model vary except the one whose multiplicative impacts are under consideration. The same is true for the concept of autonomy. To analyze the degree of autonomy is to ask the question: What are the incremental effects on Y^h of a given variation in X^h *if all the policy instruments of the foreign authority and all nonpolicy disturbances remain unaltered?*

The assumption of other exogenous forces remaining unchanged promotes analytical clarity. But there is no presumption that variation of X^h in actual practice will be unaccompanied by shocks generated by nonpolicy exogenous variables (the vector Z in chapter 11). Nor is there any presumption that the foreign authority will in fact refrain from altering the instrument settings X^f while the home authority is carrying out its policy actions.

When assessing the implications of interdependence for the overall performance of national economic policy, therefore, there is no logical basis for focusing attention solely on autonomy or solely on *policy* multipliers. It is no less relevant to analyze the impacts of the nonpolicy exogenous variables when other things are unchanged and to apply to them the label of *disturbance multipliers.*[34]

Under conditions of intermediate interdependence, analysis must distinguish among four groups of disturbance multipliers associated with nonpolicy exogenous variables. If a notation similar to that for policy multipliers is employed, these four groups may be designated as dY^h/dZ^h, the impacts of home disturbances on home variables; dY^f/dZ^h, the impacts of home disturbances on foreign variables; dY^h/dZ^f, the cross-national impacts of disturbances originating in the foreign country; and dY^f/dZ^f, the own-country impacts of foreign disturbances.[35]

The consequences of increasing interdependence for disturbance multipliers are not discussed in detail here. An analysis similar to that for policy multipliers, however, can—and in principle should—be carried out. Given some particular structural change that increases interdependence, the change in the expected values of the impact disturbance multipliers, dB, can be computed. In turn, dQ, a matrix of changes in the expected values of the final-form coefficients, can be derived.[36]

---

34. It seems inappropriate to speak of the "effectiveness" of nonpolicy exogenous shocks in influencing the various endogenous variables Y^h and Y^f. But the analytical parallel with policy multipliers is perfect.

35. All four groups of disturbance multipliers are embedded in Q, the final-form coefficient matrix defined in A-28 in appendix A.

36. As earlier, define $d\Gamma$, $d\Phi$, $d\Omega$, and $d\Lambda$ as the matrixes of changes in the original structural coefficients that define the increase in interdependence. The expected values of the impact disturbance multipliers

Comparisons can then be made of the expected values of all four groups of disturbance multipliers before and after the increase in interdependence. In principle, such comparisons can also be made of the variance-covariance matrixes for B and Q.[37]

No more evidence exists about interdependence and the international transmission of disturbances than about interdependence and autonomy. On the basis of reasoning analogous to that used in the last section, however, it seems plausible to formulate similar hypotheses. Specifically, consider the following proposition about the expected values of the disturbance multipliers:

(12-P) **The typical result of increases in interdependence is to reduce the absolute values of the means of both groups of own-country multipliers dY^h/dZ^h and dY^f/dZ^f, but to increase the absolute values of the means of the cross-national multipliers dY^f/dZ^h and dY^h/dZ^f.**

This proposition parallels hypothesis 12-C and predicts an analogous dilution of own-country effects and intensification of cross-national transmission.[38]

Next, consider a hypothesis dealing with the relative impacts of nonpolicy exogenous disturbances:

(12-Q) **Increases in interdependence will reduce the own-country impacts relative to the cross-national impacts of any given nonpolicy disturbances.**

This proposition can again be expressed more formally as a set of inequalities (the notation parallels that used in 12-E and 12-F).

(12-R) **For nonpolicy disturbances originating in the home economy:**

$$\frac{\overline{|dy^h_j/dz^h_i|}}{\overline{|dy^f_m/dz^h_i|}} < \frac{|dy^h_j/dz^h_i|}{|dy^f_m/dz^h_i|}, \qquad i = 1, \ldots, r.$$

(12-S) **For nonpolicy disturbances originating in the foreign economy:**

$$\frac{\overline{|dy^f_j/dz^f_i|}}{\overline{|dy^h_n/dz^f_i|}} < \frac{|dy^f_j/dz^f_i|}{|dy^h_n/dz^f_i|}, \qquad i = 1, \ldots, s.$$

following the increase in interdependence are given by

(12-7) $(B + dB) = -(\Gamma + d\Gamma)^{-1}(\Omega + d\Omega),$

and the change in the impact multipliers, dB, can be computed from

(12-8) $dB = [\Gamma^{-1} - (\Gamma + d\Gamma)^{-1}]\Omega - (\Gamma + d\Gamma)^{-1}(d\Omega).$

Combining 12-7 and the expression for $L + dL$ in 12-3 with the formulas for deriving the final-form coefficient matrixes (see appendix A) yields the new matrix $Q + dQ$, and hence dQ.

37. When the representation of economic structure is linear, any increases in interdependence that affect only the direct impacts of nonpolicy exogenous variables (Ω) will leave all policy multipliers unaffected. Similarly, any increases in interdependence that affect only the direct impacts of policy instruments (Φ) will not alter any of the disturbance multipliers. Presumably, however, the majority of increases in interdependence alter the interactions among the endogenous variables and hence lead to changes in Γ and Λ. In these more typical cases, the values before and after the change in interdependence are different for both the policy multipliers and the disturbance multipliers.

38. An analysis similar to that described earlier shows that proposition 12-P cannot be proved true or false independently of the signs and magnitudes of the particular coefficients in the underlying economic structure and independently of the origins of the increases in interdependence. Some types of increases in interdependence could conceivably increase rather than reduce the expected values of dY^h/dZ^h and dY^f/dZ^f. In such exceptional cases, however, the greater interdependence probably also has the effect of significantly augmenting the total, worldwide impact of the originating disturbance.

In 12-R, the inequality may not hold for every conceivable pair of home and foreign endogenous variables but is presumably correct when y_j^h and y_m^f are functionally similar variables in both countries. Similarly, the inequality in 12-S presumably holds true, if not in every case, then at least when the comparison of impacts on y_j^f and y_n^h is between functionally similar variables in the two countries.

If 12-Q through 12-S are correct, a closely related hypothesis about the comparative strengths of disturbances will probably also be true:

(12-T) **Increases in interdependence will diminish the comparative strength of disturbances that originate in the home nation relative to those that have foreign origins in influencing home target variables.**

Inequalities analogous to 12-R and 12-S can be specified to state the hypothesis 12-T more precisely.

What about the variances of the disturbance multipliers? Recall that proposition 12-K pertains to all structural coefficients. If 12-K is true, then:

(12-U) **Increases in interdependence will typically increase the variances of own-country disturbance multipliers.**

(12-V) **Increases in interdependence will typically increase the variances of cross-national disturbance multipliers.**

Despite the analytical parallelism between the hypotheses about disturbance multipliers and policy multipliers, the implications of the two sets of hypotheses for the decisions of a nation's policy authority are quite different. Other things being equal, the home authority is doubtless better off with more autonomy than with less. But the reverse is true with the own-country disturbance multipliers dY^h/dZ^h: other things being equal, the home authority will prefer to have a small, not a large, proportion of the impact of home-originating shocks remain at home. Nonpolicy shocks are troublesome to policymakers. The greater the transmission of home-originating shocks to foreign rather than home variables, the less the chances of the home authority's target variables being blown off course. On the other hand, since the home authority's target variables can be blown off course by any nonpolicy shocks wherever originating, the home authority will also prefer, other things being equal, to have low values for the cross-national multipliers dY^h/dZ^f.[39]

If propositions 12-P through 12-V are correct, the effects of increased interdependence on the disturbance multipliers are a mixed blessing for a nation's policy authority. The dissipation of own-country-originating shocks abroad *diminishes* the troublesomeness of disturbances. But an increase in the sizes of the cross-national multipliers dY^h/dZ^f *magnifies* it.

The consequences of interdependence for the impacts of nonpolicy exogenous variables require more analysis. The hypotheses ought to be refined further; and the implications of changes in the disturbance multipliers for policy decisions deserve a more systematic discussion. Even more important, analytical scrutiny

39. The qualification "other things being equal" is important in all these generalizations, for reasons discussed in chapter 13 and part 5. The beneficial aspects to an open economy of having the effects of home-originating shocks partly dissipated abroad are analyzed in chapter 23. See also, for example, Richard Cooper, "Worldwide or Regional Integration: Is there an Optimal Size of the Integrated Area?" *Economic Notes*, vol. 3 (Siena: Monte dei Paschi di Siena, 1974), pp. 28–31; and Peter B. Kenen, "The Theory of Optimum Currency Areas: An Eclectic View," in R. Mundell and A. Swoboda, eds., *Monetary Problems of the International Economy* (University of Chicago Press, 1969).

ought to be focused on the stochastic error terms, E_t and E, included as part of the original structural model in equations 11-6 and 11-13. Chapter 11 said little about the implications of these error terms for policy decisions. In practice, however, nonzero realizations of the error terms are just as much a nonpolicy "disturbance" as a change in some nonpolicy exogenous variable z_i^h or z_j^f. A complete analysis of the consequences of changes in interdependence, moreover, should ask—and try to answer—the question of whether increasing interdependence alters the properties of the stochastic processes generating E_t.[40]

Those difficult tasks, however, cannot feasibly be undertaken here. For the present, the reader must simply take the hypotheses 12-P through 12-V for what they are: a plausible, but still superficial, first pass at a complex problem.

40. When the structural coefficients in a model are treated as though they are fixed, known parameters, the stochastic error terms are then the only acknowledgment of uncertainty allowed into the analysis. In such circumstances, it is especially crucial to focus analytical attention on E_t. For a further discussion of this point, see chapter 17.

Interdependence and National Economic Policy: Controllability and National Welfare

CHAPTER 12 focuses on the consequences of increased interdependence for autonomy and for the impacts of nonpolicy disturbances. This chapter brings the discussion back to the national macroeconomic policy problem as a whole.

Interdependence and the Degree of Controllability

Controllability Constraints on National Policy Decisions

The home nation's policy authority makes use of a structural model summarizing its knowledge of the dynamic behavior of the entire world economic system. The coefficients in the final-form version of the authority's model—the policy multipliers R^h and R^f, the disturbance multipliers Q, and the other coefficient matrixes L^* and L^{**}—are a reflection of the underlying world economic structure. Given that structure, the interdependent evolution of the home and the foreign economies depends on four classes of driving forces (exogenous variables) and the original starting point (the initial conditions). Of the four types of exogenous driving forces, one—the instruments of home policy—is firmly in the hand of the home authority. The other three—the policy instruments of the foreign authority, the nonpolicy exogenous variables, and the stochastic disturbances—obviously are not controllable by the home authority. From the operational perspective of the home authority, therefore, the world economic system has the appearance:[1]

$$(13-1) \qquad Y = R^h X^h + S^h,$$

where all the "noncontrollable" aspects are grouped together as

$$(13-1a) \qquad S^h = R^f X^f + QZ + V$$

$$(13-1b) \qquad V = L^*U + L^{**}Y_0.$$

When the constraints facing the home authority are expressed as in 13-1, the main elements of the nation's policy problem stand out clearly. The authority has at its disposal certain instrument levers X^h, for which it can select whatever settings it thinks appropriate (subject to boundary conditions and instrument-variation costs). The fulcrum for transmitting the impacts of the levers to the nation's target variables is the set of multipliers dY^h/dX^h, which are embedded in R^h. The authority must be especially alert to the characteristics and reliability of this fulcrum—to the

---

1. The derivation of equations 13-1 is shown in appendix A.

degree of autonomy. But the authority must also pay close attention to the other three exogenous forces that drive the economic system. If there were no unexpected variations in S^h, there would be no need to readjust the time paths for the settings on X^h. In practice, variations in S^h occur constantly in a manner that cannot be accurately foreseen by the home authority. In particular, fluctuations in the non-policy exogenous variables (Z) cannot be unerringly forecast, and the impacts on endogenous variables of the fluctuations that do occur are especially uncertain because of uncertainty about the disturbance multipliers Q. The other nonpolicy shocks—represented in 13-1a as V, which depends on the fluctuations in the original structural disturbances (E)—are even less predictable. The final driving force—policy actions of the foreign authority—is difficult to predict because the policy multipliers R^f are uncertain and because information about X^f may be inadequate. And home authority projections for the $R^f X^f$ component of S^h are further complicated by decision dilemmas analogous to those confronting an oligopolist. There is a basic game-theoretic indeterminateness in the situation because the foreign authority as well as the home authority aspires to exert control over the interdependent economic system.

Stripped to its barest essentials, then, the home authority's decision problem at a point in time involves two tasks: (1) making the best possible projection for S^h, and then (2) choosing the particular combination of instrument settings $\hat{X}^h$ judged most likely to bring about the best, feasible time paths for national target variables. This decision problem can be characterized analytically as the minimization of the policymakers' formulation of the national loss function subject to their structural model of the national and world economy.[2]

Because the objectives embodied in the home loss function are assumed to be biased strongly, if not exclusively, in favor of the concerns of home residents, the home authority is not directly concerned about the entire equation system for the world economy. From the point of view of national welfare, the authority need only pay attention to the evolution of the home variables Y_t^h, and possibly only to the subset of those that are home ultimate-target variables. The criterion of *proximate* relevance would thus seem to permit the home authority to disregard a major part of the world equation system. Proximately, the authority need not be concerned with the effects its own policy actions will have abroad (the cross-national multipliers dY^f/dX^h) nor with the foreign own-variable multipliers dY^f/dX^f and the extent to which the foreign authority may be achieving the objectives of foreign economic policy. Proximately, any impacts on the evolution of foreign economic variables of nonpolicy disturbances that originate at home or abroad can also be ignored.

But the difficulty, of course, is that these other considerations are irrelevant to the home authority only in a proximate sense. While they do not affect national policy loss directly (because they are not proximately relevant in the equations that determine the time paths of home target variables), they do affect it indirectly. The world economy under conditions of interdependence behaves as a system; the nation's economy cannot be decoupled from the rest of the system for purposes

---

2. The decision problem at a point in time presupposes that policymakers have previously identified their loss function and have articulated the model that, in their judgment, least inadequately describes the nation's economy and its interdependencies with the rest of the world. The problem of model choice is discussed further in parts 4 and 5.

of analysis or policy control even if it is decoupled for the purpose of appraising national welfare.[3]

The game-theoretic indeterminateness stemming from the interaction of decisions by the home and the foreign authorities is the most important reason why neither national authority can afford to disregard part of the world economic system and concentrate its analytical attention on a national subsystem. Home-country choices for $\hat{X}^h$ depend critically on the projection for S^h. But the actual outcome for S^h depends critically on the instrument settings $\hat{X}^f$ selected by the foreign authority. In turn, $\hat{X}^f$ is chosen in the light of the expected behavior of foreign economic variables relative to the foreign authority's objectives. Ultimately, therefore, the home authority cannot ignore the parts of the world economic system that determine the foreign economic variables. It cannot afford to ignore the effects of its own actions on the foreign economy, and it does have to be concerned with the dY^f/dX^h and even the dY^f/dX^f groups of multipliers. Ultimately, it must be concerned with all four groups of disturbance multipliers, not just the two families dY^h/dZ^h and dY^h/dZ^f that are proximately relevant in the equations for the home target variables. An analogous argument applies to the perceptions and behavior of the foreign authority.

Just as national policymakers when formulating their decisions need to take into account the workings of the entire interdependent system and the likely decisions of its other would-be controllers, an appraisal of the overall potency of national policy must have a similarly broad scope. The degree of autonomy must somehow be assessed in relation to the other three exogenous forces that drive the world system. To put the issue in terms of the analytical framework of equations 13-1: How significant are the intensity and volatility of variations in S^h *in relation to* the national levers X^h and the fulcrum R^h which transmits the force of those levers to national target variables? Plainly, whatever the degree of autonomy, sufficiently frequent and powerful shocks generated by variations in S^h can blow the national economy off the course desired by the home authority. To appraise the overall potency of national policy, some method of analysis must be found for considering $R^h X^h$ and S^h together—for analyzing comprehensively the *degree of controllability* that a nation's policymakers have over national target variables.

Defining Controllability

The concept of controllability would be germane even in the case of a completely closed economy. Formal command over a wide range of policy instruments by the government of a closed economy would not guarantee that the government could closely control the evolution of economic activity. The existence of powerful and erratic nonpolicy exogenous disturbances, uncertainty about the general structure

3. It is not even conceptually possible to derive the final-form equation system in 13-1 unless the analysis starts from (a structural model of) the world economic system as a whole. Some important theoretical research has recently applied control theory to macroeconomic models and dealt directly with the questions of "decoupling" and "decentralization" of instrument assignment (that is, more than one controller). See, in particular, Masanao Aoki, "Noninteracting Control of Macroeconomic Variables: Implications on Policy Mix Considerations," *Journal of Econometrics*, vol. 2 (September 1974), pp. 261–81, and "On Decentralized Stabilization Policies and Dynamic Assignment Problems," *Journal of International Economics*, vol. 6 (May 1976), pp. 143–71; Nils R. Sandell, Jr., and others, "Survey of Decentralized Control Methods for Large Scale Systems," *IEEE Transactions on Automatic Control*, vol. AC-23 (April 1978), pp. 108–28.

of the economy, and uncertainty in particular about the government's policy multipliers would undermine the ability of the government to control the economy.

For a national economy that is relatively open, the number and intensity of nonpolicy exogenous shocks may be increased. Uncertainty about economic structure will certainly be increased. Policy multipliers will typically be reduced and made more uncertain. When appraising national economic policy under conditions of intermediate interdependence, therefore, there is a correspondingly greater need to raise the issue of the de facto degree of controllability.

Controllability as an analytical concept is beginning to receive attention in the economics literature. But it has been studied much more intensively in connection with the application of optimal control and systems theory in noneconomic contexts.[4] In the technical literature, a model composed of a system of dynamic equations is said to be controllable if it is possible to find a time vector of instrument settings that, over some finite interval of time, will transfer the system from some initial state to some other specified state. The conditions for controllability, if satisfied, imply that the decisionmaker who regulates the settings on the instruments can fully control the evolution of the dynamic equation system. To illustrate, an engineer can employ a dynamic equation system to describe the path of a ballistic missile from the initial moment of firing until it hits a target. An analysis of the controllability of the system will reveal whether it is possible, given the available instruments, to control the path of the missile to make it hit the correct target at the correct time.[5]

I do not know enough about control theory to write with confidence about the applicability of its concept of controllability to macroeconomics. At the moment I am inclined to agree with the view that it is of limited interest for macroeconomic theory and for most realistic macroeconomic models. Considerable work is now going forward in adapting control theory to economic problems, however, and this judgment may have to be revised.[6]

Certainly it is not sufficient when appraising the controllability of an economic system to demonstrate that it is possible to cause the system, for a momentary interval, to pass through some desired constellation of values for target variables. The relevant aim of economic policymakers is to move target variables—if they have deviated from best, feasible paths—back to those paths and then to keep them on, or close to, those paths.[7] The mathematics of control theory can apparently

4. For an early discussion of controllability in the economics literature, see Kenneth J. Arrow and Mordecai Kurz, *Public Investment, the Rate of Return, and Optimal Fiscal Policy* (Johns Hopkins University Press for Resources for the Future, 1970). For a recent summary and other bibliographical references, see Masanao Aoki, *Optimal Control and System Theory in Dynamic Economic Analysis* (American Elsevier, 1976), chap. 3.

5. This example is borrowed from Lars Nyberg and Staffan Viotti, "Controllability and the Theory of Economic Policy: A Critical View," *Journal of Public Economics*, vol. 9 (February 1978), pp. 73–81.

6. See, for example, the research and lengthy list of references cited in David Kendrick, "Applications of Control Theory to Macroeconomics," *Annals of Economic and Social Measurement*, vol. 5 (Spring 1976), pp. 171–90, and in Louis F. Pau, "Research on Optimal Control Adapted to Macro- and Microeconomics: A Survey," *Journal of Economic Dynamics and Control*, vol. 1 (August 1979), pp. 243–69. For control-theory research on economies other than that of the United States, see the papers and references in J. M. L. Janssen, L. F. Pau, and A. Straszak, *Models and Decision Making in National Economies* (North-Holland, 1979).

7. To continue with the Nyberg-Viotti example, the engineer's technical problem is solved once a launched missile explodes at the target. This is a considerably easier problem than the continuous targeting problem facing the policymakers in macroeconomics.

handle the problem of keeping target variables moving along desired paths indefinitely provided the dynamic model is one in which, among other things, the instruments are capable of continuous, unrestricted variation, and the coefficients are deterministic and known.[8] But those conditions are not characteristic of the models relevant for macroeconomic policy decisions. In policymakers' models, there is substantial uncertainty about the economic structure; continuous, unrestricted variation in some policy instruments is not feasible; and policy decisions should not be formulated solely on the basis of expected values of policy multipliers when the magnitudes of the multipliers are uncertain.

The technical concept of controllability as used in the control-theory literature seems especially inapplicable to the problems facing national policymakers under conditions of intermediate interdependence. These are preeminently situations where there are two or more would-be controllers making decisions. Given all the uncertainties and especially the game-theoretic indeterminateness that characterize these situations, the economic system is *not* completely controllable (technical definition) by just one of the controllers. Both sets of national policymakers, acting independently, cannot each move the entire world economic system to a state (much less retain such a state) where their national goals are fully achieved.

While the technical definition in the control-theory literature cannot be used, it is nonetheless important to be able to analyze the limited controllability that national policymakers do have. Here is another instance in international economics in which concepts and analysis are needed to deal with an intermediate situation, rather than an all-or-nothing approach dealing with polar cases.

Despite my current inability to provide a rigorous definition of the degree of controllability that is applicable to the analysis of national economic policy under conditions of interdependence, I nonetheless want to assume that such an analytical definition exists (and that, in due course, someone will develop it).[9]

The Consequences of Increased Interdependence

Given the hypotheses presented in chapter 12, what is the relationship between the degree of controllability of a nation's economy and its degree of openness? Specifically, does an increase in interdependence diminish controllability?

Proposition 12-N deals with the consequences of increased interdependence for the expected values and variances of national own-variable multipliers. The next

8. See the discussion of "perfect output controllability" in Aoki, *Optimal Control and System Theory in Dynamic Economic Analysis*, pp. 90–96.

9. As used in the control-theory literature—see, for example, Aoki, *Optimal Control and System Theory in Dynamic Economic Analysis*, chap. 3—"controllability," "complete controllability," and "perfect output controllability" are technical properties that dynamic equation systems either do or do not possess (unambiguously). One does not speak in this literature about "the degree of controllability." Nor are analytical techniques well developed to deal with situations of, so to speak, "very imperfect controllability." It is understandable why engineers and other users of control theory in applied contexts have concentrated on the establishment of necessary or sufficient conditions under which dynamic equation systems are controllable. In the typical applied context (for example, the ballistic missile case), models are of interest or relevance only if they are in fact controllable (technical definition). While engineers have little incentive to develop theory and analytical techniques for models that are imperfectly controllable, social scientists and particularly macroeconomists clearly do have such incentives. The concept of controllability I have in mind would be defined exclusively in terms of the structural model (that is, would not require reference to the loss function as well as the structural model). Such a definition would have the advantage of restricting the scope of the concept to technical characteristics of the model. Still broader concepts such as *policy successfulness* (see the final sections of this chapter) would be used to refer to policymakers' success in minimizing their particular loss function.

step in the logic is to specify explicitly the connection between autonomy and controllability:

(13-A)   Other things being equal, the greater is the degree of autonomy the greater the degree of control that a nation's policy authority can exert over national target variables.

This hypothesis describes, as it were, the partial derivative of controllability with respect to changes in the national own-variable multipliers. Presumably, there is little doubt about the correctness of 13-A: a reduction in autonomy with all else remaining unchanged would unambiguously worsen the prospect for controlling national target variables.

The consequences of increased interdependence for the expected values and variances of the various disturbance multipliers are identified in propositions 12-P through 12-V. From the perspective of control over the national economy by home policymakers, those consequences are a mixed blessing. Increases in interdependence magnify the likely effects on home target variables of some disturbances (particularly those originating abroad) but mitigate the likely effects of others (particularly those originating at home). Uncertainty about all the various effects is increased.

In the light of those earlier conclusions, consider next a proposition about the impacts of nonpolicy disturbances:

(13-B)   Other things being equal, changes in the impacts of nonpolicy exogenous disturbances on the various parts of the world economy may either diminish or enhance the controllability of the national economy. No broad generalization about the direction of the influences on controllability is possible because the influences vary in sign and magnitude depending, among other things, on the type and origin of the disturbances.

This hypothesis, like 13-A, is a statement about the partial derivative of controllability with respect to changes in one class of its determinants.[10]

Consider now three propositions bearing on still another set of critical determinants of the degree of controllability:

(13-C)   Other things being equal, the greater the expected impacts of foreign policy actions on the home economy and the more uncertain those impacts, the more limited the control a nation's policy authority can exert over national target variables.

(13-D)   Other things being equal, increases in interdependence exacerbate the game-theoretic uncertainties and complexities to which national policymakers are exposed.

(13-E)   Other things being equal, the more prominent the role played by game-theoretic uncertainties and complexities in the formulation of national economic policy, the more limited the control a nation's authority can exert over national target variables.

---

10. Proposition 13-B is written in broad language to cover the effects of variations in the stochastic error terms E_t as well as variations in Z_t.

The assertion in 13-C follows from propositions 12-C through 12-M. Hypothesis 13-E refers to *independent* controllability—the control that home policymakers can exert over home target variables without any coordination of decisions with foreign policymakers. Without doubt, issues of international cooperation and coordination are germane to national decisions under conditions of interdependence. The concept of controllability relevant to the discussion here, however, must refer to potential control in the absence of coordination.[11]

The degree of controllability thus depends, in principle, on all the characteristics of the world economic system 13-1. Proposition 13-A, taken in conjunction with 12-N, asserts that increases in interdependence affect the R^hX^h component of the world system in a way unfavorable to national controllability. Propositions 13-B through 13-E concern the net troublesomeness that the S^h component of 13-1 creates for controllability. In 13-C through 13-E, the ability of the home authority to control home target variables is asserted to be unambiguously weakened by the effects that increases in interdependence have on S^h; the component R^fX^f is more powerful, more uncertain, and more mutually interdependent with X^h. Hypothesis 13-B asserts that the effects of increased interdependence transmitted through S^h from the sources QZ and V could either improve the degree of controllability or further undermine it.

The relationships among the various concepts in the preceding discussion are summarized schematically in figure 13-1.

The conclusion of this analysis may be stated in a final hypothesis that builds on the earlier propositions in this and the preceding chapter:

> **(13-F) Increases in interdependence typically diminish the degree of control that a nation's policy authority can exert over national target variables. National policy decisions will therefore be more difficult to make, and more uncertain in their consequences.**

This conclusion is *not* formulated as an "other things being equal" proposition. Rather, the hypothesis refers to the *total* derivative of controllability with respect to increases in interdependence. In effect, 13-F presupposes that the consequences of increased interdependence for both the controlled (R^hX^h) and the noncontrolled (S^h) components of the equation system 13-1 have been investigated and that the various consequences have been appropriately netted in appraising the ability of the nation's policymakers to control the national economy.

Proposition 13-F is intuitively plausible. Future theoretical and empirical work, I believe, will show it to be a correct generalization. But for the time being its correctness should be regarded as moot. For certain types of increases in interdependence, other things being equal, an *improvement* in controllability could conceivably occur because of the changed impacts of nonpolicy disturbances (proposition 13-B). Furthermore, such an improvement could conceivably be large enough to outweigh the unfavorable effects on controllability of the reduction in autonomy (proposition 13-A) and the larger and more uncertain impacts of foreign policy on the home economy (propositions 13-C and 13-E).

11. The incentives to coordinate with foreign policymakers are probably inversely related to the degree of independent controllability of the home economy. Note also that the potential or actual gains from coordination cannot be analyzed without making use of a benchmark case in which national decisions are uncoordinated. Issues of international cooperation are discussed in chapter 25.

Figure 13-1. *Factors Influencing the Controllability of the Home Economy*

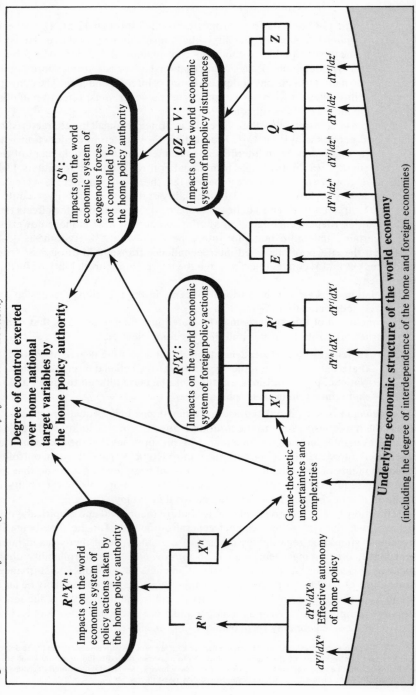

Degree of control exerted over home national target variables by the home policy authority

$R^h X^h$: Impacts on the world economic system of policy actions taken by the home policy authority

dY^f/dX^h dY^h/dX^h Effective autonomy of home policy

$R^f X^f$: Impacts on the world economic system of foreign policy actions

dY^h/dX^f dY^f/dX^f

S^h: Impacts on the world economic system of exogenous forces not controlled by the home policy authority

$QZ + V$: Impacts on the world economic system of nonpolicy disturbances

dY^h/dz^h dY^f/dz^h dY^h/dz^f dY^f/dz^f

Game-theoretic uncertainties and complexities

Underlying economic structure of the world economy
(including the degree of interdependence of the home and foreign economies)

See equation system 13-1. Arrows indicate directions of causal influence. The four types of exogenous driving forces of the world economic system—X^h, X^f, Z, and E—are enclosed in square boxes. The underlying economic structure of the world economy (see chapter 11 and appendix A for a mathematical representation) determines the coefficient matrices of the policy multipliers for home instruments (R^h), the policy multipliers for foreign instruments (R^f), and the disturbance matrix (Q).

The comments in chapter 12 pointing out the ignorance of the economics profession about the consequences of increasing interdependence for the autonomy of national economic policy apply with even greater force to the broader concept of controllability. A large amount of empirical and institutional information exists that could, if it were carefully and analytically sifted, shed light on proposition 13-F. But that sifting has not yet been done. Most of those concerned about the consequences of interdependence for national economic policy have not yet posed the question in an analytical manner, much less begun the process of accumulating the relevant evidence.

National Economic Welfare

Consider the following line of questioning: "If increasing economic interdependence typically reduces the effectiveness of a nation's policy instruments and undermines the ability of its policymakers to achieve national objectives, is that not an undesirable development? If so, is not increasing interdependence undesirable for the nation? What is more, would it not be advisable for the nation's policymakers to seek to restore a greater degree of autonomy and controllability by deliberate actions to reduce the openness of their economy?"

The last two of these questions *cannot* be answered *yes* on the basis of the analysis above. Appraising the consequences of interdependence for national welfare is an even more complex problem than appraising the consequences for autonomy and for controllability. Neither current theory nor empirical knowledge justify a generalization that increasing interdependence is likely to be harmful to a nation's economy. Nor is there a solid basis for prescriptions for reducing the degree of openness.

Because the subject is so complex, a balanced assessment of the implications of interdependence for national economic welfare will not be attempted here. What follows merely identifies several issues that inevitably arise in discussions of national macroeconomic policy.

For the purposes of this discussion, a general definition of national economic welfare will suffice. National economic welfare may be said to be greater, the greater the value of some national social welfare function—or, equivalently, the smaller the value of some national loss function. The analytical purpose of a social-welfare or loss function is to provide a normative ordering of alternative outcomes.[12] *National* loss functions refer to judgments about the aggregate well-being of those persons who reside in or are otherwise identified with "the nation." Not the least of the problems associated with the concept of national loss functions under conditions of interdependence stems from the likelihood that the nation will be somewhat better defined as a political unit than the national economy will be defined as an economic entity.

Plainly, some concept of national welfare, even if only vague and implicit, is a logical prerequisite for macroeconomic policy decisions and for normative evalu-

---

12. "Nonindividualistic" functions of the type relevant for appraising macroeconomic outcomes presuppose both interpersonal and intertemporal comparisons of individual welfares. Chapter 2 provides references on the concept of group welfare functions.

ations of what is good or bad for a nation. Therefore anyone interested in appraising national macroeconomic developments—policymaker or merely observer—must bring to that task a national loss function. So to speak, licenses authorizing the making of normative judgments about national well-being may only be issued to registered owners of a measuring stick.[13]

Measuring sticks need not have the same scales. Different appraisers may not wish to apply their measuring sticks to the same target variables. Thus different answers can be—and almost certainly will be—given to the question, What is the correct loss function to use in appraising national economic welfare? Critics may believe that the government is pursuing inappropriate objectives. If so, they will employ some loss function other than that being used by the nation's policy authority. The authority's function will itself be a complex compromise among the various loss functions preferred by the individuals or agencies making up the national authority. Uncomfortably relativistic though the conclusion may be, therefore, national economic welfare, like beauty, resides in the eye of the beholder.

Whether increasing interdependence is judged to be good or bad for a nation will thus be sensitive to the loss function used in ranking alternative outcomes. Two appraisers can reach different conclusions solely because of differences in their measuring sticks. For example, national loss functions can be nationalistic or internationalist—in the former case giving no weight, in the latter case giving a modest positive weight, to the welfare of individuals resident outside the home nation.[14] This banal point would not be worth stating here were it not so frequently ignored when generalizations are made about the implications of interdependence for national economic welfare.

Microeconomic considerations such as efficiency in resource allocation and income distribution may be at least as important in determining a nation's economic welfare as the aggregates traditionally emphasized in macroeconomics. Similarly, increasing openness of the economy will generate significant microeconomic benefits (for example, better resource allocation brought about by higher levels of international trade) and may generate microeconomic costs (for example, adverse effects on income distribution). Any balanced judgment about whether interdependence is good or bad for a nation must give prominence to microeconomic gains and losses.

The Performance of National Policymakers

Consider now the problem of appraising the overall performance of a nation's economic policy. The activities of the nation's policymakers may be judged in

13. Policymakers and their critics either do or do not want to make normative judgments. If they do, it may be a mistake to worry too much about the political and choice-theoretic niceties of whether nonindividualistic loss functions can be justified on ethical grounds. Compare Amartya K. Sen's pragmatic approach to social-welfare choices, as evidenced by his concluding observation in *Collective Choice and Social Welfare* (San Francisco: Holden-Day; London: Oliver and Boyd, 1970): "while 'pure' systems of collective choice tend to be more appealing for theoretical studies of social decisions, they are often not the most useful systems to study. . . . while purity is an uncomplicated virtue for olive oil, sea air, and heroines of folk tales, it is not so for systems of collective choice" (p. 200).

14. Some appraisers could be sufficiently cosmopolitan in outlook to use a *world* loss function that gives roughly equal weight (somehow defined) to the welfare of individual world citizens no matter where

relation to the goals specified ex cathedra by the appraiser or, alternatively, the goals that the policymakers themselves choose to pursue. Suppose an appraiser rejects the loss function used by the policymakers and substitutes a function he believes more appropriate. How then might that appraiser evaluate the performance of the policymakers? The appropriate procedures are straightforward in one sense. The appraiser should have the courage of his prejudices, superimposing his own "correct" loss function on actual or forecasted outcomes and pronouncing judgments on the basis of that measuring stick. For that particular appraiser, there is no ambiguity about which outcomes produce higher or lower levels of *welfare loss*.

But what of the contribution of policymakers in bringing about observed or forecasted outcomes? Do they deserve praise or blame for their *policy performance?* One difficulty stems from the slipperiness of the word performance. Consider the following statements:

> This nation's policymakers have the right idea about what is good for the country and they do a good job in bringing it about.

> I have nothing but admiration for the skillful way that policy is executed, but I abhor the objectives at which it is directed.

> Our policymakers have their hearts in the right place, but they are so clumsy they could botch the simplest imaginable task.

> We shudder to think how bad things could be if this lot of policymakers were adept enough to get from where they are to where they want to get to.

The differences among these evaluative statements bring out the fact that performance has, in principle, at least two dimensions. Policymakers need to be judged on their selection of the national loss function that guides policy decisions. But they also need to be judged on how well or poorly they perform in attaining the goals they have selected. The former aspect may be labeled *performance in choice of goals,* the latter *performance in technical implementation.*

For clarity in appraising the performance of policymakers, it is helpful to have still a third concept, *overall successfulness,* that refers to the degree to which economic developments conform to the objectives sought by the policymakers:

(13-G) Macroeconomic policy may be said to be more successful the smaller is the value of the particular loss function that underlies the decisions of those responsible for determining the settings on the instruments of national economic policy.[15]

Evaluation of the performance of policymakers in the choice of goals is inescapably a normative issue. Judging policymakers' performance in terms of their own chosen goals, on the other hand, has markedly less normative content. In the latter case, different appraisers may be able to agree on an objective evaluation even if they have different subjective views about the appropriateness of the chosen

---

they happen to reside. At the other extreme, some might be sufficiently hostile to foreigners to attach negative weight to the welfare of anyone resident outside the home nation.

15. The phrase "overall effectiveness of policy" is avoided in order to eliminate the confusion from using *effectiveness* in two different senses. *Effectiveness* in this book means only the effectiveness of policy instruments (the multiplier concept).

goals. It is a merit of the distinction between performance in choice of goals and the overall successfulness of policy that the obviously subjective and the more nearly objective aspects of analyzing performance are split off for separate consideration. For an appraiser who believes that the loss function used by the nation's policymakers is the correct function, the concepts "national economic welfare" and the "overall successfulness of policy" coincide. For appraisers who do not identify closely with the national government, they do not coincide.

Now consider the relationship between the overall successfulness of policy and the policymakers' performance in technical implementation. The two concepts are not coterminous even when the loss function of the national policymakers is accepted as given. When technical performance is skillful, successfulness is enhanced. Inept execution detracts from successfulness. But overall successfulness is also influenced, sometimes favorably and sometimes unfavorably, by many other factors.

The nation's economy may be likened to a ship manned by a crew of national policymakers. Suppose the objectives of a voyage have already been determined and are taken as given. The success of the ship's passage and the performance of her crew can both be evaluated in terms of the given objectives. The voyage will be more or less successful depending on, for example, whether and when the ship arrives in the designated port and whether the cargo is in good or bad condition. This evaluation of successfulness involves a straightforward comparison of goals and actual achievement. Appraising the performance of the crew, however, is more difficult. The success of the voyage depends in part on the skill of the crew in handling the ship. But for a fair evaluation of the crew's performance, it is also necessary to ascertain whether the sails and rudder were in good condition and whether the sextant and compass functioned accurately at the beginning of the voyage. Equally important, information is needed about the conditions encountered on the voyage; it is one thing to sail a ship with the benefit of fair, steady winds but quite another test of skill if the wind whips up into a typhoon.

Thus if one's analytical purpose is to appraise policymakers' performance in technical implementation, skill must somehow be isolated from the other factors that determine overall successfulness. In principle, such analysis should compare actually employed skills against best imaginable skills in the light of what best imaginable skills can feasibly accomplish.[16]

With national macroeconomic policy, there is only one ship of state and only one crew can man it at a time. Races that compare the performance of alternative crews when the weather conditions are identical are impossible. Nonetheless, an effort must be made to evaluate how well policymakers implement their chosen goals in the light of the degree of controllability of the national economy.

As seen by the policymaking crews charged with steering them, economic ships of state are poorly designed and ill equipped. The control instruments may be weak and unreliable. The degree of controllability, low in any case for a relatively closed economy, is further reduced as a nation's economy becomes more open to the rest

16. To continue the analogy, the ideal test of the relative skills of two different crews requires two identically designed and equipped ships. With each crew manning one of the ships, both should be asked to aim for the same destination and both should experience identical weather conditions. Differences in the successfulness of the two ships could then be attributed to differences in technical performance of the crews, and the former differences could be used as a measure of the latter.

of the world. Hence the overall successfulness of policy in a significantly open economy may depend much less on the skills of policymakers than on the controllability of the national ship and the weather conditions it meets on its voyages. A successful voyage may be attributable mainly to favorable winds, while an unsuccessful voyage may be caused primarily by bad weather rather than the ineptness of the crew.

Figure 13-2 schematically illustrates the relationships among the concepts of autonomy, technical performance, controllability, and overall successfulness. Note that the *foreign* policy authority's performance in choice of goals as well as its performance in technical implementation are determinants of the overall successfulness of *home* economic policy (and vice versa for the economic policy of the foreign country).

Until now, the discussion has treated the weather conditions—Z, E, and X^f—as troublesome from the point of view of home economic policy. Changes over time in Y_t emanating from these uncontrolled exogenous forces have been described as "disturbances" or "shocks." The impression may have been conveyed that it is better to have as few fluctuations over time in Z_t, E_t, and X_t^f as possible because such fluctuations, when they do occur, cause home target variables to deviate from desirable time paths.

That implicit assumption deserves more careful consideration. It is primarily *unforeseen* changes in the weather that cause difficulties. When fluctuations in Z_t, E_t, and X_t^f can be accurately predicted, some or all of their impacts may be offset through compensating changes in the time paths of the home instruments. Even more important, home target variables may already be off course at the time unforeseen changes in the weather occur. In such conditions, the unforeseen changes in the weather could help rather than hinder home policymakers in guiding their target variables back towards a preferred course.

Finally, when evaluating the consequences of changes in the weather, an analyst should distinguish between "troublesomeness" from the perspective of controllability and "badness" for overall policy successfulness or national economic welfare. Conceivably, a sequence of disturbances could *unfavorably* influence the controllability of the national economy but *favorably* influence national economic welfare.

Interdependence and Welfare

Consider now the question of whether increasing interdependence is good or bad for the overall successfulness of a nation's economic policy. Three points deserve to be stressed.

First, since unforeseen fluctuations in Z_t, E_t, and X_t^f can have either beneficial or adverse impacts on home target variables, *changes* in the impacts of those fluctuations brought about by increases in interdependence can either promote or undermine the successfulness of policy. Because a priori generalizations about the consequences for policy successfulness are not possible in the case of the original impacts and their net effects, generalizations about the net changes resulting from an increase in interdependence are also impossible.

Figure 13-2. *Factors Influencing the Overall Successfulness of Home Economic Policy*

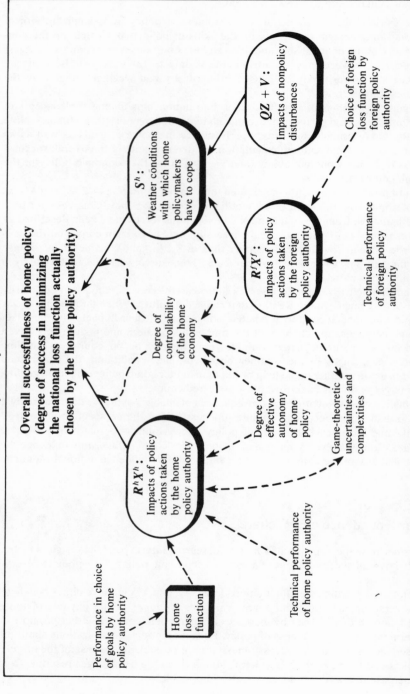

**Overall successfulness of home policy
(degree of success in minimizing
the national loss function actually
chosen by the home policy authority)**

Solid arrows represent causal influences as manifested in equation system 13-1. Dotted arrows indicate underlying causal influences. See also figure 13-1.

The second point amplifies the first. Increased interdependence alters the geographical impacts of fluctuations in Z_t, E_t, and X_t^f and thereby alters the overall successfulness of home policy. The direction of the net effects, however, is uncertain a priori. Nonpolicy disturbances originating at home are typically dissipated abroad to a greater extent after an increase in interdependence, while disturbances originating abroad have greater impacts than before on home target variables. Consider the following classification of unforeseen variations in S^h (that in turn are attributable to unforeseen fluctuations in Z_t, E_t, and X_t^f): (a) unforeseen disturbances originating at home that blow home target variables further off course; (b) unforeseen disturbances originating at home that promote the successfulness of home policy; (c) unforeseen disturbances originating abroad that impede the successfulness of home policy; and (d) unforeseen disturbances originating abroad that move home target variables back toward the preferred course.[17] When a disturbance of type a occurs, because of the openness of the home economy the successfulness of home policy is *less* adversely affected than would otherwise be the case; an increase in openness would further reduce the adverse effects of this type of disturbance. Openness of the economy is similarly helpful when disturbances of type d occur. But the reverse is true for disturbances of types b and c: increased interdependence either diminishes beneficial impacts or augments unfavorable impacts on home target variables. Are there a priori grounds for believing that disturbances of types b and c commonly predominate over types a and d, or vice versa? At this level of abstraction, agnosticism is the only reasonable position.

Third, the consequences of increased openness for the overall successfulness of policy can be influenced by the technical competence of the nation's policymakers. The theory of economic policy tends implicitly to assume that policymakers can and do turn in a satisfactory technical performance (given all the admitted difficulties). But when one's purpose is to appraise the successfulness of policy, the possibility has to be entertained that policymakers can be inept. Suppose a nation has policymakers who set sensible goals but have a propensity for varying instruments in a clumsy and highly destabilizing manner. If the technical performance of policymakers in the rest of the world is much better on average than in the home nation, the successfulness of home policy may be compromised least if the home economy is very open. Indeed, home citizens might be grateful for developments that *reduce* autonomy and controllability if they have no hope of substituting skilled policymakers for their incompetent incumbents. Analogously, if home policymakers are adept while policymakers in the rest of the world are not, an increase in interdependence might adversely influence the successfulness of home policy. Consideration of the technical performance of national policymakers thus undercuts in still another way any facile, unidirectional generalizations about the influences of economic interdependence on policy successfulness.

The three preceding points are equally relevant if an analyst changes the focus from policy successfulness and asks instead whether increasing interdependence is likely to be good or bad for a nation's economic welfare. If that most difficult of

17. Because this classification deals with unforeseen disturbances, it has limited operational significance for "today's" ex ante policy decisions. (Unforeseen disturbances occurring today and tomorrow, not yet being known, cannot influence today's decisions.) Once they become known ex post, however, "yesterday's" unforeseen disturbances can be a highly useful input into today's decisions. This point is discussed in parts 4 and 5.

questions is asked, moreover, highly normative considerations enter into the analysis at the outset. The complexity of the question is even greater, and the need for agnosticism still more evident.

Agnostic conclusions are ungratifying. This discussion of the interrelationships among economic interdependence, policy successfulness, and national economic welfare is no exception. But agnosticism is preferable to confusion. To paraphrase a comment once made by the British critic F. R. Leavis: the worst sin is to indulge in sweeping generalizations, not know what you mean, and not know that you do not know.

Part 3 has barely scratched the surface of the difficult problems associated with national economic policy in a world of several nations. And the issues discussed are merely a part of the larger set of problems associated with interdependence and national welfare broadly conceived. The economic policies of national governments are a subset of national policies. National welfare has other dimensions that may be just as important as the economic dimension. At some stage in the analysis of increasing interdependence among nations, considerations of politics, sociology, and culture must prominently enter the calculus, if not dominate it.

In the end, furthermore, economics will have to join forces with other disciplines in turning the analytical spotlight on the nation state itself. With few exceptions, this book forces the analysis into the conceptual boxes of *national* this and *national* that, treating nations as though they are well specified entities that any good practitioner of some other discipline (such as a political scientist or an anthropologist) can define.[18] But if national economies become progressively less well-demarcated as economic entities, can nations be sharply delimited as political or cultural entities? Could the concept of "nation" survive as a vigorous plant if it had to depend primarily on geographical roots for its sustenance? Today, even if a nation can be recognized as a political or a cultural entity, is it possible to say which attributes may be so normatively important that they justify preservation and which attributes may be allowed gradually to be corroded by increasing interdependence? Is it possible to preserve some national attributes while letting others be corroded—can nations get married to each other in some respects but not others?

All in all, the agenda of interdependence problems is lengthy and formidable. The appropriate approaches for tackling the problems are not clear theoretically, let alone empirically. The prospect for future research thus engenders humility. But—as when the Spanish explorer stared at the Pacific, silent, upon a peak in Darien—it also challenges analysts to revise old maps and old ideas.

18. Compare Thomas S. Kuhn's characterization of normal science as "a strenuous and devoted attempt to force nature into the conceptual boxes supplied by professional education." *The Structure of Scientific Revolutions,* 2d ed. (University of Chicago Press, 1970), p. 5.

PART FOUR

The Conduct of Monetary Policy in a Closed Economy

Macroeconomic Policy Actions
in a Closed Economy

PART 3 discussed macroeconomic policy without differentiating among policy instruments. Parts 4 and 5 refocus the analysis on monetary policy and on the ability of the central bank to use monetary instruments to achieve ultimate objectives. Two related questions command special attention: Which strategy for conducting monetary policy is likely to prove most effective? And what role should money play in the formulation and implementation of that strategy?

Part 4 returns to the closed-economy assumptions used in part 1. This expositional device facilitates the clarification of several issues in a simpler manner than is possible when both domestic and international considerations are analyzed jointly. With the conclusions of part 4 as an analytical point of departure, part 5 then reintroduces the interdependence of the nation's economy and the rest of the world.

This first chapter in part 4 states some fundamental points about monetary-policy actions, fiscal-policy actions, and their interrelationships. When appropriately modified, as will be seen in part 5, these fundamentals turn out to be especially important for the analysis of policy actions and autonomy in open economies.

Monetary-Policy Actions and Operating Regimes

What is a monetary-policy action? What are the instruments of monetary policy? A policy action is the time sequence of differences between benchmark and alternative time paths for an exogenous policy instrument (chapter 12). All exogenous policy instruments other than that involved in the policy action are assumed to remain fixed on their benchmark paths. That definition of a policy action is logically clear as far as it goes. But can it be given substantive content by specifying certain instruments as monetary-policy instruments? And is there a sound basis in actual practice to distinguish between exogenous instruments of monetary policy and endogenous noninstrument variables?

Identification of several of the instruments of monetary policy is relatively straightforward. The discount rate charged by the central bank on its lending to commercial banks and the various fractional reserve requirements imposed on the deposit liabilities of the commercial banks are examples. I use the term *straightforward* because there is usually little doubt about the appropriateness, for the purpose of analyzing policy decisions, of treating changes in the settings of these instruments as "exogenous" policy actions.[1] In most nations, changes in the

---

1. Other examples (important in some nations, absent in others) of variables that can be relatively straightforwardly identified as exogenous instruments of monetary policy include capital requirements for commercial banks, and ceilings or other limitations on the lending of commercial banks.

discount rate or in reserve-requirement ratios occur infrequently rather than daily or weekly in accordance with the central bank's routine operating procedures. Decisions to change the rate or the ratios typically occur at separate meetings called for that purpose and involve the entire decisionmaking apparatus of the central bank.[2]

Identification of the remaining exogenous instruments of monetary policy, however, involves greater conceptual difficulties. Consider the key case of open-market operations—the sale or purchase of various securities by the central bank against its own reserve liabilities. Superficially, there may not seem to be any ambiguity: open-market operations are transactions initiated by the monetary authority and may seem, self-evidently, to warrant the label "policy actions." But careful analysts must ask more probing questions. With what proximate objectives in mind does the central bank initiate its transactions? What are the normal operating procedures used to attain (or to try to attain) those objectives? How does the *operating regime*— the combination of the proximate objectives and the operating procedures—affect the volume and timing of open-market operations?

As a point of reference for a discussion of alternative operating regimes, it is helpful to use schematic representations of the budget statement and the balance sheet of the central bank. These are provided in table 14-1.[3] Note f to the table indicates the definitions of the various *reserve-money* aggregates—for example, net free reserves, the monetary base, the unborrowed monetary base—that result from the combination of several of the balance-sheet items.

Potential Instruments versus Actual Instruments

Given the schematic assumptions used in table 14-1, an open-market purchase of securities by the central bank results in an increase in security holdings (S^{CB}) matched by an equivalent increase in excess and total commercial-bank reserves (RX and RT). An open-market sale generates a decline in security holdings and an equivalent decline in excess and total reserves. Open-market purchases and sales are conducted with commercial banks or nonbank private economic units.[4]

Among the various items on the central bank's balance sheet, some are not even potential candidates for selection as an exogenous instrument of monetary policy.

2. Even with the discount rate and reserve-requirement ratios, the exogeneity of the instruments is not altogether straightforward. To grasp the conceptual ambiguity that exists, contrast three hypothetical procedures for resetting the discount rate. Under the first operating regime, acting under the instructions of the central-bank decisionmaking apparatus, a lower-level manager changes the discount rate at the beginning of every day to a level exactly 25 basis points above the previous day's closing level for some market-determined interest rate. Under the second regime, the decisionmaking apparatus agrees to review the discount rate monthly with a presumption that the discount rate will normally be set in a range some 0–50 basis points above the level of a market-determined interest rate. Under the third regime, the decisionmakers change the discount rate at irregular intervals; they give particular emphasis to their judgments about the likely "announcement effects" of a change and pay little attention to the level of market-determined interest rates. Under the first regime, and to a lesser extent under the second, the discount rate might more appropriately be characterized as an "endogenously determined policy variable" rather than an "exogenous instrument." Note, however, that the differences among all three regimes can be viewed as differences of degree rather than differences of kind. Even under the third regime, the central bank's behavior implies a so-called reaction function that makes the discount rate dependent on various "endogenous" variables and hence "endogenous" itself in some more ultimate sense. For further discussion of the exogenous-endogenous distinction, see chapter 18.

3. The balance sheet in table 14-1 is identical to that in table 5-1. Table 14-1 refers only to the central bank; later in the chapter the analysis brings in the accounts of the fiscal authority.

4. Table 14-1 assumes that all securities held by the central bank are liabilities of the fiscal authority. Although a more complex schematization would alter the details of what is said here and in the following chapters, the key points do not depend on the simplifications embodied in the schematic balance sheets.

Table 14-1. *Schematic Budget Statement and Balance Sheet of the Central Bank, Closed Economy*[a]

BUDGET STATEMENT

Receipts

$r_s(S^{CB})$ Interest earned on holdings of government debt securities[b,c]

Outlays

X^{CB} Current expenditures (for example, salaries)[d]

E^{CB} Transfer of excess interest earnings to the fiscal authority[e]

Z^{CB} Current budget surplus (plus) or deficit (minus) of the central bank

BALANCE SHEET[f]

Assets

RB Borrowings by financial intermediaries from the central bank (borrowed reserves)[c]

S^{CB} Holdings of government debt securities[g]

OA^{CB} Other assets (for example, buildings and real estate, other tangible assets)

Liabilities and capital accounts

RT Liquid claims of financial intermediaries on the central bank (total reserves),[d] subdivided into:

     RR Required reserves

     RX Excess reserves

CUR Currency in circulation

Dep^G Deposit balance of the government (fiscal authority) with the central bank[d]

NW^{CB} Surplus and capital accounts (net worth)

a. CB indicates the central bank and G, the fiscal authority. For the balance-sheet entries, a superscript on a symbol indicates the sector for which an item is an asset or net worth.

b. Other sources of central-bank income are ignored.

c. Interest payments by financial intermediaries on their borrowings and advances from the central bank are ignored.

d. For simplification, it is assumed that the central bank does not pay interest on any of its liabilities.

e. This item is assumed for expositional purposes to be positive (the typical case); the central bank could in principle have a net receipt of funds from the fiscal authority.

f. Some commonly discussed reserve-aggregate ("reserve-money") identities are defined as follows (see also chapter 5):

$$\text{Net free reserves:} \quad RF \equiv RX - RB.$$
$$\text{Unborrowed reserves:} \quad RU \equiv RT - RB \equiv RR + RF.$$
$$\text{Total reserves:} \quad RT \equiv RR + RX \equiv RU + RB.$$
$$\text{Monetary base:} \quad MB \equiv RT + CUR.$$
$$\text{Unborrowed monetary base:} \quad MBU \equiv RT + CUR - RB \equiv RU + CUR.$$

g. It is assumed that the central bank does not hold securities issued by private-sector economic units and that security holdings of the central bank are marketable liabilities of the fiscal authority.

Consider, for example, the volume of currency in circulation, CUR. Most central banks passively supply whatever amount of coins and notes the private sector wishes to hold. Therefore the item CUR is determined "endogenously" by the behavior of nonbanks and the commercial banks. Nonbanks change their holdings of coins and notes by making offsetting changes in their deposits with commercial banks. When a commercial bank experiences a significant reduction in its inventory of coins and notes, it replenishes the inventory by running down its reserve balance at the central bank; the central-bank balance sheet shows an endogenous increase in CUR offset by an equivalent decline in RX and RT.[5]

5. In principle, the central bank could decide to try to control the volume of currency in circulation precisely rather than passively supplying the amount demanded. In that event, CUR would become "exogenously" rather than "endogenously" determined.

Borrowings or discounts, RB, are another example. Given unchanged reserve-requirement ratios and an unchanged discount rate and discount policy, the amount of borrowing tends to be determined by the commercial banks. When a commercial bank initiates an increase or decrease in borrowings, excess reserves, RX, and total reserves, RT, are proximately increased or decreased by an equivalent amount.

The deposit balance of the fiscal authority, Dep^G, is yet another balance-sheet item that for practical purposes may be uncontrollable by the central bank. Decreases in the balance are proximately associated with increases in RX and RT, and vice versa for buildups. Finally, over short periods of time, changes in the other assets of the central bank, OA^{CB}, and changes in its capital accounts, NW^{CB}, are small or even zero; these magnitudes in any case are determined mainly by longer-run considerations and hence are essentially given from the point of view of alternative operating regimes.

In short, many variables on the balance sheet are uncontrollable or predetermined, at least in the short run. They cannot possibly serve as exogenous instruments.[6]

After the various endogenous items are eliminated from contention, there remain several different balance-sheet categories that are potential candidates for selection as the main exogenous instrument of monetary policy. "Potential" needs emphasis. In principle, a central bank could conduct its policy using several different operating regimes. Depending on the regime, a particular balance-sheet item could be an *actual* instrument. But not all *potential* instruments can be instruments in fact. Once a particular operating regime is chosen and used, at least one of the potentially exogenous balance-sheet categories will be endogenously determined as a by-product of the operating regime.

This last point is true simply because the actions of the central bank are limited by its budget and its balance-sheet constraints. When one category of assets on the balance sheet changes, some other category of asset or liability necessarily changes in an offsetting manner. For a central bank no less than for any other economic unit, the difference between the flow of receipts and the flow of expenditures over some time period—that is, "saving," or the current "budget surplus," or the "change in net worth"—is necessarily equal to the sum of changes in assets less the sum of changes in liabilities. In terms of the schematic budget statement and balance sheet:

$$(14\text{-}1) \qquad\qquad r_s S^{CB} - X^{CB} - E^{CB} \equiv Z^{CB}.$$

$$(14\text{-}2) \quad \Delta RB + \Delta S^{CB} + \Delta OA^{CB} - \Delta RT - \Delta CUR - \Delta Dep^G \equiv \Delta NW^{CB} \equiv Z^{CB}.$$

The budget constraint holds for flows over any discrete period of time. The balance-sheet constraint holds for stocks at every point in time, and—as in 14-2—for changes in stocks over any period of time.[7]

---

6. Institutions and procedures differ somewhat among countries. These differences influence which items on the central bank's balance sheet vary endogenously.

7. As in private-sector budget constraints, valuation effects (capital gains or losses) are assumed to be treated appropriately—that is, either excluded from both the changes in assets and liabilities and the surplus of receipts less expenditures over the period, or systematically included in both. Time subscripts are not shown explicitly for any of the variables in the identities 14-1 and 14-2, nor for the variables in any of the other identities in this chapter. The analytical frame of reference, nonetheless, is the same multiperiod, dynamic context used in part 3. The reader should think in terms of period-by-period time paths for the

The mere existence of these constraints means that it would be nonsense for an analyst to conceptualize the change in every potentially exogenous item on a central bank's balance sheet as independently exogenous in fact. The constraints also serve to alert analysts to the subtle interplay between the size and composition of a central bank's balance sheet and the central bank's ability to control financial variables that are *not* items on its balance sheet.

Consider the following rearrangement of 14-2:

(14-2a) $\Delta NW^{CB} - \Delta OA^{CB} - \Delta RB + \Delta CUR + \Delta Dep^G \equiv \Delta S^{CB} - \Delta RT.$

When each magnitude in the identity is considered individually, the only two that can potentially serve as an exogenous instrument are S^{CB} and RT. Each variable on the left side of 14-2a is uncontrollable and endogenous in the sense previously described. Suppose that the central bank wishes to designate RT as an actual exogenous policy instrument. It then follows from 14-2a as a matter of arithmetic that S^{CB}, a potential *exogenous* instrument in some other operating regime, will have to vary correspondingly (*endogenously*) by whatever amount is required to keep RT on its exogenously fixed time path. Alternatively, suppose S^{CB} is designated as an actual exogenous instrument. In that case, RT will necessarily vary endogenously. Finally, suppose the central bank conducts open-market operations in a manner that continuously fixes some variable not on its balance sheet on an exogenously chosen time path (for example an interest rate; see below). Then S^{CB} will be endogenously determined as a result of fixing that variable; determination of S^{CB} will be sufficient to determine RT (endogenously); *no* item on the central-bank balance sheet can accurately be described as an exogenous instrument of monetary policy.

How, it may be asked, can total reserves, RT, be characterized as a potential exogenous instrument and even be designated (in some operating regime) as an actual exogenous instrument? When the private sector's demand for currency changes, when commercial banks initiate changes in their borrowings, and when the fiscal authority changes its deposit balance, total reserves are proximately altered by an equivalent amount. Why does not this endogenous behavior of CUR, RB, and Dep^G make RT endogenous as well? This question underlines the necessity of being precise about alternative operating regimes and the difference between actual as opposed to merely potential exogenous instruments. Total reserves will be an endogenous variable if the central bank passively allows variations in CUR, RB, and Dep^G to induce variations in total reserves. On the other hand, it is *possible* for the central bank to convert RT into an exogenous instrument. The required procedure involves continuous monitoring of CUR, RB, and Dep^G and the execution of open-market operations sufficient to offset any of the endogenous fluctuations in those three magnitudes that would otherwise push RT off its exogenously selected path. That is, the central bank must conceptualize its balance sheet as:

(14-2b) $\Delta RT \equiv \Delta S^{CB} - (\Delta CUR - \Delta RB + \Delta Dep^G - \Delta OA^{CB} + \Delta NW^{CB}),$

it must set an exogenous time path for RT (a period-by-period sequence of ΔRTs),

---

levels of all variables (for example, S_t^{CB}, S_{t+1}^{CB}, S_{t+2}^{CB}, . . .) or, equivalently, a time sequence of changes in the variables (ΔS_t^{CB}, ΔS_{t+1}^{CB}, . . ., where Δ is the first-difference operator).

and it must then vary the amount of ΔS^{CB} (in effect, endogenously) to neutralize unwanted variations in the balance-sheet items within the parentheses in 14-2b.

By reasoning analogous to that explaining the potential exogeneity of total reserves, it is easy to see that virtually any composite aggregation of balance-sheet items *can* be an exogenous instrument if the central bank chooses to make it so. Consider, for example, the unborrowed monetary base ($MBU \equiv RT + CUR - RB \equiv RU + CUR$). In this case, the central bank must think in terms of

$$(14\text{-}2c) \qquad \Delta MBU \equiv \Delta S^{CB} - (\Delta Dep^G - \Delta OA^{CB} + \Delta NW^{CB}),$$

it must determine an exogenous path for MBU, and it must vary open-market operations to offset undesired fluctuations in Dep^G, OA^{CB}, and NW^{CB}. With the unborrowed monetary base as an exogenous instrument, the central bank does not need to neutralize endogenous fluctuations in currency demand or borrowing by commercial banks; changes in CUR or RB will affect the composition of the unborrowed base, but not its total amount.

If the central bank chooses to do so, can it control any composite of its balance-sheet items *precisely?* Technically, the answer is presumably *yes*. Accurate data on its own balance sheet are available to the central bank day by day; in principle data can be made available hour by hour. No doubt precise control of the unborrowed monetary base is an easier task than precise control of unborrowed reserves, which in turn is easier than precise control of total reserves. But it is typically feasible to attain a high degree of precision when controlling any of the composite balance-sheet aggregates—provided, of course, that the central bank devotes its energies to doing so.[8]

In the paragraphs that follow, the main alternative operating regimes of monetary policy are classified and briefly characterized. At the most general level, operating regimes may be divided into two classes: *instrument regimes* and *intermediate-target regimes*. Within each class, different families may be distinguished, which in turn may be further subdivided.

Instrument Regimes

The distinguishing characteristic of instrument regimes is that the central bank focuses its operating procedures only on variables over which it has full control— that is, on instruments per se.

Consider first the family of instrument regimes in which the central bank selects a short-term, market interest rate as its proximate focus and stands ready to conduct open-market operations in whatever volume needed to maintain this interest rate on some prespecified time path. Regimes of this type may be referred to as *interest-rate instrument regimes*. Several different interest rates—an interbank lending rate (such as the federal funds rate in the United States) or a short-dated government

---

8. Banking "float" and some other minor balance-sheet items not allowed for explicitly in table 14-1 make the question of precision of instrument control somewhat less straightforward than is implied in the text. Moreover, here again the institutional details vary somewhat among countries. A purist theorist may argue that any variable having the slightest endogenous (and therefore stochastic) component cannot be controlled "superprecisely." For such a purist, the only balance-sheet item that is a "true" instrument (potential and actual) is the central bank's portfolio of securities, S^{CB}. Practical central bankers need not, in my opinion, give much weight to this purist view. The practical definition of a potential instrument is a variable that can be controlled with a high degree of precision (but not necessarily superprecision).

security rate (such as the ninety-day Treasury-bill rate in the United States)—may be potential candidates for this exogenous instrument variable. Hence there may be several alternative regimes even among interest-rate instrument regimes.

For an interest-rate regime to qualify as an instrument regime, the central bank must have the power to control the interest rate precisely, at least over the short run. That in turn means the central bank must be willing to execute a sufficiently large volume of transactions in the particular asset whose interest rate is the instrument variable.[9]

Conceivably, the central bank may wish to focus its operating regime on an interest rate, say a long-term corporate bond rate, even though it cannot precisely control that rate. (It may not be able to control the corporate bond rate precisely because, for example, it holds few corporate bonds in its portfolio and is not willing to conduct potentially large-scale open-market operations in corporate bonds.) However, if such an operating regime is attempted, it should be characterized as an intermediate-target regime (see below) with an interest rate serving as the intermediate target.

In an interest-rate instrument regime, it is natural to define an exogenous policy action in terms of the interest-rate instrument itself—for example, a reduction of 25 basis points in the interbank lending rate (relative to the time path that would otherwise have been followed). When an interest rate is the main exogenous instrument, both the volume of open-market operations and the various reserve-money aggregates become endogenous by-products of the interest-rate instrument regime.

Consider next *reserve-aggregate instrument regimes*. The distinguishing characteristic of this family is that the central bank uses a reserve-money aggregate as its proximate operating focus. As suggested by the numerous aggregates shown in note f to table 14-1, this family includes a wide variety of alternative potential operating regimes. Although some differences among reserve-aggregate regimes are important, it is their similarities that are of interest here.[10]

Under every reserve-aggregate instrument regime, because open-market operations are directed at achieving an exogenous time path for some particular reserve aggregate, short-term market interest rates fluctuate freely to take on whatever value is dictated by demand-supply conditions in the market. The choice of a reserve-aggregate instrument regime instead of an interest-rate instrument regime permits the central bank to fix a quantity on its balance sheet, but at the expense of giving up direct control over an associated market price. Subject to minor qualifications, it is possible for the central bank to fix exogenously either an interest rate or a reserve aggregate, but both cannot be fixed exogenously at the same time.[11]

9. The central bank may not always need to execute transactions to maintain the rate at a desired level. Private-sector participants in the market may anticipate central-bank transactions to correct deviations if they are sure of the level of the rate to which the central bank is currently committed.

10. The list of alternative reserve aggregates includes (but is not restricted to) total reserves, unborrowed reserves, excess reserves, net free reserves, the monetary base, the unborrowed monetary base, unborrowed reserves plus the government deposit balance, and the unborrowed monetary base plus the government deposit balance. Conceivably, the security holdings of the central bank can be used as the instrument aggregate; S^{CB} is the balance-sheet item that can be controlled with the greatest degree of precision (see note 8 to this chapter).

11. The central bank has at its disposal other instruments: the discount rate and reserve-requirement ratios. Theoretically, the central bank could employ open-market operations to fix an interest rate exog-

Under reserve-aggregate instrument regimes, exogenous policy actions are naturally defined in terms of the instrument aggregate—for example, an increase of $500 million in unborrowed reserves (relative to the time path that would otherwise have prevailed). The central bank's balance-sheet constraint under this family of regimes is no less binding than in the case of interest-rate regimes: selection of one reserve aggregate as the exogenous instrument means that other balance-sheet aggregates necessarily become endogenous by-products of the chosen regime.[12]

The interest-rate and reserve-aggregate instrument regimes described above are pure cases: the central bank makes a once-and-for-all choice of the variable to use as its main operating instrument. Another possibility is that the central bank can alternate between the pure cases; for example, it can decide at the beginning of every month whether *for that month* it will use a market rate of interest or a reserve aggregate as its main exogenous instrument.[13] Using yet another alternative (the most technically sophisticated of all), the central bank can focus its operating procedures on, in effect, the relationship between an interest rate and a reserve aggregate; which of the two variables should be deemed the exogenous instrument under such procedures is conceptually ambiguous and in any case of minor import for monetary-policy decisions.[14] The family of operating regimes that includes the more complicated possibilities described in this paragraph may be designated *mixed instrument regimes*.

Intermediate-Target Regimes

The distinguishing characteristic of the second main class of alternative operating regimes is their use of an intermediate-target strategy. Decisions focus on a key intermediate variable and are made in two stages: first, in some manner a target time path is derived for the key intermediate variable; second, the actual instruments of policy are varied so as to try to make the key intermediate variable track as closely as possible along its target time path. Intermediate-target operating regimes differ from instrument regimes because of this two-stage method of policy implementation.

By definition a variable is an exogenous instrument if it is *possible* for policymakers to control that variable precisely, and if in fact they *actually* do so; there can be no slippage between the setting on the instrument the policymakers intend to achieve and the setting they actually achieve. In contrast, an intermediate

---

enously while simultaneously using the discount rate (proximately influencing RB) and reserve-requirement ratios (proximately controlling required reserves RR) so as to determine exogenously a reserve aggregate. In practice these two other instruments cannot be used, or at least are not used, in the continuously flexible manner that would be required. Moreover, the central bank does not have accurate, current information on the deposit liabilities of commercial banks; this information would be necessary for precision control of a reserve-money aggregate by means of the reserve-requirement ratios.

12. For example, if unborrowed reserves is chosen as the operating instrument, then open-market operations, ΔS^{CB}, are directed at attaining a prespecified time sequence of ΔRUs; total reserves, net free reserves, and the monetary base all vary endogenously.

13. See John Kareken and others, "Determining the Optimum Monetary Instrument Variable," in *Open Market Policies and Operating Procedures: Staff Studies* (Board of Governors of the Federal Reserve System, July 1971).

14. This alternative is analyzed by Stephen F. LeRoy, "Efficient Use of Current Information in Short-Run Monetary Control," Special Studies Paper 66 (Board of Governors of the Federal Reserve System, Division of Research and Statistics, September 1975).

variable is removed from instrument variables by one or more steps in a chain of behavioral causation. It can be influenced—and conceivably even controlled fairly closely—by diligent adjustment of the instrument variables. But there can be some slippage between the actual and the desired values of the intermediate-target variable, with the amount of slippage being uncertain ex ante. If a variable cannot be controlled precisely, it should be designated and analyzed as an intermediate endogenous variable.

In principle, the class of intermediate-target operating regimes contains many families. One family could focus on various long-term interest rates as the intermediate target of monetary policy. Various definitions of bank credit could be associated with another family. The key intermediate variable could be the "q" ratio emphasized by the Yale portfolio-balance approach to financial markets (that is, the ratio of the market value of financial claims on the nation's capital stock to the replacement cost of that capital stock).[15] In principle, any intermediate variable—even the stock of unsold houses or the production of television sets—could be the focus of an intermediate-target regime for monetary policy. In this book, however, the main interest in these regimes is in those that use some definition of money as the key intermediate variable.

Within the family of intermediate-target regimes that focus on a monetary aggregate, there is a need for a further two-way classification. First, some particular monetary aggregate must be selected as the key intermediate variable. Second, for any given definition of money (M), something further must be specified about the actual instruments of policy that are manipulated so as to try to keep M on its target path. The choices for the main exogenous instrument are analogous to the alternatives for instrument regimes: some short-term, market rate of interest; some reserve aggregate; or some mixed combination of an interest rate and a reserve aggregate.[16]

Policy actions in an operating regime in which a monetary aggregate serves as intermediate-target variable cannot be defined unambiguously. In particular, fluctuations in the intermediate-target variable over the short run cannot be interpreted or modeled solely as exogenous policy actions. The central bank, even if it attempts to do so, cannot achieve an intended level for M day by day or week by week. Although the central bank can indubitably exert a significant influence on (various definitions of) M, the degree of control is by no means tight enough to warrant characterization of M as an instrument. On the other hand, if the central bank works diligently at the objective of minimizing deviations of M from a target path, then M is also very different in its behavior from other intermediate endogenous variables not serving as a proximate focus of policy decisions. To describe an intermediate-

---

15. See James Tobin, "A General Equilibrium Approach to Monetary Theory," *Journal of Money Credit and Banking,* vol. 1 (February 1969), pp. 15–29; and James Tobin and William C. Brainard, "Asset Markets and the Cost of Capital," in Bela Belassa and Richard Nelson, eds., *Economic Progress, Private Values, and Public Policy: Essays in Honor of William Fellner* (Amsterdam: North-Holland, 1977), pp. 235–62. The following passage appears in William C. Brainard and James Tobin,"Pitfalls in Financial Model Building," *American Economic Review,* vol. 58 (May 1968, *Papers and Proceedings, 1967*): "the valuation of investment goods relative to their cost is the prime indicator and proper target of monetary policy. Nothing else, whether it is the quantity of 'money' or some financial interest rate, can be more than an imperfect and derivative indicator of the effective thrust of monetary events and policies" (p. 104).

16. In addition to its main operating instrument, each intermediate-target regime also employs the discount rate and reserve-requirement ratios as actual instruments.

target regime accurately, it thus is essential to specify further details of how the operating regime works in practice. For example, it is essential to specify whether—and if so, how and how often—the level or the rate of change of the target path for M is periodically adjusted in the light of past "misses" (observed deviations of M from the previously selected target path).

Why Does the Choice of Operating Regime Matter?

Some readers may be dubious about the relevance of alternative operating regimes for the analysis of the macroeconomic effects of monetary-policy actions. In fact, however, this subject has broad significance and is not merely a technical detail of concern only to those with specialized knowledge of central-bank institutions and operating procedures.

As the preceding discussion shows, it is not a trivial problem to pinpoint the actual instruments of monetary policy and to define the exogenous policy actions whose macroeconomic effects require study. The list of potential policy instruments is considerably longer than the list of actual instruments. Even more important, the identification of the actual instruments of monetary policy and the specification of the operating regime by which monetary policy is implemented are inseparable aspects of one larger analytical problem. Attempts to analyze "policy actions" without being precise about the associated operating regimes are bound to be misleading and can easily lead to incorrect conclusions.

The crucial point is that the impacts on the economy of a policy action depend critically on the operating regime used by the monetary authority. When "non-domestic" exogenous policy actions are analyzed in part 5, the interrelationships between those policy actions and the operating regime of "domestic" monetary policy will be seen to be of primary importance. Even when analysis is restricted to domestic monetary policy itself, however, the point has substantial force.

A concrete illustration helps to elucidate. Suppose the central bank announces that, as an "easing" action to stimulate the economy, it is reducing the reserve requirement it imposes on the deposit liabilities of commercial banks. Let this change be characterized as an exogenous monetary-policy action (the reserve-requirement ratio is one of the instruments of policy) and suppose one wants to analyze its effects on variables such as aggregate output, employment, and the price level.

At the preexisting levels of interest rates, prices, deposits, loans, and other endogenous variables, commercial banks in the aggregate will have more excess reserves (RX) and more borrowings from the central bank (RB) than they wish to hold in their portfolios. The banks will have an immediate inducement to alter the composition of their existing balance-sheet positions and to adjust their lending behavior. The consequences of banks' adjustments in turn will induce private nonbank economic units to change the composition of their balance sheets and to alter their borrowing, spending, and saving decisions.

Suppose as a first case that the central bank is operating with a reserve-aggregate instrument regime, with unborrowed reserves (RU) as the main instrument.[17] Under this regime, since the reduction in the reserve-requirement ratio does not give rise

17. The entire set of instruments comprises unborrowed reserves, the reserve-requirement ratio, and the discount rate.

to any change in the time path for RU, the central bank does not execute any open-market operations additional to those previously planned for the purpose of keeping RU on its exogenously determined path.[18] As a result of the banks' efforts to adjust their portfolios, and then subsequently the adjustments made by nonbanks, short-term interest rates will initially fall, the banks will begin to repay borrowings from the central bank,[19] and loans and deposits at banks will begin to rise.

Now suppose instead that the central bank implements monetary policy with an interest-rate instrument regime with the interbank lending rate as the instrument. Under this second regime, the previously planned exogenous setting for the inter-bank lending rate will remain unchanged after the reduction in the reserve-requirement ratio, and the central bank will, as always in this regime, execute whatever volume of open-market operations is required to keep the interbank lending rate at its previously planned setting.[20] Under this regime, however, the required volume of open-market operations will be different after the reduction in the reserve-requirement ratio than it otherwise would have been. The efforts by banks and nonbanks to make portfolio adjustments will lead initially to incipient downward pressure on the interbank lending rate. To keep that rate at its previously planned setting, the central bank will have to undertake additional open-market sales of securities; the volume of unborrowed reserves and excess reserves will correspondingly be reduced. Excess reserves will fall substantially further than in the first case where the central bank operates with a reserve-aggregate instrument regime. With an interest-rate instrument regime, the central bank in effect will take away with its left hand (open-market sales) a sizable portion of the excess reserves it had supplied with its right hand (the reduction in reserve requirements).

Now consider the effects of a reduction in the reserve-requirement ratio under the assumption that the central bank follows an intermediate-target regime focused on a monetary aggregate, say M_j, with the interbank lending rate as the main actual instrument. Initial incipient downward pressure on the interbank lending rate will be resisted by open-market sales of securities (as under the second operating regime). Subsequently, however, as further data for M_j accumulate and as the central bank observes deviations in M_j from its previously planned (and unchanged) target path, the central bank will be induced to alter its setting for the interbank lending rate. That revised instrument setting will in turn induce further endogenous changes in open-market operations and the supply of commercial-bank reserves. As in the second case, the central bank will be reducing excess reserves with its left hand after having initially increased them with its right hand through the reduction in reserve requirements. But the amounts of alteration carried out by the

18. This assumes that the central bank does not change its time path of settings for the instrument RU at the same time as it reduces the reserve-requirement ratio. It could change the settings on both instruments simultaneously, of course, but then one would have to analyze a package policy action rather than the single-instrument action hypothesized in the text.

19. Borrowed reserves, RB, and hence also RT, will fall "endogenously" as a result of this behavior of the commercial banks; the instrument RU, however, will not deviate from its previously planned setting.

20. Note that the previously planned setting for the interbank lending rate need not be a constant level of the rate; as for all instrument variables, it is defined as a time path. The central bank could decide to change its previously planned setting for the interbank lending rate simultaneously with the reduction in reserve requirements; but there would then be a package policy action to be analyzed rather than the action assumed in the text. Analysis of package as opposed to single-instrument actions does not change the point that the impacts of policy actions may differ greatly under different operating regimes.

left hand will obviously differ, just as the actual time paths of the interbank lending rate under the two operating regimes will differ.

Thus, under each of the three operating regimes—in the short run and, in all likelihood, over any longer run—the balance sheet of the central bank, the levels of market interest rates, and the levels of various monetary aggregates will be significantly different. Furthermore, the shorter-run and longer-run outcomes for output, employment, and the price level will be significantly different. Hence the question, What are the effects on the economy of a reduction in reserve requirements?, is not even properly defined until the operating regime for monetary policy has been fully specified.

Fiscal-Policy Actions and Budgetary Operating Regimes

In this section, which continues to deal with the nation's economy as though it is closed to the rest of the world, analogous questions are asked about fiscal policy: What are the instruments of fiscal policy? What more precisely are the fiscal-policy actions whose effects on the economy are of concern to policymakers and analysts?

As in the last section, it is helpful to anchor the discussion to a schematic representation of the relevant budget statement and balance sheet. Hence table 14-2 presents those accounts for the government (fiscal authority). Many distinctions important in actual government budgets are suppressed in table 14-2 because they would complicate the exposition without altering its conclusions. The budget and balance-sheet identities corresponding to the schematic accounts are:[21]

(14-3) $$T_d + T_n + E^{CB} - X_d - X_n - r_s S \equiv Z^G.$$

(14-4) $$\Delta Dep^G + \Delta OA^G - \Delta S \equiv \Delta NW^G \equiv Z^G.$$

Fiscal policy as usually conceived is primarily concerned with the budget flows—the various items in identity 14-3. Attention here is therefore initially confined to those receipts and outlays. The "financing" of a budget surplus or deficit—the categories in identity 14-4—is considered subsequently.

When analyzing budget flows, the first distinction to make is between items in the fiscal authority's accounts that are potentially exogenous instruments and items that will be endogenous whatever budgetary operating regime is employed. Many government expenditures and transfer payments—for example, social security retirement benefits, unemployment assistance, outlays for which obligations were made in previous periods—are relatively uncontrollable. They can be altered only if existing legislation or contractual commitments can be changed.[22] For most analytical purposes, such items have to be treated as endogenous. Interest payments on the government debt (the product of the outstanding stock of government securities, S, and the rate of interest, r_s, paid on those securities) are another

---

21. It is again assumed that capital gains and losses attributable to price changes during the period are treated appropriately. The symbols are defined in table 14-2. The balance sheet in the table is identical to that in table 5-2.

22. For illustrations in the budget of the United States, see the discussion of "relatively uncontrollable outlays" in each year's official budget documents—for example, *The Budget of the United States Government, Fiscal Year 1980*, pp. 47–48, 560–61.

category of outlays that needs to be treated as endogenous.[23] In contrast, other expenditures and transfer payments can be straightforwardly treated as discretionary, and hence potentially exogenous.

A similar situation prevails on the revenue side of the budget. Because of political or institutional constraints, many tax rates (strictly speaking, the tax functions or schedules) are unchangeable over the analytical horizon relevant for macroeconomic stabilization policy. For practical purposes, those tax rates must be taken as institutional givens; the corresponding revenues are unambiguously endogenous. It may be feasible, however, to make discretionary alterations in other tax rates. Consequently, these latter tax rates—or, conceivably but much less plausibly, the amounts of revenues that they generate[24]—are potential exogenous instruments.

To suggest these analytical distinctions, the schematic budget in table 14-2 decomposes aggregate tax revenues and aggregate outlays other than interest payments into "discretionary" (T_d and X_d) and "nondiscretionary" (T_n and X_n) groupings.

Another budget item is a potential exogenous instrument: the size of the budget surplus or deficit itself (Z^G). It may or may not be thought sensible for the fiscal authority to set a particular value for Z^G as a proximate objective (strictly speaking, a particular time path for Z^G, period by period). But some governments have done so.

Thus, in principle there are several broad budget categories, each of which, taken separately, can be utilized as an exogenous instrument of fiscal policy. A change in any of those items taken separately—a change in the time path of discretionary outlays, a change in the tax rates capable of discretionary variation, a change in the time path of the surplus itself—can be regarded as a potential fiscal-policy action.

It is again essential, however, to distinguish between *potential* and *actual* exogenous instruments. The fiscal authority can conduct its budgetary policy using several different operating regimes. Each potentially exogenous budget category can be an actual exogenous instrument in *some* operating regime. But it would be a logical contradiction to suppose that all potential instruments can be actual instruments in the same regime. Once a particular regime is selected and put into use, at least one of the potentially exogenous budget categories necessarily becomes determined endogenously as a by-product of the operating regime.

That point is of course a tautology that follows from the budget constraint. When the items in 14-3 are reordered, the identity is:

(14-3a) $$T_n - X_n - r_sS + E^{CB} \equiv X_d - T_d + Z^G.$$

23. Some of this interest is paid to the central bank (r_sS^{CB}). As suggested by table 14-1, these interest earnings may be the primary receipt item in the central bank's budget. "Excess earnings" of the central bank, E^{CB} (that is, current receipts less current expenditures less additions to capital and surplus), are shown in tables 14-1 and 14-2 as paid to the fiscal authority. From the perspective of the fiscal authority, this deposit of excess central-bank earnings reduces the net outlays for interest payments on the government debt.

24. Theoretically, one can imagine the fiscal authority exogenously fixing the intended amount of discretionary revenues, T_d, and then continuously varying the corresponding tax rates so as to keep actual T_d in line with the intended value for T_d. However, since changes in tax rates typically require legislative action and cannot be varied continuously (indeed, fiscal authorities may occasionally despair of varying any tax rates even at discrete intervals), it is more plausible to regard the discretionary tax rates as the exogenous instrument. The amount of corresponding revenue generated, T_d, is then—subject to the given exogenous tax rates selected—an endogenous quantity.

Table 14-2. *Schematic Budget Statement and Balance Sheet of the Fiscal Authority, Closed Economy*[a]

BUDGET STATEMENT	
	Receipts
T_d	Tax revenue for which the tax schedules can be discretionarily varied as an instrument of policy
T_n	Nondiscretionary revenue (associated tax schedules cannot be discretionarily varied)[b]
E^{CB}	Receipt from the central bank of excess interest earnings[c]
	Outlays
X_d	Expenditures and transfer payments that can be discretionarily varied as an instrument of policy[b]
X_n	Nondiscretionary expenditures and transfer payments other than interest payments on the government debt (cannot be discretionarily varied because of, for example, contractual commitments or existing legislation)[b]
$r_s(S)$	Interest payments on government debt securities
Z^G	Budget surplus (plus) or deficit (minus)

BALANCE SHEET	
	Assets
Dep^G	Deposit balance of the fiscal authority with the central bank
OA^G	Other assets of the government (for example, tangible assets)[b]
	Liabilities and balancing item
S	Debt securities issued by the government,[b,d] subdivided into holdings by:
S^{CB}	Central bank
S^B	Financial intermediaries
S^N	Nonbank private sector
NW^G	Balancing item[e]

a. G indicates the fiscal authority; CB, the central bank; B, the commercial bank sector (financial intermediaries); and N, the nonbank sector. For the balance-sheet entries, a superscript on a symbol indicates the sector for which an item is an asset or net worth.

b. In most countries government-owned enterprises engage in the production of "goods" as well as of conventional government "services." For simplification, the revenues, current expenditures, investment expenditures, capital assets, and financial liabilities associated with these goods-producing activities are suppressed in this schematization.

c. Assumed to be positive (see table 14-1, note e).

d. All debt securities issued by the government are assumed to be marketable; distinctions are not made among securities as to date of maturity.

e. This is usually a negative item corresponding to the net claims on the government of the private sector.

Considered individually, the magnitudes on the left side of this identity are endogenous (in the sense of being uncontrollable or predetermined) from the perspective of the fiscal authority. Two of the right-hand variables—discretionary expenditures, X_d, and the budget surplus, Z^G—are potentially exogenous. The amount of discretionary revenue generated, T_d, is endogenous but the discretionary tax rate itself is potentially exogenous. For purposes of exposition, this tax rate is designated θ. As is clear from inspection of the identity, only two out of the three variables θ, X_d, and Z^G can be actual exogenous instruments in any budgetary operating regime.

The main alternative operating regimes for budgetary policy are briefly identified below.

Consider first the regime that uses the discretionary tax rate and the magnitude of discretionary expenditures as the two exogenous instruments. Once the time paths for θ and X_d are chosen, the path of the budget surplus, Z^G, and of course the paths of the remaining budget flows are determined endogenously. This regime is the least complex of the alternatives to operate. It is also the one that analysts of fiscal policy tend to think of first when asked to be precise about how budgetary policy is implemented. "Policy actions" take the form of a specific change in the time path of θ or the path of X_d. Both θ and X_d qualify fairly well as "instruments" by the criteria given earlier, and this regime can therefore be labeled an instrument regime. I refer to this alternative as the *discretionary-expenditure regime*.

A second plausible regime uses θ and the budget surplus (or deficit), Z^G, as the two exogenous instruments of budgetary policy. In addition to a path for θ, the fiscal authority selects a time path for the intended budget surplus and conducts itself so that the actual surplus coincides with this preselected exogenous path. How can this be done in practice? The fiscal authority will continually adjust X_d so as to offset any fluctuations in other budget categories that would otherwise lead to deviations of the actual from the intended surplus. The required adjustments in X_d mean that X_d is de facto endogenous. The surplus can be described as an "instrument" in an analogous sense to total reserves being an instrument in a reserve-aggregate instrument regime for monetary policy. There, open-market operations, ΔS^{CB}, are continuously adjusted ("endogenously") to keep the reserve aggregate, RT, on an exogenously fixed path. Here, with an *exogenous-surplus regime* for budgetary policy, discretionary expenditures, X_d, are the variable that is endogenously adjusted to keep the exogenous instrument, Z^G, on path.[25]

One further family of budgetary operating regimes is of practical interest. These alternatives may be designated *composite budget-aggregate regimes;* they fall into the middle ground between a discretionary-expenditure regime and an exogenous-surplus regime. The exogenous instruments in these regimes are the discretionary tax rate and a composite budget aggregate. For example, the composite aggregate might be the sum of discretionary expenditures and interest payments on the government debt $(X_d + r_s S)$; if so, the fiscal authority will conceptualize the budget identity as:

(14-3b) $$(X_d + r_s S) - T_d \equiv T_n - X_n + E^{CB} - Z^G,$$

and will then select exogenous time paths for θ and for the composite quantity enclosed in parentheses. Discretionary expenditures, X_d, will be adjusted dollar for dollar to offset (endogenous) movements in interest payments, $r_s S$. The total of $(X_d + r_s S)$ will thereby be kept on its exogenously fixed path. In such a regime, X_d itself and also the budget surplus, Z^G, are endogenously determined. "Policy actions" take the form of changes in θ or changes in the path of $(X_d + r_s S)$.[26]

---

25. In theory an exogenous-surplus regime could employ X_d and Z^G (rather than θ and Z^G) as the two exogenous instruments of budgetary policy. In such a regime, however, the discretionary tax rate, θ, would have to be continually adjusted in an "endogenous" manner so as to keep Z^G on its exogenously fixed path. Given the practical difficulties of making frequent, closely calibrated changes in tax rates, this regime has little practical relevance in actual policymaking situations.

26. Examples of other candidates for the composite budget aggregate include the sum of nondiscretionary and discretionary expenditures $(X_d + X_n)$ and the total of all outlays including interest payments $(X_d + r_s S + X_n)$. For a theoretical study in which a composite budget-aggregate regime is contrasted with a discretionary-expenditure regime, compare Model I and Model II in James Tobin and William Buiter,

I have characterized all these budgetary regimes as *instrument regimes*. It needs to be acknowledged, however, that the difficulties encountered in using certain budget aggregates as exogenous instruments are greater than the analogous difficulties in monetary operating regimes. Strictly speaking, the instrument concept should refer only to variables for which there cannot be any slippage between the actual and the intended setting. If stringent standards of controllability are applied, some of the budgetary instruments described above fail this test.[27]

In fact, whatever budgetary operating regime may be chosen, difficulties may be encountered in controlling the "instruments" with sufficient precision. The problems of information and execution are least troublesome for the discretionary-expenditure regime but even then are not trivial.

An analyst finicky about definitions could argue that the difficulties of using the budget surplus or composite budget aggregates as instruments warrant a relabeling of the exogenous-surplus regime and the composite budget-aggregate regimes as intermediate-target regimes instead. Despite the difficulties, I believe instrument regimes is a more accurate characterization.

Are there any "genuine" intermediate-target regimes for budgetary policy? As far as I know, no economist or policymaker has recommended such alternatives. What might such regimes involve? Can one imagine the fiscal authority focusing on, say, personal disposable income as an intermediate-target variable? Would it be feasible and desirable for the fiscal authority to set a target path for personal disposable income and then to bend all its operating efforts—using (say) X_d and θ as instruments—toward achievement of that target path? Would a better intermediate variable be inventory investment in the manufacturing sector? Consumer expenditures on automobiles?

These speculations seem farfetched. Why is it, however, that intermediate-target regimes for fiscal policy seem farfetched, yet the use of money as an intermediate-target variable for monetary policy seems so intuitively correct to monetary economists as to border on orthodoxy? If intermediate-target strategies are sensible for monetary policy, why should it not be sensible to apply an analogous approach to fiscal policy? This question provides grist for the critical analysis of money strategies in the chapters to follow.

As with monetary-policy regimes, it is important in macroeconomic analysis to

---

"Long-run Effects of Fiscal and Monetary Policy on Aggregate Demand," in Jerome L. Stein, ed., *Monetarism* (Amsterdam: North-Holland, 1976), pp. 273–309. The Tobin-Buiter Model I is somewhat analogous to the use of θ and $(X_d + r_s S)$ as exogenous instruments; it assumes that when debt interest payments increase, discretionary expenditures are curtailed correspondingly. The Tobin-Buiter Model II corresponds to the model used in Alan S. Blinder and Robert M. Solow, "Analytical Foundations of Fiscal Policy" in Blinder and others, *The Economics of Public Finance* (Brookings Institution, 1974), pp. 3–115, where X_d by itself and θ are the exogenous instruments. (Actually, since Tobin and Buiter do not consider nondiscretionary expenditures and nondiscretionary tax rates, their Model I could equally well be described as an exogenous-surplus regime.) Apropos of their Model II, Tobin and Buiter comment that it "credits a given fiscal policy with expansionary effect just because interest rate increases or deficits raise outlays for debt interest. Some might regard this procedure not as constant fiscal policy but as an ever more expansionary policy" (p. 281).

27. For example, the most problematic of the potential instrument variables is the surplus Z^G. To use Z^G successfully as an exogenous instrument, the fiscal authority must have accurate, up-to-date information on every single budget category; Z^G can only be kept on an exogenously fixed path if discretionary expenditures can be continuously adjusted to offset fluctuations in other budget categories. Somewhat less information is required in a composite budget-aggregate regime, since in that case the need for information is restricted to the items making up the composite budget aggregate.

differentiate among alternative operating regimes for budgetary policy. The impacts of a particular fiscal-policy action depend critically on the budgetary regime actually used by the fiscal authority.

Institutional Procedures for the Financing of a Budget Surplus or Deficit

The options available to the fiscal authority for financing a budget surplus or deficit are evident from its balance-sheet identity:

$$(14\text{-}4) \qquad \Delta Dep^G + \Delta OA^G - \Delta S \equiv Z^G.$$

A deficit ($Z^G < 0$) must be financed through some combination of reduction in the government's deposit balance at the central bank, reduction in its other assets, or increase in its debt liabilities. A surplus must be financed through some combination of debt retirement, building up the government's deposit balance at the central bank, or accumulation of other assets.[28]

If these financing options are considered from a narrow fiscal-policy perspective, how much reliance can the fiscal authority place on each of them? And to what extent can ΔOA^G, ΔDep^G, and ΔS be construed as exogenous fiscal-policy actions?

Much of the variation in OA^G may represent changes in tangible assets. Another part of the variation may be associated with nondiscretionary expenditures, X_n, or nondiscretionary receipts, T_n. And ΔOA^G may frequently be small relative to the size of the budget surplus or deficit. Consequently, in the majority of situations ΔOA^G may be an endogenous and nondiscretionary, rather than a potentially exogenous, variable from the perspective of the fiscal authority (at least from the perspective of macroeconomic stabilization policy). Typically, little reliance can be placed on it as a contribution towards financing the surplus or deficit (indeed, ΔOA^G may often have the "wrong" sign).[29]

Institutional procedures with respect to the government's deposit balance at the central bank vary significantly across countries. But in most countries short-run fluctuations in the balance tend to be reversed over a medium run; for periods of several months or longer, ΔDep^G is thus small relative to the budget surplus or deficit. If the fiscal authority sets a narrow planned range for Dep^G and maintains the average level of the balance within that range, consistency with earlier definitions suggests that the balance (and hence the time sequence of values for ΔDep^G) should be described as both a potentially exogenous variable and an actual exogenous instrument. Under those conditions, however, Dep^G is a relatively unimportant instrument: its setting is changed little over time. Hence ΔDep^G is of only transitory significance as a method of financing the budget surplus or deficit and can, for practical purposes, be treated as an institutional datum.

---

28. The identity 14-4 holds for all time periods (with capital gains and losses appropriately excluded from or included in both sides of the identity).

29. These generalizations are less valid the more important nationalized industries are in the nation's economy. Another financing possibility excluded from the exposition in the text (because of the simplifications used in table 14-2) is that the fiscal authority may hold deposit balances with the commercial banks; these balances may move up or down with short-run changes in the budget surplus or deficit.

Given the preceding assumptions about ΔOA^G and ΔDep^G, the fiscal authority has only one significant method for financing a budget imbalance. Necessarily, the bulk of a surplus or deficit is financed with retirements or new issues of debt:

$$(14\text{-}4a) \qquad\qquad Z^G \approx -\Delta S.$$

Under these circumstances, the fiscal authority is not free to select Z^G and ΔS independently. If the fiscal authority tries to operate an exogenous-surplus budgetary regime, its choice of an exogenous path for Z^G necessarily implies a more or less closely corresponding (endogenous) path for ΔS. If the fiscal authority operates with a discretionary-expenditure regime or a composite budget-aggregate regime, the endogeneity of Z^G in those regimes necessarily implies a corresponding endogeneity for ΔS.

Changes in S can take the form of changes in the central bank's holdings of government debt (ΔS^{CB}), changes in the holdings of the private sector (ΔS^P), or both. Note that ΔS^{CB} and ΔS^P are *net* changes (over whatever period or sequence of periods is being examined). Central bank holdings can change as a result of direct transactions (new issues or retirements) between the fiscal authority and the central bank, or as a result of open-market purchases or sales by the central bank with the private sector. The holdings of the private sector can change either as a result of direct transactions with the fiscal authority or as a result of market transactions with the central bank. Hence:

$$(14\text{-}5) \qquad\qquad \Delta S \equiv \Delta S^{CB}_{direct} + \Delta S^{CB}_{market} + \Delta S^{P}_{direct} + \Delta S^{P}_{market}.$$

By definition, $\Delta S^{CB}_{market} \equiv -\Delta S^{P}_{market}$. Thus the sum of the second and the fourth terms on the right side of 14-5 is identically zero; taken individually, however, those two terms typically are not equal to zero.

Alternative institutional procedures exist for the *initial* financing of a budget imbalance. Consider first the polar case in which existing statutes or established policy prevent the fiscal authority from selling or redeeming any of its debt in direct transactions with the central bank (hence $\Delta S^{CB}_{direct} \equiv 0$). Whatever surplus or deficit exists in the budget position must then be initially financed by retirements or new issues of S with nonbanks and the banking system:

$$(14\text{-}6) \qquad\qquad \Delta S \approx \Delta S^{P}_{direct} = \Delta S^{P}_{direct} + \Delta S^{CB}_{market} + \Delta S^{P}_{market};$$

$$(14\text{-}6a) \qquad\qquad \Delta S \approx \Delta S^{P} + \Delta S^{CB}_{market}.$$

This case may be termed *initial full financing by the private sector*. When American economists think of a "pure" fiscal-policy action, they usually have in mind a combination of a change in tax rates or discretionary expenditure plus just such an initial full financing of the resulting budget imbalance by means of bond sales or retirements with the private sector.[30]

Even if a budget surplus or deficit as it occurs is initially financed entirely with the private sector, the central bank *may* decide to undertake open-market opera-

---

30. Alternatively, a "pure" fiscal-policy action is sometimes defined as a "balanced-budget increase in government spending"—that is, an increase in expenditures exactly offset by a corresponding increase in revenues. The motive behind this latter definition is often to avoid consideration of the complex analytical questions that arise in connection with financing a budget imbalance.

tions—in accordance with whatever monetary operating regime it is following. Thus, for any given period one may observe $\Delta S^{CB} \neq 0$ even though $\Delta S^{CB}_{direct} = 0$. To the extent that the central bank does conduct open-market operations, net changes in the holdings of government debt by the private sector will not correspond even approximately to the budget surplus or deficit:

$$\Delta S = \Delta S^P_{direct}$$

but

$$\Delta S^P = \Delta S^P_{direct} + \Delta S^P_{market} \neq Z^G.$$

The budget imbalance is only partially financed with the private sector *in fact* despite the institutional procedure that requires full private-sector financing *in the first instance*.[31]

In the opposite polar case, existing statutes or established policy prevent the fiscal authority from engaging in any debt transactions directly with the private sector ($\Delta S^P_{direct} \equiv 0$). All financing of a surplus or deficit in this case must initially occur through retirements or new issues of debt with the central bank:

(14-7) $$\Delta S \approx \Delta S^{CB}_{direct} = \Delta S^{CB}_{direct} + \Delta S^{CB}_{market} + \Delta S^P_{market};$$

(14-7a) $$\Delta S \approx \Delta S^{CB} + \Delta S^P_{market}.$$

This procedure, which resembles institutional practices in several European countries, may be labeled *initial full financing by the central bank*. A change in S^{CB}, even if the result of direct transactions with the fiscal authority, results in a change in commercial-bank reserves. Hence, with this institutional procedure, analysts may speak of the budget surplus or deficit being financed in the first instance entirely by the destruction or creation of "central-bank money."[32]

Of course in this case, too, the central bank may decide to conduct open-market operations with the private sector. If the government budget is in deficit and the central bank is directly acquiring additional claims on the government in the first instance, for example, some fraction of those additional claims might promptly be passed on to the private sector through open-market sales ($\Delta S^P \neq 0$ even though $\Delta S^P_{direct} \equiv 0$). Despite the *initial* full financing by the central bank, the de facto outcome can involve partial or even complete private-sector financing.[33]

The real situation with respect to initial financing in most countries falls between the two polar cases. Typically, a fiscal authority engages in some debt transactions directly with the central bank and some debt-management operations directly with

---

31. The change ΔS^{CB} and consequently the net change ΔS^P need not bear any relation to the budget imbalance. For example, a budget deficit at a rate of $10 billion could conceivably be accompanied by an increase of more than $10 billion in open-market purchases by the central bank (and hence "negative" private-sector financing of the deficit) or alternatively open-market *sales* by the central bank ("overfull" financing of the deficit by the private sector).

32. The text continues to assume that, apart from transitory fluctuations, the fiscal authority's deposit balance at the central bank is held within a narrow planned range. In many discussions of "money-financed budget deficits," it is not sufficiently emphasized that *central-bank money* is not the same thing as, and not necessarily highly correlated with, *money* in the broader sense of chapters 4 through 9.

33. Again, in principle, ΔS^{CB}_{market} need bear no relation to Z^G, so that the relevant fraction could even be greater than unity or, conceivably, negative (with the central bank adding *more* government securities to its balance sheet over a period than the amount generated by the budget deficit).

the private sector; the initial financing of a budget imbalance is therefore mixed between the private sector and the central bank. Whatever the initial financing pattern, moreover, it may be subsequently modified through open-market operations of the central bank.

It is unclear how much significance should be attached to the institutional procedures that govern the initial financing of a budget imbalance. Differences among the procedures could be unimportant: whatever the initial breakdown of ΔS between ΔS_{direct}^{CB} and ΔS_{direct}^{P}, open-market operations could be used to obtain some given ultimate division of ΔS between ΔS^{CB} and ΔS^{P}. Some analysts of macroeconomic policy also argue that differences among the initial financing procedures should be of little significance. From the perspective of the private sector, it is virtually irrelevant whether the fiscal authority, the monetary authority, or both engage in government bond transactions with the private sector so long as the net amounts of the transactions are equivalent. Furthermore, it is not the initial financing breakdown but rather the ultimate time paths for ΔS^{P} and ΔS^{CB} that matter for the evolution of the economy. Thus, according to this view, the fiscal authority and the central bank have an obligation to forge a consensus on the goals of overall macroeconomic policy and to cooperate in implementing that policy. The consensus policy should produce essentially the same ultimate financing outcome whatever the institutional details with respect to the initial breakdown of ΔS into ΔS_{direct}^{P} and ΔS_{direct}^{CB}.[34]

In what follows the phrase *fiscal-policy operating regime* is used to denote a budgetary operating regime plus the institutional procedures that characterize the initial financing of the budget surplus or deficit.

The Consolidated Government Budget Constraint

It is impossible to discuss the financing of a budget surplus or deficit without getting entangled in monetary policy. At this point, therefore, it is helpful to consolidate the budget and balance-sheet constraints faced by the central bank and the fiscal authority into a combined constraint for the government as a whole.[35]

---

34. The contrary view, that full integration of the actions of the fiscal authority and those of the central bank is *not* desirable, is considered in chapter 18. Whether or not they should have significance, in most countries the institutional procedures for initial financing of a budget imbalance probably do have a nontrivial influence on the ultimate breakdown of ΔS into ΔS^{CB} and ΔS^{P}. For an analytical study germane to this issue, see Bent Hansen, "On the Effects of Fiscal and Monetary Policy: A Taxonomic Discussion," *American Economic Review*, vol. 63 (September 1973), pp. 548–55.

35. Although the consolidated government budget constraint has more often than not been ignored in the literature on macroeconomic theory, its implications have been more widely appreciated in recent years. Important references on the subject include: Carl F. Christ, "A Simple Macroeconomic Model with a Government Budget Restraint," *Journal of Political Economy*, vol. 76 (January/February 1968), pp. 53–67; and "Econometric Models of the Financial Sector," *Journal of Money, Credit, and Banking*, vol. 3 (May 1971), pp. 419–49; Karl Brunner and Allan H. Meltzer, "Money, Debt, and Economic Activity," *Journal of Political Economy*, vol. 80 (September/October 1972), pp. 951–77; Alan S. Blinder and Robert M. Solow, "Does Fiscal Policy Matter?" *Journal of Public Economics*, vol. 2 (November 1973), pp. 319–37; and Blinder and Solow, "Analytical Foundations of Fiscal Policy"; Stein, ed., *Monetarism;* Ettore F. Infante and Jerome L. Stein, "Does Fiscal Policy Matter?," *Journal of Monetary Economics*, vol. 2 (November 1976), pp. 473–500; Alan S. Blinder and Robert M. Solow, "Does Fiscal Policy Still Matter? A Reply," *Journal of Monetary Economics*, vol. 2 (November 1976), pp. 501–10; James Tobin, "Deficit Spending and Crowding Out in Shorter and Longer Runs," in Harry Greenfield and others, eds., *Theory*

To obtain a combined budget account, the identities 14-1 and 14-3 can be consolidated:

$$(14\text{-}8) \qquad T_d - X_d + T_n - X_n - X^{CB} - r_s S^P \equiv Z^G + Z^{CB}.$$

In most countries, the current expenditures of the central bank, X^{CB}, are small relative to government-wide expenditures. Moreover, although one can theoretically imagine, say, hiring central-bank economists and typists in a recession and firing them in a boom, the current expenditures of central banks are commonly taken as nondiscretionary from the perspective of macroeconomic stabilization policy. The size of the current budget surplus or deficit of the central bank, Z^{CB}, is usually small relative to the size of Z^G. For expository purposes, it is thus useful to rewrite 14-8 as:

$$(14\text{-}8a) \qquad T_d - X_d + T_n - X_n' - r_s S^P \equiv Z^{G'},$$

where X_n' represents government-wide nondiscretionary expenditures ($X_n + X^{CB}$), and $Z^{G'}$ is the combined budget position of the government as a whole ($Z^G + Z^{CB}$).

A consolidation of the two balance sheets in first-difference form is obtained by adding 14-2 and 14-4:

$$(14\text{-}9) \qquad \Delta OA^{G'} + \Delta RB - \Delta RT - \Delta CUR - \Delta S^P \equiv Z^{G'}.$$

On the grounds argued earlier, $\Delta OA^{G'} \equiv \Delta OA^{CB} + \Delta OA^G$ can plausibly be treated as nondiscretionary from the perspective of macroeconomic policy.

Since 14-8a and 14-9 treat the government as a single entity, all intragovernmental accounts are washed out and attention is directed to the position of the private sector vis-à-vis the government as a whole. Hence it is only the change in the private sector's holdings of government debt (ΔS^P) and the interest payments on those holdings ($r_s S^P$) that appear in 14-9 and 14-8a. It is possible to write 14-9 in an even simpler form when it is remembered that the unborrowed monetary base, *MBU*, is defined as the sum of total reserves and currency less commercial-bank borrowings from the central bank. With that simplification, if 14-8a and 14-9 are combined into one identity that omits $Z^{G'}$, the result is:

$$(14\text{-}10) \qquad T_d - X_d + T_n - X_n' - r_s S^P \equiv \Delta OA^{G'} - \Delta MBU - \Delta S^P.$$

The consolidated government-wide constraint in 14-10 highlights the close links—the *inevitably* close links—between monetary policy and fiscal policy. For example, the identity makes it clear that:[36]

> It is not possible for the unborrowed monetary base to increase unless the private sector's holdings of government debt are reduced or the consolidated government budget is in deficit.

> It is not possible for the private sector's holdings of government debt to increase unless the unborrowed monetary base is reduced or the consolidated government budget is in deficit.

---

for Efficiency: Essays in Honor of Abba P. Lerner (MIT Press, 1979); and Benjamin M. Friedman, "Crowding Out or Crowding In? Economic Consequences of Financing Government Deficits," *Brookings Papers on Economic Activity, 3:1978,* pp. 593–641.

36. Each of these three statements neglects the term ΔOA^G.

A deficit in the consolidated government budget necessarily entails either an increase in the holdings of government debt by the private sector or an increase in the unborrowed monetary base.

Illogical analysis can ignore these links between monetary policy and fiscal policy, but the interrelationships can never be violated in the real world.

Identities embody essential information about the constraints that limit behavior. Yet they seldom reveal anything about behavior itself. To appreciate how the consolidated budget constraint conditions the actual practice of monetary policy and fiscal policy, it is necessary to specify the alternative operating regimes within which monetary-policy and fiscal-policy actions are implemented.

The matrix in figure 14-1 is a simple cross-classification of alternative operating regimes. Its purpose is to suggest the multiplicity of cases that would have to be analyzed in a complete taxonomy of macroeconomic policy actions. There are three dozen different combinations of operating regimes separately identified in the figure. What is more, the cross-classification shown there is only illustrative; an exhaustive taxonomy would be still larger.[37]

Each cell in figure 14-1 represents an alternative set of assumptions about the behavior of government policymakers and therefore a separate analytical conceptualization of the conduct of macroeconomic policy. A move from one cell to another—a change in either the monetary-policy operating regime, the fiscal-policy operating regime, or both—produces a different configuration of exogenous instruments and endogenous variables. It is convenient to refer to a particular combination of operating regimes (for example, one of the individual cells) as a *policy regimen.*

When identifying the exogenous instruments associated with a policy regimen, care must again be taken to distinguish between potentially exogenous variables and actual exogenous instruments. The freedom of policymakers in the government as a whole to choose exogenous instruments is restricted by yet one more degree than the freedom that seems to exist, but in reality does not, if monetary-policy and fiscal-policy operating regimes are considered in isolation from each other.

An example of an inconsistently specified regimen illustrates the point. Assume the fiscal authority has the option of initially financing its budget surplus or deficit with either the private sector or the central bank. Suppose the fiscal authority has an insular interpretation of its budgetary and debt-management responsibilities and that, looking only at its own budget and balance-sheet constraints, it decides for debt-management reasons to set a goal for the total absorption of government debt by the private sector, ΔS^P. In other words, assume the fiscal authority varies its direct transactions with the private sector (ΔS^P_{direct}) to try to generate a desired time path for ΔS^P. Can these assumptions be combined with one of the budgetary regimes and one of the monetary-policy regimes previously described to produce a plausible regimen for macroeconomic policy? Clearly not. Inspection of the consolidated constraint in 14-10 shows that it is logically inconsistent for the fiscal authority to try to employ ΔS^P as an exogenous instrument *and* for the central bank

---

37. If different institutional procedures for the initial financing of a budget surplus or deficit were specified, the number of separate cases would be a multiple of thirty-six. Compare Hansen, "On the Effects of Fiscal and Monetary Policy."

to try to implement any of its normal operating regimes.[38] The difficulty in these imagined circumstances stems from a misconception of how much scope is available to the government as a whole for choosing exogenous policy instruments. The proposed regimen is simply infeasible.

The identity 14-10 and the illustration in the preceding paragraph shed additional light on the differences between regimens using an interest-rate instrument in the operating regime for monetary policy and those regimens using a reserve-aggregate instrument. When the market interest rate on government securities is used as the major instrument of monetary policy, the amount of those securities held by the private sector, S^P, is not controlled by the central bank or the fiscal authority. (Open market operations, ΔS^{CB}_{market}, must vary endogenously to prevent the interest rate from drifting off its exogenous path, which in turn requires ΔS^P to be endogenously determined.) If S^P is endogenous and uncontrolled, the unborrowed monetary base, MBU, and all other reserve-money aggregates likewise vary in an uncontrolled manner. It matters little whether the central bank (via ΔS^{CB}_{market}) or the fiscal authority (via ΔS^P_{direct}) carries out transactions in government securities with the private sector in an effort to fix the interest rate on an exogenous path. If either successfully pegs the interest rate on government securities, the central bank loses control over (that is, cannot exogenously determine) S^P, MBU, and the other reserve-money aggregates.

In contrast, if the central bank operates a regime in which one of its balance-sheet aggregates is used as the main instrument (and provided debt-management transactions by the fiscal authority are conducted so as not to be inconsistent with that regime), then MBU or some other reserve aggregate is an exogenous magnitude in the consolidated constraint 14-10. When ΔMBU is fixed exogenously, ΔS^P is determined endogenously.

Thus, it is possible for macroeconomic policy as a whole to fix a path for a reserve aggregate exogenously, or for a market interest rate exogenously, but it is not possible to fix both together over the same time period. Policymakers in central banks and finance ministries can be confused about what their actual instruments are. They can try to implement inconsistent operating procedures. But inconsistent procedures are bound to be unsuccessful. The government as a whole can only put one policy regimen into force at any given time.

Policy Actions, Policy Regimens, and the Symbiosis between Fiscal and Monetary Policies

A policy action (to repeat the abstract definition of part 3) is an alteration in the benchmark path for one exogenous policy instrument while all other exogenous

---

38. If the central bank tries to operate with a reserve-aggregate instrument regime, it will be attempting through open-market operations to set an exogenous path for the relevant reserve aggregate (say, MBU); if the central bank is to be successful, the fiscal authority must fail in its effort to use ΔS^P as an exogenous instrument, and vice versa. Alternatively, if the central bank tries to implement an interest-rate instrument regime, it will be attempting to carry out whatever (endogenous) volume of open-market operations is required to achieve an exogenously set path for the interest rate; the central bank must fail in its effort to peg the interest rate or the fiscal authority must fail in its effort to achieve an independent path for ΔS^P.

Figure 14-1. An Illustrative Classification of Alternative Policy Regimens, Closed Economy[a]

Alternative operating regimes for monetary policy / Alternative operating regimes for fiscal policy[b]	Discretionary-expenditure budgetary regime	Composite budget-aggregate regimes		Exogenous-surplus budgetary regime
		Composite aggregate: $X_d + r_s(S)$	Composite aggregate: $X_d + X'_n + r_s(S)$	
Interest-rate instrument regimes				
Main instrument: interbank lending rate r_i	$r_i, \rho, r_d, \theta, X_d$	$r_i, \rho, r_d, \theta, (X_d + r_s S)$	$r_i, \rho, r_d, \theta, (X_d + X'_n + r_s S)$	$r_i, \rho, r_d, \theta, Z^{G'}$
Main instrument: government security rate r_s	$r_s, \rho, r_d, \theta, X_d$	$r_s, \rho, r_d, \theta, (X_d + r_s S)$	$r_s, \rho, r_d, \theta, (X_d + X'_n + r_s S)$	$r_s, \rho, r_d, \theta, Z^{G'}$
Main instrument: total reserves RT	$RT, \rho, r_d, \theta, X_d$	$RT, \rho, r_d, \theta, (X_d + r_s S)$	$RT, \rho, r_d, \theta, (X_d + X'_n + r_s S)$	$RT, \rho, r_d, \theta, Z^{G'}$
Reserve-aggregate instrument regimes				
Main instrument: unborrowed reserves RU	$RU, \rho, r_d, \theta, X_d$	$RU, \rho, r_d, \theta, (X_d + r_s S)$	$RU, \rho, r_d, \theta, (X_d + X'_n + r_s S)$	$RU, \rho, r_d, \theta, Z^{G'}$
Main instrument: unborrowed monetary base MBU	$MBU, \rho, r_d, \theta, X_d$	$MBU, \rho, r_d, \theta, (X_d + r_s S)$	$MBU, \rho, r_d, \theta, (X_d + X'_n + r_s S)$	$MBU, \rho, r_d, \theta, Z^{G'}$

Money as intermediate-target regimes	Intermediate-target variable: M_j	Interest-rate instrument: r_i	$r_i, \rho, r_d, \theta, X_d$	$r_i, \rho, r_d, \theta, (X_d + r_s S)$	$r_i, \rho, r_d, \theta, (X_d + X'_n + r_s S)$	$r_i, \rho, r_d, \theta, Z^{G'}$
		Reserve-aggregate instrument: RU	$RU, \rho, r_d, \theta, X_d$	$RU, \rho, r_d, \theta, (X_d + r_s S)$	$RU, \rho, r_d, \theta, (X_d + X'_n + r_s S)$	$RU, \rho, r_d, \theta, Z^{G'}$
	Intermediate-target variable: M_k	Interest-rate instrument: r_i	$r_i, \rho, r_d, \theta, X_d$	$r_i, \rho, r_d, \theta, (X_d + r_s S)$	$r_i, \rho, r_d, \theta, (X_d + X'_n + r_s S)$	$r_i, \rho, r_d, \theta, Z^{G'}$
		Reserve-aggregate instrument: RU	$RU, \rho, r_d, \theta, X_d$	$RU, \rho, r_d, \theta, (X_d + r_s S)$	$RU, \rho, r_d, \theta, (X_d + X'_n + r_s S)$	$RU, \rho, r_d, \theta, Z^{G'}$

a. The exogenous instruments used in a regimen are identified by the symbols in its cell. Definitions of variables: r_d = the central bank's discount rate; r_i = the interbank lending rate; r_s = the interest rate on government securities; RU = unborrowed reserves; MBU = the unborrowed monetary base; S = the outstanding stock of government securities; S^P = the stock of government securities held by the private sector; M_j = the stock of money, definition j; X_d = discretionary government expenditures; X'_n = nondiscretionary government expenditures; θ = the discretionary tax rate; $Z^{G'}$ = the government budget surplus or deficit.

b. An operating regime for fiscal policy comprises a budgetary regime plus the institutional procedures used for the initial financing of the budget surplus or deficit. Alternative institutional procedures for the initial financing of the budget imbalance are not shown in this illustrative classification.

instruments remain fixed on benchmark paths. But as this chapter emphasizes, it is no trivial matter to speak of other instruments remaining fixed on benchmark paths. Because alternative assumptions about the behavior of policymakers lead to different classifications of exogenous and endogenous variables, it becomes necessary—purely as a matter of logic—to specify alternative policy regimens and to be precise about which regimen is the one relevant for a given analytical purpose.

The crucial point is a generalization of what was said earlier about monetary policy and fiscal policy separately: the effects of a specified change in the setting of an exogenous instrument differ depending on the regimen within which the change takes place. In terms of the language of part 3, the multipliers for a policy action depend critically on the very list of other instruments in the structural model.

To illustrate, suppose an analyst wishes to study the effects on the economy of reducing the discretionary tax rate (θ) by 3 percentage points. Note first that this fiscal-policy action is essentially undefined until something more is specified about the relevant budgetary regimen. With a discretionary-expenditure regimen, X_d will remain unchanged from its exogenously fixed path; the reduction in θ with the consequent decrease in discretionary revenue, T_d, will in the first instance reduce $Z^{G'}$ and necessitate smaller debt retirements or larger new issues, ΔS. Alternatively, if the fiscal authority is operating an exogenous-surplus regimen, the time path of $Z^{G'}$ will be kept unaltered, ΔS ($\approx Z^{G'}$) will be little affected, but discretionary expenditures, X_d, will be cut back to compensate for the reduction in tax revenues. Still other shorter-run outcomes will be generated if the fiscal authority is operating with one of the composite budget-aggregate regimens.

Thus at the very least the shorter-run impacts on the economy of the cut in θ will vary significantly with the different budgetary regimens. In addition to the different impacts resulting from different time paths for X_d, X'_n, T_n, and $Z^{G'}$, note also that different paths for the stock of government debt will result, with further implications for the paths of interest paid on that debt ($r_s S^P$) and hence the paths of private-sector wealth.

If the budgetary operating regimen is specified precisely, will there be sufficient information to analyze the effects of a reduction in θ? Clearly not. The initial financing of the time sequence of values for $Z^{G'}$ associated with the relevant budgetary regimen may be relevant. Most important, since the ultimate time paths for ΔS^P and ΔS^{CB} are what matter for the analysis of the impacts of a policy action on the economy, it will be essential to specify the central bank's operating regimen for monetary policy.

If the reduction in tax rate occurs under a discretionary-expenditure regimen or any of the possible composite budget-aggregate regimens, it will generate an incrementally larger deficit (smaller surplus) in the shorter run than would otherwise have occurred. That incremental deficit in turn will set into motion both "substitution effects" and "wealth effects" as private-sector economic units rebalance their portfolios in response to the incrementally higher stock of government debt. The more direct impacts of the tax reduction on private-sector income, consumption, and saving flows can also have portfolio rebalancing consequences. Suppose the central bank is operating with an interest-rate instrument regimen, pegging the interbank lending rate. It will then be induced to carry out whatever (endogenous) amount of open-market purchases is required to keep the interbank lending rate from rising above its exogenously fixed path. The required amount will depend both on the particular budgetary regime (being greatest under a discretionary-expenditure regime) and on the initial financing breakdown between ΔS^P_{direct} and ΔS^{CB}_{direct} (being greatest when the institutional procedures require initial full financing by the private sector). Alternatively, suppose that the central bank is operating with a reserve-aggregate instrument regime. In that case, there may be no need for incremental open-market operations under initial full financing by the private sector, but a pressing need for open-market operations under initial mixed financing or initial full financing by the central bank. Still different induced monetary-policy responses will be set in motion by the reduction in θ if the central bank's operating procedures involve an intermediate-target regime with a monetary aggregate as the key intermediate variable.

The impacts on the economy of a reduction in discretionary tax rates can thus differ greatly depending on the regimen within which it occurs. Analytically, it makes no sense to speak of studying the impacts of a reduction in tax rates with ''all other aspects of government behavior remaining unchanged.'' All other aspects of government behavior remaining unchanged is a logical impossibility. It is analytically possible, however, to specify a list of other government exogenous instruments that remain unchanged. Only when that has been done—when a particular regimen has been completely specified—can it be said that the fiscal-policy action of a reduction in tax rates has been fully defined.

Consider now an illustrative monetary-policy action. Suppose an analyst wishes to study the impacts on the economy of an incremental open-market purchase of $500 million of securities by the central bank (tantamount in the first instance to an equivalent incremental increase in excess and total reserves).

Notice first that if the central bank is pursuing an interest-rate instrument regime or an intermediate-target regime in which an interest rate is used as an instrument, it would be unnatural for the analyst even to propose this question. The natural monetary-policy action to study in those cases would be not an open-market operation of a given size but a reduction (relative to what otherwise would have prevailed) of so-and-so many basis points in the interest rate—the actual exogenous instrument. Little but analytical confusion can result from postulating an ''exogenous'' open-market operation in a situation where the volume of open-market operations is determined endogenously. For the analysis of the assumed $500 million open-market purchase to be interesting in the first place, therefore, it should be presumed that the central bank operates with either some instrument regime or some intermediate-target regime in which a reserve aggregate serves as the main exogenous instrument.

It should already be evident from the earlier discussion of monetary regimes that the impacts on the economy of an incremental $500 million open-market purchase can differ significantly depending on whether the central bank pursues a reserve-aggregate instrument regime or an intermediate-target regime with a monetary aggregate as the key intermediate variable. Even when the particular monetary regime is identified, however, the effects of the open-market purchase on the economy cannot be correctly analyzed until the analyst specifies the budgetary operating regime being used by the fiscal authority.

In the very short run, under any alternative budgetary regime, the assumed policy action may have the qualitative, initial financial consequences conventionally associated with open-market purchases—for example, readjustment of private-sector portfolios, declines in market interest rates, and increases in loans and deposits at financial intermediaries. Through channels such as a reduction in the costs of borrowing relative to the costs of producing new capital goods which are substitutes for existing assets, some expansionary stimulus to aggregate output and the price level of the type predicted by conventional macroeconomic analysis may also begin to occur. But even in the short run, and a fortiori as the dynamic adjustments have a longer time to work themselves out, careful analysis of the quantitative consequences of the incremental open-market purchase will require precise specification of the relevant budgetary regime.

Suppose the fiscal authority is implementing a discretionary-expenditure regime. With both discretionary and nondiscretionary tax rates fixed and with discretionary expenditures set exogenously, the initial stimulatory effects of the open-market purchase on the economy will be likely to move the budget into a larger surplus (smaller deficit) than would otherwise have been experienced.[39] Over time, as the incrementally higher $Z^{G'}$ persists, debt will have to be retired at a faster rate from (or issued at a slower pace to) the private sector, with a consequent reduction in private-sector net worth relative to what it otherwise would have been.[40] Asset valuations in financial markets will have to adjust pari passu with the induced rebalancing of private-sector portfolios (again, via both substitution effects and wealth effects). Moreover, with S^P lower and (if only initially) r_s lower, interest payments to the private sector on the government debt $(r_s S^P)$ will probably also fall.[41] At least under some assumptions and after some period of time, the contractionary effects on the economy associated with the retirement of debt and lower interest payments on the debt can substantially mitigate if not overwhelm altogether the expansionary effects of the more traditional type.

Alternatively, suppose the fiscal authority is operating with an exogenous-surplus budgetary regime. In those circumstances, the dynamic evolution of the economy following the incremental open-market purchase will be quite different. Discretionary expenditures will be increased (endogenously) to offset any incipient upward deviations of $Z^{G'}$ from its exogenously fixed path. The incremental changes over time in private-sector holdings of government debt and the associated long-run, contractionary consequences that would play a prominent role in the evolution of the economy under a discretionary-expenditure regime will be absent under an

39. The direction of the incremental net impact on the budget surplus, $Z^{G'}$, is not certain. Although nondiscretionary and discretionary tax revenues $(T_n + T_d)$ will increase with an increase in nominal private-sector incomes and although interest payments on the government debt will probably fall (see text that follows and notes 40 and 41). some nondiscretionary government expenditures X'_n will rise endogenously.

40. The exact effects on S^P will depend on the particular operating regime for monetary policy. With a reserve-aggregate instrument regime using MBU as the instrument, for example, the entire reduction in debt occasioned by the higher $Z^{G'}$ will fall on S^P. With intermediate-target regimes keyed on a monetary aggregate, induced central-bank open-market operations will probably mitigate the fall in S^P.

41. It is evident from the simulation results in a study by Jeffrey R. Shafer—see "The Macroeconomic Behavior of a Large Open Economy with a Floating Exchange Rate" (Ph.D. dissertation, Yale University, 1976), esp. pp. 71–74, 88–95—that this result may not occur under certain types of assumptions about the formation of private expectations. In Shafer's model, which imposes one type of rational-expectations assumption, an incremental open-market purchase generates an immediate rise rather than a fall in market interest rates (even in real terms). The interest rate on government debt rises enough to more than offset the initial reduction in the supply of debt resulting from the open-market purchase: that is, $r_s S^P$ rises rather than falls. This effect is strong enough in Shafer's model, in fact, to produce an incremental net reduction in $Z^{G'}$ rather than the incremental increase postulated in the text.

exogenous-surplus regime. Hence, compared with the outcomes under a discretionary-expenditure regime, the time paths of aggregate output, employment, and the price level can be significantly higher.

Still other outcomes for the evolution of the economy—probably intermediate between the results generated by the discretionary-expenditure and the exogenous-surplus regimes—will be obtained if the fiscal authority implements one of the composite budget-aggregate regimes.

This example of an expansionary monetary-policy action again illustrates the key point that the impacts of a given policy action on the economy can differ markedly depending on the specific policy regimen within which it occurs. It would be difficult to overemphasize the importance of this proposition for the analysis of macroeconomic policy actions and their effects.

Two corollaries follow from the preceding analysis. First, it is essential when analyzing the effects of macroeconomic policy actions to be precise about the relevant policy regimen. If the various dimensions of the operating regimes being followed by the central bank and the fiscal authority are not articulated explicitly in an analysis, they are merely being assumed implicitly. But implicit assumptions are risky; they easily lead to incorrect or misleading inferences.

Second, there is simply no valid way to analyze monetary policy and fiscal policy in isolation from each other. The example of the reduction in tax rates shows that a fiscal-policy action cannot even be defined without specifying the operating objectives and procedures of monetary policy. The obverse is equally true, as illustrated by the example of the open-market purchase: a monetary-policy action cannot be defined independently of the budgetary operating regime and institutional financing procedures being followed by the fiscal authority. At the most fundamental level of analysis, the distinction between "monetary policy" and "fiscal policy" becomes blurred and somewhat arbitrary. While it may be convenient to differentiate the two semantically, a cogent analysis of macroeconomic policy must recognize that they are symbiotically joined together through the consolidated budget constraint for the government as a whole.

CHAPTER FIFTEEN

Alternative Strategies for
Conducting Monetary Policy

THE PROCEDURES followed by a central bank when formulating and implementing decisions about the settings on its instruments may be designated its *strategy* for the conduct of monetary policy. A main purpose of the chapters that follow is to compare the relative merits of alternative strategies, in particular those strategies that employ some definition of the money stock as an intermediate target. As a prerequisite for such a comparison, it is necessary to identify the entire range of potentially available strategies and to be more precise about the general characteristics of intermediate-target strategies. This chapter addresses those two tasks.

The Policy Problem prior to Strategy Choice

Before identifying the ways in which alternative strategies differ, it is useful to review the basic components of the policy problem that are not part of the problem of strategy choice per se.

The objectives that the central bank tries to promote, which in turn derive from policymakers' preferences, may not always be articulated clearly—even in policymakers' own minds, let alone in central-bank public pronouncements. Trade-offs between conflicting objectives and intertemporal comparisons of national economic welfare may not always be formulated systematically. But objectives of some sort are a logical prerequisite of any strategy. For the purposes of analysis, the objectives and preferences of policymakers—whatever they may be—can be conceptualized in terms of a policy loss function, defined over the time paths of ultimate-target variables.

In addition, all strategies presuppose the conceptual distinction between policy instruments, intermediate variables, and ultimate-target variables. As before, actual instruments are variables that the central bank can, and actually does, control precisely.

Instrument-variation costs and boundary constraints on the use of instruments may be relevant in the case of any strategy. If so, the loss function may impose inequality constraints on, or give nonzero weights to, the time paths of the instruments as well as the ultimate-target variables.

Every strategy makes use of some model that describes the interrelationships among policy instruments, intermediate variables, and ultimate-target variables. Models may differ greatly in the degree to which they try to incorporate existing structural knowledge about the economy. Some may attempt to be systemic while others may primarily emphasize one particular market or sector of the economy. Some policymakers may rely on vague rules of thumb rather than trying to specify an internally consistent analytical framework. But a model of some sort is a logical prerequisite for policy decisions.

The time horizon relevant to policy—the distance into the future that the central bank looks when making decisions about its instruments—is yet another component of the policy problem. Since the policymakers' preferences must specify how intertemporal comparisons of loss are to be made, the choice of time horizon will be influenced by the specification of those preferences. The choice of time horizon also depends on the dynamic characteristics of the policymakers' model (and thus of the economic structure the model attempts to imitate).[1]

Another component is germane for all possible strategies: the flow of new information that becomes available as time passes. Data for all the directly observable variables that figure in the policymakers' model will be available for past historical periods.[2] In the case of intermediate, ultimate-target, and nonpolicy exogenous variables, however, information on the values of the variables may not yet be available for the very recent past. Some variables, for example, may be observed at only quarterly intervals (for example, various components of gross national product) whereas many others are observed only monthly (for example, industrial production). Moreover, new "readings" on variables become available with different lengths of lag (for example, an index of January wholesale prices may be available early in February whereas data for January exports and imports may not be available before the end of February). Only for a few types of intermediate variables (for example, market interest rates and equity prices) are "yesterday's" actual values available to be an input into decisions taken at the beginning of "today."[3] Whatever may be the particular periodicities and lags with which new data for the various variables become available, all strategies confront the same pattern of accumulation of new information. Policymakers must decide, for any strategy they adopt, how to use that flow most appropriately.

Finally, all strategies for conducting monetary policy presuppose interrelations of some sort with decisions about the nonmonetary instruments of macroeconomic policy. In practice, the most important nonmonetary instruments are those of fiscal policy. The possible interrelations range from full integration of central-bank and fiscal-authority decisions at one extreme to political independence at the other.

Some of the preceding components of the policy problem tend to be common ground whatever procedures may be used for the conduct of monetary policy. Others will often need to be held invariant when comparing the relative merits of alternative procedures (see the further discussion below). Accordingly, decisions

1. If policymakers could instantly offset any undesired movements in ultimate-target variables, they would not need to look ahead over a sequence of future periods. In practice, of course, the behavior of the economy is characterized by many frictions (due to adjustment costs) and delayed responses; the impact of policy actions and nonpolicy disturbances are distributed over many future periods. These facts require policymakers to use a multiperiod horizon (see appendix A). The more complicated the dynamic behavior of the economy, the greater the distance into the future that policymakers may need to look.

2. These data will presumably have played an important role in the formulation and empirical specification of the model.

3. It follows from the definition of instruments that yesterday's and today's values of actual instrument variables are always known precisely.

about the preceding characteristics of monetary policy are regarded here as separate from the choice of a particular strategy.[4]

What Differentiates Alternative Strategies?

What characteristics differentiate one strategy from another? Four aspects stand out, and the selection of a strategy involves four corresponding sets of decisions.

First, the central bank must select those variables it will employ as actual exogenous instruments. This is the *choice of instruments* problem.

Second, the central bank must decide whether to use a single-stage or a multistage decision procedure in reasoning backward from the ultimate-target variables to the instrument settings. This is the *choice between an instrument regime and an intermediate-target regime.* The two-stage procedure used in intermediate-target regimes first requires the determination of a target path for a key intermediate variable (upper-level decision); then it requires the determination of time paths for the instrument settings designed to keep the key intermediate variable on its target path (lower-level decision). A single-stage procedure does not interpose a key intermediate variable. It presumes a continuous passage from ultimate-target variables back to instrument settings in one integrated decision.

The problem of choosing instruments is similar in both instrument and intermediate-target regimes. A decision to employ an intermediate-target regime does not obviate the need to select the actual instruments per se. The essential difference between instrument and intermediate-target regimes is that the latter require, in addition to the selection of actual instruments, the designation of a key intermediate variable to serve as the pivot for the two-stage decision process.[5] Taken together, the selection of actual instruments and the decision whether to employ an intermediate-target approach are sufficient to determine the operating regime for monetary policy.

Third, the central bank must choose procedures for altering the instrument settings as time passes. A key element here is the *frequency with which decisions are reviewed and revised.* Under instrument regimes, the central bank must decide how often to review and (possibly) adjust the instrument settings. Under intermediate-target regimes, two different periodicities for decisionmaking must be chosen. Not only must the central bank choose the frequency with which instrument settings will be reviewed; it must also specify how often the target path for the key intermediate variable will be reviewed and (possibly) revised.[6]

---

4. The definition of strategy used here does not materially influence the resolution of any substantive issue discussed below. Self-evidently, economic welfare and the overall successfulness of macroeconomic policy depend at least as critically on decisions about the nonstrategy aspects of monetary policy as on the selection and use of a particular strategy. One sometimes encounters a distinction between the "strategy" and the "tactics" of monetary-policy decisions, where "strategy" refers to an even smaller subset of monetary-policy decisions than in my connotation. A distinction between "strategy" and "tactics" tends to prejudge several substantive issues, and I have therefore avoided that terminology.

5. When policymakers try to make a key intermediate variable track along a target path, this operating strategy can be interpreted as an attempt to make an intermediate endogenous variable behave as though it were "almost" an exogenous instrument. But such an attempt cannot succeed perfectly from one short-run period to the next. The means used in such an attempt, moreover, have to be actual instruments for which there is no possibility of slippage between the realized and intended settings.

6. These frequencies of decisionmaking refer to the periodic decisions associated with implementation of the central bank's strategy. From time to time policymakers will also review the nonstrategy choices

Fourth, new data accumulating about the economy may validate or invalidate projections that were made before the availability of the new information. Depending on how policymakers choose to use them, the new data may lead to adjustments in instrument settings. The new data may also trigger revisions in the target path for the key intermediate variable (if an intermediate-target regime is in use). Thus alternative strategies may differ in the manner in which they do or do not incorporate *feedback from new information*. This aspect of a strategy is closely interrelated with the periodicity of decisionmaking.

Comparing Alternative Strategies

Views about the appropriate objectives of monetary policy can be and typically are heterogeneous, and may be so even within the central bank. If the merits of alternative strategies are to be compared analytically, however, it is essential to avoid confusion between differences in objectives and differences in strategies.

The analysis of alternative strategies in this book therefore postulates that the central bank has some given set of preferences and objectives. The loss function embodying these preferences and objectives, including its incorporation of instrument-variation costs (if any) and its embodiment of boundary constraints (if any), is assumed invariant throughout the analysis. All alternative strategies are judged against this common yardstick.

This approach to comparing strategies assumes that the relative merits of, say, strategies X, Y, and Z are fairly insensitive to the particular loss function chosen by the central bank. If Y is judged superior to X and Z for one loss function, it is assumed that Y will then also dominate X and Z for other loss functions.[7]

Analytical clarity also requires the assumption that the flow of new information about the economy, whatever its characteristics, is invariant across alternative strategies. This is not tantamount to dismissing the characteristics of information flow as irrelevant. The frequency with which various variables are observed or the timeliness of new data readings for them may well influence the choice of a strategy. The purpose of the analysis here, however, is to compare strategies on an objective basis. It would be inequitable to favor or penalize some particular strategy at the outset merely by assuming greater or lesser access to new information about the economy.

An objective comparison might also seem to require a model that remains invariant across alternative strategies. Strictly speaking, however, such a suggestion

underlying policy formulation. Now and again, for example, they will presumably reexamine their basic preferences and consider changes in the loss function that guides decisions. They must keep under continuous review the question of whether their model makes the best feasible use of existing knowledge of the economy's structure (see chapter 16). It is assumed in what follows that these nonstrategy reappraisals take place relatively independently of the periodic decisions discussed in the text.

7. This assumption could be invalid. And a superficial correlation of the apparent objectives and actual strategy recommendations of monetary economists can be cited as evidence against the assumption. For the range of policymakers' *economic* preferences and the types of alternative strategies encountered in actual practice, however, I find it difficult to imagine two plausible loss functions such that strategy Y would dominate when one loss function is used while, say, strategy Z would dominate when the other is used. Moreover, as will be seen, the analysis in chapters 16 and 17 does not rest on the idiosyncracies of any one loss function. When *political* preferences and costs are also taken into account, the comparison of strategies becomes still more difficult and the assumption in the text then probably does become invalid. See chapter 18.

involves a logical contradiction. Alternative strategies employ different operating regimes, and hence different national policy regimens. Each alternative regimen is a distinct analytical world and requires the specification of a different structural model (see chapter 14).[8]

Nonetheless, a comparison of strategies should postulate a common degree of ignorance about the functioning of the economy. A central bank needs to select those operating procedures that will most facilitate its objectives given the best available knowledge of how the economy actually works. In principle the central bank has access to that knowledge: it can hire the least ignorant economists and make use of the modeling approach that least inadequately describes the responses of the nation's economy to policy actions and nonpolicy disturbances. An inferior strategy used in conjunction with the best available modeling approach might well outperform a superior strategy if the superior strategy had to be used in association with a less accurately specified description of how the economy behaves. In principle, however, the central bank is free to take advantage of the best available modeling approach regardless of its strategy choice.

Unfortunately, the best available knowledge of the macroeconomic behavior of national economies is seriously deficient. Uncertainty may be the single most pervasive determinant of macroeconomic decisionmaking. Perhaps the most troublesome type of uncertainty is ignorance about the form, parameters, and stability over time of structural behavioral relationships; modeling approaches differ greatly in terms of how they cope with this uncertainty.[9] Worst of all, economists cannot agree on which modeling approach constitutes the least unreliable characterization of the economy's behavior. It is cheap advice, therefore, to enjoin policymakers to embody the best existing knowledge of the economy's behavior in their model, but highly problematic to give operational content to that injunction. Model choice and strategy choice need not be closely linked; in actual practice, however, a correlation can be observed between individuals' views on these two sets of choices.

Despite the preceding caveats, the most enlightening way to compare strategies is to assume that the knowledge available to policymakers and their success in incorporating it into their models are invariant across strategies. That assumption enables the analysis to concentrate on the differences among strategies for a given degree of ignorance about how the economy really works.[10]

The interrelations between monetary-policy and fiscal-policy decisions can be still another source of confusion when alternative strategies for monetary policy are compared. At the extreme of *political independence*, the central bank may be assumed to have statutory autonomy from, to communicate only at arm's length with, and to make its decisions independently of the rest of the government. "Independent" decisions mean that the central bank may pursue somewhat different

8. If structural modeling is not undertaken and the policymakers attempt to work directly with the reduced form or final form of an assumed or estimated model, each alternative regimen implies a different set of reduced-form or final-form equations. The differences among models may be only minor but can be significant—especially if the models attempt to describe the process by which private-sector economic units form expectations of the policy actions of the authorities. See chapter 18.

9. Such ignorance has even more severe implications for modeling approaches that bypass the structure and work directly with a reduced-form or final-form model.

10. Implementation of this assumption in an actual comparison implies that the strategies being compared should be evaluated in conjunction with each modeling approach regarded as a serious contender for the prize of best approach. More is said in chapter 16 about model choice and strategy choice.

objectives than the fiscal authority and may use a somewhat different model of the economy. Furthermore, since both the central bank and the fiscal authority may be concerned in such an environment to preserve flexibility for their future decisions, each may provide the other with only a vague indication of their current plans for future decisions. At the other extreme of *full integration*, the central bank may be assumed to make its decisions using a loss function and a model identical to those employed by the fiscal authority. Full integration implies intensive period-by-period coordination of decisions.

A comparison of monetary-policy strategies under conditions of political independence is a different, and analytically much more difficult, task than a comparison under conditions where monetary-policy decisions are fully integrated with the remainder of macroeconomic policy. Conditions between the two extremes— the actual situation in most countries—pose analytical problems that are different in other ways. Analytical clarity thus requires that the interrelations between monetary-policy and fiscal-policy decisions be carefully specified when monetary-policy strategies are compared. It will usually be appropriate to presume that the specified interrelations, whatever they may be, are invariant across alternative strategies.

Periodicity of Decisionmaking in Single-Stage and Two-Stage Strategies

Although the primary objective of the subsequent analysis is to evaluate strategies that use money as an intermediate target, it is instructive in the first instance to analyze intermediate-target strategies in general. It is similarly instructive to consider all strategies without regard for the identity of their actual instrument variables. That perspective thereby focuses attention only on the most general characteristics of strategies: their periodicities of decisionmaking and their manners of incorporating feedback from new information.

Accordingly, consider the classification of strategy types presented in table 15-1. The main distinction emphasized is between single-stage strategies and two-stage, intermediate-target strategies. Within each of those, a spectrum of possibilities exists.

Single-Stage Strategies

Consider first the extreme case of *nondiscretionary rules for instrument settings*. These strategies do not allow flexibility for the central bank to adjust the settings on its instruments in response to new information about the economy; instead, the time paths for the settings are specified with simple formulas or rigid rules of thumb. For example, one rule could call for the unborrowed monetary base to expand at a constant percentage growth rate. An illustrative rule for reserve-requirement ratios could stipulate that the ratios would never be changed except temporarily in a banking crisis. Periodic discretionary decisions are abjured; the rules seldom if ever are changed.

With *discretionary instrument decisions made at infrequent intervals*, a modest amount of flexibility is possible. "Infrequent" is used here to denote an interval

Table 15-1. *Alternative Types of Strategies for Conducting Monetary Policy*

Single-stage strategies using instrument operating regimes	Two-stage intermediate-target strategies using intermediate-target operating regimes
Nondiscretionary rules for instrument settings	Nondiscretionary rules for the intermediate-target variable
Discretionary instrument decisions made at infrequent intervals	Discretionary decisions focused on an infrequently revised path for the intermediate-target variable
Discretionary instrument adaptation with intermittent feedback	Discretionary decisions focused on an intermittently revised path for the intermediate-target variable
Discretionary instrument adaptation with continuous feedback	

of, say, six months to a year. During the interval between decisions, the settings of the instruments are governed by temporary rules—for example, a constant percentage growth rate of some reserve aggregate. New information accumulating in the period between decisions, however, can lead eventually to revisions in the temporarily inflexible rules.

When decisions are made infrequently, the time paths for the instrument settings to be followed in the intervals between decisions need to be formulated in the light of the average behavior of the economy over the long run. In principle, the policymakers' loss function has to be combined with a model characterizing the long-run relationships between instruments and ultimate-target variables. On the infrequent occasions when instrument settings are reviewed and revised, the new temporary rules can reflect updated judgments about the long-run, average experience.

If reviews of the instrument settings are carried out "intermittently"—say, every quarter or every other month—the resulting strategies may be described as *discretionary instrument adaptation with intermittent feedback*. Figuratively speaking, the central bank makes decisions about its instruments on a meeting day, subsequently sits on its hands for a period of two to three months, and then on its next meeting day takes new decisions that make use of the new information that has accumulated in the interim. The process has a rhythm determined by the intermittent decision interval.

At the bottom end of the spectrum of single-stage strategies in table 15-1 are strategies that may be labeled *discretionary instrument adaptation with continuous feedback*. The periodicity of decisionmaking is there reduced to an interval coincident with the period of observation for the most frequently observed variables. If many variables in the model used by policymakers are observed daily, for example, new decisions would be made—in principle—each day. Decisions are "continuous" in the sense that each new datum about the economy has the potential to trigger a revision in the settings on the policymakers' instruments.

Two-Stage Strategies

The timing of decisionmaking is more complex for two-stage strategies: two periodicities for decisions exist rather than one.

At the most inflexible end of the spectrum is a *nondiscretionary rule for the intermediate-target variable*. Such a strategy does not allow the central bank any flexibility to alter the target path of the key intermediate variable with the passage of time. Rather, that path is derived from a rule that is invariant to recent data about the economy. One simple rule, for example, could state that the intermediate-target variable should remain constant at some specified value. Alternatively, the rule could stipulate that the key intermediate variable should increase at some constant percentage rate of growth from a base value in a past period. The rule used should presumably be derived, loosely if not systematically, from the policymakers' loss function and from some model of the long-run average relationships thought to exist between the intermediate-target variable and the ultimate-target variables.

How are decisions about the actual instrument variables made in such a strategy? Proponents of this approach recommend a more or less continuous review and revision. Each new datum for the intermediate-target variable—for example, each week's reading if the variable is measured at weekly intervals—is compared with the rule-determined target value. Discrepancies between the two lead to weekly adjustments in instrument settings intended to bring the intermediate-target variable back to its target path.

The central bank has somewhat more, although still limited, flexibility under a strategy where discretionary decisions are focused on an *infrequently revised path for the intermediate-target variable*. Strategies of this type specify the target path for the key intermediate variable by means of a simple rule, but that rule is now and again recalculated in response to new data about the economy. The intervals between recalculations of the target path are, say, six months to a year (hence the designation "infrequently" revised). As in the case of two-stage strategies employing a nondiscretionary rule, the settings for the instrument variables are altered continuously.

Further along the spectrum of two-stage strategies, discretionary decisions may focus on an *intermittently revised path for the intermediate-target variable*. In these cases the intermediate-target path is recalculated at significantly shorter intervals (every quarter, or perhaps every other month). The considerations taken into account in determining the revised path are analogous to those relevant for the less discretionary two-stage strategies; the difference is that new information about the economy is used intermittently rather than infrequently or not at all. As for the instrument settings, strategies of this type are akin to their less discretionary relatives in presupposing continuous adjustment. With each new reading for the actual position of the key intermediate variable, the settings may be revised in an effort to bring the future position of the intermediate variable closer to the target path currently in force.

What if the periodicity of recalculation of the intermediate-target path were reduced still further? Instead of every quarter or every other month, suppose the intermediate-target path could be revised in response to each new reading for the ultimate-target variables, each new reading for the key intermediate variable itself, and (conceivably) each new reading for other endogenous variables. A strategy involving this "continuous" revision of the target path for the key intermediate variable would be indistinguishable for most purposes from the single-stage strategies that use discretionary instrument adaptation with continuous feedback.

As described here, all two-stage, intermediate-target strategies presuppose that the central bank makes activist, discretionary use of its policy instruments. This continuous review and revision of the instrument settings contrasts sharply with the sluggishness of recalculation of the target path for the key intermediate variable.

I describe two-stage strategies as presuming continuous instrument variation because all proponents of intermediate-target strategies have taken this position (implicitly if not explicitly). This presumption is not a logical necessity. Intermediate-target strategies could forswear continuous instrument variation just as some of them eschew frequent revisions of the path for the intermediate-target variable. In practice, despite the fact that there are other theoretically conceivable combinations of the two periodicities, the only combinations actually proposed are those that require continuous adjustment of the instruments.

Use of New Information in Revising Decisions

New data about the economy that accumulate between successive decisions are potentially the most important inputs to the process by which revised settings for the instruments are selected. How should this new information be used? Which of the various data accumulated since the prior decision should be taken into account? Different strategies answer these questions differently.

The characteristics of the policymakers' model are the most critical determinant of how new information is used. The more variables included in a model, the greater the potential ability to make use of new data. Indeed, "information" is an ambiguous concept if divorced from the notion of a "model." A new datum about the economy cannot be of any use unless it can be employed in conjunction with a model of some sort.

No feasible macroeconomic model of the economy, however, can incorporate more than a small fraction of the economic variables for which statistical data exist.[11] Hence no feasible strategy for conducting policy can claim to make use of literally all the new data about the economy that become available.

Model builders face a severe trade-off when they contemplate increasing the number of variables in their model, and hence its size. A larger model can embody more of the existing structural knowledge about the economy's behavior and can thus enable policymakers to use more of the new data that accumulate between successive policy decisions. But larger models are more difficult to understand analytically and more costly to manipulate.

11. No model could even incorporate all the variables for which aggregative data exist; disaggregation would increase the number of candidate variables exponentially further.

The model size that is chosen, whatever it may be, constrains the ability of policymakers to use new data in revising their instrument settings. If variables for automobile sales and the stock of local-government bonds appear in the policymakers' model, for example, new data for those variables can be used to condition subsequent policy decisions. If the policymakers use a small model that does not incorporate those variables explicitly, data on recent auto sales and new issues of local-government bonds are analytically irrelevant for policy decisions.[12]

As emphasized above, a comparison of alternative strategies should be kept analytically distinct from comparisons of alternative modeling approaches and of alternative ultimate objectives. The following description therefore focuses on the differences among strategies in their use of new information for some given loss function and some common modeling approach.

Single-Stage Strategies

Strategies of discretionary instrument adaptation with continuous feedback, because they presuppose that policymakers continuously contemplate the possibility of adjustments in instrument settings, are the most ambitious of all strategies in the use of new information. In principle, two features differentiate them from other strategy types: an effort is made to exploit new data for each of the model's variables, and the new data are exploited as quickly as they become available. A caricature of this approach would label such strategies "Look at and Adapt Promptly to Everything."

Strategies of discretionary instrument adaptation with continuous feedback thus presume that new data for the variables in the policymakers' model—whenever received and regardless of the specific variable to which they refer—have a potential value for current-period policy decisions. Each new datum provides a basis for making new informed projections and for revising planned instrument settings applicable to future weeks, months, and quarters. In principle, data received at the beginning of any day can lead to some adjustment in that day's settings.

Now consider discretionary instrument adaptation with intermittent feedback. Policymakers following such strategies in effect impose a self-denying ordinance on their use of new information. During the two to three month intervals between their meeting days, they ignore all new data that trickle in and adhere rigidly to the plan for the instrument settings framed on the last meeting day. On the morning of the next meeting day itself, however, all the new information that has accumulated in the interim is processed in conjunction with their loss function and their model of the economy. The meeting itself results in a new plan, which is then rigidly implemented in the ensuing intermeeting period.[13]

12. Suppose the model used by the policymakers is available only in a reduced-form or final-form version. The "St. Louis equation" for the United States (see L. C. Anderson and J. L. Jordan, "Monetary and Fiscal Actions: A Test of Their Relative Importance in Economic Stabilization," *Federal Reserve Bank of St. Louis Review*, November 1968) is an example of such a reduced-form model. In that event, the nature of the model permits the use of new data only for ultimate-target variables and exogenous variables. New data for other endogenous variables are discarded because the model itself makes no use of any information for those variables. In contrast, when a structural model is available, new readings for all its endogenous variables can be systematically used in conjunction with the model to condition new decisions (see chapter 17).

13. The plan worked out on each meeting day presumably pertains to a future period much lengthier than the two to three month intermeeting period. It is the portion of the plan referring to the immediate future that is rigidly adhered to in between meeting days.

If policymakers adopt such a strong self-denying ordinance that they refuse to schedule meeting days more frequently than once or twice a year (discretionary instrument decisions made at infrequent intervals), new information about the economy must accumulate a considerable length of time before it can have any effect in conditioning instrument settings. The temporary instrument rules decided upon at a particular meeting day stay in force unamended for some six to twelve months.

At the extreme end of the spectrum of single-stage strategies, where instrument settings are fixed with nondiscretionary rules that are seldom if ever changed, recent data about the economy are irrelevant. The new information can never be used to condition revisions in plans since discretion itself is absent.

For single-stage strategies there is thus an unambiguous correlation between the periodicity of decisionmaking and efforts to use new information. The less frequently policy decisions are reviewed and (possibly) revised, the more discontinuous is the use of new information in conditioning instrument settings.

Two-Stage Strategies

The relationship between periodicity of decisionmaking and the use of new information is more complicated under intermediate-target strategies. Because such strategies have two decision periodicities corresponding to the two stages of the decision process, the use to which new information is put depends on the specific variables to which it pertains.

If a two-stage decision process is to be logically compatible with a particular overall model of the economy, that model must be decomposable into a *lower-stage submodel* and an *upper-stage submodel*. Variables that are endogenously determined in the lower-stage submodel must be exogenous from the perspective of the upper-stage submodel. Such "lower-level" variables must include, at a minimum, the intermediate-target variable itself. If other lower-level endogenous variables exist, they may be thought of as interposed in the chain of causation in the model between the actual monetary-policy instruments and the key intermediate variable. All endogenous variables other than lower-level variables are "upper-level"; they include, at a minimum, all the ultimate-target variables.

The distinction between lower-level and upper-level variables is valid only if the overall model can be decomposed into lower-stage and upper-stage submodels. That decomposition in turn is possible only if the overall model exhibits a particular type of recursiveness. The next chapter analyzes the issue of whether actual economies exhibit the necessary recursiveness. For the remainder of the exposition here, I temporarily assume that a decomposition of the overall model into lower-stage and upper-stage submodels is analytically valid.

Consider first the use of new data for the key intermediate variable itself. Whatever their upper-level periodicity of decisionmaking, all two-stage strategies place special emphasis on these data. Each new reading for the intermediate-target variable constitutes evidence about how it is tracking relative to its target path. If a comparison of the actual and target-path values for the most recent period shows the actual value to be below (above) path, a decision is made promptly to alter the instrument settings in the direction required to raise (lower) the actual value in future periods.

New data readings for other lower-level endogenous variables (if any) are scanned and reacted to with equal promptness. Such data have, according to the lower-stage submodel, a direct bearing on the instrument settings judged to be consistent with the target path for the key intermediate variable.[14]

It is noteworthy that new data for the intermediate-target variable and for other lower-level variables trigger prompt review of the instrument settings. This prompt use of new data for lower-level variables applies not only when the intermediate-target path is intermittently recalculated, but also when that path is infrequently revised and even when it is never revised at all. Interestingly, this treatment of new data for lower-level variables under intermediate-target strategies and the actively discretionary use of the instruments with which it is associated is in principle no different from the processing of new data for those variables under a strategy of discretionary instrument adaptation with continuous feedback.

New data for upper-level endogenous variables, on the other hand, are an entirely different matter. Use of that upper-level data in an intermediate-target strategy is determined by the periodicity of upper-level decisionmaking.

For the extreme case of a nondiscretionary rule for the intermediate-target variable, the recent data for upper-level variables are completely ignored; given that the intermediate-target path is rule-determined, this new information is simply irrelevant. When two-stage strategies focus on an infrequently revised path for the intermediate-target variable, new data for upper-level variables are irrelevant most of the time (because the intermediate-target path is—most of the time—predetermined). On the occasions of the infrequent recalculations of the intermediate-target path, however, such information does become a relevant input into the recalculations.

When the target path for the key intermediate variable is revised intermittently, the extent of asymmetry in the treatment of new data for upper-level and lower-level variables is reduced. New data for upper-level variables are used as often as, say, once per quarter. This treatment is still significantly different, however, from the treatment given to lower-level variables, where new data are taken into account continuously rather than intermittently.

"Rules" and "Discretion"

In the preceding classification of strategy types, "rules" and "discretionary decisions" have connotations that correspond to the meanings of those terms in everyday discourse. The two terms, however, are potentially ambiguous. To forestall possible confusion in the subsequent analysis, a few words of additional clarification are necessary.

14. The greater the number of lower-level endogenous variables that influence the key intermediate variable, the greater the amount of new data that can be used to adjust the instrument settings to keep the key intermediate variable tracking along its target path. In a submodel that is so highly simplified that the intermediate-target variable depends on the actual instruments only through "multiplier" parameters (a lower-stage submodel collapsed into a single reduced-form relationship), there are no other lower-level endogenous variables and the only new data deemed to be relevant are observations for the intermediate-target variable itself.

Any systematic procedure for making decisions can in principle be described by its originators in a manner that permits its replication and implementation by others. Thus any systematic procedure, no matter how complex, can in some broad sense be construed as a set of decision "rules." If deviations from the systematic procedure do not occur, moreover, the decision rules could be labeled "nondiscretionary." If ordinary usage of the language is stretched in this way and applied to the preceding classification of strategies for conducting monetary policy, even a highly sophisticated version of discretionary instrument adaptation with continuous feedback could be described as a "nondiscretionary rule."

Conversely, any systematic procedure for making decisions must be initially selected from a menu of alternative procedures; if the original selection should be judged not to work well, it may be abandoned. Thus any systematic procedure, no matter how simple or rigid, presumes some degree of "discretionary" choice. Even if monetary policy were to be conducted by means of inflexible rules of thumb (in terms of the preceding classification, by nondiscretionary rules for instrument settings or by a nondiscretionary rule for an intermediate-target variable), the initial choice of the rules and the continuing decision to maintain them in force could be labeled a "discretionary" strategy. Moreover, suppose an inflexible rule of thumb were forced on the central bank because the national legislature imposed it by statute. Even then, political or economic events could lead the legislature to make "discretionary" alterations in the statute.

To label every systematic method of conducting monetary policy a "rule," or alternatively to describe every strategy as "discretionary," is more likely to foster confusion than to provide insight. Both of those procrustean usages are avoided in this book.

Recognition of the potential ambiguity in terminology, on the other hand, serves a constructive purpose. An analyst is thereby prevented from trying to draw an excessively sharp distinction between rule and discretionary strategies. Decision procedures can be classified according to the types and amounts of flexibility they permit—for example, ranked along a spectrum as in table 15-1. But the differences among strategies are a matter of degree, not of kind. No substantive issue turns on where the semantic dividing line is drawn between rules and discretion.

As used here, a procedure is termed a rule if it permits little or no flexibility for policymakers to adjust the settings on their instruments or (in the case of two-stage strategies) their target path for the key intermediate variable in response to new data, to changes in their perceptions of how the economy works, or to alterations in their ultimate objectives. The more flexibility of this sort policymakers have, the greater the degree of discretion. Both "rules" and "discretion" refer only to decisions about instruments and intermediate-target variables.

Strategies That Use Money as an Intermediate Target

Given the preceding background, *money* strategies can now be seen in better perspective in relation to other strategies. Money strategies are merely one family in the large class of two-stage strategies. The intermediate-target approach, in turn, is only one of two possible broad approaches to the formulation and implementation of monetary policy.

Some readers might have gotten the impression from chapter 6 and part 2 that the proponents of using money as an intermediate target have no differences among themselves other than those arising from the problem of choosing the best definition of the money stock. That impression would be mistaken, however; money strategies and views about them may differ on two other dimensions. Significant differences among variants may exist, first, because of different periodicities of upper-level decisionmaking about the target path for money and, second, because of differences in the choice of the actual instruments.

The first type of difference is a manifestation of the general differences among two-stage strategies focused on above. Some proponents of a money strategy advocate fixing the target path for money by a nondiscretionary rule that would never, or hardly ever, be altered. Milton Friedman's position, for example, is that the money stock should grow at a constant rate from some base value in a past period, with the precise rate of growth mattering less than the adoption of some stated and known rate.[15] The intent is to have the central bank adopt a self-denying ordinance or, if necessary, to impose the nondiscretionary rule on the central bank through statutory legislation.

Towards the opposite end of the spectrum of possibilities, other proponents recommend calculating the target money path intermittently—say, every three months. The Federal Reserve System in the United States, for example, has been making quarterly revisions in its longer-run aggregate targets in the years since those targets were first publicly announced. The language used by the Federal Reserve in its policy record emphasizes that, in principle, the target paths adopted at a particular Open Market Committee meeting are "subject to review and modification at subsequent meetings."[16]

Still other proponents of a money strategy advocate setting the target paths for money once every calendar year. The annual money targets announced in Germany and in the United Kingdom are illustrations of this "infrequent" reconsideration of the intermediate-target path.[17]

Differences among variants of money strategies in their choice of actual instruments typically receive less analytical attention than they deserve. Under some types of central-bank behavior in adjusting the actual instruments, a money strategy with a short-term interest rate as the instrument can generate outcomes very different from those generated by a money strategy with a reserve-money aggregate

15. See Milton Friedman, *The Optimum Quantity of Money and Other Essays* (Aldine, 1969), pp. 47–48, 108–10. Other sources for Friedman's position include *A Program for Monetary Stability* (Fordham University Press, 1959); and *Capitalism and Freedom* (University of Chicago Press, 1962), chap. 3.

16. See, for example, "The Implementation of Monetary Policy in 1976," *Federal Reserve Bulletin* (April 1977), pp. 323–36; "Monetary Policy and Open Market Operations in 1977," *Federal Reserve Bulletin* (April 1978), pp. 265–78; and "Monetary Policy Report to Congress," *Federal Reserve Bulletin* (March 1979), pp. 185–200. The Federal Reserve's strategy for conducting policy is complex and several alternative interpretations can be made of the role played by these longer-run aggregate targets.

17. See, for example, Deutsche Bundesbank *Annual Report 1976;* ibid. *1977,* and *1978;* and *Bank of England Quarterly Bulletin,* vol. 17 (March 1977), p. 48; ibid. (June 1977), pp. 147–55. In the spring of 1978, United Kingdom money targets began to be reviewed and rolled forward every six months; see Bank of England, *Report and Accounts for the Year Ended 28 February 1978,* pp. 6–10 and *Bank of England Quarterly Bulletin,* vol. 18 (December 1978), pp. 499–502. As in the case of the Federal Reserve's behavior with respect to its money targets, the implementation of a money strategy by the Bundesbank and the Bank of England is a complex matter open to several interpretations. These complexities cannot be considered here but could not be overlooked if the intent were to comment upon the degree to which these central banks do or do not single-mindedly pursue a money strategy in actual practice.

as the instrument. The important problems of instrument choice and instrument variation are discussed further in the chapters that follow.

When identifying differences of view among proponents of money strategies, it is also relevant to recall that the various proponents may differ in the degree of detail with which they model the behavioral relationships embodied in the upper-stage and lower-stage submodels. The most prevalent variant of a money strategy focuses on the aggregative demand and supply functions for money. It is a money-market conceptualization of macroeconomic behavior, presupposing either a version of the simplest money-income model or some version of the extended IS-LM models (see chapter 5). In principle, however, a two-stage decision procedure focused on money can be employed in conjunction with models that are more systemic in emphasis.

Evaluation of Alternative Strategies

What criteria of evaluation should be used in appraising the relative merits of alternative strategies? How should policymakers select their preferred strategy?

Suppose the loss function to be used by policymakers were accurately described to all analysts concerned with evaluating strategies and suppose each analyst agreed to use that loss function in his evaluation. Suppose further that all the analysts agreed on some particular modeling approach as the least inadequate representation of the behavior of the economy and its response to policy actions. In that event, there would in principle be a single straightforward criterion for evaluating strategies. Loosely, the criterion would be to select that strategy most likely to achieve the agreed objectives of policy. Stated more precisely, the criterion would have the analysts choose the strategy that minimizes the expected value of the agreed loss function subject to the constraints of the consensus modeling approach.

In any practical policymaking situation, it will be extremely difficult to obtain agreement on the details of a loss function and on which of the available structural modelings of the economy's behavior should be adopted as least inadequate. Even without full agreement, however, analysis could still proceed. Each strategy could be tested in conjunction with several competing modeling approaches and alternative loss functions. One strategy might well emerge from that analysis as superior to the others no matter what modeling approach and loss function are used.

A procedure of that sort is a plausible way to evaluate strategies. Among the methods currently feasible, it may be preferred in an actual policymaking situation.[18]

18. For research that illustrates how this approach could be systematically pursued, see Kenneth D. Garbade, *Discretionary Control of Aggregate Economic Activity* (Lexington Books, 1975); Gregory C. Chow, "Control Methods for Macroeconomic Policy Analysis," *American Economic Review* (May 1976, *Papers and Proceedings, 1975*), pp. 340–45; Chow, "Evaluation of Macroeconomic Policies by Stochastic Control Techniques," *International Economic Review*, vol. 10 (June 1978); and the references to various Federal Reserve studies in John H. Kalchbrenner and Peter A. Tinsley, "On the Use of Optimal Control in the Design of Monetary Policy," Special Studies Paper 76 (Board of Governors of the Federal Reserve System, Division of Research and Statistics, July 1975). Some aspects of this approach are criticized in John H. Kalchbrenner and others, "On Filtering Auxiliary Information in Short-Run Monetary Policy," Special Studies Paper 108 (Board of Governors of the Federal Reserve System, Division of Research and Statistics, February 1978); a revised version of this paper, by Kalchbrenner and Peter Tinsley, appears in Karl Brunner and Allan H. Meltzer, eds., *Optimal Policies, Control Theory, and Technology Exports*, Carnegie-Rochester Conferences on Public Policy, vol. 7 (North-Holland, 1977).

While the following three chapters adopt the spirit of that procedure, the analysis is not strictly organized along those lines. It is not feasible here to articulate a large number of alternative loss functions and competing models. Moreover, my purpose is to evaluate the relative merits of strategies in general terms, abstracting from the specifics of particular loss functions and models.

Because strategies that use money as an intermediate target are the primary concern of the analysis, the best way to proceed is to return to the fundamental issues about money strategies flagged at the end of chapter 6. Why might policy-makers be motivated to choose a money strategy? What justifications can be given for decomposing the overall decision problem into two stages, with different periodicities of decisionmaking for the two stages? And why should money rather than some other intermediate variable be selected as the surrogate target? Once the various possible answers to these questions have been identified, the subsequent analysis can then be organized around evaluation of their plausibility.

Possible Justifications for a Money Strategy

Few advocates of a money strategy have provided a systematic rationale for preferring it. But it is possible to glean as many as six conceivable justifications from the academic literature, central-bank publications, and journalistic commentary. These justifications emphasize (1) the flow of new information about the economy, (2) uncertainty, (3) resource costs, (4) game-theoretic, expectational interactions between policymakers and the private sector, (5) insulation of monetary policy from politics, and (6) insulation of monetary policy from human error. For reasons that will become clear in the next two chapters, these justifications raise issues that are independent of and more analytically significant than the "reliability" and "controllability" propositions identified in chapter 6.

Information Flow and Uncertainty

The most prevalent rationalizations of a money strategy intermingle information-flow and uncertainty considerations. The argument goes as follows: policymakers' knowledge of the behavioral relationships constituting the economy is highly uncertain. Furthermore the flow of new data about the economy is such that policymakers tend to be least well informed about the macroeconomic variables that ultimately matter most to them. Ultimate-target variables are often measured with the longest unit periods of observation (for example, quarterly or even annually for gross national product) and are subject to the longest lags between occurrence, collection of the datum, and availability of the datum to policymakers. Intermediate variables such as monetary aggregates, on the other hand, tend to have daily or weekly unit periods of observation and shorter lags between occurrence, collection, and availability.

These characteristics of existing knowledge and the flow of new information, it is argued, justify the use of an intermediate-target strategy. The thought seems to be that, since policymakers cannot directly observe many of their ultimate objectives more often than quarterly or monthly, and even then only with a sub-stantial lag, they should select an intermediate variable for which data are frequently and promptly available and use that variable as a surrogate objective. Once a target path is specified for the key intermediate variable, say money, that surrogate target can serve as the focus of policy actions. Because new data for the surrogate target become available frequently, uncertainty is minor about the behavior of money relative to its target path; policymakers can closely monitor that behavior and promptly correct incipient deviations. In contrast, the ultimate-target variables are glimpsed only intermittently and their evolution in the intervening periods is thus significantly more uncertain; it is not possible to make continuous adjustments in policy in response to observed deviations of ultimate-target variables from their desired paths.

This information-flow and uncertainty rationalization by itself does not provide a justification for the use of *money* as the intermediate-target variable. But the argument is typically supplemented by assertions that, out of all the conceivable intermediate variables, some monetary aggregate best meets the twin criteria of controllability and reliability.[19]

As an illustration of the invocation of uncertainty by proponents of a money strategy, consider these comments made by Milton Friedman in congressional testimony:

> What we observe, if we look at the record, is that, in fact, instead of using monetary fluctuations as a balance wheel, instead of using them to offset other forces, we have used them to intensify other forces. Why have we done this? We have done this because we simply do not know enough, we are not smart enough, we have not analyzed sufficiently and understood sufficiently the operation of the world so we know how to use monetary policy as a balance wheel. Therefore, what I am saying is that the first step we ought to take is to convert monetary policy from being a destabilizing force into at least being a neutral factor. . . .
>
> What I am urging is a policy of trying to have a moderate, steady, stable policy that you can live with indefinitely instead of having a world in which you go from one side to the other each time thinking you are going to offset something that is going on, but in practice, more often than not intensifying it.[20]

Karl Brunner and Allan Meltzer refer to both the uncertainty and information points together in a second example:

> From the point of view of the Account Manager executing the vague directives issued by the Board of Governors, the level of employment, prices, and the pace of economic activity are far removed from his operations and are of little use when he is deciding on his daily or hourly operations. . . . Central bankers respond to the uncertainty of knowledge about the state of the economy and the lag in receipt of information by choosing targets that reduce uncertainty and appear to increase the amount of available information. . . .
>
> The [intermediate] target problem is the problem of choosing an optimal strategy or strategies to guide monetary policy operations in the money markets under the conditions of uncertainty and lags in the receipt of information about the more remote goals of policy.[21]

19. See the discussion of propositions 6-A and 6-B in chapter 6.
20. Testimony of Milton Friedman in *The Federal Reserve System After Fifty Years,* vol. 2, Hearings before the Subcommittee on Domestic Finance of the House Committee on Banking and Currency, 88 Cong. 2 sess. (Government Printing Office, 1964), pp. 1156, 1159.
21. See Karl Brunner and Allan Meltzer, "The Nature of the Policy Problem," in K. Brunner, ed., *Targets and Indicators of Monetary Policy* (Chandler, 1969), pp. 3, 2. For additional references see, for example, the contributions of Anna Schwartz, James Tobin, Karl Brunner, and William Dewald in ibid.; Karl Brunner and Allan H. Meltzer, "The Meaning of Monetary Indicators," in George Horwich, ed., *Monetary Process and Policy: A Symposium* (Richard D. Irwin, 1967), pp. 187–217; Albert E. Burger,

Although information-flow and uncertainty considerations are often intertwined in a rationalization for a money strategy, the two ought not to be confused. The information-flow justification asserts that a money strategy is more efficient than other strategies in digesting the new data that become available about the economy and in using them to further the ultimate objectives of monetary policy. The uncertainty justification asserts that a money strategy should be preferred over other strategies because it is a superior way of coping with uncertainty about how the economy functions and about how policy actions affect the economy.

Resource Costs

Any strategy for conducting monetary policy uses up resources that have an opportunity cost—for example, the amounts of time that policymakers themselves expend in making decisions, the number of supporting staff required, the quantities of pencils, computer hours, and other supplies consumed. In principle, these costs may have an important bearing on strategy choice. All other things being equal, the strategy incurring lowest resource costs should be preferred.

It can be and has been argued that strategies using money as an intermediate target incur smaller resource costs than other strategies. Hence this argument constitutes another conceivable justification for policymakers adopting a money strategy.

Game-Theoretic, Expectational Interactions between Policymakers and the Private Sector

Private-sector economic units make their decisions in part in response to expectations of government policy actions. Alternative strategies for conducting monetary policy will generate different private-sector expectations, which in turn will differently affect the evolution of the economy. Therefore it is germane to analyze how alternative strategies may affect the formation of expectations and the decisionmaking processes of private-sector agents. An argument that some particular strategy is better than others from the perspective of favorably affecting private-sector expectations and behavior can thus constitute another set of grounds for preferring one strategy rather than another.

In recent years as increasing attention has been devoted to inflation and to expectational phenomena by the economics profession, an argument of this type has grown popular as a justification for using the money stock as the intermediate target of monetary policy. Price-setting and wage-setting decisions in the private sector, it is argued, depend on expectations of inflation, and hence on expectations of monetary-policy actions. If individual private-sector agents are uncertain about prospective monetary-policy actions, and especially if they believe that inflationary actions initiated by them are likely to be subsequently accommodated by an easier monetary policy (the central bank erring on the side of following more expansionary policies rather than risking more unemployed resources), they will feel less restraint in pushing up prices and wages. However, it is argued, if policymakers voluntarily

"Implementation Problem for Monetary Policy," *Federal Reserve Bank of St. Louis Review*, vol. 53 (March 1971), pp. 20–30; Leonall C. Andersen, "Selection of a Monetary Aggregate for Economic Stabilization," *Federal Reserve Bank of St. Louis Review*, vol. 57 (October 1975); and Benjamin M. Friedman, "Empirical Issues in Monetary Policy: A Review of Monetary Aggregates and Monetary Policy," *Journal of Monetary Economics*, vol. 3 (January 1977), pp. 87–101.

give up some of their discretion by announcing a target path for the money stock and then—credibly—holding to that path, private-sector agents can no longer expect monetary policy to accommodate any inflationary price and wage decisions. Private-sector behavior will adjust accordingly, it is believed, and policymakers can thereby achieve greater success at moderating inflation than would otherwise have been possible. More generally, the argument seems to be that policymakers should make their own behavior less unpredictable by nailing their flag to the mast of a preannounced money target, which in turn will induce better private-sector behavior and a better evolution of the economy than would occur with continuous discretionary adaptation of monetary policy.

A representative and influential statement of this justification for a money strategy may be found in the 1978 Mais lecture given by the Governor of the Bank of England:

> The main role therefore that I see for monetary targets is to provide the framework of stability within which other policy objectives can be more easily achieved. It is essential for this purpose that monetary targets should be publicly announced, and that the authorities' resolve be sufficient to make that announcement credible. . . .

> We cannot allow the economy to expand very vigorously until inflation has been brought down to a lower level and we have some assurance that this achievement will not be threatened by faster expansion. A monetary target both provides an overt public expression of this need for caution, and embodies some assurance that action will be triggered if the need for it arises. In the short term, if things go wrong adherence to an unchanged monetary target will be the equivalent of early restraining discretionary action. In the longer term, the commitment to monetary targets will also ensure a general degree of caution. One may therefore say that in a figurative sense to announce such a commitment is to serve notice on all those concerned, including those concerned with wage bargaining, how far the authorities are prepared to finance inflation.[22]

Insulation from Politics

The preceding justification raises issues that begin to spill over from economics, as traditionally defined, into politics. The last two motives that can underlie an advocacy of a money strategy are even more blatantly political.

Consider the following line of reasoning. Democratic-pluralist societies have political systems that expose government officials to pressures to discount the long run too heavily and to try to facilitate short-run political objectives (for example, ensuring the reelection of incumbent officials). It is therefore desirable to insulate macroeconomic policy decisions from the vagaries of the political process. Monetary policy in particular should be shielded from political pressures that would otherwise induce central-bank officials to pursue overly expansionary, inflationary policies. An appropriate method of providing the required insulation is to specify and announce a target path for the money stock and then to adjust the instruments of policy to adhere as closely as possible to that path.

This fifth justification for a money strategy, it should be noted, calls for a variant in which the upper-level reviews of the money path are infrequent. If the money

---

22. "Reflections on the Conduct of Monetary Policy," *Bank of England Quarterly Bulletin*, vol. 18 (March 1978), pp. 34–35. This justification for a money target has been frequently and prominently mentioned by the Deutsche Bundesbank in its monthly and annual reports. See also William Fellner, *Towards a Reconstruction of Macroeconomics: Problems of Theory and Policy* (Washington, D.C.: American Enterprise Institute for Public Policy Research, 1976).

target path were to be recalculated as often as intermittently (say, every third month), the degree of effective insulation of the decisions from political pressures might be modest, if not negligible.

The appraisal of democratic politics that underpins proposals for insulating macroeconomic policies from political pressures is well illustrated in the following comments of James Buchanan and Richard Wagner on discretionary fiscal policy:

> For most politicians, each election presents a critical point, and the primary problem they face is getting past this hurdle. . . . This is not to say that politicians never look beyond the next election in choosing courses of action, but only that such short-term considerations dominate the actions of most of them. Such features are, of course, an inherent and necessary attribute of a democracy. But when this necessary attribute is mixed with a fiscal constitution that does not restrain the ordinary spending and deficit-creating proclivities, the result portends disaster. We do not suggest that we relinquish political and public control of our affairs, but only that politicians be placed once again in an effective constitutional framework in which budgetary manipulation for purposes of enhancing short-run political survival is more tightly restrained, thereby giving fuller scope to the working of the long-term forces that are so necessary for the smooth functioning of our economic order. Just as an alcoholic might embrace Alcoholics Anonymous, so might a nation drunk on deficits and gorged with government embrace a balanced budget and monetary stability.[23]

Insulation from Human Error

A final line of reasoning justifying a money strategy relies on both political and psychological observations. Government officials, it is observed, are prone to make mistakes and yield to temptations—no less so than an average citizen of the society. In addition, because of their highly visible positions within the political system, officials are subjected to greater than average temptations. When key officials prove to be incompetent or self-serving, the argument continues, the consequences for the polity and the economy are much more serious than in the case of mistakes or turpitude on the part of the average citizen. Therefore the government should conduct economic policy, and monetary policy in particular, using procedures that minimize the scope for costly human error. A promising way of rendering the economy less vulnerable to such error than it would otherwise be is to have the central bank follow an intermediate-target strategy focused on the stock of money.

This last justification for a money strategy, like the preceding one, requires either a nondiscretionary rule for the money target path or an interim rule that is changed only infrequently.

Money Strategies versus Intermediate-Target Strategies in General

Each of the six possible justifications for a money strategy is evaluated in the chapters that follow.

---

23. James M. Buchanan and Richard E. Wagner, *Democracy in Deficit: The Legacy of Lord Keynes* (Academic Press, 1977), p. 159. See also Samuel Brittan, *The Economic Consequences of Democracy* (London: Temple Smith, 1977); William D. Nordhaus, "The Political Business Cycle," *Review of Economic Studies*, vol. 42 (April 1975), pp. 169–90; and Edward R. Tufte, *Political Control of the Economy* (Princeton University Press, 1978).

The analysis concentrates on *money* strategies rather than intermediate-target strategies in general because it is money strategies that are widely advocated and implemented. Yet a focus on money could be misleading. At bottom, as will be seen, the relative merits of intermediate-target and single-stage strategies have little to do with money per se. In some ways it would have been more revealing to ask first whether there are plausible justifications for using an intermediate-target strategy whatever may be the key intermediate variable. Then at a later point, if the answer to the prior question were affirmative, the analysis could have taken up the secondary issue of whether the money stock is the most appropriate candidate to serve as the surrogate target.

So far in the literature on monetary policy, attention has been mainly directed at the secondary issue. For example, countless regressions of nominal gross national product on various monetary aggregates and other intermediate variables have been estimated. Such evidence can be interpreted as shedding light, indirectly if not directly, on whether this or that variable will make a better intermediate target for monetary policy. Yet the secondary issue should hardly command such attention unless it can be shown that intermediate-target strategies in general are a superior strategy type. Investigations of this logically prior question are, with a few prominent exceptions, conspicuously absent from the literature.

While the following chapters conduct the analysis in terms of money strategies, therefore, they also emphasize the more general characteristics of intermediate-target strategies that are usually neglected. The argument in many places is applicable to any intermediate-target strategy, not merely those employing the money stock as the surrogate objective.

CHAPTER SIXTEEN

Model Choice and Strategy Choice

THE OBJECTIVE of chapters 16, 17, and 18 is to evaluate alternative strategies for conducting monetary policy, concentrating on the rationalizations that may be given for adopting a two-stage approach using money as an intermediate target. The analysis focuses in particular on the relative merits of money strategies and single-stage strategies of discretionary instrument adaptation.

Most proponents of a money strategy prefer to apply that strategy in conjunction with a simplified, money-market conceptualization of the economy. Most advocates of discretionary instrument adaptation prefer larger and more systemic models. In the controversies surrounding the conduct of monetary policy, the problems of strategy choice and model choice thus tend to be entangled.

For reasons given in chapter 15, a cogent evaluation of strategies is greatly helped by a differentiation between model choice and strategy choice. The analysis in chapters 17 and 18 makes that differentiation and concentrates on the latter. Because model choice and strategy choice are confused in most people's perceptions, however, this chapter begins with some further observations on the difficulties faced by policymakers when selecting their model of how the economy behaves.

The remainder of this chapter discusses three issues closely associated with model choice. One section evaluates the "reliability" and "controllability" propositions of part 1, showing that they have much greater significance for model choice than for the issue of whether to accept or reject a money strategy. The next section evaluates the resource-cost justification for a money strategy. The final sections of the chapter address the issue of whether it is logically valid, and if so under what conditions, to decompose the overall policy problem into two stages with the money stock as the fulcrum between the two.

Model Choice: Still an Unsettled and Controversial Subject

Enormous difficulties still confront those who attempt to conceptualize macroeconomic behavior. The less systematic and empirical the modeling effort, the less apparent these difficulties may be to the model builder; but they are nonetheless present. The currently preferred methods of trying to resolve these difficulties are heterogeneous and controversial—appropriately so given the meager state of existing knowledge.

This unsettled state of the art argues for avoiding too strong an attachment to any particular modeling approach and for trying to evaluate alternative approaches on their merits merely as analytical interpretations of macroeconomic behavior. It is difficult enough to judge which modeling approach constitutes the least inadequate description of the economy for the purposes of macroeconomic policymaking without also trying simultaneously to resolve the problems of how to use the policymaking model once it has been selected.

Consider the issue of the size of the policymaking model. The larger the model, the greater are the difficulties in understanding it analytically and the more costly it may be to use it. Yet larger models can embody more of the existing knowledge of behavioral relationships and in more sophisticated ways. Researchers differ on the most appropriate balance to strike between these competing considerations; no consensus on the issue is yet evident.[1]

The issue of model size is closely related to what William Fellner has termed "the problem of shortcuts."[2] Macroeconomists are in the business of making (what to them seem) plausible aggregative simplifications of microeconomic behavioral relationships. Unfortunately, one man's plausible simplification is another's unjustified assumption. Yet no analyst can avoid making shortcuts of one sort or another. Indeed, building a successful structural model of macroeconomic behavior is primarily a problem of making artful shortcuts that introduce only minor distortions into the representation of the underlying true behavior.

Some of the controversy between so-called monetarists and Keynesians is due to misunderstandings. But another substantial part is attributable to differences in judgment about the analytical appropriateness of various shortcuts. These differences in turn lead to differences in judgment about which behavioral relationships and which sectors of the economy warrant prominent emphasis in a policymaking model. Monetarists are inclined to stress the demand for and supply of money and to believe that a money-market model can capture the most important aspects of macroeconomic behavior—at least those with which they think the central bank should be concerned. Many nonmonetarists, on the other hand, believe that a more systemic approach to modeling is necessary if serious distortions are to be avoided. Although recent years have brought a narrowing of the differences between monetarists and Keynesians in their *descriptive* analysis of the economy (see below), there remain noteworthy differences of emphasis in model construction. A generally acceptable compromise model is not yet in sight.[3]

Current views in the economics profession also differ sharply about the preferred treatment of expectations in macroeconomic models (see the discussion in chapter 18).

A final controversy about model choice arises because of the difficulties of constructing a model that adequately reflects not only the existing structural

1. See, for example, the various papers collected in Lawrence R. Klein and Edwin Burmeister, eds., *Econometric Model Performance: Comparative Simulation Studies of the U.S. Economy* (University of Pennsylvania Press, 1976).

2. William Fellner, *Towards a Reconstruction of Macroeconomics: Problems of Theory and Policy* (Washington, D.C.: American Enterprise Institute for Public Policy Research, 1976), chaps. 5 and 6.

3. Compare also the Brunner-Meltzer view that a policymaking model should omit the allocative details of aggregate demand with the typical nonmonetarist view that a model should specify separate behavioral relationships for (for example) consumption, fixed investment, inventory investment, and government expenditures. See Karl Brunner and Allan Meltzer, "Aggregative Theory for a Closed Economy" and "Reply" in Jerome L. Stein, ed., *Monetarism* (Amsterdam: North-Holland, 1976), pp. 100, 181.

knowledge of the economy but also the degree of uncertainty associated with that knowledge. The most critical aspect of a model may be the manner in which it identifies (or fails to identify) the degree of confidence that can be associated with the form and parameters of its various behavioral relationships. In this dimension as well, however, the economics profession has not yet reached a wide consensus on the preferred techniques of model specification and estimation.

In these circumstances, single-minded advocacy of either large or small models to the exclusion of the other may be a defensible posture for some academic economists. And the frontiers of knowledge may get pushed outward at a faster rate if some researchers analyze specialized, nonsystemic models while others pursue a synthetic and systemic approach. But risk-averse policymakers and their staffs should not adopt any of those extreme postures. Their approach to model choice should be characterized by eclecticism and agnosticism.

Model Choice and Fiscal Policy

Agnostic policymakers might decide to use a simplified model predominantly concerned with the money market—conceivably even some version of the extended *IS-LM* models described in chapter 5. At any rate, a posture of agnosticism with respect to model choice cannot rule that possibility out a priori. But agnosticism cannot be plausibly stretched so far as to justify using a money-market model focused exclusively on the consequences of monetary-policy actions, with no provision whatsoever for the other aspects of macroeconomic policy. Even those economists who consider themselves monetarists should find that conclusion uncontroversial.

In the debates of the 1950s and 1960s, monetarism was frequently characterized as the view that money is all, or virtually all, that matters for the determination of aggregate nominal income.[4] That characterization was disputed and refined.[5] What-

4. For example, see James Tobin, "The Monetary Interpretation of History," *American Economic Review*, vol. 55 (June 1965), particularly p. 481. Tobin began an article published in 1970 with the sentences: "Milton Friedman asserts that changes in the supply of money *M* (defined to include time deposits) are the principal cause of changes in money income *Y*. In his less guarded and more popular expositions, he comes close to asserting that they are the unique cause"; see James Tobin, "Money and Income: Post Hoc Ergo Propter Hoc?" *Quarterly Journal of Economics*, vol. 84 (May 1970), p. 301. See also Karl Brunner, "The Role of Monetary Policy," *Federal Reserve Bank of St. Louis Review*, vol. 50 (July 1968); "The Role of Money in National Economic Policy," with commentary by Paul A. Samuelson, David Meiselman, James Tobin, Allan H. Meltzer, and Henry C. Wallich, in *Controlling Monetary Aggregates: Monetary Conference, June 1969* (Federal Reserve Bank of Boston, 1969); and Leonall C. Andersen, "The State of the Monetarist Debate," with commentary by Lawrence R. Klein and Karl Brunner, *Federal Reserve Bank of St. Louis Review*, vol. 55 (September 1973), pp. 9–14.

5. Milton Friedman objected to the Tobin characterizations of monetarism cited in the previous footnote; see, for example, Friedman's "Comment on Tobin" and Tobin's "Rejoinder," both in the *Quarterly Journal of Economics*, vol. 84 (May 1970), pp. 318–27, 328–29. Friedman clarified his own views as follows: "changes in the quantity of money as such *in the long run* have a negligible effect on real income, so that nonmonetary forces are 'all that matter' for changes in real income over the decades and money 'does not matter'. On the other hand, we have regarded the quantity of money, plus the other variables (including real income itself) that affect *k* [the inverse of the income velocity of money] as essentially 'all that matter' for the long-run determination of nominal income. . . . [For shorter periods of time] we have emphasized that changes in *M* are a major factor, though even then not the only factor, accounting for short-run changes in both nominal income and the real level of activity (*y*). I regard the description of our position as 'money is all that matters for changes in *nominal* income and for *short-run*

ever else they believed, however, monetarists were protesting the degree to which discussions of fiscal policy monopolized the Keynesian analysis of macroeconomic policy. Monetarists insisted, at a minimum, on the proposition that fiscal policy is not the *only* thing that matters for the determination of nominal and real aggregate income.

For a time in the late 1960s and early 1970s, some monetarists appeared to believe the even stronger proposition that fiscal policy does not matter at all, or virtually not at all. For example, a statement in one of Milton Friedman's *Newsweek* columns argued—or certainly seemed to argue—that the effects of bond-financed changes in government expenditures or tax revenues on aggregate nominal income were "certain to be temporary and likely to be minor."[6] Accordingly, analysis of monetarist views by nonmonetarist economists concentrated for several years on the question: "Does fiscal policy matter?"[7]

While many analytical details of the effects of fiscal actions on the economy remain unsettled, research in recent years has produced a substantial convergence of views about the broad question. Macroeconomists of all analytical persuasions have become progressively more sophisticated about the significance of the consolidated government budget constraint, the subtlety of the interrelationships between fiscal policy and monetary policy, and the need for a more adequate dynamic analysis of how both stocks and flows change and interact through time.[8] As a result, there are now few if any monetarists who espouse the extreme view that fiscal policy matters so little that it can safely be ignored (when discussing the determination of aggregate output, the price level, and nominal aggregate income).[9] Similarly, there are now few if any Keynesians who deny that the short-run, medium-run, and long-run impacts of a bond-financed fiscal action may differ significantly.[10]

---

changes in real income' as an exaggeration but one that gives the right flavor of our conclusions. I regard the statement that 'money is all that matters,' period, as a basic misrepresentation of our conclusions." See Milton Friedman, "A Theoretical Framework for Monetary Analysis," in R. J. Gordon, ed., *Milton Friedman's Monetary Framework: A Debate With His Critics* (University of Chicago Press, 1974), p. 27.

6. See James Tobin, "Friedman's Theoretical Framework," pp. 77–89, and Friedman, "Comments on the Critics," pp. 137–48, especially pp. 139–43, both in Gordon, ed., *Milton Friedman's Monetary Framework*.

7. See especially Alan S. Blinder and Robert M. Solow, "Does Fiscal Policy Matter?" *Journal of Public Economics*, vol. 2 (November 1973), pp. 319–37; Blinder and Solow, "Analytical Foundations of Fiscal Policy," in Blinder and others, *The Economics of Public Finance* (Brookings Institution, 1974), pp. 3–115; Albert Ando and Franco Modigliani, "Impacts of Fiscal Actions on Aggregate Income and the Monetarist Controversy: Theory and Evidence," and James Tobin and Willem Buiter, "Long-run Effects of Fiscal and Monetary Policy on Aggregate Demand," both in Stein, ed., *Monetarism*.

8. The analysis in chapter 14 of the symbiosis between fiscal policy and monetary policy omits references to the debate between monetarists and nonmonetarists over the efficacy of fiscal policy. The issues discussed in chapter 14, however, are precisely those that have figured in that debate (for example, "crowding out" and the short-run versus long-run effects of a bond-financed fiscal action).

9. See especially Karl Brunner and Allan Meltzer, "An Aggregative Theory for a Closed Economy," and "Monetarism: The Principal Issues, Areas of Agreement, and the Work Remaining," both in Stein, ed., *Monetarism;* Ettore F. Infante and Jerome L. Stein, "Does Fiscal Policy Matter?" *Journal of Monetary Economics*, vol. 2 (November 1976), pp. 473–500.

10. Blinder and Solow summarized their understanding of the convergence of analytical views about fiscal policy as of the spring of 1976 as follows: "What then is the neo-Keynesian-cum-reconstructed-monetarist view of the operation of fiscal policy? In the short run, bond financed deficit spending has its major effects on output; prices barely respond. As lags in the consumption and investment functions work themselves out, this stimulative effect reaches a peak after K (for 'Keynesian') quarters. In the meantime, wages and prices begin to rise, restricting the real money supply and otherwise depressing aggregate demands. The multiplier effect of real government spending on real GNP therefore starts to decline, while

Whatever the views of monetarists and nonmonetarists may have been in earlier stages of the controversy, therefore, the extreme views that "money and monetary policy do not matter" and "fiscal policy does not matter" need no longer be taken seriously today. Differences of analytical view now turn on the relative magnitudes and timing patterns of the impacts of the two types of actions, but not on whether one or the other can be ignored.

The implications for the problems of model choice of this convergence in analytical views are not straightforward. Few of the fundamental difficulties are resolved. Policymakers must still choose from a wide range of potential models— some predominantly emphasizing monetary policy, others incorporating analytical leanings toward the view that fiscal-policy actions are more powerful, still others striving to give prominent attention to both.

One conclusion, however, does emerge clearly from the research of recent years. The macroeconomic model used by policymakers must at a minimum include some representation of the instruments of both monetary policy and fiscal policy. Preferably, the model should be sufficiently sophisticated to take into account the manner in which monetary policy and fiscal policy interact as part of an overall national policy regimen.

Agnostic policymakers are thus on firm ground if they reject simple income-determination models that ignore financial markets and make no allowance for the effects of monetary-policy actions. They are equally justified in rejecting the simplest and smallest of money-market models. It may or may not be prudent—an impartial analyst cannot yet render a definitive verdict—to choose a small model that pays special attention to money demand and supply. But there are no good grounds for selecting a model that omits any representation of fiscal-policy actions.

The Significance of the Reliability and Controllability Propositions

As explained in part 1, advocacy of a money strategy typically rests on descriptive assertions about the reliability of the links between the money stock and ultimate-target variables (proposition 6-A of chapter 6) and the controllability of the money stock by the central bank (proposition 6-B). Criticism of a money strategy typically asserts that those reliability and controllability propositions are false; falsity of the propositions is regarded as sufficient grounds for rejecting a money strategy. Both advocates and opponents, in other words, attribute great significance to the issue of whether the propositions are correct descriptions of reality.

Neither the advocates nor the opponents, however, have discriminated between the implications of the propositions for model choice and for strategy choice. They have thereby overlooked a point of critical importance: despite the general presumption to the contrary, *the reliability and controllability propositions do not have decisive significance for strategy choice.*

---

the effect on the price level builds. Eventually, after M (for 'monetarist') quarters, the effect on real output is completely dissipated if the long-run Phillips curve is literally vertical. If not, there is a small positive effect on real output. But the effect on nominal output is not dissipated." Alan S. Blinder and Robert M. Solow, "Does Fiscal Policy Still Matter? A Reply," *Journal of Monetary Economics*, vol. 2 (November 1976), pp. 501–10.

Suppose operational definitions of some sort were supplied for "relative relia-bility" and "close controllability." Given such definitions, imagine that definitive empirical evidence became available to establish the correctness or falsity of propositions 6-A and 6-B.

If the propositions were shown to be false, what conclusions could be drawn? Most advocates of a money strategy would find such evidence unsettling because they apply a money strategy in conjunction with a small model emphasizing the demand for and supply of money. From the perspective of *model* choice, falsity of the reliability and controllability propositions would constitute sufficient grounds for eschewing a model that is predominantly money-market in focus. But now consider the implications for *strategy* choice. Falsity of the propositions would weaken any presumption in favor of using money as an intermediate target but could not logically lead to a rejection of that strategy. A money strategy could be applied in conjunction with an eclectic, systemic model; conceivably the money strategy could outperform discretionary instrument adaptation even though the money stock could not be controlled closely and the links between money and ultimate targets were as uncertain as other behavioral relationships.

Alternatively, suppose the evidence showed the reliability and controllability propositions to be empirically correct. Eclectic policymakers would then accord money demand and supply and the instruments of monetary policy a prominent role in their model. The more conclusive was that evidence (for example, the more "stable" the money demand function relative to other behavioral relationships), the stronger would be the case for giving special emphasis to the money market in *model* choice.[11] From the perspective of *strategy* choice, however, no decisive implications would follow. Just as a money strategy could be applied in conjunction with a large systemic model, discretionary instrument adaptation may be applied in conjunction with small money-market models. Even if policymakers used a simple money-income model (thereby ignoring fiscal policy), the question of whether to choose a single-stage or a two-stage strategy would still remain. The reliability and controllability propositions do not deal, one way or the other, with the analytical points at issue for strategy choice. The tendency of advocates of a money strategy to leap from those propositions to their strategy recommendation involves a logical hiatus and a confusion between the problems of model choice and strategy choice.

The reliability and controllability propositions can be kept in proper focus and their significance correctly evaluated if three related conclusions are borne in mind. First, the empirical correctness or falsity of the propositions has a primary bearing on model choice, not on strategy choice. Second, correctness of the propositions is a sufficient condition for adopting a policymaking model that gives prominent attention to money demand and supply, but does not justify the exclusion from the model of other behavioral relationships. Third, correctness of the propositions is not a sufficient condition for the appropriateness of a money strategy.[12]

---

11. There would be no compelling reason in such circumstances to have money demand and supply dominate the model altogether. Model construction need not involve simple either-or choices, such as the selection of either the money market or some other market; both may be represented in the model. Even if there is a strong predilection to keep the model small, there is no need to single out one "least unreliable" relationship and refuse to pay attention to other, somewhat more uncertain relationships. Given the resources that can be devoted to the modeling effort, the genuine challenge of model choice is to combine as much as possible of existing knowledge into an internally consistent and analytically tractable model.

12. It follows as a corollary of these conclusions that empirical correctness of the reliability and

Resource Costs of Alternative Strategies

The opportunity costs of the resources consumed in implementing various strategies are a relevant consideration when choosing among them. As the number of variables and behavioral relationships in a policymaking model are increased, the associated costs also rise—perhaps even more than proportionately.

Since money strategies tend to be applied in conjunction with small money-market models while proponents of discretionary instrument adaptation tend to prefer larger more systemic models, it may at first seem plausible to argue that money strategies incur smaller resource costs than other strategies. But further reflection reveals that this argument, too, confuses the problems of model choice and strategy choice.

Preferably, strategies should be compared for a common degree of policymakers' ignorance about the behavioral relationships constituting the structure of the economy. The lesser resource costs associated with application of a two-stage money strategy in conjunction with a small money-market model are a function primarily of the choice of model, not the choice of strategy. Hence those resource costs should have little bearing on strategy choice. Policymakers first ought to ask how well a strategy of discretionary instrument adaptation would perform if it were coupled with a comparably small model. Conversely, the greater degree of structural knowledge incorporated in a larger systemic model used in conjunction with a strategy of discretionary instrument adaptation should not be invoked as a reason for preferring discretionary instrument adaptation. Policymakers should first ask how well a money strategy could perform if it were coupled with that larger systemic model (given that all strategies incur heavier resource costs when applied with the larger model).

Properly interpreted, therefore, the resource-cost justification for a money strategy is not an argument that should critically influence strategy choice. Resource-cost considerations may constitute persuasive grounds for avoiding the use of large and complex models. They should not have a conclusive bearing on the issue of whether to use the money stock as an intermediate target in a two-stage decision process.

Agnosticism with respect to model choice and objectivity about strategy choice would in principle require analyzing how all alternative strategies would perform in conjunction with a wide range of models. Such an analysis would, for example, compare the relative performance of money strategies and discretionary instrument adaptation strategies for various types of systemic model. And it would study the consequences of applying both strategy types in conjunction with several variants of a small, money-market model. Such a comprehensive analysis of alternative strategies and models would bring the question of resource costs into proper focus: the gross benefits of each model-strategy combination would be viewed in the light of the resource costs necessary to implement it.

A comprehensive analysis of that sort is not feasible here. But chapter 17 does compare a money strategy and discretionary instrument adaptation on the basis of

---

controllability propositions is a necessary, but still not sufficient, condition for the appropriateness of a money strategy applied in conjunction with a model predominantly emphasizing the money market.

a common, simplified model. As will be seen, under those circumstances there is little difference in the resource costs associated with the two strategy types.

Recursive and Nonrecursive Models of Macroeconomic Behavior

The remainder of this chapter turns to the question first flagged in chapter 6: do the causal relationships characterizing the structures of actual economies permit the larger decision problem facing policymakers to be decomposed into two separate, subordinate problems?

Policymakers confront some technical aspects of this question, or should confront them, at the time they select their model of how the economy reacts to their policy actions. Yet the issue is not merely a technical matter of model specification. Stripped of its technical details, the question is fundamental: under what conditions will it be analytically valid to conduct monetary policy using a two-stage decision process?

The clearest way to define the issue is with the aid of a series of simplified illustrative models. The contrasts among the models bring out the differences between recursive and nonrecursive models and identify the recursiveness properties which a model must have if it is to be used in conjunction with an intermediate-target strategy. The focus of attention in each case is on the policy decisions to be made in the "current" period, referred to as period t. Decisions are assumed to be made at the beginning of the period.

Suppose first that policymakers, despite the good reasons for rejecting that approach, nonetheless conceptualize the economy in terms of the simplest of money-income models (equations 5-25 in chapter 5). That model can be rewritten as

$$M_t^s = \overline{m}(H_t)$$
$$(16\text{-}1) \qquad M_t^d = \overline{k}(Y_t)$$
$$M_t^s = M_t = M_t^d.$$

The time subscripts on the variables serve as a reminder that the model can be applied to a succession of time periods.[13]

Implementation of a two-stage money strategy within the context of that model is conceptually straightforward. The policymakers alter the setting on their instrument, the monetary base, which directly influences the money stock. The money stock, interacting with the stable demand function, influences national income, the ultimate-target variable.

The recommended process for making policy decisions involves reasoning backward from the ultimate target. First, a desired value for income, Y_t^*, may be

---

13. For simplicity in exposition, the model 16-1 is "deterministic" as presented in the text; that is, there is no acknowledgment (not even the inclusion of stochastic "error" terms) that the parameter approximations $\overline{m}$ and $\overline{k}$ will not always be exactly equal to the true definitional values m_t and k_t. The ex post identities defining the money multiplier and income velocity are $m_t \equiv M_t/H_t$ and $V_{Yt} \equiv Y_t/M_t \equiv 1/k_t$. The other models discussed in this chapter are also presented as though they were deterministic; uncertainty considerations are analyzed in chapter 17.

chosen; Y_t^* is presumably that income level judged to be the best attainable in the current circumstances. Next, the demand function for money is solved to obtain that value of the money stock, M_t^*, consistent with the ultimate target Y_t^*; this step is the upper-level calculation. Then, in a second lower-level calculation, the money-supply function is solved to obtain the particular setting for the policy instrument, $\hat{H}_t$, that is likely to keep M_t at its intermediate-target value of M_t^*.[14] Finally, the central bank implements the lower-level calculation: it adjusts the monetary base to the $\hat{H}_t$ setting and maintains that setting for the duration of period t.

Imagine that this single-period decision process is replicated over time.[15] Policymakers and private-sector economic units would then observe a sequence of values—time paths—for Y^*, Y, M^*, M, and $H = \hat{H}$. The degree of success of monetary policy could be judged in this simplified framework by some measure of the discrepancy between the paths of Y and Y^*.

The model 16-1 clearly permits a dichotomization of the decision process into two separate stages. It does so because the pattern of causation between the model's two endogenous variables is entirely unidirectional (from the money stock to income). In technical terms 16-1 is *recursive* or *consecutive* in a way that justifies decomposing the model into two parts one of which (the money-supply equation) is independent of the other.

The recursive or alternatively interdependent nature of models can be illustrated by means of so-called arrow schemes.[16] Such a diagram for the model 16-1 is shown in figure 16-1; because that model is both recursive and highly simplified, the diagram of causal interrelationships among its endogenous variables is also extremely simple.

Note that 16-1 would continue to be recursive even if it is imagined that the policymakers adjust the parameter values $\bar{k}$ and $\bar{m}$ from one period to the next (so that $\bar{k}_t$ and $\bar{m}_t$ are exogenous *variables*).[17] So long as the artificial assumption is maintained that $\bar{k}_t$ and $\bar{m}_t$ are entirely predetermined (do not depend on the current-period values of the endogenous variables Y_t and M_t), the model lends itself to decomposition into two parts and hence to a two-stage decision process.

A simple money-income model would also continue to exhibit the recursiveness required for a two-stage strategy even if the model were dynamic, that is, included lagged values of variables as determinants of income or money. Consider, for example, a model of the general form:

(16-1a)
$$M_t = m(H_t, H_{t-1})$$
$$Y_t = v(M_t, M_{t-1}).$$

This ad hoc two-equation system has no credibility as a behavioral model of money demand and supply and their interaction in a "money-market equilibrium." It is

14. The upper-level "solution" from the model is $M_t^* = \bar{k}(Y_t^*)$; the lower-level solution is $\hat{H}_t = M_t^*/\bar{m} = (\bar{k}/\bar{m})Y_t^*$.

15. Strictly speaking, as analyzed below, the lower-level calculation is replicated each period whereas the upper-level calculation is made only intermittently or infrequently.

16. For a discussion of the basic concepts of recursiveness and simultaneous interdependency, see R. Bentzel and B. Hansen, "On Recursiveness and Interdependency in Economic Models," *Review of Economic Studies*, vol. 22 (1954–55), pp. 153–68.

17. As examples of the manner in which the policymakers could adjust $\bar{k}$ and $\bar{m}$ from one period to the next, they could (a) specify that $\bar{k}_t = k_{t-1} \equiv M_{t-1}/Y_{t-1}$ and $\bar{m}_t = m_{t-1} \equiv M_{t-1}/H_{t-1}$, or (b) set $\bar{k}_t$ and $\bar{m}_t$ according to extrapolations obtained from regressing past values of k and m on a time trend.

Figure 16-1. *Causal Interrelationships in the Simplest Money-Income Model*

Endogenous variable	Behavioral dependence on other variables	Arrow scheme of causal interrelationships among endogenous variables		
		Period $t-1$	Period t	Period $t+1$
Y Nominal income	$Y_t = Y(M_t, \bar{k})$ [from money-demand function]			
M Money stock	$M_t = M(H_t, \bar{m})$ [from money-supply function]			

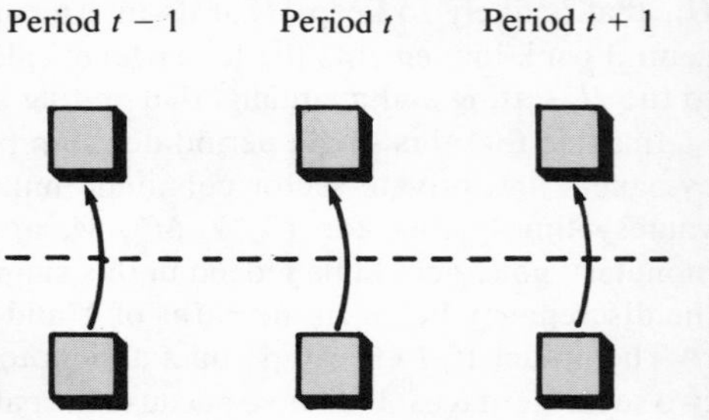

Model: Equations 16-1

Exogenous variables: H (and exogenous parameters $\bar{k}$ and $\bar{m}$)

Recursiveness properties: Model is recursive within each period and over a succession of periods; causation is unidirectional from the lower-stage money submodel to the upper-stage submodel for nominal income.

nevertheless a multiperiod model logically capable of generating time paths of the endogenous variables M and Y given an exogenous time path for H; and it is recursive in a manner that permits its decomposition into upper-stage and lower-stage submodels. Both within a single period and over a succession of periods, the money stock is an endogenous variable in the lower-stage submodel and yet an exogenous variable from the perspective of the upper-stage submodel.

Now consider the same questions about recursiveness and dichotomization of the decision process in the context of a model that is slightly less simplified, for example:

(16-2)
$$M_t^d = P_t[f(r_t, y_t)]$$
$$M_t^s = m(r_t, X_t^M)$$
$$y_t = g(r_t, Z_t, X_t^F)$$
$$P_t = h(y_t, Z_t)$$
$$M_t^d = M_t = M_t^s$$
$$Y_t = P_t(y_t).$$

This model is the extended *IS-LM* conceptualization of equations 5-30, rewritten with time subscripts on the variables. It determines the four endogenous variables y_t (real income), P_t (the price level), r_t ("the" interest rate), and M_t (the money stock) as a function of the policy instruments X_t^M ("monetary policy") and X_t^F ("fiscal policy") and a vector of nonpolicy exogenous variables Z_t.

Suppose policymakers at the central bank think of real income and the price level in 16-2 as ultimate-target variables and at the beginning of period t designate a pair of values, y_t^* and P_t^*, as the best attainable outcomes under the prevailing circumstances. Suppose further that at the beginning of the period the policymakers somehow obtain estimates, the expected values of which are contained in a vector $E(Z_t)$, of the nonpolicy exogenous variables for period t. (The symbol E here in part 4 represents the expected-value operator of the mathematics of expectations; the reader should not confuse it with the E of part 3, which represents the entire vector of stochastic error terms in a structural model.) Suppose finally that the settings for fiscal-policy instruments have already been chosen as $\hat{X}_t^F$. Then the decision problem for the central bank (for period t) is to use the estimates $E(Z_t)$, the fiscal settings $\hat{X}_t^F$, and the model 16-2 in conjunction with the targets y_t^* and P_t^* to determine the most appropriate settings for the instruments of monetary policy. Can policymakers at the central bank divide their overall decision into two separate decisions—determining an intermediate-target value M_t^* in an upper-level calculation and then, given this value M_t^*, calculating the preferred settings $\hat{X}_t^M$ at a second stage?

They cannot logically do so, because the model 16-2 does not possess the recursiveness that permits such a dichotomization.[18] The nonrecursive nature of the model is apparent from the arrow scheme in figure 16-2. When a model is recursive, it is possible to decompose it into two submodels such that the arrows are exclusively unidirectional between one submodel and the other. But no such division is possible in figure 16-2; whatever the ordering of the endogenous variables in the arrow scheme, there are always arrows running in both directions among the variables. All the endogenous variables in 16-2 are simultaneously interdependent.[19]

If the policymakers believe that 16-2 is the correct model, therefore, there is no valid way for them to calculate an intermediate-target value M_t^* in an upper-stage submodel and then, in a subsequent calculation with a lower-stage submodel, the instrument settings $\hat{X}_t^M$ designed to achieve M_t^*. A single-stage decision, on the other hand, is conceptually straightforward: the targets y_t^* and P_t^*, the estimates of nonpolicy exogenous variables $E(Z_t)$, the fiscal settings $\hat{X}_t^F$, and *all* of the model's behavioral relationships can be "solved" simultaneously to determine a set of preferred monetary settings $\hat{X}_t^M$.[20]

The distinction between models that do and do not permit a two-stage decision process can be clarified further by continuing to think in terms of models of the *IS-LM-MS-P* genre and altering the assumed behavioral relationships in various ways.

18. Policymakers could employ a two-stage decision process despite their model, but this would be "illogical" in the sense that they would thereby ignore the constraints of the analytical framework they have chosen to represent the behavior of the economy. See the further discussion below.

19. When endogenous variables in a model are simultaneously interdependent, the particular manner of drawing an arrow scheme is somewhat arbitrary (that is, it depends on which equations are "normalized" on which variables). The details of the arrow scheme do not, however, influence the conclusions about nonrecursiveness.

20. This discussion presumes that the vector X_t^M contains more than one instrument. The complications of uncertainty and coordination with fiscal policy, although suppressed here, are considered in chapters 17 and 18; incorporation of those complexities in the argument does not alter the conclusions stated in the text.

Figure 16-2. *Causal Interrelationships in the Extended* IS-LM *Model*

Endogenous variable	Behavioral dependence on other variables	Arrow scheme of causal interrelationships among endogenous variables		
		Period $t-1$	Period t	Period $t+1$
P Price level	$P_t = h(y_t, Z_t)$			
y Real income	$y_t = g(r_t, Z_t, X_t^F)$			
r Interest rate	$r_t = r(P_t, y_t, M_t)$ [from money- demand function]			
M Money stock	$M_t = m(r_t, X_t^M)$ [money-supply function]			

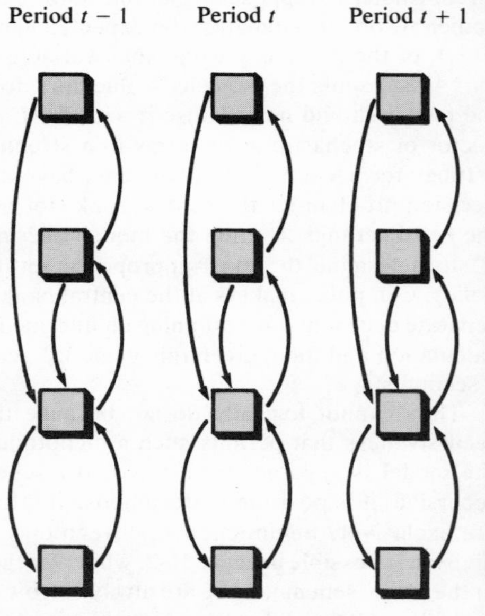

Model: Equations 16-2

Exogenous variables: X^M, X^F, Z

Recursiveness properties: Model is not recursive, either within a single period or across a succession of periods.

In particular, it is instructive to ask: what relationships between y_t, P_t, r_t, and M_t would constitute recursiveness of the appropriate type? Four further examples are given. In two of them, the models exhibit the recursiveness required for a two-stage decision; in the other two the necessary recursiveness is not present.

First, suppose the model 16-2 is altered to form a new model, 16-3, identical to 16-2 except for the fact that the money-supply function no longer depends on interest rates and is therefore influenced only by policy instruments:

(16-3, money supply) $M_t^s = m(X_t^M)$.

The resulting model is recursive with respect to the money stock; this fact is visually evident in the arrow scheme in figure 16-3. Because of that recursiveness, furthermore, policymakers could decompose their decision process into a two-stage calculation pivoting on the money stock.

How would a two-stage solution of the model 16-3 be carried out? For the upper-

Figure 16-3. *Causal Interrelationships in a Variant of the Extended* IS-LM *Model Where Money Supply Does Not Depend on Interest Rates*

Endogenous variable	Behavioral dependence on other variables	Arrow scheme of causal interrelationships among endogenous variables		
		Period $t-1$	Period t	Period $t+1$
P Price level	$P_t = h(y_t, Z_t)$			
y Real income	$y_t = g(r_t, Z_t, X_t^F)$			
r Interest rate	$r_t = r(P_t, y_t, M_t)$ [from money-demand function]			
M Money stock	$M_t = m(X_t^M)$ [money-supply function]			

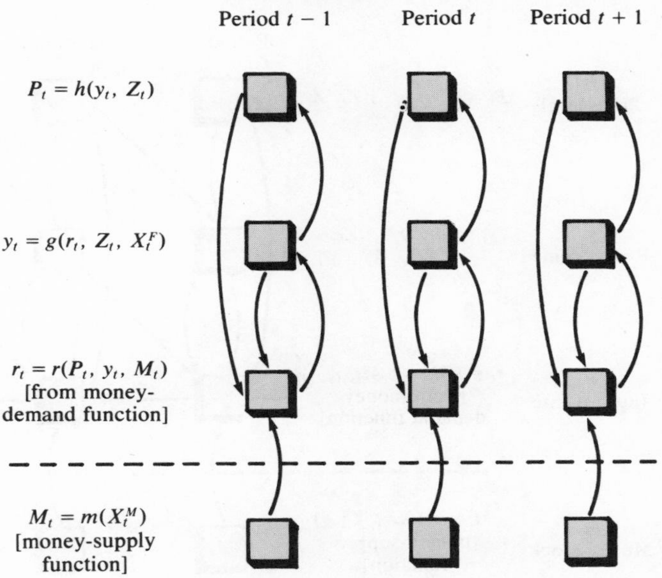

Model: Equations 16-3

Exogenous variables: X^M, X^F, Z

Recursiveness properties: Model is recursive; causation is unidirectional from a lower-stage money submodel to an upper-stage submodel determining P, y, and r.

level calculation, policymakers would use that part of the model above the dashed line in the arrow scheme in figure 16-3. In that submodel, the money stock would be treated as though it were an exogenous variable. Given designated target values y_t^* and P_t^* and values for $\hat{X}_t^F$ and $E(Z_t)$, the upper-stage submodel would be solved for an intermediate-target value of the money stock M_t^*.[21] Then, for the lower-level calculation, the remaining part of the model would be used to calculate $\hat{X}_t^M$, the appropriate settings for monetary policy. In the lower-stage submodel (in this case, simply the money-supply function), the money stock would be treated as an endogenous variable. The asymmetrical treatment of the money stock—as an

21. There are two ultimate-target variables in the example; since the value of M_t most consistent with P_t^* could differ from the value most consistent with y_t^*, the choice of M_t^* would have to reflect a trade-off in the loss function between the two ultimate objectives.

Figure 16-4. *Causal Interrelationships in a Dynamic Variant of the Extended* IS-LM *Model Where Money Supply Does Not Depend on Interest Rates*

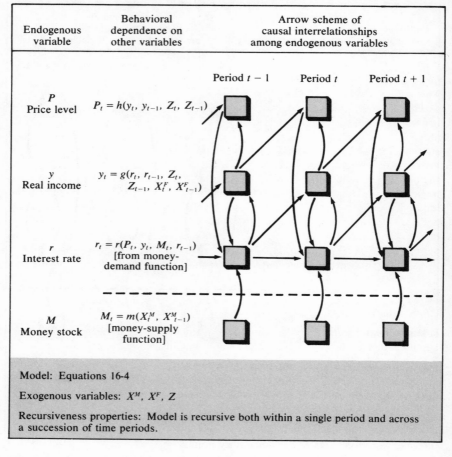

Endogenous variable	Behavioral dependence on other variables	Arrow scheme of causal interrelationships among endogenous variables
P Price level	$P_t = h(y_t, y_{t-1}, Z_t, Z_{t-1})$	
y Real income	$y_t = g(r_t, r_{t-1}, Z_t, Z_{t-1}, X^F_t, X^F_{t-1})$	
r Interest rate	$r_t = r(P_t, y_t, M_t, r_{t-1})$ [from money-demand function]	
M Money stock	$M_t = m(X^M_t, X^M_{t-1})$ [money-supply function]	

Model: Equations 16-4

Exogenous variables: X^M, X^F, Z

Recursiveness properties: Model is recursive both within a single period and across a succession of time periods.

exogenous variable in the upper-stage submodel and as an endogenous variable in the lower-stage submodel—would be analytically legitimate because of the model's recursiveness properties.

Second, consider an extended *IS-LM* model that introduces dynamic effects. Suppose private-sector behavior is assumed to adjust to policy actions and changes in nonpolicy exogenous variables with a lag so that the full impacts of changes in exogenous variables no longer take place entirely within the period in which the changes occur. Suppose further that some of the endogenous variables react to each other with lags. Finally, suppose that money supply reacts with a lag to monetary-policy instruments but, as in 16-3, does not depend on interest rates or other endogenous variables. A particular version of the extended *IS-LM* model that incorporates these ideas might be written

$$M_t^d = P_t[f(r_t, r_{t-1}, y_t)]$$
$$M_t^s = m(X_t^M, X_{t-1}^M)$$
(16-4)
$$y_t = g(r_t, r_{t-1}, Z_t, Z_{t-1}, X_t^F, X_{t-1}^F)$$
$$P_t = h(y_t, y_{t-1}, Z_t, Z_{t-1})$$
$$M_t^s = M_t = M_t^d$$
$$Y_t = P_t(y_t).$$

This model is shown in figure 16-4.

Plainly, 16-4 retains the recursiveness evident in 16-3 even though the former is a multiperiod, dynamic generalization of the latter. Both models are decomposable, within a single period and across a succession of periods, into an upper-stage submodel in which the money stock is effectively exogenous and an independent lower-stage submodel in which the money stock is determined endogenously. Given the upper-stage submodel, it is logically feasible to calculate a target path for the money stock extending over a span of several future periods. In keeping with the longer periodicity characteristic of upper-level decisions, this intermediate-target path can be kept unchanged over this succession of future periods. New lower-level decisions, on the other hand, can be taken at the beginning of each short-run period. Because of the multiperiod recursiveness of the model, no logical contradiction is involved in this asymmetry of the decision periodicities.

Now consider a third variant of the extended *IS-LM* model, identical in every respect to 16-4 except for the money supply function. Specifically, rather than

(16-4, money supply) $$M_t^s = m(X_t^M, X_{t-1}^M),$$

suppose the model incorporates the theoretically more acceptable idea that money supply depends on both interest rates and policy instruments:

(16-5, money supply) $$M_t^s = m(r_t, r_{t-1}, X_t^M, X_{t-1}^M).$$

The resulting model, 16-5, is summarized in figure 16-5. It is nonrecursive—all four endogenous variables are simultaneously interdependent—both within a single period and across a span of periods. There is no analytically valid way to decompose it into two submodels and it therefore cannot be used in conjunction with an intermediate-target strategy for monetary policy.

Finally, consider a fourth variant. Continue as in the two preceding examples to postulate the existence of lagged effects. Suppose now, however, that financial variables are assumed to have no influence on real-sector variables and the price level *within the current period* but instead only have such effects in subsequent periods. To incorporate that idea, it is necessary merely to delete the current-period value of interest rates from the real-income equation in 16-5. The new function would then be:

(16-6, real income) $$y_t = g(r_{t-1}, Z_t, Z_{t-1}, X_t^F, X_{t-1}^F).$$

Suppose that the new model 16-6 is identical to 16-5 except for this one alteration.[22]

22. If no other alteration is made, the model 16-6 continues to postulate that current-period values of real variables are relevant for current-period values of financial variables; for example, the current-period demand for money is still assumed to depend on current-period real income and current-period prices.

Figure 16-5. *Causal Interrelationships in a Dynamic Variant of the Extended* IS-LM *Model with Money Supply Dependent on Interest Rates*

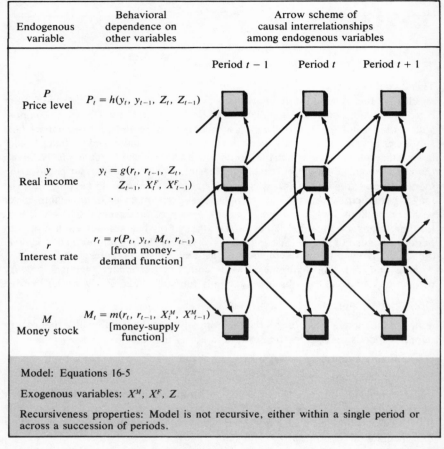

Endogenous variable	Behavioral dependence on other variables	Arrow scheme of causal interrelationships among endogenous variables		
		Period $t - 1$	Period t	Period $t + 1$
P Price level	$P_t = h(y_t, y_{t-1}, Z_t, Z_{t-1})$			
y Real income	$y_t = g(r_t, r_{t-1}, Z_t, Z_{t-1}, X_t^F, X_{t-1}^F)$			
r Interest rate	$r_t = r(P_t, y_t, M_t, r_{t-1})$ [from money-demand function]			
M Money stock	$M_t = m(r_t, r_{t-1}, X_t^M, X_{t-1}^M)$ [money-supply function]			

Model: Equations 16-5

Exogenous variables: X^M, X^F, Z

Recursiveness properties: Model is not recursive, either within a single period or across a succession of periods.

As figure 16-6 indicates, this last illustrative model is recursive within a single time period but is not recursive over a succession of time periods. Within a single period, the causation in the model runs exclusively from an income-price submodel (the "real" sector) to a money-interest rate submodel (the "financial" sector). But over a succession of periods the real and the financial submodels interact.

Models with dynamic interaction between the real and financial sectors of the sort portrayed in 16-6 are of substantial theoretical interest. Rationalizations for "point-in-time" analysis of the behavior of financial markets, for example, typically rely on the presumption that asset markets tend to adjust fairly rapidly while product markets and labor markets adjust significantly more slowly. Models of the genre of which 16-6 is a simplified example embody dynamic behavior of that sort.

But 16-6 does not have sufficient recursiveness properties to permit a two-stage decision process for monetary policy. A dichotomization of the decision process

Figure 16-6. *Causal Interrelationships in a Dynamic Variant of the Extended* IS-LM *Model That Is Recursive within a Single Time Period but Not Recursive over a Succession of Time Periods*

Endogenous variable	Behavioral dependence on other variables	Arrow scheme of causal interrelationships among endogenous variables
		Period $t - 1$ Period t Period $t + 1$
P Price level	$P_t = h(y_t, y_{t-1}, Z_t, Z_{t-1})$	
y Real income	$y_t = g(r_{t-1}, Z_t, Z_{t-1}, X_t^F, X_{t-1}^F)$	
r Interest rate	$r_t = r(P_t, y_t, M_t, r_{t-1})$ [from money-demand function]	
M Money stock	$M_t = m(r_t, r_{t-1}, X_t^M, X_{t-1}^M)$ [money-supply function]	

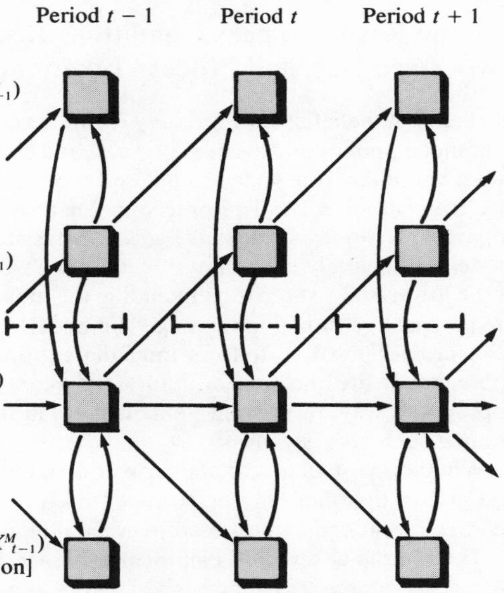

Model: Equations 16-6

Exogenous variables: X^M, X^F, Z

Recursiveness properties: Model is recursive from the income-price sector to the money-interest-rate sector *within a single period* but is not recursive and not decomposable *over a succession of time periods*.

is possible for a *single* future period. Yet it is the essence of a strategy using money as an intermediate target to fix a target path for the money stock over a succession of *several* periods. The financial-sector variables would have to be exogenous from the perspective of the real sector *over all periods* before the model could be validly decomposed into an upper-stage submodel and a lower-stage submodel. The limited recursiveness of 16-6 is thus of no help to policymakers in decomposing the model over a run of future periods. Yet such a decomposition is a logical prerequisite for calculating a multiperiod target path for the money stock that is independent of the period-by-period variation in monetary-policy instruments.

The illustrative models described in this section are highly simplified. It should be clear, however, that the same issue of recursiveness properties should be raised with respect to any model no matter how systemic or large. If a systemic model is recursive in an appropriate way, it is analytically possible to decompose it into two submodels and employ a two-stage decision process using the money stock as a pivot. If a model does not exhibit the appropriate type of recursiveness, on the other hand, it is not possible to use it in conjunction with an intermediate-target strategy focused on the money stock—or, to be strictly accurate, not possible to use it in that way without violating the analytical framework of the model itself.[23]

Are the Recursiveness Conditions Required for a Two-Stage Decision Process Likely to Be Present?

In chapter 6, belief in appropriately recursive causal links between the instruments of monetary policy and the money stock, and between the money stock and ultimate-target variables, is asserted to be a prerequisite for advocacy of a money strategy (see proposition 6-D). The preceding analysis makes the basis for that assertion apparent. A money strategy is logically consistent only if the overall policymaking model is effectively decomposable in such a way that all the endogenous variables in the lower-stage submodel, including the money stock itself, are exogenous from the perspective of the upper-stage submodel.

A crucial question follows immediately once the significance of this issue is appreciated: are the true structures of economies sufficiently recursive, in the appropriate way, to warrant policymakers in the central banks using models that assume such recursiveness?

Whether particular economies do or do not possess the necessary recursiveness is a matter that can only be resolved by bringing suitable empirical evidence to bear. Different economies, moreover, could have significantly different properties.

Even in the absence of empirical evidence, however, policymakers can safely draw a few inferences on the basis of theory alone. However money may be defined, virtually all macroeconomists postulate a dependence not only of money demand but also of money supply on interest rates (see part 1). Similarly, all theorists believe that financial-sector variables—in particular, the money stock, interest rates, or both—have an influence on real-sector variables; if this influence is not contemporaneous, then at least it occurs with the passage of time. Finally, all macroeconomic theorists believe that decisions about real-sector variables (for example, the flow of saving) have repercussions in financial markets—if not contemporaneously, then with lagged effects over time. Yet a model incorporating all three of these causal influences must, purely as a matter of logic, exhibit *some* degree of interaction among the money stock, interest rates, and real-sector variables over a succession of periods! This conclusion, which emerges clearly from the simplified models in the last section, applies no less obviously to more complex, systemic models. From a purist theoretical perspective, then, no model incorporating all three of these

23. The points made in the text about the recursiveness properties of the illustrative models can be shown more rigorously when the models are linearized and written out in matrix algebra. The final-form coefficient matrixes of a recursive model are block triangular. If the coefficient matrixes of a model are not block triangular, the model cannot be partitioned into lower-stage and upper-stage submodels. For expositional simplicity, the illustrative models used here do not include stochastic error terms. When those residuals are included in a model, even more stringent conditions must be satisfied before the model can be decomposed into two submodels: the coefficient matrixes must be block triangular *and* the variance-covariance matrix of the residuals must be block diagonal.

influences can be validly decomposed in the manner required for implementation of a two-stage money strategy.[24]

What a proponent of a two-stage money strategy must believe, therefore, is that some of these theoretically postulated interactions are sufficiently small in empirical significance that they can be safely ignored. For example, a proponent of a money strategy might claim that the behavior of financial intermediaries in supplying those deposits considered to be money depends to only a negligible extent on interest rates.

Such a position is potentially defensible so long as the available empirical evidence is still incomplete or controversial. Given that the generally accepted theory argues for the existence of endogenous interactions between the money market and the remainder of the economy, however, policymakers can reasonably place the burden of proof on those who assert that the causal dependence is essentially unidirectional in empirical practice.

24. The reader should be clear that the particular type of contemporaneous, within-period recursiveness postulated by point-in-time analysis of financial markets is *not* sufficient to validate proposition 6-D. Even if the real sector of the economy is an exogenous determinant of rapidly adjusting financial variables *in the short run*—as assumed in model 16-6 and as may well be empirically true in actual economies—the endogenous interaction of the real and financial sectors over a succession of short-run time periods prevents the decomposition of the overall model required by a two-stage strategy.

CHAPTER SEVENTEEN

The Economics of Strategy Choice

THIS CHAPTER analyzes the economic aspects of the choice of a strategy for conducting monetary policy.

Two main economic arguments are used to justify the strategy of employing the money stock as an intermediate target. The information-flow justification asserts that a money strategy is more efficient than other strategies in digesting new data about the economy and using them to further ultimate policy objectives. The second main rationale is that a money strategy is the preferred way of coping with the problems of uncertainty. The bulk of this chapter is devoted to evaluation of those two contentions.

The analysis contrasts two-stage money strategies with single-stage strategies of discretionary instrument adaptation. It concentrates on that variant of single-stage strategies in which policymakers continuously contemplate the possibility of adjustments in their instrument settings ("discretionary instrument adaptation with continuous feedback").[1]

Making the Best Use of New Data When the Policymaking Model Is Recursive

In this first section, the evaluation of the use of new data by alternative strategies is conducted with the aid of the following illustrative model:

$$Y_t = \beta_0 + \beta_1 r_t + \beta_2 r_{t-1} + \beta_3 Z_t + \beta_4 X_t^F + e_{Yt}$$

(17-1) $$M_t^d = \gamma_0 + \gamma_1 Y_t + \gamma_2 r_t + \gamma_3 r_{t-1} + e_{MDt}$$

$$M_t^s = \delta_0 + \delta_1 X_t^M + e_{MSt}$$

$$M_t^d = M_t = M_t^s.$$

1. The analysis in this chapter draws heavily on the pathbreaking work of research economists in the Federal Reserve Board's Division of Research and Statistics in applying stochastic optimization techniques to the conduct of monetary policy. See especially Stephen LeRoy and Roger N. Waud, "Observability, Measurement Error, and the Optimal Use of Information for Monetary Policy," Special Studies Paper 72 (Board of Governors of the Federal Reserve System, 1975); and John H. Kalchbrenner and Peter A. Tinsley, "On the Use of Optimal Control in the Design of Monetary Policy," Special Studies Paper 76 (Board of Governors of the Federal Reserve System, Division of Research and Statistics, July 1975); references to the underlying theoretical contributions in the optimal control and filtering literatures are given in those papers and in Peter A. Tinsley, "On Proximate Exploitation of Intermediate Information in Macroeconomic Forecasting," Special Studies Paper 59 (Board of Governors of the Federal Reserve System, Division of Research and Statistics, April 1975). Other important references include John H. Kareken, Thomas Muench, and Neil Wallace, "Optimal Open Market Strategy: The Use

This model is a linearized version of the *IS-LM-MS* framework; the three endogenous variables nominal income (Y), the interest rate (r), and the money stock (M) are determined by the exogenous instruments of monetary policy (X^M) and fiscal policy (X^F) and by nonpolicy exogenous variables (Z). To keep the exposition simple, it is convenient to interpret X^M, X^F, and Z as individual variables rather than, as hitherto, three vectors of variables. The coefficients β_1, β_2, γ_2, and γ_3 are assumed to have negative values while β_3, β_4, γ_1, and δ_1 are assumed to be positive.

The three behavioral equations in the model contain, as the minimum possible concession to the problem of uncertainty, stochastic "error" terms (e_{Yt}, e_{MDt}, and e_{MSt}). The coefficients in the equations are treated as though they are fixed and known. (Later in this chapter, when the focus is on uncertainty, this assumption is relaxed.) Lagged effects are included in two of the equations, albeit in the most rudimentary way, because several of the points made in the comparison of strategies require an illustrative model that is dynamic.

Although 17-1 suffers from all the limitations of simplified models of the *IS-LM* type, it has the decisive advantage for the purposes of the exposition here of being small and analytically tractable. All the points made below can be generalized to larger and more systemic models.

It is assumed that proponents of two-stage and single-stage strategies alike accept the relationships in 17-1 as their policymaking model. The problems of model choice are thereby held constant while the information-using characteristics of the two types of strategies are being compared.

It would be possible to analyze the illustrative model using the assumption that the interest rate r_t is chosen as the instrument of monetary policy; in that event the three endogenous variables would be Y_t, M_t, and X_t^M. But for the purposes of this section it is more revealing to assume that X_t^M is some reserve-money aggregate (for example, the unborrowed monetary base) and both a potential and the actual instrument; hence the interest rate is determined endogenously. Both the single-stage and the two-stage strategies are assumed to use X_t^M as the instrument (to avoid the difficulties of comparison that would otherwise be present if the two strategies employed different instruments). For the two-stage strategy, the intermediate-target variable is M_t.

Despite the conclusions of chapter 16, the illustrative model has been chosen to be recursive (see the arrow scheme in figure 17-1). This choice of model gives the benefit of the doubt to intermediate-target strategies and permits a comparison of the efficiency of information use under conditions when the policymakers' model can be validly decomposed into upper-stage and lower-stage submodels.

In the analysis that follows, it is assumed not only that two-stage and single-stage policymakers use the same model but also that three other aspects of decisionmaking are shared in common.

First, both sets of policymakers have the same ultimate objective. Specifically, they are assumed to have in mind the same target path for income for all future periods out to a planning horizon—a series of values Y_1^*, Y_2^*, . . ., Y_T^*—and the

of Information Variables," *American Economic Review*, vol. 63 (March 1973), pp. 156–72; Benjamin M. Friedman, "Targets, Instruments, and Indicators of Monetary Policy," *Journal of Monetary Economics*, vol. 1 (October 1975), pp. 443–73; and Benjamin M. Friedman, "The Inefficiency of Short-Run Monetary Targets for Monetary Policy," *Brookings Papers on Economic Activity, 2:1977*, pp. 293–335.

Figure 17-1. *Causal Interrelationships in the Illustrative Model 17-1*

Endogenous variable	Behavioral dependence on other variables	Arrow scheme of causal interrelationships among endogenous variables		
		Period $t - 1$	Period t	Period $t + 1$
Y Nominal income	$Y_t = Y(r_t, r_{t-1}, Z_t, X_t^F, e_{Yt})$			
r Interest rate	$r_t = r(Y_t, M_t, r_{t-1}, e_{MDt})$ [from money-demand function]			
M Money stock	$M_t = M(X_t^M, e_{MSt})$ [money-supply function]			

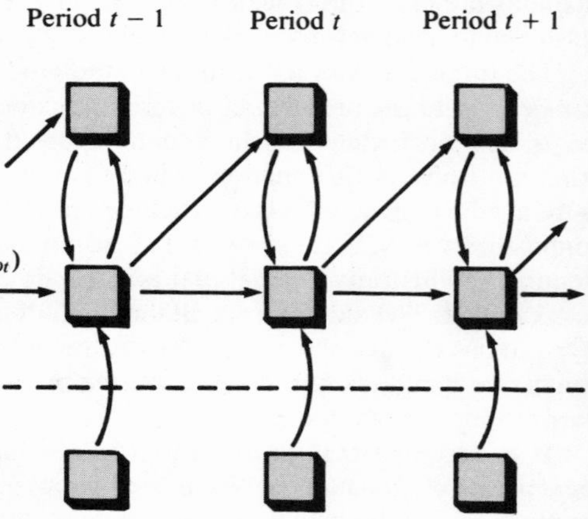

Model: Equations 17-1

Exogenous variables: X^M, X^F, Z; stochastic error terms e_Y, e_{MD}, e_{MS}

Recursive properties: Model is recursive both within a single period and across a succession of periods.

same loss function, where the loss is defined so as to depend on the deviations of actual Y from the Y^* path. As a concrete example, the loss function might be specified as:

$$(17\text{-}2) \qquad\qquad L = \sum_{t=1}^{T} (Y_t - Y_t^*)^2,$$

where the loss, L, depends both on the mean deviation of Y from the Y^* path but also on the variance of Y.[2]

Second, it is assumed that both sets of policymakers, when first observed, have the same expectations about the future values of the exogenous forces other than

2. Even when there is only a single ultimate-target variable, this type of loss function is conceptually inadequate. It fails to allow for the possibility of a time rate of discount for future losses. And policymakers might wish to give separate weights to the "bias" and "variance" of Y in relation to the Y^* path. For example, policymakers could choose to define loss as:

$$(17\text{-}2a) \qquad\qquad L = \sum_{t=1}^{T} \left(\frac{1}{1 + r^*} \right)^t [w_1(Y_t - Y_t^*) + w_2(Y_t - Y_t^*)^2],$$

where r^* is the rate of social time preference and w_1 and w_2 are weights attached to the bias and the variance components of the loss. So long as two-stage and single-stage policymakers use the same loss function, omission of these and other complications does not affect the conclusions of the analysis of the economics of strategy choice.

monetary policy that drive the economy: the nonpolicy exogenous variable Z, the instrument of fiscal policy X^F, and the three structural error terms e_Y, e_{MD}, and e_{MS}. Policymakers will probably think of these latter three exogenous forces as "unexplained model misses." Since future model misses will influence the actual outcomes for Y, r, and M, however, it is just as important for the policymakers to formulate expectations of the likely time paths for these misses as for the time paths of X^F and Z. One possible method for forming these expectations of future model misses, but of course not the only method, is to postulate that the misses will always be equal to zero. The notation $E_i(K_j)$ is used to represent the policymakers' expectations of the variable K's value in period j, with the subscript i indicating that the expectation is formed at the beginning of period i.[3]

Third, both sets of policymakers are assumed to confront the same flow of new data about the evolution of the economy. The initial comparison of information use by the two-stage and single-stage strategies assumes an idealized flow of new information: new data become available only once a month on the first morning of the month; the new data received at that time pertain to the values of the variables in the preceding month (hence the data are collected immediately at the end of the period to which they refer); and monthly data are available for all variables in the policymakers' model. With these assumptions, all variables have a uniform monthly frequency of observation; "collection lags" and "availability lags" are both uniformly zero. Policymakers do not encounter such idealized conditions in real life. The purpose of conducting the initial comparison of strategies under those conditions is to provide a benchmark case with which more complicated cases can be contrasted. The subsequent comparisons of information use by the two-stage and single-stage strategies relax the idealized information conditions, first by allowing for collection and availability lags and then by allowing for differences in frequencies of observation of the variables.

Several further assumptions facilitate the analysis. The decisionmaking process in the central bank is assumed to be first observed at the beginning of month 1 (for example, on January 1). Initially, the model 17-1 is interpreted as pertaining to monthly data. The two-stage policymakers are assumed to revise their target path for the money stock intermittently. While both two-stage and single-stage strategies have monthly periodicities of decisions for the instrument settings X^M, therefore, the two-stage policymakers review their intermediate-target objective only once every calendar quarter. When first observed on January 1, the two-stage and single-stage policymakers share in common, as potential inputs to their decisions, the target time path for income Y_t^* and the beginning-of-January forecasts $E_1(Z_t)$, $E_1(X_t^F)$, $E_1(e_{Yt})$, $E_1(e_{MDt})$, and $E_1(e_{MSt})$, for $t = 1, 2, 3, \ldots, T$.[4]

Two-stage policymakers using the money stock as an intermediate target break up the model 17-1 into two pieces. The income and the money-demand equations constitute the upper-stage submodel; the lower-stage submodel is simply the money-supply equation. When a target time path for Y^* and forecast time paths for Z, X^F,

---

3. The discussion in this chapter continues to suppress the issues of how monetary and fiscal policies are coordinated and whether they should be coordinated. Chapter 18 addresses those issues.

4. Both sets of policymakers are assumed to have a policy horizon of T periods in length and to roll this horizon forward as time passes; expectations and policy plans in period $t+1$ thus look one calendar month further ahead than in period t.

e_Y, and e_{MD} are specified, the upper-stage submodel can be used to calculate an intermediate-target path for the money stock, M^*.[5] Given an M^* path and a forecast path for e_{MS}, the lower-stage submodel can be used to calculate a time path for X^M designed to keep the actual money stock close to its target path.

Policymakers following a strategy of discretionary instrument adaptation treat the entire model 17-1 as one entity. Given a target time path for Y^* and forecast time paths for Z, X^F, e_Y, e_{MD}, and e_{MS}, they derive a time path for the instrument setting X^M by means of a single-stage calculation.[6]

So long as the two-stage and single-stage policymakers use the same loss function and the same overall model, they can only reach different decisions about the time path for their instrument setting if they use the available information in different ways. The following discussion thus focuses on the differences in inputs that the two types of policymakers use in their calculations.

Discretionary Instrument Adaptation with Idealized Information Flow

Consider first the procedures followed in connection with the single-stage strategy under the idealized information conditions where all variables have a uniform monthly frequency of observation and where collection and availability lags are absent.

At the beginning of month 1 (the first day of January), when policymakers must decide the instrument setting for that month, they have just received the new data readings for the preceding month (December). Because the essence of the single-stage approach is to reason backward from ultimate targets to instrument settings without decomposing the process into stages with different periodicities of decision, the single-stage policymakers use all the data available to them and proceed directly to the problem of determining the preferred time path for X^M. If the policymakers fully exploit the knowledge and information available to them, they combine their loss function, their path for Y^*, their model, and their forecast paths for Z, X^F, e_Y, e_{MD}, and e_{MS} and choose the future path for X^M that minimizes the expected value of the loss function.

The details of the calculations required to determine the path for X^M that

---

5. The upper-stage submodel, expressed in matrix form, is

$$\begin{bmatrix} -1 & \beta_1 \\ \gamma_1 & \gamma_2 \end{bmatrix} \begin{bmatrix} Y_t \\ r_t \end{bmatrix} + \begin{bmatrix} 0 \\ -1 \end{bmatrix} [M_t] + \begin{bmatrix} \beta_0 & \beta_3 & \beta_4 \\ \gamma_0 & 0 & 0 \end{bmatrix} \begin{bmatrix} 1 \\ Z_t \\ X_t^F \end{bmatrix} + \begin{bmatrix} 0 & \beta_2 \\ 0 & \gamma_3 \end{bmatrix} \begin{bmatrix} Y_{t-1} \\ r_{t-1} \end{bmatrix} + \begin{bmatrix} e_{Yt} \\ e_{MDt} \end{bmatrix} = \begin{bmatrix} 0 \\ 0 \end{bmatrix}.$$

The final-form solution of the submodel (the form most useful to policymakers in calculating the intermediate-target path M^*) expresses Y and r as functions of current and past values of M, Z, X^F, e_Y, and e_{MD} and of initial conditions (values for Y and r in an initial period).

6. Expressed in matrix form, the model as perceived by the single-stage policymakers is

$$\begin{bmatrix} -1 & \beta_1 & 0 \\ \gamma_1 & \gamma_2 & -1 \\ 0 & 0 & -1 \end{bmatrix} \begin{bmatrix} Y_t \\ r_t \\ M_t \end{bmatrix} + \begin{bmatrix} 0 \\ 0 \\ \delta_1 \end{bmatrix} [X_t^M] + \begin{bmatrix} \beta_0 & \beta_3 & \beta_4 \\ \gamma_0 & 0 & 0 \\ \delta_0 & 0 & 0 \end{bmatrix} \begin{bmatrix} 1 \\ Z_t \\ X_t^F \end{bmatrix}$$
$$+ \begin{bmatrix} 0 & \beta_2 & 0 \\ 0 & \gamma_3 & 0 \\ 0 & 0 & 0 \end{bmatrix} \begin{bmatrix} Y_{t-1} \\ r_{t-1} \\ M_{t-1} \end{bmatrix} + \begin{bmatrix} e_{Yt} \\ e_{MDt} \\ e_{MSt} \end{bmatrix} = \begin{bmatrix} 0 \\ 0 \\ 0 \end{bmatrix}.$$

The final-form solution of the entire model expresses Y, r, and M as functions of current and past values of X^M, Z, X^F, e_Y, e_{MD}, and e_{MS} and of values for Y, r, and M in an initial period.

minimizes expected loss are not of concern here; the algebra is tedious but conceptually straightforward.[7] The point of interest here is the manner in which new data are embodied in those calculations. This can best be illustrated by moving the focus of attention forward one month to February 1, when the January 1 procedures are repeated. In principle, the February policy decision under a strategy of discretionary instrument adaptation involves four steps, as follows.

First, the policymakers compare January's actual values of the noncontrolled exogenous variable and the fiscal-policy instrument with the values they had expected at the beginning of January. If they should find that $Z_1 \neq E_1(Z_1)$ or $X_1^F \neq E_1(X_1^F)$, those facts may lead them to revise their expectations of the future paths of those variables.[8]

Second, the policymakers use the new data for the endogenous variables—the values Y_1, r_1, and M_1—to determine how badly each relationship in the model missed in January; that is, from the model equations they calculate the actually realized values e_{Y1}, e_{MD1}, and e_{MS1}. Those values are compared with what had been expected at the beginning of January—$E_1(e_{Y1})$, $E_1(e_{MD1})$, and $E_1(e_{MS1})$—and used as an information input into new, more reliable expectations of model misses over the course of this and other future months. Various techniques are available to use in the generation of these new expectations.[9]

---

7. The basic analytical steps involve substitution of the final-form equations for each period's Y into the loss function, differentiation of the expected value of the loss function with respect to each period's setting for X^M, and solution of the resulting equations for each period's "optimum" setting $\hat{X}^M$. The procedures have already been described in general terms in chapter 11 and appendix A. The calculations yield a time path $\hat{X}_t^M$ for the entire planning period ($t = 1, 2, \ldots , T$). But only the first month of this plan, $\hat{X}_1^M$, is actually implemented; the procedures are repeated each month after new data become available. The expected value of the loss function 17-2 may be written as:

$$E \sum_{t=1}^{T} (Y_t - Y_t^*)^2 = \sum_{t=1}^{T} [E(Y_t) - Y_t^*]^2 + E[Y_t - E(Y_t)]^2 = \sum_{t=1}^{T} [(\bar{Y}_t - Y_t^*)^2 + \sigma_{Yt}^2],$$

where $\bar{Y}_t$ and σ_{Yt}^2 are, respectively, the period-t mean and variance of Y. Thus the expected value of the loss function depends not only on the means but also on the variances of each period's Y (and hence not only the means but also the variances and covariances of all the exogenous driving forces Z, X^F, e_Y, e_{MD}, and e_{MS}). Although the variance of each period's Y influences the magnitude of expected loss, its contribution to the loss cannot be offset by policy. The calculation of the optimal settings $\hat{X}^M$ thus depends only on the means $\bar{Z}$, $\bar{X}^F$, $\bar{e}_Y$, $\bar{e}_{MD}$, and $\bar{e}_{MS}$; the associated path for Y is therefore that path for which $\bar{Y}_t = Y_t^*$. This "certainty-equivalence" result (which is subjected to critical scrutiny in a later section of the chapter) follows from the treatment of the model's coefficients as fixed and known.

8. In general, because of this possibility of revising expectations after the receipt of new information, it will be the case that $E_2(Z_t) \neq E_1(Z_t)$ and $E_2(X_t^F) \neq E_1(X_t^F)$ for $t = 2, 3, \ldots , T$.

9. In general, where e is used to represent the vector of all three structural error terms in the model,

$$E_2(e_t) \neq E_1(e_t), \qquad t = 2, 3, \ldots , T,$$

because it is possible to use

$$E_2(e_t) = f(e_1, e_0, e_{-1}, e_{-2}, \ldots), \qquad t = 2, 3, \ldots , T,$$

whereas one month ago expectations of February and subsequent misses could only be formulated with less information, that is on the basis of

$$E_1(e_t) = g(e_0, e_{-1}, e_{-2}, \ldots), \qquad t = 2, 3, \ldots , T.$$

Sophisticated techniques for revising these expectations exploit knowledge of serial correlation in the past misses for particular structural equations and of nonzero covariances and autocovariances among the past misses across the model's equations. See, for example, Tinsley, "On Proximate Exploitation of Intermediate Information in Macroeconomic Forecasting."

The third step in the February decision is to calculate a revised plan for the time path of the instrument setting. This is done by repeating the procedures followed in January. The calculations use as inputs the newly formed expectations $E_2(Z_t)$, $E_2(X_t^F)$, $E_2(e_{Yt})$, $E_2(e_{MDt})$, and $E_2(e_{MSt})$, where $t = 2, 3, \ldots, T+1$.

The fourth, final step in the February decision is to adopt the initial (February) setting as calculated in this revised plan and to instruct the operational staff of the central bank to implement that setting during the course of February. (The settings in the revised plan for months subsequent to February are only tentative; they can and will be reconsidered as part of the next month's decision.)

The single-stage decision in March and in all succeeding months is taken by following identical procedures to those just described for February.

A Money Strategy with Idealized Information Flow

Now consider the procedures followed in connection with the intermediate-target strategy. Let January 1 be one of the four occasions during the year when the target path for the money stock is reconsidered. The decisions to be made on January 1 must then include the determination of a new (or a reconfirmation of the old) series of target values—M_t^* for $t = 1, 2, \ldots, T$—that will condition instrument decisions until the next reconsideration of the money path three months hence.

Various methods of calculating the money path could be followed. One possibility would be to use the average historical relationship between the growth paths of M and Y that prevailed in the past and the average growth desired for Y in the future to determine an average desired growth in M over future months. Alternatively, the upper-stage submodel could be used to calculate the target path for money that would minimize the expected value of the policymakers' loss function. Choosing the money target path by minimizing expected loss would exploit the upper-stage submodel intensively while the historical-averaging method would not; unlike the latter, however, minimizing the expected loss would not result in a smooth, constant-growth-rate path for M^*.

Because of the idealized information conditions being assumed, the two-stage policymakers have access to up-to-date data for all the variables (the December data having just been received); whatever method may be followed for making the upper-stage calculation, the policymakers presumably choose to make use of those data. Once the M^* path is chosen, however, it will be kept unchanged over the course of the next three months.

The decision on the M^* path does not by itself result in any operational policy action. The action decision—where to set the instrument—is taken in conjunction with the lower-stage submodel. In the illustration here, for example, the January 1 recommendation for the setting for the month of January follows immediately from substituting the path value for M^* into the money-supply equation:

$$(17\text{-}3) \qquad \hat{X}_1^M = \frac{1}{\delta_1} [M_1^* - \delta_0 - E_1(e_{MS1})],$$

where M_1^* is the target path value for January for the money stock and $E_1(e_{MS1})$ is the policymakers' expectation at the beginning of January of the January miss in the lower-stage submodel. The meeting of policymakers on January 1 concludes by deciding to implement the January instrument setting as calculated in 17-3.

On February 1, new data are received for all variables. Policymakers thus know the actual January values Y_1, r_1, M_1, Z_1, and X_1^F. With the exception of the new datum for the January money stock, two-stage policymakers discard this new information. The money-strategy decision to be made on February 1 is only a lower-level decision and is concerned only with minimizing expected deviations of future M from the M^* path predetermined on January 1.

To decide on a February instrument setting, two-stage policymakers need to form some expectation of future misses in the lower-stage submodel's characterization of the relationships between their instrument and the money stock. They could assume simply $E_2(e_{MSj}) = 0$ for $j = 2, \ldots, T+1$. Or they could decide to retain whatever expectations they had initially held on January 1—that is, $E_1(e_{MSj})$ where j represents February and all future months. But the new information just received about the January money stock enables them to calculate the value of the money miss, e_{MS1}, that was actually realized in January; and this may lead them to form a new set of expectations about future money misses. For example, if the money stock in January was higher than its target value because the actual error e_{MS1} was greater than the error expected on January 1, the policymakers might adjust their guesses upward about likely misses in February and subsequent months.

Assume that the expectation $E_2(e_{MS2})$ is formed in some manner. Before the two-stage policymakers can use that expectation in conjunction with the lower-stage submodel and the predetermined M^* path to decide on the instrument setting for February, they must also decide what compensation, if any, to make for the money error that occurred in January. One extreme possibility is to adjust completely for the January miss (for example, aiming for a February money stock below the M^* path by an amount equal to an overshooting in January). The opposite extreme procedure is to regard bygones as bygones and to aim for the M^* path itself without any compensation for the past miss. In any event, some decision about compensation must be made.[10] The two-stage policymakers then implement an instrument setting $\hat{X}_2^M$ for the duration of February.

On the next decision date, the beginning day of March (month 3), the policymakers receive actual data for February—Y_2, r_2, M_2, Z_2, and X_2^F. Again, the two-stage policymakers discard the new information for Y, r, Z, and X^F and focus solely on the new datum M_2. As before, they may use the new datum M_2 to formulate better-informed expectations of future money-stock errors; for example, they may abandon last month's expectation of the March error $E_2(e_{MS3})$, using instead the updated expectation $E_3(e_{MS3})$. They must again decide what compensation to make in March, if any, for past deviations of the money stock from the target path set on January 1.

Finally, consider the two-stage decision process on April 1. Unlike in February and March when the intermediate-target path determined in January was taken as given, revisions in the future target values of the money stock are now contemplated as a possibility. The upper-stage submodel can be used once again; all of the new (March) data just received are potentially relevant for this month's decisions; moreover, the January and February data for Y, r, Z, and X^F may now be retrieved

---

10. The issue of compensation adjustments in current-period decisions for discrepancies between the values of M and M^* observed in past periods only arises because lower-level decisions in a two-stage money strategy are made without reference to the policymakers' loss function.

from the cubbyhole where they were temporarily discarded. All those aspects must be different from the decision process in the two preceding months because the policymakers are reopening the question of what intermediate-target path is consistent with their ultimate objectives. The April process of determining a revised M^* target path is a replica of the procedures followed three months before in January.

Conclusions for the Case of Idealized Information Flow

Two points of contrast stand out from the preceding descriptions. First, the decision procedures under an intermediate-target strategy are discontinuous. Once a quarter an upper-level decision about the target path for the intermediate variable is made with explicit reference to the policymakers' loss function. But in between those intermittent decisions, only lower-level decisions are made. A strategy of discretionary instrument adaptation, on the other hand, is characterized by a single decision procedure that is replicated each month; there are no discontinuities in the process from one month to the next.

Second, the intermediate-target strategy discards information that discretionary instrument adaptation feeds into its regular decision process. The two-stage strategy, it is true, discards new data for the upper-stage variables only temporarily. Once a quarter when the intermediate-target path is recalculated, the two-stage strategy can use data for all the variables in the policymaking model; on those dates, moreover, the two-stage strategy can make prompt use of the then most current data. But during the intervals between recalculations of the intermediate-target path, the two-stage approach ignores all new data except for variables appearing in the lower-stage submodel. In contrast, the single-stage strategy makes no distinction between lower-level and upper-level variables; behavioral relationships for the entire model rather than just a part of it are brought into play for every decision. Once available, new information is used promptly regardless of the variables to which it pertains. Whereas the two-stage strategy involves direct use of the loss function only on intermittent occasions, every monthly decision under the single-stage strategy hinges directly on a joint use of the loss function and the policymaking model.

The discontinuity of decisionmaking and the temporary discarding of new information under an intermediate-target strategy have in turn two noteworthy consequences. First, during the interval between the intermittent upper-stage decisions the two-stage strategy does not substitute revised for out-of-date expectations of the future course of the noncontrolled exogenous driving forces. The two-stage decision in March still depends upon expectations formed at the beginning of January—for example $E_1(Z_3)$ and $E_1(e_{Y3})$. The single-stage strategy, on the other hand, is continually updating the expectations on which its decisions are based. The single-stage decision at the beginning of March depends only on expectations formed at the beginning of March with the benefit of knowledge about what actually happened in January and February. Because the data for January and February are used in addition to data for the preceding year, $E_3(Z_3)$ and $E_3(e_{Y3})$ are likely to be more reliable expectations of what will happen in March than $E_1(Z_3)$ and $E_1(e_{Y3})$.

Second, during the interval between the intermittent upper-stage decisions the intermediate-target strategy continues to depend on previously formulated expectations even after actual data have become available that can be substituted for those expectations. The two-stage policy decision in March continues to be influenced by, for example, the expectations $E_1(Z_1)$, $E_1(Z_2)$, $E_1(e_{Y1})$ and $E_1(e_{Y2})$ even though (under the idealized information conditions) the actual magnitudes of those values are already known with certainty.[11] The single-stage strategy, in contrast, immediately abandons the expectation of a magnitude once the actual datum for it has been received. It is the values Z_2 and e_{Y2} themselves—rather than $E_1(Z_2)$ and $E_1(e_{Y2})$, or even $E_2(Z_2)$ and $E_2(e_{Y2})$—that enter into the single-stage policy decision in March.

This analysis leads to an unambiguous conclusion: under idealized conditions of information flow, a money strategy is inferior to discretionary instrument adaptation in efficiently using new data to condition revisions in policy. Both strategies use the same model and loss function, but discretionary instrument adaptation exploits the available data more intensively and with greater timeliness. Hence the loss realized when the money strategy is followed can never be less than, and in between the intermittent recalculations of the intermediate-target path is unambiguously greater than, the loss realized from a strategy of discretionary instrument adaptation.[12]

The preceding comparison between two-stage and single-stage strategies focuses on the most discretionary variant of both strategy types. But suppose the intermediate-target path for the money stock is revised not once per quarter but only once per year in January. In that case, the two-stage strategy will discard new data for upper-stage variables for a much longer period of time with commensurately greater inefficiency in information use. The decision about the instrument setting in November, for example, will still depend critically on the preceding January's expectations of events during the course of the year even though most of those events would in the meantime have become known facts.

The inferiority of a two-stage money strategy to discretionary instrument adaptation with continuous feedback becomes more and more marked, therefore, the longer is the interval between recalculations of the intermediate-target path. The comparative inefficiency in information use becomes especially pronounced if two-stage policymakers cling to a money target path that is revised as infrequently as once a year or is fixed by a nondiscretionary rule.

Information Flow with Lags in Data Availability

Suppose now that new data become available, not immediately after the period to which they pertain but after one month has elapsed. For example, suppose it

11. Out-of-date expectations rather than the actual data are used because the March policy decision is merely a lower-level calculation focused on the money path value M_3^*; M_3^* was determined on January 1 when actual data for period 1 and period 2 were not available.

12. The inferiority of the two-stage strategy can be demonstrated rigorously by algebraic manipulation of the illustrative model in conjunction with the loss function. For example, one can compare each strategy's expected loss for February and March as calculated on February 1; the expected loss from the two-stage strategy is unambiguously greater. (Because of the recursive nature of the model and the illustrative assumptions used in the discussion, the expected loss for the three months January, February, and March as calculated on January 1 is identical for both strategies.) An alternative comparison can be made in terms of actual loss for the entire three-month period and yields the same conclusion so long as the plausible assumption is made for each of the noncontrolled exogenous driving forces K (that is, for $K = Z$, X^F, e_Y, e_{MD}, and e_{MS}) that $|E_3(K_3) - K_3| < |E_2(K_3) - K_3| < |E_1(K_3) - K_3|$ and $|E_2(K_2) - K_2| < |E_1(K_2) - K_2|$.

takes three weeks to collect the underlying microdata (the collection lag) and the remaining days of the month to process the data and deliver the corresponding macroeconomic observations to the policymakers (the availability lag).

When data are slow to reach them because of collection and availability lags, policymakers are worse off whatever strategy for conducting policy they choose. The new data received at the beginning of a month, say January, portray the economy not in the immediate past (December) but instead more distantly in the past (November). Not only do policymakers have to form expectations of future values of the noncontrolled exogenous variables before they can formulate policy decisions, they must form expectations of events that have already occurred in the past but are not yet known.

The best that can be done under either a two-stage or a single-stage strategy is to use—within the constraints imposed by the strategy itself—the most recent data available. Hence both strategies are implemented with procedures identical to those described above but with uncertain expected values substituted for the most recent month's data wherever those data would otherwise be used in the calculations.

Given that the two-stage and single-stage policymakers both face the worsened conditions of information flow, the same points of contrast observed under the idealized conditions are evident in these circumstances. And hence the same conclusions emerge about the relative ranking of the two strategies. Because decisions under a two-stage strategy are discontinuous and involve the temporary discarding of newly available data, the two-stage strategy does not update its expectations of the future course of the noncontrolled exogenous driving forces as soon as it becomes feasible to do so and continues to depend on out-of-date expectations well after the corresponding actual magnitudes have become known with certainty. The single-stage strategy never operates with older expectations formulated in preceding months; it always substitutes updated expectations or, as soon as it becomes possible to do so, actual data.

A uniform lag in data availability thus provides no logical reason for preferring an intermediate-target strategy instead of a single-stage approach. The reverse is true: for any uniform length of lag in data availability, discretionary instrument adaptation will always dominate a two-stage money strategy from the perspective of efficiently using the most recent factual information about the economy.

Information Flow with Differences in Frequencies
of Observation for Variables

Consider next a third set of assumed characteristics of the flow of new information. Suppose that new data are immediately collected and delivered to policymakers but that observations for the ultimate-target variable Y are recorded only quarterly. As before, let the remaining model variables be measured with a monthly frequency and policy decisions be made once a month at the beginning of the month.

Relative to the situation with idealized information flow, policymakers are again at a disadvantage whatever strategy they use. Under the idealized conditions the two-stage policymakers did not use the new monthly information for Y in between the intermittent dates for their upper-stage decisions; thus they will not now regard themselves as worse off with respect to their lower-level (monthly) decisions. But the two-stage policymakers did use the monthly data for Y in their upper-level decisions at the beginning of each quarter. Single-stage policymakers are even more adversely affected. The single-stage decision in each month t under the idealized conditions could be significantly affected by the most recent monthly data Y_{t-1} (and hence e_{Yt-1}). The now discontinuous flow of information for the ultimate-target variable thus creates obvious impediments to a straightforward implementation of the single-stage procedures described earlier.

In effect, differences in the frequencies of observation of variables drive both two-stage and single-stage policymakers to think in terms of a quarterly version of their model. Only for a quarterly version do "complete" data exist.[13] On the other hand, so long as both wish to take monthly action decisions, neither the two-stage nor the single-stage policymakers can dispense with some sort of a monthly model to use in conjunction with the quarterly model.

Development of monthly and quarterly models that are consistent with each other involves model pooling and aggregation over time. The problems encountered are technically complex and cannot feasibly be summarized here. For the purposes of this discussion, it suffices to presume that both monthly and quarterly models exist, that the best possible efforts have been made to make them mutually consistent, and that both sets of policymakers believe them to be the least inadequate models available given the current state of economic knowledge.[14]

Despite the complications posed by the differences in frequencies of observation for variables, each strategy type follows procedures closely analogous to those used under idealized information conditions.

The two-stage policymakers begin their meeting on January 1 by generating a target path for the money stock. If they aspire to make their upper-stage and lower-stage decisions compatible, they express that target path in both quarterly and monthly terms and ensure that the quarterly and monthly values are internally consistent.[15] As before, the instrument-setting decision on January 1 depends only on the lower-stage submodel—see equation 17-3. Then in February and March, again as before, the two-stage policymakers discard all newly received data except observations for the money stock and set the instrument solely in accord with the lower-stage submodel. The two-stage policymakers discard less new information in these circumstances than is discarded under the idealized information conditions.

---

13. The starting set of available information on January 1 is now characterized by actual monthly data for December and earlier months for all variables except Y; the observed data for income are quarterly (fourth quarter and earlier quarters of the year just ended). The past monthly data are used to generate quarterly observations for M, r, Z, X^F, and X^M, which in turn together with the quarterly data for Y constitute the data base for the quarterly model. The exogenous forces that drive the quarterly model, in addition to the quarterly variables Z, X^F, and X^M, are the quarterly model errors e_Y, e_{MD}, and e_{MS}. Both two-stage and single-stage policymakers are again assumed to start off the year with the same ultimate objective (target path for Y) and the same forecast paths for the five exogenous forces.

14. Appropriate procedures for handling these difficulties have been developed theoretically. For a summary of the existing technical state of the art, see LeRoy and Waud, "Observability, Measurement Error, and the Optimal Use of Information for Monetary Policy"; Tinsley, "On Proximate Exploitation of Intermediate Information in Macroeconomic Forecasting"; and J. H. Kalchbrenner and P. A. Tinsley, "On Filtering Auxiliary Information in Short-Run Monetary Policy," in Karl Brunner and Allan H. Meltzer, eds., *Optimal Policies, Control Theory, and Technology Exports*, Carnegie-Rochester Conferences on Public Policy, vol. 7 (North-Holland, 1977).

15. The quarterly path value for the first quarter of the year, for example, should be equal to the three-month average of the monthly path values for January, February, and March.

There is no essential difference, however, in the two-stage procedures. The only reason that less new information is discarded is that less is available to discard.

In contrast, single-stage policymakers still use each new datum as soon as it is received. On January 1, they incorporate all the available past data and the forecast paths for all of the exogenous forces into a January instrument decision. On February 1, they use the newly received data Z_1 and X_1^F to calculate new expectations for the future paths of those variables. And they use all the available data for endogenous variables to calculate past model misses, which in turn are used to generate revised expectations for future model misses.[16] These revised expectations become inputs into a revised plan for instrument settings for February and all subsequent months out to the planning horizon. A similar process is replicated at the beginning of March and all succeeding months.

Even under information conditions where variables have different frequencies of observation, therefore, the same points of contrast between two-stage and single-stage strategies are evident. The single-stage strategy processes new information under identical guidelines each month; decisions can be somewhat discontinuous only because the receipt of new data is somewhat discontinuous. Under the two-stage strategy, however, the recalculation of the intermediate-target path at only intermittent intervals introduces an additional element of discontinuity. Furthermore, the intermediate-target strategy continues to discard information that is used by the single-stage strategy. Two-stage decisions thus depend on out-of-date expectations of future exogenous forces and on previously formulated expectations of past events even after actual data for those events have become available.

Contrary to what is often intuitively supposed, therefore, differences in the frequencies of observation of variables do not logically justify the use of a money strategy. Even during periods when ultimate-target variables are unobserved, discretionary instrument adaptation is superior in its use of new data.[17]

Information Flow with Complex, Heterogeneous Characteristics

In actual economies, the two problems of lags in data availability and differing frequencies of observation for variables are present in heterogeneous combinations. Frequencies of observation vary from daily to quarterly, and even annually. Collection and availability lags range from zero for some variables to several months (in some cases even quarters) for variables with the longest lags. The new data that become available in a month do not arrive in a convenient package at the beginning of the month before a regularly scheduled monthly meeting of policymakers. Some new data reach policymakers every day of the month; but the volume and substantive importance of the daily flow is erratic. The day on which the first estimate of the preceding quarter's gross national product is received, for example, is obviously

16. Because an observation for Y during January is not available, it is not possible to calculate a new equation error e_Y for the income equation in the model (whereas it was possible under the idealized information conditions). There is thus greater uncertainty about the revised expectations. But the revised expectations are nonetheless formulated. Because both a monthly and a quarterly model are used in conjunction, single-stage policymakers revise their expectations of both monthly and quarterly magnitudes. So-called filtering techniques are available for carrying out these revisions in a systematic manner that best exploits the available information; again, see LeRoy and Waud, "Observability, Measurement Error, and the Optimal Use of Information for Monetary Policy."

17. The degree of dominance of a single-stage over an intermediate-target strategy is reduced compared with the idealized conditions where all variables are measured with the same unit period of observation. But that is only because the information inefficiencies of a two-stage strategy that result from the discarding of new data are relatively less costly the smaller the amount of new data there is to discard.

a more important information date than a day when the new data merely refer to yesterday's market interest rates and asset prices.

Once the heterogeneity of the characteristics of the flow of new information in actual economies is taken into account, a comparison of intermediate-target and single-stage strategies becomes still more complex. In principle, both types of policymakers require a set of mutually consistent models—one each with frequencies that are annual, quarterly, monthly, weekly, and even daily. In practice, complex problems of model pooling and data aggregation across time prevent policymakers from achieving this consistency in model specification. Coherent implementation of either a two-stage or a single-stage strategy is therefore undeniably difficult under the information-flow conditions prevailing in actual economies.

The question of interest here, however, is still the comparative one: which strategy type copes least inadequately with the flow of new data? Given the complexity of information conditions in practice, is it somehow possible to rescue the view that an intermediate-target strategy processes new data more efficiently than discretionary instrument adaptation?

No matter what the characteristics of the flow of new information, the conclusion about the relative ranking of the two strategy types as information-processing procedures remains unchanged. The degree of dominance of a single-stage over a two-stage strategy is diminished as both strategy types are compared under increasingly unfavorable information conditions. But for any given information conditions, an intermediate-target strategy will perform at least somewhat more poorly.

Making the Best Use of New Data When the Policymaking Model Is Not Recursive

Since the illustrative model 17-1 is recursive in the requisite way, it is at least logically feasible to use a two-stage money strategy in conjunction with that model. But what if the true structure of the economy is not appropriately recursive yet policymakers nonetheless employ a money strategy?

One way of considering this question analytically is to postulate two illustrative models; one of them is nonrecursive and taken to be a "true" representation of the economy's structure; the other is recursive and assumed to be used by two-stage policymakers. Continue to assume, for example, that the two-stage policymakers implement a money strategy in conjunction with the recursive model 17-1. But also assume that 17-1 incorrectly describes actual behavior and that instead the correct representation is

$$Y_t = \beta_0 + \beta_1 r_t + \beta_2 r_{t-1} + \beta_3 Z_t + \beta_4 X_t^F + e_{Yt}$$

(17-4) $$M_t^d = \gamma_0 + \gamma_1 Y_t + \gamma_2 r_t + \gamma_3 r_{t-1} + e_{MDt}$$

$$M_t^s = \delta_0 + \delta_1 X_t^M + \delta_2 r_t + \delta_3 r_{t-1} + e_{MSt}$$

$$M_t^d = M_t = M_t^s.$$

The only difference between the two models is that money supply depends positively on the interest rate in 17-4 ($\delta_2 > 0$ and $\delta_3 > 0$) whereas in 17-1 it does not (δ_2 and δ_3 are incorrectly assumed equal to zero).

Figure 17-2 illustrates the model 17-4. Unlike 17-1, 17-4 cannot be decomposed into upper-stage and lower-stage submodels. It would be logically contradictory to adopt 17-4 as the least inadequate of the available models of the economy *and* to decide to pursue a two-stage money strategy.[18]

It is a straightforward extension of the analysis in the preceding section to carry out a comparative evaluation of the two strategy types with these alterations in illustrative assumptions.[19] Not surprisingly, the results of that evaluation show a superiority of discretionary instrument adaptation even more marked than before. The use of an incorrect recursive model when the true structure of the economy is not recursive compounds the inefficiencies of information use under a two-stage strategy.

It is intuitively obvious that use of an incorrect model will, other things being equal, produce worse results than if the correct model is used. This point nonetheless warrants emphasis because the desire to use a two-stage money strategy may lead policymakers to use an incorrect recursive model even when they have grounds for believing that the least inadequate model is not recursive. Discretionary instrument adaptation does not give policymakers an analogous incentive to misspecify their model's characterization of the economy's structure.

The adverse consequences of employing a money strategy when the true economic structure is not appropriately recursive can be understood intuitively as a problem of inconsistencies between the two levels of decisions. The intent of a two-stage strategy is to determine lower-level decisions for instrument settings that will facilitate the upper-level desired outcomes for ultimate-target variables. But if behavioral relationships are not causally recursive in the required manner—if the money stock not only influences but is also influenced by some of the variables associated with the upper-stage decision—the settings actually chosen at the lower level are not in fact consistent with achievement of the upper-level desired outcomes. The inconsistencies between the upper-level and lower-level decisions occur because the two-stage procedure fails to take into account elements of simultaneity between the upper-stage and lower-stage submodels. Differing periodicities for the two levels of decisions exacerbate these inconsistencies. The policy actions implemented—the lower-level instrument decisions—are directed at the *surrogate* money target. The adverse consequences of inconsistencies between lower-level and upper-level decisions therefore tend to fall mainly on the ultimate-target variables.

18. One of two statements must be true if policymakers pursue a two-stage money strategy when the true structure of the economy is not appropriately recursive. Either the policymakers must incorrectly believe that the economy manifests the requisite recursiveness, thus formulating their model incorrectly. Or else they must knowingly violate the logic of the (nonrecursive) model that they believe to be the least inadequate representation of the economy's structure. The practical consequences of the second possibility are similar to those of the first.

19. The evaluation assumes that the two-stage policymakers make each month's decisions in conjunction with the model 17-1; hence the money target path and the recommended lower-level settings for X^M are exactly as described in the preceding section. The single-stage policymakers make decisions using 17-4 as their model; although the results of each month's single-stage calculation of the setting for X^M differ from those made in the preceding section in conjunction with the model 17-1, the procedures for making the calculations are the same. The monthly settings for X^M derived via discretionary instrument adaptation can be substituted back into the loss function and the model 17-4 to calculate an expected loss from the single-stage strategy. The expected loss from the two-stage strategy can be evaluated by substituting the two-stage settings for X^M into the loss function and the "correct" model 17-4. The relative magnitude of the losses associated with the two strategies is a measure of their relative performance.

Figure 17-2. *Causal Interrelationships in the Illustrative Model 17-4*

Endogenous variable	Behavioral dependence on other variables	Arrow scheme of causal interrelationships among endogenous variables
		Period $t - 1$ Period t Period $t + 1$
Y Nominal income	$Y_t = Y(r_t, r_{t-1}, Z_t, X_t^F, e_{Yt})$	
r Interest rate	$r_t = r(Y_t, M_t, r_{t-1}, e_{MDt})$ [from money-demand function]	
M Money stock	$M_t = M(r_t, r_{t-1}, X_t^M, e_{MSt})$ [money-supply function]	

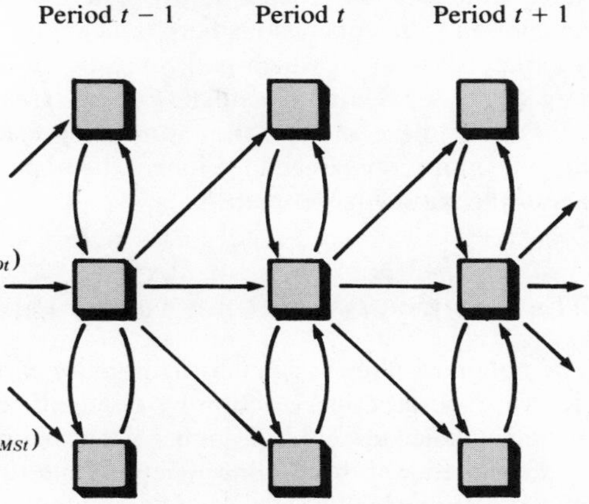

Model: Equations 17-4

Exogenous variables: X^M, X^F, Z; stochastic error terms e_Y, e_{MD}, e_{MS}

Recursiveness properties: Model is not recursive either within a single period or across a succession of periods.

Conclusions about the Information-Flow Justification for a Money Strategy

In sum, money strategies are *less* efficient than discretionary instrument adaptation in digesting available new information and using it to further the objectives of macroeconomic policy. When policymakers use the money stock as an intermediate target, they ignore large amounts of new data that can profitably be used to condition the action decisions of monetary policy. Even the new information about the money stock itself is used less efficiently in a two-stage than in a single-stage strategy. This conclusion holds unambiguously even when the benefit of the doubt is given to money strategies by assuming that the policymaking model can legitimately be decomposed into upper-level and lower-level submodels. When the policymaking model is not recursive in the manner required for an intermediate-target strategy to be logically valid, the conclusion holds with even greater force.

Far from justifying an intermediate-target approach to monetary policy, therefore, analysis of how information is used in alternative strategies calls the two-stage approach into serious question. Certainly there are no grounds for adopting a money strategy simply because it permits policymakers to react to financial variables (for example, the money stock) that are observed frequently and promptly. Single-stage strategies also react to frequently and promptly observed variables, and in a more efficient manner.

Because of its focus on the most discretionary variant of both strategy types, the preceding comparison of procedures for using new information has placed two-stage strategies in the least unfavorable light relative to discretionary instrument adaptation. The conclusions here thus apply with still greater force to variants of a money strategy in which policymakers adhere for long periods to an unaltered target path for the money stock. For any given characteristics of the flow of new data about the economy, the information-use inefficiencies of a money strategy become more pronounced the longer the upper-level periodicity of decisionmaking about the money target path.

The Controversy of Rules versus Discretion

The notion of efficiency in information use carries with it the presumption of some degree of discretionary action by policymakers. For that reason the analysis of strategy choice up to this point has been somewhat biased against rule strategies.[20]

Proponents of discretionary action tend to perceive the economy as akin to a poorly equipped sailing ship that may encounter many changes in weather conditions on its voyage. The crew of the ship, macroeconomic policymakers, are fallible sailors with only limited knowledge of how the ship functions. Conceivably, the crew at the beginning of the voyage could put on moderate sail, lock the helm in one place, and lash themselves to the deck for the duration of the voyage. But such forbearance from discretionary action regardless of the prevailing winds encountered on the voyage is not, it is argued, a sensible strategy for reaching the port of destination as promptly and safely as possible.

Proponents of rules, however, contend that governmental discretion in macroeconomic policy is undesirable rather than salutary. Seen from their perspective, the greater the efforts made by policymakers to react promptly to new data and to adapt their policy decisions accordingly, the worse off the economy and the polity may be.

Why might an individual be antipathetic to discretionary action by government policymakers? Four classes of reasons can be distinguished.

First, an opponent of discretionary policy may believe that existing knowledge about macroeconomic behavioral relationships and about the impacts of policy actions is so meager that discretionary decisions are likely to do as much harm as good. According to this view, no reliable way may exist to forecast the weather conditions even immediately ahead. Worse yet, no reliable way may exist to predict whether the ship will bear to port or starboard if the helm is turned to the right. The least dangerous thing to do in such circumstances, it may be argued, is to lash oneself to the deck and take no action at all. This reason for opposing discretion appeals to uncertainty considerations. It asserts that the adverse consequences of uncertainty can best be minimized by adhering to a simple policy rule.

20. Both "rule" and "discretion" continue to be used in accordance with the definitions given in chapter 15.

Second, an individual may be opposed to discretionary policy because of a belief that announced policy rules will prove more conducive to stable and desirable private-sector behavior. For example, it may be argued that private-sector expectations of government policy actions will be formulated with less uncertainty and with less of an inflationary bias if policymakers announce simple rules for their behavior and then credibly stick to those rules. Proponents of this view emphasize that the behavior of the ship's passengers, including especially their responses to actions by the crew, can importantly influence the outcome of the voyage. This case for rules instead of discretion appeals to propositions about the interrelationships between government and private-sector decisions analogous to those that need to be analyzed in connection with the game-theoretic, expectational justification for a money strategy.

Third, an opponent of discretion may believe that government officials in a democratic-pluralist society are exposed to irresistible political pressures to pursue incorrect policies. In this view, the political system itself tends to generate deficient macroeconomic policies by sacrificing long-run well-being to short-run political expediency. The example typically given is the alleged proclivity of governments and central banks to impart an inflationary bias to the economy when monetary and fiscal policies are made in a discretionary way. The remedy for this political malaise, it may be argued, is to substitute statutory rules or rigid self-denying ordinances in place of discretionary decisions. The ship's crew must have wax put in their ears or, like Odysseus, be lashed to the mast in order to resist the allurement of the Sirens' call.

The fourth class of reasons for opposing discretionary policy appeals to deficiencies not in the workings of the polity at large but rather in the behavior of government officials themselves. Those subscribing to this last perspective may believe that the ship's crew are likely to be incompetent or to succumb to the temptation to be knaves. Given human frailty, according to this view, it is better severely to limit the discretion of policymakers, thereby reducing the likelihood of mistakes and rascality.

Analysis of the third and fourth classes of reasons for antipathy to discretionary government action falls outside the scope of economics as conventionally defined and into the domains of political science and sociology. The issues raised are the same as those to be analyzed in connection with the insulation-from-politics and the insulation-from-human-error justifications for a money strategy.

Uncertainty and Model Choice

The uncertainty rationalization for eschewing discretionary policy actions has especially important implications for model choice. An appreciation of these implications is a prerequisite for cogent analysis of the implications of uncertainty for strategy choice.

Because of the pervasiveness of uncertainty about the macroeconomic behavior of the economy and the salience of uncertainty for policy decisions, the specification of a policymaking model should represent not only what is thought to be known about macroeconomic behavior but also the confidence with which that knowledge is held. Rather than suppressing the various uncertainties associated with the behavioral relationships incorporated in a model, a model builder should systematically highlight the *relative* importance of those uncertainties. Broadly speaking, if one relationship in the model is thought more reliable than another, or one coefficient estimate in an equation more trustworthy than the other coefficient estimates, the model specification should incorporate such judgments explicitly.

In practice, few model builders and users follow this advice. Two types of formal model dominate the macroeconomics literature. The first, deterministic models, suppress uncertainty aspects altogether. Models of the second prevalent type make a minimum concession to uncertainty by including stochastic error terms in their behavioral equations. The parameters in a model of this second type, once estimates of them have been obtained, are treated as though they are fixed and known with certainty. The illustrative models earlier in this chapter, as well as the conceptual framework in part 3, are of this second type. The uncertainties attributable to the additive stochastic terms are often labeled "errors in the equations."

Although models incorporating stochastic error terms in the behavioral relationships are a marked improvement over deterministic models, they fail to represent uncertainty considerations adequately. The behavioral parameters in most model equations, and even the forms of the equations, are themselves quite uncertain. An adequate incorporation of uncertainty considerations thus requires that the *coefficients* of the structural model be represented as random variables having probability distributions. Treatment of the model's coefficients as stochastic can be interpreted in two ways. The underlying population parameters may be thought of as stochastic; alternatively, the uncertainty about the coefficients may be regarded as a consequence of the need to rely on estimates of unknown parameters whose "true" values are fixed. In either case, the structural behavioral parameters cannot be known with certainty, which in turn means that reduced-form and final-form policy multipliers for the model cannot be known with certainty.

Coefficient uncertainty poses much greater difficulties for model formulation and use than do the uncertainties associated with errors in the equations and with forecast values of nonpolicy exogenous variables. The requisite model technology is less well-developed, less familiar to most economists, and less easy to use. But it does exist. The basic concepts and theoretical points were stated clearly more than a decade ago in a one-period, comparative-statics context.[21] Subsequent work has extended the theory to less simplified and dynamic models.[22] Research on the subject is still proceeding actively, including work designed to ease the computa-

21. See William C. Brainard, "Uncertainty and the Effectiveness of Policy," *American Economic Review,* vol. 67 (May 1967, *Papers and Proceedings, 1966*), pp. 411–25.
22. See, for example, Gregory C. Chow, *Analysis and Control of Dynamic Economic Systems* (Wiley, 1975), chaps. 10–11; Roger Craine and Arthur Havenner, "Optimal Monetary Policy Under Uncertainty," Special Studies Paper 101 (Board of Governors of the Federal Reserve System, Division of Research and Statistics, May 1977); Stephen J. Turnovsky, "Optimal Choice of Monetary Instrument in a Linear Economic Model with Stochastic Coefficients," *Journal of Money, Credit and Banking,* vol. 7 (February 1975), pp. 51–80; Edward C. Prescott, "The Multi-Period Control Problem Under Uncertainty," *Econometrica,* vol. 39 (November 1972); Richard M. Young, "Deterministic and Stochastic Policy Decisions: Some One-Period Simulation Results," *Journal of Public Economics,* vol. 5 (April–May 1976), pp. 209–24; Franklin R. Shupp, "Uncertainty and Optimal Stabilization Policy," *Journal of Public Economics,* vol. 6 (October 1976), pp. 242–53.

tional burdens that presently inhibit the implementation of existing techniques in practical policymaking applications.[23]

It is not feasible to include an analysis of the complex implications of uncertainty for model choice in this book. As a foundation for the discussion of strategy choice, however, three points about model choice need to be kept clearly in mind.

First, the specification of a policymaking model should emphasize uncertainty considerations regardless of the size of the model. The smaller a model, the more the representation of macroeconomic behavior is compressed into a few relationships containing a handful of variables and coefficients; hence the greater may be the implausibility of modeling those relationships as deterministic, or as deterministic except for the presence of additive stochastic terms. Even in the case of large models, however, the preferred model specification is one that incorporates coefficient uncertainty as well as additive stochastic terms.

Second, policymakers should emphasize the uncertainty aspects of their model regardless of the strategy they use for conducting policy. As with other aspects of model choice, the objective should be to select the least inadequate representation of the economy's uncertain behavior and its uncertain responses to policy actions.

The third point, although obvious, is often overlooked: because uncertainty about the policymaking model is bound to be great for any model, no strategy for conducting monetary policy can prevent nonpolicy disturbances from buffeting the economy or ensure that policy mistakes are never made. To hope for consistently excellent results from any strategy would be especially quixotic if major uncertainties about the model are not represented in the model and hence not factored into decisions made in conjunction with the model. Blood cannot be squeezed from a turnip.

The Uncertainty Justification for a Money Strategy

When considering the implications of uncertainty for strategy choice, the appropriate procedure is to compare two-stage and single-stage strategies for a comparable degree of uncertainty about how the economy behaves. As earlier in the chapter, therefore, suppose that a set of model-choice decisions has already been made. In addition, however, suppose now that the relative uncertainties associated with the various behavioral relationships included in the model—coefficient uncertainties as well as stochastic errors in the equations—have been explicitly specified. The model will then be "least inadequate" in two respects. It will incorporate the best available representation of what is known about macroeconomic behavior. But it will also take advantage of the best available model technology to represent what is *not* known about that behavior.

Given such a model, if uncertainty and the consequent risk of mistaken policy actions were to constitute a sound justification for a money strategy, two conclusions would have to be established. A two-stage strategy applied in conjunction with the

23. See Roger Craine and Arthur Havenner, "A Stochastic Optimal Control Technique for Models with Estimated Coefficients," *Econometrica*, vol. 45 (May 1977), pp. 1013–21, and the additional references to the literature mentioned there.

model would need to be shown to produce better decisions than other strategies. And policymakers would have to be able to cope better with the uncertainties associated with the model if the money stock were the intermediate-target variable.

Recall the conclusion reached earlier in the chapter for models incorporating uncertainty only in the form of stochastic error terms and forecast values for nonpolicy exogenous variables: a money strategy employs information less efficiently than a single-stage strategy and accordingly results in larger expected loss ex ante and larger realized loss ex post. Indirectly, therefore, that earlier analysis has already cast doubt on the uncertainty justification for a two-stage money strategy. If anything, the presumption about uncertainty in those models contradicts the intuitive supposition made by proponents of a money strategy. If a money strategy copes less efficiently with limited information in a context where uncertainty is assumed to exist only in the form of errors in the equations and in forecast values of nonpolicy exogenous variables, what reason is there for presuming that a money strategy can cope better with any aspect of uncertainty?

In fact, neither coefficient uncertainty nor any other manifestation of uncertainty provide an analytical basis for preferring a money strategy instead of discretionary instrument adaptation. There is no refinement in model technology available for dealing with uncertainty that, if beneficial when following a money strategy, cannot be at least as beneficial when used in conjunction with discretionary instrument adaptation. To the extent that the characteristics of the policymakers' loss function and their uncertainty about their model dictate caution in their conduct of monetary policy, a single-stage strategy can heed that dictum at least as effectively as a money strategy. Whatever degree of technical skill or commonsense judgment in coping with uncertainty may be possessed by policymakers can be used to at least as good effect under a single-stage as under an intermediate-target strategy. In sum, despite the widespread intuitive view to the contrary, there is not a single logical argument based on uncertainty considerations that justifies the pursuit of a money (or any intermediate-target) strategy instead of discretionary instrument adaptation.

A rigorous demonstration of this conclusion even for simple illustrative models would require the presentation of considerable algebra. The discussion that follows tries to convey the key points of such an analysis without including its technical details.

Suppose both two-stage and single-stage policymakers make decisions in conjunction with the following model:

(17-5)
$$Y_t = \lambda_t M_t + u_t$$
$$M_t = \eta_t H_t + v_t,$$

where Y_t represents income and is an ultimate-target variable, M_t is the money stock, and H_t is the monetary base and used as an exogenous policy instrument. The terms u_t and v_t are additive stochastic errors. The coefficients λ_t and η_t are treated as random variables rather than fixed parameters; loosely speaking, λ_t is a "velocity multiplier" linking income and money and η_t is a "money multiplier" linking money and the policymakers' exogenous instrument.

Although 17-5 has no good foundation in theory and presumably would never be used in practice by either two-stage or single-stage policymakers, it can facilitate the exposition here. It incorporates coefficient uncertainty as well as stochastic error terms in the simplest conceivable model that also permits a stylized representation of some aspects of a two-stage decision process.[24]

A commensurately simplified loss function for use in evaluating the two strategy types may be specified as a one-period counterpart of 17-2. The loss, L, is

$$(17\text{-}6) \qquad L_t = (Y_t - Y_t^*)^2,$$

where Y_t^* is a target value for income; expected loss is then

$$(17\text{-}6a) \qquad E(L_t) = E(Y_t - Y_t^*)^2 = (\overline{Y}_t - Y_t^*)^2 + \sigma_{Yt}^2,$$

where $\overline{Y}_t$ is the mean (expected value) and σ_{Yt}^2 is the variance of income.

The reduced-form equation for the ultimate-target variable is

$$(17\text{-}7) \qquad Y_t = \lambda_t \eta_t H_t + u_t + \lambda_t v_t.$$

Four uncertain forces determine income: the two random coefficients and the two equation errors. Define $\pi_t \equiv \lambda_t \eta_t$ and $w_t \equiv u_t + \lambda_t v_t$ so that the reduced-form equation for income may be expressed more simply as

$$(17\text{-}7a) \qquad Y_t = \pi_t H_t + w_t.$$

From the perspective of the single-stage policymakers, the entire model 17-5 is regarded as a unity, summarized by 17-7a. The "policy multiplier" for their actions is the uncertain parameter π_t, which in turn is a composite of the two random structural coefficients; income is also influenced in an additive way by a term that depends on the two equation errors and one of the structural coefficients. In contrast, from the perspective of the two-stage policymakers, 17-5 is regarded as two submodels.

Given the model, the correct expected value of Y conditional on the instrument setting for H is[25]

$$(17\text{-}8) \qquad \overline{Y} = E(\pi H + w) = \overline{\pi} H + \overline{w}.$$

It is shown in appendix B that $\overline{\pi}$, the expected value of the policy multiplier, depends not only on the expected values of λ and η but also on their covariance ($\sigma_{\lambda\eta}$); the mean of w, $\overline{w}$, depends not only on the means of u, v, and λ but also on the covariance of λ and v ($\sigma_{\lambda v}$).

---

24. The discussion of the model presumes a one-period, comparative-statics frame of reference in order to focus on the problem of coefficient uncertainty; the complications of multiperiod aspects of the policy problem are thereby suppressed. The most important feature of a two-stage decision process—the different periodicities of lower-level and upper-level decisions—obviously cannot be represented in a one-period framework.

25. In the remainder of this section a bar over a variable is used to denote its expected value. Since the exposition deals with only a single time period, the time subscripts are henceforth omitted for notational simplicity.

The correct variance of Y conditional on the instrument setting for H is given by

(17-9) $$\sigma_Y^2 = \sigma_\pi^2 H^2 + \sigma_w^2 + 2\sigma_{\pi w} H,$$

where σ_π^2 and σ_w^2 are the variances of π and w and $\sigma_{\pi w}$ is their covariance. If σ_π^2, σ_w^2, and $\sigma_{\pi w}$ are evaluated in terms of the underlying variances and covariances (see appendix B), it can be shown that the variance of income depends on fourteen different parameters associated with the joint probability distributions of λ, η, u, and v; these are the four expected values ($\bar{\lambda}$, $\bar{\eta}$, $\bar{u}$, $\bar{v}$), the four variances (σ_λ^2, σ_η^2, σ_u^2, σ_v^2) and, if they should have nonzero values, the six covariances ($\sigma_{\lambda\eta}$, $\sigma_{\lambda u}$, $\sigma_{\lambda v}$, $\sigma_{\eta u}$, $\sigma_{\eta v}$, σ_{uv}).

Because the expected value and variance of the ultimate-target variable depend on the expected values, variances, and covariances of λ, η, u, and v, the expected loss in 17-6a depends on all those parameters as well. Policymakers thus need to incorporate in their model not only their estimates of the means $\bar{\lambda}$, $\bar{\eta}$, $\bar{u}$, and $\bar{v}$ but also their estimates of or judgments about the variances and covariances. To be able to specify judgments about the relative importance of the various variances and covariances is the policymakers' opportunity to incorporate what they do *not* know into their model and thereby to let the relative importance of their uncertainties influence their decisions in an intelligent manner. Suppose, for example, that the policymakers feel reasonably confident about their mean estimate for the money multiplier $\bar{\eta}$ but are much less confident about the mean estimate of the velocity coefficient $\bar{\lambda}$; in that event they would postulate a small value for the variance σ_η^2 but a much larger value for σ_λ^2. Again, both two-stage and single-stage policymakers have equally strong incentives to approach the problem of model specification in this way.

Consider now the approach of single-stage policymakers to a decision about the instrument setting for H. In principle, the single-stage policymakers combine 17-8 and 17-9 with their loss function and find the instrument setting that minimizes expected loss (see appendix B). If expressed in terms of the target value of income Y^*, the "policy multiplier" π, and the combined error term w, that preferred single-stage setting, $\hat{H}_{1S}$, is

(17-10) $$\hat{H}_{1s} = \frac{\bar{\pi}(Y^* - \bar{w}) - \sigma_{\pi w}}{\bar{\pi}^2 + \sigma_\pi^2}.$$

The expression 17-10 indicates the importance of policymakers' taking coefficient uncertainty into account in their model and instrument decisions. The preferred setting in 17-10 depends on the variance of π and on the covariance $\sigma_{\pi w}$. For example, 17-10 says that policymakers should, other things being equal, choose a smaller instrument setting the greater is the uncertainty about the policy multiplier (the greater the variance of π).

The result in 17-10 may be contrasted with the instrument setting that would be chosen if policymakers treated λ and η in their model as though those coefficients were fixed and known rather than uncertain:

(17-11) $$\hat{H}_{NRC} = \frac{Y^* - \bar{w}}{\bar{\pi}}.$$

The setting chosen with nonrandom coefficients, $\hat{H}_{NRC}$, depends only on the policymakers' expected values of the coefficients. In effect, policymakers would think solely in terms of the means of the model coefficients, suppressing their variances and covariances. Given the loss function 17-6 and the model 17-5, the policy suggested in 17-11 is clearly inferior to the policy 17-10 that takes into account the implications of coefficient uncertainty.[26]

The difference between 17-10 and 17-11 is a manifestation in this simplified model of the presumption, already discussed in part 3, that greater uncertainty about the impacts of their policy actions should lead policymakers to be more cautious in taking policy actions. The presumption is equally relevant for single-stage and two-stage strategies.[27]

Consider next, in contrast to the instrument setting in 17-10 chosen under a single-stage procedure, the calculations associated with a money strategy. The two-stage policymakers regard the equation for income in 17-5 as the upper-stage submodel and treat the money stock as though it were exogenous in that submodel. This treatment ignores simultaneous interdependencies between the upper-stage and lower-stage submodels, including interdependencies in uncertainty such as a nonzero covariance between the velocity coefficient λ and the money multiplier η.[28] Because two-stage policymakers incorrectly treat the money stock as exogenous in the upper-stage submodel, they use incorrect expressions for the expected value and the variance of their ultimate-target variable (see appendix B) rather than the correct expressions 17-8 and 17-9. To calculate their intermediate-target value for the money stock, M_{2S}^*, the two-stage policymakers combine those incorrect expressions for $\bar{Y}$ and σ_Y^2 with the loss function and obtain the value

$$(17\text{-}12) \qquad M_{2S}^* = \frac{\bar{\lambda}(Y^* - \bar{u}) - \sigma_{\lambda u}}{\bar{\lambda}^2 + \sigma_\lambda^2}.$$

This result, because the policymakers take coefficient uncertainty into account (within the limitations of the two-stage procedure), makes the target value for the money stock depend on one of the two underlying coefficient variances (σ_λ^2) and one of the covariances ($\sigma_{\lambda u}$) in addition to the means $\bar{\lambda}$ and $\bar{u}$.

At the lower level of the calculations, several options exist for deriving the two-stage instrument setting, $\hat{H}_{2S}$. For example, that setting might be derived either by

26. For a more detailed exposition of this point, see Brainard, "Uncertainty and the Effectiveness of Policy." The expression in 17-10 becomes identical with 17-11 if the variance of the policy multiplier and the covariance $\sigma_{\pi w}$ are both zero.

27. The presumption in favor of greater caution does not extend to greater uncertainty of all types but applies only to uncertainty about policy multipliers (which in turn stems from uncertainty about the model's coefficients). Even the presumption about policy multipliers may sometimes prove an unreliable guide to policy decisions. In the illustrative model in the text, for example, with certain values of $\bar{w}$, $\sigma_{\pi w}$, and σ_w^2 (produced in turn by particular combinations of the means, variances, and covariances of the underlying random variables), an increase in the variance of the policy multiplier π could paradoxically lead to a larger recommended dose of policy action. On this point, see Brainard, "Uncertainty and the Effectiveness of Policy," pp. 422–24; Chow, *Analysis and Control of Dynamic Economic Systems*, pp. 247–51; Craine and Havenner, "Optimal Monetary Policy Under Uncertainty"; Young, "Deterministic and Stochastic Policy Decisions"; and Shupp, "Uncertainty and Optimal Stabilization Policy."

28. Negative interest elasticity of the demand for money and a positive interest elasticity of money supply would, other things being equal, generate an observed (positive) correlation between λ and η. Other variables omitted from the model that influence both λ and η could likewise produce a nonzero covariance $\sigma_{\lambda \eta}$.

choosing the value of H that would set the expected value of the money stock equal to the target M_{2S}^* or, alternatively, by choosing the value of H that would minimize the expected value of the squared deviations of the money stock from its target value. To give the benefit of the doubt to the money strategy, suppose the two-stage policymakers choose the latter option;[29] in that event, the calculation using the lower-stage submodel results in

$$(17\text{-}13) \qquad \hat{H}_{2S} = \frac{\bar{\eta}(M_{2S}^* - \bar{v}) - \sigma_{\eta v}}{\bar{\eta}^2 + \sigma_\eta^2}.$$

The differing implications of the single-stage and two-stage policy decisions can be most readily compared if both decisions are expressed entirely in terms of the underlying means, variances, and covariances of λ, η, u, and v. When this is done, the single-stage decision 17-10 may be written (see equation B-12a in appendix B):

$$(17\text{-}10a) \qquad \hat{H}_{1S} = \frac{J - (2\bar{\lambda}\bar{v}\sigma_{\lambda\eta} + 2\bar{\lambda}\bar{\eta}\sigma_{\lambda v} + \bar{\lambda}\sigma_{\eta u} + \bar{u}\sigma_{\lambda\eta} + \sigma_{\lambda\eta}\sigma_{\lambda v} - Y^*\sigma_{\lambda\eta})}{K + 2(\sigma_{\lambda\eta})^2 + 4\bar{\lambda}\bar{\eta}\sigma_{\lambda\eta}}.$$

Combination of 17-12 and 17-13 shows that the two-stage decision is equivalent to

$$(17\text{-}14) \qquad \hat{H}_{2S} = \frac{J - \sigma_\lambda^2 \sigma_{\eta v}}{K}.$$

The symbols J and K, identical in both 17-10a and 17-14, represent complicated expressions given in appendix B.

Inspection of the settings for the two strategies in 17-10a and 17-14 brings out the central point of relevance here and illustrates the conclusion asserted at the beginning of the section. Both strategies make use of a common model that incorporates coefficient uncertainty as well as stochastic errors in the equations; both strategies thus avoid the pitfalls of "certainty-equivalence" recommendations. Yet the two-stage approach ignores possible interdependencies in the uncertainties associated with the two submodels. Only for the special case in which all four of the covariances $\sigma_{\lambda\eta}$, $\sigma_{\lambda v}$, $\sigma_{\eta u}$, and $\sigma_{\eta v}$ are equal to zero (that is, where there are no interdependencies between the submodels) do the two-stage and single-stage approaches yield identical recommendations for the setting on the policy instrument.

Because single-stage policymakers can take interrelationships between the upper-stage and lower-stage submodels into account as a regular part of their decisionmaking, they can always choose a setting for policy at least as appropriate as the setting resulting from two-stage calculations. By itself, therefore, great uncertainty about the policymaking model does *not* constitute a valid analytical reason for choosing a money strategy. Indeed, the opposite conclusion is the correct one: for equivalent assumptions about the form of the policymaking model and the joint

---

29. The latter option is analogous, at the level of the lower-stage submodel, to the specification of the loss function itself (see 17-6). If the two-stage policymakers choose the former instead of the latter option, the comparison between the two-stage and single-stage strategies shows an even greater inferiority for the two-stage procedure.

probability distributions of its coefficients and equation errors, the expected loss from pursuing a money strategy is never smaller, and in the general case is unambiguously greater, than the corresponding expected loss from a strategy of discretionary instrument adaptation.

The exposition in this section relies on an extremely simplified model that is of no intrinsic interest in a practical policymaking situation. The conclusion that emerges from the analysis, however, is not an idiosyncrasy of that model. A comparison of a money strategy and discretionary instrument adaptation using a one-period, random-coefficient model less simplified than 17-5 would involve even more cumbersome algebraic expressions but would yield the same conclusion. There is every reason to suppose, furthermore, that the results of a comparison of the two strategies would be still more unfavorable for the money strategy if the random-coefficient model were dynamic rather than one-period and if the money target path were revised only intermittently rather than in every period.[30]

Summary of the Economic Case against Intermediate-Target Strategies

This chapter has evaluated and rejected the economic arguments cited in favor of using the money stock as a proximate focus of monetary policy. But the reader should be clear that rejection of those arguments cannot validly be used as a justification for focusing policy on some intermediate variable other than money— for example, a market interest rate or some "credit" aggregate constructed from the asset side of the balance sheets of financial intermediaries.

The basic conclusion of the analysis in this chapter is that preoccupation with any one intermediate variable, *whatever that variable may be,* is an inferior discretionary approach to conducting monetary policy. The argument against the two-stage approach may be summarized in six points.

First, any intermediate-target strategy discards potentially useful information and thus involves unnecessary inefficiencies in the use of new data about the economy. Second, no intermediate-target strategy copes as well with uncertainty as a single-stage strategy. Third, in order for any intermediate-target strategy to be valid, the network of macroeconomic behavioral relationships for the economy would have to exhibit a particular type of causal recursiveness with respect to its key intermediate variable; yet no less than in the case of any definition of the money stock, there are strong grounds for doubting that economies are structured in the requisite manner.

Fourth, as in the money case, any intermediate-target strategy encounters difficulties in selecting the "correct" or "best" empirical definition of the intermediate-target variable. The more an intermediate variable may be reliably linked

30. When a dynamic rather than one-period, comparative-statics context is assumed, it is less clear conceptually how to organize a comparison of two-stage and single-stage strategies. Given that the two types of policymakers behave differently from period to period, it may seem problematic to assume that the probability distributions characterizing the coefficients and the equation errors in the model are identical for both strategies (and hence that both strategies share a common model). This problem, although making a comparison more difficult, provides no reason for supposing that a two-stage strategy could cope better with uncertainty than a single-stage strategy.

to the ultimate targets of policy, the less amenable it is to close control. The more precisely it can be controlled, the greater the uncertainty about its impacts on ultimate targets.

The fifth point is a corollary of the points about use of new information and treatment of uncertainty. Intermediate-target strategies in which the target path for the key intermediate variable is intermittently recalculated are discretionary and adaptive to some degree. But the only continuous adaptation that occurs is the lower-stage adjustment of the instruments to keep the key intermediate variable close to its target path. The target path itself is adapted only discontinuously. This discontinuity in the upper-stage decisions of an intermediate-target strategy creates two types of risk. On the one hand if the intermediate-target path has to be altered drastically at the time of its periodic recalculation, the instrument settings themselves may have to be altered drastically to push the key intermediate variable on to its new target path. As a consequence, the instruments may influence the ultimate targets in a jerky, discontinuous manner. Alternatively, and this may be the greater of the two risks, the instruments may get progressively out of line with the settings that are optimal for influencing ultimate targets. This could occur, for example, if there is reluctance to make large changes in the intermediate-target path at any one point in time and as a consequence the path (and the derived instrument settings used to try to attain it) are adjusted less promptly than warranted by the underlying economic situation. In this second case, timidity or myopia generate an excessive preoccupation with the surrogate intermediate target which in turn leads policy-makers to violate what even their own two-stage approach recommends they ought to do. These risks are inherent in the discontinuity of the upper-stage decision process. And the avoidance of one risk inevitably courts the other.[31]

Sixth and finally, the root cause of the deficiencies in all intermediate-target strategies is that a lower-level, surrogate objective is inappropriately substituted for higher-level, fundamental objectives. Macroeconomic policy decisions cannot be satisfactorily decomposed into monetary decisions and fiscal decisions, with monetary decisions further dichotomized into upper level and lower level, each level to be made separately and with different periodicities. The interactions between the decision levels are too strong. If made separately, lower-level decisions even when first derived can inadvertently be inconsistent with upper-level criteria. Lower-level decisions are in any case sure to become suboptimal for influencing ultimate targets as time passes.

Lower-level decisions, although "lower" in a chain of logical reasoning leading backward from the upper-level criteria, determine what the central bank actually does. They are the only decisions that lead directly to policy *actions*. As time passes, therefore, the inconsistencies between lower-level and upper-level decisions tend to be worked out in a way that favors attainment of the lower-level, surrogate objective at the expense of upper-level criteria—an outcome that reverses real priorities.[32]

31. As with a money strategy, the risks associated with discontinuous adaptation of the intermediate-target path in any two-stage strategy are correspondingly greater the longer the periodicity of upper-stage decisionmaking.

32. The inconsistencies are especially troublesome if the true structure of the economy is not appropriately recursive, and yet policymakers nevertheless impose the recursiveness property on their model (as they must if they are to use a two-stage strategy).

Virtually all government decisionmaking requires some form of "suboptimization"—breaking down a larger problem into smaller, more manageable chunks. The concept of "macroeconomic stabilization policy" itself, for example, presumes a higher-level decision integration between, say, economic policy and national defense policy. Even so, the key to good decisionmaking is to avoid dichotomization and suboptimization when the interactions between decision levels are especially strong. In such cases, of which macroeconomic stabilization policy is a prime example, the only way to avoid serious suboptimization errors is to make the decisions at the various levels simultaneously in the light of the interactions.[33]

Popular support for intermediate-target strategies is no doubt partly attributable to the greater visibility of intermediate than ultimate-target variables. Because new data for many intermediate variables are received fairly continuously, use of such a variable as a surrogate target enables policymakers to ascertain more or less continuously whether a target path for the surrogate is being achieved. With new observations for ultimate-target variables received much less frequently, continuous tracking of the performance of the ultimate targets is not possible. And these facts can be superficially interpreted as an argument in favor of an intermediate-target strategy.

But only superficially! It is not sensible to use an intermediate variable as a surrogate target rather than aim at the genuine objectives merely because the former is always visible while the latter are not. The problem is analogous to that facing a ship's captain who must navigate into a dangerous harbor at night. It would not be logical to steer into a channel marked by buoys flashing every ten seconds rather than one marked by buoys flashing every two minutes merely because the former can be followed more easily. Useful information is obtained from a frequently flashing buoy; the captain can thereby establish his current location more frequently, and thus more exactly. But he should steer the ship into the channel marked by the ten-second buoys only if he believes that to be the correct route to his destined berth in the harbor.

33. A general discussion of suboptimization issues in decisionmaking is contained in Roland N. McKean, *Efficiency in Government Through Systems Analysis* (Wiley, 1958), chap. 2.

CHAPTER EIGHTEEN

Money Strategies and the Politics of Monetary Policy

THIS CHAPTER continues the analysis of strategy choice. In contrast to the last chapter that evaluated arguments of a primarily economic nature, however, the discussion here ventures beyond the confines of economics as conventionally understood.

Any attempt to discuss the politics or sociology of monetary policy quickly becomes embroiled in the pros and cons of political independence for the central bank. This chapter does not try to resolve that difficult issue but does put it in clearer perspective and indicates its relationship to the debate about rules versus discretion.

A primary aim of the chapter is to evaluate the remaining justifications advanced in support of a strategy that uses the money stock as an intermediate target. Thus the first sections that follow analyze the contention that a money strategy can perform better than other strategies in favorably conditioning the expectations of private-sector economic units and thereby promoting a more satisfactory evolution of the economy. Subsequent sections ask whether a cogent case can be made for adhering to a money strategy in order to insulate monetary policy from political pressures, from the human frailty of policymakers, or from both.

The pros and cons of political independence for the central bank are closely related to the costs and benefits of integrating monetary policy into macroeconomic stabilization as a whole. Thus the chapter also comments on the desirability of coordinating the settings on the instruments of monetary policy and fiscal policy and on whether, given the extent of integration of monetary-policy and fiscal-policy decisions that actually exists, a money strategy performs better or worse than other strategies in facilitating that coordination. The final section of the chapter discusses the problem of "target myopia" to which a money strategy is prone: that is, the danger that policymakers and private-sector opinion become preoccupied with the surrogate money target, thereby blurring perception of the genuine objectives of economic policy.

Interrelationships between Policy Actions and Private-Sector Decisionmaking

The concept of economic structure is a basic constituent of any analytical approach for studying macroeconomics; so, too, is the distinction between endogenous and exogenous variables in a structural model designed to represent that economic structure. But the discussion of structural models and their use in policymaking has so far glossed over some important complications inherent in those concepts. As a prelude to evaluating the game-theoretic, expectational justification for a money strategy, those complications need to be identified.

Without qualification, previous chapters have treated government policy actions as "exogenous" in the structural models presumed to be used by policymakers. Changes in the settings of policy instruments have influenced the evolution of the economy but, according to the models, the economy has not influenced the changes in those settings. Yet in a fundamental sense the analysis has presumed that causation between instruments and the economy operates in both directions. The policymakers have been assumed to react to movements in the economy, for example trying to dampen undesirable cyclical fluctuations. The more discretionary the policy decisions, the greater the extent to which the policymakers have been presumed to try to stabilize the economy's fluctuations.

Even though policy instruments are treated as exogenous variables in the structural models, therefore, the behavior of the policymakers is, in an important sense, "endogenous." An outside observer of the nation's economic system would presumably regard that system as composed of *both* the structural model of the economy and the policymakers' loss function, and would consider the decision procedures of the policymakers as they react to the economy no less endogenous than the behavior of private economic units (whose decision procedures are, in the aggregate, embodied in the behavioral relationships of the structural model).

The notion of an outside observer and the earlier distinction between descriptive and prescriptive analysis can help to bring this complication into focus. From the point of view of an observer whose motive is to describe or explain the evolution of the economic system as a whole, the government's policy instruments should not be modeled as exogenous variables. From the perspective of the observer, the *reaction function* of the government's policymakers to the economy is a major part of the phenomena to be explained.

The policymakers, however, cannot adopt the perspective of an outside observer. Their job is to decide, somehow, what to do with the government's policy instruments. Since they have to make prescriptive decisions, they must characterize their instruments and the corresponding policy actions as exogenous. Anyone proferring advice about policy decisions must likewise adopt this perspective.

In principle, then, the question of whether government policy actions are exogenous or endogenous has at least two correct answers. Different theoretical perspectives can justify quite different analytical procedures.

Although there is no ambiguity about the appropriate treatment of instruments as exogenous variables when the purpose of the analysis is prescriptive, policymakers and their staffs should be careful not to lose sight of the endogenous aspects of their behavior. In particular, they need to make a sharp distinction between *constructing* (for example, specifying and econometrically estimating) their model of how the economy responds to policy actions and *using* the model for the purpose of making policy decisions. It is when using the model to determine instrument settings that the instruments are unambiguously exogenous (that is, "decision" variables). When constructing their model, however, policymakers will presumably rely heavily on data indicating how the economy evolved in the past. Those data will have been determined in part by their own past policies. If no allowance is made in constructing the model for the endogenous aspects of government policy, the resulting structural model is likely to be seriously misspecified. In effect, policymakers have to be careful not to confuse the *conceptual exogeneity* of their decisions ex ante with *statistical exogeneity* of their actions ex post. Their behavior is exogenous in the former sense, but definitely not in the latter.[1]

Acknowledgment of the potential ambiguity about whether government policy actions are exogenous or endogenous leads naturally to recognition of a second, more serious difficulty. Not only did the analysis in earlier chapters treat government policy actions as simply exogenous; it omitted any discussion of private-sector expectations of those actions. Yet the game-theoretic elements in the interrelationships between government and private-sector behavior may be highly significant.

The problem has been lucidly stated in general terms by Robert Lucas.[2] As typically constructed by practicing econometricians and (albeit often less formally) policymakers, a structural model pays little attention to private-sector expectations—in particular, expectations of policy actions. Moreover, the model is employed for the purpose of determining "optimum" policy actions or predicting the consequences of alternative policy actions *on the presumption that the structural model itself is not affected by the policy actions that are implemented.* But if private-sector expectations are largely or wholly ignored in the structural model, this presumption is wrong in principle. Private-sector decisions no less than government policy decisions will be formulated on the basis of expected future values of variables of concern to the decisionmakers. Private decisions will therefore adapt to expected and actually observed policy actions. Macroeconomic policy is not merely a game against nature but, first and foremost, a game against other rational economic agents. The behavioral relationships in the structural model used by the policymakers are supposed to be a representation (in the aggregate) of the decision rules of private-sector agents. If the model makes no allowance for the adaptations of private decisions to policy actions, however, the model is misspecified; if used for policymaking, it may well lead to incorrect decisions.

This criticism of the structural models commonly used in policymaking deserves serious attention from policymakers. It is undeniably true that most existing models either ignore the expectational and game-theoretic interrelationships between government and private-sector decisions or characterize them in an ad hoc, inadequate manner. Research attempting to redress this oversight has recently begun to appear in substantial volume—much of it under the banner of "rational expectations" (see below). Whether the interrelationships are of sizable or only modest importance empirically remains for the time being an unsettled and controversial issue.

1. For a further discussion of this complication and its implications for model construction and interpretation, see Stephen M. Goldfeld and Alan S. Blinder, "Some Implications of Endogenous Stabilization Policy," *Brookings Papers on Economic Activity, 3:1972,* pp. 585–640; Alan S. Blinder and Robert M. Solow, "Analytical Foundations of Fiscal Policy," in Blinder and others, *The Economics of Public Finance* (Brookings Institution, 1974), pp. 69–71; James R. Crotty, "Specification Error in Macro-Econometric Models: The Influence of Policy Goals," *American Economic Review,* vol. 63 (December 1973), pp. 1025–30.

2. Robert E. Lucas, Jr., "Econometric Policy Evaluation: A Critique," in Karl Brunner and Allan H. Meltzer, eds., *The Phillips Curve and Labor Markets,* Carnegie-Rochester Conference Series on Public Policy, vol. 1 (North-Holland, 1976). See also Thomas J. Sargent and Neil Wallace, "Rational Expectations and The Theory of Economic Policy," *Journal of Monetary Economics,* vol. 2 (April 1976), pp. 169–83.

Although policymakers should formulate their model so as to incorporate expectational considerations, the inevitably prescriptive nature of their task must nonetheless be the dominant factor conditioning their conceptualization of the economy and their own role in it. During any given short-run period, policymakers must already have formulated *some* structural model that can be taken as given while that period's policy decisions are being made. Furthermore, although persistent efforts should be made to capture the complexities of the expectational aspects of private-sector decision rules in the policymaking model, policymakers cannot postpone decisions while they try to refine their model; today's prescriptive decisions must be based on today's least inadequate model.[3] The given structural model need not be "unaffected by policy actions" to the degree that policymakers have succeeded in incorporating private-sector expectations of policy actions in the model. But the model itself—in particular, the specific manner in which private-sector decisions vary with respect to expectations of policy actions—necessarily has to be given from the point of view of policy decisions.

Self-Imposed Limits on Discretion by Means of Announcements of Policy Intentions

Some analysts give such great emphasis to the expectational and game-theoretic interrelationships between the government and the private sector that they conclude that the government should follow rules for its actions rather than exercising its ability to make discretionary adaptations in policy. Rules rather than discretion, it is argued, will induce private-sector agents to make better decisions and hence lead to a more favorable evolution of the national economy.

A general statement of this view appears in a recent article by Finn Kydland and Edward Prescott.[4] These authors emphasize that when policy actions fail to take into account private-sector expectations of future policy actions, policy will be suboptimal over the course of several periods even though each period's policy decision may be reached using the analytic techniques of control theory. As an illustration of an area where a rule would dominate a posture of discretionary action, Kydland and Prescott discuss flood-control and flood-protection policy. Suppose the government's loss function indicates that houses should not be built in a particular flood plain but, if they are built anyway, that costly flood-control measures should be implemented. Kydland and Prescott argue that

> if the government's policy were not to build the dams and levees needed for protection and agents knew this was the case, even if houses were built there, rational agents would not live in the flood plains. But the rational agent knows that, if he and others

---

3. Private-sector expectations depend on government actions, which depend on government expectations of the private-sector expectations; the private-sector expectations in theory can depend on what the private sector thinks the government sector expects the private sector to be doing; and so on. As a practical matter, the problem of this infinite regress requires policymakers to choose some arbitrary cutoff point in their modeling of expectational interaction between government and private-sector decisions.

4. Finn E. Kydland and Edward C. Prescott, "Rules Rather than Discretion: The Inconsistency of Optimal Plans," *Journal of Political Economy*, vol. 85 (June 1977), pp. 473–91. See also Edward C. Prescott, "Should Control Theory Be Used for Economic Stabilization?" and John B. Taylor, "Control Theory and Economic Stabilization: A Comment," both in Karl Brunner and Allen H. Meltzer, eds., *Optimal Policies, Control Theory, and Technology Exports*, Carnegie-Rochester Conference Series on Public Policy, vol. 7 (North-Holland, 1977).

build houses there, the government will take the necessary flood-control measures. Consequently, in the absence of a law prohibiting the construction of houses in the flood plain, houses are built there, and the army corps of engineers subsequently builds the dams and levees.[5]

By analogy with the flood-control example, is there a persuasive case for the government employing rules rather than discretion for the instruments of macroeconomic policy? In particular, given that private-sector anticipations of inflation depend on (among other things) expectations of the future course of monetary policy, should the central bank announce some simple rule it intends to follow and then conduct policy accordingly?

Kydland and Prescott confidently answer those questions in the affirmative, as do Robert Lucas and a number of other economists associated with the rational expectations approach to macroeconomics.[6] The staunchest proponents of the rational expectations view support their preference for a rule by citing a "policy ineffectiveness proposition" that is derivable from their analytical models, namely, that discretionary government actions can be completely undone by offsetting private behavior.[7] William Fellner likewise stresses the game-theoretic interrelationships between private decisions and government policy actions; Fellner's conclusions are more cautiously drawn, but he too advocates clear statements of government policy intentions and credible actions to adhere to those intentions.[8]

The merits and deficiencies of this general argument in favor of rules rather than discretion for macroeconomic policy have yet to be analyzed and evaluated satisfactorily. The issues that require resolution are essentially the same as those being intensively investigated in the research on rational expectations. It is not feasible here to summarize the current state of that research or to try to predict the outlines of an eventual consensus. The following comments therefore do no more than register five relevant observations.

First, it is essential when describing private-sector expectations and their interrelationships with government policy to define the expectational concepts carefully.

5. Kydland and Prescott, "Rules Rather than Discretion," p. 477. Government policy with respect to patents is given as another microeconomic example.

6. The papers and comments presented at two recent conferences—the first sponsored by the National Bureau of Economic Research in October 1978 and the second sponsored by the American Enterprise Institute in January 1980—provide a good overview of the research literature on rational expectations; see Stanley Fischer, ed., *Rational Expectations and Economic Policy* (University of Chicago Press, forthcoming); and Bennett T. McCallum and William G. Dewald, eds., *Journal of Money, Credit and Banking*, vol. 12, no. 4 (November 1980), pt. 2. Robert E. Lucas, Jr., summarizes his policy views in "Rules, Discretion, and the Role of the Economic Advisor," in Fischer, ed., *Rational Expectations and Economic Policy*. For a helpful survey of the issues, favorable to the rational expectations view, see Bennett T. McCallum, "Rational Expectations and Macroeconomic Stabilization Policy: An Overview," in McCallum and Dewald, eds., vol. 12, *Journal of Money, Credit and Banking*.

7. See, for example, Thomas J. Sargent and Neil Wallace, " 'Rational' Expectations, the Optimal Monetary Instrument, and the Optimal Money Supply Rule," *Journal of Political Economy*, vol. 83 (April 1975), pp. 241–54; Robert J. Barro, "Rational Expectations and the Role of Monetary Policy," *Journal of Monetary Economics*, vol. 2 (January 1976), pp. 1–32; and Bennett T. McCallum, "Price Level Adjustments and the Rational Expectations Approach to Macroeconomic Stabilization Policy," *Journal of Money, Credit and Banking*, vol. 10 (November 1978), pp. 418–36. In these models, private-sector decisions adapt to monetary-policy actions in such a way that the actions can have no impacts on the economy's real output.

8. William Fellner, *Towards a Reconstruction of Macroeconomics: Problems of Theory and Policy* (Washington, D.C.: American Enterprise Institute for Public Policy Research, 1976). See also William Fellner, "The Valid Core of Rationality Hypotheses in the Theory of Expectations," in McCallum and Dewald, eds., vol. 12, *Journal of Money, Credit and Banking*.

The phrase "rational expectations" has been used loosely in connection with several different assumptions of how private-sector agents formulate expectations. The most basic hypothesis associated with rational expectations is that each microeconomic unit makes optimal use of all the information available to it given its preferences, the constraints it faces, and its model of how the economy functions. That general hypothesis is undoubtedly the right place to start in modeling microeconomic behavior. Nor is it controversial among macroeconomists (even though most of them fail to give it sufficient emphasis in their theoretical and empirical models). "Rational expectations" in the sense used in recent theoretical research, on the other hand, is a concept that goes well beyond the general hypothesis to the specific assumptions that each economic unit employs the same model of how the economy functions and that the common model is, apart from zero-mean stochastic disturbances, a correct representation of how the economy functions. These latter assumptions, unlike the basic hypothesis, are very strong and decidedly controversial.[9]

Second, the policy ineffectiveness proposition derivable from some theoretical models is not a conclusion derivable from all theoretical models making use of the basic hypothesis of rational expectations. Indeed, that proposition does not even follow from all models incorporating the strong, controversial form of the rational expectations assumptions. Future research may show that the drastic policy inferences drawn by early workers in this area are attributable to other features of their models (for example, the assumptions about the speed with which prices and wages adjust to clear markets) rather than to their expectational assumptions.[10]

Third, analysts should use identical assumptions about the ultimate objectives of policymakers when comparing the game-theoretic aspects of alternative approaches to conducting monetary policy. The contention that rules rather than

9. The importance of distinguishing among the different connotations of rational expectations is stressed by Robert Barro and Stanley Fischer, "Recent Developments in Monetary Theory," *Journal of Monetary Economics*, vol. 2 (April 1976), pp. 133–67, and by Benjamin M. Friedman, "Optimal Expectations and the Extreme Information Assumptions of 'Rational Expectations' Macromodels," *Journal of Monetary Economics*, vol. 5 (January 1979), pp. 23–41. See also Stephen J. Turnovsky, "Structural Expectations and the Effectiveness of Government Policy in a Short-Run Macroeconomic Model," *American Economic Review*, vol. 67 (December 1977), pp. 851–66.

10. Rational expectations models that lead to less extreme conclusions about the effectiveness of discretionary macroeconomic policy include John B. Taylor, "Monetary Policy During a Transition to Rational Expectations," *Journal of Political Economy*, vol. 83 (October 1975), pp. 1009–21; Edmund S. Phelps and John B. Taylor, "Stabilizing Powers of Monetary Policy Under Rational Expectations," *Journal of Political Economy*, vol. 85 (February 1977), pp. 163–90; Stanley Fischer, "Long-term Contracts, Rational Expectations, and the Optimal Money Supply Rule," *Journal of Political Economy*, vol. 85 (February 1977), pp. 191–205; J. Peter Neary and Joseph E. Stiglitz, "Towards a Reconstruction of Keynesian Economics: Expectations and Constrained Equilibria," National Bureau of Economic Research Working Paper 376 (Cambridge, Mass.: NBER, August 1979); and John B. Taylor, "Estimation and Control of a Macroeconomic Model with Rational Expectations," *Econometrica*, vol. 47 (September 1979), pp. 1267–86. An appraisal of the current status of the debate about the policy effectiveness proposition is provided by McCallum, "Rational Expectations and Macroeconomic Stabilization Policy: An Overview," by James Tobin, "Discussion," and by Arthur M. Okun, "Rational-Expectations-with-Misperceptions as a Theory of the Business Cycle," in McCallum and Dewald, eds., vol. 12, *Journal of Money, Credit and Banking*. On the general issue of rules versus discretion raised in this literature, see also Martin Neil Baily, "Stabilization Policy and Private Economic Behavior," *Brookings Papers on Economic Activity, 1:1978*, pp. 11–50; Stanley Fischer, "On Activist Monetary Policy with Rational Expectations," in Fischer, ed., *Rational Expectations and Economic Policy;* and Willem H. Buiter, "The Macroeconomics of Dr. Pangloss: A Critical Survey of the New Classical Macroeconomics," *Economic Journal*, vol. 90 (March 1980), pp. 34–50.

discretion will promote "better" private-sector decisions and therefore a "more favorable" evolution of the economy obviously presumes an underlying loss function against which alternative evolutions of the economy can be evaluated. As before, it is important to try to avoid the analytical confusion that results if advocates of rules and of discretion assess outcomes with different yardsticks. When game-theoretic and political considerations begin to play a prominent role in the analysis, however, it becomes more difficult to avoid this confusion. In principle, the agreed loss function used for evaluating both rules and discretion strategies needs to incorporate *political* values and trade-offs among those values. Yet it is even more difficult to obtain a consensus on the noneconomic than on the economic aspects of social welfare. When proponents of rules and proponents of discretion dispute about the relative merits of their strategies as a way of coping with the game-theoretic, expectational elements in policymaking, therefore, there is a commensurately greater risk that differences in basic values and objectives will become confused with the problems of strategy choice.[11]

Fourth, when contemplating the possibility of self-imposed limits on discretionary policy action, policymakers are not faced with an all or nothing choice. Suppose it could be demonstrated that a strategy of the fullest possible exercise of discretion would generate great uncertainty for private-sector expectations of policy actions and would also undermine the credibility of the government's resolve to avoid high rates of inflation. That demonstration alone would scarcely justify the conclusion that discretionary policy adjustments should be forsworn altogether. It might be that a middle course could be announced and adhered to—so to speak, a part-rule, part-discretion policy—that would be better than either untrammeled discretion or the adoption of rigid rules. To illustrate: the central bank might announce its intent to pursue given paths for its instrument settings, subject to discretionary adjustments for a list of contingent possibilities; crop failures and unexpectedly weak investment in plant and equipment might be designated as disturbances warranting discretionary responses, for example, whereas the announcement would exclude an unexpectedly rapid advance in wage rates as a disturbance justifying discretionary adjustment. Subsequent policy actions would have to adhere to announced intentions if such a middle-course policy were to be credible. But credibility problems with self-imposed limitations on discretion might be no greater for the middle-course policy than for rigid rules.

Fifth, when analysts conceptualize macroeconomic policy as a problem in game theory and expectational interactions, more attention should be devoted to modeling the policy authority of the government as the *dominant* player. Indeed, it may be justifiable to go further and conceptualize the policy authority as a "Stackelberg leader" and the various private-sector agents as "followers." In that event it would be assumed that the policy authority tries to incorporate the decision rules of the

11. Consider William Fellner's emphasis on the political undesirability of direct wage and price controls and his conviction that the "intermediate area" in between the comprehensive controls of the police state and complete abstention from the use of direct controls "is highly objectionable, even if not objectionable in precisely the same sense as a well-organized and thoroughly policed system of political and economic control" (*Towards a Reconstruction of Macroeconomics*, p. 16). Fellner notes that other analysts do not share in equal measure his aversion to this intermediate area. For the purposes of comparing Fellner's recommendations on strategy choice with the views of others, it would be analytically preferable to distinguish between differences over the appropriate loss function and differences over the consequences of pursuing alternative strategies given some common loss function.

private agents into its policymaking model (including the responses of the private agents to government actions), but that each private agent, as a follower, ignores the effects of its own decisions on the decisions of the government and of other private agents. This Stackelberg formulation of the problem treats the various players in the game asymmetrically, but that asymmetry may be justified by actual behavior in the real world.[12]

The preceding observations leave moot the difficult issue of whether game-theoretic considerations may justify some form of self-imposed limit on policymakers' discretion. Pending further theoretical and empirical research that will help resolve the issue, policymakers have no alternative but to rely on their subjective judgments about the likely expectational responses of the private sector to different types of discretionary policies and different types of announced rules.

If a Rule, Why a Money Rule?

A sharp distinction should be drawn between acknowledging the possibility that game-theoretic considerations may justify some preannounced limitations on discretionary actions for monetary policy and making the specific recommendation that the central bank should announce and pursue a rule with respect to an *intermediate-target variable,* the stock of money.

Unfortunately, that distinction has been ignored in discussions about the use of money in the conduct of monetary policy. Those who advocate a money strategy on game-theoretic, expectational grounds take it for granted that no further analysis of their case would be required if it could be established that announced limits on discretionary action would engender better private-sector decisions. But further analysis is necessary. The general game-theoretic case for limits on discretion does not depend on propositions about money supply and demand. Quite the contrary: that case can be evaluated without any mention of the money stock. An unexplained leap of logic is involved in jumping from the general case to the specific advocacy of a money strategy.

One benefit of preannounced limits on discretionary action, if they were credible, would be a reduction in private-sector uncertainty about future policy actions. But the greatest reduction in that uncertainty could be achieved by announcements of limits applying to the actual instruments of policy, to the ultimate objectives of the policymakers, or to both. The instruments are controlled precisely; when an instrument setting is observed to change, the private sector knows the change has occurred because the policymakers have made an explicit decision. Instrument settings will be expected to change in the future only because of explicit policy decisions. Similarly, the policymakers unambiguously determine the ultimate objectives at which they aim. Without doubt, credible announcements of the policymakers' loss function and planned instrument settings would give private decisionmaking units a firmer basis for formulating expectations and decisions.[13]

12. The difference between Nash-Cournot and Stackelberg conceptualizations of games is discussed further in chapter 25.
13. In theory, the policymakers could even go so far as to announce their loss function, the details of their policymaking model, the analytical procedures used in deriving the plans ("rules"?) for the instrument settings, and the contingencies, if any, that would cause them to change their instrument plans.

Intermediate variables such as the money stock, on the other hand, cannot be unambiguously determined by the policymakers. No matter how vigorously policymakers pursue an intermediate-target strategy, some deviations are inevitable between the actual path of the variable and a preannounced target path. When deviations are observed, moreover, private-sector agents cannot discern how much of the deviations to attribute to factors outside the control of policymakers and how much to the policymakers' failure to adhere conscientiously to their preannounced target path. Private-sector agents should therefore value an announcement of an intermediate-target path less highly than correspondingly truthful announcements of instrument plans and ultimate objectives. The latter would reduce their uncertainty about future policy actions more than the former. Note, too, that a potential for private-sector incredulity inevitably exists with respect to announcement of an intermediate-target path. In principle, this potential can be eliminated if announcements refer only to instruments and ultimate objectives.

The purpose of preannounced limits on discretion would be to condition private-sector decisions, thereby fostering more socially desirable behavior than would otherwise prevail. In theory, that conditioning would take place pari passu with the reduction in private-sector uncertainty about future policy actions. At a time when inflationary decisions about prices and wages threaten to become widespread, for example, policymakers would try to convince private economic units that a continuation of their inflationary behavior would not be validated by discretionary easing of monetary policy. The monetary policy deemed appropriate for the evolution of the economy in the absence of inflationary behavior would be preannounced and then credibly adhered to (even if private-sector decisions initially failed to adapt accordingly).

For any given degree of policymakers' resolve to stand firm, what monetary policy would perform that conditioning function most effectively? If the policymakers announce limits on their discretion in terms of instrument paths, the private-sector decisionmakers need only decide whether to believe that the policymakers will adhere to the announced limits. If the announcement runs in terms of an intermediate-target path for the money stock, however, there is yet a further element of doubt about whether the intermediate-target path can be and therefore will be achieved. Private decisionmakers know, furthermore, that the ultimate objectives of the policymakers are a basic determinant of policy actions. If policymakers announce their ultimate objectives, private decisionmakers need to decide whether the objectives are truthfully characterized and whether they will remain unchanged. But a truthful statement of objectives seems likely to have an especially powerful conditioning influence on private-sector decisions.

These points lead to an important conclusion. Game-theoretic and expectational considerations may or may not provide a justification for self-imposed limits on discretionary action implemented by announcements about *some* aspect of monetary policy. But no persuasive case exists on those grounds for announcing and adhering to a target path for the money stock or some other intermediate variable. The announcements, if made at all, should be made in terms of actual instruments, ultimate objectives, or perhaps both.[14]

14. If the central bank were determined to pursue an intermediate-target strategy based on the money stock, an announcement of the money target path being followed would be important information for

The Politics of Monetary Policy within the National Government

Economists have used the abstraction of a unified policy authority in virtually all their work on the prescriptive theory of economic policy. The national government is treated as though it were a single decisionmaker that seeks to achieve consensus objectives subject to the constraints of a model consensually judged to be the least inadequate representation of the economy's behavior. Most of this book, including the preceding discussion of the game-theoretic interrelationships between private-sector agents and "the government," continues that tradition.

Yet the concept of a single policy authority and the consequent assumption of an integrated approach to macroeconomic policy within a national government are false abstractions of the political and bureaucratic facts of life. In all countries, for better or for worse, the ship of state has more than one captain and stabilization decisions are not fully coordinated.

All theory must do violence to reality. Lack of realism is thus not, by itself, a damaging criticism of the traditional theory of economic policy. But economists' exclusive use of the abstraction of a single decisionmaker is open to criticism on a more fundamental point: the abstraction has inhibited analytical study of the politics of macroeconomic policy. Because economists have failed to ask analytic questions about the political aspects of the subject, moreover, the prescriptive recommendations derived from their theory of economic policy are of uncertain applicability. In effect, the theory of policy as developed by economists is a theory of *what* decisions should be made divorced from an analysis of *who* should (and does) make them. Little wonder, then, that many political scientists and sociologists regard the theory as naive.

The degree of disaggregation appropriate for conceptualizing decisionmaking units is in itself an issue that merits careful deliberation. For which purposes can an analyst safely ignore the multiplicity of policy agencies within a national government and merely work with the abstraction of a single policy authority? And when can an analyst safely work with the abstractions of several different policy agencies—for example, "the fiscal authority" and "the central bank"—without disaggregating still further and acknowledging the existence of subsidiary units or individual actors within the several policy agencies? Questions of this nature, rather than being suppressed, are highlighted in organization theory and other branches of sociology. Analysts of economic policy ought to address them at the outset of their work, but seldom do.

The greater the degree of disaggregation of decisionmaking units within the national government, the more difficult the analytical task. With several policy agencies, the possibility has to be entertained that each has different ultimate objectives. Each may have a different model of how the economy functions. In any case, each agency has actions it can take (instruments under its control) that influence the economy. Decisionmaking merely *within* the national government becomes a subtle, highly complex problem in game theory.

---

private economic agents. But it would be circular to use that argument here. The relevant issue for the purposes of this analysis is whether game-theoretic, expectational considerations themselves constitute an independent justification for pursuing a money strategy.

The analytical difficulties encountered as soon as the problem contains several decisionmaking units explain why economists have avoided a disaggregated perspective. Considerable progress has been possible using the abstraction of a single decisionmaker, whereas virtually any disaggregated abstraction—even the two-agency case of "the fiscal authority" and "the central bank"—mires the analysis in a game-theoretic swamp at the outset.

Formidable though the analytical difficulties may be, they are no longer a persuasive justification for deferring a decentralized approach to the theory of policy. Unlike the situation several decades ago, the case of the single policy authority has now been explored in some detail. And, if anything, the need for analysis of the decentralized case has become more compelling.[15]

From the perspective of a political scientist, it is not sufficient merely to disaggregate the government into separate policy agencies each having its own objectives, instruments, and model. It becomes important to ask how each agency comes to have the goals it pursues. If the agencies perceive the economy differently and thus employ different structural models of the economy, it is also important to know why they select the models they use and what political factors impinge on that choice. To ask questions of this type is to recognize not only the diversity of objectives, models, and instruments associated with the various decisionmaking units but also their endogeneity from the perspective of the political process.

Indeed, the political theorist and the sociologist try to ask fundamental questions about "the state," the interrelationships among its component agencies, and the most appropriate concepts to use in analyzing it. Economists tend to assume, often only implicitly, a simple democratic-pluralist model of the national political process. Yet pluralist models are only one of the possible classes of conceptualizations entertained in political theory. Elitist and class theories deserve serious consideration as alternative, or complementary, models of the organization of the polity.[16] In principle, the choice of a model to represent the functioning of the political and social system and, within that system, the organization of the national government could have an important bearing on the type of analysis to be used for modeling the decisions of the various economic-policy agencies and their interaction within the government.[17]

Finally, some further fundamental questions about decisionmaking deserve mention. How are decisions reached within government agencies? And how may they best be modeled for the purposes of analyzing macroeconomic policy? The deep-seated tradition in economics, continued in this book, is to postulate that decisionmakers are "rational" in the sense of systematically studying all feasible

15. For examples of research that begin to address this task, see Robert S. Pindyck, "The Cost of Conflicting Objectives in Policy Formulation" and Finn Kydland, "Decentralized Stabilization Policies: Optimization and the Assignment Problem," in *Annals of Economic and Social Measurement*, vol. 5 (Spring 1976), pp. 239–47 and 249–60; Finn Kydland, "Noncooperative and Dominant Player Solutions in Discrete Dynamic Games," *International Economic Review*, vol. 16 (June 1975), pp. 321–35; and Nils R. Sandell, Jr., and others, "Survey of Decentralized Control Methods for Large Scale Systems," *IEEE Transactions on Automatic Control*, vol. AC-23 (April 1978), pp. 108–28.

16. See, for example, Robert R. Alford, "Paradigms of Relations Between State and Society," in Leon N. Lindberg and others, eds., *Stress and Contradiction in Modern Capitalism: Public Policy and the Theory of the State* (Lexington Books, 1975).

17. For a discussion of the different approaches of economists and sociologists to theories of the social and political system, see Brian M. Barry, *Sociologists, Economists, and Democracy* (London: Collier-Macmillan, 1970).

courses of action open to them and then choosing that course which best achieves their objectives. Yet many political scientists, sociologists, and psychologists neither share nor accept this tradition; they propose other models of decisionmaking—particularly for the decisionmaking process in large bureaucracies.

Several of the possible alternative conceptualizations of government decisionmaking have been articulated in Graham Allison's study of the Cuban missile crisis.[18] The approach that presumes a national policy authority behaves as a centralized decisionmaking unit corresponds to Allison's "Rational Actor" (or "Classical") model. This model is traditional not only in economics but in the literature on international politics and diplomatic relations. But an analyst might employ instead, Allison observes, an "Organizational Process" model that emphasizes the institutional processes and procedures of component agencies that make up the national government.[19] Conceptual approaches of this second variety are analyzed further by John Steinbruner; he identifies a "cybernetic paradigm" and a "cognitive paradigm," both of which are to be sharply contrasted with the "analytic paradigm" used in economics and international relations.[20] Still a third conceptual approach, the "Governmental or Bureaucratic Politics" model, emphasizes the different perceptions, motivations, and powers of the various component agencies within the government and the results of bargaining among them. It attempts to combine some insights stressed in organization theory with some of the analytic perspective of the rational-actor model.[21]

The most unrealistic aspects of the rational-actor model, as already noted, may be avoided by abandoning the abstraction of a single policy authority for the national government and adopting a more disaggregated schematization of the decisionmaking process. In effect, game-theoretic analysis of the interrelationships among the separate policy agencies involves application of the rational-actor model to each agency individually rather than to the government as a whole. The rationalist and the governmental politics approaches to the analysis of decisionmaking may therefore be less incongruent than might seem at first glance.[22] The gulf that separates the rationalist and the cybernetic approaches, however, cannot be closed merely by adopting a more disaggregated perspective on the relevant decisionmaking units. Those two traditions look at decisionmaking through conceptual lenses that are fundamentally different.

18. Graham T. Allison, *Essence of Decision: Explaining the Cuban Missile Crisis* (Little, Brown, 1971).

19. See ibid., chap. 3; Herbert A. Simon, "Theories of Decision-Making in Economics and Behavioral Science," *American Economic Review*, vol. 49 (June 1959), pp. 253–83; and James G. March and Herbert A. Simon, *Organizations* (Wiley, 1958).

20. John D. Steinbruner, *The Cybernetic Theory of Decision: New Dimensions of Political Analysis* (Princeton University Press, 1974). Steinbruner's "cognitive paradigm" refers to the cybernetic conceptualization of decision processes as amended by propositions from cognitive theory.

21. See Allison, *Essence of Decision*, chap. 5. Other studies in the tradition of this third conceptualization include Morton H. Halperin with Priscilla Clapp and Arnold Kanter, *Bureaucratic Politics and Foreign Policy* (Brookings Institution, 1974); and Richard E. Neustadt, *Presidential Power: The Politics of Leadership* (Wiley, 1960).

22. Furthermore, the rationalist assumptions can be applied at a still more disaggregated level to the behavior of the individual people who are the actors within each policy agency; see, for example, Anthony Downs, *Inside Bureaucracy* (Little, Brown, 1967). An earlier book by Downs, *An Economic Theory of Democracy* (Harper Brothers, 1957), applies rationalist assumptions to explain the political behavior of government officials at a more aggregative level.

The various issues that have been broached in this section are all germane to the analysis of the politics of monetary policy. An analyst's views about these issues determine how the central bank is conceptualized, how its objectives are defined, how it is perceived as modeling the economy, how its decisions are or are not perceived as being coordinated with fiscal-policy decisions, and how the decisions even within the central bank itself are conceptualized. When these issues are not addressed explicitly, assumptions are merely being made about them implicitly.

Political Independence of the Central Bank

The interrelationships between monetary-policy and fiscal-policy decisions may vary, in principle, from the extremes of political independence to full integration. Where on the spectrum between the two extremes do central-bank decisions fall in practice?

Central banks, at least those in industrial countries, probably have objectives that are somewhat independent of those pursued by their counterpart fiscal authorities. To a lesser extent, the central banks probably also employ somewhat different models of how the various economies function. Evidence supporting these generalizations includes the widespread perception that central banks are "more conservative" (for example, give more weight to the costs and dangers of inflation) than heads of government and fiscal authorities.

The point of greatest interest, however, is whether differences in objectives between the central bank and fiscal authority actually become translated into monetary-policy actions that are significantly different from what the fiscal authority would prefer. If central-bank preferences for the ultimate objectives are different but yet systematically overridden by a politically dominant fiscal authority, the de facto relationship between monetary policy and fiscal policy is characterized by full integration of decisions—regardless of any public rhetoric that may give a contrary impression. Conversely, the central bank may choose and be able to sustain settings for the instruments of monetary policy different from the settings preferred by the fiscal authority even while publicly professing to support the objectives of the fiscal authority.

It is thus difficult in practice to make judgments about the degree of *effective* independence of a nation's central bank. The fiscal authority, the central bank, or both may find it convenient to characterize their interrelationships in ways not altogether faithful to the facts. The head of the government and the fiscal authority may wish to preserve the fiction of a semi-independent central bank even when the degree of its effective independence is slight. Equally important, the greater the degree of effective independence, the stronger the incentives may be to discourage public rhetoric about that independence. A further complication in appraising the relationships arises because the central bank may (even in internal discussions within the government) disguise differences in ultimate objectives as though they were differences in judgments about the appropriate model or the future paths of nonpolicy exogenous variables; differences in "technical" judgments call attention to the political consequences of independence much less prominently than do differences in objectives.

The limited evidence available suggests that the degree of effective independence of the central bank varies significantly across countries. The range of ultimate objectives thought germane to monetary policy differs; some central banks much more than others pursue allocative objectives (for example, facilitating credit flows to particular sectors of the economy) in addition to the more traditional macroeconomic objectives (for example, high employment and price stability for the economy as a whole). A similar diversity across countries is evident in the types and numbers of monetary-policy instruments. These differences seem in turn to be correlated with the apparent degree of political independence of nations' central banks. Central banks that pursue allocative as well as economy-wide objectives with not only general but also selective instruments seem to be less politically independent of their fiscal authorities and heads of government.[23]

Many nations have parliamentary forms of government that merge the legislative and administrative functions of government. In those nations there is accordingly little need to raise the question, Independence of the central bank *from what?* In a political system with a sharp distinction between the legislative and executive branches of national government, however, that question inevitably arises. In the United States, for example, a recommendation to eliminate the degree of independence enjoyed by the Federal Reserve System would need to specify whether the control of a nonindependent central bank should be assigned primarily to the Congress or to the President. Day-to-day control of a central bank by the legislative branch of government would pose practical difficulties; but control of a previously independent central bank by the executive branch of government would strengthen still further the power of the executive relative to the legislature. These complexities in a federal system help to explain the vigor and persistence of central bank independence in the United States.

The determinants of the degree of effective independence and the role of central banks in nations' political processes deserve more descriptive analysis than they have so far received from any social science discipline. Such analysis, although a precondition for sound prescriptions for how monetary policy should be conducted, is beyond the scope of this book.

Arguments For and Against Central Bank Independence

As background for an evaluation of the two "insulation" justifications for a money strategy, it is helpful first to broach the broad and explicitly normative question: Is political independence for the central bank good or bad for the nation?

Some insight into this question can be gained by specifying why central bank independence may be advocated. In particular, note that virtually all those who advocate independence do so because they want the central bank to pursue, or at

---

23. This interesting correlation is studied by John T. Woolley, "Monetary Policy Instrumentation and the Relationship of Central Banks and Governments," *Annals of the American Academy of Political and Social Science,* vol. 434 (November 1977), pp. 151–73. The causal relationships underlying this correlation are unclear: greater selectivity in objectives and instruments might lead to reduced independence; a lesser degree of independence might explain why a central bank can be pressured into pursuing selective objectives with selective instruments; or some more fundamental factors may condition both the degree of independence and the degree of selectivity in goals and instruments.

least to be able to pursue, fundamentally different objectives from those pursued by the rest of the government. Conversely, opponents of independence object to the idea of the central bank pursuing different objectives. The issue of political independence is thus primarily a controversy about which loss function should condition monetary-policy decisions and which individuals should determine that loss function. The relevant concept of loss function is one that incorporates not only economic preferences but political and social values as well.[24]

Consider, therefore, six possible views about the normative desirability of political independence.

A first position asserts that the political process in democratic-pluralist societies generates pressures on government officials to adopt policies inimical to long-run welfare (for example, policies that foster excessive monetary expansion and hence inflation). To correct this failing in the political system, it is argued, an independent central bank should be insulated from political pressures so that it can pursue the appropriate long-run objectives. Those holding this view typically emphasize the timing of the elections in which national policymakers try to get themselves or their political party reelected and argue that the need to insulate monetary policy from "partisan politics" is especially great during the year or two immediately preceding national elections.[25]

A second, contrary view asserts that the political process in democratic-pluralist societies works reasonably well and that the objectives pursued by political leaders are as accurate an approximation as is obtainable of the appropriate goals for the society's evolution. According to this view, the loss function used by the central bank should be identical to that used by the duly elected head of government and his fiscal authority; any other loss function, for example one giving more weight to the costs of inflation, would be "undemocratic." Thus not only would no beneficial purpose be served by political insulation of the central bank. To allow such insulation, it is argued, could result in a technocratic minority's views about the society's goals being imposed on the will of the majority.

A third position agrees with the allegation that the political process may work badly in the sense of sacrificing long-run welfare to short-run political expediency. But this view, like the second, attaches great importance to the preservation of political accountability in a pluralist-democratic political process. Accordingly, the recommended solution to the problem of a deficiently functioning political system

24. Conceivably, someone could hold the view that the central bank should be required to adopt the same objectives pursued by the remainder of the government but yet should be "operationally" independent because decisions will be "technically superior" under conditions of independence. If all controversy over ultimate objectives were ruled out, however, it is difficult to understand why technical implementation of policy should be greatly affected by different administrative relationships. Thomas Mayer, in his 1976 essay on reforming the Federal Reserve System in the United States, advocates a "compromise" solution in which the central bank would have its objectives specified by the President but would nevertheless retain substantial independence from partisan politics; see "The Structure and Operation of the Federal Reserve System: Some Needed Reforms," in House Committee on Banking, Currency, and Housing, *Financial Institutions and the Nation's Economy* [FINE], Papers prepared for the FINE Study, 94 Cong. 2 sess. (GPO, 1976), pt. 3, pp. 669–724. Mayer's compromise, however, seems contradictory; it is not clear whether the Federal Reserve would or would not pursue separate objectives; Mayer's discussion blurs the issue and implicitly argues the matter both ways. The discussion of political independence for the Federal Reserve in G. L Bach, *Making Monetary and Fiscal Policy* (Brookings Institution, 1971), pp. 209–13, also blurs the basic issue of differences in objectives.

25. See, for example, James M. Buchanan and Richard E. Wagner, *Democracy in Deficit: The Legacy of Lord Keynes* (Academic Press, 1977).

is not to delegate strong powers to nonpartisan technocrats insulated from political pressures (for example, at an independent central bank) but rather to try to improve the manner in which the political process translates the real interests of the society's individual members into the collective objectives pursued by accountable government officials.[26]

Fourth, an individual might advocate political independence for the central bank on grounds of "dispersion of power." According to this view, a fragmentation of decisionmaking power among government agencies is inherently desirable as a political end. The exercise of separate and limited powers by various competing agencies will, it is alleged, produce a better political and economic outcome than would result with a concentration of power in a single location. The recommended "competition" is preeminently a competition in goals: the intent is to leave the central bank free to seek somewhat different objectives than would otherwise be sought if decisionmaking power were more concentrated.[27]

Each of the four preceding views, implicitly if not explicitly, posits a pluralist-democratic conceptualization of the political process. An elitist conceptualization can lead to quite different views. For example, a fifth position asserts that the central bank should be effectively responsive to an elite group whose members control the society's financial organizations. The economic and social interests of this elite would not be adequately protected, it is argued, if the central bank were fully exposed to all the caprices of the electoral process and the political pulling and hauling among the various bureaucracies in the remainder of the government.[28]

Finally, consider a sixth position that accepts an elitist diagnosis of the political and social system but, because of different normative values, reaches an opposite recommendation. According to this view, the financial community already enjoys excessive political power in the society. The influence of that elite group needs to be counteracted by the political bargaining power of other elites, it is argued, and therefore the central bank should be fully exposed to political and bureaucratic pressures instead of being granted independence.

Monetary-Policy Rules and Central Bank Independence

The six positions just identified indicate the range of possible views about central bank independence. The political aspects of the rules versus discretion controversy

26. For a discussion of issues germane to these first three positions, see Brian M. Barry, "Does Democracy Cause Inflation? A Study of the Political Ideas of Some Economists," paper prepared for the conference on "The Politics and Sociology of Global Inflation," Brookings Institution, December 1978. Leon Lindberg and Charles Maier are editing the conference papers for publication.

27. See, for example, Arthur F. Burns, "The Independence of the Federal Reserve System," *Reflections of an Economic Policy Maker, Speeches and Congressional Statements: 1969–78* (Washington, D.C.: American Enterprise Institute for Public Policy Research, 1978), where he argues: "The concept of independence of the monetary authority within the structure of government is congenial to the basic principles of our Constitution. As Alexander Hamilton put it in one of the Federalist Papers, our system of government is based on the precept that partitions between the various branches of government 'ought to be so contrived as to render the one independent of the other.' Such a division of power, according to another of the Federalist Papers, is 'essential to the preservation of liberty' " (p. 381).

28. Fred Hirsch, "The Ideological Underlay of Inflation," in Fred Hirsch and John H. Goldthorpe, eds., *The Political Economy of Inflation* (Harvard University Press, 1978), pp. 263–84, discusses some reasons why business and moneyed interests, having lost direct control of the state to the mass electorate, have an incentive to insulate the central bank from the rest of government.

are identified in chapter 17. Juxtaposition of those two issues helps to bring both into clearer focus.

A desire to insulate monetary policy from the political process, it will be recalled, is a conceivable reason for opposition to discretionary actions by government policymakers as well as a rationalization for central bank independence. Hence alleged deficiencies in the political process can serve as an argument for monetary-policy rules, for independence, or for both together.

While monetary-policy rules and central bank independence may be advocated in combination, there is no necessary link between them. An individual may favor independence for the central bank without being a proponent of rules, and vice versa. The typology in figure 18-1 emphasizes this point by cross-classifying views on the two issues.

The supporters of a high degree of independence for the central bank tend to have polarized views about discretionary adaptation of monetary policy, being either antipathetic or strongly in favor.

The group favoring discretion (those with the views labeled B in figure 18-1) contains the majority of the supporters of independence, in part because this group includes most central bankers. The typical individual in this group regards rules as a dangerously inflexible way to conduct monetary policy because rules prevent policymakers from responding promptly to new information about the economy. On the other hand, this view endorses the value judgment that responsibility for monetary-policy decisions should be lodged with technically competent but non-partisan individuals motivated by considerations of the long-run public interest. The nonpartisan technocrats, it is believed, should be able to pursue—and when necessary should pursue—a different definition of the public interest than that espoused by incumbent politicians. The alleged need to elevate monetary-policy decisions "above politics" is the main argument typically used to support this position, but the dispersion-of-powers argument is often invoked as well.[29]

The second, smaller group supporting central bank independence (the views labeled A in figure 18-1) is more heterogeneous. Individuals holding this position share a conviction that central banks should follow predetermined rules as a way of limiting discretionary policy actions but reach that conclusion by different routes. Some use the argument that monetary policy should be insulated from politics to advocate, in effect, double insurance. Even if the central bank should be statutorily independent, they argue, central bankers with discretionary powers would still be prone to yield too much to the vagaries of short-run political pressures. Hence the

---

29. The following quotations from Burns, *Reflections of a Policy Maker*, provide a representative expression of this position. "The Federal Reserve has thus been able to fashion monetary policy in an impartial and objective manner—free from any sort of partisan or parochial influence. While the long history of the Federal Reserve is not faultless, its policies have consistently been managed by conscientious individuals seeking the nation's permanent welfare—rather than today's fleeting benefit (p. 420)." "I doubt that the American people would want to see the power to create money lodged in the presidency—which may mean that it would in fact be exercised by political aides in the White House. Such a step would create a potential for political mischief or abuse on a larger scale than we have yet seen. Certainly, if the spending propensities of Federal officials were given freer rein, the inflationary tendency that weakened our economy over much of the past decade would in all likelihood be aggravated. The need for a strong monetary authority to discipline the inflationary tendency inherent in modern economies is evident from the historical experience of the nations around the world (p. 383)." See also Mayer, "The Structure and Operation of the Federal Reserve System: Some Needed Reforms"; and Bach, *Making Monetary and Fiscal Policy*, pp. 161–68, 209–22.

Figure 18-1. *Typology of Normative Positions on the Two Issues of Rules versus Discretion and Political Independence for the Central Bank*

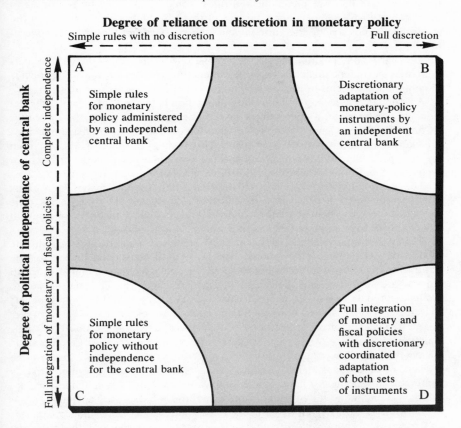

Degree of reliance on discretion in monetary policy

Simple rules with no discretion ────────── Full discretion ➤

Degree of political independence of central bank

Complete independence ↑

Full integration of monetary and fiscal policies ↓

A

Simple rules
for monetary
policy administered
by an independent
central bank

B

Discretionary
adaptation of
monetary-policy
instruments by
an independent
central bank

C

Simple rules
for monetary
policy without
independence
for the central bank

D

Full integration
of monetary and
fiscal policies
with discretionary
coordinated
adaptation
of both sets
of instruments

conclusion that rules limiting discretion are at least as important as, and are required in addition to, formal political independence. Others place greater emphasis on the need to insulate monetary policy from human error or to disperse the powers of government. According to these individuals, government officials in general and central bankers in particular seldom turn out to be skilled technocrats selflessly seeking the public interest; nonindependent central bankers can be easily manipulated to seek bad ends or to follow incompetent policies, yet independent central bankers still have ample scope to make mistakes on their own. Thus the least dangerous way to organize the government and its policymaking is to decentralize decisionmaking power and to restrict the scope for discretionary error by imposing policy rules—in other words, to the maximum extent feasible, a "government of laws, not of men."

A third conceivable stance with respect to the issues juxtaposed in figure 18-1 is advocacy of monetary-policy rules but rejection of, or at least indifference to, central bank independence (the views labeled C). Only a few economists and others espouse this position in practice.[30] Why this should be so is somewhat puzzling. One might think, for example, that those persuaded by the game-theoretic, expectational case in favor of preannounced rules would be as likely to oppose as to favor central bank independence; no part of that case hinges on the nature of the interrelationships among the various policy agencies within the national government.[31]

The fourth polar position represented in figure 18-1 (the views labeled D) rejects both rules and independence, favoring full integration of monetary and fiscal policies in conjunction with discretionary adaptation of both sets of instruments.

As emphasized in chapter 15, a sharp distinction between "rules" and "discretion" is not possible; a spectrum of possibilities exists between two extremes. "Complete independence" and "full integration of monetary with fiscal policies" are likewise polar positions on a spectrum. The typology in figure 18-1 leaves room for intermediate positions along both spectra. The polar combinations have been emphasized here to highlight the major differences of view on the issues.

The values, ideologies, and behavioral assumptions underlying the various positions identified in figure 18-1 need further refinement. They then need to be evaluated with the benefit of the concepts and analytical methods of political science, sociology, jurisprudence, and perhaps even psychology.

Evaluation of those positions is especially difficult. The questions triggering the evaluation—Is political independence for the central bank good or bad for the nation? and Is the nation better or worse off if monetary policy is conducted with rules?—are normative and elicit highly normative responses. The analysis has to evaluate ultimate objectives and preferences, or at least political and social beliefs that are closely related to ultimate objectives and preferences. Unlike in earlier chapters where alternative positions could be evaluated using some given loss function, the essence of the problem here is to evaluate alternative loss functions themselves. But how should "ultimate" preferences be evaluated? Prescriptive analysis of alternatives logically requires some basis for ranking one alternative as preferable to another. Yet no consensual yardstick exists. Again, inescapably, national economic welfare resides in the eye of the beholder (see chapter 13).

As with the more descriptive aspects of the politics of monetary policy, analysis of these prescriptive aspects is not feasible here. For the purposes of this book, the broad noneconomic issues that arise in connection with the conduct of monetary policy have to be regarded as unresolved. No decisive political or sociological reasons have been given for either rejecting or espousing discretionary monetary policy. Nor has any decisive political or sociological case been presented for opposing or supporting the integration of monetary-policy and fiscal-policy deci-

---

30. One example is Milton Friedman, "Should There Be an Independent Monetary Authority?" in Leland B. Yeager, ed., *In Search of a Monetary Constitution* (Harvard University Press, 1962), pp. 219–43. Another example may be Harry G. Johnson, "Should There Be an Independent Monetary Authority?" in Warren L. Smith and Ronald L. Teigen, eds., *Readings in Money, National Income, and Stabilization Policy,* 3d ed. (Richard D. Irwin, 1974), pp. 276–78 (reprinted from *The Federal Reserve System after Fifty Years,* Hearings before the House Committee on Banking and Currency, 88 Cong. 2 sess. [GPO, 1964], pp. 970–73); in this paper Johnson unambiguously rejects central bank independence and advocates a strategy basically similar to a fixed rule of monetary expansion.

31. Similarly, the assertion that monetary policy needs to be insulated from the consequences of human frailty is an argument against discretion but does not bear directly on the issue of central bank independence.

sions. Pending further analysis of the politics of monetary policy, an impartial analyst should have an open mind on the subject.

"Insulation" Justifications for a Money Strategy

Suppose the benefit of the doubt is given to those who advocate monetary-policy rules on the basis of political and sociological considerations. Specifically, suppose policymakers accept the arguments that monetary policy should be insulated from the political process, from human error, or from both. What implications would follow for the specifics of strategy choice?

If policymakers wished to conduct monetary policy with some type of rule strategy, two families of such strategies would be available (see chapter 15). Rules could be formulated in terms of an intermediate-target variable. In a money strategy the rule might be to keep the money stock growing at a constant rate of x percent indefinitely. Alternatively, rules could be formulated in a single-stage strategy in terms of the instrument settings. In a policy regimen where unborrowed commercial-bank reserves were used as an instrument, the rule might be to keep unborrowed reserves indefinitely growing at a constant rate of y percent.

Advocates of rules for monetary policy argue for the former type and almost always propose the money stock as the rule variable. But why a rule in terms of an intermediate variable? That preference seems especially paradoxical if the intent is to restrain discretionary decisions for political or sociological reasons. Under a money strategy, even if the money target path were fixed indefinitely by a nondiscretionary rule, policymakers would have to exert continuous discretion to refix their instrument settings to try to keep the money stock on its target path. Thus political pressure might still be applied in an effort to get the central bank to aim its discretionary actions at political goals; the central bank could subtly yield to such pressures while still professing to be "trying" to adhere to the money rule. A money strategy would also provide leeway for policymakers to make mistakes because of incompetence. With an instrument rule, on the other hand, an unambiguous check would exist on whether the rules were being followed; actual instrument settings would merely have to be compared with the settings dictated by the rule. Thus insulation either from politics or from human frailty would be better assured. In short, instrument rules would restrain discretionary policy mistakes altogether whereas a money stock rule leaves the door partly open to discretionary errors. If discretion is undesirable, why not shut the door completely?

Recognition of this paradoxical inconsistency in the antidiscretion case for a money strategy is sufficient to establish an important conclusion: the political grounds for preferring monetary-policy rules do not provide a valid justification for a two-stage instead of a single-stage strategy, nor for a money strategy in particular. Although an impartial analyst has to admit the possibility that one or both of the insulation arguments may provide a justification for monetary-policy rules of some sort, he can without compunction disallow the two insulation justifications as convincing rationalizations for a *money* strategy. As with the case of the game-theoretic, expectational justification discussed earlier in the chapter, proponents of a money strategy overlook a logical gap in their reasoning when they jump from a general argument against discretion to the specific recommendation of a money strategy.

Monetary Policy's Role in Macroeconomic Stabilization Policy as a Whole

Thus far this chapter has focused on arguments in favor of central bank independence and monetary-policy rules and against full integration of monetary-policy and fiscal-policy decisions. But an uncoordinated approach to macroeconomic policy would have significant negative aspects as well. Such costs need to be weighed alongside the alleged political and sociological benefits before reaching an overall conclusion on the desirability of decentralized decisionmaking.

Suppose the central bank has a loss function significantly different from that of the fiscal authority and sufficient independence to act on the basis of its different preferences. Suppose as a consequence that the central bank and the fiscal authority fail to coordinate policy decisions. To illustrate: the central bank might pay less attention to the effects of monetary-policy actions on certain ultimate-target variables—for example, the aggregate level and the regional distribution of employment—than does the fiscal authority. The fiscal authority might take policy actions attaching less importance to the impacts on the inflation rate than does the central bank.

Such a competition in policy goals, whatever political merits it might have as a reflection of a constitutional separation of powers, has to be judged from the analytical perspective of chapter 14. The separate agencies of the government are inescapably linked through the constraints of the economic structure—especially through the consolidated budget and balance-sheet constraint for the government as a whole. The fiscal authority and the central bank can exercise formal sovereignty over a subset of the instruments of macroeconomic policy; that is, each can independently determine the settings for its own subset. But neither of the two can enjoy a high degree of *effective* autonomy: neither can be sure of using the instruments at its command to control the ultimate-target variables important in its own loss function.[32]

The difficulties that can arise when the components of macroeconomic policy are not integrated into a coherent whole can be likened to the problems that would occur on a sailing ship manned by two crews, each under the separate command of its own captain and each adjusting the instruments under its control to influence the outcome of the voyage in accordance with its captain's preferences for the ship's route, speed, and final destination. A satisfactory voyage in a sailing ship requires an agreed navigation plan and a coordinated use of the ship's instruments; what is done with the rudder depends on which sails are rigged, and vice versa. The holistic unity of all the components of macroeconomic stabilization policy requires a similar integration of decisions. Because the instruments of fiscal policy as well

32. If different parts of the national government have different loss functions and act without coordination, the analytical situation is formally similar to the two-nation, two-decisionmaker conceptualization of part 3. Instead of interdependence among nations, two interdependent agencies within the national government seek separate goals making decentralized decisions about the settings on policy instruments.

as monetary policy influence ultimate-target variables, the choice of settings for monetary instruments is logically contingent on projected paths for the fiscal instruments—and vice versa. When the fiscal instruments deviate from previously projected paths, the settings for monetary instruments should be reconsidered (and vice versa). Even if the fiscal authority and a semi-independent central bank have different loss functions, therefore, it is highly desirable to forge a working consensus before venturing out on the open seas. In the absence of a consensus, neither the fiscal authority's nor the central bank's objectives may be attained; some altogether different port may be reached. In any case, the voyage is likely to be erratic. One crew's mistakes may at times be offset by the other's prudence. But another possibility is shipwreck.

To argue that monetary policy needs to be an integral part of a coherent macroeconomic stabilization policy need not imply that monetary policy be subservient to fiscal policy. No one part of the overall policy requires or warrants primacy.[33] The logic of this argument merely demands that an effort be made to reach a consensus on objectives and to determine jointly the settings for all policy instruments.

Coordination with Fiscal Policy under Alternative Strategies

For some given set of ultimate objectives, the fewer obstacles a monetary-policy strategy places in the way of coordination with fiscal-policy decisions, the stronger the grounds (other things being equal) for adopting that strategy. Given whatever degree of central bank independence exists, which monetary-policy strategy performs best in facilitating coordination with fiscal policy? How does a money strategy compare with discretionary instrument adaptation?

An analytical basis for comparing alternative strategies in terms of their amenability to coordination with fiscal policy is implicit in the analysis of chapter 17.

The illustrative models in that chapter took fiscal policy as exogenously given to the central bank. The settings on the monetary-policy instrument (X^M) were chosen on the basis of, among other things, expectations of the settings on the fiscal instrument (X^F). The central bank's policymakers were assumed to have no influence over the time path of values for X^F. Nor did monetary-policy decisions take into account the likely effects of monetary-policy actions on the decisions of the fiscal policymakers.

The analysis in chapter 17 thus pertains to the case in which fiscal policy and monetary policy are not closely coordinated. The loss function and the model of the economy in that analysis should be interpreted as belonging to the central bank. Implicitly, the fiscal authority has a different loss function and a different model; its decisionmaking procedures are out of sight behind the scenes.

---

33. Compare Arthur M. Okun, in "Fiscal-Monetary Activism: Some Analytical Issues," *Brookings Papers on Economic Activity, 1:1972:* "Whether good fiscal policy is more or less effective than good monetary policy for stabilization purposes is like the question of whether good headlights are more or less important than good brakes for night driving. Fortunately, neither the stabilization policy maker nor the driver has to make such a choice" (p. 125). Okun's article is consistent with my stress on the holistic unity of macroeconomic policy but does not address the additional issues stemming from the possibility of two noncoordinating drivers of the same vehicle.

With a strategy of discretionary instrument adaptation and fiscal-policy decisions exogenously given to the central bank, the preferred settings for X^M were altered whenever expectations of future fiscal actions were altered or whenever a new datum was observed for some period's actual fiscal action that differed from previous expectations of it. Each month's decisions for monetary policy were adapted promptly to the exogenously given course of fiscal policy. Although those adaptations did not represent mutual coordination of monetary and fiscal policies, they did constitute, under the assumed circumstances, the most efficient possible response of monetary policy to fiscal actions. In effect, discretionary instrument adaptation was the best feasible "one-way coordination," given that the monetary policymakers were intent on achieving the separate objectives embodied in their own loss function.

Under the two-stage money strategy in chapter 17, however, the central bank was not able to adjust efficiently to the exogenously given fiscal actions. At the times of recalculation of the money target path, to be sure, the monetary policymakers were assumed to take the expected course of fiscal policy into account in setting that path. Thus the logical interdependence of the money path and the instrument settings for fiscal policy was recognized *intermittently*. In between the intermittent recalculations of the money path, however, that interdependence was ignored. Any deviations of fiscal policy from what was expected in January or any changes in the expected course of future fiscal policy had to be ignored in February and in March because of the invariance of the money target path and the exclusive preoccupation of lower-stage decisions with that path. Compared with discretionary instrument adaptation, therefore, a two-stage money strategy was a more sluggish, less efficient way of adjusting monetary policy to the exogenously given decisions of the fiscal authority.

Now consider the case of full integration of macroeconomic policy in which the central bank and fiscal authority share a common loss function and use the same policymaking model. Under those assumptions, the central bank would not need to formulate expectations about the fiscal authority's plans for fiscal policy, and vice versa. Each policy agency would reach its decisions jointly with the other, fully coordinating their use of both the fiscal and the monetary instruments.[34] Under such conditions, which type of strategy for monetary policy would best facilitate the incorporation of monetary policy into a coherent unity for macroeconomic stabilization policy as a whole?

Single-stage strategies are well designed to cope with the mutual interdependence among several policy instruments and their various impacts on the economy. Integration of monetary-policy and fiscal-policy decisions poses no analytical obstacles over and above those fundamental difficulties—for example, uncertainties about the magnitudes and timing of the impacts of policy actions—that beset any decisionmaking procedure for macroeconomic policy. A conceptually straightforward approach exists for combining the policymakers' loss function and model in order to select preferred settings for the entire array of available policy instruments.

If a money strategy is pursued, however, the resulting dichotomization of the decision process and the differing periodicities associated with its two levels of

---

34. This implicitly assumes that differences of judgment about either objectives or the model are resolved by the emergence of a consensus or by appeal to the final authority of the head of government.

decisionmaking introduce an additional set of complications. Taking the mutual interdependence of fiscal and monetary actions into account is not straightforward. If the intermediate-target path of the money stock is to be consistent with the best feasible outcome for ultimate-target variables, that path must be chosen simultaneously with projected paths for the fiscal instruments. The money target path should be reconsidered whenever the fiscal instruments deviate from earlier projected paths (and vice versa). The intermediate-target approach thus confronts a serious dilemma. If the money target path is kept unchanged as the economy evolves and as discretionary changes may be made in fiscal policy, fiscal and monetary policies can get progressively out of coordination with each other. Even if efforts to *re*integrate fiscal and monetary policies are made on the periodic occasions when the money target path is recalculated, a *dis*integration reappears during the intervals between recalculations. The longer the interval between recalculations, the greater the degree of disintegration that may develop. If emphasis is given to the coordination of monetary and fiscal instruments, on the other hand, the money target path cannot be kept unchanged for lengthy intervals. Yet it is the essence of the intermediate-target approach *not* to recalculate the money path frequently. If the money path recalculations are carried out more or less continuously, the approach can no longer be construed an intermediate-target strategy in a meaningful sense.

The preceding paragraph presupposes a sophisticated application of a money strategy in which, *albeit only intermittently,* the interaction of the impacts of monetary and fiscal instruments on ultimate-target variables is taken into account. This presumption, as with the analysis of the illustrative models in chapter 17, presents the intermediate-target approach in the most favorable light possible. The lack of coordination of monetary and fiscal decisions would be exacerbated significantly further if the target path for the money stock were reconsidered less often than intermittently or if a cruder procedure were used for calculating that target path (for example, a procedure ignoring part or all of the policymaking model).[35]

Analysis of how alternative strategies compare in facilitating the systematic integration of macroeconomic policy thus produces an unambiguous conclusion. A two-stage decision procedure focused on money makes coordination of monetary policy and fiscal policy considerably more difficult than if monetary policy is conducted by discretionary instrument adaptation. This conclusion applies for any given degree of effective independence of the central bank from the rest of the government. It takes on progressively greater practical significance the stronger is the desire within the national government to use monetary and fiscal instruments in a unified discretionary approach to macroeconomic policy as a whole.

Chapter 16 briefly reviewed the range of views in the recent theoretical literature on fiscal policy and noted that knowledgeable differences of view about the relative importance of monetary policy and fiscal policy now turn on the magnitudes and timing patterns of the impacts of the two types of actions, not on whether one or the other can be ignored altogether. That fact has a corollary: latter-day monetarists

35. Difficulties of integrating monetary policy and fiscal policy when the former employs money as an intermediate target would be troublesome even if the economy's behavioral relationships were recursive in the manner postulated by the two-stage decision process. If the postulated recursivity does not exist, as it probably does not, these difficulties become still more troublesome.

and nonmonetarists alike need to devote serious attention to the problems of coordinating monetary policy and fiscal policy. It is certainly not an acceptable response to the issue discussed in this section to argue that "fiscal policy matters so little for the macroeconomic evolution of the economy that a money strategy can safely ignore fiscal actions." That point of view has a political attraction for individuals who for quite separate reasons wish to pretend that the macroeconomic impacts of fiscal actions can be forgotten.[36] But it does not merit attention in a serious discussion of the most appropriate strategy to use for the conduct of monetary policy.

Surrogate Targets and Policy Myopia

One last set of considerations remains to be put into the balance when weighing the relative merits of money strategies and discretionary instrument adaptation.

The money stock in all but the most rigid, nondiscretionary variants of an intermediate-target strategy is merely a surrogate for ultimate targets. In theory, policymakers implementing the strategy are always looking through the intermediate target to the ultimate targets. In theory, private-sector agents correctly interpret the significance of the money target path and evaluate the performance of policymakers only in terms of the degree to which best, feasible paths of the ultimate-target variables are attained. From the perspective of both policymakers and private-sector agents, it is not the surrogate but only the ultimate targets that "genuinely matter."[37]

When a money strategy is pursued in practice, however, policymakers or private-sector agents or both may be strongly tempted to give disproportionate emphasis to the money stock. Under such a strategy, money is the focus of day-to-day decisions. New data for the money stock are reported with greater frequency and a shorter lag than for ultimate-target variables. It becomes easy for attention to be diverted from the genuine objectives of policy to the surrogate objective. The more heed paid to the surrogate target in policymaking discussions, in journalistic reporting of policy, and in simplified expositions of macroeconomic policy for laymen, the greater the risks that individuals both in and out of the policymaking process may allow their perception of the ultimate objectives to become blurred. At worst,

36. Arthur M. Okun observes: "What is most important and most dangerous about the monetary rule is its implicit precept: Ignore fiscal policy. . . . Carried to its ultimate conclusions, the monetarist position would justify a totally unconstrained federal fiscal policy. Now I know a few people in Washington who would love an intellectual justification for fiscal irresponsibility. Some day they are going to discover the most important message of the monetarist view. And then we will see some fireworks" (*The Political Economy of Prosperity* [Brookings Institution, 1970], pp. 116–17). Henry Wallich makes a similar observation: "Increasingly, monetarist prescriptions play a role in political discussions. Policy objectives are being expressed and debated in terms of growth targets of the money stock. The elected representatives of the people have discovered the attraction of monetarist doctrine because it plays down the effects of fiscal policy"; see "From Multiplier to Quantity Theory," in Bela Belassa and Richard Nelson, eds., *Economic Progress, Private Values, and Public Policy: Essays in Honor of William Fellner* (North-Holland, 1977), p. 279.

37. Individual private-sector agents may appraise outcomes with a loss function different from that of the policymakers and hence have different views about which time paths for ultimate-target variables are "best feasible." But from the perspective of virtually any plausible loss function, the money stock, however defined, is merely an intermediate variable.

preoccupation with the surrogate may lead to perception of the money target path as an end in its own right.[38]

The phenomenon of policy myopia—greater attention being paid to a surrogate target because the surrogate is near at hand and highly visible—is the cognitive, perceptual analogue of the substantive problems with an intermediate-target strategy analyzed in chapter 17. As in the old joke, if a man loses his house key in the dark across the street, he ought to be judged a fool for looking for it under the lamp post even though that is where the light is. Yet individuals and public opinion are impressionable. Many do not know where to look and thus take their guidance from others; once some people are observed to be looking under a particular lamp post, many others may come along and do so too. In practice, great potential exists for disproportionate attention to be lavished on the surrogate objective.

Single-stage strategies have less potential for inducing policy myopia. Individuals and public opinion could conceivably become preocccupied with instrument settings themselves, perceiving them as ends in their own right. Yet severe myopia of that sort is less likely. The substantial risk of confusion in the case of intermediate-target strategies arises because of the coexistence of two types of targets, one genuine and the other surrogate. Discretionary instrument adaptation dispenses with surrogate targets altogether.

No doubt policy myopia under an intermediate-target strategy is likely to occur mainly because of inadvertence. Disproportionate emphasis may be given to the surrogate goal but without the perceptual distortion being recognized.

Even if private-sector decisionmakers are the only ones whose attention is diverted from ultimate objectives, some adverse consequences may result. Although policymakers try to execute the two-stage strategy without losing sight of their ultimate objectives, faulty public understanding can make it more difficult for them to alter course when circumstances call for a change in the surrogate target. If the attention of private-sector agents is diverted from ultimate targets, moreover, there will be less pressure on policymakers to articulate those ultimate targets and to specify how conflicting targets are being traded off against one another. If policymakers themselves inadvertently allow their vision of the ultimate targets to become blurred, it becomes a virtual certainty that the surrogate goal will be achieved at the cost of sacrificing the goals that really matter.

Policy myopia, if that disability develops among policymakers themselves, will no doubt usually be attributable to inadvertence. But two alternative, more subtle hypotheses also deserve mention.

Clear articulation of ultimate goals and systematic reasoning about the channels of transmission between policy actions and ultimate goals are extremely difficult tasks. And the job of a policymaker can be less taxing if he can successfully avoid being specific about his trade-offs among ultimate goals, remain vague about his model of the relationships between policy actions and ultimate goals, focus others' attention on a target time path for a surrogate goal that can be attained fairly readily, and avoid frequent respecification of the surrogate goal. Thus a strategy of using the money stock as an intermediate target, it can be argued, is well-designed to tempt central bankers already disposed towards the easy life to give in to those

38. This risk of confusion between surrogate and genuine objectives is not peculiar to *money* strategies; it could arise with the use of any intermediate variable as a surrogate target.

inclinations. From the perspective of such central bankers, policy myopia outside the central bank would be convenient and a phenomenon to be encouraged.

Still another possibility suggests itself. Suppose a nation's central bank has a substantial but still limited degree of political independence and the central bank governor intends to use that independence to the full by pursuing different ultimate objectives from those desired by the head of government and the fiscal authority. To pursue his different objectives as successfully as possible, the central bank governor might decide to avoid specification of his ultimate goals and the trade-offs among them, to focus attention instead on a target path for a surrogate goal such as the money stock, and to avoid clear articulation of his judgments about the relationships between ultimate goals, surrogate targets, and policy actions. Better yet, the central bank governor might heighten the confusion still further by offering up several surrogate targets (for example, several different definitions of the money stock). By obfuscating policy in that way, the central bank governor might enhance his freedom to implement those settings for the monetary-policy instruments he thinks most likely to achieve his ultimate goals. Such a strategy would not be a two-stage money strategy. But it would travel in that disguise. In such a case, policy myopia outside the central bank might again be deliberately fostered. The value of the surrogate targets to the central bank governor would lie precisely in the assistance they give him in dissembling with the fiscal authority and with private-sector agents about the true objectives of monetary policy.

Policymakers disposed toward the easy life could elect to pursue a single-stage strategy instead of a money strategy. A strong-willed, independent governor of the central bank might try to dissemble about his ultimate objectives even as he conducted monetary policy by means of discretionary instrument adaptation.

It is nonetheless true that an intermediate-target strategy provides greater opportunities for the deliberate encouragement of policy myopia. And those opportunities are an additional reason for doubting the presumption that insulation of monetary policy from human error could be achieved unambiguously better by one type of strategy rather than another. As noted earlier, most of those who espouse monetary-policy rules because of concern about potential incompetence or deceit of policymakers leap without justification to the conclusion that the rule should be a money rule. One hopes that central bankers are neither concerned with leading an easy life nor inclined to deceive those outside the central bank, but rather wish only to make good decisions. If that were an imprudent hope, however, is it self-evident that one should prefer the central bank to conduct policy with the money stock as a surrogate target rather than with a single-stage strategy? If anything, perhaps the presumption ought to go the other way.

Lack of clarity in publicly available information about the ultimate goals of monetary policy, whether that lack is inadvertent or deliberate, is a serious political issue that deserves more attention than it typically receives. There is much room for improvement on this score quite apart from the particular strategy used for conducting policy.[39] More precise, truthful information about the ultimate targets

---

39. Compare Bach, *Making Monetary and Fiscal Policy:* "Evaluation of the Federal Reserve's goal-setting and its success in achieving these objectives is difficult because the goals are stated only in general terms, without specification of the weights being given to each, and because there is substantial disagreement on what the goals should be" (p. 164). . . . "Neither fiscal nor monetary policymakers [in the Eisenhower years] specified their goal structures, except in very general terms. Thus, evaluation of the policy process

of monetary policy would also be beneficial from the perspective of the expectational interaction between the central bank and private-sector decisionmakers. Those benefits would accrue, again, quite apart from whether a money strategy or a single-stage strategy were chosen for conducting monetary policy.

The trend in recent years toward formulating monetary policy in terms of money stock targets has been associated with an increased volume of information about central bank behavior, most of it made available by the central banks themselves. That increase in information has been all to the good, and in turn may have engendered an improvement in private-sector understanding of the role of monetary policy in macroeconomic developments.[40]

Yet there need be no correlation between availability of more information and the pursuit of a money strategy. Central banks can, and should, make more information available about their ultimate objectives and their operating procedures, whatever strategies they may follow.

---

is difficult. Insofar as the results seem unacceptable, it is hard to distinguish clearly how much of the shortfall was due to differences among the policymakers' preferred goal structures, and how much to unsatisfactory use of monetary and fiscal policy instruments'' (p. 108).

40. In the United States, one stimulus to the central bank to provide more information came from House Concurrent Resolution 133, passed in March 1975. This resolution required the Federal Reserve to testify quarterly before the Congress on its "objectives and plans with respect to the ranges of growth or diminution of monetary and credit aggregates in the upcoming twelve months." Some regard the resulting quarterly hearings as significant because of the monetary-aggregate targets themselves; see, for example, Robert Weintraub, "Monetary Policy and Karl Brunner," *Journal of Money Credit and Banking*, vol. 9 (February 1977), pp. 255–57. Others have a more dubious view about the money targets; see, for example, William Poole, "Interpreting the Fed's Monetary Targets," *Brookings Papers on Economic Activity*, 1:1976, pp. 247–59; James Pierce, "The Myth of Congressional Supervision of Monetary Policy," *Journal of Monetary Economics*, vol. 4 (April 1978), pp. 363–70; and Steven M. Roberts, "Congressional Oversight of Monetary Policy," *Journal of Monetary Economics*, vol. 4 (August 1978), pp. 543–56. In my view, the most significant aspect of the quarterly hearings is not the announcement of money targets but rather the increase in more general information about the objectives and conduct of monetary policy that has resulted.

CHAPTER NINETEEN

Instrument Choice
and Instrument Variation

THE CONCLUSIONS about strategy choice in the preceding chapters are controversial because of their incompatibility with the increasingly influential view that
a money strategy is the preferred means of conducting monetary policy. It is
especially important, then, that those conclusions not be misinterpreted. In particular, my advocacy of discretionary instrument adaptation does not constitute an
endorsement of the monetary policies followed in the decades before the 1970s
when central banks paid little attention to the money stock. Nor is my rejection of
money strategies tantamount to an embrace of interest-rate strategies.

Because the chances of misinterpretation might otherwise be substantial, this
chapter begins by amplifying these points about what the preceding analysis does
not imply. That discussion then leads naturally to analysis of the problems of
instrument choice and instrument variation in single-stage strategies.

The chapter summarizes the conclusions about instrument choice that have
come to be widely accepted by monetary economists. But it then stresses a more
important and less familiar conclusion: the central bank's decisions about instrument
choice are of only secondary importance relative to its continuing decisions about
instrument variation. The final sections of the chapter highlight the differences
between "fine tuning" and discretionary instrument adaptation and emphasize the
analytical weakness of the argument that uncertainty justifies a nonactivist policy.

Stabilizing Interest Rates

The analysis in chapters 15 through 18 avoids the alleged issue of "money versus
interest rates" and most other trappings of the debate between monetarists and
Keynesians. It will nonetheless displease those who accept the policy recommendations of monetarism. Less obviously perhaps, but no less surely, the analysis
should also displease any nonmonetarist who construes monetary policy as a
straightforward matter of fixing the appropriate level of interest rates.

Monetarist economists have insistently, and correctly, pointed out that the
stabilization of interest rates for an extended period while ignoring the behavior of
monetary aggregates is a pernicious strategy for conducting monetary policy. When
real economic activity is expanding strongly, central bank open-market purchases
of securities to prevent nominal interest rates from rising stimulates the economy
procyclically compared with a policy that refrains from open-market purchases and
permits interest rates to rise pari passu with the strength in activity. Conversely,

central-bank sales of securities to prevent interest rates from falling when output and employment are weak have a *procyclical* contractionary effect compared with a policy that permits or encourages nominal interest rates to fall. Stabilizing interest rates can therefore exacerbate inflation in an expansion and intensify losses of output and employment in a recession. Such consequences are the antithesis of the *contracyclical* influences that, in theory, central banks should be trying to exert.[1]

The potential dangers of central-bank stabilization of interest rates over an extended period, or of merely leaning too heavily against changes the market would otherwise bring about, have been appreciated by perceptive monetary economists since at least the middle of the nineteenth century.[2] Wicksell emphasized the procyclical expansion of money and credit attributable to stickiness in market rates of interest.[3] "Real bills" and "needs of trade" conceptualizations of bank credit (which have been closely associated with arguments for stabilizing interest rates) may have become widely discredited only after the Great Depression and World War II; but many economists long before that time had pointed out the risks of the central bank operating on the basis of those views.[4] Even so, it is also true that enthusiasm in the 1930s and 1940s for the ideas of Keynes produced many naive Keynesians who paid little attention to monetary policy and, when they did so, thought only of choosing and then maintaining an appropriate level for interest rates. In recent decades it has been primarily monetarist economists who have called attention to the dangers of interest-rate stabilization.[5]

Viewed with hindsight, monetary history contains many instances in which central banks undesirably stabilized the level of interest rates for a protracted period or adjusted it much too sluggishly. The most infamous episodes in the United States were the early years of the Depression (when the Federal Reserve permitted a large absolute contraction of the money supply)[6] and the period between the end of World War II and March 1951 (when the Federal Reserve, under pressure from the Treasury Department, stabilized the prices of government securities).[7] But instances can also be cited in the United States during the 1950s and 1960s.[8] Experience in other countries offers many additional examples.

1. Central banks "peg" or "stabilize" interest rates if they use some short-term interest rate as the primary actual instrument of policy (buying or selling whatever volume of securities may be required to maintain the interest-rate instrument at the desired "exogenous" level) *and* if they keep that interest rate relatively unchanged for an extended period. The interest rate being stabilized by the central bank then strongly influences other market-determined interest rates. When a central bank stabilizes interest rates, it necessarily loses control over the quantities on its own balance sheet, including the outstanding amounts of its reserve-money liabilities (see chapter 14).

2. See Jacob Viner's discussion of the English bullionist and currency controversies in *Studies in the Theory of International Trade* (London: Harpers, 1937; Allen and Unwin, 1960); and Walter Bagehot, *Lombard Street* (London: Kegan, Paul, 1873; reprinted by John Murray, 1924), chap. 7.

3. Knut Wicksell, "The Exchange Value of Money," *Lectures on Political Economy* (London: Routledge and Sons, 1935), pt. 4.

4. See Lloyd W. Mints, *A History of Banking Theory in Great Britain and the United States* (University of Chicago Press, 1945).

5. See, for example, Milton Friedman, "The Role of Monetary Policy," *American Economic Review*, vol. 58 (March 1968), reprinted in Friedman, *The Optimum Quantity of Money and Other Essays* (Aldine, 1969), esp. pp. 99–101. Paul Wonnacott, *Macroeconomics*, rev. ed. (Richard D. Irwin, 1978), chaps. 11 and 12, summarizes the issues from a middle ground, between the monetarist and Keynesian extremes.

6. Milton Friedman and Anna Jacobson Schwartz, *A Monetary History of the United States, 1867–1960* (Princeton University Press for the National Bureau of Economic Research, 1963), pp. 299–419.

7. Ibid., pp. 620–36.

8. See William Poole, "Rules-of-thumb for Guiding Monetary Policy," in *Open Market Policies and Operating Procedures—Staff Studies* (Board of Governors of the Federal Reserve System, 1971).

Popular opinion usually fails to perceive the potentially pernicious consequences of stabilizing interest rates. Many parts of the electorate seem simply to want interest rates kept "low." Central banks are thus exposed to strong political pressures which can reinforce any proclivities they may already have to try to stabilize interest rates.

Monetarist critics of central banks and monetarist educators of public opinion therefore perform a valuable service by stressing the pitfalls in a policy of stabilizing interest rates. Nonmonetarist economists who favor the use of an interest rate as an operating instrument of policy but who appreciate the dangers of rigidity in the setting for that instrument would be well-advised in public utterances to emphasize the pitfalls as well.

Let there be, then, no misunderstanding: the arguments in this book against a policy preoccupation with the money stock are not arguments for a policy preoccupation with interest rates, and most especially not for the stabilization of interest rates. I am strongly opposed to any strategy involving either the use of an interest rate as an intermediate-target variable or the sluggish adaptation of an interest-rate instrument over an extended succession of short-run periods. Nowhere in the book do I even take the position that an interest rate is preferable to some quantity aggregate as the primary operating instrument used for the implementation of policy from one short-run period to the next.

Stabilizing a Financial Aggregate versus Stabilizing an Interest Rate

Monetarists tend to jump without further ado from the commandment "thou shalt not stabilize interest rates" to the recommendation that monetary policy focus on the money stock as an intermediate target. Many monetarists make a still bigger leap, recommending that the money stock be pegged as closely as possible along a seldom-altered target path characterized by a constant percentage rate of growth. Such leaps in reasoning, however, are tantamount to a decision by the judge in a beauty contest to award the prize to the second contestant after seeing only the first.

As earlier chapters have shown, the practical choices facing a central bank are considerably wider than stabilizing an interest rate or adhering to an infrequently changed intermediate-target path for the money stock. And if the central bank is inclined to peg a "quantity" instead of a "price," it need not look so far away as some definition of the money stock. It would be more straightforward simply to peg some quantity variable on its own balance sheet that can be an instrument (one or another of the reserve-money aggregates) rather than to try to peg an intermediate variable that cannot be controlled precisely.

Given the compelling arguments against intermediate-target strategies, many monetarists may eventually agree that a money strategy is an inferior way to conduct discretionary monetary policy. However, monetarists will continue—justifiably—to object to a policy of stabilizing interest rates. "Reformed" monetarists who reject a money strategy may then fall back on a policy of pegging a quantity such as the monetary base or unborrowed reserves. Such a position would be immune from the criticisms that apply to intermediate-target strategies.

Is it preferable, then, for the central bank to stabilize a quantity rather than a price, merely being careful to pick a quantity it can control precisely? Again, caution is desirable; the judge should not award the prize to the third contestant merely because both the first and the second have deficiencies. Can there be circumstances, it must be asked, when it would *not* be a superior policy to peg a financial aggregate rather than an interest rate?

In fact, there are potential dangers associated with stabilizing a financial aggregate. Suppose, for example, that private-sector economic units unexpectedly alter their asset preferences so that they wish to hold larger amounts of currency and bank deposits and smaller amounts of bonds and equities. Central-bank stabilization of a financial aggregate in such circumstances imparts an undesirable contractionary impetus to economic activity compared with a policy of central-bank open-market purchases of securities ("unpegging" of the financial aggregate) carried out to prevent nominal interest rates from rising. Conversely, an autonomous shift of private asset preferences away from bank deposits toward bonds results in an inflationary stimulus under stabilization of a financial aggregate that would be avoided if the central bank were to stabilize an interest rate instead.

Because there are dangers in stabilizing either a financial aggregate or an interest rate, it may seem natural to pose the two choices as alternative evils and to recommend that the central bank choose the less dangerous of the two. Indeed, many discussions of central bank decisionmaking have characterized the options for policy in that simple way. Even after it is acknowledged that the money stock is an intermediate variable and even if attention is restricted to financial aggregates that are potential instruments, however, that antipodal characterization is misleading. The apparent necessity to choose between stabilizing some price (interest rate) *or* some quantity (reserve-money aggregate) is a false dilemma.

Instrument Choice in a Comparative-Statics Context

The relative merits of the two alternative pegging strategies have been analyzed in an influential theoretical article by William Poole.[9] The conclusions in the preceding sections about the potential dangers of stabilizing interest rates and financial aggregates emerge clearly from the type of analysis used by Poole. It is therefore instructive to begin the discussion of instrument choice with a review of that analysis and its supposed implications for the conduct of monetary policy.

Poole's analysis is often interpreted as a discussion of whether to use an interest rate or the *money stock* as a policy instrument. But that interpretation is incorrect. Poole's theoretical model includes three variables represented by the symbols Y, r, and M; the variable M, moreover, is called "money" in the textual discussion. But the M in his model, as Poole himself points out, is assumed to be precisely

9. William Poole, "Optimal Choice of Monetary Policy Instruments in a Simple Stochastic Macro Model," *Quarterly Journal of Economics*, vol. 84 (May 1970), pp. 197–216. See also John H. Kareken, "The Optimum Monetary Instrument Variable," *Journal of Money, Credit, and Banking*, vol. 2 (August 1970), pp. 385–90; Stephen F. LeRoy and David E. Lindsey, "Determining the Monetary Instrument: A Diagrammatic Exposition," *American Economic Review*, vol. 68 (December 1978), pp. 929–34; Stephen F. LeRoy, "Efficient Use of Current Information in Short-run Monetary Control," Special Studies Paper 66 (Board of Governors of the Federal Reserve System, September 1975).

controllable by the central bank; the policymakers can, if they wish, choose M instead of r as their exogenous control variable—their instrument.[10] If Poole's analysis is interpreted carefully, therefore, it really addresses the issue of whether to choose an interest rate or a financial aggregate as the instrument *for a single-stage decision process*. Despite superficial appearances to the contrary, it sheds no light on the pros and cons of conducting monetary policy with a two-stage money strategy.[11]

It is important to be clear about another aspect of the theoretical context assumed in Poole's paper: the method of analysis is comparative statics. The model, in effect, deals with a single time period of uncertain length. Decisionmaking in this simplified context involves only the selection of an actual instrument from the menu of potential instruments and the choice of an instrument setting at the beginning of the period that will be maintained unchanged thereafter.

Consider the following illustrative model which, like Poole's, suppresses time subscripts on the variables and requires a comparative-statics analysis:

(19-1)
$$Y = \beta_0 + \beta_1 r + \beta_3 Z + \beta_4 X^F + e_Y$$
$$M^d = \gamma_0 + \gamma_1 Y + \gamma_2 r + e_{MD}$$
$$M^s = \delta_0 + \delta_1 H + \delta_2 r + e_{MS}$$
$$M^s = M = M^d.$$

The variables include nominal income (Y), the money stock (M), an exogenous fiscal-policy instrument (X^F), and a nonpolicy exogenous variable (Z); e_Y, e_{MD}, and e_{MS} represent stochastic error terms. Assume that each of the other variables, the interest rate (r) and a reserve-money aggregate (H), is a potential monetary-policy instrument. The central bank must choose which of these two to use as its actual instrument.[12] Suppose the values of the parameters in the model are treated as fixed and known, with β_3, β_4, γ_1, δ_1, and δ_2 having positive values while β_1 and γ_2 have negative values. Again assume that policymakers regard Y as their ultimate-target variable and make decisions on the basis of the loss function:

(19-2)
$$L = (Y - Y^*)^2,$$

so that the expected loss is given by

(19-2a)
$$E(L) = E(Y - Y^*)^2 = (\bar{Y} - Y^*)^2 + \sigma_Y^2,$$

where Y^* represents a target level of income and $\bar{Y}$ and σ_Y^2 are the expected value

10. See Poole, "Optimal Choice of Monetary Policy Instruments in a Simple Stochastic Macro Model," p. 198; and William Poole and Charles Lieberman, "Improving Monetary Control," *Brookings Papers on Economic Activity*, 2:1972, pp. 293–335.

11. While Poole has a perceptive understanding of the problems of imperfect controllability of the money stock (see "Improving Monetary Control"), his writings show an insufficient sensitivity to the weaknesses of two-stage money strategies compared with single-stage strategies employing a reserve-money aggregate as the primary instrument of monetary policy.

12. In the models 17-1 and 17-4 of chapter 17, which are similar to 19-1, r is assumed to be endogenous and the reserve-money aggregate to be exogenous; the symbol X^M rather than H is used for the reserve-money aggregate. All of these illustrative models are extremely simplified; they contain only a single interest rate and only one other asset in addition to the reserve-money aggregate. In practice, if the policymakers select an interest rate as their instrument it will be a short-term rate such as the interbank lending rate for short-term funds; other interest rates will be market determined. Those other rates would be the relevant ones to include in behavioral equations for real-sector variables in a model including several assets and several interest rates as endogenous variables.

and variance of income. Assume that the setting for the fiscal-policy instrument is already given as $\hat{X}^F$. Suppose finally that policymakers generate forecasts—$\overline{Z} = E(Z)$, $\overline{e}_Y = E(e_Y)$, $\overline{e}_{MD} = E(e_{MD})$, and $\overline{e}_{MS} = E(e_{MS})$—of the noncontrolled exogenous forces that affect their ultimate-target variable.[13]

If the policymakers choose the reserve-money aggregate as their instrument, a "quantity instrument" version of the model is the result; it determines income, the interest rate, and the money stock as the three endogenous variables. When this version of the model is solved, the reduced-form equation for Y may be written:

$$(19\text{-}3) \qquad Y = a_0 + a_1 H + a_2 Z + a_3 X^F + a_4 e_Y + a_5 e_{MD} + a_6 e_{MS},$$

where the coefficients a_1, a_2, a_3, a_4, and a_6 have positive signs and a_5 has a negative sign.[14] If the policymakers calculate their "optimal" setting for the reserve-money aggregate under these circumstances, the resulting policy $\hat{H}$ depends on the target value for income, the given setting for fiscal policy, the forecasts for each of the noncontrolled exogenous forces, and the values of the reduced-form coefficients from 19-3:[15]

$$(19\text{-}4) \qquad \hat{H} = \frac{(Y^* - a_2\overline{Z} - a_3\hat{X}^F - a_4\overline{e}_Y - a_5\overline{e}_{MD} - a_6\overline{e}_{MS} - a_0)}{a_1}.$$

Alternatively, if the policymakers select the interest rate as their instrument, the resulting "price instrument" version of the model determines income, the money stock, and the reserve-money aggregate as the three endogenous variables. Because the basic model is so simplified, this version has a reduced-form equation for Y identical to the "structural" equation:

$$(19\text{-}5) \qquad Y = \beta_0 + \beta_1 r + \beta_3 Z + \beta_4 X^F + e_Y.$$

The "optimal" setting for the interest rate, $\hat{r}$, that minimizes the expected value of the loss function depends on the target value for income, the given setting for fiscal policy, the forecasts $\overline{Z}$ and $\overline{e}_Y$, and the four coefficients $\beta_1, \beta_3, \beta_4$, and β_0:

$$(19\text{-}6) \qquad \hat{r} = \frac{(Y^* - \beta_3\overline{Z} - \beta_4\hat{X}^F - \overline{e}_Y - \beta_0)}{\beta_1}.$$

Imagine that policymakers fix their instrument setting at the value thought to be optimal, either pegging the reserve aggregate at $\hat{H}$ or the interest rate at $\hat{r}$. This

13. The forecasts for the stochastic errors could be $\overline{e}_Y = \overline{e}_{MD} = \overline{e}_{MS} = 0$; as emphasized in chapter 17, however, the policymakers may often have additional information suggesting nonzero values for these expectations.

14. Expressed in terms of the structural coefficients, the reduced-form coefficients are:

$$a_1 = \frac{\beta_1 \delta_1}{\Delta} > 0; \quad a_2 = \frac{\beta_3(\gamma_2 - \delta_2)}{\Delta} > 0;$$

$$a_3 = \frac{\beta_4(\gamma_2 - \delta_2)}{\Delta} > 0; \quad a_4 = \frac{\gamma_2 - \delta_2}{\Delta} > 0;$$

$$(19\text{-}3a)$$

$$a_5 = \frac{-\beta_1}{\Delta} < 0; \quad a_6 = \frac{\beta_1}{\Delta} > 0;$$

$$a_0 = \frac{\beta_0(\gamma_2 - \delta_2) - \beta_1\gamma_0 + \beta_1\delta_0}{\Delta}; \quad \Delta = \beta_1\gamma_1 + \gamma_2 - \delta_2 < 0.$$

15. Because "certainty-equivalence" obtains under the given assumptions, the setting that minimizes the expected value of the loss function can be found simply by taking the expected value of 19-3, setting $E(Y) = Y^*$, and solving for the resulting value of H.

policy action occurs at the beginning of the period being analyzed (after making of the forecasts $\bar{Z}$, $\bar{e}_Y$, $\bar{e}_{MD}$, and $\bar{e}_{MS}$, and after receipt of the information about the fiscal setting $\hat{X}^F$). Now let time pass, but suppose the instrument setting for monetary policy remains unchanged. What can be said about the consequences of the alternative instrument choices?

Consider the effects of an unforeseen disturbance occurring in the real sector of the economy. Within this theoretical context, such an event can be represented as a surprise in the error term in the model's income equation. Instead of the expected error $\bar{e}_Y$, for example, suppose the actual value of the error turns out to be $e_Y = \bar{e}_Y + \epsilon_Y$.

If the policymakers have chosen to keep the interest rate unchanged at $\hat{r}$, the unforeseen disturbance ϵ_Y affects income adversely by an equivalent amount (see equation 19-5). The interest-rate peg, although intended to be consistent with the target value of income Y^*, in fact is associated with an income level of $Y^* + \epsilon_Y$. An expansionary disturbance ($\epsilon_Y > 0$) causes an unwanted spurt of income above its desired level, and vice versa for a contractionary disturbance.

If the policymakers have chosen to keep the reserve-money aggregate unchanged at $\hat{H}$, the consequences of the real-sector disturbance are less adverse. The impact of the surprise on income (see equation 19-3) is $a_4 \epsilon_Y$. Since the reduced-form coefficient a_4, while positive, is unambiguously less than unity, an income value of $Y^* + a_4 \epsilon_Y$ is less distant from the target than the value $Y^* + \epsilon_Y$.[16]

If the real-sector disturbance takes the form of an unanticipated change in the nonpolicy exogenous variable Z, an analogous conclusion holds. Income drifts further away from its target value in response to a surprise in Z if the authorities peg the interest rate than if they peg the reserve aggregate.[17]

Consider also the consequences of a surprise in fiscal policy. For example, suppose there is an unanticipated shortfall of discretionary government expenditures from the planned level, causing the setting for fiscal policy to fall below the expected policy $\hat{X}^F$. Here, too, the adverse consequences for the ultimate-target variable are greater—in this case aggregate demand contracts by a larger amount—if the policymakers in the central bank are pegging the interest rate rather than the reserve aggregate.[18]

Now, however, consider the consequences of unexpected disturbances occurring in the financial sector of the economy. Within the context of the illustrative model, these disturbances can be represented as surprises—ϵ_{MD} and ϵ_{MS}—in the error terms of the money-demand and money-supply equations.[19]

The reduced-form equation for the ultimate-target variable when the interest rate is the instrument (equation 19-5) indicates that surprises in money demand have no adverse effects on income. Nor do unexpected changes in money supply

16. The value of the coefficient a_4 (see 19-3a) is given by the ratio $(\gamma_2 - \delta_2)/(\beta_1 \gamma_1 + \gamma_2 - \delta_2)$. Since $\gamma_2 < 0$, $\delta_2 > 0$, $\beta_1 < 0$, and $\gamma_1 > 0$, it follows that $0 < a_4 < 1$.

17. Suppose the surprise in Z is $\tilde{Z}$ (so that $Z = \bar{Z} + \tilde{Z}$). Comparison of the two reduced-form equations shows that the impact of $\tilde{Z}$ on income is $\beta_3 \tilde{Z}$ when the interest rate is pegged and $a_2 \tilde{Z}$ when the aggregate is pegged. The coefficient a_2 (see 19-3a) is equal to $\beta_3(\gamma_2 - \delta_2)/(\beta_1 \gamma_1 + \gamma_2 - \delta_2) = \beta_3 a_4$. Since $0 < a_4 < 1$, it follows that $0 < a_2 < \beta_3$.

18. By reasoning analogous to that in the preceding footnotes, it follows that $0 < a_3 < \beta_4$, where a_3 is the coefficient governing the impact of the fiscal surprise under the aggregate regime and β_4 is the corresponding coefficient under the interest-rate regime.

19. By definition, $e_{MD} = \bar{e}_{MD} + \epsilon_{MD}$, and $e_{MS} = \bar{e}_{MS} + \epsilon_{MS}$.

have adverse effects. Maintenance of the interest rate unchanged facilitates accommodation within the financial sector of the shifts in asset-demanding and liability-supplying behavior underlying the surprises.

If the policymakers keep the reserve aggregate unchanged, however, the financial-sector disturbances do have adverse consequences for the ultimate objective of policy. An unanticipated increase of ϵ_{MD} in the demand for money generates a larger rise or smaller fall in the interest rate than would otherwise occur and thus transmits a contractionary impetus to income (and vice versa for $\epsilon_{MD} < 0$).[20] An unexpected increase of ϵ_{MS} in money supply causes a smaller rise or larger fall in the interest rate than would otherwise occur and thereby pushes income above its target level.[21]

To summarize: when policymakers peg an interest rate, the impacts of unforeseen real-sector disturbances on economic activity are exacerbated compared with the outcome that would result from pegging a financial aggregate. In contrast, when unforeseen disturbances originate within the financial sector, a policy of pegging an interest rate instead of a financial aggregate mitigates the adverse consequences of the disturbances on economic activity.[22]

Most analysts and policymakers who have worked their way through the preceding argument tend next to ask themselves the question, Which types of disturbances occur more frequently and are more quantitatively significant? The idea implicit in the question is to assess the relative frequencies and magnitudes of the two broad types of disturbances *on the average.*

A majority of analysts and policymakers would probably judge that—on the average—unforeseeable real-sector disturbances are more prevalent or larger in magnitude than unforeseeable financial-sector developments. When the problem of instrument choice is raised within the limitations of the preceding frame of reference, therefore, many analysts and policymakers conclude that monetary policy should peg a financial aggregate rather than an interest rate because the balance of risks associated with the aggregate policy is smaller. Sometimes the argument is reinforced with a related nuance. A "wrong" setting for a financial aggregate, it is claimed, does not carry as great a risk of an unwanted cumulative expansion or contraction of (nominal) aggregate demand. It can be argued, for example, that a wrongly fixed setting for an interest rate could facilitate an unlimited inflationary explosion, whereas the adverse consequences of a wrongly fixed setting for a financial aggregate could not cumulate in this manner.[23]

---

20. The effect of the surprise on income is $a_5\epsilon_{MD}$, where $a_5 = -\beta_1/(\beta_1\gamma_1 + \gamma_2 - \delta_2) < 0$.

21. The size of the impact on income is $a_6\epsilon_{MS}$, where $a_6 = \beta_1/(\beta_1\gamma_1 + \gamma_2 - \delta_2) > 0$.

22. As demonstrated here, these generalizations about the consequences of alternative instrument pegs are derived from an illustrative model that is greatly simplified. When Poole gave prominence to them in 1970 ("Optimal Choice of Monetary Policy Instruments in a Simple Stochastic Model"), he used a still more simplified model. But the basic conclusion emerges from analysis of much more complex, systemic models: a given setting for an instrument, compared with other policy alternatives, facilitates adjustment to some types of disturbances but aggravates the adverse consequences of other types.

23. See, for example, Henry C. Wallich, "From Multiplier to Quantity Theory," in Bela Belassa and Richard Nelson, eds., *Economic Progress, Private Values, and Public Policy: Essays in Honor of William Fellner* (Amsterdam: North-Holland, 1977), esp. pp. 285–87. Despite its inclusion of a number of analytical insights, Wallich's paper discusses the "money supply" as though that intermediate variable can be an instrument. As with so many other discussions of the role of money in monetary policy, therefore, it fails to acknowledge the serious weaknesses of a two-stage money strategy compared with single-stage strategies that use a reserve-money aggregate as an instrument.

Suppose the alternative pegging strategies are defined as (a) keeping a nominal interest rate unchanged at a constant level and (b) keeping the nominal amount of a reserve-money aggregate growing along a constant-growth-rate path with the growth rate chosen so that it is equal to the economy's trend growth in productivity.[24] If forced to choose between only these two alternatives, the central bank undoubtedly should select the policy of stabilizing the reserve-money aggregate. That policy would not so frequently have such highly adverse consequences as the policy of stabilizing a nominal interest rate.[25]

Instrument Choice and Instrument Variation in a Dynamic Context

Comparative-statics contests between rate-pegging and quantity-pegging strategies of the sort described in the preceding section generate some important insights and therefore have a pedagogical value. If properly interpreted, however, *they have no operational implications for policymakers*. Policy decisions are not taken within a one-period, comparative-statics frame of reference. Central banks therefore have no practical need to choose between pegging a financial aggregate, pegging an interest rate, or pegging any other variable for an extended period of time. All such strategies are mechanical rules of thumb that abstract from the possibility of period-by-period discretionary decisions.

Under any strategy for conducting policy, it is true, those variables selected for use as instruments are "pegged" in the very short run (momentarily). By definition, an instrument is a variable for which, day by day or even hour by hour, there is no slippage between the actual (pegged) setting and the intended setting; its value is controlled exogenously at each point in time. But use of a variable as a policy instrument in no way presupposes rigidity of the setting with the passage of time—

24. Stabilization of either a reserve-money aggregate or an interest rate has a straightforward connotation in a theoretical context where neither real activity nor the price level exhibit secular growth: "pegging" can be equated with maintenance of the instrument setting at a fixed value. In an economy where output or the price level or both are growing over time, however, nontrivial problems occur in trying to specify an operational definition of "pegging." There are obvious difficulties with defining a financial-aggregate peg as an unchanged nominal magnitude (for example, $x billion of unborrowed reserves). Yet what criteria should be used to choose a particular expansion path? As soon as one makes the distinction between nominal and real interest rates in a growing economy subject to inflation, the appropriate definition of an interest-rate peg is not self-evident either. Nothing in the preceding illustrative model, it should be noted, sheds light on these important questions.

25. This criterion for choosing between the two pegging strategies can be developed more formally in terms of the illustrative model and loss function by comparing the expected losses associated with the setting $\hat{H}$ in 19-4 and with $\hat{r}$ in 19-6. That comparison shows that the policymakers' choice should depend on the relative magnitudes of the variances of the underlying exogenous disturbances; an interest-rate peg results in smaller loss if financial-sector disturbances are relatively more important but is the wrong choice if the dominant source of disturbances is the real sector. The algebra shows that the choice between the pegs should also depend on any nonzero covariances of the disturbances. Finally, and no less important, the detailed analysis shows that the choice between pegs can be critically influenced by the values of the structural coefficients of the model. For Poole's analysis, see "Optimal Choice of Monetary Policy Instruments in a Simple Stochastic Macro Model," pp. 203–09; see also Poole and Lieberman, "Improving Monetary Control," pp. 296–99; Benjamin M. Friedman, "Targets, Instruments, and Indicators of Monetary Policy," *Journal of Monetary Economics*, vol. 1 (October 1975), pp. 445–49; LeRoy and Lindsey, "Determining the Monetary Instrument"; Roger Craine and Arthur Havenner, "Optimal Monetary Policy with Uncertainty," Special Studies Paper 101 (Board of Governors of the Federal Reserve System, July 1977); and Craine and Havenner, "The Optimal Monetary Instrument: An Empirical Assessment," Special Studies Paper 100 (Board of Governors of the Federal Reserve System, July 1977).

that is, pegging *for an extended period*. If an interest rate is employed as the main operating instrument, it can be discretionarily varied from one day to the next or one week to the next. Similarly, if a reserve-money aggregate is the instrument, the peg can be revised from one short-run period to the next.[26]

When the artificial frame of reference of one-period comparative statics is abandoned, therefore, monetary-policy decisions involve the problems of *instrument variation* as well as *instrument choice*. Whatever operating regime may be chosen by the central bank, decisions can be made more or less continuously. Whatever the operating regime, moreover, the passage of time affords an opportunity for instrument variation to offset some of the disadvantages that would otherwise be associated with the operating regime if the instruments were to be kept pegged over a succession of short-run periods. The opportunity need not be seized. A decision to maintain an instrument setting unchanged, however, is not merely a matter of instrument choice. It also constitutes a decision to forswear instrument variation.[27]

The distinction between instrument choice and instrument variation can be highlighted by contrasting four different instrument operating regimes: a short-term interest rate used as an exogenous instrument and kept rigidly on a predetermined path over a succession of periods (interest-rate peg), a reserve-money aggregate used as the instrument with its quantity maintained on a predetermined path (reserve-aggregate peg), an interest rate used as the exogenous instrument but with its setting discretionarily adjusted from period to period (discretionary interest-rate regime), and finally an operating regime in which a reserve-money aggregate is selected as the instrument but used in a discretionary manner from period to period (discretionary reserve-aggregate regime).

Because the time paths for their instrument settings are predetermined, the interest-rate peg and the reserve-aggregate peg may be said to use instrument rules. The selection of one of those two regimes, if they were the only alternatives, would involve choosing between a predetermined path for a price or a quantity. A choice between the other two regimes, however, cannot accurately be characterized as a choice between price-pegging or quantity-pegging except over the very short run. Under both discretionary regimes, some variability in both the interest rate and the reserve-money aggregate could occur over a longer period, and presumably would.

The antipodal choice between the interest-rate peg and the reserve-aggregate peg can be avoided by selecting a discretionary operating regime. The greater the period-by-period discretionary variation in instrument settings, moreover, the less consequential may be the choice between a discretionary interest-rate regime and a discretionary reserve-aggregate regime. Instrument choice as opposed to instrument variation is not a trivial problem even under discretionary instrument adaptation. But instrument choice cannot be an overriding concern in its own right unless policymakers wish to follow instrument rules.[28]

26. Whether the time path for the setting for a "quantity" instrument such as a reserve-money aggregate is expressed as a sequence of levels for each short-run period or as a sequence of rates of change from each period to the next is purely a matter of semantic taste.

27. See James Tobin, "Discussion," in Federal Reserve Bank of Boston, *Controlling Monetary Aggregates* (Federal Reserve Bank of Boston, 1969), pp. 78–82.

28. The points stressed in this section are discussed in LeRoy, "Efficient Use of Current Information in Short-run Monetary Control." If the central bank were to adopt LeRoy's technically sophisticated suggestion for a mixed instrument regime (discussed in chapter 14), the problem of instrument choice

Pegging Rules versus Discretionary Adaptation

The preceding discussion once again raises the issues at stake in the controversy over rules versus discretion.[29] What posture should policymakers adopt vis-à-vis their opportunities for discretionary instrument variation? Are there convincing reasons why they should forswear discretion and adopt one or another form of instrument rule—for example, some variant of a reserve-aggregate peg?

Recall first that the rules versus discretion controversy has expectational and political-sociological dimensions that may well be as important as the uncertainty and efficiency aspects traditionally stressed in economics. Thoughtful analysis of those other dimensions is a precondition for a balanced view of the controversy as a whole, yet much of the requisite analysis and evidence is not yet at hand. Conceivably, the arguments for insulating monetary policy from politics and from human error could be honed into a persuasive justification for adopting an instrument rule—persuasive, at least, to people with certain types of ultimate preferences. After considerably more research into the game-theoretic interactions between the government and the private sector, moreover, it is conceivable that a majority of macroeconomists will come to espouse self-imposed limits on discretionary monetary-policy action—for example, through an announcement of some type of instrument rule. For the moment, however, an impartial analyst can only suspend judgment about the expectational and noneconomic dimensions of the choice between instrument rules and discretionary adaptation.

A conclusion with respect to the uncertainty and efficiency dimensions of the choice, however, does not need to be deferred until further research is completed.

One systematic method of analyzing these uncertainty and efficiency issues would be to use multiperiod analogs of the illustrative model and loss function 19-1 and 19-2. For example, one could employ the loss function 17-2 and the model 17-4 of chapter 17. All four of the instrument regimes in the preceding section could be compared over a horizon of several periods—for example, the "months" of January, February, and March as in chapter 17. In the case of the reserve-aggregate peg and the interest-rate peg, predetermined paths for the instrument setting for the whole three-month period would be specified at the outset (on January 1). Instrument settings under the discretionary reserve-aggregate and discretionary interest-rate regimes would be revised each month in response to newly received data about the evolution of the economy. Evaluation of the strategies could take the form of comparing their expected losses as of the various decisionmaking dates

---

would become still less important than suggested in the text. Poole's "Optimal Instrument Choice in a Simple Stochastic Macro Model" can be interpreted as making use of the distinction between instrument choice and instrument variation in the section where a "combination policy" is shown to be superior to either a pure interest-rate peg or a pure financial-aggregate peg (see pp. 208–09). Poole fails to emphasize, however, that his combination policy cannot be executed unless new data become available *during the course of the comparative-statics period being analyzed;* when the interest rate is the instrument under a combination policy, it must be possible to observe the financial aggregate during the period (and vice versa when the financial aggregate is the instrument). The critical point stressed by LeRoy and omitted by Poole is that when new observations become available for *any* endogenous variable, instrument variation can respond to the new information regardless of which way the instrument choice has been made.

29. The rules to be considered here, however, are only instrument rules, since a rule for an intermediate-target variable such as the money stock has already been rejected on the grounds of the analysis in chapters 16 through 18.

(for example, on February 1), or comparing their actual losses under specified assumptions about discrepancies between the policymakers' expectations of non-policy exogenous forces and actual outcomes for those forces.

Various alternative assumptions could be made about the nature of nonpolicy exogenous disturbances. One set of comparisons could postulate unexpected disturbances occurring exclusively in the real sector of the model; a second set could postulate only financial-sector disturbances; a third could consider both types of disturbances in combination. As in chapter 17, the analysis could also vary the assumptions about the flow of new information available to policymakers.[30]

Several questions could be illustratively answered by such an analysis. First, it would be possible to compare the consequences of a reserve-aggregate peg and an interest-rate peg over a horizon of several periods and thereby ascertain how the results of the comparative-statics evaluation of pegging strategies should be modified in a dynamic context. Second, it would be possible to compare the outcomes under the two discretionary operating regimes and thus shed light on the relative importance of the problem of instrument choice under conditions of discretionary instrument variation. Finally, and most interesting, such an analysis could compare the two pegging regimes with the two discretionary regimes and thereby shed some light on the relative merits of instrument rules versus discretionary adaptation.

I have carried out some, although not all, of these suggested comparisons. That work leads me to be confident of the overall conclusions that result. The discussion that follows omits the comparative analysis entirely but presents five generalizations based on the conclusions.

First, the outcomes of all the various comparisons are sensitive to the postulated pattern of unforeseen exogenous disturbances. Other things being equal, as in the comparative-statics comparisons, a reserve-aggregate peg results in smaller (greater) losses than an interest-rate peg when the unforeseen disturbances occur primarily in the economy's real (financial) sector. Analogously, a discretionary reserve-aggregate regime proves superior (inferior) to a discretionary interest-rate regime when the unforeseen disturbances are mainly in the real (financial) sector.

Second, when unforeseen disturbances occur mainly in the real sector, the difference in loss between the two discretionary regimes is markedly smaller than the difference in loss between the pegging regimes. When the unforeseen disturbances are primarily in the financial sector, the discretionary interest-rate regime dominates the discretionary reserve-aggregate regime by a markedly smaller amount than the interest-rate peg dominates the reserve-aggregate peg.

These results provide illustrative corroboration for the earlier assertions that instrument choice under conditions of discretionary instrument variation tends to be a much less significant matter than under instrument pegging rules, but that instrument choice is not a negligible issue even under conditions of discretionary instrument variation.[31]

30. The illustrative analysis suggested in the text would take into account two out of three types of uncertainty afflicting policymaking: uncertainty about the forecast values for nonpolicy exogenous variables and uncertainty due to equation errors (nonzero values for the stochastic error terms in the model's behavioral equations). Uncertainty about the model's structural coefficients (and hence uncertainty about the final-form multipliers relevant for policy actions) would not be taken into account; coefficient uncertainty is discussed further in the following section.

31. The poorer the information about the economy available to policymakers, the more important is instrument choice per se.

Third, the discretionary reserve-aggregate regime always dominates the reserve-aggregate peg, and the discretionary interest-rate regime always has at least as small a loss as the interest-rate peg. The degree of the superiority of discretionary adaptation over the counterpart pegging rule is influenced by the pattern of unforeseen disturbances and the information-flow conditions. Regardless of the type of disturbances and the availability of data, however, the ranking of the adaptive and the pegging strategies is not altered. Rigidity of an instrument's settings on a predetermined time path consistently generates suboptimal outcomes compared with what is otherwise possible with discretionary adaptation of the settings in response to new information.

Fourth, a discretionary interest-rate regime can dominate a reserve-aggregate peg for many assumed patterns of unforeseen disturbances—including specifically cases where sizable disturbances occur in the real sector of the model. The ability of discretionary interest-rate variation to outperform the reserve-aggregate pegging rule in the presence of real-sector disturbances is greatest under the "idealized" conditions of information flow where collection and availability lags are absent and where all variables have the same frequencies of observation. Even with less-than-ideal information, however, this ranking can still persist.

Finally, a discretionary reserve-aggregate regime can dominate an interest-rate peg even when sizable unforeseen disturbances occur in the financial sector.[32] This superiority of the discretionary reserve-aggregate strategy can be observed even under less-than-ideal conditions of information flow.

The last three generalizations taken together suggest the conclusion that an adaptive approach to instrument decisions can virtually always dominate an instrument rule when the two are evaluated on an otherwise comparable basis (that is, for the same loss function, the same model, access to the same flow of new information, and exposure to the same unforeseen disturbances).

Because the preceding generalizations are based on the analysis of a highly simplified model and loss function, they cannot be accepted as definitive evidence. The use of different illustrative models and loss functions as well as alternative assumptions about unforeseen disturbances and information availability could conceivably generate outcomes that would contradict the fourth and fifth generalizations. The first three generalizations, however, are likely to hold for any model and any assumptions. I conjecture that even the fourth and the fifth will prove to be robust.

The few studies that have examined these issues in the context of empirical models have come to similar conclusions. For the economy of the United States, for example, Gregory Chow with a small annual model and Kenneth Garbade with a moderately large quarterly model have compared pegging rules and discretionary instrument variation; both conclude that discretion can reduce the loss associated with pegging rules by orders of magnitude of some 30–80 percent.[33] Roger Craine,

32. Given the simplified model 17-4, financial-sector disturbances have no effect on the ultimate-target variable when the interest rate is the instrument. A discretionary reserve-aggregate regime therefore cannot do better than an interest-rate peg under the (artificial) assumption that unforeseen disturbances occur exclusively in the financial sector.

33. Gregory C. Chow, "How Much Could Be Gained by Optimal Stochastic Control Policies?" Annals of Economic and Social Measurement, vol. 1 (October 1972), pp. 391–406; the results from this research are also summarized in Chow's book, Analysis and Control of Dynamic Economic Systems (Wiley and Sons, 1975), pp. 216–24. Kenneth D. Garbade, Discretionary Control of Aggregate Economic Activity (Lexington Books, 1975).

Arthur Havenner, and James Berry compare alternative strategies for the volatile period of the large increases in oil prices in 1973–75 and reach a more equivocal but still favorable verdict about the benefits of feedback strategies.[34] Craine and Havenner have studied the problem of instrument choice under conditions of instrument variation;[35] Garbade's book also addresses this issue. Both studies conclude that the choice between an interest rate or a financial aggregate as the main operating instrument of monetary policy is a second-order problem so long as the chosen instrument is discretionarily varied in response to the evolution of the economy.[36]

On the basis of the analysis and evidence so far available, then, the economic arguments lead to a clear conclusion: policymakers should avoid pegging rules of thumb for monetary policy. Pegging rules have the advantage of being simple to describe and understand. But they have little else to recommend them. The economically preferable approach to instrument decisions is to digest new information about the economy promptly and to keep the instrument settings under continuous review.

When the policymakers have information about specific disturbances that are currently affecting the economy or are likely to affect it in the future, they can and should respond differentially. Their model of the economy and their loss function will indicate the appropriate response. For many disturbances it will be appropriate for interest rates to do most of the adjusting while financial aggregates change less. In other cases the bulk of the adjustments should fall on financial aggregates. These responses will be appropriate regardless of whether the policymakers use a reserve-money aggregate or an interest rate as their instrument.

At times when the policymakers have little or no information about specific disturbances currently or prospectively affecting the economy, they cannot do much to tailor their responses to the types of disturbances and should not try to do so. Even in those circumstances, however, they are better off eschewing either extreme pegging rule. Instead, they should follow the discretionary policy they think best at the moment, reevaluating the situation period by period.[37]

34. Roger Craine, Arthur Havenner, and James Berry, "Fixed Rules versus Activism in the Conduct of Monetary Policy," *American Economic Review*, vol. 68 (December 1978), pp. 769–83.

35. Craine and Havenner, "The Optimal Monetary Instrument."

36. The models used in both the Garbade and Craine-Havenner analyses treat the money stock as though it can be perfectly controlled by the central bank. The choice between a financial aggregate or an interest rate as the main exogenous instrument of monetary policy is seen as a choice between using the money stock or the short-term Treasury bill rate. This simplification is a serious defect in the two models. One would like to know how the results of their studies would be modified if the money stock were treated endogenously and, say, the unborrowed monetary base were used as the financial-aggregate instrument. I conjecture that the conclusion emphasized in the text would not be altered even if the two models were amended in that manner.

37. The best policy under those circumstances is likely to be a course intermediate between the two pegging rules. Suppose the policymakers find themselves in a situation where unexpected and as-yet-unexplainable market pressures require *either* a rise in short-term interest rates (compared with earlier expectations) *or* a larger volume of reserve-supplying open-market purchases (compared with earlier expectations). Those market pressures could be consistent either with unforeseen expansionary disturbances in the real sector of the economy (for example, an autonomous spurt in investment demand) or with unforeseen shifts in asset preferences (for example, an autonomous increase in the demand for money). If no information yet exists to help identify the source of the disturbances (because, for example, new data are not yet available for the variables in the relevant parts of the policymaking model), the least inappropriate middle course for "today" may be a combination of allowing interest rates to rise somewhat and the reserve-money aggregate to expand somewhat (relative to earlier plans). The situation can and should be reevaluated "tomorrow" when further information may be available. Notice again that it may matter relatively little what variable is used as the actual instrument; whatever the instrument may be, it is discretionarily adjusted from one short-run period to the next.

Discretionary Adaptation
versus Fine Tuning

At the opposite extreme from pegging rules, policymakers could continuously and energetically adjust the settings on policy instruments in an effort to "fine tune" the economy. This observation leads naturally to a final set of questions: Is "fine tuning" undesirable? Is discretionary instrument adaptation merely a euphemism for fine tuning? If not, what are the differences between the two? Just how discretionary should an adaptive strategy be?

In answering these questions, it is essential to distinguish between two types of active discretionary behavior. Policymakers may digest new information about the economy as soon as it is received and decide promptly what, *if any,* policy action to take in response. Alternatively and quite differently, policymakers may invariably adjust their instrument settings in response to each new piece of information, basing their decisions solely on the expected impacts of their actions and ignoring uncertainty about those impacts.

The first type of behavior is unquestionably activist. It entails promptly looking at and adapting to all new data about the economy. However, it does not presuppose ignoring any of the uncertainties that afflict policymaking. Activist behavior in this first sense involves only the continuous processing of new data and the prompt *contemplation* of possible actions in response. Whether or not actions will be taken, and if so of what size, depends critically on the degree of the policymakers' risk aversion and the extent of their uncertainty about the impacts of their actions. Looking at and adapting to all new information—promptly but also cautiously—is a fortiori a sensible approach when risk aversion is intense and uncertainty about the model is great.

The second type of behavior goes considerably further. It entails aggressive instrument manipulation: sizable changes in the settings may occur continuously, with frequent changes in direction. Policymakers who are activist not only in the first but also in this second sense feel confident of their ability to calibrate the impacts of their actions on the economy precisely.

Activist behavior of the first, but only the first, type is the essential characteristic of discretionary instrument adaptation as advocated in this book. "Fine tuning" implies activist behavior of both sorts.

The difference between fine tuning and discretionary adaptation is that the former accepts whereas the latter rejects a "certainty equivalence" approach to all aspects of policy decisions. Fine tuners ignore uncertainty in the sense of setting uncertain variables and uncertain coefficients at their expected values ("best guesses") and then proceeding as if those values were known and certain. This treatment of uncertainty has two consequences. First, policy actions are unaffected by the relative severity of the various uncertainties associated with the policymaking model. For example, the settings deemed appropriate for a pair of instruments are unaffected by whether the policy multipliers associated with the instruments are regarded as equally uncertain or whether one set of multipliers is regarded as five times more uncertain than the other set.[38] Second, policymakers' attitudes toward risk tend to have little or no effect on their policy decisions. The instrument settings determined under a fine-tuning policy could remain unaffected, for example, even if policymakers decided to alter their loss function so as to associate five times as much loss with deviations of particular ultimate-target variables from their desired paths.

In contrast, discretionary adapters do not frame their decisions as if the values of variables and coefficients were known with certainty. The relative sizes of their policy actions are influenced by the relative degrees of uncertainty associated with policy multipliers. Whatever preferences with respect to risk may be embodied in the loss function, moreover, those preferences also influence the sizes of the discretionary variations in instrument settings.[39]

Any policymaker or economist who claims that existing knowledge of the economy is sufficient to permit accurate calibration of the impacts of policy actions is either naive or a charlatan. Anyone willing to make decisions solely on the basis of the expected impacts of policy actions without regard for the uncertainty of those impacts is a dangerous man to have at the helm. Thus if fine tuning is defined as aggressive, certainty-equivalent manipulation of policy instruments, fine tuners merit the opprobrium typically associated with the label. Their putatively best policy can be the enemy of the good policy.[40]

It would be wrong, however, to attribute the vices of fine tuning to discretionary instrument adaptation. Discretionary adaptation is compatible with any degree of policymakers' risk aversion and any degree of uncertainty about the macroeconomic behavioral relationships characterizing the economy. Indeed, it can outperform other strategies the most when uncertainty is great—precisely because it provides an objective procedure for conditioning instrument decisions in accordance with policymakers' judgments of the various types and degrees of uncertainty.

When policymakers have a loss function exhibiting a very high degree of risk aversion and when they sufficiently emphasize coefficient uncertainty in their model, the decisions made under a strategy of discretionary instrument adaptation may be cautious in the extreme. Although continuous consideration is given to whether actions are warranted, few changes in instrument settings—and very few large changes—may actually be made.

The pervasiveness of uncertainty is not a sound justification for instrument rules for essentially the same reasons that the uncertainty justification for a two-stage money strategy cannot be supported analytically. Conceivably, instrument rules may dominate fine tuning because of the failure of the latter approach to take uncertainty adequately into account. But rejection of fine tuning need not imply

---

38. As measured by, say, the judgments of the standard deviations of the multipliers expressed as a percentage of their expected values (their coefficients of variation).

39. As conventionally and loosely used, "fine tuning" may connote something about the *preferences* of policymakers as well as about their choice of operating *strategy*. For example, whereas "conservative" policymakers may have loss functions exhibiting a high degree of risk aversion, "fine tuners" may attach much smaller negative weights to the variance of outcomes. The comparison of fine tuning and discretionary adaptation in the text, as with the rest of the analysis in part 4, abstracts from differences in loss functions in order to evaluate strategies on a common basis. For any given loss function, the distinction in the text permits fine tuners to be differentiated from discretionary adapters.

40. On the origins and subsequent fortunes of the term "fine tuning," see Arthur M. Okun, *The Political Economy of Prosperity* (Brookings Institution, 1970), p. 110.

forswearing discretion. It need only mean avoidance of certainty-equivalent instrument manipulation.

Activism versus Lack of Action

In apparent contradiction to the preceding conclusion, there exists a superficially appealing argument that "doing something" can easily be worse than "doing nothing." When the effects of policy actions are uncertain, this argument alleges, policy actions may on balance *add* to the variance of the outcome rather than perform a stabilizing function. Merely to keep their actions from being destabilizing, this argument continues, policymakers have to take actions in the "right" direction to stabilize the economy, and in the "right" amounts, not just half the time but considerably more than half the time. The classic statement of this argument appears in an article by Milton Friedman.[41]

Earlier chapters have already emphasized that when policy multipliers are uncertain, the appropriate policy actions will probably be more cautious and in any case will differ from certainty-equivalent actions. It is undeniably true, moreover, that the variances of the ultimate-target variables are increased, *other things being equal*, by the variances of the uncertain policy multipliers.

In response to those correct points, it may seem tempting to propose that policymakers fix their instrument settings at a value of "zero" so as to eliminate that part of the variances of ultimate-target variables attributable to the uncertain impacts of the policy instruments. Such a proposal, however, has no practical relevance for most policy instruments. For the cases of reserve-requirement ratios, reserve-money aggregates, or interest rates such as the interbank lending rate and the central bank's own discount rate, for example, it would be nonsensical to set those instruments at zero values and to define the resulting situation as "doing nothing" with monetary policy.

For most instruments, settings at some nonzero value must be in force at every point in time. "Doing nothing" can therefore mean in practice only one of two things. Either the instrument settings must be kept literally unchanged at constant values; or the settings at each point in time must be fixed by predetermined rules— for example on a constant-growth-rate path. "Doing nothing" is thus tantamount to *pegging* the instrument. In neither case is there any reasonable basis for arguing that the time paths of the instrument settings have no effect on the economy and do not add to the variance of ultimate-target outcomes.[42] For reasons already given, moreover, in neither case are pegging rules of thumb likely to do as well as a discretionary adaptive strategy in achieving policymakers' objectives.

---

41. Milton Friedman, "The Effects of a Full-Employment Policy on Economic Stability: A Formal Analysis," in *Essays in Positive Economics* (University of Chicago Press, 1953), pp. 117–32.

42. This fundamental point is overlooked in Friedman's essay in ibid. Friedman implicitly considers only the variance in the outcome due to the deviation of a discretionary countercyclical policy from a "nondiscretionary" benchmark peg. This nondiscretionary policy, however, is never defined. "Doing nothing" in the sense of the Friedman article does not eliminate the uncertain, "destabilizing" effects of macroeconomic policy on the variance of the outcome. Policymakers presumably have an interest in both the expected values and the variances of their ultimate-target variables. Friedman's analysis considers only the variance of the outcome and ignores the expected value—another point that vitiates his conclusions.

If "doing something" were to involve certainty-equivalent instrument manipulation, that policy could adversely affect the variance of the outcome by an amount large enough to more than offset any gains in bringing the expected value of the outcome closer to the desired target value. The caution, "Don't just do something, stand there," may thus be good advice to give to fine tuners. When advising policymakers who are inclined to adjust the settings on their instruments very sluggishly, on the other hand, the more traditional exhortation, "Don't just stand there," is still likely to be appropriate.

Which is the greater practical danger: the Scylla of fine tuning or the Charybdis of overly sluggish use of policy instruments? Accidents may occur somewhat more often, it seems to me, when the ship drifts too close to Charybdis. The politics of macroeconomic policy on balance probably impart too much inertia to decision-making. Quite apart from the politics, moreover, policymakers confronted with great uncertainty may often choose to act with *excessive* hesitancy. The history of the postwar period in many countries certainly seems to exhibit a high degree of autocorrelation in the settings of policy over time.

Other pressures, it is true, tend to push the ship too close to Scylla. For example political pressure groups, concerned about a particular aspect of the overall macroeconomic situation, will frequently urge new policy actions to deal with that one aspect. If the pressures from one group are not politically neutralized by counter-pressures from others, policymakers may be pushed into taking action even though their best judgment counsels against it.

Whichever of the two dangers is regarded as more troublesome in practice, both must be avoided to achieve a safe passage. The best hope for doing so is the middle course of discretionary instrument adaptation.

The Conduct of Monetary Policy in an Open Economy

CHAPTER TWENTY

Monetary-Policy Actions
in an Open Economy

THIS CHAPTER begins the analysis of the open-economy aspects of monetary policy, focusing on what are traditionally referred to as exchange-market-intervention policy and alternative exchange-rate regimes. It analyzes essentially the same questions as those discussed in chapter 14—What are monetary-policy actions? What are the instruments of monetary policy?—but highlights their international features.

Exchange rates and the balance of payments are frequently discussed as a separate compartment of macroeconomic policy, and even as a separate compartment of monetary policy. "International" financial policy is taken to be concerned with capital flows in the balance of payments, with official intervention in exchange markets, with holdings by the government of international reserve assets, and with commitments (or lack of them) to keep exchange rates unchanged. "Domestic" monetary policy is considered independently of international complications and is taken to be concerned with, for example, discount-rate changes, open-market operations, and the supply of commercial bank reserves.

There is a danger of going seriously astray, however, if exchange-market intervention is analyzed in isolation from other government policy actions. As this chapter shows, there is no valid way to segregate the "external" and "domestic" aspects of national monetary policy for separate analysis.

This and subsequent chapters draw heavily on several recent contributions to the literature of international economics that modify the earlier conventional emphasis of balance-of-payments and exchange-market analysis on the relative prices of goods, the relative levels of national incomes, and the price and income elasticities of trade and other current-account flows. Each new approach—the portfolio-balance approach to international capital flows, the asset-market approach to exchange-rate determination, and the monetary approach to the balance of payments—emphasizes the capital account in the balance of payments and stock equilibrium in financial markets. A fully adequate macroeconomic theory for open economies—something not yet achieved—must combine a flow-equilibrium analysis of goods and labor markets and a stock-equilibrium analysis of financial markets into an integrated, general-equilibrium theory.[1]

1. On the portfolio-balance approach to capital flows, see Ralph C. Bryant, "Empirical Research on Financial Capital Flows," in Peter B. Kenen, ed., *International Trade and Finance: Frontiers for Research* (Cambridge and New York: Cambridge University Press, 1975). For the asset-market approach to exchange-rate determination, see Peter Isard, *Exchange-Rate Determination: A Survey of Popular Views and Recent Models*, Princeton Studies in International Finance 42 (Princeton University Press, 1978). References for the monetary approach to the balance of payments are given in chapter 9 above. I owe an especially heavy

Official Intervention in Foreign-Exchange Markets

What is an "exchange-market-intervention action"? How should its impacts on the home economy be analyzed?

Consider first some facts. (1) A market purchase or sale of "foreign exchange" by the home central bank is an exchange of assets with a private economic unit resident either in the home nation or abroad—that is, with some member of the world private sector. (2) If the central bank sells foreign exchange, the world private sector acquires more assets denominated in foreign currency and gives up assets denominated in the home currency. (3) From the perspective of the central bank, a purchase or sale of foreign exchange is merely one type of open-market operation. (4) Central-bank purchases or sales of foreign exchange—as with any other open-market operation—necessarily involve either offsetting changes in other asset categories or offsetting changes in the central bank's liabilities.

An appreciation of the significance of these facts is the beginning of wisdom about central-bank intervention in foreign-exchange markets. But what is "foreign exchange"? What particular type of open-market operation is carried out? *Which* assets in the two currencies are exchanged?

Schematic Budgets and Balance Sheets for the Central Bank and Fiscal Authority

Analytical discussion of the preceding questions requires the aid of schematic representations of the budgets and balance sheets of the central bank and fiscal authority of the home nation. Accordingly, table 20-1 adds international items to the domestic ones already shown in the central-bank accounts in table 14-1. Table 20-2 is an open-economy version of the accounts of the fiscal authority shown in table 14-2.

As in parts 2 and 3, the "world" is theoretically collapsed into two interdependent nations, the "home" country and the "foreign" country. Transactions, assets, and liabilities may be denominated in either the home or the foreign currency. An asterisk is used to denote foreign variables that are the analogues of home variables, and π represents the exchange rate, expressed as the price of foreign currency in home-currency units.[2]

---

debt to Lance Girton and Dale Henderson, whose pathbreaking work relates to all three of these areas. Their research first appeared as "A Two-Country Model of Financial Capital Movements as Stock Adjustments with Emphasis on the Effects of Central Bank Policy," International Finance Discussion Paper 24 (Board of Governors of the Federal Reserve System, March 1973). Subsequent papers include "Financial Capital Movements and Central Bank Behavior in a Two Country, Short-run Portfolio Balance Model," *Journal of Monetary Economics*, vol. 2 (January 1976), pp. 33–61; "Critical Determinants of the Effectiveness of Monetary Policy in the Open Economy," in M. Fratianni and K. Tavernier, eds., *Bank Credit, Money, and Inflation in Open Economies*, supplement to *Kredit und Kapital* (3: 1977), pp. 231–83; "Central Bank Operations in Foreign and Domestic Assets Under Fixed and Flexible Exchange Rates," in P. Clark, D. Logue, and R. Sweeney, eds., *The Effects of Exchange Rate Adjustments* (Government Printing Office, 1977), pp. 151–79.

2. In the notation used in part 5, the currency denomination of variables and the identity of liability issuers is implicit, rather than explicit as in part 2 (for example, S^* rather than Sf_{FG} is used to represent the total nominal stock of securities issued by the foreign government denominated in the foreign currency).

Table 20-1. *Schematic Budget Statement and Balance Sheet of the Home-Country Central Bank*[a]

Home-currency units

BUDGET STATEMENT	
	Receipts
$r_s(S^{CB})$	Interest earned on holdings of debt securities of the home government
$\pi(r_{s*})(S^{*CB})$	Interest earned on external reserve assets held in the form of debt securities of the foreign government[b]
	Outlays
X^{CB}	Current expenditures (for example, salaries)[c]
E^{CB}	Transfer of excess interest earnings to the fiscal authority
Z^{CB}	Current budget surplus (plus) or deficit (minus)

BALANCE SHEET	
	Assets
RB	Borrowings by commercial banks from the home central bank (borrowed reserves)
S^{CB}	Holdings of debt securities of the home government
FA^{CB}	External reserve assets,[d] subdivided into:
$\pi(Dep^{*CB})$	Foreign-currency deposit balance of the home central bank with the foreign central bank[b]
$\pi(S^{*CB})$	Holdings of debt securities (denominated in foreign currency) of the foreign government[b]
$\zeta(J^{CB})$	Holdings of world outside reserve assets[b,e]
OA^{CB}	Other assets (for example, tangible assets)
	Liabilities and capital accounts
RT	Liquid claims of commercial banks on the home central bank (total reserves),[c] subdivided into:
RR	Required reserves
RX	Excess reserves
CUR	Currency in circulation
Dep^{G}	Deposit balance of the home fiscal authority with the home central bank[c]
Dep^{FCB}	Deposit balance of the foreign central bank (denominated in home currency) at the home central bank[c]
NW^{CB}	Surplus and capital accounts (net worth)

a. *CB* indicates the home central bank, *G*, the home fiscal authority, and *FCB*, the foreign central bank. For the balance-sheet entries, a superscript on a symbol indicates the sector for which an item is an asset or net worth. For notes on "domestic" items and for definitions of the various identities for reserve-money aggregates, see table 14-1.

b. S^{*CB} represents that part of the total nominal stock of securities issued by the foreign government held by the home central bank. All securities issued by the foreign government are assumed to be denominated in the foreign currency unit. The symbol r_{s*} represents the interest rate paid by the foreign government on its debt. It is assumed that the foreign central bank does not pay interest on its deposit liabilities and that no interest is paid on world outside reserve assets. Outside reserve assets are discussed in chapter 20, note 4.

c. It is assumed that the home central bank does not pay interest on any of its liabilities.

d. FA^{CB} is the symbol used for the total value, expressed in home-currency units, of the three components of the home country's external reserve assets. That is,

$$FA^{CB} \equiv \pi(Dep^{*CB}) + \pi(S^{*CB}) + \zeta(J^{CB}),$$

where π is the exchange rate (home-currency price of one unit of the foreign currency).

e. J^{CB} represents an amount of outside reserve assets, for example ounces of gold or numbers of special drawing rights, and ζ is the home-currency price of outside reserve assets. For the relationship between π and ζ, see chapter 20, note 4.

Table 20-2. *Schematic Budget Statement and Balance Sheet of the Home-Country Fiscal Authority*[a]

Home-currency units

BUDGET STATEMENT	
Receipts	
T_d	Discretionary tax revenue[b]
T_n	Nondiscretionary tax revenue[b]
E^{CB}	Receipt from the central bank of excess interest earnings
Outlays	
X_d	Discretionary expenditures and transfer payments[b]
X_n	Nondiscretionary expenditures and transfer payments other than interest payments on the home-government debt[b]
$r_s(S)$	Interest payments on home-government debt securities
Z^G	Budget surplus (plus) or deficit (minus)

BALANCE SHEET	
Assets	
Dep^G	Deposit balance of the fiscal authority with the home central bank
OA^G	Other assets (for example, tangible assets)
Liabilities and balancing item	
S	Debt securities issued by the home government (denominated in home currency),[c] subdivided into holdings by:
S^{CB}	Home central bank
S^{Ph}	Members of the world private sector resident in the home country
S^{Pf}	Members of the world private sector resident in the foreign country
S^{FCB}	Foreign central bank
NW^G	Balancing item (net worth)

a. G indicates the home fiscal authority, CB, the home central bank, FCB, the foreign central bank, Ph, private-sector economic units resident in the home country, and Pf, private-sector economic units resident in the foreign country. For the balance-sheet entries, a superscript on a symbol indicates the sector for which an item is an asset or net worth. For further explanation of "domestic" items, see table 14-2.

b. It is assumed for expositional simplicity that the home government does not collect revenue from foreign-country residents, does not make expenditures on foreign-produced goods and services, and does not make transfers to foreign residents.

c. $S \equiv S^{CB} + S^{Ph} + S^{Pf} + S^{FCB}$; $S^P \equiv S^{Ph} + S^{Pf}$, where P indicates the world private sector. All securities issued by the home government are assumed to be denominated in the home currency unit.

The most important change in table 20-1 relative to table 14-1 is the addition of external reserve assets, FA^{CB}, to the asset side of the central bank's balance sheet.[3] External reserve assets may be held in three forms: a foreign-currency deposit balance at the foreign central bank (πDep^{*CB} when expressed in units of home currency); holdings of securities denominated in foreign currency issued by the foreign government (πS^{*CB} valued in home currency); and holdings of world "outside" reserve assets such as gold or special drawing rights (ζJ^{CB} valued in home currency, where ζ is the home-currency price of outside reserve assets).[4] For

3. In some nations (for example, the United States) a substantial fraction of external reserves is held by the fiscal authority rather than the central bank; accordingly, substantial amounts of exchange-market intervention are carried out for the account of the fiscal authority. These institutional complexities, which are unimportant for many analytical purposes, are ignored here.

4. "Outside" reserve assets are those assets accepted for settlements between national monetary authorities that are not at the same time a liability of some governmental or private economic unit resident in a particular nation. Gold and SDRs are the main examples in practice. The distinction between "inside" and "outside" reserves is suggested by the analogous distinction between inside and outside money in

simplicity, it is assumed that the home central bank does not hold deposit balances with foreign commercial banks and does not hold any securities denominated in foreign currency except those issued by the foreign fiscal authority.

The other new items in table 20-1 are the central bank's interest earnings on its holdings of foreign-currency securities, $\pi(r_s{}^*)(S^{*CB})$, and a deposit liability to the foreign central bank, Dep^{FCB}. The latter constitutes a home-currency cash balance for the foreign central bank and is the analogue of the foreign-currency cash balance, Dep^{*CB}, held by the home central bank.

In most open economies, the government makes expenditures for foreign-produced goods and services, makes transfer payments to foreign residents, and collects revenues from foreign residents. These international transactions of the government are ignored in table 20-2. Thus the only difference between tables 20-2 and 14-2 is on the liability side of the fiscal authority's balance sheet. The relevant private sector that may hold the home government's debt is now a *world* private sector that includes foreign residents (superscript Pf) as well as home residents (superscript Ph). Home government debt may also be held by the foreign central bank.[5]

Initial Asset Exchanges Resulting from Exchange-Market Intervention

Suppose the home central bank is a seller of foreign exchange—that is, delivers assets denominated in foreign currency in exchange for assets denominated in home currency.[6] Let the amount of the illustrative sale be 100, measured in units of the home currency ($100/\pi$ in foreign-currency units).

In the simplest type of exchange-market intervention—case A—the home central bank enters into a "spot" contract to sell foreign currency in the market and settles the contract by drawing down its deposit balance with the foreign central bank.[7] The settlement transfers demand claims on the foreign central bank (denominated in foreign currency) to the member of the world private sector on the other side of the exchange-market contract. The private sector pays for its acquisition of foreign-currency demand claims on the foreign central bank by drawing down balances denominated in home currency at the home central bank. As a result of the asset exchange, an equivalent amount of assets ($\pi\Delta Dep^{*CB}$) and liabilities (ΔRT) disappears from the balance sheet of the home central bank. From the perspective of

---

closed-economy monetary theory originally made by John G. Gurley and Edward S. Shaw in *Money in a Theory of Finance* (Brookings Institution, 1960). When a change in the exchange rate π occurs, this must be reflected in ζ, the home-currency price of outside reserve assets, in ζ^*, the foreign-currency price of outside reserve assets, or in both ζ and ζ^* ($\pi = \zeta/\zeta^*$). For the necessary interrelationships among changes in π, ζ, and ζ^* and the treatment of associated capital gains or losses on the central bank balance sheet, see Girton and Henderson, "Critical Determinants of the Effectiveness of Monetary Policy in the Open Economy," esp. p. 238, note 9.

5. Tables 20-1 and 20-2 could be marginally simplified if the home nation were assumed to be either a pure "reserve-center" country or a country without any of the attributes of a reserve center. In the former case, S^{*CB} could be eliminated from the external reserve assets of the home central bank; in the latter case, the foreign central bank would not hold any of the home government's debt ($S^{FCB} = 0$).

6. All the examples that follow use this assumption; except for obvious changes in signs, the analysis is identical for the reverse case of central-bank purchases of foreign exchange.

7. In practice, contracts in the exchange market are made by telex or telephone; "spot" transactions are typically settled on the second business day following the making of the contract. For a description of the detailed mechanics of exchange-market transactions, see Roger M. Kubarych, *Foreign Exchange Markets in the United States* (Federal Reserve Bank of New York, 1978). These details are ignored in the text where it is assumed for simplicity that settlement occurs immediately after the contract commitment.

the world private sector, the external open-market operation destroys 100 units of home-currency reserve money and creates $100/\pi$ units of foreign-currency reserve money.[8]

Before considering other cases, it is worth noting that the asset exchange just described is always a component of an intervention action in the exchange market by the home central bank. Transactions in the foreign-exchange market, between any two participants, are always *proximately* a sale of legal tender ("cash") denominated in one currency for legal tender denominated in another currency. When it conducts an open-market "sale" of foreign exchange, the home central bank sells foreign-currency cash. It must therefore have such cash in its possession immediately before making payment for the transaction. When the home central bank conducts an open-market "purchase" of foreign exchange, increasing the volume of home-currency reserve money, it receives foreign-currency cash in payment.

Given its requirements for settling exchange-market transactions, the home central bank must maintain a means-of-payment account through which it can route payments and receipts denominated in foreign currency.[9] But the average size of the balance in that account can be, and typically is, kept quite small. Central banks hold the bulk of their external reserves in some form other than foreign-currency cash—either outside reserve assets, for which risks are judged to be lower, or foreign-currency securities, which earn interest.

Thus consider case A', in which the exchange-market intervention by the home central bank involves not only (1) the sale of foreign-currency reserve money for home-currency reserve money but (2) a simultaneous sale of gold or SDRs to the foreign central bank (a reduction in holdings of J^{CB}). The second transaction is the means by which the home central bank acquires sufficient foreign-currency means of payment to honor the exchange-market contract entered into in the first transaction. Although two separate transactions are involved in case A', for purposes of analysis it is the net result that is relevant. From the perspective of the world private sector, the relative supplies of assets change as in case A: a reduction in the volume of home-currency reserve money and an increase in the volume of reserve money denominated in foreign currency. From the perspective of the foreign central bank, on the other hand, cases A and A' are different: two liability items change in an offsetting manner in case A, whereas the *assets* of the foreign central bank increase in case A'. When analyzing the effects of an exchange-market-intervention action, it would be correct to treat cases A and A' as equivalent only if all other associated behavior of the two central banks were identical.

---

8. It is of secondary interest whether the member of the world private sector that acquires the foreign reserve money in the first instance is a bank or a nonbank, and whether it resides in the home country or abroad. As used here, "reserve money" comprises all the liabilities of the central bank to the private sector—in other words, the monetary base ($MB = RT + CUR$). Since in practice the foreign-exchange transactions of central banks are hardly ever carried out in currency notes or coin and since the transactions are primarily with commercial banks or other central banks, case A would directly result in an increase in the reserves (denominated in foreign currency) held by commercial banks at the foreign central bank and a reduction in commercial-bank reserves (denominated in home currency) at the home central bank. Even if the member of the private sector were a nonbank, the indirect result (after additional transactions) would be the same changes in the relative supplies of commercial-bank reserves in the two currencies.

9. Hence the balance-sheet item πDep^{*CB} (the foreign-currency means-of-payment account of the home central bank) in table 20-1. The analogous (home-currency) account of the foreign central bank is Dep^{FCB} (a liability of the home central bank).

Table 20-3. *Initial Asset Exchanges Involved in a Sale of Foreign Exchange by the Home Central Bank before Any Offsetting "Domestic" Transactions* [a]

Exchange-market intervention	Changes in the balance sheet of the home central bank (amounts in units of home currency)		Changes in the balance sheet of the world private sector (amounts in units of home currency)
	Assets	Liabilities	Assets
Type A	Deposit account at foreign central bank: -100	Home reserve money: -100	Home reserve money: -100 Foreign reserve money: $+100$
Type A'	Outside reserve assets: -100 Deposit account at foreign central bank: 0 (net)	Home reserve money: -100	Home reserve money: -100 Foreign reserve money: $+100$
Type B	Foreign-currency securities: -100 Deposit account at foreign central bank: 0 (net)	Home reserve money: -100	Home reserve money: -100 Foreign-currency securities: $+100$

a. See text for discussion.

In case B, the home central bank, simultaneously with (1) its exchange-market sale of foreign reserve money, replenishes its foreign-currency cash balance by (2) the sale of foreign-currency securities to the world private sector.[10] The net result of these two open-market operations is an exchange of foreign-currency securities for home-currency reserve money. Equivalent amounts of assets and liabilities are eliminated from the balance sheet of the home central bank; 100 units of home-currency reserve money are destroyed in case B as in cases A and A'. From the perspective of the world private sector, however, case B results in a significantly different change in the relative supplies of assets. Though in all three cases the private sector holds a smaller total stock of assets denominated in the home currency and a larger total stock of foreign-currency assets, the increment to the stock of foreign-currency assets in case B takes the form of interest-bearing securities rather than reserve money.

Table 20-3 contains a schematic summary of the preceding discussion that highlights the differing balance-sheet consequences of the three types of intervention.

Type B intervention by the home central bank (case B) would be more common than either type A or type A' (cases A and A') if the foreign country played the role of a reserve-center nation. Type A' intervention would be the typical form under institutional arrangements requiring so-called full asset settlement of international payments imbalances.

10. In practice, this second open-market transaction would usually occur in the foreign country's securities market (often with the foreign central bank acting as agent for the home central bank).

Interaction with Domestic Operating Regime

Whichever type of intervention is used in a particular situation, a definition of an exchange-market-intervention action by the home central bank must go beyond the initial asset exchanges to specify the "domestic" operating regime being followed during and after the period when the exchange-market intervention occurs.

Suppose first that the home central bank operates a reserve-aggregate instrument regime, using one of the home-currency reserve-money aggregates as an exogenous instrument. In each of the three cases, A, A', and B, the setting for the domestic instrument will be disturbed by the exchange-market intervention (reduced by 100 units) unless additional open-market transactions are carried out. The home central bank's routine procedures will therefore lead it to carry out "defensive" or "sterilizing" operations (simultaneously with the exchange-market intervention) to maintain the home-currency reserve aggregate at its previously set exogenous level. A "domestic" open-market purchase of 100 units of home-currency-denominated securities by, as it were, the left hand has to be made to offset the 100 unit decline of home-currency reserve money resulting from the "external" open-market sale by the right hand. If the external open-market operation takes the form of drawing down outside reserve assets or the central bank's foreign-currency cash balance (cases A and A'), the net outcome of all the operations for the world private sector is a reduction in private holdings of home-currency securities and an increase in private holdings of foreign-currency reserve money. If the external open-market operation involves the sale of foreign-currency securities (case B), the net outcome of the external and domestic operations is that the world private sector is forced to hold fewer securities denominated in the home currency and correspondingly more securities denominated in the foreign currency, with no change in the available supplies of reserve money in either currency. Subsequent market adjustments of the exchange rate and asset valuations and yields in response to portfolio rebalancing decisions of the private sector will differ depending on which combination of asset exchanges the home central bank carries out. Table 20-4 illustrates the balance-sheet consequences of the combined external and domestic operations for this assumption of a domestic reserve-aggregate regime.[11]

Alternatively, suppose the home central bank operates an interest-rate instrument regime. The postulated initial exchange-market intervention, having reduced the supply of home reserve money and increased the supply of foreign reserve money (cases A and A') or of foreign-currency securities (case B), sets into motion a different pattern of market adjustments of the exchange rate and asset valuations

---

11. If the home central bank's foreign-exchange intervention is type A or type A', the home currency appreciates against the foreign currency but interest rates on home-currency securities may either decline or increase. The larger the responsiveness of private demands for home-currency and foreign-currency securities to exchange-rate changes relative to the responsiveness of demands for home-currency money to exchange-rate changes, the more likely the home interest rate is to increase rather than decrease. If the foreign-exchange intervention is type B, the home currency appreciates and interest rates on home-currency securities decline unambiguously. These conclusions assume that the foreign central bank is "passive" in the sense of conducting no external or domestic open-market operations of its own; further analysis is needed to deal with the more realistic cases in which the foreign central bank is not passive (see text that follows). For the analytical apparatus needed to derive these conclusions about the short-run adjustments of interest rates and the exchange rate to asset exchanges initiated by central banks, see Girton and Henderson, "Central Bank Operations in Foreign and Domestic Assets Under Fixed and Flexible Exchange Rates."

Table 20-4. *Combined "External" and "Domestic" Asset Exchanges Involved in a Sale of Foreign Exchange When the Home Central Bank Uses a Domestic Reserve-Aggregate Regime*[a]

Exchange-market intervention	Changes in the balance sheet of the home central bank (amounts in units of home currency)		Changes in the balance sheet of the world private sector (amounts in units of home currency)
	Assets	Liabilities	Assets
Type A	Deposit account at foreign central bank: −100 Home-currency securities: +100	Home reserve money: 0 (net)	Home-currency securities: −100 Foreign reserve money: +100 Home reserve money: 0 (net)
Type A	Outside reserve assets: −100 Home-currency securities: +100 Deposit account at foreign central bank: 0 (net)	Home reserve money: 0 (net)	Home-currency securities: −100 Foreign reserve money: +100 Home reserve money: 0 (net)
Type B	Foreign-currency securities: −100 Home-currency securities: +100 Deposit account at foreign central bank: 0 (net)	Home reserve money: 0 (net)	Home-currency securities: −100 Foreign-currency securities: +100 Home reserve money: 0 (net) Foreign reserve money: 0 (net)

a. It is assumed that the foreign central bank is "passive" (does not conduct any "external" or "domestic" open-market operations in response to actions of home central bank); see text for discussion.

and yields. These adjustments will in turn evoke "domestic" (endogenous) open-market operations by the home central bank in whatever amounts may be required to keep the interest-rate instrument on its (exogenous) time path. In the absence of domestic operations, this interest rate would otherwise tend to rise or fall with the market adjustments of the exchange rate and asset yields. The possible balance-sheet consequences of the combined external and domestic operations under an interest-rate regime are summarized in table 20-5.[12] As suggested by the illustrative numbers in tables 20-4 and 20-5, there is no a priori presumption that the domestic

12. When the foreign-exchange intervention is type A or A', the home currency appreciates but the direction of the incipient pressure on the home interest rate is ambiguous. If the home interest rate would increase in the absence of "domestic" actions to keep it from rising, the central bank will engage in open-market purchases of home-currency securities; these purchases partially offset the destruction of home reserve money associated with the foreign-exchange intervention. If the incipient pressure on the home interest rate is downward, the central bank engages in open-market sales of home-currency securities. When the foreign-exchange intervention is type B, the home currency appreciates and the incipient pressure on the home interest rate is unambiguously upwards (calling forth "domestic" open-market purchases of home-currency securities). These conclusions again assume "passive" behavior by the foreign central bank and are based on the Girton-Henderson analytical model of short-run financial behavior.

Table 20-5. *Combined "External" and "Domestic" Asset Exchanges Involved in a Sale of Foreign Exchange When the Home Central Bank Uses a Domestic Interest-Rate Regime*[a]

Exchange-market intervention	Changes in the balance sheet of the home central bank (*amounts in units of home currency*)		Changes in the balance sheet of the world private sector[b] (*amounts in units of home currency*)
	Assets	*Liabilities*	*Assets*
Type A' when home interest rate would *rise* in the absence of offsetting domestic action[b]	Outside reserve assets: -100 Home-currency securities: $+50^c$ Deposit account at foreign central bank: 0 (net)	Home reserve money: -50 (net)[c]	Home reserve money: -50 (net)[c] Foreign reserve money: $+100$ Home-currency securities: -50^c
Type A' when home interest rate would *fall* in the absence of offsetting domestic action[b]	Outside reserve assets: -100 Home currency securities: -25^c Deposit account at foreign central bank: 0 (net)	Home reserve money: -125^c	Home reserve money: -125^c Foreign reserve money: $+100$ Home-currency securities: $+25^c$
Type B (home interest rate would unambiguously rise in the absence of offsetting domestic action)	Foreign-currency securities: -100 Home-currency securities: $+50^c$ Deposit account at foreign central bank: 0 (net)	Home reserve money: -50 (net)[c]	Home reserve money: -50 (net)[c] Foreign-currency securities: $+100$ Home-currency securities: -50^c Foreign reserve money: 0 (net)

a. It is assumed that the foreign central bank is "passive"; see text for discussion.
b. The balance-sheet consequences for the world private sector of type-A and type-A' intervention are identical when the foreign central bank is assumed to be passive.
c. These specific numbers are illustrative only. The sizes of actual changes (and the direction of the incipient pressure on the home interest rate itself) depend on, among other things, the detailed characteristics of private portfolio preferences.

open-market operations carried out under an interest-rate regime would be equivalent in amount to the domestic operations under a reserve-aggregate regime.

Yet other outcomes will result if the home central bank follows the domestic operating procedures characteristic of a mixed instrument regime or some variant of an intermediate-target regime. The amounts and timing of domestic open-market operations and hence the relative supplies of various assets available to the world private sector will differ, however, compared with the domestic operations and asset supplies that result when the volume of some home-currency reserve aggregate or some home interest rate serves as the main instrument of domestic monetary policy.

The domestic operating regime of the home central bank thus plays a crucial role in the working out of the effects of an exchange-market initiative in monetary policy. Strictly speaking, it is not possible even to define an exchange-market-intervention action, much less systematically analyze its consequences, without reference to domestic operating procedures and objectives.

The analysis so far has postulated an initial "external" open-market operation. The unstated presumption has been that exchange-market intervention by the home central bank—whether of type A, type A', or type B—constitutes an exogenous policy action. But why begin the analysis at that point? Perhaps exchange-market intervention, although a *potentially exogenous* policy variable, would more accurately be characterized as *endogenous?* Why not begin with, for example, an exogenous change in the exchange rate instead? Alternatively, why not begin with an exogenous "domestic" policy action (for example, a domestic open-market operation or a change in an interest-rate instrument), and then attempt to provide a logically consistent description of that action—including its implications for exchange-market intervention?

As these questions suggest, before the analysis can be carried further there is a need to identify the operating procedures and proximate objectives—the "external" operating regimes—with which exchange-market intervention may be associated.

Alternative Operating Regimes for External Monetary Policy

Although instrument-variation costs and boundary conditions that constrict the ranges within which instruments may be used can exist for any of the alternative operating regimes for domestic monetary policy, they do not play a primary role in the specification of the regimes. The instrument-variation costs that exist, moreover, are those judged by the national policymakers to be worthy of being taken into account; the cost-benefit calculus is, so to speak, self-imposed by the policymakers. When present, boundary conditions are by-products of national laws, economic institutions, or political pressures.

Costs or constraints of the self-imposed type may also be relevant to external monetary policy. But there is an additional dimension not present on the domestic side: intergovernmental treaties and nonstatutory commitments may further constrain the freedom of action of national policymakers. Most notably, supranational law may impose one or another form of boundary condition on the movement of the exchange rate.

It is instructive first to compare alternative regimes for external monetary policy under the hypothetical assumption that the supranational dimension is absent. For the moment, therefore, suppose that there are no international institutions such as the International Monetary Fund, no internationally imposed boundary conditions constraining the movement of exchange rates—indeed, no international rules or understandings of any sort. Furthermore, suppose that the home central bank chooses its external operating regime from a myopic national perspective, disregarding the possible consequences of its actions for decisions made in the rest of the world.

Consider the budget and balance-sheet identities of the home central bank that follow from table 20-1:

(20-1) $[r_s(S^{CB}) + \pi(r_s*)(S^{*CB})] - [X^{CB} + E^{CB}] \equiv\quad Z^{CB}.$

Budget receipts   Budget outlays   Budget surplus
or deficit

(20-2) $[\Delta RB + \Delta S^{CB} + \Delta FA^{CB} + \Delta OA^{CB}]$

Changes in assets

$\qquad - [\Delta RT + \Delta CUR + \Delta Dep^G + \Delta Dep^{FCB}] \equiv \Delta NW^{CB} \equiv Z^{CB}.$

Changes in liabilities   Budget
surplus
or deficit

For reasons given in chapter 14, most of the "domestic" items in these identities are endogenous—that is, not directly controllable—from the perspective of discretionary stabilization policy. Specifically, when considered in isolation, none of the magnitudes ΔRB (changes in commercial-bank borrowing), ΔOA^{CB} (changes in "other assets"), ΔCUR (changes in currency in circulation), ΔDep^G (changes in the home fiscal authority's deposit balance), and $\Delta NW^{CB} \equiv Z^{CB}$ (changes in the central bank's surplus and capital accounts) can be characterized as potential (much less actual) exogenous instruments of monetary policy. On the other hand, domestic open-market operations (ΔS^{CB}) and the change in total bank reserves (ΔRT) are potentially exogenous.[13] One of the "international" items in the identity 20-2, ΔDep^{FCB} (changes in the foreign central bank's deposit balance at the home central bank), is unambiguously an endogenous variable from the perspective of the home central bank; decisions about that balance are made by the foreign central bank. The home central bank's external reserve assets (FA^{CB}), however, are under its own potential control; FA^{CB} could be an exogenous policy instrument in some operating regimes.

To emphasize the division of balance-sheet items into these two groups, 20-2 may be rearranged so that the potentially exogenous variables are on the right side of the identity:

(20-2a) $\Delta NW^{CB} - \Delta OA^{CB} - \Delta RB + \Delta CUR + \Delta Dep^G + \Delta Dep^{FCB}$

$$\equiv \Delta S^{CB} + \Delta FA^{CB} - \Delta RT.$$

From the perspective of the home central bank, at most two out of the three quantities on the right can be independently chosen as exogenous instruments.[14]

Suppose the home central bank were to treat the exchange rate as an exogenous instrument, conducting whatever volume of purchases or sales of foreign exchange were required to fix the exchange rate on a specified time path. In that event, the path of external reserves, FA^{CB}, would be endogenously determined. Alternatively, FA^{CB} could be an exogenous instrument if the central bank allowed the exchange

---

13. So, too, are the other reserve-money aggregates (for example, unborrowed reserves, the monetary base); see chapter 14.

14. As in chapter 14, note that several alternative *combinations* of balance-sheet quantities could be designated as exogenous (for example, $\Delta RU \equiv \Delta RT - \Delta RB$ could be substituted for ΔRT), but the maximum number of exogenous magnitudes is still two.

rate to vary endogenously. As a third possibility, suppose the central bank were to determine both the exchange rate and a home interest rate exogenously. In that event both domestic and external open-market operations would be endogenously determined; *no* item on the central-bank balance sheet would be an exogenous instrument for monetary policy.

When identifying alternative operating regimes for external monetary policy, it is again useful to contrast instrument regimes with intermediate-target regimes. Within the class of instrument regimes, a further distinction can be made between exchange-rate regimes and external-reserves regimes.

Exchange-Rate Instrument Regimes

When the exchange rate is used as an instrument, external open-market operations are conducted in whatever volume may be required to maintain the exchange rate on some exogenously specified path.[15] Exogenous policy actions take the form of a change in the time sequence of settings for the exchange-rate instrument (for example, a 2 percent depreciation of the home currency relative to the path that would otherwise have been maintained). In the absence of supranational constraints, the central bank may either keep the exchange rate unchanged at a pegged level or discretionarily reset the level at frequent intervals. In the latter case, the exchange rate can exhibit substantial variability despite the fact that the central bank is using it as an instrument.

Close parallels exist between an external regime of this type and a domestic regime that uses an interest rate as an instrument. The operating procedure is the same in both cases: carrying out asset exchanges with the private sector large enough to keep a market price on an exogenously set path. In both the domestic and external cases, an asset quantity on the central-bank balance sheet becomes an endogenous by-product of the operating regime (S^{CB} and FA^{CB}, respectively).[16]

Can the home central bank control the exchange rate precisely enough to warrant use of the "instrument" label? Fundamentally, there are great difficulties.[17] So long as the analysis focuses myopically on the options available to a single nation, however, there is virtually as much justification for treating the exchange rate as an instrument as there is for regarding an interest rate as an instrument in a domestic operating regime.

Domestically, the exogenous fixing of an interest rate could induce balance-sheet changes that would be deemed unacceptable. This would be particularly likely if the interest rate were kept unchanged for long periods regardless of the evolution of economic and financial activity. It is a conceivable, though unlikely,

---

15. Since the exposition here assumes only two countries and two currencies, there is only one exchange rate. With more than two countries and hence more than one exchange rate, an important new range of problems emerges. It becomes necessary to distinguish, for example, between exchange-rate instrument regimes in which the exogenous exchange rate is a bilateral exchange rate vis-à-vis a single foreign currency (perhaps the currency of the home country's largest trading partner) and those in which it is some weighted average of exchange rates. In actual practice, for many countries this range of problems may be as difficult as the broad choice among external operating regimes discussed in the text.

16. External reserve assets have three components, and as noted earlier it can be important to distinguish among exchange-market intervention of the three corresponding types.

17. With two central banks in the world but only one exchange rate, it is obviously impossible for each central bank to fix the single rate at a different exogenous level. With n central banks there are only $n - 1$ independent exchange rates. These difficulties are discussed in chapter 25.

possibility that the central bank could run out of home-currency securities in an effort to keep an interest rate from falling below an exogenous peg. By and large, however, it is within the technical power of the central bank—if it chooses to do so—to fix an interest rate precisely over a short run.

Likewise, the home central bank could precisely fix the exchange rate over a short run if the foreign central bank acquiesced. The required volume of exchange-market intervention might prove unacceptably large, especially if the exchange rate were held unchanged regardless of economic developments. Moreover, the probability of the central bank running out of external reserves in an effort to prevent the home currency from depreciating is much higher than the probability of its running out of home-currency assets in an effort to prevent an exogenous interest-rate instrument from falling. Even so, over the short run the required market operations and the problems of precise control are remarkably similar for the use of a "domestic" interest rate and the "external" exchange rate as instruments.

External-Reserves Instrument Regimes

In these operating regimes, the total amount of external reserve assets (or, alternatively, some subcomponent) is the exogenous instrument of external monetary policy. Accordingly, the exchange rate fluctuates endogenously to take on whatever value is dictated by market supply and demand conditions.[18] Exogenous policy actions are naturally defined in terms of the instrument (for example, an increase in external reserves of $100 million relative to the time path that would otherwise have been maintained). Exchange-market intervention can be type A, type A', or type B, corresponding to the three types of external reserve assets; for many analytical purposes, specification of an external-reserves regime will need to include particulars about holdings of the three types of assets and their use in external open-market operations. Since external reserves are a balance-sheet item, little difficulty arises in controlling their time path precisely.

The parallels between domestic and external regimes are instructive here also. Just as the choice of a reserve-aggregate regime instead of an interest-rate regime domestically permits the exogenous fixing of a balance-sheet quantity at the expense of surrendering direct control over an associated market price, the choice of an external-reserves regime requires the central bank to give up the possibility of exogenously setting the exchange rate. The offsetting gain is control over the volume of external reserves. Even if the foreign central bank were passive, it would not be possible for the home central bank to have it both ways: either the exchange rate or the volume of external reserve assets can be determined exogenously in the short run, but not both at the same time.

In an unconstrained external-reserves regime the central bank could either peg the volume of external assets for some extended period or revise the instrument setting discretionarily from one short-run period to the next. If the setting is adjusted discretionarily, external reserves could exhibit substantial variability and exchange-rate fluctuations could be dampened despite the exogeneity of the former and the endogeneity of the latter.

---

18. Provided the foreign central bank is not pursuing an exchange-rate instrument regime and setting the rate exogenously (see text that follows).

External Intermediate-Target Regimes?

The language of "intermediate targets" is alien to the literature on the external aspects of macroeconomic policy just as it is absent (see chapter 14) from discussions of fiscal policy. The conventional focus in international economics on one or another measure of balance-of-payments "equilibrium," however, could conceivably be reinterpreted as an advocacy of an external-sector intermediate variable as a proximate policy objective. Under such an interpretation, the controversy over the correct ex post measurement of "the" balance-of-payments surplus or deficit could be regarded as a dispute about the most appropriate intermediate-target variable for external economic policy. Alternative candidates for such an intermediate target include the "balances" that result when the double-entry bookkeeping accounts of the balance of payments are arbitrarily divided into "above-the-line" and "below-the-line" categories in the conventional ways; the gamut runs from the official settlements balance to the trade balance, with contenders in between such as the liquidity balance, the basic balance, and the balance on current account.[19]

An application of the intermediate-target strategy to external economic policy would involve specifying a target time path for one of these balance-of-payments measures and then adjusting policy instruments—for example, either the exchange rate or the volume of external reserves—to try to keep that particular measure on its target path.

No one to my knowledge has consistently advocated setting some measure of the balance-of-payments surplus or deficit as an *intermediate* target, and I have no brief for such a strategy myself. Accordingly, external intermediate-target regimes for monetary policy are not mentioned further in what follows. As in the case of fiscal policy, however, note how this lack of interest provokes a question: Why is an intermediate-target strategy for the conduct of domestic monetary policy widely regarded as valid and necessary while no interest exists in applying an intermediate-target approach to the conduct of external monetary policy?

Supranational Constraints

This chapter has thus far assumed that the central bank has a myopic national perspective, that it is free to choose any one of the preceding external regimes, and that any boundary conditions on the variation of instruments are self-imposed or dictated by purely national considerations. Those assumptions bring out the fundamental similarities between the unconstrained options available to external and domestic monetary policy—similarities that deserve much greater attention than they usually receive.

Because nations have subjected themselves to international treaties and understandings, however, supranational constraints may inhibit national freedom to

19. For the controversy about definitions as it pertains to the U.S. balance of payments, see Review Committee for Balance of Payments Statistics, *The Balance of Payments Statistics of the United States: A Review and Appraisal* (GPO, April 1965); "Report of the Advisory Committee on the Presentation of Balance of Payments Statistics," *Survey of Current Business*, vol. 56 (June 1976), pp. 18–27. On the lack of a sound rationale for focusing on *any* single measure of surplus or deficit in the balance of payments, see Ralph C. Bryant, "Dollar Balances and The United States Balance of Payments: A Conceptual Review" (Ph.D. dissertation, Yale University, 1966).

choose external regimes for monetary policy. To identify the regimes actually available for choice, it is necessary to supplement the preceding account with a summary of the supranational constraints that have been or could be imposed.

At an abstract level, supranational constraints may be divided into two groups: those restricting the movement of exchange rates and those restricting the national accumulation or decumulation of external reserve assets. The main supranational legal restrictions since the end of World War II have been codified in the Articles of Agreement of the International Monetary Fund (particularly Article IV) and the associated Selected Decisions and Bylaws, Rules and Regulations. Proposed constraints that have not been adopted—at least those that have received serious governmental attention—are described in other International Monetary Fund documents.[20]

Possible supranational constraints on movements in exchange rates can be located along a spectrum from the extreme of absolute prohibition of rate movements to the extreme of no limitations whatsoever. It is convenient to oversimplify by highlighting only three positions along the spectrum: an infrequently adjustable peg, limits specifying the maximum permissible speed for peg adjustment, and the complete absence of limitations.[21]

With an infrequently adjustable peg system, the intention of the supranational restrictions is to prohibit exchange-rate fluctuations during "normal" times. The peg can be adjusted if a "fundamental disequilibrium" emerges, but only by a discrete jump to a new peg thought to be sustainable for the next longish run. Constraints of essentially this form were embodied in Article IV of the original IMF Articles of Agreement and for the most part were adhered to by member nations throughout the years 1945–73. Most proponents of this system of supranational restrictions (at the least its original proponents) presumed that fundamental disequilibriums, and hence the need to change pegs, occur only infrequently.

At the extreme of no limitations on exchange-rate movements, supranational law would be completely permissive about rate fluctuations. A nation would not be constrained from allowing exchange rates to be determined entirely by private-sector demands and supplies. But neither would it be discouraged from adopting any other position about exchange-rate movements. This situation of national freedom of choice with no supranational constraints is somewhat like the actual world situation since March 1973. The revised version of Article IV, in force since April 1978, contains exhortations to international cooperation and injunctions to the International Monetary Fund to "exercise firm surveillance over the exchange-rate policies of members," but does not contain effective constraints on exchange-rate movements.[22]

20. See, for example, International Monetary Fund, *International Monetary Reform: Documents of the Committee of Twenty* (Washington, D.C.: IMF, 1974); and *Annual Report of the International Monetary Fund, 1974*, app. 2; ibid., *1975;* and ibid., *1976.* For a history of actual and proposed changes in international monetary arrangements in the postwar period, see Robert Solomon, *The International Monetary System, 1945–76* (Harper and Row, 1977).

21. This summary description omits mention of margins around pegs within which no limitations on rate movements are imposed, different possible widths of these margins, and several other complexities that have been significant in actual practice.

22. The most important exception to the general absence of supranational constraints on exchange-rate movements since 1973 has been the "snake" arrangements linking certain European currencies, transformed in 1979 to the European Monetary System.

In the middle ground between an infrequently adjustable peg and the absence of any limitations it would be possible to have many types of restrictions that would partially constrain peg adjustment. For example, the rate at which pegs were adjusted might be subject to limitations specifying a maximum permissible speed. So-called crawling pegs (gliding parities) would be allowed under this form of supranational traffic regulation so long as the rate of crawl did not exceed the speed limit.

Much less attention has been devoted to supranational constraints on accumulation and decumulation of external reserve assets. But restrictions can be envisaged analogous to those that have been or could be imposed on exchange-rate movements. Rigid rules could limit all changes in reserve assets, but with provision for temporary suspension of the constraint during an "abnormal" or emergency period. As a middle-ground set of rules, constraints could take the form of a limit specifying the maximum allowable rate of change of reserve assets.[23] At the opposite extreme from rigid rules, supranational law and understandings could be entirely permissive about changes in nations' external reserves.

In 1945–78 there existed virtually no supranational constraints on reserve movements. Subject to the constraints on exchange-rate movements (before 1973), nations were formally free to run down their external reserves or to accumulate additional reserves without limit. For the post-1978 period, it remains to be seen whether the International Monetary Fund will adopt explicit decisions or rules about reserve movements as part of an implementation of the revised Article IV of the amended Articles of Agreement. As of this writing, it has not done so.[24]

Since national central banks have the options of using a quantity (external reserves) or a price (an exchange rate) as their external instrument and since a variety of combinations of supranational constraints are conceivable, there are in principle a large number of possible operating regimes for external monetary policy. It seems natural to assume that most national governments will choose to use the exchange rate as an exogenous instrument in the presence of supranational constraints on exchange-rate movements; that instrument choice will, among other things, make it easier to abide by the supranational constraints. Conversely, national governments would be likely to operate with external reserves as an exogenous instrument if supranational constraints limited movements in external reserves. But it is conceivable that some form of supranational constraints could apply to both exchange rates and reserves (although not rigid constraints of both types) and that nations would still have considerable latitude for choice of an external operating regime.

When observing the external regimes that national governments employ when supranational constraints exist, an analyst should not automatically presume that the constraints are *binding*. The important question is whether the constraints

23. Proposals for the use of "reserve indicators" were discussed intensively during the 1972–74 Committee of Twenty meetings on international monetary reform. See, for example, IMF, *International Monetary Reform: Documents of the Committee of Twenty*, esp. pp. 24–30, 51–75, and 141–58.

24. Article IV, Section 3 of the amended Articles not only enjoins the International Monetary Fund to "exercise firm surveillance over the exchange rate policies of members" but also states that it "shall adopt specific principles for the guidance of all members with respect to those policies." The "Statement on the Surveillance Over Exchange Rate Policies," adopted by the Executive Directors in April 1977, does not contain explicit constraints on reserve movements.

inhibit choice in the sense that the national government abides by the supranational traffic regulations, even though it would prefer not to do so. A national government, after all, can voluntarily forswear certain policy choices or impose boundary conditions on itself because it believes such behavior will facilitate national objectives.

Once again the parallels with domestic operating regimes need to be recognized. No supranational authority has ever proposed to limit the fluctuations in interest rates or the magnitude of open-market operations in home-currency securities. Nonetheless, had chapter 14 described domestic regimes in greater detail, it could have discussed the voluntary establishment by the national policymakers themselves of an "adjustable peg" for the interbank lending rate or the government security rate.[25] Similarly, the central bank could impose a speed limit on the pace at which it would allow itself to expand the volume of the monetary base under a reserve-aggregate domestic regime. No central bank in practice has deemed it appropriate to impose constraints on the use of domestic instruments as rigid as those it accepted under the Bretton Woods system during 1945–73 on the use of external instruments. But boundary conditions and instrument-variation costs can be relevant in choosing among domestic regimes. And there can be self-imposed constraints on the external side quite independent of the presence or absence of supranational constraints. To cite only the most obvious example, since March 1973 there have been no effective supranational constraints on exchange-rate movements, yet many countries have voluntarily chosen to peg their currencies to the currency of a major trading partner.[26]

Four Archetypal External Regimes

At several points in the analysis that follows it is necessary to compare the consequences of a policy action or a nonpolicy disturbance under different assumptions about the operating regime for external monetary policy. Hence four archetypal external regimes are identified here for use in those comparisons.

Under the first regime, an *exchange-rate peg*, the exchange rate is used as an exogenous policy instrument and is held unchanged over a succession of short-run periods. Under the second regime, an *external-reserves peg*, the quantity of external reserves is used as an instrument and held unchanged over a succession of periods. A nation might adopt one of these pegging regimes to abide by supranational constraints. Alternatively, it might choose such a regime voluntarily in the absence of supranational constraints. In a third case, a *discretionary exchange-rate regime*, the exchange rate is used as an exogenous instrument but may be adjusted from one short-run period to the next rather than kept unchanged at a given setting. Finally, under a *discretionary external-reserves regime* the quantity of external reserve assets is selected as the external instrument but may be adjusted from period to period. For a nation to be able to adopt one of these discretionary regimes,

25. In the early postwar period in the United States, before the so-called Treasury-Federal Reserve Accord of March 1951, an adjustable peg policy for the yield on government securities was imposed on the Federal Reserve by the Treasury.

26. The actual exchange-rate practices followed by member countries of the International Monetary Fund are now tabulated in the introductory pages of each month's issue of the Fund's statistical publication, *International Financial Statistics*; see, for example, vol. 32 (December 1979), pp. 4, 5, and 11. See also H. Robert Heller, "Determinants of Exchange Rate Practices," *Journal of Money, Credit and Banking*, vol. 10 (August 1978), pp. 308–21.

supranational constraints must be loose enough not to inhibit the exercise of a substantial degree of national discretion.

The first two of these external regimes correspond to the conventional polarization between fixed and flexible exchange rates. The latter two cannot so naturally be characterized as one or another sort of "exchange-rate regime." Both are merely external analogues of discretionary domestic operating regimes. Some degree of exchange-rate variability—and variability in external reserve assets—could and would occur under both.[27]

"Domestic" and "External" Monetary Policy

The domestic operating regime of the home central bank plays a crucial role in the working out of the effects of an exchange-market-intervention action. The external operating regime plays an equally crucial role in conditioning the impacts of a domestic monetary-policy action.[28]

To illustrate the latter proposition, this section contrasts the initial sequence of events following a domestic policy action using three different assumptions about the external operating regime. For the first alternative, it is supposed that the home central bank adopts a rigid external-reserves peg. For the second, the central bank is assumed to follow an exchange-rate instrument regime and supranational constraints are assumed to require an infrequently adjustable peg; at least for the time being, therefore, the operable regime is a rigid exchange-rate peg. For the third alternative, it is assumed that there are no supranational constraints on exchange-rate fluctuations and that the home central bank follows a discretionary exchange-rate regime; the level of the exchange rate is fixed exogenously at some constant value during each week, but may change from one week to the next; if the central bank finds its external reserves (FA^{CB}) falling by a large amount, the exchange rate for subsequent weeks is adjusted, depreciating the home currency somewhat (and vice versa for rapid increases in FA^{CB}).[29]

Domestic Policy under a Reserve-Aggregate Regime

Suppose the home central bank is following a reserve-aggregate instrument regime domestically, with the unborrowed monetary base (MBU) as the exogenous instrument. Suppose further that one wants to analyze the impacts on the home economy of an incremental domestic open-market purchase (an increase in S^{CB}) of 500 home-currency units. The intention of the home central bank's policy action

27. The differences among the four external regimes precisely parallel the differences domestically among an interest-rate peg, a reserve-aggregate peg, a discretionary interest-rate regime, and a discretionary reserve-aggregate regime.

28. Now that alternative regimes for external monetary policy have been described, the discussion in the first section of the chapter can be put into clearer perspective. Three varieties of exchange-market intervention (types A, A', and B) were described and the analysis was initiated presupposing that one of those types was an exogenous policy action. That presupposition would be natural if the home central bank were operating an external-reserves instrument regime. If the home central bank were operating an exchange-rate instrument regime, on the other hand, it would be analytically confusing to postulate an "exogenous" exchange-market-intervention action. In exchange-rate instrument regimes, the volume of exchange-market intervention is determined endogenously.

29. The phrase "depreciation of the home currency" always means an increase in the home-currency price of foreign currency (a fall in the foreign-currency price of the home currency).

is to raise the time path of home reserve money 500 units above what it otherwise would be.[30]

The case in which the home central bank uses an external-reserves peg for its external operating regime is the most straightforward to analyze. After the initial domestic policy action, which reduces the world private sector's holdings of home-currency-denominated securities by 500 home-currency units and correspondingly increases its holdings of home reserve money, the central bank in effect sits on both its left and right hands. Both the domestic instrument, MBU, and the external instrument, FA^{CB}, remain fixed at their desired settings, so there is no need for further operations. Given its domestic and external regimes, the home central bank is willing to allow domestic interest rates and the exchange rate to adjust endogenously. Because of the change in relative asset supplies forced on them, members of the world private sector seek to adjust their asset portfolios. At least in the first instance there will be a downward movement in domestic interest rates and a depreciation of the home currency.

Under the exchange-rate peg, the change in relative asset supplies brought about by the domestic open-market purchase likewise puts incipient downward pressure on domestic interest rates and incipient pressure on the home currency to depreciate. Under this external regime, however, exchange-market intervention is (endogenously) called forth to prevent the depreciation of the home currency. This exchange-market intervention produces a decline in home reserve money and an increase in one or another form of foreign-currency assets held by the world private sector (table 20-3). Some part of the incremental reserve money the home central bank had (exogenously) provided with its domestic left hand is thus taken away (endogenously) with its external right hand. But then the left hand is required to take further action. Additional domestic open-market purchases are carried out, and continue to be carried out so long as the domestic exogenous instrument, MBU, threatens to fall below the desired time path (500 units higher than before any of the operations began). As the left hand continues to act, the right hand will also be forced to carry out further amounts of exchange-market intervention. Provided the whole sequence of left-hand and right-hand actions settles down reasonably promptly (see below), one would expect to observe, at least in the first instance, a larger fall in domestic interest rates than would occur under the external-reserves peg. External reserve assets will have fallen, perhaps by a sizable fraction of the central bank's gross purchases of home-currency securities.

For the third alternative, in which the home central bank uses a discretionary exchange-rate regime, the analysis of effects becomes still more complicated. During the first week the situation is essentially the same as under the exchange-rate peg. External reserves fall as a result of the exchange-market support of the home currency, while home-currency securities (S^{CB}) rise not only by the 500 increment associated with the initial domestic action but also by whatever additional amount may be needed to offset the fall in external reserves. On the first weekend, however, a new decision about the exogenous setting for the external instrument is made. As a result of the observed decline in external reserves during the first week, suppose the home central bank changes the exchange rate for the subsequent

30. The following discussion again draws on the analytical apparatus developed by Girton and Henderson in "Central Bank Operations" and "Critical Determinants."

week, devaluing the home currency by a small amount (say, one quarter of one percent). The central bank's open-market operations in the subsequent week, both domestic and external, therefore differ from operations that would occur under the rigid exchange-rate peg. Similarly, the time paths for domestic interest rates take a different course. Suppose similar small adjustments in the exchange rate are made on successive weekends. After the passage of several weeks, this third case probably produces a smaller decline in domestic interest rates than would occur under the exchange-rate peg, but a larger decline than under the external-reserves peg. The fall in external reserves is less under the discretionary exchange-rate regime than under the exchange-rate peg. The time path of the exchange rate, of course, is also different in this third case from what it would be under either of the two pegging regimes.

An analysis of the effects of a domestic open-market purchase under the three preceding assumptions about the external regime can go no further without bringing in a number of additional considerations, four of which are identified here. (Others are discussed in subsequent chapters.)

First, can one even be sure that each of the three combinations of domestic and external regimes is viable—viable in the narrow sense that the home central bank can actually achieve both of the desired exogenous instrument settings? For example, what if in the second case (the exchange-rate peg) the right hand of the home central bank were called upon to conduct foreign-exchange intervention so promptly after the initial left-hand domestic action and in such large quantities that the left hand could never manage to push the unborrowed monetary base all the way up to its 500-unit higher path? Even if the exchange-rate peg were viable, moreover, would the home central bank tolerate large declines in external reserves without feeling impelled to take still further actions? Questions of this sort lead directly to the issues of autonomy and controllability discussed in part 3.

Second, to what extent do private-sector residents of one nation hold assets and incur liabilities denominated in the currency of the other? How different are the portfolio preferences of home and foreign residents? To what degree do the home and foreign private sectors regard the various home-currency-denominated and foreign-currency-denominated assets and liabilities as good substitutes for each other? Answers to this category of questions are crucial in analyzing the interest-rate and exchange-rate consequences of the portfolio rebalancing behavior of the private sector. They also are important for the issues of autonomy and controllability.[31]

Third, the endogenous exchange-market interventions carried out by the home central bank under the exchange-rate peg and the discretionary exchange-rate regime are incompletely defined. The effects of exchange-market intervention on the relative supplies of assets available to the world private sector depend critically on whether the intervention by the home central bank takes the form of reductions in its holdings of foreign-currency securities (type B) or in its holdings of outside reserve assets or deposits at the foreign central bank (types A' and A). Since different relative asset supplies available to the private sector engender different adjustments in portfolio behavior and thus different changes in domestic and foreign

---

31. Note that these questions are essentially requests for information about those structural characteristics of private economic behavior that bear most closely on the degree of financial interdependence.

interest rates and different (actual or incipient) changes in the exchange rate, a careful comparison of the three external regimes would need to specify the asset composition of the exchange-market intervention.

Fourth, the illustrative comparison presumes a myopic national perspective and fails to allow for the behavior of the foreign central bank. It is assumed, first, that the foreign central bank takes no interest in the subject of external operating regimes, leaving the home central bank a completely free hand in this area; and second, that the analysis can safely ignore whatever the foreign central bank does about its domestic operating regime. The first assumption is altogether unrealistic. Suppose, however, that the foreign central bank were willing to leave the selection of the external regime solely to the home central bank. Even then, the outcomes under the three external regimes would differ according to whether the foreign central bank operates domestically with a reserve-aggregate regime, an interest-rate regime, or an intermediate-target regime focused on the foreign money stock (see chapter 25 for further discussion).

Domestic Policy under Other Operating Regimes

The illustrative domestic action whose consequences are analyzed in the preceding discussion—the raising of the unborrowed monetary base to a new exogenous path above the level of the path that would otherwise have been followed—is only one possible type of domestic action. Imagine instead that the analysis starts with a different assumption about the domestic operating regime; suppose, for example, it postulates an interest-rate instrument regime with the interbank lending rate as the exogenous instrument and asks about the effects of a 25-basis-point reduction in that interest rate relative to the path that would otherwise have been followed. What would a comparison of the impacts on the economy under the three alternative external regimes reveal?

Under the external-reserves peg, the analysis would sketch out one set of initial results for the exchange rate, for noncontrolled domestic interest rates, and for the (endogenous) variations in such aggregates on the central-bank balance sheet as home-currency security holdings (S^{CB}) and the unborrowed monetary base (MBU). Under the exchange-rate peg, it would sketch out a quite different set of initial results for noncontrolled domestic interest rates and for the aggregates on the central bank's balance sheet; for example the central bank would have to increase S^{CB} by a much larger amount (and correspondingly experience a decline in external reserve assets FA^{CB}) than it would under the external-reserves peg. Under the discretionary exchange-rate regime, a still different set of initial results would be predicted—for example, an expansion of S^{CB} and a fall of FA^{CB} intermediate between the results of the exchange-rate peg and the external-reserves peg. Furthermore, the analysis would run up against similar stumbling blocks. Questions about the viability of the regime combinations would have to be raised (particularly in the case of the exchange-rate peg). The degree of financial interdependence would be highly relevant to predicting the outcomes. It would be similarly artificial to conduct the analysis without bringing in explicit facts or assumptions about the type of foreign-exchange intervention and the behavior of the foreign central bank.

Now imagine yet another comparison of the effects of a domestic policy action under the three alternative external regimes. Suppose the analysis starts by assuming that the home central bank pursues an intermediate-target regime, with some definition of the home money stock as the key intermediate variable. Suppose the analysis specifies a target path for that money stock and the detailed procedures by which the central bank uses the interbank lending rate as an exogenous instrument to try to keep the money stock on its target path. Suppose, finally, the analysis assumes some given increase in the target money path (for example, an increment of 500 units above what it would otherwise have been) and an initial "exogenous" reduction in the interbank lending rate thought to be consistent with that new target path.

Of the illustrative domestic actions hypothesized, this last one would be the most complex to analyze. The domestic intermediate-target regime would interact with each of the three alternative external regimes in an especially intricate way because of the frequent adjustment of the interbank lending rate (designed to keep the money stock from drifting off course). The "external" behavior of the home central bank and the endogenous movements of "external" variables (for example, the exchange rate, external reserve assets, foreign interest rates) would have "domestic" effects on both the demand for and supply of the money stock.[32] The effects would be *different*, however, under each of the three external regimes. Note again that the analysis would quickly run up against stumbling blocks requiring the introduction of additional information and analytical tools.

Symbiosis between Domestic and External Monetary Policy

The preceding illustrations do not provide a comprehensive analysis of the initial impacts, much less the longer-run consequences, of domestic policy actions. The purpose of including them here is to emphasize a conclusion that emerges sharply even from a sketchy analysis: a domestic monetary-policy action cannot even be fully defined, and certainly not systematically analyzed, without specifying the relevant operating regime for external monetary policy.

Seen from one perspective, this conclusion is banal. For many years, careful analysts of domestic monetary-policy actions under "fixed exchange rates" have emphasized the possibility of dissipation of those actions through the balance of payments.[33] But banalities deserve reexamination when their implications are not fully appreciated. The conclusion stressed here—together with its obverse, that external monetary-policy actions cannot be defined and systematically analyzed without specification of the relevant operating regime for domestic monetary policy—do have such implications. In particular, because these conclusions apply for *any* degree of variability in exchange rates and *any* type of external regime,

---

32. This of course is one of the main points emphasized in part 2. Effects of some sort occur regardless of the definition of the money stock and regardless of the nature of the external operating regime.

33. The basic analytical insights about the endogeneity of domestic monetary aggregates under fixed exchange rates go back at least to the "Political Discourses, 1752" of David Hume. For a discussion of Hume's analysis, see Jacob Viner, *Studies in the Theory of International Trade* (Harpers, 1937; Allen and Unwin, 1960), esp. pp. 290–387; excerpts from Hume are reprinted in Richard N. Cooper, ed., *International Finance: Selected Readings* (Penguin, 1969), pp. 25–37. For recent reviews of the historical literature, see Jacob A. Frenkel and Harry G. Johnson, "Essential Concepts and Historical Origins," in Frenkel and Johnson, eds., *The Monetary Approach to the Balance of Payments* (University of Toronto Press, 1976), pp. 21–45; Jacob A. Frenkel, "Adjustment Mechanisms and the Monetary Approach to the Balance of Payments: A Doctrinal Perspective," in Emil-Maria Claassen and Pascal Salin, eds., *Recent Issues in International Monetary Economics* (North-Holland, 1976), pp. 29–48.

they have great significance not only for the case of so-called fixed exchange rates, but also for the analysis of the effects of monetary policy under external regimes and international institutional arrangements permitting a high degree of exchange-rate flexibility.

Much remains to be said on the subjects of exchange-market intervention and the relationships between external and domestic monetary policy. Even so, enough has already been said to demonstrate the proposition with which the chapter began: it is impossible to draw a sharp, analytical distinction between "domestic monetary policy" and "external monetary policy." The two aspects of central bank behavior are much too symbiotic to be disentangled and analyzed in isolation.

CHAPTER TWENTY-ONE

The Unity of National Macroeconomic Policies

AN IMPORTANT guideline for analysis grows out of the discussion in chapter 20: to be able to assess correctly the effects of monetary-policy actions in an open economy, the analyst must specify precisely both the domestic and external operating regimes and treat monetary policy as an integrated whole. Given different combinations of operating regimes, there can be many different "endogenous" open-market operations and many different outcomes for other endogenous variables that occur in response to an initial "exogenous" policy action; this is true whether the initial action is domestic or external. These subtle interrelationships arise out of the interplay of the central bank's operating behavior and its balance-sheet identity.

But why restrict this line of reasoning to monetary policy? There exists a holistic unity not just of monetary policy per se, but of all national macroeconomic policy. In chapter 14 the symbiosis of monetary and fiscal policies is emphasized without reference to international considerations. That analysis is combined here with the analysis of chapter 20 to outline an integrated view of national macroeconomic policy for an open economy.

Fiscal-Policy Actions and Budgetary Financing in an Open Economy

Open-economy versions of the budget and balance-sheet identities for the home central bank have been presented in equations 20-1 and 20-2. The corresponding identities for the home country's fiscal authority (based on the schematic accounts in table 20-2) are

(21-1) $\quad [T_d + T_n + E^{CB}] - [X_d + X_n] - [r_s(S^{CB} + S^{Ph} + S^{Pf} + S^{FCB})] \equiv Z^G.$

$[T_d + T_n + E^{CB}]$	$- [X_d + X_n]$	$- [r_s(S^{CB} + S^{Ph} + S^{Pf} + S^{FCB})]$	$\equiv Z^G$
Budget receipts	Budget outlays other than interest payments	Interest payments on the government debt	Budget surplus or deficit

(21-2) $\quad [\Delta Dep^G] + [\Delta OA^G] - [\Delta S^{CB} + \Delta S^{Ph} + \Delta S^{Pf} + \Delta S^{FCB}] \equiv \Delta N W^{iG} \equiv Z^G.$

$[\Delta Dep^G]$	$+ [\Delta OA^G]$	$- [\Delta S^{CB} + \Delta S^{Ph} + \Delta S^{Pf} + \Delta S^{FCB}]$	$\equiv \Delta N W^{iG} \equiv Z^G$
Change in government's deposit balance	Change in other assets	Change in government debt securities outstanding	Budget surplus or deficit

The net change in the stock of the home government's debt in 21-2 is the sum of four components: changes in the holdings of the home central bank, of private-sector economic units resident in the home country, of private economic units resident abroad, and of the foreign central bank. Interest payments on all four components appear in the budget identity 21-1. Note that, since they are "international" transactions, the last two magnitudes on the left sides of 21-1 and 21-2 appear as entries in the home country's balance-of-payments accounts.

As in chapter 20, there is as yet no need to distinguish among members of the private sector according to whether they reside at home or abroad. Hence for the time being the discussion needs to consider only the total of the world private sector's holdings of home government debt ($S^P \equiv S^{Ph} + S^{Pf}$).

The fiscal authority in an open economy has available essentially the same choices for a budgetary operating regime as those identified in chapter 14: a discretionary expenditure regime, an exogenous-surplus regime, or some variety of composite budget-aggregate regime.[1]

In an open economy, the home fiscal authority may retire or issue debt directly with the foreign central bank as well as with the home central bank and the (world) private sector. Hence some amendments are necessary to the account in chapter 14 of alternative institutional procedures for the initial financing of a budget surplus or deficit. As before, a distinction between direct transactions (new issues or redemptions) with the fiscal authority and market asset exchanges results in the identity

$$(21\text{-}3) \quad \Delta S \equiv \Delta S^{CB}_{direct} + \Delta S^{P}_{direct} + \Delta S^{FCB}_{direct} + \Delta S^{CB}_{market} + \Delta S^{P}_{market} + \Delta S^{FCB}_{market}.$$

Since every purchase by one market participant is a market sale by another, the sum of the last three magnitudes in 21-3 is equal to zero. Hence

$$(21\text{-}4) \quad \Delta S^{CB}_{market} + \Delta S^{FCB}_{market} \equiv -\Delta S^{P}_{market}.$$

In the absence of "market" transactions between the two central banks, every market purchase or sale of home-government debt by the foreign central bank affects the supply of home-government debt available to the world private sector.

For reasons given in chapter 14, it is justifiable here to ignore fluctuations in the home government's deposit balance at the home central bank (ΔDep^G) and changes in its other assets (ΔOA^G) and therefore write

$$(21\text{-}5) \quad Z^G \approx -\Delta S.$$

That is, the bulk of a budget surplus or deficit must be financed with retirements or new issues of home-government debt. As in the closed economy, the institutional arrangements that may be used by the fiscal authority to finance budget surpluses or deficits in the first instance include the polar extremes of initial full financing by the central bank ($\Delta S^{P}_{direct} \equiv \Delta S^{FCB}_{direct} \equiv 0$) and initial financing without any direct recourse to the home central bank ($\Delta S^{CB}_{direct} \equiv 0$). For most countries, the relevant set of institutional procedures is somewhere in between (initial mixed financing).

The *ultimate* breakdown of ΔS between net acquisitions or sales by the home central bank (ΔS^{CB}) and net acquisitions or sales by the world private sector and

---

1. At a less extreme level of abstraction than used here, a distinction could be made between (for example) government expenditures on domestically produced versus foreign produced goods and services. Discretionary expenditures for the two types of goods and services could then be regarded as two (potential or actual) instruments rather than one.

the foreign central bank ($\Delta S^P + \Delta S^{FCB}$) does not have to bear any relation to the *initial* breakdown of ΔS between ΔS^{CB}_{direct} and $\Delta S^P_{direct} + \Delta S^{FCB}_{direct}$. In principle, domestic open-market operations by the home central bank (ΔS^{CB}_{market}) could be carried out in sufficiently large volume, short-run period by short-run period, to render the procedures for initial financing an irrelevant detail for macroeconomic outcomes. In actual practice, however, the institutional procedures for initial financing probably do exert a nontrivial influence on the ultimate financing outcome.

The Consolidated Government Budget Constraint in an Open Economy

Because analysis of the financing of a surplus or deficit in the fiscal authority's budget inescapably brings monetary policy into the discussion, it is again revealing to combine the accounts of the central bank and the fiscal authority into one consolidated set of accounts for the home government as a whole. Using the same definitions as in chapter 14, one can obtain the consolidated budget identity by adding 20-1 and 21-1 together:

$$(21\text{-}6) \quad [T_d + T_n] - [X_d + X'_n] + [\pi(r_{s*})(S^{*CB})] - [r_s(S^P + S^{FCB})] \equiv Z^{G'}.$$

Consolidated budget receipts	Consolidated budget expenditures	Interest receipts on external reserve assets	Interest payments on government debt	Consolidated budget surplus or deficit

The corresponding consolidated balance-sheet identity in first-difference form, the sum of 20-2 and 21-2, is

$$(21\text{-}7) \quad [\Delta OA^{G'}] + [\Delta FA^{CB}] + [\Delta RB - \Delta RT - \Delta CUR]$$

Change in other assets	Change in external reserve assets	Net changes in borrowed reserves, total reserves, and currency in circulation

$$- [\Delta Dep^{FCB}] - [\Delta S^P + \Delta S^{FCB}] \equiv Z^{G'}.$$

Changes in foreign central bank's balance at home central bank	Change in government debt outstanding	Consolidated budget surplus or deficit

Since the unborrowed monetary base of the home country is defined as the sum of total reserves and currency less borrowed reserves, the balance-sheet identity can be simplified to

$$(21\text{-}7a) \quad [\Delta OA^{G'}] + [\Delta FA^{CB}] - [\Delta Dep^{FCB} + \Delta S^{FCB}] - [\Delta MBU] - [\Delta S^P] \equiv Z^{G'}.$$

Change in other assets	Change in external reserve assets	Change in external reserve liabilities to foreign central bank	Change in unborrowed monetary base	Change in government debt held by world private sector	Consolidated budget surplus or deficit

If desired, 21-6 and 21-7a can be combined into one identity that omits the consolidated budget imbalance $Z^{G'}$:

$$(21\text{-}8) \quad T_d + T_n - X_d - X_n' + \pi(r_{s*})(S^{*CB}) - r_s(S^P) - r_s(S^{FCB})$$
$$\equiv \Delta OA^{G'} + \Delta FA^{CB} - (\Delta Dep^{FCB} + \Delta S^{FCB}) - \Delta MBU - \Delta S^P.$$

What is different about the consolidated constraint facing the home government once the open-economy aspects are introduced? As schematized here, there are four differences. (1) Interest earnings on external reserve assets contribute to combined budget receipts $(\pi r_{s*}S^{*CB})$. (2) Interest on the home government's debt is paid to the foreign central bank $(r_s S^{FCB})$ and also to private-sector foreigners (the latter payment being part of $r_s S^P$, the total interest paid to the world private sector). (3) Changes in the home government's "reserve liabilities" to the foreign central bank (ΔDep^{FCB} and ΔS^{FCB}) appear in the constraint as an additional financing item. A budget deficit, for example, can be financed by a building up of the foreign central bank's deposit balance at the home central bank or by increased holdings of home-government securities by the foreign central bank.[2] (4) Changes in the home government's external reserve assets (ΔFA^{CB}) also constitute an additional source or use of funds generated in association with the budget imbalance. Accumulations of external reserve assets, for example, can be an alternative use of budget-surplus funds, reducing the need to retire government debt or home-currency reserve money.[3]

All the major components of national macroeconomic policy—fiscal policy, domestic monetary policy, external monetary policy—can be seen to be intertwined in the consolidated budget constraint for the home government. The identities 21-6 and 21-7a, or alternatively 21-8, knit the three components together so closely that a change in any component necessarily has consequences for one or both of the others.

When discussing the interactions between external and domestic monetary policies, chapter 20 emphasized the ways in which central-bank operations change the relative supplies of assets available to the world private sector. Changes in asset stocks other than those due to asset exchanges initiated by the central bank were left in the background and ignored. The most thorough theoretical studies of the short-run consequences of monetary-policy actions in open economies approach the analysis in just that way. Those studies assume that income and saving flows are exogenously fixed, that the wealth of the private sector and total asset stocks are constant except for changes brought about by central-bank operations and market adjustments of asset valuations, and that financial markets are promptly equilibrated by changes in interest rates and (when it is allowed to move) the exchange rate. Use of these assumptions and theoretical time horizon, often referred

---

2. For reasons similar to those given in chapter 20 in the discussion of the home central bank's deposit balance at the foreign central bank, the normal practice of the foreign central bank would be to maintain Dep^{FCB} at a small average level, using the account essentially as a transactions balance. Apart from transitory fluctuations, therefore, ΔDep^{FCB} can be assumed to be small; from the point of view of the home government, it would not play a major role in the constraints on policies represented by 21-8.

3. The schematization used here allows room for both the home country and the foreign country to be "reserve centers," that is, to have reserve liabilities that are the counterpart to external reserve assets of the other nation. If instead the home country were schematized as a "periphery" country, the home government would have no debt obligations to foreign monetary authorities; ΔS^{FCB} and $r_s S^{FCB}$ would be eliminated from 21-8.

to as point-in-time analysis, presumes that asset markets tend to adjust rapidly while product markets and labor markets adjust more slowly.[4]

To discuss fiscal policy and its interactions with monetary policy, it is necessary to lengthen the horizon of analysis to at least an intermediate run and, among other things, to incorporate all sources of changes in asset stocks and wealth portfolios. *Flows* of saving, investment income, and other income-account transactions occurring during short-run periods must be consistently integrated with an analysis of *stock* (balance-sheet) demands for and supplies of assets at particular moments (as it were, at the beginnings or ends of the short-run periods).[5] Private-sector saving flows lead to increases in net worth over time. Investment flows add to the stocks of physical capital and (modified by the financing decisions of firms) the stocks of corporate bonds and equities available in financial markets. Surpluses or deficits in the home government's budget subtract from or add to the stock of home government debt or home reserve money available to the private sector. Surpluses or deficits in the current account of the balance of payments change the distribution over time of the world private sector's wealth between home and foreign residents.[6] When these additional sources of changes in asset stocks are considered, it is apparent that open-market operations (domestic and external) by the central bank are only one—though important—reason why private-sector economic units continually rebalance their portfolios in response to changing relative supplies of assets and liabilities.

Home-government policy actions have direct effects on the income-account flows of the world private sector primarily through fiscal policy—government expenditures, transfer payments, tax collections, and interest payments on the government debt. Home-government policy actions have direct effects on the various asset stocks available to the world private sector through asset exchanges and the financing of budget imbalances: domestic monetary policy alters the relative supplies of different types of assets denominated in the home currency; external monetary policy alters the stocks of assets denominated in the home currency relative to those denominated in foreign currency. As highlighted by the consolidated

4. Lance Girton and Dale Henderson explore this point-in-time analysis thoroughly; see, for example, "Financial Capital Movements and Central Bank Behavior in a Two Country, Short-run Portfolio Balance Model," *Journal of Monetary Economics*, vol. 2 (January 1976), pp. 33–61 and "Central Bank Operations in Foreign and Domestic Assets Under Fixed and Flexible Exchange Rates," in P. Clark, D. Logue, and R. Sweeney, eds., *The Effects of Exchange Rate Adjustments* (Government Printing Office, 1977), pp. 151–79. See also Stanley W. Black, *International Money Markets and Flexible Exchange Rates*, Princeton Studies in International Finance 32 (Princeton University Press, 1973); Charles Freedman, ".'A Model of the Eurodollar Market," *Journal of Monetary Economics*, vol. 3 (April 1977), pp. 139–61; John Hewson and Eisuke Sakakibara, *The Eurocurrency Markets and Their Implications* (Lexington Books, 1975); Dale W. Henderson, "Macroeconomic Theory: Modeling the Interdependence of National Money and Capital Markets," *American Economic Review*, vol. 67 (February 1977, *Papers and Proceedings, 1976*), pp. 190–99; and Peter Isard, *Exchange-Rate Determination: A Survey of Popular Views and Recent Models*, Princeton Studies in International Finance 42 (Princeton University Press, 1978). The presumption that asset markets adjust more rapidly than product and labor markets is a main theme of the so-called asset-market approach to exchange-rate determination.

5. Theoretical modeling of this dynamic process poses intricate questions of specification. See, for example, Duncan K. Foley, "On Two Specifications of Asset Equilibrium in Macroeconomic Models," *Journal of Political Economy*, vol. 83 (April 1975), pp. 303–24; Willem H. Buiter and Geoffrey Woglom, "On Two Specifications of Asset Equilibrium in Macroeconomic Models: A Note," *Journal of Political Economy*, vol. 85 (April 1977), pp. 395–402; Douglas D. Purvis, "Dynamic Models of Portfolio Behavior," and Gary Smith, "Dynamic Models of Portfolio Behavior: Comment on Purvis," *American Economic Review*, vol. 68 (June 1978), pp. 403–16.

6. These points are discussed further in chapter 22.

budget constraint, however, home-government actions affecting income-account flows ineluctably have implications for home-government policies concerned with asset stocks, and vice versa.

The interactions between fiscal policy and domestic monetary policy have already been discussed in chapter 14. In an open economy the "external" manifestations of the interactions among the components of macroeconomic policy—the inevitably close links between external monetary policy and domestic (fiscal as well as monetary) policies—are no less important.

The interrelationships that constrain macroeconomic policy as a whole can be stated, mechanically but revealingly, in all the following ways:[7]

> It is not possible for the unborrowed monetary base of the home country to increase unless the world private sector's holdings of home-government debt are reduced, or foreign-government claims on the home government are reduced, or the home government's external reserve assets are increased, or the home government's budget is in deficit.

> It is not possible for the holdings of home-government debt by the world private sector to increase unless foreign-government claims on the home government are reduced, or the home government's external reserve assets are increased, or the unborrowed monetary base of the home country is reduced, or the home government's budget is in deficit.

> An increase in the home government's external reserve assets necessarily entails an increase in foreign-government claims on the home government, or an increase in the world private sector's holdings of claims on the home government (unborrowed monetary base or government securities), or a surplus in the home government's budget.

> If the external reserve liabilities of the home government (foreign-government claims on the home government) are to be increased, then the world private sector's holdings of home-government debt must be reduced, or the external reserve assets of the home government must rise, or the unborrowed monetary base of the home country must decline, or the home government's budget must be in deficit.

> A surplus in the home-government's budget necessarily entails an increase in the home government's external reserve assets, or a decrease in foreign-government claims on the home government, or a decrease in the world private sector's holdings of government debt, or a decrease in the unborrowed monetary base of the home country.

No one of these statements is more accurate than any other. Each merely restates the identity 21-7a in words. Still, the identity is no trifling matter. Just as the American writer Margaret Fuller accepted the universe, so should national policymakers accept the consolidated budget constraint. The constraint inevitably holds no matter what policies are pursued by the home central bank and the home fiscal authority. It can be ignored when policy is made or analyzed, but can never

---

7. Each of these five statements neglects the term ΔOA^G (changes in the "other assets" of the consolidated home government).

be violated. If it *is* ignored, policy actions may have results very different from what the policymakers intend.[8]

Judging from the consolidated government budget constraint alone, a policymaker might think that the openness of an economy provides an extra degree of flexibility for national macroeconomic policy. In contrast with the hypothetical situation of a closed economy, for example, the policymaker might interpret the possibility of increases in the home government's external reserve assets as providing elbow room for a government budget surplus without a concomitant need for reducing the private sector's holdings of home reserve money or government securities. Or the policymaker might argue that the openness of the economy permits the supply of home reserve money to be expanded without the necessity of the home government running a budget deficit or retiring debt securities in the hands of the private sector.[9] Strictly speaking, these statements are true; no restatement of an ex post identity can render it false. As part 3 shows and chapter 25 further emphasizes, however, the issue of policy flexibility for an individual nation appears in a different light when policymakers abandon a myopic national perspective.

The Holistic Unity of National Macroeconomic Policy

Although analysis of macroeconomic policy should be disciplined by an awareness of the consolidated government budget identity, the only way to ascertain the particular manner that identity binds is to specify the operating regimes through which policy actions are implemented. The concept of *policy regimen* (see chapter 14) refers to the complete collection of operating regimes and procedures that characterizes the macroeconomic policy behavior of the home government (central bank plus fiscal authority). For an open economy, a policy regimen has four components: a budgetary operating regime, a set of institutional procedures for the initial financing of a budget surplus or deficit (these first two constituting the fiscal-policy operating regime), an operating regime for domestic monetary policy, and finally an operating regime—together with supranational constraints, if any—for external monetary policy.

When the options for external monetary policy are added to the wide range of options for domestic policies shown in figure 14-1, the number of policy regimens that are theoretically conceivable becomes very large.

Analysts of national policy actions and their effects need to be aware of this multiplicity of alternative regimens. A national government can adopt, or at least try to adopt, any one of the potentially available regimens. To predict or study the consequences of the government's policy actions, therefore, it is first essential to identify fully and carefully the regimen within which the actions take place.

8. The story goes that when Margaret Fuller's comment, "I accept the universe," was reported to Thomas Carlyle, he retorted: "By God, she'd better!"

9. Germany in the period after World War II provides a concrete example. Policymakers did not wish to run a deficit in the government budget (indeed, in the early years of the period they were constrained from doing so by constitutional sanctions), and there was only a small amount of marketable government debt outstanding to the private sector. German policymakers wanted the monetary base to expand pari passu with the expanding economy. Fairly steady increases in Germany's external reserve assets provided an escape valve for the German economy that permitted policymakers to expand the monetary base and avoid budget deficits without making major alterations in the institutions and practices of debt management.

All parts of the policy regimen within which a home-government policy action occurs are analytically germane. Hence it is not sufficient to recognize that the consequences of an exchange-market-intervention action or a devaluation of the home currency cannot be correctly analyzed without specifying the operating regime for domestic monetary policy. Nor is it sufficient merely to specify the external monetary regime before analyzing the consequences of a domestic open-market operation or a change in the level of an interest-rate instrument. The logic of chapter 20 applies with equal force to fiscal policy. The effects of a given change in an exogenous instrument of either external or domestic monetary policy depend critically on the fiscal-policy operating regime followed by the home government. The consequences of a reduction in tax rates or an increase in discretionary government expenditures cannot be correctly analyzed without first specifying the relevant operating regimes for both domestic and external monetary policy.

A careful analyst is thus driven to the conclusion that *any division of national macroeconomic policy into compartments labeled "fiscal policy," "domestic monetary policy," and "external monetary policy" is fundamentally arbitrary and disguises the holistic unity of the whole.* In principle, an analytical compartmentalization is impossible.

This conclusion should not be misinterpreted: the issues highlighted in chapters 14 and 20 are neither linguistic nor taxonomic. Nothing important turns on where the semantic boundaries between the various facets of national macroeconomic policy are drawn; analysts can name or classify the different facets anything they like.[10] The critical point is that, wherever the semantic boundaries are drawn, *analysis* has to integrate across them.

To emphasize the symbiosis among the components of macroeconomic policy is not to claim that national fiscal and monetary authorities make decisions in a unified, coordinated manner. A nation's fiscal authority and central bank can—unwittingly or deliberately—work at cross-purposes (see chapter 18). Even within the central bank, the international department's foreign-exchange trading desk may operate somewhat independently of the domestic department; the domestic department may react to the actions of the international department, with neither being sufficiently sensitive to the implications of the operating procedures.

Regardless of the presence or absence of self-conscious analytical integration across institutional boundaries, however, there is a residual "unifier": the budget and balance-sheet constraints. Individual members of the crew working a sailing ship are, inescapably, in the same boat. The sailors trimming the jib and manning the helm can certainly work at cross-purposes. On a disorganized ship, they can act on different estimates of the weather conditions and even seek to direct the ship towards different destinations. If an observer studies the consequences of the crew's actions for the behavior of the ship, however, he can scarcely analyze the effects of what is done with the rudder without taking into account the way the sails are trimmed. No more so in macroeconomics can analysts appraise the consequences of policy actions ignoring the holistic unity of overall national policy.

10. If it seems convenient, for example, analysts may without any harm define a "pure" fiscal-policy action, a "pure" domestic monetary-policy action, and a "pure" exchange-market-intervention action. With such definitions and terms, however, it is essential not to let semantic purity be a stumbling block to correct analysis.

CHAPTER TWENTY-TWO

Fixed versus Flexible Exchange Rates

GIVEN the background in chapters 20 and 21, the analysis now turns to the controversial issue of whether the objectives of a nation's monetary policy may be better promoted by permitting or preventing variability in exchange rates.

Traditionally, questions about exchange-rate variability have been debated in terms of the polar cases of perfectly "fixed" exchange rates (an exchange-rate peg) and perfectly "flexible" exchange rates (an external-reserves peg). As this chapter shows, however, adequate analysis of the external aspects of monetary policy is not possible so long as attention is restricted to those two pegging regimes. What is worse, the points of greatest practical relevance for policymakers are lost sight of altogether when the debate about exchange-rate variability is forced into that procrustean bed.

Greater Variability in Exchange Rates

The preeminent requirement for avoiding analytical confusion when discussing greater variability in exchange rates is to attach a precise meaning to "greater." Greater compared to what? Over what time period should the comparison be made? Until a benchmark situation in which exchange rates are "less variable" is carefully specified, propositions about greater variability are amorphous and incapable of being proved either true or false.

Careless comparisons of "fixed" and "flexible" exchange rates use a hypothetical benchmark situation in which exchange rates are locked together, permanently and successfully. But that benchmark is a never-never land.

If the permanent locking of exchange rates is postulated as taking place while other existing characteristics of nations remain unchanged, the analytical implications of that assumption are highly implausible. Given that the economic interdependence of most nations is significant but still only intermediate, given that political sovereignty drives governments to pursue unabashedly national objectives, and given that private economic units form expectations of exchange-rate changes and alter the currency denomination of their assets and liabilities in anticipation of actual changes, the likelihood for most nations of a rigid pegging of exchange rates being successfully maintained over an indefinitely long period is small enough that it can be neglected. Indeed, an analyst verges on nonsense to postulate a benchmark situation in which "everything else is unchanged" among a group of nations except for a rigid pegging of their currencies to each other.[1]

On the other hand, if the permanent locking of exchange rates is postulated as occurring simultaneously with hypothetical changes in many other characteristics of nations—including structural changes that render the nations' economies much more homogeneous and the objectives of their governments much more compatible—the benchmark situation may have theoretical interest but has no practical relevance to the real world economy and polity of the 1970s and 1980s.[2]

It is easier to dismiss implausible or irrelevant benchmark situations for "less variability" than to specify an appropriate benchmark. The difficulties in making practical comparisons among different types of exchange-rate variability may be illustrated with a diagram. Consider figure 22-1, in which four different hypothetical evolutions of some nation's economy are postulated. Each evolution is assumed to start on the same initial date (t_0) and with identical initial conditions throughout the home economy and the world economy. The diagram plots the time paths for the exchange rate and the quantity of external reserve assets associated with each evolution.

All four evolutions assume a set of events occurring at and subsequent to t_0 that put pressure on (among other variables) the exchange rate or external reserve assets or both. The structure of the home economy, the national objectives of the home policymakers, and the finite size of home external reserves make it impossible to maintain the exchange rate "permanently" at the initial level. The differences among the four cases result from different assumptions about the external operating regime used by the home central bank. In case A, the external regime is an exchange-rate peg and the exchange rate is thus held rigidly unchanged until the large loss in external reserves forces a devaluation of the home currency (at time t_2); subsequent to the devaluation, the rate is again held unchanged at the new depreciated level. In case B, external reserve assets are held rigidly unchanged (an external-reserves peg) while the exchange rate floats freely. In case C, the exchange rate is

1. The comparison criticized in the text is an example of a logical error to which John Stuart Mill drew attention over a century ago in his *A System of Logic, Ratiocinative and Inductive*, published in 1843, reprinted in J. M. Robson, ed., *Mill's Collected Works* (University of Toronto Press, 1974), vols. 7 and 8: "In order to apply . . . the most perfect of the methods of experimental inquiry, the Method of Difference, we require to find two instances, which tally in every particular except the one which is the subject of inquiry. If two nations can be found which are alike in all natural advantages and disadvantages; whose people resemble each other in every quality . . .; whose habits, usages, opinions, laws and institutions are the same in all respects, except that one of them has a more protective tariff . . .; if one of these nations is found to be rich, and the other poor, or one richer than the other, this will be an *experimentum crucis:* a real proof by experience, which of the two systems is most favourable to national riches. But the supposition that two such instances can be met with is manifestly absurd. . . . Two nations which agreed in everything except their commercial policy, would agree also in that" (Book VI, chap. 7, pp. 881–82).

I learned of this quotation from Brian M. Barry, who points out the analogous error some observers make in asking "what would have happened if everything else had been the same in a country except the inflation rate"; see his "Does Democracy Cause Inflation? A Study of the Political Ideas of Some Economists," paper prepared for the conference on "The Politics and Sociology of Global Inflation," Brookings Institution, December 1978. Leon Lindberg and Charles Maier are editing the conference papers for publication.

2. Association of exchange-rate "flexibility" with a hypothetical situation in which the amounts of external reserve assets and liabilities are permanently frozen poses similar, if less severe, difficulties. Present-day central banks have the *ability* to refrain altogether from market purchases or sales of foreign-currency assets and from issuance or repayments of external liabilities. Yet in practice no central bank does refrain completely. The polar case of "pure" flexible exchange rates maintained "permanently" is thus also of interest primarily for theoretical and pedagogical purposes.

Figure 22-1. *Time Paths of the Exchange Rate and External Reserve Assets for Four Different Evolutions of a Nation's Economy*

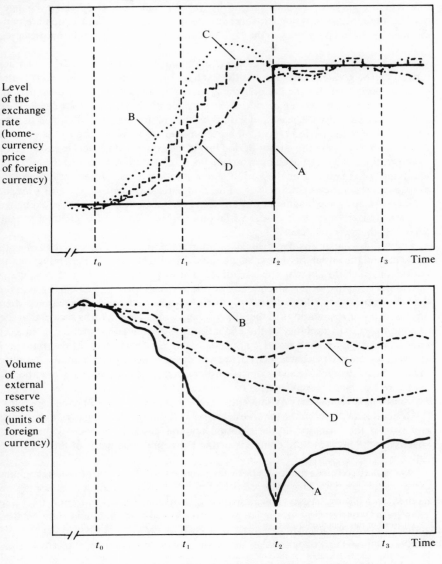

held unchanged within each short-run period but is varied, partly in response to market pressures, from one short-run period to the next (a discretionary exchange-rate regime). Case D is characterized by variable amounts of official exchange-market intervention within each short-run period, decisions about which are conditioned by market pressures on the exchange rate (a discretionary external-reserves regime).

Which of the four evolutions of the economy assumed in figure 22-1 is characterized by the greatest variability in the exchange rate, and which the least? If the comparison is made for the period from t_0 to t_1, both the end-of-period and period-average levels of the exchange rate differ significantly among the four cases; case A is characterized by the least and case B by the greatest amount of exchange-rate variability. For the period t_1 to t_2, the period-average levels of the exchange rate differ much more than the end-of-period levels; customary statistical measures (for example, the variance of each time series) would rank case A as having the *greatest* variability of the four. For the period t_2 to t_3, both the end-of-period and period-average levels of the rate differ little. If the comparison is made for the entire longer run period t_0 to t_3, the beginning-of-period and end-of-period levels of the exchange rate are similar for all four cases; variability within the period is greatest for the "fixed-exchange-rate" case.[3]

Figure 22-1 illustrates five critically important points. (1) Comparisons of both the level and the variability of exchange rates can differ markedly depending on the period for which the comparison is made. (2) The ex post variability of the exchange rate under a regime of an infrequently adjusted exchange-rate peg can be *greater* than the ex post variability under freely flexible exchange rates during periods when devaluations or revaluations of the "fixed" peg occur. That in turns means that the ex ante expected variability of the exchange rate can be either greater or smaller under "fixed" rates than under "flexible" rates. (3) Either type of discretionary external regime can be characterized, even in shorter runs, by substantial variability in *both* the exchange rate and external reserve assets. (4) Compared with either an exchange-rate peg ("fixed" rates) or an external-reserves peg ("flexible" rates), a discretionary regime may exhibit either more or less variability in exchange rates. (5) Generalizations about the relative degree of variability of exchange rates between any two of the four archetypal external regimes cannot be made without first specifying the period of the comparison and the actual time paths of the exchange rate.[4]

Again note the close analogies between external and domestic operating regimes for monetary policy. The polar case of "pure" flexible exchange rates may be likened to a "pure" reserve-aggregate peg in which the central bank fixes the quantity of some home-currency aggregate on its balance sheet and refrains altogether from intervening in home-currency securities markets. The issue of exchange-rate variability is analogous to the "domestic" issue of variability in interest rates.

___

3. This and the following paragraph leave open the difficult (and usually ignored) issue of whether the statistical variances of different time series of the exchange rate are the most appropriate measures to use in comparing their "variability."

4. These points are usually obscured in theoretical analyses of exchange-rate flexibility because that literature concentrates on the polar cases of a rigid fixing of the quantity of external reserves or a rigid fixing of the exchange rate. Since *permanent* pegging of the exchange rate is an implausible assumption if the analysis purports to deal with nonhomogeneous nations with differing national objectives, the traditional theoretical analysis of fixed exchange rates must be construed as presuming pegging of the rate *for the time being* (see text that follows for further discussion).

Compared with either an interest-rate peg ("fixed" interest rates) or a reserve-aggregate peg ("flexible" interest rates), the discretionary interest-rate and discretionary reserve-aggregate regimes may exhibit either more or less variability in interest rates; the outcome of the comparison depends on the time period selected and the specific paths followed by the interest rate.[5]

Undeniably, dissimilarities exist between external and domestic regimes. Though supranational treaties or understandings may constrain a nation's freedom of action with respect to external regimes, no supranational constraints have been applied to interest-rate variability or to fluctuations in home-currency quantities on the balance sheets of central banks. Such supranational constraints on domestic regimes have not even been seriously proposed.[6]

Although once of great significance, this first source of dissimilarity is no longer important; individual national governments now have wide latitude to try to implement external regimes of their own choosing and to encourage or discourage exchange-rate variability. Accordingly, at least for the time being, supranational constraints do not provide a rationale for analyzing a single nation's choice of external regime by criteria different from those used to select the domestic regime.

A more important dissimilarity between external and domestic regimes arises from the fact that all nations cannot *successfully* implement external regimes of their own independent choosing. Even in the absence of supranational constraints, a single nation's policymakers have effective freedom of choice only to the extent that policymakers in one or more foreign nations are willing to remain passive.

This second dissimilarity, and more generally the nonindependence of national monetary policies, is emphasized in chapter 25. Until then, however, a myopic national perspective is retained and it is therefore *assumed* that an individual nation can successfully implement any external regime it deems will best facilitate national objectives. Given that assumption, there is *no* valid reason for a nation's central bank to treat the problems of external instrument choice and external instrument variation any differently from the corresponding domestic problems.

Instrument Options for Monetary Policy in a Comparative-Statics Framework

An analytical framework of some sort is a prerequisite for evaluating alternative views about exchange-rate variability and, more broadly, about instrument choice and instrument variation for monetary policy. Thus the discussion will again make use of simplified illustrative models. Here in part 5, it is essential that the analytical framework incorporate, if only in highly schematic form, the key macroeconomic relationships that link a nation's economy with the rest of the world. Appendix C describes the relationships included in the illustrative models and outlines briefly how those relationships interact.[7]

5. The fact that these analogies are seldom appreciated is testimony to the asymmetrical manner in which the external aspects of monetary policy have been traditionally perceived and described.
6. Zealous recommendations early in the century for an "ideal" gold standard are a possible exception.
7. The limited purpose of appendix C is to summarize an internally consistent framework for studying macroeconomic outcomes in an open economy. It omits most descriptive details that would merit elaboration in a more technical theoretical treatment; and it does not present a rigorous analysis of the models based on that framework. Many readers may find it a help to read the first portion of appendix C (Comparative-Statics Relationships) before continuing the discussion in the text.

The models are in the tradition of the small and open paradigm and thus ignore the influences of events in the home nation on economic variables in the rest of the world. In other respects, however, the illustrative framework allows for the conditions of intermediate interdependence specified in part 3. Each nation imports a tradable good from the other because spending units in each nation, in addition to consuming nontradable and tradable goods produced within the nation, are accustomed to consuming goods produced abroad. The framework allows for the possibility, however, that most residents of each nation are less familiar with or do not prefer imported goods and thus (at prevailing relative prices) allocate the bulk of their expenditures to goods produced at home. Nonbanks and banks in the home nation are assumed to hold securities denominated in the foreign currency. Foreign economic units invest in home-currency securities. Yet this financial interdependence is also intermediate; neither home nor foreign economic units regard the securities issued in the two currencies as perfect substitutes.

As described in the first portion of appendix C, the time horizon of analysis for which the illustrative models are relevant is the short run and the method of analysis is comparative statics. Most financial and many nonfinancial variables are assumed to have time to adjust to policy actions or to nonpolicy exogenous disturbances. The period considered is assumed to be short enough, however, for the analysis to ignore changes in asset stocks and wealth due to saving, investment in new capital goods, imbalances in the government budget, and imbalances in the current account of the balance of payments. Those dynamic changes in asset stocks and their repercussions are discussed later in the chapter, after the conclusions of the comparative-statics analysis have been presented.

The various components of the comparative-statics framework in appendix C may be combined into a small number of key relationships. The financial-sector equations may be summarized in terms of excess demand conditions in the "markets" for home deposit money, for the home monetary base, and for securities denominated in the home currency. The real-sector equations may be consolidated into supply functions and excess-demand conditions for nontradable goods and home-produced tradable goods, a function for real national potential to consume, an equation for the government budget position, and definitions of real national product and nominal national product. Taken together, those relationships constitute an internally consistent system of eleven equations in the following thirteen endogenous (or potentially endogenous) variables:

y_N home output of nontradable goods
p_N price of nontradable goods
y_T home output of tradable goods
p_T price of home-produced tradable goods
y real national product
Y nominal national product
$\bar{y}_d$ real potential to consume
Z^G government budget surplus or deficit
M home money stock (home-currency deposits in home banks)
π exchange rate (home currency price of foreign currency)
XA^{CB} home-currency value of external reserve assets
r interest rate on home-currency securities
H home monetary base

In the context of the illustrative framework, the home policymakers have the choice of using either the interest rate r or the monetary base H as their domestic monetary instrument. Under the assumption that the home policymakers can successfully select their preferred external operating regime, they can also choose between using the exchange rate π or the quantity of external reserves XA^{CB} as their external instrument. When these instrument choices are made, the comparative-statics relationships become a complete system of eleven equations capable of determining eleven endogenous variables.

Because the frame of reference of the analysis is comparative statics, these instrument options are the choice between an interest-rate peg and a reserve-aggregate peg and the choice between an exchange-rate peg and an external-reserves peg. There are thus four possible combinations of operating regimes:

(1)   a "flexprice" approach to both domestic and external policy (reserve-aggregate peg with external-reserves peg)

(2)   a "fixprice" approach to both domestic and external policy (interest-rate peg with exchange-rate peg)

(3)   a "fixprice" domestic policy and a "flexprice" external policy (interest-rate peg with external-reserves peg)

(4)   a "flexprice" domestic policy and a "fixprice" external policy (reserve-aggregate peg with exchange-rate peg)

The first and third options correspond to the case traditionally emphasized in the theoretical literature of "freely flexible exchange rates." The second and fourth represent the case of "exchange rates fixed for the time being."

The fact that four different monetary-policy regimens are possible in the context of the common illustrative framework means, strictly speaking, that an analysis of instrument choice must work with four models rather than one (see appendix C). The behavior of such endogenous variables as the prices p_N and p_T and the outputs y_N and y_T differ significantly among the four models.

Pegging External Reserves versus Pegging the Exchange Rate

This section of the chapter uses the four models based on the illustrative framework to extend the closed-economy analysis of chapter 19. It shows that unforeseen disturbances have different impacts on the ultimate-target variables of the home policymakers for different external as well as domestic operating regimes. Some types of disturbances have the least unfavorable consequences if the exchange rate adjusts while external reserve assets and liabilities remain unchanged. But other types of disturbances have the least unfavorable consequences if the exchange rate remains unchanged while external reserve assets and liabilities respond to the disturbance. This section thus concludes that *neither of the pegging rules of thumb— "price" adjustment of the exchange rate or "quantity" adjustment of external reserve assets—can possibly be the preferred means for coping with all types of disturbances.*

This conclusion has far-reaching implications for macroeconomic policy decisions. Despite the fact that it is merely an extension of a proposition whose validity for "domestic" policy is now widely accepted among economists, few macroeconomists and policymakers as yet appreciate its significance.[8]

"Optimal" Policy in the Comparative-Statics Framework

In the comparative-statics context presumed here, the decision facing the policymakers in the home central bank is to choose instrument settings at the beginning of the period being analyzed. Those settings are then maintained unchanged during the period of analysis.

Assume as before that home policymakers have certain macroeconomic magnitudes they select as ultimate-target variables and that they formulate their preferences in terms of a loss function defined over targeted and actual levels of those variables. For example, suppose the policymakers specify real national product y and the consumption price index P_C as their target variables.[9] Assume that the settings for the instruments of home fiscal policy have already been chosen. Suppose finally that the home policymakers have made forecasts of all the noncontrolled exogenous forces that influence their ultimate-target variables. In the illustrative framework here, those forces include foreign real and nominal income (y^* and Y^*), the foreign-currency price of home imports (p^*), the foreign interest rate (r^*), the medium-run expected exchange rate ($\hat{\pi}$), and the various stochastic errors representing other "disturbances" (for example, exogenous shifts in the saving function of home nonbanks and exogenous shifts in asset demands).

For each of the four monetary-policy regimens—for each variant of the common analytical framework—there exists a different set of reduced-form equations for the ultimate-target variables. Given any one of the four sets of reduced-form equations and given the loss function and forecasts of noncontrolled exogenous forces, the reader can imagine the policymakers selecting "optimal" values of the settings for the instruments used in that regimen. (See chapters 11 and 19 for discussions of the analytical procedures involved.)

The question of immediate interest here is to compare the consequences of choosing one monetary-policy regimen rather than another—and in particular the differing consequences associated with fixprice versus flexprice external operating regimes. For that purpose, suppose the instrument settings have been chosen optimally for each of the four regimens at the beginning of the period being analyzed

---

8. Some notable exceptions in the recent literature are Russell S. Boyer, "Optimal Foreign Exchange Market Intervention," *Journal of Political Economy*, vol. 86 (December 1978), pp. 1045–55; Willem Buiter, "Optimal Foreign Exchange Market Intervention with Rational Expectations," Research Memorandum 216 (Princeton University, Econometric Research Program, November 1977) and in J. Martin and A. Smith, eds., *Trade and Payments Adjustments under Flexible Exchange Rates* (Macmillan, forthcoming); and Dale W. Henderson, "Financial Policies in Open Economies," *American Economic Review*, vol. 69 (May 1979), pp. 232–39. See also Jerome L. Stein, "The Optimum Foreign Exchange Market," *American Economic Review*, vol. 53 (June 1963), pp. 384–402; Edward Tower and Thomas D. Willett, "The Theory of Optimum Currency Areas and Exchange-Rate Flexibility," Special Paper in International Economics 11 (Princeton University, 1976); and Stanley W. Black, *Floating Exchange Rates and National Economic Policy* (Yale University Press, 1977).

9. The price of imports is relevant both for appraising inflation and for measuring the real purchasing power (over foreign as well as home goods and services) of the nation's current real output. An example of a simple loss function for the comparative-statics case, like that used in part 4, would be

$$L = w_1(y - y^\circ)^2 + w_2(P_C - P_C^\circ)^2,$$

where y° and P_C° denote specific target values for national output and the national consumption price index and w_1 and w_2 are weights indicating the relative importance attached to the two components of loss.

but that, as time passes, one or another sort of unforeseen disturbance occurs. For a variety of such disturbances, the question is then asked, Which of the four regimes best mitigates the adverse consequences of the disturbance for the policymakers' ultimate-target variables?[10]

Exogenous Asset Shift out of Home Securities into Home Money

Consider first an unforeseen once-for-all shift in asset preferences by home nonbanks out of home-government securities into deposit money. This financial-sector disturbance might be labeled as "internal" in origin, since it stems from a change in the behavior of home economic units and since the home-government securities and the deposit money are both denominated in the home currency.[11]

The unexpected shift in asset preferences puts *incipient* pressures on financial variables. The *actual* adjustments in those variables depend on how domestic and external monetary policy are implemented. The incipient pressures include tendencies for the home interest rate to rise and for the home currency to appreciate.

Under the interest-rate peg with exchange-rate peg, neither the home interest rate nor the exchange rate can move in response to the disturbance. The incipient pressures on them are countered by central-bank open-market operations: the central bank purchases home securities in the "domestic" security market and purchases one or another form of foreign-currency asset through its intervention in the exchange market. Both external reserves and the home monetary base rise (the latter more than the former), accommodating the exogenous shift in private asset preferences through offsetting quantity adjustments on the central bank's balance sheet. As a result, the disturbance has no effect on the goods markets; the prices of nontraded goods, home-produced traded goods, and imports remain unchanged and there is no fall in output.

If the home central bank implements an interest-rate peg with external-reserves peg, the exogenous increase in the demand for money cannot move the interest rate, but it does push the home currency to appreciate. This appreciation tends to create excess supply in both home goods markets; other things being equal, home and foreign consumers wish to switch expenditures away from home-produced goods, while home producers may wish to increase production because of the initial fall in the price of the imported good relative to home-produced goods.[12] Prices of home-produced goods thus fall, which in turn tends to impart a net contractionary impetus to home output.[13]

Under a reserve-aggregate peg with exchange-rate peg, the incipient pressure on the exchange rate to appreciate is resisted by "external" open-market purchases

---

10. If the behavioral coefficients in the common analytical framework are specified as fixed parameters rather than as uncertain random variables and if the instrument settings are chosen optimally for each of the four regimes, the expected values of the outcomes for ultimate-target variables (before the occurrence of unforeseen disturbances) do not differ among the four regimes. The variances of the outcomes, and hence the expected loss associated with each regime, do of course differ.

11. In the illustrative models, the disturbance can be represented as an unforeseen increase in the "error" disturbance e_{MD}^N and an offsetting decrease of equal size in e_{SD}^N; see equations C-9a and C-10a, appendix C.

12. See appendix C, equations C-39 through C-41, C-43 through C-45, C-24, and C-25.

13. The downward move in prices occurs regardless of the magnitudes of structural parameters in the behavioral relationships. The direction of movement of output may be sensitive to the relative magnitudes of supply responses to the various price changes.

of foreign-currency assets. The home interest rate is allowed to move upward, however, so that excess supply in the home goods markets is created through consumption and investment responses to the interest rate.[14] In this case too, therefore, the prices of home goods fall and home output tends to contract.

Under the fourth regimen, the reserve-aggregate peg with external-reserves peg, the unforeseen shift in home asset preferences can generate excess supply in the home goods markets in both of the ways just described. The appreciation of the home currency leads, other things being equal, to expenditure switching and supply responses, while any upward movement in the interest rate lowers the total of aggregate demand for home goods.[15] Once again, therefore, the price and output magnitudes that are the ultimate-target variables of the home policymakers fall below the levels at which the policymakers are aiming.

For an unforeseen, once-for-all shift in private asset preferences into home money out of home securities, therefore, the home policymakers' ultimate-target variables will be least adversely affected if the central bank institutes an interest-rate peg with exchange-rate peg. Either of the regimens with a flexprice external operating regime permits the financial-sector disturbance to impart a contractionary impetus to the ultimate-target variables in the short run through an appreciation of the home currency. A fixprice external regime combined with a flexprice domestic regime still permits the exogenous increase in money demand to have an impact on prices and output in the short run. For this type of disturbance, the preferable regimen allows all financial quantities to adjust—including, of course, the money stock—holding both the exchange rate and the interest rate at their predisturbance levels.[16]

Exogenous Asset Shift out of Home Securities into Foreign Securities

Now consider a different type of financial-market disturbance, an unforeseen once-for-all shift by private economic units out of home-currency securities into foreign-currency securities. This exogenous shift could be initiated by home nonbanks or by home banks; or it could be initiated by foreign nonbanks or by foreign banks. In the first two cases, the disturbance could conceivably be labeled internal in origin and in the last two cases, external.[17] For the purposes of the discussion

---

14. See appendix C, equations C-36 and C-42.

15. While the home currency definitely appreciates under the reserve-aggregate peg with external-reserves peg, there may be some uncertainty whether the interest rate rises, and if so to what degree. (The falls in output and prices generated by the exchange-rate appreciation lead, other things being equal, to a reduction in the transactions-related demand for money; this source of downward pressure on the home interest rate works against the other pressures tending to make the interest rate rise.)

16. Among the three regimens that are inferior from the point of view of protecting ultimate-target variables from adverse impacts of an exogenous increase in money demand, the reserve-aggregate peg with external-reserves peg probably affords the least protection. The precise ranking of the three depends on the structural characteristics of the behavioral relationships in the economy. Some combinations of characteristics associated with the level of the reserve requirement imposed on home banks' deposit liabilities, with the transactions-related demands for money and securities of home nonbanks, and with the portfolio preferences of home banks, for example, might conceivably render the outcome less adverse under a reserve-aggregate peg with external-reserves peg than under an interest-rate peg with external-reserves peg. The ranking also depends on dynamic effects that are not captured in the comparative-statics models.

17. In the illustrative models in appendix C, the disturbance can be represented as an unforeseen increase in the exogenous term e^i_{FD} offset by an equivalent decrease in e^i_{SD}, where the superscript i can be any one of N, B, FN, and FB.

here, however, the residence and the identity of the asset owners are of no intrinsic interest; the consequences for home economic variables are identical regardless of the particular asset-holder responsible for initiating the disturbance.

The incipient pressures on financial variables resulting from this private-sector switch out of home-currency into foreign-currency securities include tendencies for the home interest rate to rise and for the home currency to depreciate.

Under the regimen of the interest-rate peg with exchange-rate peg, external reserve assets decline by the amount of the private asset shift. The home central bank's intervention in the exchange market and domestic financial markets results de facto in an exchange of assets with the private investors whose portfolio preferences have changed. The central bank buys home securities in a "domestic" transaction and sells foreign-currency assets in an "external" transaction; both open-market operations are equivalent in size to the initial private asset shift. The consequence of this central-bank accommodation of private asset preferences at an unchanged interest rate and exchange rate is to leave home goods markets, and hence home prices and output, undisturbed.

The outcome is essentially the same under a reserve-aggregate peg with exchange-rate peg. External reserve assets decline by the amount of the private asset shift. Although the central bank pegs the home monetary base rather than the home interest rate, the home interest rate does not need to move to clear asset markets. The exogenous pegging of the exchange rate and the endogenous lack of movement in the home interest rate prevent the initial disturbance from having any effects on home prices and output.

The effects of the shift out of home-currency into foreign-currency securities are quite different, however, if the home policymakers adopt a flexprice external regime instead of pegging the exchange rate. Under the interest-rate peg with external-reserves peg, the increased demand for foreign-currency-denominated assets and the increased supply of home-currency-denominated assets (at the predisturbance exchange rate) require a depreciation of the home currency to clear asset markets. Because of incipient upward pressure on the home interest rate, the central bank is obliged to increase the home monetary base (conduct "domestic" open-market purchases) to keep the interest rate pegged. The depreciation of the currency has the effect of creating excess demand in both home goods markets; thus the prices of both home-produced goods rise, which in turn tends to induce an expansion in home output.

Under the reserve-aggregate peg with external-reserves peg, the private asset shift triggers both a depreciation of the home currency and a rise in the home interest rate. These developments have contrary implications for home prices and outputs. The depreciation of the currency tends, other things being equal, to generate excess demand in home goods markets. The rise in the interest rate, however, tends to dampen excess demand. The rise in the interest rate thus works to mitigate the adverse inflationary consequences that would otherwise be associated with the currency depreciation.

To summarize: an exogenous private shift out of home-currency into foreign-currency securities is a second example of a disturbance for which the adverse effects on home ultimate-target variables are greater under a flexprice external regime than under a fixprice external regime. In the case of this disturbance, it happens that the interest-rate peg with exchange-rate peg and the reserve-aggregate peg with exchange-rate peg perform equally well in buffering the consequences of the disturbance. Variability in the exchange rate, on the other hand, transmits the disturbance to prices and output.[18]

Exogenous Shift in Saving by Home Residents

Next consider a quite different type of disturbance. Suppose home residents unexpectedly reduce the amount of disposable income they save, correspondingly increasing their consumption expenditures. Suppose the saving rate persists at the new lower level. For simplicity, assume that underlying tastes for the three goods are unchanged, so that consumption expenditures on the home nontraded good, on the home tradable good, and on imports go up proportionately to their weights in total consumption.[19] The initial effects of this exogenous "internal" disturbance are to create excess demand in the markets for both home-produced goods and to put incipient upward pressure on the home interest rate. As before, the subsequent effects depend on the operating regimes of the home central bank.

Under the interest-rate peg with exchange-rate peg, neither the interest rate nor the exchange rate can move to help eliminate the initial excess demand in home goods markets. That excess demand must therefore be eliminated by a combination of (1) upward movements in the prices of both home-produced goods, (2) an increase in imports (both consumption and investment expenditures on the imported good tend to rise due to expenditure switching), (3) a reduction in exports (expenditure switching by foreigners as the price of the home-produced tradable rises), and (4) increases in the outputs of both home goods (supply responses as the prices rise). The combination of these adjustments leads to a deficit in the current account in the balance of payments.[20] Under this dual fixprice regime, therefore, the unexpected exogenous reduction in saving raises home prices and output. Home ultimate-target variables get pushed above the levels desired and expected by the policymakers at the outset of the period.

Under the regime in which the exchange rate is pegged but the home interest rate is permitted to adjust, the excess demand in home goods markets also pushes up prices and output; but the increase in aggregate demand pulls up the home interest rate at the same time. The rise in the interest rate helps to mitigate the excess demand in goods markets (by inducing increased saving to offset some of the earlier exogenous reduction in saving, and by reducing investment expenditures)

18. A comparison of the outcomes under the two regimes permitting exchange-rate flexibility warns against the generalization that the regime incorporating flexibility in both the interest rate and the exchange rate is the worst of the four in coping with asset-market disturbances. In the example here, the regime generating the most adverse consequences for home prices and output could be the interest-rate peg with external-reserves peg.

19. In the illustrative models in appendix C, the disturbance can be represented as an unforeseen negative change in e_s in equation C-36, with $de_{cN} = de_{cT} = de_{cM} = 0$ in equations C-39 through C-41.

20. Over the short-run period for which the comparative-statics framework is relevant, the home central bank can either lose or gain external reserves. The direction of short-run change in external reserves depends on the relative strengths of the transactions-related demands for money and securities of home nonbanks, on the level of the reserve requirement imposed on home banks' liabilities, and on the portfolio preferences of home banks in allocating their investable assets. The current-account deficit does not put downward pressure on external reserves in the short-run comparative-statics model because the model ignores intercountry transfers of wealth (see text that follows).

and therefore serves to dampen somewhat the rise in prices and outputs. The adverse effects of the exogenous reduction in saving on home ultimate-target variables are therefore smaller under the reserve-aggregate peg with exchange-rate peg than under the interest-rate peg with exchange-rate peg. Although the current account in the balance of payments moves into deficit, the size of that deficit, unlike the deficit under the interest-rate peg with exchange-rate peg, is curbed somewhat by the rise in the home interest rate (because home absorption of imports is somewhat dampened and because real exports fall less as a result of the smaller rise in the home-currency price).

Under the interest-rate peg with external-reserves peg, the excess demand in goods markets created by the exogenous fall in saving again leads to an upward push on home prices and outputs. The interest rate, being pegged, cannot rise to help choke off the excess demand or to dampen the tendency toward a current-account deficit. The exchange rate is free to move, and the home currency depreciates. Other things being equal, however, this depreciation reinforces the excess demand in home goods markets (through expenditure switching and supply reduction effects). Simultaneously with these effects, the tendency toward a deficit in the current account of the balance of payments is somewhat alleviated. Loosely speaking, the depreciation of the home currency tends to bottle up the goods-markets effects of the disturbance within the home country rather than allow the consequences to spill over into other nations' goods markets through the current account in the balance of payments.[21]

Under the reserve-aggregate peg with external-reserves peg, both the exchange rate and the interest rate are free to adjust to the initial disturbance. The home interest rate rises but the home currency depreciates.[22] Thus the movements in these two key variables have opposite consequences for the demand for and supply of home-produced goods. The rise in the interest rate serves to choke off the excess demand while the currency depreciation tends to exacerbate it. Both "price" variables, on the other hand, have the same directional effect on the current-account deficit created by the exogenous reduction in saving; the rise in the interest rate reduces home absorption of imports, while the currency depreciation stimulates

21. Consequences of exchange-rate variability analogous to those highlighted here were studied by Svend Laursen and Lloyd A. Metzler, "Flexible Exchange Rates and the Theory of Employment," *Review of Economics and Statistics,* vol. 32 (November 1950), pp. 281–99; the Laursen-Metzler model, however, completely suppresses the capital account in the balance of payments and domestic financial markets. For other sources in which similar points are discussed, see Gottfried Haberler, "Comment," in Harry G. Johnson and Alexander K. Swoboda, eds., *The Economics of Common Currencies* (Allen and Unwin, 1973); Peter B. Kenen, "The Theory of Optimum Currency Areas: An Eclectic View," in Robert A. Mundell and Alexander K. Swoboda, *Monetary Problems of the International Economy* (University of Chicago Press, 1969); and Tower and Willett, "The Theory of Optimum Currency Areas and Exchange-Rate Flexibility."

22. Since the underlying comparative-statics model ignores long-run stock effects, the home currency can conceivably appreciate rather than depreciate (depending on the relative strengths of the transactions-related demands for money and securities of home nonbanks, on the level of the reserve requirement imposed on home banks' liabilities, and on the portfolio preferences of home banks in allocating their investable assets). The bottling up of the exogenous disturbance discussed in the text occurs only if the home currency depreciates. When the longer run stock effects are taken into account (see the discussion in text that follows), there seems little doubt that the home currency depreciates. These points about the direction of movement of the exchange rate also apply to the discussion of outcomes under the interest-rate peg with external-reserves peg in the preceding paragraph.

exports and dampens imports. Although home prices and output get blown off course under this regimen, the size of the deviation is less than under the interest-rate peg with external-reserves peg.

For the case of an exogenous reduction in the saving of home residents, therefore, the objectives of the home policymakers are likely to be best protected in the short run with an asymmetrical posture toward the domestic and the external operating regimes. Because the interest rate is free to rise to help dampen the excess demand for home-produced goods, home ultimate-target variables are less adversely affected, whatever the external regime, under the flexprice domestic regime of a reserve-aggregate peg. Because the home currency is free to depreciate, on the other hand, home ultimate-target variables are more adversely affected in the short run under the external-reserves peg than under the fixprice external regime of an exchange-rate peg, whatever the domestic regime. Flexibility of the exchange rate works to force more of the consequences of the exogenous shock on the home country (permitting less to be transmitted to the rest of the world through goods flows in the current account of the balance of payments). The preferred regimen for this type of disturbance, at least in the short run, is therefore the reserve-aggregate peg with exchange-rate peg; the worst of the four is the interest-rate peg with external-reserves peg.[23]

The qualification "in the short run" is important. Under both regimens employing the exchange-rate peg, external reserve assets will unambiguously decline as longer run stock effects influence the outcome (see below). If the nation's external reserves are small relative to that decline, the exchange-rate peg may be infeasible over a longer run regardless of its less unfavorable impacts on home prices and output.[24]

Exogenous Shift in Saving by Foreign Residents

The three disturbances so far analyzed have all been of a type best handled, at least in the short run, by the maintenance of an unchanged exchange rate. But there are many other types of disturbances for which a fixprice external regime can be inferior. Consider, for example, an "external" disturbance like the preceding "internal" shift in saving behavior: suppose foreign residents unexpectedly reduce the amount of their disposable income that is saved, correspondingly increasing their consumption both of foreign goods and of home-nation exports.

The initial effects of the increased foreign consumption are to create excess demand not only in goods markets abroad but also (through increased export

23. It can be shown that the *relative* prices of the two home-produced goods are altered by the exogenous reduction in home residents' saving.

24. As noted in appendix C, the analysis here implicitly holds the medium-run expected exchange rate ($\hat{\pi}$) unchanged. If, instead, this expected exchange rate were to change as well (for example, if the home currency is expected to be devalued under an exchange-rate peg or to remain at a depreciated level or even to depreciate further under an external-reserves peg after the effects of the initial exogenous excess demand begin to be observed in goods markets), the conclusions would have to be substantially modified. Under either regimen with the exchange-rate peg, declines in external reserves would be more severe and would persist over a succession of periods (reflecting both the capital-account consequences of the shift in expectations and the current-account deficit associated with the initial downward shift in saving). Hence there could be even greater doubts about the sustainability of the short-run policy of maintaining the exchange rate unchanged. If the expected exchange rate were to change (for example, if $\hat{\pi}$ were to rise) when an external-reserves peg was in force, the actual depreciation of the home currency would be larger than otherwise and hence the bottling up effects would also be exacerbated.

demand) in the market for home-produced tradable goods. The excess-demand pressure is also transmitted to the market for home nontraded goods as the price of the home-produced tradable good increases. The incipient pressures on financial variables include tendencies for the home currency to appreciate and for the home interest rate to rise.[25]

Under the interest-rate peg with exchange-rate peg, the home country's goods markets have the greatest exposure to the foreign shock. The home interest rate cannot rise and the home currency cannot appreciate to help choke off the excess demand. Home prices and outputs thus rise and the current account of the balance of payments moves into surplus as the foreign disturbance spills over strongly into home goods markets.

Under a reserve-aggregate peg with exchange-rate peg, the exchange rate still cannot move and the exogenous rise in foreign consumption again pushes the home country's current-account balance toward surplus. Since the home interest rate can adjust under this regimen, however, a rise in the interest rate serves to dampen the upward push on home prices and outputs that would otherwise occur.

When the exchange rate is free to move, the outcome for the home country can be quite different. Especially over a longer run, the exogenous reduction in foreign saving causes the home currency to appreciate. Other things being equal, this appreciation works against the upward forces on home prices and outputs stemming from the original disturbance. The flexibility in the exchange rate serves, as it were, to buffer the home goods market against the foreign shock. An appreciation of the home currency also serves to hold down the size of the current-account surplus in the home country's balance of payments. Conceivably, the home currency could appreciate by a large enough amount and the effects of the appreciation on the home goods markets could be strong enough to produce *declines* in home goods prices and a *contraction* in home output.[26] Between the two regimens using the flexprice external regime, the reserve-aggregate peg with external-reserves peg will probably perform better than the interest-rate peg with external-reserves peg in buffering home ultimate-target variables against the disturbance originating abroad. With the home policymakers pegging a domestic reserve aggregate, the home interest rate is free to move either up or down—whichever is needed—to complement the effects resulting from the adjustment in the exchange rate. If the home-currency appreciation would otherwise be large enough to cause a fall in home prices and output, for example, the interest rate can decline, thereby mitigating that contractionary impetus.

When an unexpected exogenous reduction in saving occurs abroad, therefore, the target variables of home policymakers tend to be blown furthest off course

---

25. In one-country models making use of the small and open paradigm, all major foreign macroeconomic variables are taken as exogenous. In principle, an exogenous reduction in saving by foreign residents would raise both foreign prices and foreign output. If the foreign central bank pursued a reserve-aggregate peg domestically, the reduction in foreign saving would also lead to a rise in the foreign interest rate. For the purposes of the discussion here, the exogenous reduction in foreign saving is assumed to result in a rise in foreign prices, real output, and real income, which in turn leads to an increased demand for home exports. The foreign interest rate, however, is assumed to be held constant at its predisturbance level; that is, the foreign central bank pursues an interest-rate peg as its domestic operating regime.

26. In other words, the effects of the appreciation could conceivably be so strong as to more than offset the initial excess-demand pressure from the foreign spurt in demand, thereby creating net excess supply in home goods markets (at the predisturbance levels of home output and prices).

under an interest-rate peg with exchange-rate peg. The smallest adverse consequences occur under the dual flexprice regimen of the reserve-aggregate peg with external-reserves peg. From a myopic national perspective, it is best to allow prompt "price" adjustment in response to real-sector disturbances originating abroad, thus bottling up the disturbances as much as possible within the foreign domain where they first occur.[27]

Summary Generalizations

For ease of reference and comparison, table 22-1 recapitulates the results of the preceding discussion in tabular form.

A more comprehensive and technical analysis of the comparative-statics models underlying the preceding discussion, including the analysis of still other types of disturbances, would be out of place here. In any case, the results in table 22-1 are sufficient to support the main conclusion of interest here, namely, that neither exchange-rate variability nor exchange-rate fixity can provide the best possible protection for home target variables against all types of disturbances.

Comparison of the illustrative cases summarized in table 22-1 suggests three important generalizations about the consequences of variability in exchange rates. First, when home policymakers let the exchange rate float freely, the impacts on goods prices and real output of unforeseen shifts in asset preferences among home-currency assets or between home-currency and foreign-currency assets ("financial-sector" disturbances) are more adverse than when the exchange rate is pegged. Second, for many unforeseen disturbances originating internally within the "real sector" of the home economy, the adverse effects on home economic activity are greater with variability of the exchange rate, at least in the short run, than when the exchange rate is pegged. Third, for many other unforeseen disturbances—for example, those originating abroad within the real sector of the foreign economy— the adverse impacts on home economic activity are greatest when home policymakers peg the exchange rate.

Although suggestive, these generalizations need to be supplemented or qualified with further observations. For one thing, as the analysis makes clear, it is not possible to determine which *external* pegging regime best facilitates home economic objectives in the face of a given disturbance without simultaneously studying the consequences of the two *domestic* pegging alternatives.

For another, the distinction between disturbances originating within the home country ("internal") and those originating abroad ("external") is not as straightforward as it might at first seem (recall the example of the switch in asset preferences between home-currency and foreign-currency assets in which the internal or external residency of the private investor was irrelevant). Furthermore, the classification of disturbances as originating within the "financial sector" or the "real sector" is also problematic. Consider, for example, the case of an exogenous shift in asset preferences by foreign nonbanks out of foreign-currency securities into foreign money. If foreign central banks operate with a reserve-aggregate peg domestically, this disturbance will alter foreign interest rates, goods prices, and real output, and hence have impacts on home goods markets through increased

---

27. The analysis of real-sector disturbances originating in the rest of the world is, if anything, more complex than the analysis of other types of disturbances. As suggested in note 25, conclusions are sensitive to the precise manner in which the small and open paradigm specifies foreign variables to be exogenous.

Table 22-1. *Short-Run Comparative-Statics Effects of Illustrative Nonpolicy Disturbances under Alternative Regimens for Home Monetary Policy*[a]

Type of nonpolicy disturbance	Summary of consequences under the four different monetary-policy regimens				Preferred regimen for coping with disturbance in short run
	Interest-rate peg with exchange-rate peg (1)	*Reserve-aggregate peg with exchange-rate peg (2)*	*Interest-rate peg with external-reserves peg (3)*	*Reserve-aggregate peg with external-reserves peg (4)*	
Exogenous asset shift out of home-currency securities into home deposit money (by home nonbanks)	External reserves and monetary base increase; prices and output unchanged	Interest rate rises; external reserves increase; prices and output decline	Home currency appreciates; prices and output decline	Home currency appreciates; interest rate probably rises; prices and output decline	Interest-rate peg with exchange-rate peg
Exogenous asset shift out of home-currency securities into foreign-currency securities	External reserves decline; monetary base, prices, and output unchanged	External reserves decline; interest rate, prices, and output unchanged	Home currency depreciates; monetary base increases; prices and output rise	Home currency depreciates; interest rate rises; prices and output are changed (probably rise)	Interest-rate peg with exchange-rate peg or reserve-aggregate peg with exchange-rate peg
Exogenous reduction in saving by home residents	External reserves decline; prices and output increase	Interest rate rises and external reserves decline; prices and output increase but less than under 1	Home currency depreciates; prices and output increase more than under 1	Home currency depreciates; interest rate rises; prices and output increase less than under 3 but probably more than under 2	Reserve-aggregate peg with exchange-rate peg
Exogenous reduction in saving by foreign residents	External reserves and monetary base increase; prices and output rise more than under other regimens	Interest rate rises and external reserves increase; prices and output rise but less than under 1	Home currency appreciates; prices and output probably rise (but could fall?)	Exchange rate and interest rate both change; prices and output change modestly (could rise or fall?)	Reserve-aggregate peg with external-reserves peg

a. This summary omits mention of the qualifications discussed in the text notes.

exports. Although in one sense the disturbance is unambiguously external and originates in the foreign financial sector, it will nonetheless be a complex combination of real-sector and financial-sector disturbances as it is transmitted to the home economy.

The preceding generalizations omit any explicit mention of the degree of openness of the national economy. Yet some aspects of the degree of openness—for example, the importance of the two tradable goods relative to the nontraded good in home production and in home consumption, and the degree of substitutability between home-currency and foreign-currency assets—can have a critical bearing on the quantitative significance of the generalizations.

For still another caveat, recall that this analysis views the problems of macro-economic policy exclusively from the perspective of the home policymakers. The external regime that best facilitates *home* economic objectives in the face of a given disturbance can easily be inferior from the perspective of the rest of the world. The examples of the exogenous changes in saving behavior illustrate this point vividly. When the exogenous increase in demand for goods originates abroad, the home country's price and output objectives are damaged least if the exchange rate is variable and an appreciation of the home currency helps to bottle up more of the disturbance abroad. But the bottling up of the disturbance abroad exacerbates the adverse consequences in the short run for foreign countries. Conversely, if the home policymakers maintain the exchange rate unchanged when an exogenous spurt in the demand for goods originates at home, the maximum spilling over of the disturbance into other countries through an enlarged current-account deficit means that home ultimate-target variables are blown off course less in the short run than they would be under a flexible exchange rate. Yet this outcome must be regretted by policymakers in the rest of the world as a failure to confine as much of the disturbance as possible to the home nation.

Dynamic Evolution of an Open Economy

The preceding analysis fails to incorporate some dynamic aspects of macroeconomic behavior of critical importance. The shortcomings in the analysis parallel deficiencies in the illustrative framework outlined in the first part of appendix C. The latter portion of appendix C thus supplements the comparative-statics framework with a discussion of stock-flow interactions that play a key role in the dynamic evolution of an open economy.

The first of these interactions is the accumulation of capital assets: nonzero flows of net investment result in changes in the nation's capital stock. Of all the dynamic processes that generate growth and cycles in macroeconomic activity, this one may be preeminently important.

Second, as the counterpart of investment flows adding to the capital stock, the flow of saving results in an accumulation of wealth. Nominal wealth at the end of a period is the sum of wealth at the beginning of the period plus net saving and the net value of capital gains and losses during the period.

The interactions of the government's budget flows with the stocks of assets and liabilities on the balance sheets of the fiscal authority and the central bank are the third dynamic process identified in the latter portion of appendix C. Those interactions, already discussed in chapters 14 and 21, are embodied in the consolidated budget and balance-sheet constraint for the government as a whole.

In an open economy, transactions with the rest of the world critically influence, and are critically influenced by, all three of the preceding stock-flow interactions. An understanding of the interdependence of the saving-wealth nexus and the balance of payments is therefore essential for an understanding of the macroeconomic dynamics of open economies.[28]

An imbalance in the current account of the balance of payments is, necessarily, the counterpart of any discrepancy between net domestic investment and the sum of saving by the home private sector and the home government. Hence a flow current-account imbalance and the stock of home private-sector wealth are also necessarily linked. As explained in appendix C, changes in home private wealth can be attributed to four sources: (1) changes in the private economy's capital stock brought about by domestic private investment; (2) saving or dissaving by the government, which changes the stock of home-currency securities; (3) a nonzero current account in the balance of payments; and (4) capital gains or losses resulting from changes in the exchange rate. The first two of these sources are widely understood and would be regularly present in completely closed economies. The second two sources are less widely appreciated; they can occur only in open economies.

When the flow of exports exceeds the flow of imports and the current-account balance is in surplus, home private wealth increases along with the surplus (other things being equal). Conversely, a current-account deficit transfers wealth from the home country to foreigners as the counterpart of the flow of net imports of goods and services. From the perspective of the private sector in the rest of the world, the changes in wealth are in the opposite direction; for example, a surplus in the home nation's current account (a current-account deficit for the rest of the world) drains wealth away from foreigners.

Home residents tend to have different asset preferences from those of foreigners. In particular, the bulk of the assets in home portfolios tend to be denominated in the home currency, while foreigners prefer assets denominated in foreign currency. These differences parallel differences in goods preferences: home-produced goods bulk larger in home residents' consumption than foreign-produced goods, and vice versa. The more open an economy, it is true, the less marked these differences may be. Indeed, the similarities or differences in asset and goods preferences provide the analytical content for definitions of the degree of openness or interdependence (see part 3). Even so, for present-day open economies the differences among nations are a prominent fact of economic life.[29]

Because home and foreign residents have dissimilar asset preferences, the intercountry redistributions of wealth associated with current-account imbalances

---

28. In the same spirit as the description of the comparative-statics framework, the exposition in the latter portion of appendix C is nontechnical and omits details. Many readers may wish to read that part of appendix C before continuing with the text.

29. The illustrative analytical framework used in this chapter embodies these differences in a stark form. By virtue of the simplifying assumptions, home residents do not hold foreign money or titles to the foreign capital stock; foreign residents do not hold home money or titles to the home capital stock; and foreigners do not consume the "nontraded" good produced at home.

have major implications for the time path of the exchange rate. When the current-account balance of the home country is in deficit, for example, the counterpart transfer of wealth from the home private sector to foreign wealth-owners generates portfolio rebalancing both at home and abroad. Because the current-account deficit is a flow and may be spread over many periods, the intercountry redistribution of the total world stock of wealth and the consequent implications for asset markets as foreign and home wealth-owners allocate the changes in their wealth may also be a protracted process. Other things being equal, however, the reduction in home wealth (which primarily takes the form of a reduced demand for assets denominated in home currency) and the increase in foreign wealth (which primarily takes the form of an increased demand for assets denominated in foreign currency) put pressure on the home currency to depreciate—gradually if the process goes smoothly, more suddenly if expectations of the future exchange rate react strongly to the current-account deficit. The other-things-equal pressure on the exchange rate is in the reverse direction—the home currency tends to appreciate—when the home country runs a current-account surplus.[30]

Alternative External Pegging Regimes over a Longer Run

Because the comparative-statics analysis of alternative external pegging regimes did not take into account the dynamic aspects of macroeconomic behavior that have just been identified, the conclusions of that analysis need to be reevaluated.

A comprehensive reevaluation is impractical here. Even without a detailed analysis, however, it is possible to make informed conjectures about the ways in which comparative-statics conclusions will be modified by a dynamic respecification of the illustrative models. The brief discussion that follows makes a few such conjectures. The broader purpose of including this discussion is to point out the dangers of relying solely on short-run, comparative-statics conclusions and to indicate the lines along which future research will have to extend the analysis summarized in this chapter.

Exogenous Shift in Saving by Home Residents

Consider again the illustrative disturbance of an unexpected exogenous spurt in the consumption expenditures of home residents. The conclusion of the earlier analysis of this disturbance was that the home ultimate-target variables would be least adversely affected in the short run under a reserve-aggregate peg with exchange-rate peg and most adversely affected under an interest-rate peg with external-reserves peg. Explicitly dynamic variants of the models might not alter this conclusion per se. The dynamic analysis would indicate, however, the critical signif-

---

30. Intercountry redistributions of wealth through current-account imbalances and their implications for the exchange rate over the long run are analyzed in Pentti Kouri, "The Exchange Rate and the Balance of Payments in the Short Run and in the Long Run: A Monetary Approach," *Scandinavian Journal of Economics*, vol. 78 (May 1976), pp. 280–304; Pentti Kouri and Jorge Braga de Macedo, "Exchange Rates and the International Adjustment Process," *Brookings Papers on Economic Activity*, 1:1978, pp. 111–57; and Dale W. Henderson, "The Dynamic Effects of Exchange Market Intervention Policy: Two Extreme Views and a Synthesis," in Helmut Frisch, ed., *The Economics of Flexible Exchange Rates*, supplement to *Kredit und Kapital* (6:1980).

icance of the phrase "in the short run" and would raise pertinent questions about the sustainability of the short-run choice of an exchange-rate peg as the external operating regime.

For example, suppose the policymakers operate the "preferred" regimen of the reserve-aggregate peg with exchange-rate peg. The initial excess demand in goods markets set off by the exogenous shift in saving behavior puts upward pressure on the prices and outputs of home goods and induces an increase in imports, a reduction in exports, and a deficit in the current account of the balance of payments. The home interest rate is pulled up by the increase in prices and outputs and therefore helps to moderate somewhat the unexpected expansionary stimulus. In the comparative-statics model, the direction of the short-run change in the external reserve assets of the home central bank is ambiguous (because of transactions-related demands for money and securities).[31] The comparative-statics model, however, does not acknowledge the intercountry transfer of wealth associated with the current-account deficit. Once this transfer of wealth and the consequent portfolio rebalancing that it engenders are incorporated in the analysis, the likelihood of the central bank gaining rather than losing reserves in the short run is reduced. Moreover, the central bank is virtually certain to lose reserves over a longer run. Even if in the short run there are modest upward pressures on external reserves attributable to the increased transactions demand for money, this transactions-related change in portfolios is a once-for-all adjustment to higher levels of transactions. The transfer of wealth out of domestic portfolios into foreign portfolios associated with the current-account deficit, on the other hand, involves a continuing downward pressure on external reserves so long as the current account remains in deficit.

Now recall the consequences of the shift in saving behavior under the regimen of the reserve-aggregate peg with external-reserves peg. The home interest rate rises, helping to choke off some of the excess demand created by the initial disturbance. The home currency depreciates, however, which (other things being equal) serves to exacerbate the excess demand in home goods markets.[32] Both the rise in the home interest rate and the depreciation of the home currency mitigate the tendency of the current account to move into deficit; conceivably, the current account could even move in the direction of a surplus. The home country therefore has a smaller current-account deficit but larger upward deviations of its prices and outputs from desired, target levels than under the reserve-aggregate peg with exchange-rate peg.

31. The increases in prices and outputs of home-produced goods have the effect, other things being equal, of increasing home nonbanks' transactions demand for money and reducing their demands for both home-currency and foreign-currency securities. The increases in nonbanks' demand for money in turn raise the investable assets of home banks (see equations C-4 through C-8 in appendix C). If home nonbanks satisfy their increased transactions demand for money to a sufficient degree by reducing their demands for foreign-currency securities rather than for home-currency securities and if home banks allocate a sufficiently small proportion of their investable assets to foreign-currency securities, the home central bank may have to buy rather than sell foreign-currency assets (increase rather than decrease its external reserves) in order to keep the exchange rate pegged.

32. The comparative-statics model does not rule out the possibility of an appreciation rather than a depreciation of the home currency. The presence in the model of transactions-related demands for money and securities is again responsible for introducing this possibility. Once the dynamic stock-flow interactions are incorporated in the model, there will presumably no longer be any ambiguity about the direction of movement in the exchange rate. At the initial exchange rate, the current account would move into deficit; the ensuing transfer of wealth to foreigners would constitute an additional source of pressure on the exchange rate, adding to the other forces tending to cause the home currency to depreciate.

In the comparative-statics analysis of this disturbance, a regimen using an exchange-rate peg was preferable to one using an external-reserves peg, because the former promotes a larger spilling over of the domestic disturbance into the rest of the world through goods flows in the current account of the balance of payments. Depreciation of the home currency serves to confine more of the goods-market consequences of the domestic disturbance to the home country, thereby pushing home target variables further off course than under the exchange-rate peg. This basic point about the short-run consequences of the disturbance is not overturned when the analysis is altered to take into account the dynamics of the saving-wealth nexus and the transfer of wealth between countries through current-account imbalances. But consideration of the dynamics brings out the fact that the preferred regimen of the reserve-aggregate peg with exchange-rate peg implies a continuing current-account deficit and a continuing decline in external reserves. These trends can be sustained in a short run. Over a longer run, on the other hand, their persistence could force a discrete devaluation of the home currency. The size of a nation's external reserves is finite; the further external reserves are drawn down, moreover, the greater the likelihood that private economic units will revise their expectations of the medium-run exchange rate, thereby adding still more downward pressure on the reserves.[33]

Bringing dynamic considerations into the analysis thus creates doubt about the validity of the comparative-statics conclusions for a longer run. To moderate the adverse impacts of the disturbance on home ultimate-target variables, no doubt it would be preferable over a long run as well as a short run to have the disturbance spill over as much as possible into the rest of the world. But the home country may not be able to foster that result over a long run unless it holds very large amounts of external reserves at the onset of the disturbance. The more open the economy and, in particular, the greater the substitutability of home-currency and foreign-currency assets in private portfolios, the larger the required level of external reserves is likely to be. Remember also that the holding of a large quantity of external reserves in anticipation of possible disturbances has a sizable opportunity cost for the nation.

Note finally that if a devaluation of the home currency should prove necessary under either of the regimens using an exchange-rate peg, the comparative-statics comparison of outcomes under the four regimens has to be completely reevaluated. The regimen of the reserve-aggregate peg with exchange-rate peg generates the least adverse impacts on home ultimate-target variables *only when the initial exchange rate is successfully maintained.* Comparison of the consequences of the domestic disturbance for home prices and outputs under an external-reserves peg and under an exchange-rate peg, for cases in which a devaluation occurs under the latter, creates even more complex analytical problems than the comparisons already discussed. But there is certainly no a priori presumption that the adverse consequences are worse under the external-reserves peg than under the temporarily fixed but subsequently adjusted exchange-rate peg.

33. The comparative-statics analysis held the medium-run expected exchange rate unchanged. This unrealistic assumption biased the comparison of the regimens in favor of those using an exchange-rate peg. Recognition that exchange-rate expectations would respond endogenously to the current-account deficit and the decline in external reserves thus further reinforces the point that pegging of the exchange rate may prove sustainable only for a short run.

Other Types of Exogenous Disturbances

Incorporation into the analytical framework of dynamic stock-flow relationships and differential speeds of behavioral response could significantly modify any of the earlier conclusions.[34] In practice, the conclusions that seem likely to be modified the least are those pertaining to unexpected disturbances taking the form of once-for-all shifts in asset preferences.

For the case of the once-for-all shift by home nonbanks out of home securities into home money, for example, the earlier reasoning requires little amendment. Among the four regimens being compared, home ultimate-target variables would be best protected against the disturbance, both in the short run and over a longer run, under an interest-rate peg with exchange-rate peg. None of the dynamic forces would make an exchange-rate peg unsustainable over the longer run; the private-sector asset shift merely requires a finite, once-for-all increase in external reserves and the home monetary base. Similarly, in the case of the once-for-all asset shift out of home-currency securities into foreign-currency securities, the preferred regimen remains one in which the exchange rate is kept unchanged. The private-sector disturbance does lead to a decline in external reserves under an exchange-rate peg. This change is again, however, of finite size and duration; unless home external reserves are small relative to the size of the exogenous asset shift, home policymakers can best protect their ultimate objectives by absorbing the disturbance through offsetting quantity changes on their own balance sheet rather than by allowing it to induce changes in either interest rates or the exchange rate.

Dynamic considerations are likely to alter the comparative-statics analysis in more important ways, however, for the cases of persisting flow disturbances—particularly those that originate in the real rather than the financial sectors of the home and foreign economies. The case of a persisting reduction in the saving rate of home nonbanks provides one illustration of this general point. The intercountry transfer of wealth through current-account imbalances would also play a significant role in determining the dynamic consequences of an exogenous shift in saving by foreign residents. Incorporation of stock-flow relationships into the analysis of that case would cast doubt on the longer run sustainability of the outcomes under an exchange-rate peg; the home country's current-account surplus and increases in external reserves could continue only so long as the drain on foreign nations' external reserves could be sustained; in the longer run, the currency of the home country might have to appreciate even under an exchange-rate peg.[35]

Summary Conclusion

The extent of economists' knowledge about the dynamic transmission of disturbances within a single open economy and from one open economy to another is still distressingly meager. Even after all dynamic relationships and differential speeds of behavioral response have been correctly incorporated into the analysis, however, the outcomes for home ultimate-target variables under alternative mon-

34. Because the preceding example suggests many of the points that arise in reevaluating the comparative-statics conclusions about other types of exogenous disturbances, none of the other illustrative disturbances analyzed earlier are discussed here in detail.

35. The dual flexprice regimen of the reserve-aggregate peg with external-reserves peg would provide the best protection for home target variables, in both the short run and the long run.

etary-policy regimens are sure to be different and to be sensitive to different patterns of unforeseen exogenous disturbances. Those differences may be more extreme for shorter-run outcomes, but exist for the longer run as well (to some extent even if devaluations or revaluations occur under an exchange-rate peg). The fundamental point thus stands unchallenged: regimens using a flexprice external regime sometimes provide better buffering for target variables against disturbances, while for other types of disturbances they provide less effective buffering than regimens with a fixprice external regime. Neither of the external pegging rules can possibly be the preferred means for coping with all types of disturbances.

Choosing between Fixed and Flexible Exchange Rates in a Comparative-Statics Context

At this point in the analysis, as in chapter 19, the next step that may seem natural to many readers is to stage a contest between fixprice and flexprice strategies for the exchange rate.

For any given national economy with its given degree of openness, it may be asked, Which types of disturbances occur more frequently and are more quantitatively significant *on the average?* For example, is the home economy buffeted more often by unforeseen shifts in private-sector asset preferences or by unexpected changes in the saving and spending behavior of home residents? How do the frequencies and magnitudes of unexpected changes in the saving and spending decisions of home residents compare on average with the frequencies and magnitudes of unforeseen shifts in foreigners' saving and spending decisions? Answers to questions such as these, it may be thought, could lead naturally to a rational resolution for that economy of the controversy over fixed versus flexible exchange rates. Should not policymakers choose either an exchange-rate peg or an external-reserves peg, depending on which types of disturbances are greatest and most prevalent?

It can be argued that unforeseeable financial-sector disturbances (occurring initially either at home or abroad) are—on the average—less frequent and less quantitatively significant than unforeseeable real-sector disturbances (occurring initially either at home or abroad). If true, that assertion tends to weigh in favor of pegging the quantity of external reserves and against pegging the exchange rate.

For economies with a significant but not an extreme degree of openness, it can also be argued that the risks of policymakers making a large mistake tend to be smaller if they let the exchange rate float freely rather than try to peg the rate. Suppose, for example, that the home central bank chooses an external-reserves peg and experiences a wide variety of unforeseen disturbances, both real-sector and financial-sector in nature. Although this view acknowledges that unexpected shifts in asset preferences would generate worse outcomes than would be observed under an exchange-rate peg, it also notes that the adverse consequences for ultimate-target variables of once-for-all asset shifts would not be cumulative. By contrast, it is claimed, an exchange-rate peg would permit other types of unexpected disturbances—for example, a persisting reduction in the propensity to save of economic units in the rest of the world—to exert large cumulative, and hence very damaging, inflationary pressure on home ultimate targets; the adverse consequences of such disturbances could not cumulate in so dangerous a manner under an external-reserves peg.

Suppose the home central bank were forced to choose between the external pegging alternatives of (a) keeping the exchange rate pegged indefinitely at some initial rate and (b) pegging the quantity of external reserves along a constant-growth-rate path with the growth rate chosen to be equal to the trend growth in the nation's international transactions.[36] Considerations such as the foregoing, not to mention practical experience with the Bretton Woods system, might then constitute a sound rationale for choosing the external-reserves peg rather than the exchange-rate peg.

Once again, the resemblances are compelling between the external and the domestic aspects of monetary policy. If the choice of domestic operating regime is restricted to the polar cases of an interest-rate peg or a reserve-aggregate peg, theory and practical experience suggest that the latter may prove less damaging to home ultimate-target variables on the average. Similarly, if the central bank of a moderately open economy insists on pegging some external financial variable, the external-reserves peg would probably be—*on the average*—the less dangerous and crisis prone of the two polar possibilities. To most observers looking back on the postwar period in which the Bretton Woods supranational constraints were in force, it seems miraculous that the system held together as long as it did, given its limited and rigid provisions governing exchange-rate changes.[37]

Instrument Choice and Instrument Variation in a Dynamic Context

The logic in the preceding section is acceptable within its own limited terms of reference. Yet such a comparison of external pegging regimes has virtually no practical relevance. Home policymakers do not have to make the artificial choice between pegging the exchange rate and pegging external reserve assets. To peg

36. As in the case of domestic pegging regimes, there are nontrivial problems in specifying an operational definition of "pegging" in an economy in which output, the price level, international transactions, or all three are growing over time.

37. As in chapter 19, it is straightforward to make these points more formally in terms of a linear specification of the illustrative comparative-statics framework and an illustrative loss function. If the expected value of the policymakers' loss function were minimized subject to the four models based on the common framework, a comparison of the resulting expressions for the four pegging regimens would show that the "correct" choice of external pegging regime depends on the relative magnitudes of the variances of the exogenous driving forces. Such an analysis would also show the choice among the external pegging rules to be dependent on any nonzero covariances of the exogenous factors and on the structural coefficients of the behavioral relationships. Since the degree of the economy's openness is, by definition, a function of many of these structural coefficients, the analysis would emphasize that the quantitative differences between the alternative choices for the external pegging regime, if not the "correct" choice itself, depend on the extent of the nation's economic interdependence with the rest of the world. If the analysis were to treat the structural coefficients of the model as uncertain rather than known parameters, the choice among the four regimens would depend not only on the means of the parameters, but also on their variances and covariances (see chapter 17 and appendix B). Finally, note that this analytical procedure would provide a basis for *jointly* selecting the appropriate combination of domestic and external instruments for monetary policy (instead of choosing the external operating regime separately). For a pioneering discussion of how the degree of openness might influence the choice between the polar cases of fixed and flexible exchange rates, see Ronald I. McKinnon, "Optimum Currency Areas," *American Economic Review*, vol. 53 (September 1963), pp. 717–25.

any external variable for an extended period is to follow a mechanical rule of thumb rather than to take advantage of the possibility of period-by-period discretionary decisions.

As in the case of domestic operating regimes, the variable selected for use as the actual external instrument will always be "pegged" in the very short run, its setting fixed exogenously. But use of a variable as an instrument—controlling its value exogenously at every moment—need not involve rigidity in its setting *over an extended period*. Regardless of whether the exchange rate or the quantity of external reserves is the external instrument, the setting can be discretionarily revised from one short-run period to the next.

Externally as well as domestically, the practical problems of decisionmaking involve *instrument variation* much more than *instrument choice*. The instrument-choice problem for the external operating regime is not trivial when the policymakers pursue discretionary instrument adaptation. But it is secondary. Only if the home policymakers reject discretionary adaptation of their instrument setting can the problem of external instrument choice become an overriding concern in its own right.

Within the comparative-statics frame of reference earlier in the chapter, it was possible to consider only four monetary-policy regimens, each a combination of an external and a domestic pegging rule of thumb. With a dynamic, multiperiod frame of reference, however, the choice of a monetary-policy regimen requires consideration of discretionary as well as pegging operating regimes. The relevant array of possibilities for instrument regimes is summarized in figure 22-2. As indicated there, the regimens characterized by instrument pegging are "corner choices": they involve not merely the choice of a variable as an instrument but also a decision to forswear discretionary variation in its setting. In the dynamic context in which real-world policymakers can make decisions more or less continuously, the choice of an exchange-rate peg is the choice of an instrument rule. The same statement applies with equal force to freely floating exchange rates; although an external-reserves peg is a rule of thumb for fixing a quantity instead of a price, it is nonetheless a mechanical, nondiscretionary rule.

Pegging Rules versus Discretionary Adaptation for External Monetary Policy

The long-standing debate about exchange-rate variability in the literature of international economics presents the issue as one of fixed *versus* flexible exchange rates—that is, choosing one or the other of the external pegging regimes. There has been surprisingly little questioning, by advocates of either side, of the traditional lines along which the debate has been drawn.

As is clear from the preceding discussion, that debate needs at the very least to be broadened so that it considers discretionary as well as pegging alternatives to external monetary policy. Preferably, less attention should be paid to the issue of whether the exchange rate or the quantity of external reserves should be selected as the external instrument. Instead, the focus should be shifted to the relative merits of pegging rules and discretionary adaptation. Most important of all, analysis of the

Figure 22-2. *Alternative Regimens for National Monetary Policy in the Absence of Supranational Constraints*

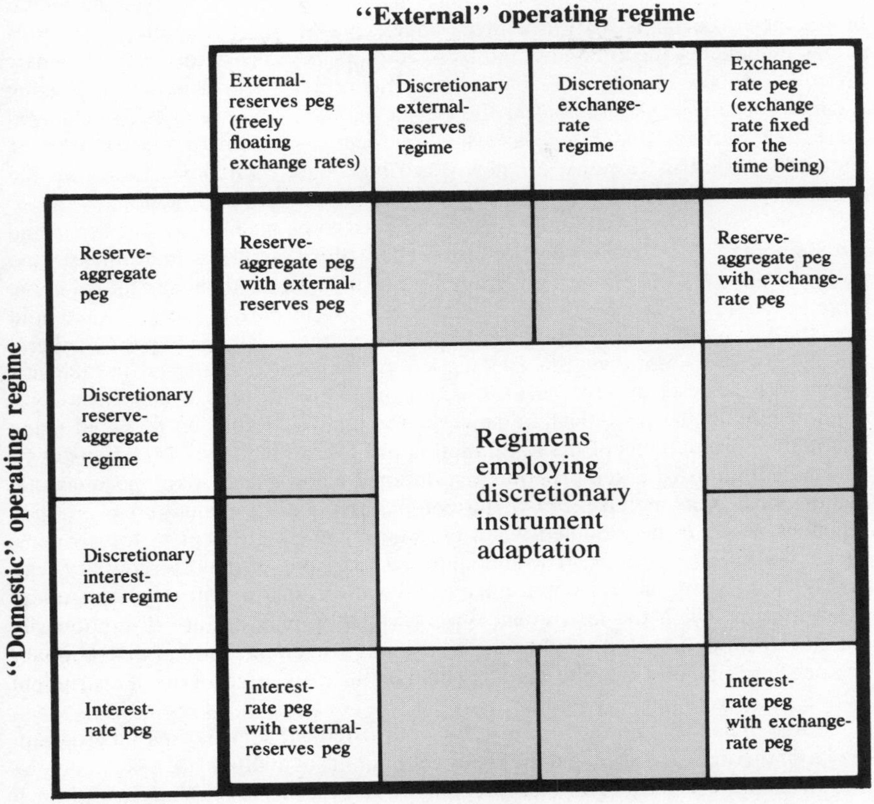

"External" operating regime

"Domestic" operating regime	External-reserves peg (freely floating exchange rates)	Discretionary external-reserves regime	Discretionary exchange-rate regime	Exchange-rate peg (exchange rate fixed for the time being)
Reserve-aggregate peg	Reserve-aggregate peg with external-reserves peg			Reserve-aggregate peg with exchange-rate peg
Discretionary reserve-aggregate regime		Regimens employing discretionary instrument adaptation		
Discretionary interest-rate regime				
Interest-rate peg	Interest-rate peg with external-reserves peg			Interest-rate peg with exchange-rate peg

consequences of exchange-rate variability should evaluate pegging rules and discretionary adaptation for the domestic as well as the external aspects of monetary policy, with "monetary policy" considered as a unity.[38]

How might a systematic analysis proceed that avoids the artificial preoccupations of the conventional debate?

The chief requirements would be an analytical framework for modeling a given nation's economy and a summary description of its policymakers' loss function; both the framework and the loss function would have to be specified dynamically. A comprehensive comparison of alternative monetary-policy regimes could be tedious, because in principle there are at least sixteen possibilities (see figure 22-2). For practical purposes, the number of regimens might be reduced to no more

38. The failure of the conventional debate about fixed versus flexible exchange rates to perceive the issues as part of the larger question of whether to conduct policy by "rules" or "discretion" is another manifestation of the bifocal lenses through which analysts customarily view the domestic and the external aspects of macroeconomic policy separately.

than eight—the four pegging regimens and the four regimens employing discretionary operating regimes. All regimens would be compared over the same time horizon. Similarly, the hypothetical policymakers operating each regimen would be assumed to begin the analysis with the same expectations of nonpolicy exogenous forces influencing the economy and to have the same access to the flow of new information about the economy. Paths for the instrument settings under the pegging regimens would be determined at the outset of the analysis and left unchanged thereafter. Settings under the discretionary regimens would be revised in each short-run period in response to newly received data. Outcomes under all the regimens would be evaluated on the basis of the common loss function.

A variety of different assumptions would need to be made about the types and sizes of nonpolicy exogenous disturbances. The analysis could postulate unexpected policy actions by the foreign government and investigate their effects on home target variables under the alternative regimens. As in part 4, the analysis could vary the assumptions about the flow of new information available to policymakers. Finally, to the extent that the conclusions of the analysis seemed particularly sensitive to the description of the loss function or the specification of some behavioral relationships in the analytical framework, the analysis could be repeated using alternative formulations of the loss function or of those behavioral relationships.

The ambitious research program just outlined could clarify many questions. It could reveal more precisely how the comparative-statics evaluation of pegging regimens needs to be modified when pegging regimens are kept in force over a succession of time periods. It would allow comparisons of the discretionary regimens, showing the relative importance of the various instrument selections under conditions in which the instruments, whatever they may be, are discretionarily varied. Most important, it would permit the analytical comparison of discretionary and pegging regimens, thereby shedding light on the respective merits of instrument rules and discretionary adaptation.

Although neither I nor anyone else has yet carried out such a research program, the basic theoretical issues and the required methods of analysis are essentially the same as those discussed in the closed-economy analysis in part 4. Therefore, though final judgment must be reserved until the research is done, a sound basis exists for anticipating what the results will show.

First, the outcomes for home ultimate-target variables under the alternative regimens for monetary policy are once again certain to be different and to be sensitive to the pattern of unforeseen exogenous disturbances postulated in the analysis. Regimens characterized by more rather than less variability of exchange rates will provide the best possible protection against some disturbances, while for others they prove inferior.

Second, the results will surely show that (1) choice of the exchange rate or external reserves as the instrument under conditions of discretionary instrument variation tends to be much less important than under a pegging rule, but (2) instrument choice (external and domestic) is not a negligible issue even under conditions of discretionary instrument variation.

Finally, the results will surely show that an adaptive approach to instrument decisions can always dominate the use of instrument rules when the two are evaluated on a comparable basis. For example, a regimen consisting of a discretionary reserve-aggregate regime and a discretionary external-reserves regime can always dominate a reserve-aggregate peg with external-reserves peg if the two regimens are evaluated using the same loss function, the same model framework, access to the same flow of new information, and exposure to the same unforeseen disturbances. Likewise, a regimen combining a discretionary reserve-aggregate regime and a discretionary exchange-rate regime can probably always dominate a reserve-aggregate peg with exchange-rate peg.

The conclusion that policymakers should avoid pegging rules for external as well as domestic monetary policy holds for the same general reasons stressed in part 4: the best way to incorporate new information about the economy into policy decisions, and to cope with uncertainty about the impacts of policy decisions, is to digest the new information promptly and to keep the instrument settings under continuous review.

Managed Fixing or Floating

The next chapter continues the analysis of whether the objectives of a nation's monetary policy can be better promoted with a little or a lot of exchange-rate variability. But one key policy conclusion stands out already and will remain unaltered by what follows: *the choice between fixed versus flexible exchange rates, as traditionally understood, is an artificial choice that does not have to be made and should not be made.* The preferable approach is to avoid pegging either the exchange rate or external reserves, discretionarily varying whichever of the two is used as an instrument in response to economic developments within the nation and in the rest of the world.

This discretionary approach involves application to external monetary policy of the same principles and procedures used in making decisions about domestic policy. It asserts that there is no valid reason, so long as the policymakers' perspective is myopically national, for treating external open-market operations in an analytically different way from domestic open-market operations.

Use of either a discretionary exchange-rate regime or a discretionary external-reserves regime implies substantial variability over time in *both* the exchange rate and external reserve assets. This joint variability may be labeled either "managed fixing" or "managed floating" of exchange rates, or, alternatively, "managed pegging" or "managed variations" of external reserves. The label itself obviously makes little difference. The key word, in any case, is "managed."

The essence of the discretionary approach to instrument variation, for both the external and domestic instruments, is to respond differentially to different disturbances affecting the economy. For many types of exogenous disturbances (for example, those known to take the form of shifts in asset preferences), home policymakers should wish most of the adjustment in the external sector of the economy to fall on external reserves while the exchange rate changes little. For many other disturbances (for example those originating in markets for goods and services outside the home nation), it will be preferable for the exchange rate to do most of the adjusting while external reserves remain relatively unchanged. The appropriateness of these responses depends little on whether the policymakers use the exchange rate or external reserves as their instrument. If the exchange rate should do most of the adjusting in response to particular disturbances, the instrument setting for external policy will have to be changed if the exchange rate is the instrument but may not need to be changed at all if external reserves are the instrument. The converse applies, of course, when particular disturbances call for most of the adjustment to fall on external reserves.

When data is not yet available to identify the sources and intensities of disturbances creating divergences between the actual and best feasible paths for home target variables, policymakers cannot do much to tailor their responses to the types of disturbances. Nor should they try to do so. In those circumstances, however, neither should they adhere rigidly to a pegged instrument setting for the exchange rate or for external reserves. Rather, they should still pursue the discretionary policy they think best at the moment, reevaluating the settings for both external and domestic instruments period by period as additional data accumulate. This approach, though of course uncertain, is nonetheless a more conservative, risk-avoiding response than adherence to a pegged value of either the exchange rate or external reserves.[39]

Such joint discretionary management of the exchange rate and external reserves is not a "fine tuning" policy and should not be confused with it. Everything said in chapter 19 about fine tuning and its differences from discretionary instrument adaptation is equally applicable here in part 5.

---

39. Suppose the home central bank finds itself in a situation in which unforeseen and as-yet-unexplainable market pressures require *either* a depreciation of the home currency (relative to earlier projections of the exchange rate) *or* a greater volume of exchange-market support of the home currency (larger sales of foreign-currency-denominated assets relative to earlier projections). Those market pressures could be consistent with a wide variety of unforeseen changes in factors taken as exogenous in the central bank's policymaking model. To take two examples with contrary implications for policy, the underlying disturbances could be either autonomous shifts out of home-currency assets into foreign-currency assets or autonomous reductions in the demands for goods in the rest of the world. If no information yet exists to help identify the source of the disturbances (because, for example, recent data for capital flows in the balance of payments and for foreign industrial production are not yet available), the least inappropriate course for "today" may be a combination of allowing the home currency to depreciate somewhat and external reserves to fall somewhat (relative to earlier plans). As further information becomes available "tomorrow," the setting for the external instrument can and should be reconsidered. When the external instrument is discretionarily adjusted from one short-run period to the next, note again that it may matter relatively little which of the two—the exchange rate and external reserves—is the actual instrument and which the "endogenous" variable.

CHAPTER TWENTY-THREE

Exchange-Rate Variability,
Autonomy, and Controllability

THE LARGER in absolute value and the less uncertain are the impacts of national monetary-policy actions on national ultimate targets, the greater is the autonomy of national monetary policy (see chapter 12). The autonomy of monetary policy has a major influence on the degree of controllability that policymakers have over national ultimate targets, which in turn is a critical determinant of the overall successfulness of national economic policy (see chapter 13). Autonomy and controllability can be affected by any aspect of the world economic structure. This chapter focuses on only one—the external operating regime of monetary policy—and analyzes how autonomy, controllability and, ultimately, national welfare are affected by the manner and degree of variability in exchange rates.

The traditional view is that flexible exchange rates permit greater independence for a nation's monetary policy than do fixed exchange rates. It has also traditionally been believed that flexibility in exchange rates insulates a nation's economy from the rest of the world. At best, however, those propositions are incomplete and misleading. This chapter argues that exchange-rate variability plays only a secondary role in determining what can and cannot be accomplished with discretionary monetary policy in an open economy.

Supranational Constraints and National Independence

When analyzing the proposition that greater variability in exchange rates is associated with greater independence for national monetary policy, it is best to begin with a tautological but nonetheless highly important point.

Imagine a world economy in which nations are constrained by supranational restrictions on exchange-rate movements. Suppose each nation is obliged to declare a par value for its currency in terms of an outside reserve asset (for example, gold) and to restrict movements of the exchange rates of its currency within very narrow margins around the cross rates implied by national par values. Now suppose that a period of increasingly frequent and traumatic changes in par values ("fundamental disequilibria") leads national governments to scrap the international treaty imposing the supranational restrictions.

If a binding constraint on a nation's discretionary decisions is lifted, the choices open to the national government increase. Whatever could be done before can still be done; and additional choices are available. In the assumed case of the withdrawal of supranationally enforced par-value obligations, rather than having to use the exchange rate as its external instrument and keeping the setting for the exchange rate unchanged until the advent of a "fundamental disequilibrium," an individual monetary authority can now choose either the exchange rate or the quantity of external reserves as its external instrument. It can now carry out any amount of exchange-market intervention at national discretion. The amount could be zero or very large; or it could be precisely the amount required to maintain the exchange rate within the old par-value limits.[1]

After the abandonment of the supranational constraints, an individual nation's authority thus gains greater maneuverability in using national policy instruments. Greater maneuverability of instruments enhances the authority's ability to influence national ultimate-target variables. Hence the nation's authority, and by implication the nation itself, could be significantly better off than when forced to operate within the old supranational constraints.

This truth had great practical relevance from World War II through 1973, when the Bretton Woods system of adjustable par values was in force. The obligation to declare and maintain a par value was then a binding constraint on the external open-market operations of central banks.[2] The effective abandonment of par-value obligations in 1973 significantly increased the scope for discretionary decisions in each nation. To the extent that greater flexibility in exchange rates in the 1970s can be attributed to the withdrawal of supranational constraints on exchange-rate movements, therefore, this greater flexibility can unambiguously be said to have enhanced the independence of each nation's monetary authority.[3]

Practically important though it has been, this truth scarcely exhausts the subject of monetary independence and exchange-rate variability. First, even from the perspective of a single nation the truth has to be stated conditionally; although elimination of supranational constraints *could* make that nation better off, it is also conceivable that the benefits to that nation from greater maneuverability of its own policy instruments could be more than offset by costs associated with *other* nations in the world no longer being subject to the supranational constraints. Second, as soon as one abandons a myopic national perspective, matters appear in a rather different light: an individual nation can enjoy greater maneuverability and independence, but the world as a whole cannot (see chapter 25).

Most important, the truth is essentially a tautology. To say that the lifting of supranational constraints on exchange-rate movements permits greater independence for one nation's monetary policy is implicitly to define "independence" in terms of the number and severity of constraints on the use of national policy instruments for national ends. Although that definition is no doubt reasonable, the

1. In effect, the old "international monetary system" required that all nations uniformly implement an exchange-rate peg. The new international monetary arrangements leave each nation free to try to implement an exchange-rate peg, an external-reserves peg, a discretionary exchange-rate regime, or a discretionary external-reserves regime.

2. Except for countries (for example, Canada in 1950–62 and 1970–73) which failed to comply with the International Monetary Fund Articles of Agreement.

3. Compare Fred Hirsch, "The Ideological Underlay of Inflation," in Fred Hirsch and John H. Goldthorpe, eds., *The Political Economy of Inflation* (London: Martin Robertson, 1978): "The break-up of the [Bretton Woods monetary order] in the early 1970s and its replacement by a regime of flexible exchange rates, subject to national management and only the loosest international influence, can be seen as a declaration of national independence in the monetary sphere" (p. 266).

proposition that greater exchange-rate flexibility permits greater "independence" is then less substantive than it might at first appear.

National Autonomy and Controllability in the Absence of Supranational Constraints: Five Issues

To decide how to behave in an environment in which supranational constraints on exchange-rate movements are largely absent, a nation's government needs to know whether the effects of its domestic policy actions may be more or less potent under alternative assumptions about exchange-rate variability. More broadly, it needs to know the implications of exchange-rate variability for its capacity to exert control over national ultimate targets.

The required analysis must probe deeply into the interrelationships of exchange-rate variability, autonomy, controllability, and the openness of the nation's economy. Merely formulating an appropriate frame of reference within which to conduct the analysis is a difficult matter. In principle, a careful study of the consequences of policy actions should specify (a) the macroeconomic policy regimen of the home country (domestic monetary policy, external monetary policy, fiscal policy); (b) the policy regimen in force in the rest of the world; (c) the expected behavior of the foreign policy authorities; and (d) the nonpolicy exogenous "weather conditions." Adoption of the small and open paradigm as a frame of reference, as in the illustrative analysis in the last chapter, somewhat reduces the complexity—but not by enough to make the analysis readily manageable.

The rest of this chapter, like chapter 22, postulates a world economy without explicit supranational constraints on the freedom of nations to choose external regimes. The discussion is organized around five questions, all viewed from the perspective of a single nation's monetary authority:

(1)   Are some national policy regimens less viable than others—viable in the narrow sense that the central bank can successfully implement desired settings for the monetary-policy instruments?

(2)   What are the implications of exchange-rate variability for the ability to attain *ultimate* policy objectives?

(3)   Does variability in exchange rates insulate the national economy?

(4)   Does variability in exchange rates free macroeconomic policy to focus on the domestic economy?

(5)   Are nations "dis-integrated" when exchange rates are more variable?

These questions avoid use of the term *independence*. If a nation's authority is unconstrained by supranational rules and understandings, if it therefore can try to implement any type of external regime, and if it *voluntarily* chooses an exchange-rate peg, its ability to take independent policy actions is not thereby restricted. It can voluntarily abandon the exchange-rate peg at any time, reversing its earlier choice. If independence means *ability to act independently,* therefore, it is silly to argue that a nation's monetary policy can be more independent if the monetary authority chooses, say, an external-reserves peg rather than an exchange-rate peg.

The preceding questions could be phrased in terms of "independence" if independence were defined differently—if, for example, greater independence were taken to mean a greater degree of *autonomy for national monetary policy* or a greater degree of *controllability of the national economy*. The traditional conclusion that flexible exchange rates permit greater independence for a nation's monetary policy is customarily interpreted as though *independence* and *autonomy* are synonyms. Confusion easily results, however, when two very different meanings are associated with the same word. Unlike the traditional literature, therefore, the analysis here uses *independence* to mean only the unconstrained freedom to take policy actions. *Autonomy* or *controllability* are used if the issue is de facto ability to influence intermediate or ultimate targets rather than merely de jure command over a set of policy instruments.

Viability of Alternative National Policy Regimens

The issue of the viability of alternative monetary-policy regimens—the first question—logically precedes the others. Unless the central bank can successfully implement a particular regimen *in the narrow sense of being technically able to attain desired combinations of the settings for its instruments,* there is little point in its considering such a regimen further.

Comparison of the Four Pegging Regimens

Under the dual flexprice regimen of the reserve-aggregate peg with external-reserves peg, home policymakers can presumably attain desired settings for both quantity instruments with little difficulty. To be sure, the desired levels of the pegs must be plausible. A small, open economy can readily peg its external reserves at their existing level, for example, but cannot feasibly fix the quantity at a level twice or half that amount—at least not until after a transition period has passed. More important still, the policymakers must be willing to tolerate whatever "price" changes result from their decisions to peg the instrument quantities. In principle, the exchange rate and interest rates must be allowed to fluctuate without limit. If extreme fluctuations occur, neither private-sector opinion nor the policymakers might be comfortable with rigid adherence to the quantity pegs. Nonetheless, from the standpoint of viability in the narrow sense of technical ability to implement the regimen, a reserve-aggregate peg with external-reserves peg does not present major difficulties.

Matters are somewhat less straightforward with the dual fixprice regimen of the interest-rate peg with exchange-rate peg. Here the policymakers must fix two prices and allow market forces to determine the associated adjustments in quantities. Formally, the situation is similar to the dual flexprice regimen. The level of the price pegs—the fixed values of the interest rate and the exchange rate—must be plausible in the light of the economy's recent history. And the policymakers must merely be willing to tolerate whatever quantity changes result from their decisions to peg the prices. In practice, however, this "merely" can sometimes prove to be an insuperable difficulty. Policymakers may not be able—able in a narrow, technical sense—to allow reserve-money aggregates and external reserves to fluctuate without limit. Not only is there the problem that, if the required quantity changes should turn out to be very large, public opinion and the policymakers may come to regard them as intolerable. There is the added difficulty that quantity changes in one direction have a limit; the policymakers may experience "quantity exhaustion." Once the home central bank has exhausted its external reserve assets (and its ability to borrow abroad) in exchange-market intervention to prevent the home currency from depreciating, it will be forced to abandon the particular value of the exchange rate it had been pegging. In theory, the central bank could also run out of home-currency assets in domestic open-market operations required to prevent the interest rate from falling below its pegged level.[4] The sheer technical ability of policymakers to implement the regimen of an interest-rate peg with exchange-rate peg can therefore be in doubt in certain circumstances.

Each of the two other pegging regimens involves fixing one price and one quantity. They fall between the dual flexprice and dual fixprice regimens in possible difficulties with implementation. From least to most problematic in terms of technical viability, the four pegging regimens can be ranked as (a) the reserve-aggregate peg with external-reserves peg, (b) the interest-rate peg with external-reserves peg, (c) the reserve-aggregate peg with exchange-rate peg, and (d) the interest-rate peg with exchange-rate peg.

Interaction of Domestic and External Regimes

The issue of viability cannot be assessed without taking into account the pervasive interaction of the domestic and the external operating regimes. Suppose the home central bank uses the regimen of the reserve-aggregate peg with exchange-rate peg and wishes to take the "domestic" expansionary action of raising the monetary base by an incremental amount above some benchmark path (see chapter 20). An initial open-market purchase of home-currency securities will expand the monetary base and put downward pressure on home interest rates. But suppose private economic units (home or foreign) respond by promptly purchasing foreign-currency assets (having just sold home-currency securities to the central bank). To that extent, the central bank will find itself carrying out "external" open-market operations (sales of foreign-currency assets to prevent the home currency from depreciating) that reduce the monetary base and undermine its initial domestic action. Further domestic open-market purchases will therefore be required to restore the setting for the monetary base to its incrementally higher level; but then private economic units may respond by purchasing still further amounts of foreign-currency assets. Under conditions of high substitutability between home-currency and foreign-currency assets in private portfolios, the central bank may thus have difficulty in pushing the monetary base up to its new path and keeping it there; at the very least, a sizable reduction in external reserves may have to be tolerated.[5]

---

4. In practice, the probability of quantity exhaustion occurring in domestic open-market operations is much lower than in external open-market operations. Domestically the central bank might also have the option of *borrowing* from the market in the form of long-term securities.

5. Comparable feedbacks between the domestic and external operating regimes of this regimen could occur if the home central bank attempted to reduce the monetary base below a formerly determined benchmark path. The policymakers then might have to tolerate a large increase in external reserves before successfully achieving the new lower setting for the monetary base.

External open-market operations coincident with maintaining the pegged value of the exchange rate could similarly threaten the viability of domestic policy actions taken under the regimen of the interest-rate peg with exchange-rate peg. Raising (lowering) the setting for the interest-rate instrument might require, at a minimum, very large increases (decreases) in external reserves. These difficulties in achieving desired settings for the interest rate would probably be at least as severe as the analogous difficulties of achieving settings for the monetary base under a reserve-aggregate peg with exchange-rate peg.

In general, the more open the national economy, the greater the substitutability between home-currency assets and foreign-currency assets in private behavioral functions (for both home and foreign residents). The greater the degree of that substitutability, the more severe the difficulties of implementing domestic monetary policy in association with an exchange-rate peg. In the limiting case of "perfect" substitutability, the home authority could find it impossible to change the setting on its domestic instrument under a regimen with an exchange-rate peg so long as the fixed value of the exchange rate was successfully maintained.

Comparison of Pegging and Discretionary Regimens

Even if monetary policy is conducted with a regimen combining discretionary operating regimes, the issue of viability can arise.

Suppose the policymakers in a very open economy adopt a regimen with a discretionary exchange-rate regime. They may encounter difficulties in achieving desired settings for their domestic instrument if at the same time they discretionarily keep the exchange rate unchanged for an extended period. Analogous difficulties could arise even under a regimen with a discretionary external-reserves regime if the policymakers discretionarily vary the quantity of external reserves in such a manner as to keep the exchange rate effectively unchanged from an initial level.

The key point is that it may not be viable in a very open economy—using either an instrument rule or discretionary adaptation—to maintain a constant exchange rate and at the same time achieve settings for domestic instruments greatly out of line with financial conditions prevailing in the rest of the world.

Nevertheless, for any given degree of openness the issue of viability is less important when monetary policy is conducted under a discretionary rather than a pegging regimen. The period-by-period reconsideration of the external instrument setting under a discretionary exchange-rate regime, and a fortiori under a discretionary external-reserves regime, permits policymakers to abandon an initial value of the exchange rate as soon as their discretionary external actions threaten to undermine the attainment of desired settings for the domestic instruments. Discretionary settings for the external instrument can be similarly abandoned if changes in external reserves threaten to become intolerably large. At the very least, the use of a discretionary external regime helps the policymakers avoid the exchange-market crises and jerky stops and starts for domestic policy that can be characteristic of an exchange-rate peg.

To summarize: when the economy is extremely open or when external reserves are small, a nation's policymakers may experience substantial difficulty in achieving desired settings for their domestic instruments if they also maintain an unchanged value of the exchange rate. The greatest doubts about technical viability in such circumstances attach to regimens using an exchange-rate peg.

This conclusion does not deny the possibility that even an exchange-rate peg may prove to be viable for many nations over an extended period. The issue of technical viability may often be unimportant in practice—especially when policymakers pursue discretionary instrument adaptation.

Although technical viability is necessary if a regimen is to be used by policymakers, a ranking of regimens in terms of their viability, under either normal or extreme circumstances, provides no basis for choosing among them. The task of a nation's policymakers is to influence national ultimate-target variables, not merely to be sure of achieving settings for their policy instruments.

Exchange-Rate Variability and Influence over Ultimate Targets: Comparative-Statics Analysis

Theoretical research on the implications of variability in exchange rates for the ability of home policymakers to influence their ultimate-target variables has so far been conducted almost exclusively in the context of one-period comparative statics. That analysis has thus compared only the two archetypal external regimes that involve pegging rules; and it has neglected dynamic interactions of flows and stocks—for example, the intercountry transfer of wealth resulting from current-account imbalances.

To review the existing theoretical literature, the following discussion at first accepts the limitations of the conventional analysis. Later in the chapter the issues of autonomy and controllability are considered in a broader, dynamic context.

Autonomy

In the context of comparative statics, an analyst can study the implications of exchange-rate variability for the autonomy of a nation's policy instruments merely by examining the single-valued policy multipliers for the "one period" to which the analysis refers. Comparison of alternative external regimes is restricted to the two pegging rules. Hence the analyst simply compares the multipliers of a "domestic" action with respect to home ultimate-target variables under the exchange-rate peg and the external-reserves peg to ascertain which of the two impacts is greater.[6]

The conventional analysis of the impacts of *monetary-policy* actions under an exchange-rate peg and under an external-reserves peg is easily summarized. When the exchange rate is pegged, an expansionary domestic action lowers interest rates (either directly under an interest-rate peg or indirectly—as a result of increases in the quantity of central-bank liabilities—under a reserve-aggregate peg), which in turn stimulates aggregate demand and leads to increases in output and prices.[7] The fall in interest rates and an induced increase in imports together result in a current-

6. In principle, the analysis should treat policy multipliers as uncertain and therefore compare not only their means but also their variances and covariances (see chapters 12, 17, and 19). The discussion here, in keeping with the existing literature and with the especially great ignorance that exists about the other aspects of the multipliers' probability distributions, refers only to their means.

7. Most of the existing theoretical literature casually employs one or the other of the two alternative definitions of a "domestic" action—a change in an interest-rate instrument (under an interest-rate peg) or a change in the quantity of a financial aggregate (under a reserve-aggregate peg)—without worrying about possible differences between them. The extent to which output as well as prices rise depends on the degree of slack in resource utilization; see the discussion in appendix C.

account deficit and declines in external reserves. Depending on the economy's degree of openness, a modest or a sizable proportion of the expansionary stimulus of the domestic action can leak abroad through changes in the flows of imports and exports. When the policymakers operate an external-reserves peg, on the other hand, the same expansionary domestic action brings about a reduction in interest rates and a depreciation of the home currency. Both forces generate increased demand in home goods markets. The consequent increases in home output and prices, therefore, are greater than the increases under the exchange-rate peg. External reserves are of course unchanged, and any tendency toward a deficit in the current account of the balance of payments is mitigated by the depreciation of the home currency. More of the expansionary stimulus of the domestic action is bottled up at home as a result of the currency depreciation.

This conventional conclusion, that domestic monetary-policy actions have a larger impact on home output and the home price level under flexible than under fixed exchange rates, was initially put forward in the early 1960s by Marcus Fleming and Robert Mundell.[8] The models used by those authors in deriving the conclusion were later shown to embody troublesome deficiencies inconsistent with a stock-equilibrium theory of asset demands and supplies.[9] Subsequent reworking of the analysis correcting those deficiencies suggested that the conventional conclusion might not apply in all circumstances. In particular, in comparative-statics models in which stock demands for financial assets depend not only on expected returns and wealth but also on the flow of aggregate demand as a proxy for the volume of transactions, it was shown that in the short run the home currency can conceivably appreciate rather than depreciate under an external-reserves peg following an expansionary domestic monetary-policy action. An appreciation of the home currency, were it to occur, would result in a *smaller* impact on home output and prices than under an exchange-rate peg.[10]

Consideration of the multipliers for domestic monetary policy in the comparative-statics framework used in chapter 22 suggests the same potential ambiguity. An expansionary domestic monetary-policy action in that framework pushes up home prices and outputs under regimes with either an exchange-rate peg or an external-reserves peg. Complexities stemming from the sensitivity of demands for financial assets to the volume of transactions (the nominal value of national product) make it theoretically conceivable, however, for the home currency to appreciate rather

8. See J. Marcus Fleming, "Domestic Financial Policies Under Fixed and Floating Exchange Rates,"*IMF Staff Papers*, vol. 9 (November 1962), pp. 369–80; Robert A. Mundell, "Flexible Exchange Rates and Employment Policy," *Canadian Journal of Economics and Political Science*, vol. 27 (November 1961), pp. 509–17; and Robert A. Mundell, "Capital Mobility and Stabilization Policy Under Fixed and Flexible Exchange Rates," ibid., vol. 29 (November 1963), pp. 475–85. The Mundell papers appear in Robert A. Mundell, *International Economics* (Macmillan, 1968).

9. See, for example, Ronald I. McKinnon and Wallace E. Oates, *The Implications of International Economic Integration for Monetary, Fiscal, and Exchange-Rate Policy*, Princeton Studies in International Finance 16 (Princeton University Press, 1966); Ronald I. McKinnon, "Portfolio Balance and International Payments Adjustment," in Robert A. Mundell and Alexander K. Swoboda, eds., *Monetary Problems of the International Economy* (University of Chicago Press, 1970); Thomas D. Willett and Francesco Forte, "Interest Rate Policy and External Balance," *Quarterly Journal of Economics*, vol. 83 (May 1969), pp. 242–62.

10. See Dale W Henderson, "Modeling the Interdependence of National Money and Capital Markets," eview, vol. 67 (February 1977, *Papers and Proceedings, 1976*), p. 194. This paper ices in comparative-statics models and conclusions between the Fleming-Mundell he portfolio-balance view of the 1970s.

than depreciate. Accordingly, in the models based on that framework it is possible for the impacts on home prices and outputs to be larger under an exchange-rate peg than under an external-reserves peg—the reverse of the conventional conclusion.

Further research is required before this possibility can be put into proper perspective. But I conjecture that the conventional conclusion is much the more likely outcome for present-day industrial economies. An expansionary monetary-policy action seems especially likely to lead to a depreciation of the home currency under an external-reserves peg once dynamic stock-flow interactions are brought into the analysis (see below). The contrary theoretical possibility cannot be dismissed out of hand, however; the aspects of behavior that give rise to this possibility in the newer models—the sensitivity of the stock demands for money and other financial assets to the flow of economic activity—are a critical link between financial markets and goods markets.

Comparative-statics analysis of the relative magnitudes of the multipliers for *fiscal-policy* actions under an exchange-rate peg and an external-reserves peg raises analogous issues.[11] Even in the 1960s, theoretical analysis generated ambiguous conclusions. One of Mundell's papers, for example, argued that fiscal policy as well as monetary policy would have larger impacts on home variables under an external-reserves peg than under an exchange-rate peg.[12] Other models, including one of Mundell's that uses the assumption that home and foreign interest rates cannot differ, generated the conclusion that fiscal policy can have *smaller* impacts on home variables under an external-reserves peg when capital is internationally mobile.[13] The ambiguity in results stemmed from the fact that under the external-reserves peg the home currency could either depreciate or appreciate after an expansionary fiscal action, thus either reinforcing or mitigating the direct effects of the fiscal stimulus.

Theoretical reworking in the 1970s of the Fleming-Mundell model (replacing its inappropriate treatment of asset demands and the capital account in the balance of payments with a portfolio-balance approach) has not resolved this ambiguity. In some of the newer comparative-statics models, the home currency unambiguously appreciates under an external-reserves peg, and home external reserves unambiguously increase under an exchange-rate peg; in those models the multipliers for fiscal actions are unambiguously smaller under the external-reserves peg than under the exchange-rate peg.[14] In other models, however, the relative magnitudes of the fiscal policy multipliers under the two external pegging regimes remain ambiguous.[15] The differences among model results are partially explainable by their different

11. The summary generalizations about fiscal policy that follow gloss over the critical differences in alternative specifications of budgetary operating regimes and financing procedures and hence in alternative specifications of fiscal-policy actions (see chapters 14 and 21). Most of the conventional theoretical literature on the impacts of fiscal policy under fixed and flexible exchange rates has been insufficiently sensitive to these issues.

12. *International Economics*, chap. 17.

13. Ibid., chap. 18; in this model, in fact, fiscal policy becomes altogether ineffective in influencing home variables when the country is small and very open and the exchange rate is freely flexible.

14. See, for example, the discussion in Henderson, "Modeling the Interdependence of National Money and Capital Markets."

15. See, for example, Betty C. Daniel, "Analysis of Stabilization Policies in Open Economies under Conditions of Inflation and Inflationary Expectations" (Ph.D. dissertation, University of North Carolina, 1976).

specifications of fiscal-policy actions.[16] Even when this source of difference is removed, however, some ambiguity remains.

On the basis of the literature using comparative-statics models, therefore, it is not yet possible to make reliable generalizations about the consequences of exchange-rate variability for the autonomy of fiscal policy.

One additional point about the autonomy of both monetary policy and fiscal policy needs to be stressed. The preceding comparisons of the two external pegging regimes assume that an exchange-rate peg can be successfully maintained. As already noted, however, adoption of a policy regime incorporating an exchange-rate peg can imply very large fluctuations in external reserves. If the changes in external reserves should become intolerably large, the exchange rate that was pegged for the time being will have to be altered by a discrete devaluation or revaluation. To take this possibility into account in theoretical analysis of an exchange-rate peg is difficult. Yet it can scarcely be ignored in practical comparisons of the multipliers for domestic policy instruments under an exchange-rate peg and an external-reserves peg. The conclusion that domestic policy actions have more powerful impacts on home ultimate targets under an external-reserves peg than under an exchange-rate peg is valid, if at all, only so long as the pegged exchange rate under the latter is successfully maintained.[17]

Controllability

Suppose the comparative-statics impacts of domestic monetary-policy actions on a nation's target variables could be definitely shown to be larger under an external-reserves peg than under a successfully maintained exchange-rate peg. Suppose the same were true of fiscal-policy actions (contrary to the preceding discussion). The autonomy of the nation's macroeconomic policy, as defined in theoretical comparative-statics analysis, would then have been shown to be greater under perfectly flexible exchange rates than under rigidly pegged exchange rates. What conclusions would follow for policy decisions?

In principle, no definitive conclusions would follow! The characteristics of the policy multipliers relating national instruments and national ultimate targets may be the single most important determinant of the controllability of the nation's economy (see chapter 12). But they are nonetheless only one of several critical determinants (see chapter 13). Even within the limits of comparative-statics analysis, therefore, appraisal of the relative merits of fixed and flexible exchange rates

16. Some analyses, for example, model an expansionary fiscal stimulus as a bond-financed increase in government expenditures, whereas in other analyses the stimulus takes the form of a balanced-budget increase in government expenditures.

17. Imagine that figure 22-1 portrays four hypothetical evolutions of the home economy, in each of which the home government takes an identical expansionary monetary-policy action at time t_0. The consequences of the domestic stimulus for home prices and output will obviously differ between the exchange-rate peg and external-reserves peg during the period t_0 to t_2; under the external-reserves peg, the depreciation of the currency bottles up more of the stimulus at home and raises prices and output by a larger amount. Now, however, alter the time horizon of the analysis, and ask about the relative sizes of the impacts of the domestic action at the end of the entire period t_0 to t_3. Given that policymakers are forced to accept a discrete devaluation of the home currency on the date t_2 in the case of the exchange-rate peg and that the levels of the exchange rate during the subsequent period t_2 to t_3 are roughly similar under both the exchange-rate peg and the external-reserves peg, only minor differences in impacts on home prices and output under the two pegging regimes might be observable by the date t_3. If that were the case, moreover, it would be inappropriate to make unqualified statements asserting a greater autonomy for domestic monetary policy under "flexible" than under "fixed" exchange rates.

in promoting controllability must also consider the effects of nonpolicy exogenous forces on home ultimate targets and differences in those effects under alternative policy regimens.

Chapter 22 outlines an analysis of the latter sort. It shows that an external-reserves peg provides better protection for home ultimate targets against certain types of disturbances but inferior protection against others. Thus no sweeping generalization in favor of one or the other external operating regime can be analytically justified. To decide whether an external-reserves peg or an exchange-rate peg will provide the better protection on the average, a nation's policymakers must take into account the structure of their economy, including its degree of openness, and must form judgments about the frequencies and magnitudes of the various nonpolicy disturbances the economy will encounter.

Unambiguous conclusions that the home impacts of home policy actions are larger under freely flexible exchange rates would constitute a powerful *other-things-equal* argument for choosing an external-reserves peg rather than an exchange-rate peg. But the advantages of greater autonomy under an external-reserves peg would also be coupled with greater short-run exposure to financial-sector disturbances and to disturbances originating within the real sector of the home economy. The more prevalent these types of disturbances, the stronger (other things being equal) is the argument against the external-reserves peg. The various benefits and risks thus have to be weighed against each other. There is no reason to expect the net balance of the benefits and risks to work out the same way for all national economies.

Analysis of the autonomy of a nation's policy instruments, even if its results were unambiguous, would therefore not qualitatively alter the conclusions of chapter 22 about the appropriate procedure for choosing an external pegging rule in the analytical context of comparative statics. The "correct" choice for home policymakers between an external-reserves peg and an exchange-rate peg still depends ultimately on the variances and covariances of the nonpolicy exogenous forces that drive the home economy and on the characteristics of the economic structure itself (which are also, of course, the ultimate determinants of the absolute values and variances of the multipliers for monetary policy and fiscal policy).

Imagine a nation with relatively sophisticated policymakers, with a relatively stable institutional environment, and with an economy in which relatively few disturbances originate in home financial markets and in the home real sector. Suppose that most of the major disturbances experienced by this economy originate in the rest of the world. If the autonomy of monetary policy for this nation were greater under an external-reserves peg than under an exchange-rate peg, that fact would reinforce an already strong presumption that the nation would be better off on the average under an external-reserves peg.

Now consider a nation whose policymakers are relatively inept by world standards, whose institutional environment is relatively unstable, and whose economy tends to be more strongly buffeted by internal than by external disturbances. In such a case, the home economy on the average would be in greater trouble under an external-reserves peg than under an exchange-rate peg. This verdict might well be valid even if the autonomy of monetary policy and fiscal policy were much greater under an external-reserves peg. For a nation with those characteristics, the greater autonomy associated with exchange-rate variability would be a very mixed blessing.

Policy Impacts and Controllability in a Dynamic Context

The preceding analysis of autonomy and controllability is deficient in two respects. It does not take into account dynamic interactions between asset stocks and current-period flows. And it fails even to mention the possibility of discretionary external operating regimes.

Policy Impacts with Stock-Flow Interactions

Chapter 22 emphasizes the importance of broadening a comparative-statics analysis to incorporate dynamic changes in asset stocks due to saving, investment in new capital goods, imbalances in the government budget, and imbalances in the current account of the balance of payments. Those same stock-flow relationships can have a significant bearing on the analytical issues discussed in the preceding section.

A policy multiplier in a comparative-statics context is merely a single number; in a multiperiod context, it is an entire time series expressing, period by period, the changes in the time path of an endogenous variable attributable to a specified pattern of changes in the time path of a policy instrument. Comparisons of the degree of autonomy associated with alternative policy regimes therefore become much more complex as soon as the analysis abandons a comparative-statics frame of reference (see chapter 12).

Recall that more recently formulated comparative-statics models allow for the possibility of the home currency appreciating rather than depreciating as a result of an expansionary monetary-policy action taken by the home central bank, which in turn would imply a lesser rather than greater degree of autonomy for domestic monetary policy under an external-reserves peg than under an exchange-rate peg. The possibility of this outcome seems unlikely to survive in a dynamic respecification of comparative-statics models. Over a medium or long run, if not in the short run, the dynamic processes ignored in comparative-statics models are likely to move the exchange rate in the direction predicted by conventional theorizing.

The unconventional result that expansionary domestic monetary policy might appreciate the home currency under an external-reserves peg occurs in the newer comparative-statics models because those models allow for transactions-related demands for money and securities. A higher level of nominal income brought about by the expansionary monetary policy has the effect, other things being equal, of raising the transactions demand for money and correspondingly reducing the demands for other home-currency assets and for foreign-currency assets. The more this other-things-equal increase in the transactions demand for money is met by reductions in foreign-currency rather than home-currency assets, the more likely is an appreciation of the home currency.[18]

18. The comparative-statics framework in appendix C endogenizes the behavior of home banks. In that framework, therefore, the direction of movement of the exchange rate following an expansionary domestic monetary policy also depends on the reserve requirement imposed on the deposit liabilities of home banks and on the proportion of the banks' investable assets allocated to foreign-currency securities. The larger is the reserve requirement and the smaller is the proportion of foreign-currency assets in the banks' desired portfolio, the more likely the unconventional result of an appreciation of the home currency.

But the comparative-statics models ignore the intercountry transfer of wealth through current-account imbalances. With an expansionary monetary policy and an unchanged exchange rate, the current account would tend to move into deficit simultaneously with the expansion in home outputs and prices. Any short-run tendency for the home currency to appreciate would make the current account swing even further in a deficit direction. The transfer of wealth to foreigners from home residents associated with the current-account deficit would gradually reduce worldwide private demand for home-currency assets and increase the demand for foreign-currency assets. If it should occur at all, therefore, any shorter-run tendency for the home currency to appreciate after an expansionary monetary-policy action is likely to be reversed over the longer run by the cumulating downward pressure on the currency resulting from the wealth transfer associated with the current-account deficit.[19]

Pending the results of further research, the preceding argument provides grounds for discounting the unconventional possibilities encountered in comparative-statics models and relying instead on the traditional conclusion that the autonomy of domestic monetary policy is greater under an external-reserves peg than under an exchange-rate peg.

A dynamic respecification of comparative-statics models will also help resolve the current theoretical ambiguity about the relative magnitudes of fiscal-policy multipliers under fixed and flexible exchange rates. I conjecture that such research will tip the balance in favor of the view that expansionary fiscal policy generates, in the medium or long run if not in the short run, a *depreciation* of the home currency under an external-reserves peg and a *decline* in reserves under an exchange-rate peg.[20]

The reasoning behind this conjecture again appeals to the dynamics of wealth transfer through the current account of the balance of payments. An expansionary fiscal-policy action, regardless of how fiscal policy is defined, pushes up the home price level and (at least in the shorter run) home output. Other things being equal, the current account is also pushed in the direction of a deficit. The home currency can appreciate in the shorter run under an external-reserves peg (or external reserves can increase under an exchange-rate peg) because of two forces working through the capital account of the balance of payments. Private economic units can make net shifts in their portfolios away from foreign-currency assets toward home-currency assets (a) because of the higher level of home nominal income, which induces an increased transactions demand for home money and hence also a higher level of banks' investable assets, and (b) because of rises in home interest rates induced by the increases in transactions demand for home money.[21] Those two

19. If the home currency depreciates promptly in the shorter run (the more probable outcome), there is less of a tendency toward a current-account deficit and less ensuing transfer of wealth abroad. But there is also no unconventional outcome to explain.

20. Those working toward such a dynamic analysis of fiscal-policy impacts include Stephen J. Turnovsky, "The Dynamics of Fiscal Policy in an Open Economy," *Journal of International Economics*, vol. 6 (May 1976), pp. 115–42; and Donald J. Mathieson, "The Impact of Monetary and Fiscal Policy Under Flexible Exchange Rates and Alternative Expectations Structures," *IMF Staff Papers*, vol. 24 (November 1977), pp. 535–68.

21. The second of these forces can operate under a monetary-policy regimen in which the policymakers use a reserve-aggregate peg for their domestic regime, but cannot operate (or at least not to the same degree) when the domestic regime is an interest-rate peg.

forces, however, are shorter run portfolio shifts. They can only exert pressure on the home currency to appreciate (under an external-reserves peg) or on external reserves to increase (under an exchange-rate peg) as long as home nominal income and home interest rates are in the process of moving to higher levels. In contrast, the transfer of wealth out of home into foreign portfolios because of the current-account deficit exerts pressure on the home currency to depreciate over the entire period that the current account continues in deficit. That persisting downward pressure on the home currency will eventually more than offset any net upward pressure in the shorter run.

If the expansionary fiscal-policy action results in a budget deficit (for example, an increase in government expenditures financed by issuance of new debt), the likelihood is still greater that the home currency—eventually, if not in the shorter run—will depreciate from its initial level. A government budget deficit adds to the stock of private net wealth; the increment to private wealth must take the form of home-currency assets if the new government debt is denominated in home currency. Since private asset holders will wish to diversify any increments to their wealth among foreign-currency as well as home-currency assets, however, the debt-financed expansionary fiscal policy has the effect (other things being equal) of creating an excess supply of home-currency assets and thereby putting pressure on the home currency to depreciate.[22] This source of downward pressure on the home currency, like the transfer of wealth through the current-account deficit, is a continuing force. It persists so long as the government budget remains in deficit with new debt securities issued as financing.[23]

The foregoing comments have significance for more than the direction of movement of the exchange rate. If expansionary fiscal-policy actions under an external-reserves peg lead if not initially then at least over a longer run to a depreciation of the home currency (and vice versa for contractionary fiscal policy), then the impacts of fiscal policy on home ultimate targets will if not initially then at least over a longer run be greater under an external-reserves peg than under an exchange-rate peg. As with monetary policy, movements of the exchange rate would eventually help to bottle up more of the thrust of government actions within the home country.[24]

Discretionary versus Pegging External Regimes

Comparative-statics analysis of autonomy and controllability encourages a focus on the polar cases of the two pegging rules for external monetary policy. Chapter 22 emphasizes the artificiality of the traditional preoccupation with fixed versus

22. A government budget deficit financed by increases in reserve money rather than government debt (a combination of expansionary fiscal policy and expansionary monetary policy as those policies are often defined) a fortiori leads to depreciation of the home currency and to upward pressure on the home price level.

23. The exchange-rate effects of a debt-financed fiscal expansion would obviously be different if the government denominated its new debt in *foreign* rather than home currency; see Peter Isard, *Exchange-Rate Determination: A Survey of Popular Views and Recent Models*, Princeton Studies in International Finance 42 (Princeton University Press, 1978), pp. 28–29.

24. Differences in the time profile of the monetary-policy and fiscal-policy multipliers can be of critical significance for short-run macroeconomic policy. Suppose that expansionary domestic monetary-policy actions under an external-reserves peg were to lead promptly to depreciation of the home currency and hence promptly to upward pressures on the home price level (through the currency depreciation), but only with a lag to increases in real output. Suppose further that expansionary fiscal-policy actions under an external-reserves peg were to lead reasonably promptly to short-run increases in output and only over a

flexible exchange rates and its dysfunctional contribution to analysis of discretionary macroeconomic policy. The points made there are equally applicable to the subject of this chapter. Thus the only need here is to expand on the implications of those points for controllability and policy successfulness.

Consider first the narrower question of autonomy. By definition, the degree of autonomy depends on the characteristics of policy multipliers. The differences between discretionary and pegging operating regimes do not, to a first approximation, involve differences in the impacts of a given change in an instrument setting on target variables. Rather, the differences come from the presence or absence of an adaptive variation in the instrument settings. To a first approximation, therefore, the policy multipliers relevant for a discretionary regimen are the same as those relevant for the counterpart pegging regimen.[25] As specific examples, the multipliers for the home price level and national output with respect to a given-sized expansion in the monetary base under a reserve-aggregate peg with external-reserves peg might be roughly equivalent to those under a regimen combining a discretionary reserve-aggregate regime with a discretionary external-reserves regime; and the analogous multipliers under a reserve-aggregate peg with exchange-rate peg might be roughly equivalent to those under a regimen combining a discretionary reserve-aggregate regime with a discretionary exchange-rate regime.

Consequently, if the autonomy of domestic monetary policy is greater under an external-reserves peg than under an exchange-rate peg, it will presumably also be greater under a discretionary external-reserves regime than under a discretionary exchange-rate regime. What chiefly matters for autonomy is the presence or absence of movement in the exchange rate following a domestic policy action; exchange-rate movement facilitates a more powerful impact of home policy actions on home ultimate targets. Whether the movement comes about discretionarily or through pegging the quantity of external reserves is a secondary matter.

Now, however, consider the broader issues of controllability and policy successfulness. For those issues, the differences between discretionary and pegging regimens are highly significant. A period-by-period adaptive approach to policy decisions makes it possible to respond differentially to different types of nonpolicy disturbances. Home policymakers can try, with both their domestic and external instruments, to promote "price adjustment" when price adjustment seems appropriate, and conversely, to promote "quantity adjustment" when price adjustment does not seem appropriate.

Discretionary instrument adaptation therefore has a clear potential to outperform instrument rules as a means of helping policymakers exert control over home ultimate-target variables. This proposition, valid in general, applies no less forcefully to the problem of choosing an operating regime for external monetary policy. Policymakers wishing to exert the maximum possible control over the nation's

---

longer run to increases in prices and a depreciation of the home currency. In such an economy, policymakers might want to rely more heavily on fiscal policy than monetary policy for short-run management of the real economy. An argument along these lines is advanced in Rudiger Dornbusch and Paul Krugman, "Flexible Exchange Rates in the Short Run," *Brookings Papers on Economic Activity, 3:1976*, pp. 537–84.

25. The multipliers can be the same only "to a first approximation" because private-sector expectations of government policy actions will differ depending on whether the government employs pegging rules or discretionary adaptation; those differences in turn imply differences in economic structure, and hence different policy multipliers (see chapter 18).

economy will thus reject both of the external pegging rules and implement external monetary policy with either a discretionary exchange-rate regime or a discretionary external-reserves regime.

The choice between the two discretionary external regimes involves difficulties similar to those affecting the domestic choice between a discretionary interest-rate regime and a discretionary reserve-aggregate regime. Whether the exchange rate or external reserves is selected as the external instrument is undoubtedly less important than the issue of how the instrument settings are varied. But instrument choice per se may well have a significant bearing on controllability.

Substantially more research is required before one can safely generalize about the relative merits of the two discretionary external regimes in promoting controllability and policy successfulness. The only general conclusions about external operating regimes that seem warranted so far are negative conclusions about the nondiscretionary pegging alternatives. These negative conclusions follow from the analysis in chapter 22 and can be stated succinctly. There is no theoretical presumption whatever that a nation's policymakers can exert the maximum possible control over their ultimate-target variables simply by refraining from interfering with market determination of freely floating exchange rates. Nor is there any analytical basis for believing that more rather than less variability in exchange rates always promotes controllability and policy successfulness. A fortiori, maximum control and maximum overall success in achieving policy objectives is not possible when the exchange rate is held fixed with a pegging rule.

The awkward fact is that an open national economy is sometimes better off when the exchange rate is allowed to move and at other times better off when it is not allowed to move. The more that policymakers preoccupy themselves with the traditional choice between the exchange-rate peg and the external-reserves peg, the less progress they can make in dealing with this awkward fact.

Does Variability in Exchange Rates Insulate the National Economy?

According to a widespread influential view, "flexible exchange rates are a means of combining interdependence among countries through trade with a maximum of internal monetary independence" and "they are a means of permitting each country to seek for monetary stability according to its own lights, without either imposing its mistakes on its neighbors or having their mistakes imposed on it."[26] A careless version of this view asserts that flexible exchange rates bottle up policy actions and nonpolicy disturbances within the nation where they originate, thereby completely insulating other nations from their consequences. A somewhat less sweeping version (such as the preceding quotation) asserts only that flexible rates completely insulate nations from each other's "monetary" disturbances.

26. Milton Friedman, "The Case for Flexible Exchange Rates," in Friedman, *Essays in Positive Economics* (University of Chicago Press, 1953), p. 200. Note that "independence" is used in this quotation to mean autonomy or controllability rather than merely ability to act independently. For another illustration in the literature of the view that exchange-rate variability tends to insulate national economies, see W. M. Corden, *Inflation, Exchange Rates and the World Economy* (University of Chicago Press, 1977), chap. 4.

Current macroeconomic theory, however, cannot be made to support either assertion—not for the extreme case of a rigid external-reserves peg and not for any other external operating regime. Nor is there any convincing empirical evidence for it. Monetary-policy actions in foreign countries affect the home economy—including specifically ultimate targets like aggregate output and the price level—whatever external operating regime may be in force. The effects of home monetary-policy actions are not completely confined to the home nation regardless of the manner and degree of exchange-rate variability; home policy actions always have significant impacts on the rest of the world. Similar conclusions apply to the international consequences of fiscal-policy actions and nonpolicy disturbances. Incontrovertibly, *the interdependencies among significantly open economies are much too pervasive to be neutralized by any degree or form of variability in exchange rates.*

"Domestic" policy actions taken by national governments are not independent. Domestic monetary-policy actions taken by one nation necessarily alter either interest rates or domestic financial aggregates (or more likely both) in the rest of the world, and vice versa for domestic actions taken by monetary authorities in the rest of the world. The specific home variables affected by foreign monetary-policy actions and the size of the effects depend on exchange-rate movements, if any, and on the domestic responses, if any, by the home policymakers. But no type of external operating regime and no type of offsetting domestic response can prevent *some* kind of impact on the home economy.

Consider the short-run impacts in home financial markets of an expansionary domestic open-market operation by a foreign central bank (for example, a purchase of foreign-currency-denominated securities resulting in an expansion of the foreign-currency monetary base). If the monetary-policy regimen of the home nation is an interest-rate peg with exchange-rate peg, home external reserves and the home-currency monetary base will be increased. If the home regimen is a reserve-aggregate peg with exchange-rate peg, external reserves will increase and interest rates on home-currency securities will rise. Under an interest-rate peg with external-reserves peg, the home currency will appreciate and the home-currency monetary base will be altered. If the home policymakers use a reserve-aggregate peg with external-reserves peg, the home currency will appreciate and home interest rates will be altered.[27] Under any of the regimens using discretionary operating regimes, some combination of the above effects will occur. In no conceivable case can all key variables in the home financial sector remain unchanged after the monetary-policy action taken abroad. Indeed, regardless of the manner and degree of exchange-rate variability, interdependence between home and foreign financial markets is sufficiently pervasive for the domestic operating regime chosen by the foreign policymakers to condition the effects of *home* monetary-policy actions on the *home* economy. (See chapter 25 for further discussion.)

Similar conclusions about the insulating properties of exchange-rate variability follow when analysis is extended to cover the financial and real sectors of the home

27. Whether the home central bank will be required to carry out domestic open-market purchases or sales to keep the interest rate at its exogenous setting under the interest-rate peg with external-reserves peg, and whether home interest rates will rise or fall under the reserve-aggregate peg with external-reserves peg, depends on the characteristics of the asset-demand equations of private home and foreign residents.

economy together. There is no conceivable way that the prices and quantities of goods produced and consumed in the home economy can be completely insulated from policy actions taken in the rest of the world. In particular, regardless of the external operating regime, *monetary-policy* actions taken abroad get transmitted to home outputs and prices. No theoretical model of "flexible exchange rates" can be made to yield a complete-insulation outcome without using implausible simplifying assumptions directly responsible for that outcome.[28]

There is nevertheless an element of truth in the conventional wisdom about the insulating properties of flexible exchange rates. The consequences for the home economy of policy actions and nonpolicy disturbances originating abroad do vary in magnitude under different home policy regimes. For most, if not all, domestic macroeconomic policy actions taken abroad and for many types of nonpolicy disturbances, the effects spill over *less* into the home country under an external-reserves peg or an external regime in which discretionary decisions keep external reserves unchanged than under an exchange-rate peg or an external regime in which discretionary decisions prevent the exchange rate from moving.

Support for this conclusion may be derived from analysis of the theoretical framework outlined in chapter 22 and appendix C.[29] In that framework, foreign policy actions and nonpolicy disturbances in the real sector of the foreign economy have smaller impacts on home ultimate-target variables under an interest-rate peg with external-reserves peg than under an interest-rate peg with exchange-rate peg, and smaller impacts under a reserve-aggregate peg with external-reserves peg than under a reserve-aggregate peg with exchange-rate peg. The policy actions and nonpolicy disturbances are bottled up to a greater degree within the rest of the world under an external-reserves peg because of exchange-rate movements and their effects on demands and supplies in goods markets. A policy action or nonpolicy disturbance abroad that has expansionary (contractionary) implications for foreign prices or output brings about, if not in the short run at least in a medium or long run, an appreciation (depreciation) of the home currency. The other-things-equal effects of this exchange-rate movement on home goods markets mitigate the excess demand (excess supply) that exists at the initial exchange rate. Relative to the outcome under an exchange-rate peg in which the initial exchange rate is maintained unchanged, therefore, the external-reserves peg moderates the ensuing impacts of the foreign events on home ultimate targets like employment and inflation. Con-

28. The view that flexible exchange rates insulate each nation's economy evolved during a time when theoretical analysis of international macroeconomics tended to ignore *financial* interdependence. Analyses that focus exclusively on the current account of the balance of payments and the direct interdependence of real sectors through exports and imports of goods and services (implicitly or explicitly assuming an absence of all international capital flows except changes in official reserve assets) can yield the complete-insulation outcome. The model in Murray C. Kemp, *The Pure Theory of International Trade* (Prentice-Hall, 1964), chaps. 19 and 20, also generates the complete-insulation result. Kemp's model, however, considers only a single asset ("money") in each country and therefore does not have endogenous interest rates and a plausible capital account in the balance of payments; those features of the model in turn permit the implausible conclusion that total spending in each country is invariant to changes in the exchange rate.

29. The illustrative framework in appendix C represents all key foreign macroeconomic variables as exogenous and does not contain an explicit representation of the instruments of either foreign fiscal policy or monetary policy (with the possible exception of the foreign interest rate). It therefore cannot be used in a careful analysis of the consequences of policy actions by the foreign government. But if foreign policymakers take expansionary (contractionary) action with either domestic monetary policy or fiscal policy, that action can be assumed to raise (lower) foreign prices and output. In the context of that framework, therefore, the consequences for the home economy of foreign policy actions can be approximated by postulating an "exogenous" rise or fall in foreign prices and output.

ceivably, the appreciation (depreciation) of the home currency could even go so far as to produce a net contractionary (expansionary) impact on home ultimate targets, more than offsetting the initial expansionary (contractionary) impetus of the foreign events at the initial exchange rate. I conjecture, however, that the typical impacts on the home economy under an external-reserves peg are in the same direction as the corresponding impacts under an exchange-rate peg. A definitive verdict on the direction of the effects on the home economy, and a better understanding of their size, are contingent on further research.[30]

Similar generalizations apply to policy regimens in which home policymakers use a discretionary external regime. Whether that regime has external reserves or the exchange rate as the instrument, moreover, is probably a secondary matter. The impacts on home ultimate targets of foreign policy actions and nonpolicy disturbances originating in the real sector of the foreign economy are likely to be smaller if the home policymakers discretionarily keep the quantity of external reserves fairly constant and allow the exchange rate to adjust than if they discretionarily engage in large amounts of foreign-exchange intervention to keep the exchange rate relatively unchanged.

These generalizations reinforce what was said earlier in the chapter about the autonomy of home macroeconomic policy. Another way of stating those earlier conclusions would have been to point out that home monetary-policy and fiscal-policy actions tend to spill over to the rest of the world more under an exchange-rate peg than under an external-reserves peg, and more under a discretionary external regime in which the exchange rate is kept relatively unchanged than under one in which the home currency is allowed to depreciate or appreciate.

The preceding analysis of the insulating properties of external operating regimes may be summarized in a single proposition: although complete insulation of the nation's economy through exchange-rate variability is impossible, policymakers can provide the maximum attainable degree of buffering against most policy actions of foreign governments and against many types of disturbances originating in the real sector of foreign economies by allowing the home currency to appreciate in response to external stimuli that are expansionary and to depreciate in response to those that are contractionary.

This proposition does not, it should be clear, constitute an unqualified recommendation in favor of more rather than less exchange-rate variability. The "partial insulation" resulting from variability must be viewed in the light of two further, equally important points.

First, the buffering tendencies associated with exchange-rate variability do *not* apply to every type of disturbance originating abroad. For example, suppose foreign nonbanks or foreign banks decide, for reasons not stemming from changes in their

---

30. Several theoretical models in the literature yield the result that under an external-reserves peg an expansionary (contractionary) event occurring abroad contracts (expands) home output or prices. See, for example, Mundell, *International Economics*, chap. 18, p. 269. For discussion of this result and some empirical research that contradicts it, see John F. Helliwell, "Adjustment Under Fixed and Flexible Exchange Rates," in Peter B. Kenen, ed., *International Trade and Finance: Frontiers for Research* (Cambridge University Press, 1975) and John F. Helliwell, "Trade, Capital Flows, and Migration as Channels for International Transmission of Stabilization Policies," in Albert Ando and others, eds., *International Aspects of Stabilization Policies* (Federal Reserve Bank of Boston, 1974). In the models based on the illustrative framework in appendix C, an actual contraction (expansion) of home output or prices following an expansionary (contractionary) impetus originating abroad appears to be a possible but not necessary outcome.

expectations of interest yields and the future exchange rate, to reduce the proportion of home-currency assets and to increase the proportion of foreign-currency assets in their portfolios; a policy permitting the exchange rate to adjust in response to that changed behavior of foreign economic units would not provide the maximum degree of buffering for the home economy (see chapter 22). More generally, in circumstances in which financial-market disturbances originate abroad, home policymakers may be *least* effective in buffering the effects of the disturbances if they refrain from exchange-market intervention and permit the exchange rate to float.

Second, the buffering tendencies associated with exchange-rate variability are not always beneficial. Home policymakers should not want their nation to be buffered against the rest of the world, for example, in periods dominated by disturbances originating within the real sector of the home economy. If home policymakers take policy actions that turn out to have been mistakes, moreover, they will be less unhappy in retrospect to have had as much as possible of the consequences of their mistakes spill over into the rest of the world.

Does Variability in Exchange Rates Free Macroeconomic Policy to Focus on the Domestic Economy?

The idea that exchange-rate variability insulates a nation's economy is frequently associated with another idea, that flexible exchange rates unshackle monetary policy and fiscal policy from international constraints, freeing them to concentrate on domestic economic developments. To those who advance that idea, "monetary policy" means *domestic* monetary policy.

Consider, for example, the following passage from Harry Johnson's essay on "The Case for Flexible Exchange Rates, 1969":

> The fundamental argument for flexible exchange rates is that they would *allow countries autonomy with respect to their use of monetary, fiscal, and other policy instruments,* consistent with the maintenance of whatever degree of freedom in international transactions they chose to allow their citizens, by *automatically ensuring the preservation of external equilibrium.* Since, in the absence of balance-of-payments reasons for interfering in international trade and payments, and given autonomy of domestic policy, there is an overwhelmingly strong case for the maximum possible freedom of international transactions to permit exploitation of the economies of international specialization and division of labor, the argument for flexible exchange rates can be put more strongly still: *flexible exchange rates are essential to the preservation of national autonomy and independence* consistent with efficient organization and development of the world economy.[31]

Later in the essay, Johnson states that "the adoption of flexible exchange rates would have the great advantage of *freeing* governments to use their instruments of domestic policy for the pursuit of domestic objectives, while, at the same time, removing the pressures to intervene in international trade and payments for balance-of-payments reasons" (p. 100).

Johnson himself was doubtless aware of many of the complexities associated with this argument. But numerous others are not. Popular advocacy of flexible

31. In George N. Halm, ed., *Approaches to Greater Flexibility in Exchange Rates: The Burgenstock Papers* (Princeton University Press, 1970), pp. 91–92; the italics are my addition. Note that the meanings Johnson attaches to "autonomy" and "independence" are problematic in the way pointed out earlier in this chapter.

exchange rates, for example, frequently involves the flat-footed claim that, since exchange-rate movements automatically satisfy the balance-of-payments constraint, governments are free to forget about the balance of payments and to worry merely about the domestic economy.

Although there is a kernel of truth in conventional views about the "policy-liberating" properties of flexible exchange rates, that kernel is customarily surrounded by a great deal of chaff. Worse still, careless acceptance of the conventional view fosters a dangerous attitude toward the conduct of national economic policy. The injunction to let the exchange rate float freely and to focus attention on the domestic economy can easily be interpreted to mean that economic developments abroad can be ignored; by implication, flexible exchange rates provide complete insulation.

But complete insulation is an illusion. In any case, home policymakers should not always want to be insulated. "Forgetting" about the external sector of the economy, therefore, can never be appropriate and can be especially silly in situations in which the insulating tendencies of exchange-rate variability are detrimental.

Consider a situation in which the home economy experiences an unwanted expansionary shock generated internally—for example, an unexpected spurt in investment spending. If home policymakers happen to be holding the exchange rate unchanged at the time the inflationary stimulus occurs, they will experience a loss in external reserves but will to the maximum extent possible share the adverse consequences of the shock with the rest of the world. But imagine now that the policymakers reason as follows: "We can shut off the decline in our external reserves by refraining from exchange-market intervention. If we maintain the 'discipline' of the fixed exchange rate, however, further declines in our external reserves will probably force us to take restrictive actions with fiscal policy or monetary policy. Let us therefore simply let the currency float and avoid having to subjugate our domestic policies to the shackles of the balance of payments."

Such an attitude would be very wrongheaded. In the hypothesized circumstances of an unexpected spurt in home spending, the resulting inflationary impetus will affect the economy, including its external sector, in one way or another. The short-run response that will best advance the selfish interests of the home nation is to resist or at least to moderate the tendency for the currency to depreciate, thereby allowing more of the inflationary shock to spill over abroad, while simultaneously altering the settings on domestic policy instruments to try to offset the disturbance. The "freedom" to maintain the initial settings on the domestic instruments is a freedom that should not be exercised. The *worst* thing the home policymakers can do is to adhere to their original domestic policies and to let the exchange rate float freely. The resulting depreciation of the home currency will exacerbate the domestic consequences of the inflationary shock.[32]

As the earlier analysis shows, there is no meaningful sense, under any conceivable operating regime, in which a nation's policymakers can safely ignore the economy's interdependence with the rest of the world. Since the balance of payments is nothing

---

32. For discussion of instances in the post-1973 period in which national policymakers compounded their problems by a false belief that floating the exchange rate would relax the constraints on their policies, see Stanley W. Black, *Floating Exchange Rates and National Economic Policy* (Yale University Press, 1977), chaps. 4 and 5.

more than a record of the consequences of that interdependence, moreover, there is no meaningful sense in which policymakers can safely ignore the balance of payments. Events abroad always affect the home economy—sometimes favorably, sometimes unfavorably. The impacts on the home economy of events occurring at home are always conditioned by interdependencies with the rest of the world— sometimes favorably, sometimes unfavorably. These international influences can be ignored in the same sense that an airplane pilot flying under conditions of low visibility can look merely at his plane's compass and speedometer and choose to ignore the altimeter. If prudent, however, neither pilots nor policymakers behave in that manner.

Are Nations Dis-integrated When Exchange Rates Are More Variable?

The idea that flexible exchange rates insulate a nation's economy is first cousin to the idea that greater flexibility in exchange rates causes a "dis-integration" of all nations' economies. For people especially troubled by the undermining of national economic policy brought about by increasing interdependence, this supposed consequence of greater exchange-rate flexibility is seen as desirable. Conversely, ardent advocates of the benefits of international economic integration view greater flexibility as damaging to further progress.

"Economic integration," like "openness" and "interdependence," is a subtle concept. Most people use it without giving it clear analytical content. An analytical definition must be rooted in the behavior patterns of microeconomic units and in their technological, institutional, and social environments. Changes in integration imply changes in those underlying behavior patterns and environments.[33]

Although behavior patterns and environments change over time, most such changes occur in a slow evolutionary way rather than abruptly. That is why analysis of many economic issues can fruitfully postulate an "unchanged" economic structure—constant behavior patterns and environments—and investigate the consequences of policy actions and nonpolicy disturbances within that unchanging structure. In particular, analysts can postulate a structural model of the world economy with some given degree of economic integration among nations and nonetheless analyze exchange-rate variability within that unchanged structure. Such a method of analysis seems especially natural for the polar case in which all nations agree to use external-reserves-peg regimes (so that exchange rates are, unambiguously, endogenous variables). But the method is only a little less plausible for other assumptions about external operating regimes.

These observations imply that the behavior patterns of microeconomic units and the other fundamental determinants of the degree of economic integration may not be much affected, especially in the short run, by the form and degree of exchange-rate variability.[34]

33. See chapter 11's definition of interdependence. Definitions of "integration" for financial markets are discussed in Peter B. Kenen, *Capital Mobility and Financial Integration: A Survey*, Princeton Studies in International Finance 39 (Princeton University Press, 1976).
34. There is no inconsistency between this statement and the assumption used throughout part 5 that microeconomic behavior, under *any* external operating regime, is sensitive to expected changes in exchange

Exchange-rate variability, on the other hand, cannot help but be strongly influenced by the degree of economic integration. When interdependence and integration are only intermediate, when policymakers in each nation try to pursue diverse and independently formulated objectives, and when nations experience different types of nonpolicy disturbances, the probability is high that exchange rates will have to be variable *in some way or another* over a medium or at least the long run. Myopic policymakers of a significantly open economy have a full range of choice among external operating regimes in the short run, including specifically the exchange-rate peg and the maintenance of an unchanged initial value of the exchange rate under a discretionary external regime. Unless home external reserves are very large and unless there exists a willingness to abandon independently formulated national objectives, however, the home policymakers will not be able, or will not want, to keep the exchange rate at some initial level indefinitely, regardless of the external regime they use in the short run.

Hence the analysis of economic integration and exchange-rate variability should avoid not only the artificial comparison of a rigid external-reserves peg and a successfully maintained exchange-rate peg. It should guard against excessive emphasis on the differences among *any* of the external operating regimes. Over a medium and long run, such differences can be unimportant.

The perspective on exchange-rate variability summarized here differs significantly from the conventional wisdom. This perspective emphasizes the institutional and behavioral characteristics that determine the degree of integration of national economies. It emphasizes that the degree of integration strongly influences exchange-rate movements over time, particularly the longer run trends in the levels of exchange rates. It observes that the amount of adjustment in the levels of exchange rates required in the medium and long run can be relatively insensitive to the form and degree of exchange-rate variability in any short run. This perspective therefore tends to reverse the conventional wisdom that flexible exchange rates promote dis-integration of national economies. From this perspective, exchange-rate variability neither causes dis-integration nor strongly deters a more extensive integration of national economies. Rather, the causal links run in the *opposite* direction—from the existing degree of integration to the amount of variability in exchange rates.

A nation's policymakers, it is true, are capable of mistakenly letting the maintenance of a particular exchange rate become an end in itself. (Note the resemblance to the problem of allowing a surrogate target path for money to become an end in itself!) And a nation's policymakers can be severely constrained by supranational obligations. If the policymakers of most nations energetically use their policy instruments to pursue fixity of exchange rates as an end in itself (some of them thereby sacrificing basic national goals) and then subsequently decide to abandon that preoccupation, an observer could conceivably argue that a dis-integration of the world economy had occurred. Even for those circumstances, however, it would not be correct to say that the initially fixed exchange rates were responsible for integrating national economies and that the subsequent variability brought about

---

rates. The issue is not whether exchange rates and exchange-rate expectations appear as arguments in behavioral functions—which of course they do—but whether in the shorter run the functions themselves change significantly in response to exchange-rate variability.

dis-integration. The exchange-rate variability would still be more a consequence than a cause. An analytical interpretation would give prominence to the change in the objectives and policy actions of the national governments and to the withdrawal of supranational constraints as the fundamental causes of the dis-integration.

Imagine a world economy characterized by extensive but still incomplete integration between a large home nation and the rest of the world. Suppose initially there is no net pressure on the exchange rate, external reserves, and the current account of the balance of payments. Then imagine an extreme change in the policy behavior of foreign governments, with the instruments of both foreign fiscal policy and monetary policy altered to highly expansionary settings; in particular, suppose foreign monetary authorities use the monetary base as the main instrument in their domestic operating regimes and try to make their monetary bases grow at a rate of 20 percent a year. In contrast, suppose home policymakers try to hold to their noninflationary ultimate objectives and therefore wish to permit expansion of the home monetary base at a rate of only 3 percent a year. In these circumstances, to what extent and in which respects is it possible for the evolution of the home economy to differ from that of the rest of the world? For example, to what extent can the home economy maintain a degree of slack in the utilization of resources and experience an inflation rate different from those in the rest of the world?

Consider first an artificial case in which the home policymakers have an exchange-rate peg in force and are rigidly maintaining the peg. The pegging of the exchange rate facilitates the spilling over into the home economy of the expansionary policy actions and the resulting inflation in the rest of the world. Home external reserves rise so rapidly that home policymakers find themselves unable to prevent the home monetary base from increasing at a much faster rate than 3 percent a year. Through this monetary channel as well as directly through higher export demands, powerful forces thus reduce the slack in resource utilization in the home economy and boost the home inflation rate toward the higher rate prevailing abroad. So long as the exchange rate is held unchanged, the home nation cannot prevent being driven toward a higher inflation rate, just as the rest of the world cannot prevent having its inflationary monetary policy moderated by the conservative policy of the home policymakers.

Next suppose the home policymakers rigidly adhere to an external-reserves peg and resolutely follow their 3 percent expansion path for the home monetary base, while foreign policymakers continue to expand their monetary bases at a 20 percent rate. The inflationary stimulus abroad will trigger large exchange-rate changes. The home currency will appreciate—more or less continuously, though probably not smoothly. The home nation will therefore be able to maintain a greater slack in resource utilization and experience a lower inflation rate than under the rigidly maintained exchange-rate peg. Even for this extreme example, one should guard against the oversimplification that exchange-rate changes will insulate the home nation from the excessive monetary expansion and inflation occurring abroad. The rate of growth in the home price level is still likely to be higher than it would have been without the acceleration in foreign inflation. The home nation will not be "free to choose its own rate of inflation." Relative to its position in the hypothetical case in which the exchange rate is locked in place, however, the home economy will be much better buffered against the foreign inflation.

The home policymakers could feasibly adhere to an external-reserves peg in these hypothetical circumstances. But it strains credulity to imagine the home and foreign governments indefinitely maintaining an unchanged exchange rate while pursuing highly diverse monetary and fiscal policies. The first scenario with the rigid exchange-rate peg is therefore of purely theoretical interest. The practical alternatives under the operating regime of an exchange-rate peg would involve (a) periodic adjustments in the pegged level of the exchange rate, or (b) abandonment by foreign governments of their excessively expansionary policies as their external reserves and borrowing capabilities ran out, or (c) acquiescence by the home policymakers in more expansionary instrument settings and more home inflation than they earlier had desired.[35]

As this example suggests, *extreme differences among national economies in macroeconomic conditions—especially in secular trends—can persist for lengthy periods, if they can exist at all, only when exchange rates are variable in some way or another.* The phrase "in some way or another" is an essential part of the proposition. The exchange-rate changes need not occur continuously or smoothly. They could occur under any external operating regime. The proposition by itself cannot, therefore, be taken as a brief for freely flexible exchange rates.

Substantial differences exist among nations: in the ultimate objectives of their economic policies, in their experiences with internally originating nonpolicy disturbances, in the microeconomic behavior patterns of their residents, and in their institutional, social, and legal environments. If policymakers of heterogeneous nations seek to bring about greater integration among their economies solely by trying to lock their currencies together with unchanged exchange rates, therefore, the attempt is certain to prove abortive. So long as the more basic differences in national objectives, behavior patterns, and institutions remain, the locking of the exchange rates will have to be abandoned long before the greater integration has been achieved.[36]

In response to this conclusion, it may be said that if the policymakers of a group of nations were to lock the exchange rates of their national currencies together *irrevocably,* the result would be to force an increasing homogeneity in national policy objectives and hence a much greater degree of integration. But of course. *If* exchange rates were irrevocably locked together, nations could not have widely divergent macroeconomic conditions. And if storks brought babies, procreation would not be necessary for bringing children into the world.

35. Analogous conclusions would apply if one assumes home policymakers use a discretionary external operating regime rather than one of the external pegging rules.

36. The postwar history of attempts at "monetary integration" in Europe provide some notable illustrations. On the earlier years and the European Payments Union, see Robert Triffin, *Europe and the Money Muddle* (Yale University Press, 1957). For the later years of the Bretton Woods system, the period of the "snake in the tunnel," the snake without the tunnel, and other serpentine episodes, see Lawrence B. Krause and Walter S. Salant, eds., *European Monetary Unification and Its Meaning for the United States* (Brookings Institution, 1973); Robert Solomon, *The International Monetary System, 1945–76* (Harper and Row, 1977); and Stanley W. Black, *Floating Exchange Rates and National Economic Policy* (Yale University Press, 1977). On the European Monetary System inaugurated in 1979, see the papers and comments (including some of my own that elaborate on the point in the text) in Philip H. Trezise, ed., *The European Monetary System: Its Promise and Prospects* (Brookings Institution, 1979).

CHAPTER TWENTY-FOUR

Strategies for Domestic Monetary Policy under Conditions of Interdependence

PART 5 has so far concentrated on the external aspects of national monetary policy. This chapter returns briefly to the domestic aspects of strategy choice.

Because of the interdependencies between a nation's economy and the rest of the world, a central bank cannot be assured that the national money stock, however defined, will be reliably linked to the ultimate objectives of national economic policy and at the same time amenable to close control (see part 2).

Yet international interdependencies prove troublesome for any strategy for conducting a nation's monetary policy. Regardless of the central bank's choice of instruments, regardless of the acceptance or rejection of a two-stage decision process, regardless of the choice of analytical model to be used in the formulation of policy, regardless of the frequency with which decisions are reviewed and revised, and regardless of whether decisions incorporate feedback from newly available data, economic openness undermines the controllability of the nation's economy (see part 3).

When a nation's central bank decides how to conduct monetary policy, therefore, the practical issue it faces is not whether a strategy of using some definition of the national money stock as an intermediate-target variable may perform poorly in an absolute sense, but whether that strategy performs more or less poorly than the other feasible strategies.

When money strategies were compared with discretionary instrument adaptation in part 4 and shown to be inferior, the analysis suppressed open-economy complications. The discussion here asks how the conclusions about strategy choice reached in part 4 should be modified when the nation's interdependence with the rest of the world is taken into account.

Information-Flow and Uncertainty Justifications for a Money Strategy

National policymakers have inadequate information about current and past economic developments, and have still less analytically useful knowledge about macroeconomic behavioral relationships. Marginal improvements in information and knowledge, even if possible, are costly. The more open the nation's economy, the more serious these difficulties will be.

National policymakers face more uncertainty not only because of the economy's openness; their ultimate objectives are buffeted by additional forces—nonpolicy

442

disturbances originating abroad and the policy actions of foreign governments—over which they have no control. Because the exogenous forces with which they have to cope (the "weather conditions" of part 3) can change more drastically, and probably more suddenly, the risks of getting blown substantially off a desired course are commensurately greater. To make matters worse, the autonomy of the nation's monetary and fiscal policies is reduced, rendering still more problematic any efforts by the policymakers to steer the economy back to a desired course. At times, responsibility for fixing the settings on the nation's policy instruments can seem as difficult as managing a sailboat in a typhoon.

All the more reason, then, for policymakers to exploit efficiently whatever the limited resources at their disposal. Because the uncertainty about economic structure and the impacts of policy actions is exacerbated by the economy's openness, they have a more urgent need to use existing knowledge systematically. Because the risks are greater of being unpredictably blown about by the weather, they have even stronger incentives to extract clues from recent data to make the best possible weather predictions.

Comparison of alternative strategies under closed-economy assumptions shows that use of the money stock as an intermediate target results in inefficiencies in the use of new data about the economy. A money strategy deliberately discards new data—the more so the longer the intervals between recalculations of the target money path. This inefficiency cannot be plausibly justified for a hypothetical closed economy (see chapter 17). For open economies, in which the opportunity cost of throwing away useful information is higher still, such an approach has even less justification.

A central bank using a strategy of discretionary instrument adaptation is less likely to ignore, or postpone reacting to, new disturbances that have unfavorable consequences for the nation's ultimate targets. If the autonomy of national monetary policy is limited, the most the central bank can achieve may be a small mitigation of such consequences. If great uncertainty exists about the impacts of the disturbances and the impacts of its own policy actions, moreover, the central bank should be very cautious in trying to offset the disturbances. Even so, it will always be preferable for the central bank to consider the *possibility* of offsetting action rather than to continue to aim at an unchanged money target path.

The only continuous adaptation carried out under a money strategy is the lower-stage adjustment of the instruments to keep the money stock close to its target path. In an open economy, the new data fed into those instrument decisions are a small subset of the available new data about national and global developments. The upper-stage money path is adapted discontinuously—in many variants at infrequent intervals. That discontinuity in the decision process cannot improve, and is likely to undermine, the contribution of monetary policy to the achievement of national objectives. The money path may be adjusted more sluggishly than the evolving world or domestic economic situation requires; if so, the instrument settings as time passes get increasingly out of line with the settings that are most appropriate for achieving the ultimate objectives. If, instead, the money target path is altered drastically at the time of its recalculation (which may be justified if it has been inappropriately adhered to for a long time), there may then occur jerky, potentially disruptive impacts of the instruments on the ultimate targets. Both types of risks due to the discontinuity in a money strategy are greater when the nation's economy is open than when it is nearly closed.

Discretionary instrument adaptation with continuous feedback avoids these problems. Given the policymakers' model, new data are promptly evaluated for *all* variables in the chains of causation from instruments and nonpolicy exogenous variables to national ultimate targets. If judged appropriate, adjustments in instrument settings are made. Because events in the rest of the world significantly influence the nation's ultimate-target variables, many of the new data pertain to developments outside the domestic economy. In principle, data for foreign variables should be processed no differently from other new information.[1]

A discretionary approach to monetary policy of the type discussed here does not presuppose policymakers who are confident they know how the national economy works and who can calibrate the impacts of their actions precisely; it is not the certainty-equivalent approach of "fine tuning" (see chapter 19).

Any reasonable strategy for monetary policy must emphasize the fact that knowledge and information about the national economy are uncertain—the more open the economy, the more uncertain. The only controversial economic issue is how to conduct policy in the least unreliable way in the face of that fact. Advocates of a money strategy place their faith in a procedure that ignores, temporarily if not permanently, the bulk of the available knowledge and information. An advocate of discretionary adaptation argues that, precisely because the conditions under which decisions have to be made are so adverse, it is important to make the best possible use of whatever knowledge and information are available.[2]

Do Open Economies Have the Recursive Structure Required by a Money Strategy?

The two-stage decision process of a money strategy is contingent on a policymaking model that can be decomposed into two submodels. Even when the openness of a nation's economy is ignored, substantial doubt exists that "domestic" macroeconomic behavior is sufficiently recursive to warrant policymakers using a model that assumes such recursiveness (see chapter 16).

The appropriateness of this assumption is still more doubtful when account is taken of the economy's interdependence with the rest of the world. Monetary theory for an open economy suggests that the behavior of private economic units in demanding and supplying money depends on the exchange rate and foreign

1. The extent to which the majority of the foreign variables can be represented as simply exogenous rather than endogenous in the analytical model used for policymaking depends on, among other things, the appropriateness for the particular nation's circumstances of the small and open paradigm.
2. A rigorous analysis demonstrating this extension to open economies of the conclusions reached earlier about the information-flow and uncertainty justifications for a money strategy would be similar to the analysis in chapter 17. Whatever illustrative model was used in the analysis would include external-sector as well as domestic endogenous variables. Policy actions of foreign governments and nonpolicy disturbances originating abroad would be added to the list of exogenous magnitudes for which home policymakers make ex ante projections and to which they react ex post when new data are received. The analysis could incorporate differing degrees of uncertainty for the external-sector and domestic relationships in the model (by specifying differing variances for stochastic error terms or, if the model allowed for coefficient uncertainty, for both stochastic errors and random coefficients). In such an analysis, however, no new analytical points would be raised about information use or the treatment of uncertainty. Nor would the logic of the comparison of strategies be altered in its essentials. An extension of the detailed analysis in chapter 17 to the modeling framework of appendix C or to some other open-economy model is therefore omitted here.

interest rates as well as on home interest rates; this theoretical presumption holds true regardless of how the national money stock may be defined (see part 2). The home money stock, the exchange rate, and home and foreign interest rates may all have an influence on such real-sector variables in the national economy as prices, output, employment, and consumption—perhaps contemporaneously, but at least with the passage of time. The influence of the exchange rate on exports and imports, for example, is an important channel for such effects in open economies. The real-sector variables in turn influence the money stock and the other financial variables— if not contemporaneously, then at least with lagged effects. For example, the exchange rate is influenced by an imbalance in the current account in the balance of payments (through its redistribution of wealth between home and foreign residents).

Interdependence of the home and foreign economies, with the exchange rate and foreign financial variables playing an especially prominent role, thus strongly reinforces those interactions of the home money stock, home financial variables, and home real-sector variables that would occur anyway in a closed economy. Those interactions may even be simultaneous within short-run periods; for example, within a given month real economic activity may help to determine interest rates, the exchange rate, and the money stock while within the same month those financial variables may influence real spending decisions. But the interactions definitely occur over a succession of short-run periods. This month's interest rates, exchange rate, and monetary-policy actions, for example, are sure to influence real spending decisions sometime during the next twelve months even if, because of lags in behavioral responses, they do not influence this month's spending decisions. Similarly, this month's spending decisions are sure to influence financial variables during future months, if not also this month.

Policymaking models incorporating *two-way* interactions of financial variables (including the home money stock) and home ultimate-target variables do not have the recursiveness properties required for splitting an overall model into two sub-models. The necessary properties do not exist even if causal influences are uni-directional within a short run. As shown in chapter 16, the only models that can be validly decomposed into lower-stage and upper-stage submodels in the manner required by a money strategy are those in which causal influences between the submodels are exclusively unidirectional *over every time period*.

All the more in an open economy, therefore, the theoretical validity of a two-stage decision process focused on the money stock is called into question. Whether the instruments-money links can validly be broken off from and operated on independently of the links between money and ultimate-target variables is—even for a highly open economy—an empirical issue. The more interdependent the nation's economy with the rest of the world, however, the greater the burden of proof on those who assert that such a decomposition is legitimate.

Integrating the Domestic and External Aspects of Policy Decisions

Macroeconomists have conventionally regarded the problem of strategy choice as a matter of selecting *domestic* operating objectives and procedures. They have asked, What exchange-rate regime best facilitates the conduct of monetary policy? "Monetary policy" has been understood to mean domestic monetary policy. Decisions about "the exchange-rate regime" have been acknowledged to bear importantly on (domestic) strategy choice, but have nevertheless been treated as separate, ancillary decisions.

This traditional compartmentalized way of looking at external monetary policy is flawed in its basic premise. "Exchange-rate arrangements" or "the exchange-rate regime" are no less an integral part of the problem of strategy choice than domestic operating regimes. The exchange-rate regime and official exchange-market intervention *are* monetary policy every bit as much as, say, "the interest-rate regime" and (domestic) "open-market operations" (see chapters 20 through 23).

A nation's central bank should therefore feel as uncomfortable about making a once-for-all decision on "the optimal degree of exchange-rate flexibility" as about being asked to decide on "the optimal degree of interest-rate variability." The problem of selecting optimal amounts of foreign-exchange intervention is fundamentally the same problem as deciding on optimal amounts of domestic open-market operations. So-called dirty floating of exchange rates should occasion little more comment than the dirtying of purely flexible interest rates that occurs every time the central bank engages in purchases or sales of domestic-currency securities.

The preferable approach for the central bank is to regard domestic and external regimes as components of a single overall strategy. Unless the political or sociological arguments for central bank independence (see chapter 18) are accepted, moreover, that strategy for monetary policy should in turn be combined with a fiscal operating regime and with institutional procedures for financing the government budget imbalance to produce an integrated policy regimen for national macroeconomic policy.

Discretionary instrument adaptation lends itself well to such an integrated approach to the domestic and external aspects of policy decisions. The logic of the strategy treats the external instrument like domestic instruments. All instruments are jointly aimed at a common specification of national ultimate objectives. To the maximum extent feasible within the constraints of analytical knowledge about the economy, the impacts of each instrument on all the ultimate-target variables are systematically taken into account.

For reasons summarized in the next section, a nation's central bank will probably not even attempt to integrate the domestic and external aspects of policy decisions if it uses a two-stage money strategy.

Purist and Inward-Looking Variants of a Money Strategy

In an open economy, several conflicting approaches exist for implementing an intermediate-target strategy focused on (some definition of) the national money stock. Proponents of money strategies, having thought less about the external than the domestic aspects of their recommendations, tend to be insensitive to these alternatives.

Consider first a "purist" approach that would carry the two-stage reasoning of the intermediate-target decision process to its logical conclusion. All monetary-policy instruments would be subordinated to the surrogate objective of keeping the national money stock on its target path. Hence, as a routine part of its conduct of the lower stage of the two-stage strategy, aiming exclusively at the money stock, the central bank would continuously and discretionarily vary not merely the domestic instruments *but the external instrument as well.* Suppose, for example, the central bank uses the quantity of external reserves as its external instrument and an interest rate as its chief domestic instrument. Then the central bank would promptly engage in exchange-market sales (purchases) of foreign currency in addition to raising (lowering) its interest-rate instrument whenever the money stock strayed above (below) its target path. Alternatively, if the exchange rate were the external instrument, deviations of the money stock above (below) its target path would promptly call forth not only variation in the domestic instrument but also a revaluation (devaluation) of the home currency.

Because such operating procedures would systematically direct the external instrument toward the same surrogate target aimed at with the domestic instruments, this purist variant would at least be internally consistent. Advocates of this variant could justifiably argue that it would integrate the domestic and external aspects of monetary policy. The internal consistency of the purist variant, however, would make it especially subject to the rigidities and inefficiencies resulting from the differing periodicities for the two levels of the intermediate-target decision process.

In practice, advocates of a money strategy do not pursue the intermediate-target approach to its logical conclusion. Rather, they favor one or another "inward-looking" variant that focuses only on the relationships between domestic instruments and the national money stock. Decisions about the settings for the external instrument, instead of being directed at the money path, are dissociated from "domestic" decisions.[3]

A schizoid treatment of external and domestic instruments is especially pronounced when advocacy of a money strategy is coupled with a recommendation that the central bank use an external-reserves peg. While domestic instruments are to be dexterously adjusted to keep the money stock on a target path, the setting for the external instrument is to be rigidly locked in place to let the exchange rate float freely. Other inward-looking variants likewise downplay or ignore the interrelationships of domestic and external operating regimes. In contrast to the rigid variant using the external-reserves peg, however, they permit the external instrument to be discretionarily adjusted from time to time.[4]

All inward-looking variants involve an arbitrary assignment of the instruments of monetary policy. The domestic instruments are directed toward the surrogate money target. The external instrument is assigned some objective other than the money target path. But *what* other objective? Those few advocates of a money

3. Significantly, there seem to be no published references to the purist variant, either in newspapers or in the academic literature. Nor have critics of money strategies pointed out the failure of the inward-looking variants to treat the use of domestic and external instruments in a consistent way.

4. No proponent of a money strategy seems to favor an exchange-rate peg for the external regime, with good reason. Conclusions similar to those reached in chapter 23 about the technical viability of alternative combinations of instrument regimes apply to situations in which the central bank uses some definition of the national money stock as an intermediate target. In particular, policymakers will encounter greater difficulties keeping the money stock on a target path if they maintain an unchanged value of the exchange rate rather than let the rate vary. Ability to control the money stock is poorest of all when the external regime is a rigid exchange-rate peg.

strategy who have not overlooked the question believe that the external instrument should be assigned the goal of maintaining "equilibrium" in the balance of payments. Some appear to believe this is automatically accomplished under floating exchange rates; they therefore simply recommend an external-reserves peg. Others believe official intervention in the foreign-exchange market may periodically be necessary; they recommend, in effect, one of the discretionary external regimes.

Whether balance-of-payments "equilibrium" should be regarded as an ultimate policy objective is a controversial issue, in part because the concept itself is so slippery. In my view, if "equilibrium" is given a clear analytical definition, there is no justification for regarding it as a separate objective of national macroeconomic policy. A nation's economy is always subject to the constraint of the balance of payments—independently of the presence or absence of exchange-rate variability (see chapter 23). But a constraint should not be elevated to the status of an ultimate objective.

This thorny issue cannot and need not be resolved here.[5] Suppose the nation's policymakers accept equilibrium in the balance of payments, somehow defined, as an ultimate objective. And suppose they aim external monetary policy at that objective, as recommended under inward-looking variants of a money strategy. The point requiring emphasis here is the possible incompatibility of "domestic" and "external" policy decisions when monetary policy is compartmentalized in that way.

The assignment of the external instrument to the balance of payments alone tends to deflect policymakers' attention from the impacts of the external instrument on the money stock (and on the "domestic" ultimate targets for which the money-stock target is supposed to be a surrogate). Similarly, because the domestic instruments are aimed exclusively at the money target path, policymakers are likely to be insufficiently aware of the impacts of their domestic actions on the balance of payments and the exchange rate. When these interactions are downplayed or ignored, both external and domestic actions may have consequences different from what the policymakers intend.[6]

The possibility that an inward-looking money strategy will have unintended adverse consequences is greatest under an external-reserves peg. Chapter 22 analyzes illustrative situations in which a rigid pegging rule for external reserves generates more adverse consequences for ("domestic") ultimate-target variables than would occur if policymakers adjusted their external instrument setting to take domestic repercussions into account. Those examples presume that domestic monetary policy is conducted with an instrument regime rather than with an

5. For a discussion of different concepts of "equilibrium" in the balance of payments and their use in economic policy, see Ralph C. Bryant, "Balance of Payments Adjustment: National Targets and International Inconsistency," in American Statistical Association, *Proceedings of the Business and Economic Statistics Section* (Washington, D.C.: ASA, 1968). Some part of the controversy about balance-of-payments concepts and their use as goals is in any case semantic. A nation's citizens are certainly not indifferent among various levels and rates of change of the exchange rate, external reserves, and the balance of payments. All macroeconomic analysts should therefore be able to agree that *something* about an economy's relationships with the rest of the world belongs as an argument in the policymakers' loss function, either as an ultimate objective or a constraint. Moreover, even those who regard balance-of-payments "equilibrium" as an ultimate objective would presumably not regard it as equivalent in importance to, say, price stability or high output and employment.

6. If the nation's policymakers paid systematic attention to the interactions, yet adhered to a money target path, the strategy would be a purist variant.

intermediate-target regime. When the exchange rate is freely flexible *and* the domestic instruments are aimed exclusively at a surrogate money target, the interactions of the external sector of the economy and the domestic ultimate targets are even less likely to be adequately considered. In effect, policymakers put themselves under a double handicap. Externally they tie their hands with a rigid rule. Domestically they expose themselves to the rigidities of a decision process under which lower-stage and upper-stage decisions can become inconsistent and a surrogate target can win out at the expense of genuine objectives.[7]

If an inward-looking strategy is coupled with a discretionary external regime instead of an external-reserves peg, remedial action may be taken more promptly when incompatibilities between external and domestic decisions occur *and are recognized.* But will they be recognized? The very notion of assigning an "external objective" to the external instrument and looking inward with the other instruments predisposes the nation's policymakers not to make conscious trade-offs between their external and domestic decisions.

In short, even with a purist variant but especially with an inward-looking variant of a money strategy, policymakers are unlikely to integrate their decisions about the settings for domestic and external instruments into a coherent national monetary policy.

The Role of Monetary Aggregates in a Strategy of Discretionary Instrument Adaptation

Proponents of a money strategy believe that existing knowledge about the behavioral relationships underlying the demand for and supply of money is more reliable than knowledge about other aspects of the economy's structure. They blame the critics of money strategies for attaching little importance to those relationships and ignoring new data for monetary aggregates.

That accusation, however justified in other cases, is clearly not applicable to the criticism of money strategies in this book. None of the analysis in earlier chapters argues that the demand for and supply of money are less important or less well understood than other parts of the economy's structure. Discretionary instrument adaptation is not antipathetic to money or other financial aggregates. On the contrary, the basic idea of discretionary adaptation is to use as much of existing knowledge and as much of the new data about the economy as feasible. Thus that strategy neither jettisons the behavioral relationships nor ignores the new data to which a money strategy gives such prominence. The more reliable existing knowledge about money demand and supply is thought to be (relative to the extant knowledge of other behavioral relationships), the more prominent a role money will play in the model used in conjunction with a single-stage discretionary strategy and the greater will be the value attached to new data for the money stock.

In contrast to the models used by many advocates of money strategies, however, the models used by advocates of discretionary adaptation do not exclusively

---

7. Each source of rigidity, as explained in earlier chapters, is problematic in itself. In some circumstances—for example, if money demand should change for reasons not attributable (judging from past behavior) to changes in interest rates, the exchange rate, prices, or real activity—the adverse consequences of the two rigidities can reinforce one another.

emphasize aggregative demand and supply functions for money. Instead, they try to make eclectic use of a larger number of the macroeconomic relationships for which useful analytical knowledge is available.

In a strategy of discretionary adaptation, money and other financial aggregates serve as *information variables*.[8] Their function is not qualitatively different from that of other endogenous variables. Because new data for financial aggregates become available more quickly than for most nonfinancial variables, however, they have a special value as early warning indicators.

Finding the "best" definition of the national money stock, a problem that must be resolved before implementing a money strategy, is not an issue for a strategy of discretionary instrument adaptation. The subtotals of different types of assets or liabilities owned or issued by various groupings of economic units can be important information variables in their own right. The separate bits of information contained in new data for the subtotals can be summarized by aggregating the subtotals into one or more composite bundles. But aggregation decisions are a matter of analytical modeling and convenience. Consolidation of subtotals into an aggregate is appropriate so long as the individual components contain little or no useful information beyond that contained in the aggregate itself. If the components of a broad aggregate systematically behave differently, however, policymakers lose potentially useful information by looking at the aggregate and ignoring its components.

The more important the *international* debtor-creditor relationships are in an economy, the more probable the need for policymakers to go behind new observations of broad financial aggregates to examine the information contained in their key components. The total national money stock is an important example of this proposition.[9]

Imagine an economy in which home nonbanks hold sizable amounts of foreign-currency as well as home-currency deposits in financial intermediaries. Suppose foreigners also hold sizable amounts of home-currency deposits in home banks. Even if the home central bank neglects complications resulting from different maturities of deposits, from the issuance of foreign-currency deposits by home intermediaries, and from the issuance of home-currency deposits by foreign intermediaries, it could define the home money stock in several alternative ways (see chapter 8). But no matter how it defines the money stock, it will be able to profit from the information contained in the separate components as it filters new data and considers revisions in its instrument settings.

A new observation of the home-currency deposits of home nonbanks, for example, may provide an early warning of an unexpected change in domestic economic activity or an unforeseen autonomous change in home nonbanks' asset preferences. In contrast, a new observation of the home-currency deposits of foreigners in home banks may signal an unexpected change in international transactions or foreign economic activity or an unforeseen autonomous shift in foreigners'

8. The first clear articulation of the point is due to John H. Kareken, Thomas Muench, and Neil Wallace, "Optimal Open Market Strategy: The Use of Information Variables," *American Economic Review*, vol. 63 (March 1973), pp. 156–72.

9. The proposition applies with equal force to other "national" aggregates defined broadly. Total credit extended by home banks, total liquid assets owned by home households, and total debt securities issued by home nonfinancial corporations are three additional examples.

asset preferences. If the home-currency deposits of foreigners in home banks are counted along with the home-currency deposits of home nonbanks as part of the home nation's money stock, the central bank will not want to ignore the independent information contained in the two disaggregated components; to focus merely on the new observation of the total money stock would be to throw away clues about possibly important differences in behavior of the national economy's domestic and external sectors. If the home-currency deposits of foreigners in home banks are not counted as part of the national money stock, the central bank will nonetheless want to evaluate new data for those deposits when revising its instrument settings.

Whether the deposits of foreign residents in home financial intermediaries and the deposits of home residents in foreign financial intermediaries are included in the home nation's money stock is, in itself, an issue of no consequence for a strategy of discretionary instrument adaptation. What *is* important is that data for such deposits be used as an information input into policy decisions.

Game-Theoretic Interactions between the Nation's Central Bank and the World Private Sector

Expectational phenomena, particularly the game-theoretic interactions of private-sector decisions and those of the central bank, are likely to be even more important in a highly open than in a relatively closed economy.

Unless capital controls successfully inhibit substitution, the composition of private-sector portfolios will be altered in response to changes in the expected returns on home-currency and foreign-currency assets. For home residents, the expected returns on foreign-currency assets depend critically on, and at times can be dominated by, expected changes in the exchange rate; for foreign residents, the expected returns on home-currency assets depend in an equally critical way on expected changes in the exchange rate (see chapter 7). Private-sector expectations of changes in the exchange rate will always be based in part on expectations of the actions of the home central bank.

For one thing, private expectations of the exchange rate depend directly on the external operating regime of the central bank. If the central bank uses the exchange rate as an instrument, private expectations will focus on the likely variation in the instrument setting itself. If external reserves are the instrument, private expectations will nevertheless pay great attention to external monetary policy; official exchange-market intervention, if and when it occurs, has an immediate, direct influence on the exchange rate.

Less directly but almost as strongly, private expectations of the exchange rate depend on the domestic monetary policy of the central bank. Prospective or actual expansionary (contractionary) changes in the settings on the domestic instruments will, other things being equal, engender private projections of a depreciation (appreciation) of the home currency relative to previous expectations, a decline (increase) in external reserves, or both.

Private economic units in foreign countries, not merely residents of the home economy, form expectations of national monetary policy and substitute between home-currency and foreign-currency assets accordingly. The central bank in an open economy thus must be concerned about game-theoretic interactions with the *world* private sector.

The more open a nation's economy, the more powerful a constraint on its monetary policy will be the tendency of private decisionmakers to substitute foreign-currency assets for home-currency assets, or home-currency assets for foreign-currency assets, in response to actual and anticipated policy actions. Greater substitutability between goods produced at home and abroad and greater mobility of people across the nation's borders—partly in response to national policy actions—will likewise prove to be a greater constraint on the central bank. These expectational, game-theoretic phenomena are another manifestation of the weaker controllability of the national economy associated with increased openness.

Open-economy considerations apart, a nation's central bank needs to pay close attention to private-sector expectations of its policy actions. The most serious weakness of the traditional theory of economic policy is its failure to cope adequately with this problem (see chapter 18). Most of the recent research on expectational interactions of government and private decisions has ignored the external sector of the economy. Future research, even if it concentrates only on domestic macroeconomic behavior, may ultimately justify some form of limitation on policymakers' discretion to react to new data and knowledge. If so, taking open-economy considerations into account will undoubtedly strengthen such a case against unlimited discretion.

Suppose future research were to show that a nation's central bank could better facilitate national economic objectives by preannouncing and adhering to self-imposed limits on its discretionary actions. Even then, no convincing grounds would exist for stating such announcements in terms of the national money stock or any other intermediate-target variable. For the reasons given in chapter 18, which become still more persuasive when international considerations are incorporated in the analysis, announcements of "partial rules" would better be made in terms of the nation's actual policy instruments, its ultimate objectives, or perhaps both.

CHAPTER TWENTY-FIVE

International Cooperation

THIS BOOK analyzes the conduct of monetary policy from the myopic outlook of policymakers in an individual nation. No other perspective would be pragmatically relevant in a world in which nation states are the dominant political entities. Just as one must treat ocular myopia with corrective eyeglasses, however, a nation's policymakers, to facilitate national goals intelligently, must modify their myopic perspective with an appreciation of the behavior of other nations' policy authorities and of the world economic system as a whole.

The Non-Independence of Policy Actions of National Governments

Some nations may be sufficiently small and open to warrant a substantial degree of national myopia in analytical perspective. Policymakers in those nations can concentrate on the dependence of the home economy on policy actions and other events abroad; for most purposes, they can ignore the (small) effects of home-government policy actions on the rest of the world. For such nations, the theme of interrelationships among policy actions stressed in chapters 20 and 21 could be, figuratively speaking, cut off at the geographical borders of the home country.

Under conditions of intermediate interdependence, however, the logic of the argument in those earlier chapters applies even across national borders. Because the decisions of the policy authorities in the home and foreign nations are fundamentally interrelated, the behavior of each constrains that of the other (see part 3).

Everything said thus far about macroeconomic policies in the home nation can be said with equal validity about other nations. In particular, each foreign government will implement its policies within the context of a policy regimen. Each nation's fiscal authority will follow some budgetary operating regime and some pattern of institutional procedures for the initial financing of its budget surpluses or deficits. Each foreign central bank will adopt proximate objectives and operating procedures for the domestic aspects of monetary policy. Each foreign government will also, in contrast with the assumption hitherto employed, have definite preferences about the external operating regime for national monetary policy.

In principle, intermediate interdependence requires analysis of macroeconomic policy actions within a framework that fully specifies the regimen in force in the home nation *and* the policy regimens being used in the rest of the world.

If the analysis of national macroeconomic policy is carried out in such a framework, a key fact becomes apparent: *the policy regimens of the home and the foreign*

453

nations cannot be chosen independently. The de facto freedom of nations' governments to take independent exogenous policy actions is more restricted than the
freedom that seems to exist, but in reality does not, when each nation's choices are
contemplated in isolation.

External Policy Actions

The constraints on national freedom manifest themselves most clearly in the
choice of external operating regimes. In the theoretical world of two nations there
are two currencies but only one exchange rate. Two central banks cannot act
independently to set one exchange rate at different exogenous levels. In the real
world, the number of independent exchange rates is one less than the number of
national monetary authorities; n central banks cannot act independently to set
$n - 1$ exchange rates at n exogenous levels. On logical grounds alone, therefore,
home policymakers can only successfully adopt an exchange-rate instrument regime
if foreign policymakers also adopt such a regime *and* if the two can mutually agree
on an exogenous time path of the exchange rate.

The commonality in external regimes goes well beyond the exchange rate per
se. Apart from increases in the world total stock, one nation cannot acquire (spend)
outside reserve assets without another nation simultaneously using (receiving)
them. Nor can one nation accumulate or run down external reserve assets in
currency-denominated form without generating counterpart changes in external
reserve liabilities for another nation. These truisms are reflections of a *world*
balance-of-payments identity. Home policymakers thus cannot successfully adopt
an external-reserves instrument regime unless foreign policymakers also adopt
such a regime and the two can select exogenous time paths for their external-reserve
positions that are mutually compatible.

The inevitable commonality of external operating regimes can be revealingly
highlighted by restating the consolidated balance-sheet identity for the *home* nation
in terms of changes in the external reserve assets and external reserve liabilities
of *foreign* nations.

In the two-nation world of chapters 20 and 21, for example, let FA^{*FCB} represent
the external reserve assets of the foreign central bank, and πFA^{*FCB} the same
magnitude expressed in units of the home nation's currency.[1] Assume that the
foreign central bank, like the home central bank, holds its external reserves in three
components.[2] Let ΔJ^W represent the change in the world stock of outside reserve
assets, and $\zeta \Delta J^W$ the same magnitude in terms of home-currency units; this change
might be zero, but need not be.[3]

---

1. Symbols have the same definitions as in earlier chapters; the analysis is based on the schematic
income statements and balance sheets given in tables 20-1 and 20-2. An asterisk indicates the foreign-
country analogue of home-country variables previously defined.

2. The three components of ΔFA^{CB}, changes in the home country's external reserve assets, are (see
table 20-1) $\pi \Delta Dep^{*CB}$, $\pi \Delta S^{*CB}$, and $\zeta \Delta J^{CB}$. The analogous components of ΔFA^{*FCB}, changes in the external
reserve assets of the foreign country (expressed in units of foreign currency), are $(1/\pi)(\Delta Dep^{FCB})$, the
home-currency deposit balance of the foreign central bank at the home central bank; $(1/\pi)(\Delta S^{FCB})$, home-
currency securities issued by the home government held by the foreign central bank; and $\zeta^* \Delta J^{FCB}$, the
foreign central bank's holdings of outside reserve assets, where ζ^* is the foreign-currency price of outside
reserve assets. The first two components of the foreign nation's external reserve assets are the external
reserve liabilities of the home government.

3. Changes in the world stock of outside reserve assets could arise from changes in the stocks of
monetary gold owned by the central banks or from new allocations or cancellations of SDRs. The stocks

With these definitions, the consolidated balance-sheet identity for the home government, equation 21-7a, can also be written as

(25-1) $[\zeta \Delta J^W]$ $-$ $[\pi \Delta FA^{*FCB}]$ $+ [\pi(\Delta Dep^{*CB} + \Delta S^{*CB})]$

Change in world outside reserve assets	Change in external reserve assets of foreign central bank	Change in external reserve liabilities of foreign central bank to home central bank

$+$ $[\Delta OA^{G'}]$ $-$ $[\Delta MBU]$ $-$ $[\Delta S^P]$ $\equiv$ $Z^{G'}$.

Change in other assets of home government	Change in home unborrowed monetary base	Change in home government debt held by world private sector	Consolidated budget surplus or deficit of home government

The balance-sheet constraint facing the *home* government is thus linked directly, through the world balance-of-payments identity, to changes in the external reserve assets of the *foreign* government, changes in the external reserve liabilities of the *foreign* government, and the changes, if any, in the *world* stock of outside reserve assets. As with the identities in previous chapters, 25-1 is no more than a statement of what must be true ex post. But it dramatizes the limited scope that one nation has to choose an external operating regime independently.

Attempted implementation of an external regime by one nation can easily be frustrated by incompatible intentions and actions of foreign policymakers. Suppose, for example, home policymakers try to implement an external-reserves peg, expecting to observe the exchange rate adjust endogenously in response to the market supplies and demands of the world private sector. Suppose, however, that foreign policymakers decide to use a discretionary exchange-rate regime and intervene in the exchange market to keep the exchange rate on an exogenously determined path of their choosing. The attempt of the home policymakers to implement their preferred external regime will be frustrated, both because the exchange rate will not move freely to equilibrate market demands and supplies and because the exchange-market intervention of the foreign policymakers will generate unexpected and undesired changes in the external reserve position of the home nation. For the home policymakers to implement a regime in which the exchange rate adjusts freely, they must first persuade their foreign counterparts to do the same.

More generally, no nation can implement any external operating regime without the affirmative agreement or, at the least, the passive acquiescence of other nations. If not by ex ante agreement, then de facto through the interplay of the inconsistent behavior of national governments, incompatible intentions are necessarily reconciled ex post. One way or another, there will be a common, *world* external regime.

The impossibility of nations' independently choosing external operating regimes is masked in the actual world economy of many countries. Individual nations can act without taking into account the consequences of their actions for other nations. And because most nations are small in relation to the world as a whole, they can *appear* to be acting independently. But at least one of the n nations must passively

---

and their valuations are related by the following identities: $J^{CB} + J^{FCB} \equiv J^W$ (total stock of outside reserve assets); $\zeta \Delta J^{CB} \equiv \zeta \Delta J^W - \pi \zeta^* \Delta J^{FCB}$ (changes expressed in home-currency units); $\pi \equiv \zeta/\zeta^*$ (relationship between exchange rate and the two currency valuations of outside reserve assets).

acquiesce in the outcome of the other $n - 1$ nations' choices of external regimes if the combination of the $n - 1$ choices is to be effectively sustained. Even with a "passive" nth country, moreover, the actual world external regime as it affects a single small country depends critically on the choices of all the $n - 2$ "nonpassive" nations. A small country acting "quasi-independently," for example, may be able exogenously to peg the bilateral exchange rate of its currency against the currency of a major trading partner; but it is powerless to set exogenous values for several of its bilateral exchange rates simultaneously.

Because all nations cannot successfully implement external regimes of their own independent choosing and because the possible consequences of anarchy may be feared by all, national governments feel under substantial pressure to reach agreement on supranational "traffic regulations" to govern their non-independent choices. This pressure accounts for the actual or proposed supranational constraints on external regimes discussed in chapter 20.

When a common, world external regime exists by design—as the result of ex ante agreement among nations about their individual external regimes—the resulting exchange-rate and external-reserves arrangements are often labeled "the international monetary system."[4] When such ex ante agreement is lacking or partially lacking, the world external regime is more a happenstance resulting from the interplay of inconsistent national policy regimens. Advocates of explicit traffic regulations complain about this happenstance outcome and label it an "international monetary non-system."[5]

Domestic Policy Actions

The non-independence of national policy actions extends well beyond the choice of operating regimes for external monetary policy.

The central banks of foreign nations have the same potential choices for an operating regime for domestic monetary policy as those available to the home central bank (see chapter 14). Whatever domestic regimes and instrument settings are selected, foreign central banks will presumably adhere to them when disturbances occur that, if not offset, would undermine their policies. If a foreign central bank follows a reserve-aggregate regime with the unborrowed monetary base as the exogenous instrument, any incipient pressure that would otherwise push the unborrowed base off its exogenous path will be resisted by domestic open-market purchases or sales. Similarly, under an interest-rate instrument regime, the foreign central bank will conduct domestic open-market operations as necessary to keep its interest rate on the policy-determined exogenous path.

The choice of domestic regime by foreign central banks can have important consequences for the home nation and for the decisions of the home central bank. Under conditions of intermediate interdependence, the domestic monetary regimes in foreign nations not only condition the impacts of home monetary-policy actions on the foreign economies, *but even the impacts of home actions on the home economy!*

---

4. Compare Robert Solomon, *The International Monetary System 1945–1976: An Insider's View* (Harper and Row, 1977), chap. 1.
5. See, for example, John Williamson, *The Failure of World Monetary Reform, 1971–1974* (New York University Press, 1977).

This important conclusion can be readily demonstrated for the theoretical world of two nations, using the point-in-time analysis in which asset stocks are assumed constant except for changes brought about by central-bank operations and the consequent market adjustments of asset valuations. Consider again the example of an incremental domestic open-market purchase by the home central bank intended to raise the level of the exogenous path of the home unborrowed monetary base 500 units above what it would otherwise be (see chapter 20). As before, consider a comparison of a rigid external-reserves peg, a rigid exchange-rate peg, and a discretionary exchange-rate regime. Assume that the foreign central bank passively acquiesces in the home central bank's choice of external regime; hence the comparison is, in effect, of three alternative "world" agreements on the international monetary system. Finally, make some explicit assumptions about the type of exchange-market intervention used to support the exchange rate, if and when it is supported. For example, purchases of home-currency assets to prevent or moderate the depreciation of the home currency could be carried out by the home central bank using outside reserve assets (type A' intervention) or securities denominated in the foreign currency (type B intervention). Alternatively, the foreign central bank could be assumed to carry out any required exchange-market intervention.[6]

What happens in the foreign nation as a result of the home nation's decision to revise the instrument setting for the home unborrowed monetary base? The interest rates on foreign-currency-denominated securities will change in the absence of offsetting action by the foreign central bank. Except when both central banks completely refrain from exchange-market intervention (under the external-reserves peg), domestic reserve aggregates in the foreign country such as the unborrowed monetary base (MBU^*) will be increased in the absence of offsetting action by the foreign central bank. Broader monetary aggregates in the foreign country will also be altered in the absence of efforts by the foreign central bank to keep them unchanged (probably even despite such efforts).

The foreign central bank will not wish to have its instrument settings or inter-mediate-target variables pushed off course. It will therefore carry out domestic open-market operations to try to prevent, or at least to reverse, those unwanted impacts. The required "sterilizing" operations depend both on the domestic regime followed by the foreign central bank and on the world external regime. Sterilizing actions are required, regardless of the nature of the external regime, if the foreign

---

6. In the analysis in chapters 20 through 24, any exchange-market intervention is assumed to be conducted by the home central bank. But one could, with equal justification, adopt the opposite extreme assumption. When the foreign central bank conducts exchange-market intervention, it becomes necessary to differentiate three ways in which the intervention may be financed. These three types—cases C, C', and D, respectively—are analogous to exchange-market intervention by the home central bank of types A, A', and B (see chapter 20). Intervention of type C involves the foreign central bank altering the level of (in the example in the text, increasing) its deposit balance with the home central bank pari passu with the change (expansion) of foreign-currency reserve money. Intervention of type C' involves changes (an increase) in the holdings of outside reserve assets by the foreign central bank. Type D intervention involves changes in the foreign central bank's holdings of home-currency securities (an increase in S^{FCB}) as the counterpart of a change (expansion) in foreign-currency reserve money. From the perspective of the world private sector, exchange-market intervention of types A and A' by the home central bank and types C and C' by the foreign central bank all result—*proximately*—in an exchange of home-currency reserve money against foreign-currency reserve money. Type B intervention by the home central bank results, proximately, in an exchange of home-currency reserve money against foreign-currency securities. Type D intervention by the foreign central bank changes the relative supplies available to the world private sector of home-currency securities and foreign-currency reserve money.

central bank follows an interest-rate instrument regime or an intermediate-target regime. Such actions are also required when the foreign central bank follows a reserve-aggregate instrument regime if the external regime is an exchange-rate peg or a discretionary exchange-rate regime.[7] The required operations also depend on the particular type of exchange-market intervention (when the external regime is the exchange-rate peg or the discretionary exchange-rate regime).

Regardless of whether the foreign central bank remains passive or conducts sterilizing operations to maintain its instrument settings or intermediate targets at their previous levels, the expansionary monetary action in the home nation will influence the ultimate-target variables of the foreign policymakers. Foreign prices and output will unambiguously rise if the external regime is the exchange-rate peg or if the foreign currency is kept from appreciating very much under the discretionary exchange-rate regime.[8] Foreign prices and output will probably rise if the exchange rate is permitted to float freely under the external-reserves peg, but to a smaller extent than under the exchange-rate peg.[9]

Consider now the impacts on home financial variables of the original home policy action. When the external regime is the external-reserves peg, the magnitudes of the depreciation of the home currency and the fall in home interest rates vary according to whether the foreign central bank uses a foreign interest rate or a reserve aggregate (for example, MBU^*) as its exogenous instrument.[10] Under either of the external regimes in which exchange-market intervention occurs, the sizes of the fall in home interest rates and the decline in home external reserves are sensitive to the domestic regime of the foreign central bank; given the incrementally higher level of the home unborrowed monetary base, larger declines in home interest rates and home external reserves will occur if the foreign central bank employs a reserve aggregate rather than an interest rate as its exogenous instrument.[11]

The impacts of the home policy action on such home ultimate-target variables as home prices and output likewise vary with the foreign central bank's choice of domestic regime. Under the exchange-rate peg, home prices and output rise by an unambiguously larger amount (and foreign prices and output increase less) when the foreign central bank pursues domestic monetary policy with a reserve-aggregate peg rather than an interest-rate peg. If the external regime is the external-reserves peg or if a substantial depreciation of the home currency is permitted under the

7. The only case in which the foreign central bank will not be prompted to carry out sterilizing domestic actions is when it pursues a reserve-aggregate regime domestically and when both central banks eschew all exchange-market intervention (that is, under the external-reserves peg).

8. As in chapters 22 and 23, it is assumed here that an increase in aggregate nominal demand will call forth not only an increase in prices but also some increase in output. If the increase in demand occurs when there is no slack in resource utilization, only prices will rise.

9. Foreign prices and output could conceivably fall rather than rise under the external-reserves peg (see chapter 23).

10. The structural characteristics of the asset-demand equations of home and foreign private economic units determine whether the home currency depreciates more or less when the foreign central bank uses a foreign interest rate rather than a reserve aggregate for its domestic instrument. The greater is the depreciation of the home currency, the smaller is the fall in home interest rates (for either choice of foreign domestic regime). See Lance Girton and Dale W. Henderson, "Critical Determinants of the Effectiveness of Monetary Policy," in M. Fratianni and K. Tavernier, eds., *Bank Credit, Money and Inflation in Open Economies,* supplement to *Kredit und Kapital* (3:1977), pp. 231–83.

11. When exchange-market intervention mitigates or prevents the depreciation of the home currency and the foreign central bank uses a reserve aggregate for its domestic instrument, foreign interest rates tend to rise as a result of the home monetary-policy action. For detailed discussion, see ibid.

discretionary exchange-rate regime, it cannot be stated unambiguously which of the two domestic regimes of the foreign central bank will engender the larger rise in home prices and output; the comparison could go either way depending, among other things, on the characteristics of the portfolio preferences of home and foreign asset owners.[12] The conclusion that the relative magnitudes of the effects on the home economy can be significantly influenced by the domestic policy of the foreign central bank, however, is not in doubt even for the cases when the exchange rate is variable.[13]

The example just discussed illustrates the sensitivity of the home impacts of home monetary-policy actions to monetary policy abroad. In principle, the budgetary regime and debt financing procedures of the foreign government are conditioning factors as well. In the same manner that the changes in asset stocks of the private sector resulting from changes in the home government's budgetary position shape the further evolution of home economic activity after an initial policy action (see chapter 14), the changes in the asset stocks of the world private sector resulting from surpluses or deficits in the budget of the foreign government require, so long as they continue, adjustments in portfolio composition and asset yields. Under conditions of intermediate interdependence, a home policy action can induce a change in the foreign budget position; consequent changes in the stock of foreign-government securities and the associated adjustments they entail can in turn have feedback influences on the home economy.

This analysis again highlights the critical importance of national policy regimens. The "effectiveness" of a monetary-policy action taken by the home central bank is sensitive to the home nation's regimen, the international monetary system, and even the domestic aspects of the policy regimen in the rest of the world. Likewise, the sizes of the impacts of foreign-government policy actions, on both the foreign and the home economies, depend on the domestic aspects of the policy regimen in the home nation.

The Governmental Budget Constraint for the World as a Whole

Further insight into the non-independence of policy actions can be obtained by focusing on a consolidation of national governments' budgets and balance sheets— a *world* government budget constraint.

Tables 20-1 and 20-2 provide schematic representations of the accounts of the home central bank and fiscal authority. Corresponding budget statements and balance sheets of the foreign central bank and fiscal authority have analogous items and may be schematized in a similar way. Those foreign accounts are expressed in units of foreign currency; most variables are also denominated in foreign currency.

---

12. If private demands for the monetary bases of both countries were relatively independent of the level of the exchange rate and demands for home-currency and foreign-currency securities were strongly dependent on it, the larger rise in home prices and output would occur when the foreign central bank uses the reserve-aggregate peg; compare ibid., pp. 256–57. Other combinations of assumptions about private asset-demand equations, however, can produce the opposite result.

13. Given the choice of domestic regime by the foreign central bank, home prices and output will increase by larger amounts when the home currency depreciates than when the exchange rate is kept unchanged (see chapter 23).

The consolidated budget and balance-sheet constraints for the foreign government, expressed in terms of foreign-currency units, may be written as

(25-2) $[T_d^* + T_n^*] - [X_d^* + X_n^{*\prime}] + \dfrac{1}{\pi}[r_s (S^{FCB})] - \dfrac{1}{\pi}[r_{s*} (S^{*P} + S^{*CB})] \equiv Z^{*FG\prime}$

| Consolidated budget receipts | Consolidated budget expenditures | Interest receipts on external reserve assets | Interest payments on government debt | Consolidated budget surplus or deficit |

(25-3) $[\Delta OA^{*FG\prime}] + [\Delta FA^{*FCB}] - [\Delta Dep^{*CB} + \Delta S^{*CB}]$

| Change in other assets | Change in external reserve assets | Change in external reserve liabilities to home central bank |

$\qquad\qquad\qquad\qquad\qquad - [\Delta MBU^*] - [\Delta S^{*P}] \equiv Z^{*FG\prime}.$

| Change in unborrowed monetary base | Change in government debt held by world private sector | Consolidated budget surplus or deficit |

The symbols in 25-2 and 25-3 have analogous definitions to those used in the home-government constraints 21-6 and 21-7 (see chapter 21). An asterisk continues to indicate a foreign analogue to the corresponding home variable; the superscripts *FCB, CB, FG′,* and *P* denote, respectively, the foreign central bank, the home central bank, the consolidated foreign government, and the world (home plus foreign) private sector.

The consolidated constraints for the foreign and the home governments can be combined by expressing 25-2 and 25-3 in terms of home currency and then adding the two national sets of constraints together. Such a consolidation cancels out not only intragovernmental transactions within each nation but all *intergovernmental* transactions between the two nations as well. The resulting governmental budget constraint for the world, expressed in home-currency units, is

(25-4) $[(T_d + T_n) - (X_d + X_n' + r_s S^P)]$
Home government receipts and outlays
vis-à-vis world private sector

$\qquad\qquad + \pi[(T_d^* + T_n^*) - (X_d^* + X_n^{*\prime} + r_{s*} S^{*P})] \equiv [Z^{G\prime} + \pi Z^{*FG\prime}].$

| Foreign government receipts and outlays vis-à-vis world private sector | Consolidated budget surplus or deficit of the two governments combined |

The counterpart balance-sheet constraint for the world, in home-currency units, is

(25-5) $[\Delta OA^{G'} + \pi\Delta OA^{*FG'}] + [\zeta\Delta J^W] - [\Delta MBU + \pi\Delta MBU^*]$

Changes in other assets of the two governments	Change in world outside reserve assets	Changes in home reserve money and foreign reserve money

$$- [\Delta S^P + \pi\Delta S^{*P}] \equiv [Z^{G'} + \pi Z^{*FG'}].$$

Changes in world private sector's holdings of home-government and foreign-government securities	Consolidated budget surplus or deficit of the two governments combined

These two identities thus embody all the impacts of both national governments on the budget and balance sheets of the world private sector.[14]

Evaluation of government policy actions in the light of 25-4 and 25-5 forces an analyst to keep track of the subtle intertwining of national macroeconomic policies and brings the net effects of government actions on the world private sector more clearly into view.

As an illustration of the analytical discipline imposed by recognition of the consolidated government constraint for the world as a whole, consider again the question, What is an exchange-market-intervention action? From the perspective of members of the world private sector who, at some levels of interest rates and the exchange rate, have to hold the asset stocks made available by the national governments, the significant thing about an exchange-market intervention by the home central bank is that it proximately raises or lowers the home unborrowed monetary base, MBU, with offsetting effects either on the foreign unborrowed base, MBU^*, or the stock of foreign-currency debt liabilities of the foreign government, S^{*P}. An exchange-market intervention by the foreign central bank proximately raises or lowers the foreign unborrowed base, MBU^*, with offsetting effects either on the home unborrowed base, MBU, or the stock of home-currency government debt, S^P. Furthermore, since both central banks actively implement some type of domestic operating regime, any exchange-market intervention necessarily gives rise to still other asset exchanges affecting the supplies of assets that must be held by the world private sector. The home central bank will conduct domestic operations producing offsetting changes in the quantities of MBU and S^P; the foreign central bank will engage in domestic operations forcing the world private sector to accept offsetting changes in MBU^* and S^{*P}. Causation also operates in the opposite

---

14. Indeed, it would be equally accurate to describe the two identities as the result of a grand consolidation of the accounts of every private economic unit in the world economy, where all intra-private-sector transactions have been netted out. The symbol π should be interpreted as the average exchange rate ruling during the period to which the identities refer. As in earlier chapters, capital gains and losses due to revaluations of asset and liability stocks must be appropriately treated for the identities to be valid.

direction. For example, a domestic asset exchange initiated by the foreign central bank between MBU^* and S^{*P} will often trigger some form of external asset exchange, which may then induce domestic asset exchanges by the home central bank. Domestic actions in the home country may give rise to exchange-market intervention, which in turn will often necessitate domestic action abroad.

All these monetary interrelationships must conform to 25-5. That identity is a straitjacket constraining the movement in the world financial system of all governmental assets and liabilities vis-à-vis the world private sector. It thus provides an internally consistent frame of reference within which to analyze the complex interrelationships that characterize that system.

The world consolidated constraint provides a similar discipline for analyzing fiscal-policy actions and the budget-financing implications of monetary-policy actions. From 25-4 and 25-5 it is clear that a change in any discretionary expenditure magnitude, any discretionary tax rate, or any other exogenous fiscal variable—at home or abroad—will bring about changes over time in one or more of the asset stocks of home reserve money (MBU), home government securities (S^P), foreign reserve money (MBU^*), or foreign government securities (S^{*P}).[15] Such changes themselves deserve to be called "monetary"—and they have monetary consequences—just as much as any of the domestic or external asset exchanges conducted by the two central banks. Likewise, because of the many budgetary magnitudes in 25-4 that are individually endogenous and because one or both governments will probably allow endogenous variations in the size of their budget surpluses, an initial exogenous monetary-policy action (for example, one that alters MBU and S^P in offsetting directions) will generate changes in both governments' budget positions. These changes will bring about additional changes in the asset stocks MBU, S^P, MBU^*, and S^{*P}, which in turn will generate still further monetary consequences.

Whenever one or more of the stocks of home reserve money, home government securities, foreign reserve money, and foreign government securities change *for any reason*, portfolio rebalancing by the world private sector generates alterations in the market valuations and yields of assets and changes in the pattern of asset ownership. The asset stocks MBU, S^P, MBU^*, and S^{*P} are affected. But the valuations and ownership distributions of all other asset stocks—those that are tangible assets and those that are financial claims on private economic units—are altered as well. These in turn have effects on nonfinancial variables.

Portfolio rebalancings by the world private sector, as both cause and response, are typically associated with changes in the exchange rate and in international transactions. Those international transactions alter the ownership distribution of asset stocks between private home and private foreign residents (see chapter 22 and appendix C). The world consolidated identities 25-4 and 25-5 do not directly illuminate those international transactions between home and foreign members of the world private sector. Nonetheless, such changes in the *national* ownership of asset stocks in general, and of the asset stocks S^P and S^{*P} in particular, are strongly conditioned by the existence of the straitjacket on relative asset supplies embodied in those constraints.

In short, *any type of policy action either by the home or by foreign governments*

---

15. This statement abstracts from changes in the "other assets" of both governments and from changes in the world stock of outside reserve assets.

inevitably has "monetary" consequences for both the home nation and the rest of the world. Conventional analyses of macroeconomic policies for open economies suppress the close links between policies in the home nation and in the rest of the world. Many even suppress the holistic unity of monetary and fiscal policies within each nation. Attention to the consolidated governmental constraint for the world as a whole, on the other hand, ensures that any such suppression is a deliberate simplifying assumption rather than an inadvertent omission.

Policy Flexibility: The Individual Nation versus the World as a Whole

Judged solely on the basis of the constraints facing each nation individually, the openness of each economy might seem to provide extra freedom of choice to each nation's policymakers—for example, permitting them to expand the supply of home reserve money without having to run a budget deficit or retire debt securities from the private sector (see chapter 21).

Once a myopic national perspective is abandoned and the question of national policy flexibility is considered in the light of the analytical discipline of the world consolidated governmental constraint, however, an important conclusion becomes immediately evident. Any extra room for maneuver in one nation's macroeconomic policies attributable to the openness of its economy must come at the expense of policy flexibility for other nations. All countries cannot enjoy additional flexibility simultaneously.

As an illustration, suppose the home government does not wish to run a budget deficit (it wants to observe $Z^{G'} \geq 0$), either does not want to reduce or is institutionally constrained from reducing the stock of its own debt in the hands of the private sector ($\Delta S^P \geq 0$), and yet does want to see home reserve money grow ($\Delta MBU > 0$) at a rate commensurate with the growth in home economic activity. Such an outcome is possible—see the national constraint 21-7a—provided only that home external reserve assets grow over time ($\Delta FA^{CB} > 0$) or home external reserve liabilities are reduced ($\Delta Dep^{FCB} + \Delta S^{FCB} < 0$). It is evident from the world constraint 25-5, however, that such an outcome necessarily implies a *reduction* over time in foreign reserve money ($\Delta MBU^* < 0$), a *reduction* in foreign-government debt available to the private sector ($\Delta S^{*P} < 0$), a *depreciation* of the foreign currency relative to the home currency (a smaller value of π), or a *deficit* in the foreign government's budget ($Z^{*FG'} < 0$).[16] If the home government's desired outcome is to be achieved, in other words, that outcome will inevitably impose constraints on the foreign government's freedom of policy choice and entail a loss of room for maneuver by foreign policymakers.

In contrast with the widely held view that flexible exchange rates insulate domestic macroeconomic policies, the conclusion that one nation's enjoyment of additional policy flexibility always constrains the options available to other nations holds true whatever may be the degree of exchange-rate variability.

16. This statement abstracts from changes in the "other assets" of both governments and changes in the world stock of outside reserve assets. The identity 25-5 is expressed in home-currency units; a depreciation of the foreign currency reduces the home-currency value of changes in foreign reserve money, in foreign-currency securities, and the foreign government's budget position.

The root cause of the non-independence of nations' policy actions is the non-independence of the national economies themselves. Under conditions of intermediate interdependence, the world (home plus foreign) economy itself has a holistic unity. An exchange rate links two currencies, but there is only one exchange rate; a transaction across national borders cannot be a receipt for the resident of one nation without being a payment by a resident of another nation. Trivial facts those may be. Yet with what ramifications for the choice of national policy regimens and the analysis of national macroeconomic policies!

Game-Theoretic Analysis of National Policy Decisions

National targets and policy actions can easily be inconsistent ex ante. Each nation's policymakers can *try* to enjoy additional flexibility at the expense of other nations. But there can be only one record of past history. Somehow, a reconciliation of inconsistencies takes place: some, if not all, ex ante national targets and policy actions go unrealized ex post.

Which nations are forced to endure the greatest disappointments? Are ex post outcomes for the world economy Pareto optimal, so that one nation's ultimate objectives could be better achieved only if another's were less fully achieved? Or does the process of reconciliation typically generate "inefficient" outcomes that, in retrospect, are judged disappointing by all nations? If the process of reconciliation is inefficient, can it be made more efficient by improving communication and cooperation among national policy authorities? How should a single nation's policymakers appraise the costs and benefits from yielding some political sovereignty in exchange for a more coordinated international formulation of national policies? What role can be played by supranational traffic regulations and supranational institutions? Answers to these questions require game-theoretic analysis of nations' policy decisions.

Game theory deals with situations in which two or more interacting agents make decisions. The situations traditionally emphasized in economic theory and in applications of control theory to macroeconomic policy contain only one decisionmaker (implicitly if not explicitly). As von Neumann and Morgenstern emphasized over three decades ago, problems with two or more decisionmakers have elements in common with the constrained maximum or minimum problems confronted by a Robinson Crusoe, yet they also contain some—very essential—elements of an entirely different nature:

> . . . the result for each [participant] will depend in general not merely upon his own actions but on those of the others as well. Thus each participant attempts to maximize a function . . . of which he does not control all variables. This is certainly no maximum problem, but a peculiar and disconcerting mixture of several conflicting maximum problems. Every participant is guided by another principle and neither determines all variables which affect his interest. . . .
>
> One would be mistaken to believe that [the difficulty] can be obviated, like the difficulty in the Crusoe case . . . by a mere recourse to the devices of the theory of probability. Every participant can determine the variables which describe his own actions but not those of the others. Nevertheless those "alien" variables cannot, from his point of view, be described by statistical assumptions. This is because the others are guided, just as he himself, by rational principles—whatever that may mean—and

no *modus procedendi* can be correct which does not attempt to understand those principles and the interactions of the conflicting interests of all participants.[17]

Systematic analysis of the game-theoretic elements in the decisions of national governments about macroeconomic policy has not progressed very far. Lack of development in the analytic techniques of game theory may partly explain that fact. But another, more important part of the explanation is the failure of macroeconomists to become acquainted with the techniques that already exist and to apply them to the situation of intermediate interdependence.[18]

Interactions of the policymakers of different nations can be modeled with emphasis on either the cooperative or the noncooperative aspects. In *cooperative* games the policymakers are assumed to enter into binding and enforceable agreements. "Coordination" (or synonymously "cooperation") thus has a more precise meaning than is typical in ordinary usage and casual analysis; it implies agreements among national authorities to implement instrument settings different from those that would be chosen in the absence of the agreements. If on the other hand national authorities eschew binding commitments, with each merely adapting its decisions to what it observes or expects the others to do, no coordination takes place and the game is *noncooperative*. Noncooperative modeling of the interactions emphasizes the strategies of the individual national authorities and focuses on what each nation's authority may be able to attain independently as a function of its own strategy and the strategies of others.[19]

Noncooperative behavior and outcomes associated with it can in turn be modeled on the basis of either Cournot-Nash or leader-follower assumptions. In a *Cournot-Nash solution* (so named because Cournot originated and Nash generalized the underlying assumptions), each nation's authority ignores the effects of its own decisions on the behavior of the other authorities and simply takes the others' decisions as given. A *leader-follower solution* to a noncooperative game (sometimes called a Stackelberg solution after the German economist who first investigated it) postulates an asymmetry in behavior: one authority is a dominant player and attempts to model the reaction functions of the others. Since the leader authority takes into account the dependence of others' behavior on its own decisions, it can thereby exploit the interaction of the decisions to its own benefit.[20]

17. John von Neumann and Oskar Morgenstern, *Theory of Games and Economic Behavior*, 5th ed. (Princeton University Press, 1944, 1953), p. 11. See also Oskar Morgenstern, "Thirteen Critical Points in Contemporary Economic Theory: An Interpretation," *Journal of Economic Literature*, vol. 10 (December 1972), pp. 1165–67.

18. The brief summary that follows contains references to the main exceptions. For general references on game theory itself, see R. Duncan Luce and Howard Raiffa, *Games and Decisions: Introduction and Critical Survey* (Wiley, 1957); Martin Shubik, *Strategy and Market Structure: Competition, Oligopoly, and the Theory of Games* (Wiley, 1959); Thomas C. Schelling, *The Strategy of Conflict* (Galaxy Books, Oxford University Press, 1963); and Martin Shubik, "Game Theory Models and Methods in Political Economy," in Kenneth Arrow and Michael D. Intriligator, eds., *Handbook of Mathematical Economics* (North-Holland, forthcoming). James W. Friedman, *Oligopoly and the Theory of Games* (North-Holland, 1977) is a recent textbook.

19. When account is taken of information availability (for example, the exchange of projections and model specifications) and of other dynamic aspects, the sharp distinction between cooperative and noncooperative analytical "solutions" to games tends to become blurred. Compare M. Shubik, "Game Theory Models and Methods in Political Economy," section 2.

20. Conceivably, all authorities could try to model the reaction functions of the others; one might then speak of "leader-leader" assumptions and (if they exist) solutions. On the difference between Cournot-Nash and Stackelberg formulations of games, see the discussion and references in James M. Henderson

Suppose national authorities exchanged enough knowledge and information to reach a consensus on a common structural model of the world economy. In principle they could then isolate a set of ex ante outcomes that would be "efficient" for attaining the independent objectives of each nation's authority. Each outcome within that efficient set would be Pareto optimal (ex ante): no nation's authority could expect to reduce its own policy loss from such an outcome without increasing the policy loss for another authority.

Even if national authorities could agree on a set of efficient expected outcomes, intense bargaining would be required to reach cooperative agreement on one particular outcome in that set (with its associated settings for each nation's instruments). Some index of relative bargaining strengths or political power would be required to settle this choice. No authority, however, would have a rational interest in pursuing, or forcing on other nations, an outcome outside the efficient set. So long as the projected configuration of nations' instrument settings threatened to produce an inefficient expected outcome, further efforts at cooperative bargaining by disadvantaged authorities could in principle induce the others to move toward a "better coordinated" configuration that would leave each nation at least as well off as before.

Cooperative agreement among national authorities to aim for a particular ex ante outcome could not guarantee the achievement of that outcome ex post because of the many uncertainties inherent in macroeconomic policymaking. Even so, the instrument settings resulting from ex ante coordination would be as "efficient" as possible under the circumstances.

How are noncooperative outcomes likely to compare with the set of Pareto-optimal outcomes realizable with coordination?[21] Jürg Niehans and Koichi Hamada have analyzed this question. And although Cooper, Roper, Levin, De Grauwe, and Aoki do not employ the techniques of game theory, they have addressed similar issues.[22]

---

and Richard E. Quandt, *Microeconomic Theory*, 2d ed. (McGraw-Hill, 1971), pp. 222–35 and James W. Friedman, "Cournot, Bowley, Stackelberg, and Fellner, and The Evolution of the Reaction Function," in Bela Belassa and Richard Nelson, eds., *Economic Progress, Private Values, and Public Policy: Essays in Honor of William Fellner* (North-Holland, 1977). For an application of these solution concepts in international resource economics, see Stephen W. Salant, "Exhaustible Resources and Industrial Structure: A Nash-Cournot Approach to the World Oil Market," *Journal of Political Economy,* vol. 84 (October 1976), pp. 1079–93.

21. This question may be asked from both an ex ante and an ex post perspective. If cooperation is not attempted, the relevant comparison ex post is between actual noncooperative outcomes and the outcomes that would have been realizable with (ex ante) coordination.

22. Jürg Niehans, "Monetary and Fiscal Policies in Open Economies Under Fixed Exchange Rates: An Optimizing Approach," *Journal of Political Economy,* vol. 76 (July/August 1968, pp. 893–920); Koichi Hamada, "Alternative Exchange Rate Systems and the Interdependence of Monetary Policies," in Robert Z. Aliber, ed., *National Monetary Policies and the International Financial System* (University of Chicago Press, 1974); Koichi Hamada, "A Strategic Analysis of Monetary Interdependence," *Journal of Political Economy,* vol. 84 (August 1976), pp. 677–700; Koichi Hamada, "On the Political Economy of Monetary Integration: A Public Economics Approach," in Robert Z. Aliber, ed., *The Political Economy of Monetary Reform* (Macmillan, 1977); Richard N. Cooper, "Macroeconomic Policy Adjustment in Interdependent Economies," *Quarterly Journal of Economics,* vol. 84 (February 1969), pp. 1–24; Don E. Roper, "Macroeconomic Policies and the Distribution of the World Money Supply," *Quarterly Journal of Economics,* vol. 85 (February 1971), pp. 119–46; Jay H. Levin, "Decentralization vs. Coordination of Monetary Policies Between the United States and the Rest of the World Under Flexible Exchange Rates," Wayne Economic Papers, 4 (Department of Economics, Wayne State University, January 1977); Paul De Grauwe, *Monetary Interdependence and International Monetary Reform* (Lexington Books, 1976); Paul De Grauwe, "The

A basic conclusion emerges from this still limited theoretical analysis: *noncooperative decisions can lead to outcomes far outside the efficient, Pareto-optimal set.*

Hamada's approach in developing this conclusion is to specify a greatly simplified model of the world economy based on the interaction of demand and supply functions for national money stocks. Exchange rates are assumed to be fixed. Each nation has different objectives for its rate of inflation and the change in its external reserves, and each has a policy instrument wielded independently. Game-theoretic interplay among the separate national decisions is studied explicitly.[23]

Hamada shows that noncooperative decisions tend to generate inefficient outcomes under either Cournot-Nash assumptions or when one of the nations is assumed to be a Stackelberg leader. While the outcome reached under the leader-follower assumptions is typically more and is never less favorable for the dominant player than the Cournot-Nash result, it does not seem possible to generalize a priori about which type of noncooperative outcome deviates by the larger amount from a Pareto-optimal outcome dependent only upon the relative bargaining strengths of the nations.[24]

The original discussion by Niehans of the likely inferiority of noncooperative outcomes employed an example where failure to cooperate imparted a recessionary bias to world economic activity. But examples with different biases are easy to construct. Even in Hamada's highly simplified model, noncooperative decisionmaking can lead to either overly expansionary or overly contractionary outcomes relative to the efficient set realizable with policy coordination.[25]

Analytical support for the conclusion that noncooperative behavior can generate serious inefficiencies is provided by some control-theory research on decentralized decisionmaking. Although this research has been concerned only with closed-economy models (the several decisionmakers are, for example, the fiscal authority and the monetary authority within a single nation's government), the analytical issues are formally similar.[26]

Interaction of Monetary Policies in a Group of European Countries," *Journal of International Economics,* vol. 5 (August 1975), pp. 207–28; Masanao Aoki, "A Note on the Stability of the Interaction of Monetary Policies," *Journal of International Economics,* vol. 7 (February 1977), pp. 81–94. For a recent contribution, about which I learned too late to incorporate in my drafting, see Koichi Hamada, "Macroeconomic Strategy and Coordination under Alternative Exchange Rates," in Rudiger Dornbusch and Jacob A. Frenkel, eds., *International Economic Policy: Theory and Evidence* (Johns Hopkins University Press, 1979).

23. The simplicity of Hamada's model permits its algebraic solution for the case of *n* countries; following the lead of Niehans, Hamada also uses Stackelberg diagrams to present a geometrical analysis of the two-country case; see Hamada, "A Strategic Analysis of Monetary Interdependence." Hamada's earlier paper ("Alternative Exchange Rate Systems") considers only two countries, using a variant of the model in Robert A. Mundell, *International Economics* (Macmillan, 1968), chap. 18.

24. Hamada, "A Strategic Analysis of Monetary Interdependence," pp. 692–94.

25. Growth in the *world* stock of reserve assets is an important determinant of the direction of bias, both in real life and in the Hamada model (see the discussion below).

26. See Robert S. Pindyck, "The Cost of Conflicting Objectives in Policy Formulation," *Annals of Economic and Social Measurement,* vol. 5 (Spring 1976), pp. 239–48; Finn Kydland, "Noncooperative and Dominant Player Solutions in Discrete Dynamic Games," *International Economic Review,* vol. 16 (June 1975), pp. 321–35; Finn Kydland, "Decentralized Stabilization Policies: Optimization and the Assignment Problem," *Annals of Economic and Social Measurement,* vol. 5 (Spring 1976), pp. 249–61. For other control-theory references on decentralized decisionmaking (unrelated to the international aspects), see the bibliographies in N. R. Sandell, Jr., and others, "Survey of Decentralized Control Methods for Large Scale Systems," *IEEE Transactions in Automatic Control,* vol. AC-23 (April 1978), pp. 108–28; J. B. Cruz, Jr., "Survey of Nash and Stackelberg Equilibrium Strategies in Dynamic Games," *Annals of*

Further support for the conclusion can be found in economic theory itself. Studies of "market failures" have long since established the result that noncooperative competition can in some circumstances lead to socially suboptimal outcomes.[27] Numerous instances have been identified in which unconstrained maximization by individual economic units, while rational for each individual, can be irrational for all individuals together.[28]

The inferiority of noncooperative outcomes in world macroeconomic decision-making is easiest to demonstrate theoretically for models in which exchange rates are fixed. But the same general conclusion holds even when exchange rates are variable. Just as exchange-rate variability permits greater differences among national macroeconomic conditions than would otherwise be possible, the deviations of noncooperative outcomes from the Pareto-optimal set are likely to be smaller when exchange rates are variable than when rigidly fixed. The analytical justification for believing that noncooperative behavior produces Pareto-optimal outcomes under flexible exchange rates, however, is as weak as the case for believing that flexible exchange rates completely insulate one national economy from another.[29]

Explanations for Noncooperative Behavior

Noncooperative behavior is the norm in the world economy, notwithstanding the theoretical case that each nation could better achieve its national objectives by entering into cooperative agreements. Why? What inhibits the "supply of cooperation" from increasing to a level that would prove mutually beneficial?

Economic and Social Measurement, vol. 4 (Spring 1975), pp. 339–44; Michael Athans, "Theory and Applications: Survey of Decentralized Control Methods," *Annals of Economic and Social Measurement,* vol. 4 (Spring 1975), pp. 345–56. For a pioneering discussion of the application of control-theory methods to decentralized instrument decisions in an international context, see Masanao Aoki, "On Decentralized Stabilization Policies and Dynamic Assignment Problems," *Journal of International Economics,* vol. 6 (May 1976), pp. 143–72.

27. See, for example, Francis M. Bator, "The Anatomy of Market Failure," *Quarterly Journal of Economics,* vol. 72 (August 1958), pp. 351–79; Kenneth J. Arrow, "Uncertainty and the Economics of Medical Care," *American Economic Review,* vol. 53 (December 1963), pp. 941–73; Alfred E. Kahn, "The Tyranny of Small Decisions: Market Failures, Imperfections, and the Limits of Economics," *Kyklos,* vol. 19 (1966), pp. 23–47; Kenneth J. Arrow, "The Economics of Moral Hazard: Further Comment," *American Economic Review,* vol. 58 (June 1968), pp. 537–39; Kenneth J. Arrow, "Limited Knowledge and Economic Analysis," *American Economic Review,* vol. 64 (March 1974).

28. Compare Fred Hirsch, *Social Limits to Growth* (Harvard University Press, 1976), chaps. 5, 6, and 10; and Thomas Schelling, "On the Ecology of Micromotives," in Robin Marris, ed., *The Corporate Society* (Macmillan, 1974). In "The Bagehot Problem," *Manchester School,* vol. 45 (September 1977), pp. 241–55, Hirsch applies similar ideas to the "lender of last resort" problem in commercial banking.

29. Hamada, "Alternative Exchange Rate Systems," pp. 25–29, considers the two-country case under floating exchange rates. For his simplified model and for some simplified characterizations of national objectives, Hamada concludes that "the system of floating exchange rates allows each country to pursue its independent monetary policy" (p. 26). Hamada fails to point out, however, that his simplified example attributes only one objective (the level of income) to each nation's authority under floating exchange rates, whereas under fixed exchange rates each authority is assumed to have *two* ultimate-target variables (the level of income and the change in external reserves). There is no convincing rationale for assuming that national policymakers care about the evolution of the external sector of their economies under fixed exchange rates (for example, have a target for external reserves) but are indifferent to the evolution of the external sector under floating rates (for example, are indifferent to the level of the exchange rate). If the floating rate case were analyzed in Hamada's model under the assumption that each authority has both an internal and an external objective, the same divergence between noncooperative and Pareto-optimal outcomes would still be evident.

One explanation for this ostensible paradox is that the distinction between Pareto-optimal and inefficient outcomes cannot be given operational content in real-life policymaking. Nations' policy authorities cannot isolate a set of ex ante outcomes that is Pareto-optimal, much less bargain about which member of the set to aim for, unless they can use a common, agreed model of the world economy. In practice, each nation's policymakers have so rudimentary a knowledge of macroeconomic behavior—in particular of the transmission of economic stimuli between their own economy and the rest of the world—that they (rightly) regard the concept of a *world* structural model as visionary. The notion of all nations' policymakers undertaking a systematic comparison of differing world models and reaching agreement on a common, least-inadequate model is still more visionary.

Even if existing knowledge of the world economy were adequate enough to permit nations' authorities to distinguish operationally between Pareto-optimal and inefficient outcomes, a shared political resolve to coordinate policies would still be lacking, for two related reasons.

First, each nation's authority tends to have a biased perception when assessing the ex ante trade-off between loss of national political sovereignty and the potential gains from greater international cooperation. Government officials can readily imagine the discomforts of more intensive bargaining with their foreign counterparts, would experience many of those discomforts personally, and might be held politically accountable for any adverse consequences (real or imagined).[30] The benefits that could accrue to the nation's economy, on the other hand, are widely diffused and necessarily uncertain. A tendency exists, inside a nation's government as well as in the private sector, to underestimate the disparity between formal sovereignty to manipulate instruments and effective ability to control national target variables.[31] No matter how anachronistic, this tendency is likely to persist because of the continuing dominance in domestic politics of ideas, symbols, and institutions that are exclusively national in orientation.

Second, quite apart from anachronistic perceptions, the "supply of cooperation" is likely to fall short of what would be mutually beneficial because international cooperation is in essence a public good. Mancur Olson's analysis of the logic of collective action explains why members of a group sharing an objective can individually behave rationally yet collectively produce a suboptimal outcome.[32] In the context here, a nation's policymakers will decide to coordinate instrument settings with foreign counterparts to the extent that the marginal benefit of the coordination

30. More generally, bargaining entails costs that cannot be ignored when asserting that nations' policymakers have incentives to continue bargaining until they achieve a Pareto-optimal outcome.

31. Richard Cooper has observed: "Widespread reluctance to make the required political commitments [to greater cooperation] reflects in part a confusion between formal sovereignty and real freedom of action. Autonomy may have been lost long before the public recognizes it and is prepared to yield the sovereignty which can actually restore a certain freedom of action." *The Economics of Interdependence* (McGraw-Hill, 1968), p. 264.

32. See Mancur Olson, *The Logic of Collective Action: Public Goods and the Theory of Groups*, 2d ed. (Harvard University Press, 1971). A public good is often defined as having one or both of the following properties: if the public good is supplied (if any common goal or the satisfaction of any common interest is achieved), all who value the good tend to benefit whether or not they contribute to the cost of supplying it; if the public good is available to any one person in a group, it is or can be made available at little or no marginal cost to the other members of the group. In addition to *The Logic of Collective Action*, see also Mancur Olson and Richard Zeckhauser, "An Economic Theory of Alliances," *Review of Economics and Statistics*, vol. 48 (August 1966), pp. 266–79, where the theory is applied to international organizations.

to the home nation exceeds the marginal costs of supplying the coordination. Because each nation ignores the potential benefits of the greater coordination for others, however, the degree of coordination actually supplied is suboptimal. A "globally optimal" supply of a public good would involve equating the marginal costs of supplying an additional unit to the sum of all nations' benefits.

Olson's theory also predicts that participation in the supply of public goods will depend upon the number of members in the relevant group. The larger the group, the greater the probability that some members will be "free riders" and the less likely the group will further its common interests. Furthermore, the largest members of a group—those who would on their own provide the largest amount of the public good—tend to bear a disproportionate share of the costs of providing it.[33]

These last points warn against focusing exclusively on the two-nation case in theoretical analysis of the interactions of nations' policymakers. The number of national authorities making interdependent decisions may critically influence both the determinateness of the outcome and the tendency to reach cooperative agreements. If only two nations were involved, each nation's authority could learn from experience whether the other would be cooperative; each could perceive reasonably clearly the value of coordination, and the bargaining outcome of the game-theoretic interaction would probably be determinate. With, say, five to ten nations' authorities interacting, a learning process would be more protracted; the mutual benefits of coordination would be perceived less clearly, and the deviation of noncooperative outcomes from the set of Pareto-optimal possibilities would be markedly greater. With a large number of nations involved in the interdependent decisions (for example, the more than 130 member nations of the International Monetary Fund), outcomes may well be analytically indeterminate; in any case, the policymakers of many of the nations will have weak incentives to coordinate the settings on national policy instruments.[34]

Supranational Traffic Regulations

The international monetary system, to the extent a "system" exists, is the set of traffic regulations followed by national governments, most notably the supranational constraints imposed on the external operating regimes of national authorities. Some of those regulations may be informal conventions or bilateral understandings. Others, the most important ones, are typically embodied in legal documents—for example, the Articles of Agreement of the International Monetary Fund.[35]

Supranational traffic regulations exist outside the financial area. The main

---

33. Olson, *The Logic of Collective Action*, pp. 22–36. Hamada, "On the Political Economy of Monetary Integration," contains a useful summary of the "rational theory of participation" in the context where nations choose whether or not to join a monetary union.

34. For two recent papers that draw on the theory of public goods as an explanation for noncooperative behavior among national governments, see Charles P. Kindleberger, "Dominance and Leadership in the International Economy: Exploitation, Public Goods, and Free Rides," in *Hommage à Francois Perroux* (Presses Universitaire de Grenoble, 1978), and "Government and International Trade," Princeton Essays in International Finance 129 (Princeton University Press, July 1978). For an application of the public goods literature to the military expenditures of the North Atlantic Treaty Organization, see Jacques M. van Ypersele de Strihou, "Sharing the Defense Burden Among Western Allies," *Yale Economic Essays*, vol. 8 (Spring 1968), pp. 261–320.

35. On the legal foundations and history of the International Monetary Fund, see Joseph Gold, *The International Monetary Fund and International Law: An Introduction*, pamphlet 4 (IMF, 1965); Hans

constraints pertain to international trade in goods and services. The General Agreement on Tariffs and Trade, for example, embodies exhortations and rules dealing with national restrictions and subsidies selectively affecting international trade.[36] The financial and nonfinancial traffic regulations taken together may be said to constitute "the international economic system."

When the international economic system is construed in this manner, intergovernmental economic relations might be characterized as a two-stage game. In the first stage, nations' policy authorities agree on a covenant defining the environment within which they will interact with each other; in the second stage, they play out the game under the agreed rules with each nation's authority making its instrument decisions noncooperatively.[37]

The pressures that lead nations' governments to adopt and abide by traffic regulations are readily understandable. A supranational rule of law is one form, albeit limited, of cooperation—an insurance policy against the worst excesses of untrammeled noncooperative behavior.

How much insurance can be expected from traffic regulations alone? Is it feasible to design systemic rules at a first stage that will render any further international cooperation unnecessary during the second-stage interaction of national macroeconomic policies? Unfortunately, government officials and economists probably expect too much of systemic rules, while they unduly neglect opportunities for mutually beneficial cooperation at the second stage.

Consider the roles and limitations of laws within a single nation's legal system. Legal rules outlaw certain activities altogether—those regarded as "criminal" and certain others that impinge adversely on another individual's rights. For example, ordinances forbid a man to dump his garbage on his neighbor's lawn. Ordinances or conventions also outlaw activities associated with public bads if the activities sufficiently affect others' well-being for everyone to agree that "negative presumptions," universally applied, are desirable. It is not legal to dump one's garbage on one's *own* lawn; by convention if not ordinance, flowers should not be picked in a public park.

However, many areas of activity and most types of interactions among individuals are not directly regulated, despite the fact that many of them involve noncooperative behavior where the individuals' interests are in conflict. Unregulated bargaining

---

Aufricht, *The International Monetary Fund: Legal Bases, Structure, Functions* (Praeger for the London Institute of World Affairs, 1964); J. Keith Horsefield and Margaret de Vries, *The International Monetary Fund, 1945–1965: Twenty Years of International Monetary Cooperation* (IMF, 1969); Margaret de Vries, *The International Monetary Fund, 1966–1971: The System Under Stress* (IMF, 1977).

36. Kenneth W. Dam, *The GATT: Law and International Economic Organization* (University of Chicago Press, 1970). The text of the Agreement is available in an appendix.

37. The two-stage characterization is due to Hamada, "Alternative Exchange Rate Systems" and "On the Political Economy of Monetary Integration." Intergovernmental economic relations in modern history conform moderately well with this characterization. Long periods of relative stability in the systemic environment have been interrupted by intervals of crisis in which the rules themselves have been reevaluated. The gold standard for many years before World War I constituted a common-law code of behavior. The 1920s and the Great Depression brought turbulence and some anarchy, but created pressures for the development of better traffic regulations. The codification of new rules in the Bretton Woods agreement that set up the International Monetary Fund and the World Bank, combined with the Marshall Plan and other postwar recovery efforts, again allowed the second-stage game to be played reasonably smoothly for two decades. The progressive breakdown of the Bretton Woods system generated new pressures for "reform" of the international monetary system. While an extensive reform could not be negotiated in 1971–75, such modifications to the traffic regulations as could be agreed were embodied in the amendments to the IMF Articles of Agreement officially adopted in April 1978.

occurs continuously, within the framework of the legal system and social conventions. The bulk of economic activity in most societies fits this description.

A third type of activity is also important: if public goods are to be supplied or public bads ameliorated, positive collective action is required. A city needs to pick up and dispose of garbage so that it will not be on *anyone's* lawn. Although additional legislation may be required to facilitate the supply of public goods, such legislation is ancillary to the positive collective action. Mere evolution of the legal system is not sufficient.

The legal system within a single nation, therefore, does not (and could not) determine all the economic, political, and social interactions of its citizens. A balance is struck—at least in those societies attaching a high value to pluralism and the protection of minority rights—between a pure government of laws and a government of men who dispense with the rule of law. The need for collective action to provide public goods precludes passive reliance on a legal system alone.[38]

Within a nation, externalities and public goods are becoming more numerous and conspicuous over time. On the frontier or in low-density agricultural areas, no ordinances are required restricting the picking of flowers or the disposal of garbage. The shared desires to have public parks and to cperate a garbage collection service arise in high-density urban areas. So long as recent secular trends in population, urbanization, and congestion continue, the relative importance of intra-national cooperative behavior, above and beyond that necessary to devise new laws, is also likely to increase.[39]

The preceding summary of the roles and limitations of the legal system within a single nation illuminates what can and cannot be expected from supranational laws that regulate the interactions of nations themselves.

First, if sufficient international consensus exists, certain types of activities can be outlawed or declared presumptively undesirable. Restrictions or subsidies applied exclusively to a nation's exports or imports, for example, may be analogous to the picking of flowers in a public park. If one nation adopts a few such measures, others may be hurt only a little. But many nations cannot simultaneously behave that way without bringing about a major change in the environment adverse to all. Hence sound grounds, and perhaps also sufficient collective will, may exist for adopting a supranational ordinance presumptively prohibiting everyone.

---

38. Great emphasis on legal rules and legislation frequently accompanies a naive view of the law. Two versions of that preoccupation are widespread: legalism and pragmatism. "Both view law as substance—as substantive rules prescribing rights and obligations for all parties for all future problems. Legalists view substantive rules as inherently desirable—and the more detailed and comprehensive, the better. Pragmatists are more likely to view detailed and comprehensive substantive rules as obstacles to the accomplishment of commonly held, long-term objectives. This jointly held view of the nature of the law tends to obscure the importance of procedures—or, if you will, of the legal process. Law is not solely, or even primarily, a set of substantive rules. It is also a set of procedures, adapted to the subject matter and designed to resolve disputes that cannot be foreseen at the moment when those procedures are established. Perhaps more important than serving to settle disputes, law viewed as procedures and process serves to identify the common interest in complex situations and to formulate short-term policies for the achievement of long-term objectives." Ironically, "the importance of legal procedures and the insufficiency of substantive rules alone are more clearly recognized in domestic legal systems than in the primitive and decentralized international legal order." See Dam, *The GATT,* pp. 4–5.

39. This point is a major theme in Hirsch, *Social Limits to Growth.* Mancur Olson stresses the point in "The Plan and Purpose of a Social Report," *The Public Interest,* vol. 4 (Spring 1969), pp. 85–97. See also Olson, *The Logic of Collective Action,* pp. 172–73, and Schelling, "On the Ecology of Micromotives."

Second, the great bulk of economic interactions of nations will be organized on the basis of decentralized decisions—by individuals, by groups within the nations, or by the national governments. To arrange for coordinated, international decisionmaking in those cases would be prohibitively costly. Even if coordination were attempted and the costs borne, the results could easily be inferior to the noncooperative market outcomes.

But then finally, a third category of interactions will warrant international collective action because noncooperative behavior, by ignoring externalities and the public-goods dimension of the interactions, would otherwise produce greatly inferior outcomes. In those cases, just as within a nation's society, the problem cannot be dealt with by traffic regulations alone. Positive cooperation to supply a public good or suppress a public bad will be necessary. Although collective action within transnational private groups may be appropriate in many cases, the burden of cooperation if it is taken up at all will most frequently fall on national governments.

Externalities and public goods are probably becoming more numerous and conspicuous over time in the economic interactions of nations. Increases in population, economic growth, continued urbanization, and the more intensive exploitation of natural resources generate external diseconomies not only within but across national boundaries (for example, air and ocean pollution). External economies where benefits spill across national jurisdictions probably also increase in importance (for example, the gains from basic research and from control of communicable diseases). Issues about use of the international "commons" (for example, exploitation of fisheries and the sea bed) become more urgent. Economies of scale realizable from international cooperation may seem more compelling (for example, in a joint U.S.-Soviet effort in scientific space research).

Of greatest relevance here, the autonomy of nations' macroeconomic policies and the controllability of nations' economies are undermined by increasing interdependence. As each nation's policy instruments have stronger impacts abroad relative to the impacts at home, the potential costs of ignoring the external impacts become correspondingly greater and the presumptive case becomes stronger for international collective action to take account of system-wide consequences.[40]

These observations show that it is not possible, *even in principle,* to design good supranational traffic regulations at a "first stage" of intergovernmental relations and then to rely solely on noncooperative national decisions within those systemic rules during a "second stage." In fact, the distinction between first and second stages is itself called into question as soon as public goods and positive collective action are admitted into the analysis.

Supranational traffic regulations, as traditionally conceived, are subject to another serious limitation. Rules for the international monetary system have been

---

40. Most of the externalities that arise in connection with economic interdependence among nations not only generate pressures for intergovernmental collective action but also undermine the jurisdictional authorities of the national governments themselves; see the discussion in Richard N. Cooper, "Worldwide or Regional Integration: Is there An Optimal Size of the Integrated Area?" *Economic Notes,* vol. 3 (Siena: Monte dei Paschi di Siena, 1974), pp. 21–36. The major consideration that argues against the enlargement (and possibly even for a diminution) of the jurisdictions supplying some types of public goods is the desirability of accommodating diversity in preferences; on this important point, see Mancur Olson, "The Principle of 'Fiscal Equivalence': The Division of Responsibilities Among Different Levels of Government," *American Economic Review,* vol. 59 (May 1969, *Papers and Proceedings 1968*), pp. 479–87.

designed to pertain primarily to exchange rates and external reserves—that is, to only the external operating regimes of national central banks. Similarly, regulations in the nonfinancial areas pertain only to the external sector of national economies—for example, to exports and imports. Transactions between domestic residents are regarded as outside the purview of the supranational rules.

Article IV of the amended IMF Articles of Agreement and the ancillary guidelines for the surveillance of exchange rates illustrate the problem. Although section 1 of Article IV mentions some general obligations of member nations and affirms that "each member undertakes to collaborate with the Fund and other members to assure orderly exchange arrangements and to promote a stable system of exchange rates," the *operational* emphasis of Article IV is on the exchange-rate (and by implication external-reserves) policies of member countries. The closest resemblance to an effective constraint on national policies is contained in section 3(b) where the Fund is given a mandate to "exercise firm surveillance over the *exchange rate* policies of members" and to "adopt specific principles for the guidance of all members with respect to *those policies*"; members are also enjoined in section 3(b) to "provide the Fund with the information necessary for *such surveillance*" and, when requested by the Fund, to "consult with it on the member's *exchange rate* policies" (emphasis added). The Fund's guidelines for the surveillance over exchange rate policies also focus narrowly on the external operating regimes of central banks; with the exception of a caveat and one important reference that gets the camel's nose into the tent, the guidelines do not even mention nations' domestic macroeconomic policies.[41]

From the perspective of a single nation's policymakers, however, there is no logically valid dividing line between the external and the domestic operating regimes for monetary policy, nor between the external and the domestic sectors of the nation's economy. Similarly, an analytically consistent appraisal of world macroeconomic developments must acknowledge the non-independence of nations' domestic as well as external policies.

Supranational traffic regulations applying exclusively to the external sectors of nations' economies, therefore, are bound to be analytically unsound. Systemic regulations concerned only with exchange rates and external reserves, for example, will be some version of the nondiscretionary external rules that have been shown in earlier chapters to be inferior for the conduct of national monetary policy. Strong pressures exist to adopt regulations that can apply uniformly to all nations, with departures mandated only in extreme circumstances. At worst, therefore, inter-

---

41. For the text of the guidelines for Surveillance over Exchange Rate Policies, see the *IMF Survey,* vol. 6 (May 2, 1977), pp. 131–32, and vol. 7 (April 3, 1978), pp. 97–107. The caveat, contained in the "General Principles" of the guidelines, acknowledges that "there is a close relationship between domestic and international economic policies." The camel's nose gets into the tent when the document later states that the Fund's appraisal of a member's exchange rate policies, its balance of payments, its reserve position, and its external indebtedness "shall be made within the framework of a comprehensive analysis of the general economic situation and economic policy strategy of the member, and shall recognize that domestic as well as external policies can contribute to timely adjustment of the balance of payments." Despite these references, the operational procedures in the guidelines concentrate only on exchange-rate policies and the external sector. For example, the Managing Director is empowered to "maintain close contact with members *in connection with their exchange arrangements and exchange policies*"; if he "considers that a member's *exchange rate* policies may not be in accord with the *exchange rate* principles, he shall raise the matter informally and confidentially with the member" (emphasis added).

national monetary regulations may prescribe that all nations follow one of the rigid external pegging rules.[42]

Supranational traffic regulations applying only to the external sectors of nations' economies will become progressively less appropriate over time as interdependence in the world economy increases.

If traffic regulations were written to conform to the realities of the interdependence of nations' economies, at a minimum the scope of the regulations would have to be extended to the entire range of domestic as well as external macroeconomic policies. Should national governments then be urged to develop such a comprehensive rule of law for the world economy and to subject their domestic policy actions to corresponding enforcement responsibilities of supranational institutions? Even if it were economically sensible to try to accomplish so much with a supranational legal system, political logic would hopelessly conflict with economic logic. A sufficient reason for rejecting such a recommendation is its obvious impracticality.

One is thus inevitably driven to the conclusion that it is not possible to devise supranational traffic regulations that are both politically feasible and analytically sound, and not wise to rely upon conformity with agreed traffic regulations as the main form of cooperative behavior among nation states.

A "World" Instrument of Macroeconomic Policy: Changes in Outside Reserves

Just as many people think only of supranational traffic regulations when considering international cooperation, many also regard supranational institutions primarily as enforcers of the traffic regulations. In fact, the more important challenges facing supranational institutions lie elsewhere.

In a limited way, supranational institutions can be the locus of actions analogous to changes in the settings on national policy instruments. In the decade of the 1970s, the most important "world instrument" was the stock of outside reserve assets. To the extent that national governments cooperate to make deliberate decisions about changes in that stock, the International Monetary Fund is the organization through which such cooperation occurs.[43] Credit tranche lending of "conditional liquidity" by the International Monetary Fund may also be likened to a world policy instrument.[44]

42. The central feature of the Bretton Woods regulations was the rule of thumb "do not change the exchange rate except in case of fundamental disequilibrium" (the exchange-rate peg with an escape hatch). The other simple rule for the international monetary system that could be uniformly applied to all nations is "do not dirty the float unless exchange-market conditions become very disorderly" (the external-reserves peg with an escape hatch).

43. Until the activation of the agreement creating Special Drawing Rights (SDRs) at the beginning of 1970, the only form of world outside reserves was monetary gold. Before the closure of the London Gold Pool and the establishment of the two-tier system in March 1968, the world stock of monetary gold was determined by a complex combination of private market forces, central bank transactions, and national regulations. "Deliberate" management of world outside reserves was thus not even attempted before 1968.

44. The budgetary expenditures of supranational institutions—for example, the specialized agencies of the United Nations—could become sufficiently important in future decades to require macroeconomic analysis to treat such expenditures analogously to the fiscal-policy instruments of national governments. Even in the present-day world economy, development financing extended by the World Bank group of

The significance of changes in the world stock of outside reserves for world macroeconomic outcomes was analyzed extensively in the 1960s and early 1970s. Economists and government officials gradually came to a consensus that such changes are very important in an international monetary system in which supranational constraints require nations to operate infrequently adjusted pegs for exchange rates and enjoin them from imposing restrictions on international trade and capital movements. Under those conditions, each nation must be concerned with the level of its external reserves in relation to other national macroeconomic variables. Transitory declines in external reserves will be desirable from time to time, but most nations will seek to have their external reserves grow secularly. Nations having reserve liabilities ("reserve centers") will be concerned with their *net* external reserve position and will seek to have their holdings of outside reserve assets grow secularly—the more so the faster their reserve liabilities increase over time. These macroeconomic preferences and behavior patterns will be translated into effective "demands" for external reserves (including the composition of reserves between outside reserves and inside-reserve claims on reserve centers). With no change or a decline in the world stock of outside reserves, individual nations will not be able to experience "desired" increases in external reserves except to the extent that other nations experience "desired" or "undesired" declines.[45] An incremental growth in the world stock of outside reserves, however, makes it possible for many more nations to achieve their ex ante preferences for reserve increases without forcing other nations to experience unwanted declines. Insufficient growth in world outside reserves will impart a contractionary bias to the world economy. Excessive expansion in world outside reserves will foster world inflation. Deliberate international management of the change in world outside reserves can thus significantly mitigate the tendency for noncooperative national decisions to produce macroeconomic outcomes that deviate by a large amount from Pareto-optimality.[46]

The analysis summarized in the preceding paragraph has yet to be comprehensively reevaluated for a world monetary environment in which supranational constraints on exchange-rate movements are largely absent. The important issue is whether changes in the stock of world outside reserves continue to have significant impacts on world macroeconomic outcomes under conditions in which many nations practice managed floating.

The broad outlines, if not the details, of the managed-flexibility analysis are reasonably clear. Even with substantial variability in exchange rates, the preferences

---

lending institutions and by the regional development banks (for example, the Asian Development Bank) may have large macroeconomic impacts within particular developing countries. None of these other "world instruments" can feasibly be discussed here.

45. The preferences of reserve-center countries need to be expressed for the purposes of the analysis in terms of changes in net reserve positions (official settlements balances).

46. The debate about deliberate management of world reserves and the creation of a new form of outside reserve asset began with Robert Triffin, *Gold and the Dollar Crisis* (Yale University Press, 1960). The argument summarized in the text can be found in International Monetary Fund, *International Reserves: Needs and Availability* (IMF, 1970); see particularly the contributions of Kemp, Niehans, and Salant. See also J. Marcus Fleming, "The SDR: Some Problems and Possibilities," *IMF Staff Papers*, vol. 18 (March 1971), pp. 25–47, and Fred Hirsch, "SDRs and the Working of the Gold Exchange Standard," *IMF Staff Papers*, vol. 18 (July 1971), pp. 221–53. A discussion of world reserve growth in the context of game-theoretic interactions among national authorities is presented in Hamada, "A Strategic Analysis of Monetary Interdependence."

and behavior patterns of nations' policymakers give rise to effective demands for external reserves. Inconsistencies between ex ante national demands at some initial level of world outside reserves generate pressures for changes in the then-ruling levels of interest rates, exchange rates, and prices; those changes in turn have consequences for real economic activity. Given the initial effective demands for external reserves of each nation's authority, moreover, an increase in world outside reserves exerts an expansionary effect on prices and output (and a decline a contractionary effect) relative to the macroeconomic outcome that would otherwise have resulted. The size of the change in world outside reserves needed to bring about any given balance between expansionary and contractionary forces in the world as a whole is presumably smaller than it would have been under the Bretton Woods system. In principle, however, international management of world outside reserves is still capable of contributing to better world macroeconomic outcomes than would otherwise be possible.

The setting for the "world" policy instrument of outside reserves must be determined somehow, if not deliberately then by default. Nations' governments have a strong *collective* incentive to cooperate in determining that setting. As with public goods in general, however, nations' governments may not perceive and further their mutual interest.

International Coordination of National Policy Decisions

Some nations' policy authorities make bilateral or multilateral efforts to cooperate with each other above and beyond the cooperation implicit in adherence to systemic traffic regulations. Policymakers within some regional groupings of nations, for example in the European Economic Community or the Central American Common Market, have frequent occasion to discuss the region-wide consequences of each nation's policies. The Economic Policy Committee and its Working Party Three in the Organization for Economic Cooperation and Development (OECD) provide periodic forums in which developed countries exchange information and views about each other's macroeconomic policies. Some degree of consultation occurs within the Executive Board and the Interim Committee of the International Monetary Fund. Economic "summit" meetings of the largest industrial countries were held in the latter years of the 1970s.

With the possible exception of some regional groupings, however, such cooperative efforts are very limited. The discussions frequently involve little more than an exchange of recently available national data and their interpretation by each nation's policymakers.

Even that limited activity, it is true, can have significant impacts on noncooperative decisions. If each nation's policymakers acquire better information on recent developments in other countries, their projections of (what are from their perspective) nonpolicy exogenous variables can be improved, which will in turn alter their own instrument decisions (see part 3).

Multilateral consultations about national policies could be still more informative if policymakers frankly revealed their ultimate objectives, their current plans for instrument settings, and their current projections of national economic developments. Even with the existing rudimentary understanding of the transmission of economic stimuli among nations, such exchanges could highlight gross ex ante inconsistencies in nations' policies.

The exchanges of plans and projections that occur in practice tend to be hesitant and less than fully candid because policymakers fear that divulgence of their goals and instrument plans might result in premature or distorted public disclosure, or give other governments greater leverage to pressure them into altering their plans. Defending one's policies in a critical forum of other policymakers involves some de facto surrender of the freedom to implement national policy independently of other nations' preferences. As predicted in Olson's analysis of collective behavior, the benefits of a candid exchange of projections may well be less than the expected costs *as rationally perceived by a single nation*. Despite the likelihood that externalities are sufficiently great so that all nations could profit from adoption of a different attitude, the actual benefits realized from the international consultations turn out to be very modest.[47]

Existing international consultations about macroeconomic policy give little emphasis to exchanges of knowledge about the structural behavior of the world economy and possible steps to augment that knowledge. Basic research in this area is an international public good par excellence. Given the large number of nations in the world, however, the presumption here, too, is that the actual supply falls well short of the socially optimal supply of such research and that a disproportionate share of the costs of supplying the suboptimal amount falls on the largest nations.

All things considered, would it be feasible to intensify the international coordination of macroeconomic policies? And would it be desirable? Five different answers to these questions have been given.

First, some economists and government officials believe it would not be desirable to broaden the efforts at cooperation—whatever the feasibility—because to do so would rely less on free markets and more on central planning. According to this view, proposals for better coordination of national instrument settings are merely one more manifestation of the dangerous tendency to want to substitute centralized for decentralized decisionmaking and would be equally as wrong as many of the unnecessary encroachments on the free-enterprise system observed within national economies. A second group takes the opposite view, on equally general grounds. Greater coordination is both feasible and highly desirable, it is claimed, for essentially the same reasons that argue in favor of relying on government-coordinated, socialist planning of domestic economic activity rather than on capitalist free enterprise.

47. The periodic discussions in the Economic Policy Committee and Working Party Three of the OECD, and possibly also in an occasional "summit" meeting, are the least inadequate of the existing exchanges of plans and projections that do occur. An important reason for the somewhat better result of OECD discussions is the staff work associated with the meetings. For example, the OECD staff prepares an overview—using as a basis national policymakers' discussions of the outlook in their individual countries—of total demand within the OECD countries and of world trade. An effort is made to judge the consistency of national projections—for example whether the sum of ex ante national exports is approximately consistent with the sum of ex ante imports. A cautiously worded version of the OECD staff's analysis has been publicly available since mid-1967 in the semi-annual publication *OECD Economic Outlook*. The forecasting procedures used by the OECD staff are described in the "Sources and Methods" section of the *Economic Outlook;* see also Lee Samuelson and others, "The OECD International Linkage Model," in *Occasional Studies: January 1979*, supplement to *OECD Economic Outlook* (Paris: OECD, 1979).

Despite a widespread tendency to think in those terms, both views deserve to be dismissed summarily. The issues involved are much too complex to be profitably debated, much less resolved, on the basis of broad preferences for social and economic arrangements.[48]

A third view argues that greater efforts at coordination would not be desirable because each nation's domestic policies should be its own concern. If national policymakers interfere with each other's sovereignty by proferring advice on domestic matters, it is claimed, political tensions will be exacerbated. Furthermore, nations differ in their ultimate objectives and national policymakers differ in their analytical understanding of macroeconomic behavior. Those differences, it is argued, should be respected rather than challenged in international relations.[49] Many of those holding this view may also believe that domestic economic developments in one nation can be insulated from those in other nations through appropriate flexibility in exchange rates.

This view, too, deserves to be rejected. Each nation's domestic policies and the political constraints that determine them warrant no less respect internationally than the respect accorded within a country to the preferences and perceptions of each individual. But a nation's preferences and perceptions, as translated into decisions about the settings for its domestic policy instruments, have consequences that cannot possibly be confined within its borders. The greater the degree of interdependence, the less one nation's domestic economy can be insulated from domestic policy actions taken elsewhere in the world. Furthermore, "noninterference" in each others' domestic policies does not maximize the chances of each nation achieving its independent objectives. The theoretical analysis of noncooperative behavior and collective action summarized earlier in fact argues the reverse. Exchange-rate variability provides some scope for divergences among national economic conditions but is no panacea for the problems of interdependence. Regardless of whether national governments recognize it or chafe under its yoke, the non-independence of domestic economic developments is a fact. Thus each nation can no more treat its domestic policies as just its own concern than each sailor in the crew can decide independently whether to sit on the port or starboard side of a longboat.

A fourth view maintains that further coordination of nations' policies, while desirable, is not feasible. Existing institutions and procedures (such as those of the OECD, the IMF, and summit meetings of the largest nations) are not able to support more intensive efforts, it is argued, while the political will to set up new institutions or procedures is lacking. Sophisticated versions of this position invoke the expla-

48. Thoughtful consideration of the problems of public goods and collective action in supplying them is sufficient to lead one to this conclusion. As Mancur Olson notes in *The Logic of Collective Action*, "both the ideology that calls for thoroughgoing centralization of government and the ideology that calls for maximum possible decentralization of government are unsatisfactory [since] efficient government demands many jurisdictions and levels of government," pp. 170–72; see also Olson, "The Principle of 'Fiscal Equivalence.' "

49. See, for example, Gottfried Haberler, "The International Monetary System after Jamaica and Manila," in William Fellner, ed., *Contemporary Economic Problems, 1977* (Washington, D.C.: American Enterprise Institute for Public Policy Research, 1977); Gottfried Haberler, "Reflections on the U.S. Trade Deficit and the Floating Dollar," in William Fellner, ed., *Contemporary Economic Problems, 1978* (AEI, 1978); Herbert Stein, "International Coordination of Domestic Economic Policies," *The AEI Economist* (Washington, D.C.: American Enterprise Institute for Public Policy Research, June 1978).

nations for noncooperative behavior given earlier and assert that any initiatives for more coordination cannot succeed.

Although this view rests on cogent analytical arguments and cannot be shown to be wrong, it nonetheless seems too pessimistic. I favor a fifth view—that the potential gains are great enough, and the opportunities for realizing them sufficiently realistic, to warrant more intensive efforts.

The existing degree of economic cooperation among nations' policymakers has probably changed little, if at all, in the last two decades.[50] Since economic interdependence has grown significantly in that time, an underlying basis for more extensive cooperative efforts has been created on that account alone.[51]

The chief reason for not accepting the pessimistic view, however, is its failure to give adequate emphasis to the potential role of leadership. As critics of the "free rider" explanation of the suboptimal supply of public goods have emphasized, imaginative political entrepreneurship can sometimes circumvent the inability of unorganized groups to act by integrating individual benefits into a collective action.[52] That point has obvious applicability to officials of national governments. If their perceptions of national well-being are not distorted by an excessive preoccupation with political sovereignty and if they are alert to opportunities for gains from coordination, they may be able to exert leadership as international political entrepreneurs.

Richard Cooper has likened the outcome of noncooperative intergovernmental behavior to the situation in which each member of a crowd, wishing to see better, rises to his tiptoes to view a passing parade, with the result that all are more uncomfortable but no one sees better than before.[53] The potential contribution of political leadership is analogous to the role of a parade official who, grasping the collective problem and taking the initiative to propose a solution, uses a megaphone to persuade everyone to sit down simultaneously.

A Catalytic Role for Supranational Institutions

For reasons given earlier, the job of supranational institutions as enforcers of traffic regulations is limited because such regulations can themselves play only a modest role in resolving international economic conflicts and promoting a healthy world economy. But supranational institutions can play a vital catalytic role in facilitating international cooperation in other ways.

Above all, supranational institutions can be a major source of the political entrepreneurship that helps nations' governments perceive opportunities for beneficial collective action. The perspectives and immediate responsibilities of supranational organizations encourage recognition of such opportunities in any case.

50. The European Economic Community is an exception.
51. Conceivably but less likely, cooperation was abnormally high in the 1940s and 1950s given the then-existing extent of interdependence, while the relationship between the two at the end of the 1970s was the normal relationship.
52. See, for example, Norman Frohlich, Joe Oppenheimer, and Oran Young, *Political Leadership and Collective Goods* (Princeton University Press, 1971). Olson acknowledges the validity and importance of the criticism in *The Logic of Collective Action*, app. pp. 176–77.
53. *The Economics of Interdependence*, pp. 160–73.

Imaginative use of their capabilities can magnify the influence of this leadership role.

The desirability of obtaining international agreement on the settings for "world" policy instruments provides especially salient opportunities for leadership by the management and staffs of supranational institutions. In the important case of changes in the world total of outside reserves, for example, skillful use of the administrative resources of the International Monetary Fund can help to catalyze national decisions on SDR allocations or cancellations and on treatment of national gold stocks that pay due attention to world externalities.[54]

Leadership showing how to make better use of existing knowledge and institutional procedures is likely to be the most readily apparent contribution of supranational institutions. They can also exert political entrepreneurship in suggesting or implementing new procedures or new institutions when those alternative routes show promise of facilitating greater coordination of national macroeconomic policies.

Finally, supranational institutions can play a key role in pushing back the frontiers of knowledge about how the world economy functions. Their research staffs, for example, can take the lead in developing alternative structural models of the world economy and encouraging national policymakers to make better use of the analytical models that already exist. At the current stage of evolution of the world economy, leadership of this latter sort, although less glamorous than other activities, may well be the single most important role for supranational institutions like the International Monetary Fund, the World Bank, and the Organization for Economic Cooperation and Development. Improved analytical understanding of the world economy is a precondition for the success of any substantial effort to improve international cooperation.

54. If supranational governmental jurisdictions should gradually acquire increasing political authority in the decades to come, supranational leadership with respect to world instruments could likewise evolve from an exclusively catalytic role to direct participation and, conceivably, to eventual substantive control.

Concluding
Summary

CHAPTER TWENTY-SIX

Guidelines for the Conduct of
National Monetary Policy

THE ANALYSIS in this book is theoretical. But it is inspired by a practical motive: to enhance the understanding of monetary macroeconomics under conditions of interdependence and thereby to improve the conduct of monetary policy by nations' central banks. In keeping with that motive, this concluding chapter begins by proposing thirteen guidelines for policy decisions. The guidelines are a condensed statement of the recommendations, positive and negative, that flow from the earlier analysis. The chapter then summarizes the principal conclusions of the book that constitute the rationale for the guidelines.

Basic Guidelines for National Monetary Policy

To conduct monetary policy in the best way possible, the policymakers of a nation's central bank should first articulate, as precisely as they can, their ultimate objectives and the relative weights attached to them. Clear specification of goals is a necessary condition for sensible policy decisions.

Second, subject to the degree of consensus that can be reached within the national government on the ultimate goals of the nation's economic policies, the policymakers in the central bank should integrate their decisions about monetary policy with the decisions made in the rest of the government about fiscal policy and about other policy areas. Hence the policymakers in the central bank should pay close attention to the effects of monetary-policy actions on *all* ultimate-target variables.

Third, policymakers in the central bank should acquire the least unreliable knowledge about macroeconomic behavioral relationships that is available and incorporate that knowledge in the analytical framework used in making their decisions. That framework—the policymaking "model"—should systematically stress the uncertainties associated with the behavioral relationships and the relative importance of those uncertainties, not merely the single most probable form of each relationship based on current imperfect knowledge. The model must specify not only the relationships for all important aspects of "domestic" macroeconomic behavior, but also the key relationships linking the nation's economy to the global economy.

Fourth, policymakers should constantly focus, as best they can, on their ultimate-target variables. All available data for the variables in the policymaking model should be used to monitor how the ultimate targets are behaving. Because the

485

ultimate targets often cannot be observed directly, available data for intermediate variables should be used to make informed inferences about the contemporaneous evolution of the ultimate-target variables.

Fifth, policymakers should not focus their monitoring activity on just one or a few intermediate variables, and should not use an intermediate variable as a surrogate target in a two-stage strategy. In particular, policymakers should not specify a target time path for the national money stock, somehow defined, and direct the instruments of monetary policy at the objective of minimizing deviations of the actual money stock from that target path.

Sixth, policymakers should conduct monetary policy using a strategy of discretionary instrument adaptation with continuous feedback. The essence of that strategy is to respond differentially to the different types of disturbances affecting the nation's economy through prompt processing of newly available data and continuous contemplation of possible adjustments in instrument settings.

Seventh, whatever variables policymakers may choose as the actual instruments of monetary policy, they should avoid fixed "pegs" and predetermined time paths for instrument settings. This negative guideline applies to all instruments, domestic and external, and regardless of whether "price" or "quantity" in nature. Hence variability in exchange rates and interest rates should not be analyzed in the artificial terms of "fixed versus flexible" extremes. And neither the presence nor the absence of variability in exchange rates should be regarded as a goal of national monetary policy. The polarization between "fixprice" and "flexprice" external operating regimes that is conventional in international economics is an impediment to clear analysis of discretionary alternatives for monetary policy.

Eighth, policymakers should abandon ingrained habits of mind that artificially compartmentalize the analysis of macroeconomic developments into "domestic-sector" and "external-sector" categories. Instead, they should formulate their decisions about domestic monetary policy and external monetary policy as integrated components of one unified set of decisions.

Ninth, although policymakers should continuously review their instrument settings, they should eschew aggressive instrument manipulation based on certainty-equivalent decisionmaking. Given the great uncertainties associated with policy decisions in an open economy, discretionary adaptation should be a middle course between the extremes of "fine tuning" and rigid nondiscretionary rules.

Tenth, policymakers should obtain (or develop) the least unreliable appraisal that is possible of the autonomy of their instruments and of the controllability of the nation's economy. Their instrument decisions should in turn be conditioned by that appraisal.

Eleventh, policymakers should not confuse autonomy and controllability with national welfare. Nonpolicy developments and policy measures that alter the degree of economic interdependence with the rest of the world should be evaluated in terms of their nationwide benefits and disadvantages, not merely how they change autonomy and controllability.

Twelfth, unless the nation's economy is sufficiently small and open to warrant completely ignoring the impacts of national policy actions on the rest of the world, policymakers should try to project those impacts, the possible reactions to them by foreign policymakers, and the resulting feedback effects on the nation's economy.

Thirteenth, policymakers should be alert to opportunities for potentially beneficial cooperation with policymakers in other nations' central banks and governments. The natural bias against yielding any of the nation's political sovereignty should not obscure the perception of problems caused by a lack of international coordination of nations' macroeconomic policies, and should not be allowed to inhibit collective action when net benefits would accrue to the nation as a result.

Interdependence and National Policy Decisions

The theory of economic policy has traditionally been focused on the hypothetical case of a closed economy. This book modifies that theory to allow for the circumstances in which a nation's economy exhibits intermediate interdependence with the rest of the world. Each of the preceding guidelines is conditioned by the book's analysis of interdependence and the constraints it imposes on national policy decisions.

The central dilemma confronting policymakers in interdependent nations is the contrast, heightened by economic openness, between de jure sovereignty over policy instruments and de facto control of ultimate targets. When a nation's economy is significantly open, its ultimate targets are influenced not only by its own government's policy actions and by nonpolicy disturbances originating domestically. The nation's ultimate targets are also buffeted by nonpolicy disturbances originating abroad and by the purposive actions taken by foreign governments to influence foreign ultimate targets (chapters 10 and 11).

The *autonomy* of a nation's economic policy should be identified with the effectiveness of its policy instruments in influencing national target variables. The larger in absolute value and the less uncertain are the impacts of its instruments on national targets, the greater the degree of autonomy. Increases in the openness of a nation's economy tend to reduce autonomy (chapter 12).

The degree of *controllability* that policymakers can exert over the nation's target variables, a much broader concept, depends importantly on autonomy. But it also depends on such factors as the impacts on the nation's economy of nonpolicy disturbances and of the policy actions of foreign governments. Increases in interdependence tend to diminish controllability. As a result, national policy decisions are more difficult to make and more uncertain in their consequences; the ability of the nation's policymakers to achieve national objectives is undermined (chapter 13).

The financial aspects of interdependence have especially important consequences for national monetary policy. If financial interdependence is extensive and increasing, a nation's central bank will have increasing difficulties in bringing about conditions in domestic financial markets that diverge greatly from financial conditions in the rest of the world (part 5).

Forming judgments about autonomy and controllability and ensuring that those judgments help to shape policy decisions—guideline 10—are essential aspects of conducting a sensible monetary policy in an open economy. Policymakers should particularly guard against the tendency to presume a greater degree of autonomy and controllability than exists in fact. If policy is formulated on the basis of exaggerated perceptions of the ability to control national targets, decisions may have consequences very different from those intended and serious policy mistakes may result.

Although controllability is important for a nation's policymakers, maximizing controllability should not be an end in itself. Substantial benefits accrue to a nation from interdependence through the more efficient allocation of resources brought about by international trade and capital movements and the resulting ability of the nation's residents to enjoy a higher standard of living. Those benefits may—for most nations at most times probably do—more than offset any disadvantages associated with diminished controllability. This fundamental point gives rise to the admonition in guideline 11 not to confuse controllability and national welfare.

Ultimate Objectives and the Unity of National Policy

Guidelines 1 and 2 are concerned with the selection of the ultimate objectives sought by policymakers (in more technical terms, the choice of "loss function"). Goal selection depends on the workings of the nation's political processes, both outside the national government (electoral and party politics) and within it (inter-agency and bureaucratic politics).

Should the ultimate goals of the nation's monetary policy be coterminous with the ultimate goals of its fiscal policy? Normatively, the answer to that thorny question depends on the desirability of political independence for the central bank, views about which depend on fundamental value judgments concerning the political and social system. As a practical matter, the answer is determined for each nation by its political institutions and by those individuals who at the moment head its government and administer its fiscal authority and central bank (chapter 18).

Defining objectives and the trade-offs among them is problematic enough within the central bank. Forging an explicit consensus about a unified set of goals for the nation as a whole is exceedingly difficult. Without a reasonably clear specification of national objectives, however, a coherent national monetary policy is impossible.[1]

Given the extent of political independence of the central bank and given whatever consensus can be reached about the nation's ultimate goals, monetary-policy decisions should be formulated in an integrated way with decisions about the rest of macroeconomic policy. National macroeconomic policy has a holistic unity that prevails whether or not policymakers in the central bank and in the fiscal authority acknowledge it. Sound policy decisions require that the unity be acknowledged by an integration of decisionmaking (chapters 14, 18, and 21).

The Money Stock as an Intermediate Target of Monetary Policy

One of the main conclusions of this book is that policymakers should reject an intermediate-target strategy focused on the national money stock and instead

---

1. The most lucid gloss on guidelines 1 and 2 has been provided by Lewis Carroll: "Would you tell me, please," said Alice, "which way I ought to go from here?" "That depends a good deal on where you want to get to," said the Cheshire Cat. "I don't much care where. . . ." said Alice. "Then it doesn't matter which way you go," said the Cat. "So long as I get *somewhere*," Alice added as an explanation. "Oh, you're sure to do that," said the Cat, "if you only walk long enough" (*Alice in Wonderland*, chap. 6).

conduct monetary policy using a strategy of discretionary instrument adaptation. Guidelines 4 through 6 embody that conclusion and the recommended treatment of intermediate and ultimate-target variables that it implies.

The key characteristics of an intermediate-target strategy are its dichotomization of policy decisions into two separate stages and its use of different periodicities of decisionmaking for the two stages. The upper-stage decision that determines the target path for the money stock is revised only intermittently (in an extreme variant, never); lower-stage decisions about instrument settings are revised more or less continuously in response to observed discrepancies between the actual money stock and its target path (chapters 6 and 15). In contrast, discretionary instrument adaptation has no need for a surrogate target to substitute for the genuine ultimate targets. It derives preferred time paths for instrument settings in a single-stage, integrated decision that is kept under continuous review (chapter 15).

Choosing the "Best" Definition of the National Money Stock

Advocacy of the strategy of using the money stock as an intermediate target typically rests on two assertions:

> There exists for the economy as a whole a bundle of financial assets— a particular definition of the money stock—reliably linked through one or more behavioral relationships to the ultimate-target variables of national economic policy; knowledge about these relationships is markedly less uncertain than knowledge about the other macroeconomic behavioral relationships constituting the structure of the economy (the "reliability" proposition).

> Policymakers are able to manipulate the actual instruments of monetary policy so as closely to control that definition of the money stock (the "controllability" proposition).

At least two criteria are relevant, therefore, if policymakers feel compelled to choose a "best" definition of money to use as an intermediate target. The reliability proposition argues for selecting that definition for which the causal links between money and ultimate-target variables are least uncertain. The second proposition suggests choosing the financial aggregate that can be most closely and easily controlled.

The two criteria, however, point in opposite directions. If policymakers search for the financial aggregate most reliably linked by behavioral relationships (for example, the demand for money function) to ultimate-target variables, they tend to move along the chains of causal relationships in the behavioral functions characterizing the economy in the direction of ultimate targets. The more reliable is an aggregate in its links to ultimate targets, the less easily and closely it can be controlled by adjustment of the instruments of monetary policy. Conversely, the more closely an aggregate is tied to policy instruments, the more complex and numerous the behavioral relationships between it and the ultimate-target variables. Thus the price paid for selecting an aggregate that can be controlled closely is to accept increasing uncertainty about the links between that aggregate and the ultimate targets.

This trade-off between reliability and controllability is especially acute for national economies significantly open to the rest of the world. If a definition of the national money stock is chosen to maximize the predictability and dependability of the relationships between money and national ultimate targets, the central bank may have very poor control over the money stock. If a definition is chosen to maximize the central bank's ability to control national money, the relationships linking that money to national ultimate targets may be weak and highly uncertain. For most definitions of the national money stock, reliability *and* controllability are problematic.

Defining the national money stock as a subset of the liquid assets owned by nonbank residents of the nation's economy does not produce an "ideal" definition suitable for use as an intermediate target. And it is an illusion to hope that some definition of national money can be found that will purge international interdependencies from the demand for and supply of money, thereby leaving the central bank free to operate on an uncontaminated relationship between "domestic money" and the volume of "domestic transactions." Indeed, a careful analysis of alternative definitions of the national money stock leads to two impossibility theorems: under conditions of interdependence, (1) the national money stock cannot be defined in such a way that it will be impervious to interactions between the home economy and the rest of the world, and (2) there is no national monetary aggregate that the central bank can control closely and that has a direct, reliable relationship with the ultimate targets of national economic policy (chapters 8 and 9).

A nation's central bank has no straightforward basis for trading off reliability and controllability when selecting a definition of the national money stock to use as an intermediate-target variable. Yet use of a money strategy requires the selection of some single definition as least problematic.

A strategy of discretionary instrument adaptation does not require settling on a single definition of national money. Monetary aggregates (strictly speaking, the various components of the aggregates) are valuable to such a strategy because of their information content; policymakers do not in any sense ignore monetary quantities. But the aggregation of the quantities into broad summary measures is an issue of minor importance (chapter 24).

Putative Justifications for a Money Strategy

Regardless of how national money may be defined, an intermediate-target strategy focused on the money stock can be justified only if there are good reasons to decompose the complete decision problem facing policymakers into two separate stages having different periodicities of decisionmaking.

Six types of justification are conceivable. They assert that a money strategy (1) uses the flow of new information about the economy more efficiently, (2) copes more successfully with policymakers' uncertainty about how the economy functions, (3) incurs smaller resource costs, (4) takes better advantage of game-theoretic, expectational interactions between policymakers and the private sector, (5) provides better insulation for monetary policy from the vagaries of the political process, and (6) affords better protection for the economy from errors due to incompetence or mistakes in judgment on the part of central bankers.

Each of those justifications, however, is analytically inadequate. None of the last four is an acceptable rationale for a two-stage decision process. And the first two are flatly wrong: a money strategy is demonstrably *less* efficient in processing new data about the economy and *less* successful in coping with uncertainty than a single-stage strategy of discretionary instrument adaptation.

The putative case for using a money strategy on information grounds appeals to the facts that data for the surrogate money target become available frequently and promptly whereas ultimate-target variables are glimpsed only intermittently (gross national product being observed, for example, only quarterly and with a substantial lag). Because of the better flow of data about the money stock, it is argued, the central bank can closely monitor the behavior of money relative to its target path and promptly correct any incipient deviations. The central bank cannot make continuous adjustments in policy in response to observed deviations of ultimate-target variables from their desired paths.

Although the facts about the flow of data cited by the advocates of a money strategy are correct, only in a superficial analysis can those facts be used to justify a two-stage decision procedure. The central bank does not have a valid reason for using an intermediate variable as a surrogate target rather than aiming at its genuine objectives merely because the former is continuously visible while the latter are not. To recommend pursuit of a surrogate target because of its better visibility is no more logical than to advise a ship's captain navigating into a dangerous harbor at night to steer into a channel marked by buoys flashing every ten seconds rather than one marked by buoys flashing every two minutes merely because the ten-second buoys can be followed more easily.

The essence of the two-stage decision procedure is *not* to recalculate the upper-stage target path for the key intermediate variable with each arrival of new information. Temporarily (or in the extreme variant permanently), an intermediate-target strategy thus discards a large fraction of the available new data about the economy. And it does not react more promptly or more efficiently to any of the non-discarded data than does a strategy of discretionary instrument adaptation with continuous feedback. A careful analysis of how information is used in alternative strategies, far from supporting a money strategy, exposes serious inefficiencies inherent in the two-stage decision procedure (chapter 17).

When existing knowledge about behavioral relationships is very imperfect (the policymaking model thus poorly imitating the true behavior of the economy) and when the flow of new data about the economy is inadequate and unreliable, all strategies for conducting monetary policy will be problematic. The more deficient the information flow, the smaller may be the degree of superiority of a single-stage over an intermediate-target strategy. No conceivable flow of new information, however, could reverse the relative ranking of the two strategies from the perspective of efficiency in information processing.

A similar fallacy underlies the contention that a money strategy copes more successfully with uncertainty. The existence of uncertainty about how the economy functions, and in particular how it reacts to the central bank's policy actions, is a compelling argument for making policy decisions cautiously. But uncertainty does not constitute a valid reason for splitting the policy problem into two stages with different periodicities for the two levels of decisions. A two-stage approach necessarily ignores interdependencies between the uncertainties associated with upper-level and lower-level decisions. For equivalent assumptions about the forms and intensities of uncertainties confronting policymakers, about the policymakers' ultimate objectives, and about their skills in making decisions, the results from pursuing a money strategy can never be better, and in the general case are unambiguously worse, than the results from following a strategy of discretionary instrument adaptation (chapter 17).

The inefficiencies in using new data and coping with uncertainty that are inherent in a two-stage decision process are even more troublesome in a significantly open than in a nearly closed economy. Autonomy and controllability are more limited, and the information loss resulting from the discarding of new data during the intervals between reconsiderations of the target money path therefore has an even higher opportunity cost. Uncertainty about economic structure and about the impacts of policy actions is heightened by the economy's openness, and policymakers thus have an even more urgent need to make the best possible use of existing knowledge and information (chapter 24).

Resource-cost considerations, although an important factor in choosing a policymaking model, do not have decisive implications for strategy choice. The putative justification for a money strategy based on resource costs is not a convincing reason for using a surrogate money target in a two-stage decision process (chapter 16).

The rationales for a money strategy that appeal to game-theoretic interactions with the private sector and that advocate insulation of monetary policy from the political process and from human error are essentially arguments against the exercise of discretion by policymakers. The game-theoretic argument emphasizes the private sector's expectations of policy actions and asserts that self-imposed limits on policymakers' discretion, implemented by credible announcements of a policy rule, will induce private-sector agents to make better decisions and hence lead to a more favorable evolution of the nation's economy. The insulation arguments rely on political and sociological observations about the potentially adverse effects on the economy of permitting monetary-policy decisions to be made discretionarily.

These arguments against discretion, it may be granted, are conceivable justifications for a monetary-policy rule.[2] But they are not analytically valid justifications for a rule *based on an intermediate-target variable*. If game-theoretic and expectational considerations were to justify the central bank imposing limits on its discretionary actions by announcements of some sort of rules, the announcements should be made in terms of actual instruments, ultimate objectives, or conceivably both. Similarly, even if the political and sociological arguments for espousing monetary-policy rules were accepted, they would not justify a two-stage strategy focused on a *money* rule. Advocates of rules for the money stock overlook a logical gap in their reasoning when they leap from their general arguments against discretion to the specific recommendation of pegging the money stock on an intermediate-target path (chapter 18).

Further Reasons for Rejecting a Money Strategy

Three additional considerations argue against the central bank conducting monetary policy with an intermediate-target strategy.

2. Any "rule" must be adopted, and may be amended, by discretionary action. Any "discretionary" procedure for making decisions systematically may be described as a complex rule. The terms rule and discretion as used throughout this book have the same meanings as in ordinary discourse (see chapter 15).

First, the use of a surrogate target can easily divert attention from ultimate targets, with undesirable consequences for policy decisions. Private-sector opinion may more readily misperceive monetary policy; as a result, desirable adjustments in policy may at times be more difficult. At worst, policymakers themselves may slip into the habit of treating the money target path as an end in its own right (chapter 18).

Second, an intermediate-target strategy for monetary policy makes coordination of monetary policy and fiscal policy more difficult than it would otherwise be with monetary policy conducted by discretionary instrument adaptation. This consideration becomes progressively more important the stronger is the desire within the national government to use monetary and fiscal instruments in a unified discretionary approach to macroeconomic stabilization policy as a whole (chapter 18).

Third, the two-stage decision process of an intermediate-target strategy requires a policymaking model that can validly be decomposed into two submodels. In effect, the central bank must be able to segregate the causal links between its policy instruments and money from the causal links between money and ultimate-target variables and operate on the former independently of the latter. Economic theory raises substantial doubts, however, that macroeconomic behavior is sufficiently recursive to warrant policymakers using a model that assumes the required decomposability. This problem is a fundamental analytical weakness that has been overlooked by advocates of intermediate-target strategies (chapters 6, 16, and 24).

Instrument Choice and Instrument Variation in a Single-Stage Strategy

Guidelines 7 through 9 are concerned with decisions about instrument choice and instrument variation under a single-stage strategy (on the assumption that policymakers reject the inferior approach of intermediate-target strategies).

The problem of *instrument choice* under a single-stage strategy involves selection of an instrument operating regime for domestic monetary policy and an instrument operating regime for external monetary policy. The selection of operating regimes is typically a one-time decision not subjected to continuous reevaluation. *Instrument variation* is the changing of the settings on the instruments once the operating regimes have been chosen. The problem of whether to vary the instrument settings, and if so by how much, is an ongoing decision that policymakers face every day.

Some variables controlled directly by the central bank—for example, reserve-requirement ratios and the central bank's discount rate—are instruments in any operating regime. In addition, policymakers have a choice, for both domestic and external monetary policy, between using a "quantity" and a "price" as an operating instrument. Domestically, they can choose the quantity of a reserve-money aggregate as the primary domestic instrument, letting short-term interest rates fluctuate endogenously; or they can select an interest rate as the instrument, letting the quantity of reserve money be determined endogenously (chapters 14, 19, and 22). Externally, if their actions are not opposed by policymakers in foreign governments, they can choose the quantity of external reserves as their instrument, letting the

494

exchange rate fluctuate endogenously; or they can use the exchange rate as the instrument, permitting the quantity of external reserves to be determined endogenously (chapters 20 and 22).

The problem of instrument choice lends itself more readily to theoretical analysis than the problem of instrument variation and has therefore enjoyed the lion's share of attention in monetary theory. The alternative decisions about instrument choice most often analyzed in the theoretical literature, however, are in fact decisions embodying a combination of instrument choice and instrument variation: policymakers choose whether to use a quantity or a price as their instrument at the beginning of the comparative-statics period of analysis and then leave the instrument "pegged" at its initial setting thereafter.

The traditional theoretical analysis has the unfortunate by-product of greatly exaggerating the significance of instrument choice while deflecting attention from ongoing decisions about instrument variation. In operational practice, decisions about instrument variation are much more important. Central banks have no practical need to choose whether to peg a price or peg an associated quantity for an extended period of time; either type of behavior implies use of a mechanical rule and ignores the possibility of period-by-period discretionary decisions. When the central bank is prepared to vary its instrument settings from one short-run period to the next, furthermore, the question of whether a quantity or a price is used as the instrument becomes an issue of secondary importance. Instrument choice cannot be an overriding concern in its own right unless policymakers wish to use predetermined rules for the time paths of instrument settings (chapters 19 and 22).

Arguments supporting the use of instrument rules instead of discretion can usefully be divided into two categories. Some economic arguments assert that policymakers can cope better with uncertainty and can otherwise achieve their objectives more efficiently by pegging instrument settings on predetermined time paths (chapters 17, 19, and 24). A second group of arguments, broader in scope and going beyond economics, supports the case for rules by invoking game-theoretic interactions between the policymakers and the private sector, political-sociological considerations, or both (chapters 18 and 24).

The economic arguments in favor of instrument rules do not stand up to analysis.[3] Instrument rules do not make efficient use of new data about the economy and are an inferior way for policymakers to respond to uncertainty. Judged on the basis of economic considerations, therefore, policymakers should avoid predetermined time paths for instrument settings. They should especially avoid pegging rules of thumb that fix instrument settings and then leave them unchanged for an extended period. The preferable approach is to keep the instrument settings under continuous discretionary review.

Different types of nonpolicy disturbances affect the nation's economy differently. A strategy of discretionary instrument adaptation permits policymakers to respond differentially to the different disturbances. At times when little information is available about the sources and magnitudes of specific disturbances currently affecting the economy, policymakers cannot do much to tailor their responses to the types of disturbances and should not try to do so. The more uncertain the

3. A summary evaluation of the second group of arguments is given in a subsequent section.

policymaking model, the more cautious the responses should be. Even when information is poor and uncertainty is great, however, policymakers are better off eschewing instrument rules and following instead the cautious discretionary policy that seems best at the moment, reevaluating the situation period by period (chapters 19 and 22).

Discretionary Adaptation for External Monetary Policy

The injunction against pegged instrument settings in guideline 7 applies no less to external than to domestic monetary policy. That unconventional treatment of the external aspects of monetary policy stems from two important differences between current orthodoxy and the conceptual approach advocated in this book.

First, the analysis here abandons the artificial characterization of "exchange-rate regimes" that has become traditional in international economics. Just as the central bank does not have to make the artificial choice between pegging an interest rate and pegging a reserve-money aggregate domestically, its choices for external monetary policy need not and should not be restricted to pegging the exchange rate or pegging the quantity of external reserves. The principles and procedures used in making "myopic" national decisions about external monetary policy should be essentially the same as those used for domestic policy: pegging rules of thumb should be rejected in favor of discretionary instrument adaptation.[4]

The traditional focus on "fixed versus flexible exchange rates" has always had the undesirable consequence of diverting attention from the period-by-period discretionary use of the external instrument. Such a focus is especially inappropriate in an era when supranational constraints on exchange-rate variability have been largely abandoned.

Discretionary variation of the external instrument helps policymakers respond differentially to the different types of disturbances affecting the economy. It is especially helpful in permitting a differentiated response to disturbances that originate within the nation's economy and those that originate abroad. Such an approach implies substantial variability over time in *both* the exchange rate and the external reserve position (just as, domestically, both interest rates and reserve-money aggregates exhibit variability). That joint variability should occur independently of whether policymakers use the exchange rate or the quantity of external reserves as their instrument (chapters 22, 23, and 24).

Second, the analysis here departs from conventional thinking by breaking down the traditional compartmentalization between "monetary policy" and "exchange-rate regimes," with the former understood to mean *domestic* monetary policy and the latter regarded as a specialized subject in international finance about which decisions can be made on separate principles. The compartmentalized approach is flawed in its basic premises. Not only are there conspicuous parallels between domestic and external policy actions. The interactions between domestic and external actions require that they be analyzed concurrently. A domestic action cannot be defined or systematically analyzed unless the external operating regime

---

4. Myopic national decisions focus solely on the home nation's objectives and actions. Sound policy requires that international cooperation modify this myopic perspective.

is specified. Nor can one define an exchange-market-intervention action or systematically analyze its consequences without reference to domestic operating procedures and objectives.

The correct approach for policymakers in the central bank, as emphasized in guideline 8, is to treat domestic monetary policy and external monetary policy as integrated components of one unified set of decisions (chapters 20 through 24). The strategy for monetary policy should in turn be combined—see guideline 2—with a fiscal operating regime and with institutional procedures for financing the government budget imbalance to produce an integrated policy regimen for national macroeconomic policy (chapters 14, 21, and 24).

Discretionary instrument adaptation facilitates an integration of decisions about the settings for domestic and external instruments into a coherent national monetary policy. A two-stage money strategy, especially an "inward-looking" variant of the type commonly espoused, does not (chapter 24). This consideration is one more good reason why the central bank should conduct monetary policy with discretionary instrument adaptation rather than with an intermediate-target strategy.

Fine Tuning, Rules, and Discretion

Discretionary instrument adaptation is not a euphemism for "fine tuning." Fine tuning involves aggressive, certainty-equivalent manipulation of policy instruments: new data about the economy invariably lead to adjustments in instrument settings, with policymakers basing their decisions solely on best estimates of the impacts of their actions and ignoring uncertainty about those impacts. In sharp contrast, discretionary adaptation involves merely a prompt processing of newly available data and a continuous contemplation of possible actions; whether actions are taken in response to new data, and if so the sizes of the actions, depends critically on the degree of the policymakers' aversion to risk and the extent of their uncertainty about the impacts of their actions.

Certainty-equivalent manipulation of instrument settings is dangerous. Fine tuning thus merits the opprobrium it generally receives. But its vices should not be attributed to discretionary instrument adaptation. Discretionary adaptation is compatible with any degree of policymakers' risk aversion and any degree of uncertainty about the macroeconomic behavioral relationships characterizing the nation's economy and its links with the rest of the world. If used in conjunction with the best available techniques for incorporating uncertainties into the policymaking model (as recommended in guideline 3), a strategy of discretionary adaptation can be especially helpful to policymakers when uncertainty is great; it then provides a way of conditioning instrument decisions in accordance with policymakers' judgments about the sources and relative intensities of different types of uncertainty (chapters 17 and 19).

Although criticism of discretionary adaptation on the grounds that it represents fine tuning is mistaken, two other lines of criticism—the "rational expectations" challenge to the theory of economic policy and the political-sociological arguments against discretion—cannot be so readily dismissed.

The greatest weakness of the traditional theory of economic policy is its failure to deal adequately with expectational phenomena, particularly game-theoretic interactions between policymakers and the private sector. When the openness of the economy and private-sector expectations of exchange rates and the external reserve position are taken into account, the weakness is even more glaring. The game-theoretic argument in favor of instrument rules rather than discretion, most often made in the context of the research on rational expectations, derives its force from recognition of that weakness.

The merits and deficiencies of the game-theoretic case for policy rules are currently undergoing intensive analysis by the economics profession. It is conceivable that future research—the issue is moot at the time of this writing—will show that a nation's central bank could better facilitate national objectives by preannouncing and adhering to some form of self-imposed limits on its discretionary actions.

The criticisms of discretionary decisions and the corresponding arguments for instrument rules that can be advanced on political and sociological grounds—for example, that instrument rules would facilitate a desirable insulation of monetary policy from the political process and would provide a needed protection against the possibility of policymakers' errors—are even more difficult to evaluate than the game-theoretic criticism. This is in part because value judgments and ideologies necessarily play a prominent role in the evaluation.

This book discusses the game-theoretic and political arguments against a strategy of discretionary adaptation but does not try to render judgment on them. Objective judgments about those arguments must await further analysis of the issues, incorporating insights drawn from the other social sciences even more than from economics (chapters 18 and 24).

Strategy Choice: False and Genuine Issues

Debate about the conduct of monetary policy has typically been preoccupied with the differences between "monetarist" and "Keynesian" views. Whether the central bank should emphasize money or interest rates in its policy decisions is widely thought to be the central issue in the debate.

Conventional monetarist and conventional Keynesian views about monetary policy, however, are both inadequate. The typical result of casting the debate in those terms is to generate heat, not light. Worse still, the alleged issue of money versus interest rates is a red herring that diverts the debate from the issues that genuinely merit attention.

Issues of genuine importance exist in all three areas of *goal selection, model choice,* and *strategy choice.* When selecting its goals, the central bank must decide how to specify the trade-offs among its ultimate-target variables (the issue of specification of the loss function). It must decide on the appropriate degree of coordination of its decisions with those of the rest of the nation's government (the issue of central bank independence). When choosing the analytical framework to use in shaping its decisions, the central bank must decide between conflicting views on the best approaches to macroeconomic modeling (for example, the issues of model size and treatment of uncertainty). When choosing its strategy, the central bank must take a position on two central issues. It must decide whether or not to use an intermediate-target approach (the issue of two-stage versus single-stage decision procedures). And it must decide how discretionary an approach to adopt in its ongoing decisions about instrument variation (the issue of instrument rules versus discretionary adaptation).

None of those genuine issues, in my view, can be fruitfully described as requiring a choice between monetarism and Keynesianism. If the labels monetarist and Keynesian continue to be used, participants in the debate at the very least should distinguish among the issues of goal selection, model choice, and strategy choice.

The remaining differences that divide thoughtful macroeconomists willing to be regarded as monetarists and Keynesians are primarily controversies about ultimate objectives and the politics of monetary policy. To a lesser extent, views also continue to differ about model choice (chapters 16 and 18).

The two central issues of strategy choice are illuminated least of all by the conventional debate between monetarists and Keynesians. That debate has scarcely shown a sensitivity to the differences between intermediate-target and single-stage decision procedures, much less commented cogently on their relative merits. The controversial aspects of the issue of rules versus discretion are noneconomic and can scarcely be settled by invoking alternative approaches to macroeconomic theory; if monetarism and Keynesianism are associated with different views of the political process and with different social values, it is those latter differences that should receive emphasis.

The insensitivity of the monetarist-Keynesian controversy to the issue of two-stage versus single-stage decision procedures is illustrated by the emphasis customarily given to the reliability and controllability propositions about the money stock. Both the advocates and the critics of a money strategy attribute great significance to the question of whether the reliability and controllability propositions are correct descriptions of reality. In fact, no decisive implications for strategy choice would follow *even if* some definition of the national money stock existed that could be closely controlled by the central bank and was predictably and dependably related to national ultimate targets. The empirical correctness or falsity of the propositions has significance primarily for the specification of the analytical model used in policymaking. The tendency of advocates of a money strategy to leap from the reliability and controllability propositions to their strategy recommendation involves a logical hiatus and a confusion between the problems of model choice and strategy choice (chapter 16).

The genuine issues of model choice and strategy choice are badly distorted if posed as a choice between emphasizing money *or* interest rates. More broadly, the genuine issues do not require the central bank to choose between emphasizing "quantities" *or* "prices."

The fundamental problem with a money strategy is its two-stage decision procedure, not its selection of a quantity as the surrogate target. A two-stage strategy using a "price" variable as the surrogate target (for example, the interest rate on long-term bonds) would in most circumstances be even worse than a money strategy.

When the central bank selects its operating regimes, it must choose whether to use quantities or prices as its actual instruments. But those instrument choices are secondary issues if the instrument settings are discretionarily varied. And no matter how the instrument choices are made, quantities *and* prices are important in policy decisions.

Monetarists who argue against stabilizing interest rates are right—some of the time. Keynesians who argue against stabilizing financial quantities are right—some of the time. The key point, however, is that neither a price-stabilization nor a quantity-stabilization presumption is the appropriate guideline for domestic monetary policy in all circumstances.

Similarly, those who argue against minimizing the variance of the exchange rate are right—some of the time. Those who argue against untrammeled floating of the exchange rate are right—some of the time. But neither the fixprice nor the flexprice presumption is an appropriate external monetary policy for all circumstances.

Awkward though the truth may be, no good reason exists for the central bank to emphasize quantities instead of prices, or prices instead of quantities. As operas require a libretto and a score, a sensible approach to national monetary policy requires an integrated perception of both prices and quantities, combined with a discretionary differentiation of decisions in accordance with the current and prospective circumstances of the nation's economy.

The Nation and the Global Economy

The analysis in this book not only discards the traditional focus on fixed versus flexible exchange rates. It rejects the conventional view that variability in exchange rates insulates national economies from each other.

When a nation's economy is financially open, monetary-policy actions in foreign nations affect financial and real-sector variables in the home economy whatever happens to the exchange rate. Monetary-policy actions taken by the central bank of the home nation are not completely bottled up at home regardless of the form and degree of exchange-rate variability. Similar conclusions apply to the international consequences of fiscal-policy actions and nonpolicy disturbances.

The impacts on a nation's economy of policy actions and nonpolicy disturbances originating abroad vary in magnitude under different home policy regimens. For most policy actions and many types of nonpolicy disturbances, the impacts spill over less into the home economy if the nation's currency is permitted to appreciate in response to external stimuli that are expansionary and to depreciate in response to those that are contractionary. But that "partial" insulation does not argue for always encouraging rate variability. The buffering tendencies do not apply to every type of disturbance originating abroad. And policymakers should not always want their nation to be buffered against the rest of the world.

In a nirvana designed for nationally myopic policymakers, they would be able simultaneously to retain within the home economy the benefits of good things originating at home, to export as much as possible of their own nation's bad things to the rest of the world, to import good things from the rest of the world, and to insulate the home economy from all bad things originating in the rest of the world. But such a nirvana is illusory. Any dream of achieving it by means of some once-for-all decision about the form and degree of exchange-rate variability is a still more forlorn hope (chapters 22 and 23).

The conventional view of the insulating properties of exchange-rate variability is frequently associated with the idea that flexible exchange rates free nations' governments to forget about their balances of payments and to worry only about their domestic economies. Greater flexibility in exchange rates is also thought to cause a "dis-integration" of nations' economies. Those ideas, too, are misleading if not flatly wrong. The interdependencies among significantly open economies are much too pervasive to be neutralized by variability in exchange rates.

Indeed, the differences between alternative forms and degrees of exchange-rate variability have less importance for macroeconomic policy issues than has traditionally been presumed in international economics. Such differences may not even be the most critical determinant of the autonomy of national monetary policy. They are certainly not the decisive factor influencing the controllability of the national economy or its integration with the rest of the world (chapter 23).

The only conceivable way for a nation's policymakers to dis-integrate the nation's economy from the global economy, or even to inhibit its further integration, would be to place impediments in the way of movement of goods, assets, people, or information across the national borders. But such actions would simultaneously reduce the benefits to the nation's residents that result from interdependence. Again, therefore, contemplation of such actions should carefully distinguish national welfare from autonomy and controllability (guideline 11). If dis-integration is either impossible or excessively costly, which is the probable case for most nations at most times, the nation's policymakers have no effective choice but to accept increasing interdependence and to try to make the best possible policy decisions in the face of it.

The economies of most industrialized nations are not small enough in relation to the global economy to justify a posture of forgetting altogether about the impacts of the nation's economy on the rest of the world. The more closely actual conditions correspond to intermediate interdependence, the greater the attention that policymakers must devote to feedback effects on the national economy (part 3, chapter 25, guideline 12).

It is debatable whether policymakers in *any* nation can legitimately ignore the need for some amount of cooperative decisionmaking among nations about macroeconomic policies. As with other public goods, it is true, the supply of international cooperation is likely to fall short of what would be mutually beneficial; many nations in the world have strong incentives to behave as "free riders," with the result that the world as a whole fails to further its common interests. Yet each nation has an interest in preventing unsatisfactory outcomes for the global economy resulting from untrammeled noncooperative behavior. Enlightened policy for a single nation must therefore increasingly confront the difficulties and potentialities of international cooperation, including the promotion of supranational institutions that can catalyze that cooperation. In essence, national governments will gradually have to learn the lessons of collective action on an international scale that have been learned, or in some cases are still being learned, within their individual nations (chapter 25, guideline 13).

Theory and Common Sense

The guidelines at the beginning of this chapter, like the book itself, are abstract—merely a skeleton. They lack the flesh and blood of real political and economic institutions, and of actual macroeconomic behavioral relationships. They thus provide no detailed guidance for the formidable difficulties that a central bank encounters in actual practice.

Those who yearn for easy solutions for the problems of conducting monetary policy may complain that the guidelines are little more than common sense. In effect, it may be said, the guidelines urge a nation's policymakers to "do what is intelligent and prudent" without defining, simply and concretely, what such a course of action would be.

Undeniably, the analysis here goes only a short way toward resolving the practical problems facing the central bank of a specific nation at specific times. It nonetheless represents a sound framework within which policymakers can begin to tackle those problems. And a sound analytical framework, after all, is no small matter. Edifices with wobbly superstructures do not hold up well when the rains come and strong winds blow.

It is even more true that this book fails to propose simple and concrete "solutions." But it is a disservice to prescribe simple nostrums for complex problems that will not yield to nostrums. When dealing with complex problems, furthermore, policymakers should not underestimate the value of an analytical framework that is merely common sense. In monetary policy as in so many other areas, things would go better if common sense were more common.

Appendixes

Further Notes to Chapter 11: The Mathematical Representation of a Two-Nation World Economy

THIS APPENDIX supplements the discussion in the corresponding sections of chapter 11.

Representation of Structural Model and Its Reduced Form for a Single Period

As shown in definitions 11-1 through 11-5, the variables of a two-nation world economy may be represented as an $n + m$ vector of endogenous variables Y_t (n labeled as home, m as foreign); as a $k + l$ vector of policy instruments X_t (k home, l foreign); as an $r + s$ vector of nonpolicy exogenous variables Z_t (r home, s foreign); as an $n + m$ vector of lagged values of endogenous variables Y_{t-1}; and as an $n + m$ vector of additive stochastic error terms E_t. If the structural model is assumed to be linear, a representation of the system of $n + m$ equations for a single time period may be written

$$(A\text{-}1) \qquad \Gamma Y_t + \Phi X_t + \Omega Z_t + \Lambda Y_{t-1} + E_t = 0,$$

where the coefficient matrixes Γ and Λ are of order $(n + m) \times (n + m)$, Φ is of order $(n + m) \times (k + l)$, and Ω is of order $(n + m) \times (r + s)$.[1]

The reduced-form equations of this system for period t are:

$$(A\text{-}2) \qquad Y_t = AX_t + BZ_t + LY_{t-1} + U_t.$$

The reduced-form coefficient matrixes are given by

$$(A\text{-}3) \qquad A = -\Gamma^{-1}\Phi$$

$$(A\text{-}4) \qquad B = -\Gamma^{-1}\Omega$$

$$(A\text{-}5) \qquad L = -\Gamma^{-1}\Lambda,$$

and the reduced-form error terms are

$$(A\text{-}6) \qquad U_t = -\Gamma^{-1}E_t,$$

where the matrix Γ^{-1} is the inverse of the nonsingular matrix of structural coefficients Γ.

As emphasized in chapter 11, each reduced-form coefficient in the interdependence submatrixes of A, B, and L usually has a nonzero value even if many of the

---

1. For convenience, some of the equations in chapter 11 are repeated in the appendix; for example, equations A-1 appear in chapter 11 with the number 11-6.

structural coefficients in the interdependence submatrixes of Γ, Φ, Ω, and Λ have values of zero. Strong links between the home and foreign economies in only a few structural equations may be sufficient to generate indirect interdependence (that is, links in the reduced-form equations) for virtually all endogenous variables.

However, if all the coefficients in the interdependence submatrixes in the structural model are very small in the sense of approaching the limiting case of zero, each of the elements in the corresponding submatrixes in the reduced-form equations also approach the value of zero. To see that this assertion holds, note that (from A-3 through A-5) the inverse of the matrix Γ plays a key role in determining the interdependence coefficients in A, B, and L. Let M be any $(n + m) \times (n + m)$ nonsingular matrix partitioned as

$$M = \begin{bmatrix} \pi & \rho \\ \sigma & \tau \end{bmatrix},$$

where π is an $n \times n$ submatrix, ρ an $n \times m$ submatrix, σ an $m \times n$ submatrix, and τ an $m \times m$ submatrix. The inverse matrix M^{-1} exists and is partitioned in the same way as M, that is,

$$M^{-1} = \begin{bmatrix} P & R \\ S & T \end{bmatrix},$$

where P is $n \times n$, R is $n \times m$, S is $m \times n$, and T is $m \times m$. It is shown in matrix algebra texts that:[2]

$$P = (\pi - \rho\tau^{-1}\sigma)^{-1}$$
$$R = -P\rho\tau^{-1}$$
$$S = -\tau^{-1}\sigma P$$
$$T = \tau^{-1} - \tau^{-1}\sigma R.$$

From these identities it can be seen that all the elements of R and S will be zero or small in absolute value if all the elements of ρ and σ are zero or very small in absolute value. Finally, recall that the matrix product of two block-diagonal matrixes is itself block diagonal (for example, the product $\Gamma^{-1}\Phi$ if each of the interdependence submatrixes of Γ and Φ is a null submatrix).

The generalization in the preceding paragraph is valid only if *all* of the elements of *each* of the interdependence submatrixes in the structural model are "small." Suppose, for example, that the policy instruments of each nation have little or no direct impact on the other country (that is, the elements of the interdependence submatrixes of Φ are all very small or zero) but that there is considerable interaction between home and foreign endogenous variables (that is, many of the elements of the interdependence submatrixes of Γ are nonzero with "large" absolute values). In this case it is clearly not true that the elements of the interdependence submatrixes of the reduced-form matrix $A = -\Gamma^{-1}\Phi$ are all small or zero.

The presumption that *nearly completely decomposable* equation systems (that is, those with coefficient matrixes that are "almost" block-diagonal) will behave, especially in the short run, much as though they actually are *completely decom-*

2. See, for example, G. Hadley, *Linear Algebra* (Addison-Wesley, 1961), pp. 107–11.

posable systems is articulated and proved by Herbert A. Simon and Albert Ando.[3] In a companion paper, Franklin Fisher and Albert Ando discuss the case of systems that are *nearly decomposable* ("almost" block-recursive) and *decomposable* (perfectly block-recursive) and prove that nearly decomposable systems behave, especially in the short run, much as if they are actually decomposable.[4] Applied in the context of the discussion here, the Ando-Simon paper provides theoretical support for treating a nearly closed economy as though it is completely closed (especially in the short run), while the Fisher-Ando paper provides support for ignoring any two-way interaction between a home economy and the rest of the world if the home economy has "almost no effect" on the rest of the world. Note, however, that for a sufficiently great degree of interdependence (the intermediate case) neither the Ando-Simon nor the Fisher-Ando results are applicable.

It is helpful for some purposes to rewrite the reduced-form equations as

$$(A-7) \qquad Y_t = A^h X_t^h + A^f X_t^f + BZ_t + LY_{t-1} + U_t,$$

where the policy instruments of the home and the foreign nations are shown separately. The relationship between A, A^h, and A^f, where A^h is of the order $(n + m) \times k$ and A^f is of the order $(n + m) \times l$, is as follows:[5]

$$(A-8) \qquad A \equiv \begin{bmatrix} & | & \\ & | & \\ A^h & | & A^f \\ & | & \\ & | & \end{bmatrix} \equiv \begin{bmatrix} A_1^h & | & A_1^f \\ A_2^h & | & A_2^f \\ \hline A_3^h & | & A_3^f \\ A_4^h & | & A_4^f \end{bmatrix} \equiv \begin{bmatrix} A_{11} & | & A_{12} \\ A_{21} & | & A_{22} \\ \hline A_{31} & | & A_{32} \\ A_{41} & | & A_{42} \end{bmatrix}.$$

Simple Analytics of the National Policy Problem

The subset of n^* reduced-form equations for the ultimate-target variables of the home policy authority is (for period t)

$$(A-9) \qquad y_t^{*h} = A_1^h X_t^h + S_t^{*h},$$

where S_t^{*h}, the vector of influences not controllable by the home authority, is given by

$$(A-9a) \qquad S_t^{*h} = A_1^f X_t^f + B_{11} z_t^h + B_{12} z_t^f + L_{11} y_{t-1}^h + L_{12} y_{t-1}^f + u_t^{*h}.$$

The corresponding m^* equations for the ultimate-target variables of the foreign authority are

$$(A-10) \qquad y_t^{*f} = A_3^f X_t^f + S_t^{*f},$$

3. "Aggregation of Variables in Dynamic Systems," in Albert Ando, Franklin Fisher, and Herbert A. Simon, eds., *Essays on the Structure of Social Science Models* (MIT Press, 1963), esp. p. 75.
4. "Near-Decomposability, Partition and Aggregation, and the Relevance of Stability Discussions," in ibid.
5. For example, A_1^h and A_{11} are equivalent ways of referring to the $n^* \times k$ submatrix of coefficients relating home instruments to home ultimate-target variables; A_2^f and A_{22} are equivalent notations for referring to the $(n - n^*) \times l$ submatrix relating foreign instruments to home intermediate variables.

where

(A-10a) $\qquad S_t^{*f} = A_3^h X_t^h + B_{32} z_t^f + B_{31} z_t^h + L_{32} y_{t-1}^f + L_{31} y_{t-1}^h + u_t^{*f}$

is the vector of influences on the foreign target variables not controllable by the foreign authority.[6]

The home authority in principle wishes to solve the subset of n^* equations A-9 in terms of its own instrument variables. For example, if the home authority has as many instruments as ultimate targets, it can calculate $(A_1^h)^{-1}$, the inverse of A_1^h, and write

(A-11) $\qquad X_t^h = (A_1^h)^{-1} y_t^{*h} - (A_1^h)^{-1} S_t^{*h}.$

Suppose the home authority makes predictions of (or has reliable information about) the values of X_t^f, z_t^h, z_t^f, y_{t-1}^h, y_{t-1}^f, and u_t^{*h}. From equations A-9a it can then generate the vector of predicted values $\hat{S}_t^{*h} = \hat{S}_{1,t}^{*h}, \ldots, \hat{S}_{n^*,t}^{*h}$. Given $\hat{y}_t^{*h}$, a vector of fixed values for its ultimate-target variables, the home authority can use A-11 to derive

(A-12) $\qquad \hat{X}_t^h = (A_1^h)^{-1} \hat{y}_t^{*h} - (A_1^h)^{-1} \hat{S}_t^{*h},$

where $\hat{X}_t^h$ is the vector of k instrument settings appropriate for achieving the target values $\hat{y}_t^{*h}$.

In an analogous way, if the foreign authority specifies a vector $\hat{y}_t^{*f}$ of fixed values for its ultimate-target variables, if it has as many instruments as ultimate targets, and if it can generate a vector of predicted values $\hat{S}_t^{*f}$ for the noncontrollable influences on its targets, it can use the equations A-10 and the inverse of the matrix A_3^f to calculate the vector of l instrument settings:

(A-13) $\qquad \hat{X}_t^f = (A_3^f)^{-1} \hat{y}_t^{*f} - (A_3^f)^{-1} \hat{S}_t^{*f}.$

Optimizing Determination of Target Values

General quadratic forms of a loss function for the home and the foreign authorities, as shown in chapter 11, can be written respectively as

(A-14) $\qquad W_t^h = w_0^h + c' Y_t + d' X_t^h + \tfrac{1}{2} Y_t' C Y_t + \tfrac{1}{2} X_t^{h\prime} D X_t^h$

and

(A-15) $\qquad W_t^f = w_0^f + g' Y_t + p' X_t^f + \tfrac{1}{2} Y_t' G Y_t + \tfrac{1}{2} X_t^{f\prime} P X_t^f$

Y_t, c, and g are $(n + m) \times 1$ column vectors; X_t^h and d are $k \times 1$ column vectors; C and G are $(n + m) \times (n + m)$ matrixes; X_t^f and p are $l \times 1$ column vectors; D is a $k \times k$ matrix; and P is an $l \times l$ matrix. While the home authority's loss function includes the home instrument settings (to allow for boundary constraints and instrument-variation costs that may directly affect home welfare), the home authority is assumed not to attach direct importance to the settings on foreign

6. This discussion abstracts from the fact that each nation's authority has differing perceptions of the world economic structure (leading in turn to different estimates of the structural coefficients and hence of the reduced-form matrixes A^h, A^f, B, and L).

instruments and not to worry about direct costs associated with variation of those settings.[7]

For ease of exposition, the vectors Y_t, X_t^h, and X_t^f in W_t^h and W_t^f are the original vectors defined in equations 11-1 and 11-2. Alternatively, the elements of Y_t, X_t^h, and X_t^f could be expressed as deviations of each y_{it} and x_{jt} from some prespecified preferred values $\hat{y}_{it}$ and $\hat{x}_{jt}$ (where "preferred" has the sense "preferred without regard being paid to the values of any other variables"). For example, let T_t^* be an $(n + m) \times 1$ vector of prespecified values $\hat{y}_{it}$ and X_t^{h*} be a $k \times 1$ vector of instrument settings $\hat{x}_{jt}^h$ preferred by the home authority. The home loss function might then be written

$$
\begin{aligned}
\text{(A-14a)} \quad W_t^h = w_0^h &+ c'(Y_t - T_t^*) + d'(X_t^h - X_t^{h*}) \\
&+ \tfrac{1}{2}(Y_t - T_t^*)' C(Y_t - T_t^*) + \tfrac{1}{2}(X_t^h - X_t^{h*})' D(X_t^h - X_t^{h*}).
\end{aligned}
$$

The pure quadratic form is an undesirably restrictive specification of the loss function.[8] For example, it implies "satiation" at the preferred target values. And it treats positive and negative deviations of variables from desired levels symmetrically when in fact policymakers would not regard such deviations as equally undesirable. The satiation difficulty, however, may be avoided by setting the preferred target values unrealistically high or low. One way around the undesirable symmetry of the pure quadratic form is to make the loss function *piecewise* quadratic.[9]

The home policy authority is likely to skew its preferences strongly towards home variables. Consider, for example, the weighting coefficients in c and C. A plausible specification of the home authority's preferences might set the majority of these coefficients equal to zero; in particular, all coefficients associated with foreign variables might be assigned the value of zero. Thus

$$
\text{(A-14b)} \qquad c'Y_t = \begin{bmatrix} c_1' & | & 0 & | & 0 & | & 0 \end{bmatrix} \begin{bmatrix} y_t^{*h} \\ \hline y_t^h \\ \hline y_t^{*f} \\ \hline y_t^f \end{bmatrix}
$$

and

$$
\text{(A-14c)} \qquad Y_t' CY_t = \begin{bmatrix} y_t^{*h'} & | & y_t^{h'} & | & y_t^{*f'} & | & y_t^{f'} \end{bmatrix} \begin{bmatrix} C_{11} & 0 & | & 0 & 0 \\ 0 & 0 & | & 0 & 0 \\ \hline 0 & 0 & | & 0 & 0 \\ 0 & 0 & | & 0 & 0 \end{bmatrix} \begin{bmatrix} y_t^{*h} \\ \hline y_t^h \\ \hline y_t^{*f} \\ \hline y_t^f \end{bmatrix},
$$

7. If that assumption is considered implausible, the home loss function could contain the additional terms $d^{f'}X_t^f + \tfrac{1}{2}X_t^{f'}D^fX_t^f$. Analogous considerations explain the inclusion of X_t^f and exclusion of X_t^h from the loss function of the foreign authority.

8. Quadratic forms for loss functions are discussed in Theil, *Economic Forecasts and Policy*, 2d. rev. ed. (Amsterdam: North-Holland, 1961); and Theil with P. J. M. van den Bogaard, *Optimal Decision Rules for Government and Industry* (Amsterdam: North-Holland, 1964).

9. This procedure is described in Benjamin M. Friedman, *Economic Stabilization Policy: Methods in Optimization* (Amsterdam and Oxford: North-Holland, 1975; New York: American Elsevier, 1975), esp. chap. 7.

where C_{11} is the $n^* \times n^*$ diagonal submatrix

$$C_{11} = \begin{bmatrix} c_{11} & 0 & 0 & \cdot & \cdot & \cdot & 0 \\ 0 & c_{22} & 0 & \cdot & \cdot & \cdot & 0 \\ 0 & 0 & c_{33} & \cdot & \cdot & \cdot & 0 \\ \cdot & \cdot & \cdot & \cdot & \cdot & \cdot & \cdot \\ \cdot & \cdot & \cdot & \cdot & \cdot & \cdot & \cdot \\ \cdot & \cdot & \cdot & \cdot & \cdot & \cdot & \cdot \\ 0 & \cdot & \cdot & \cdot & \cdot & \cdot & c_{n^*n^*} \end{bmatrix}$$

This particular form of c and C assumes that the home loss function does not attach direct importance to any of the home intermediate variables. The majority of the coefficients in D might also be equal to zero:

(A-14d)
$$D = \begin{bmatrix} d_{11} & 0 & 0 & \cdot & \cdot & \cdot & 0 \\ 0 & d_{22} & 0 & \cdot & \cdot & \cdot & 0 \\ 0 & 0 & d_{33} & \cdot & \cdot & \cdot & 0 \\ \cdot & \cdot & \cdot & \cdot & \cdot & \cdot & \cdot \\ \cdot & \cdot & \cdot & \cdot & \cdot & \cdot & \cdot \\ \cdot & \cdot & \cdot & \cdot & \cdot & \cdot & \cdot \\ 0 & \cdot & \cdot & \cdot & \cdot & \cdot & d_{kk} \end{bmatrix}$$

In the case of the foreign authority's loss function, the weighting coefficients tend to be biased in an opposite manner. The matrix G, for example, might take the form

(A-15a)
$$G = \begin{bmatrix} 0 & 0 & \vdots & 0 & 0 \\ 0 & 0 & \vdots & 0 & 0 \\ - & - & - & - & - & - \\ 0 & 0 & \vdots & G_{33} & 0 \\ 0 & 0 & \vdots & 0 & 0 \end{bmatrix},$$

where G_{33} is the $m^* \times m^*$ diagonal submatrix:

$$\begin{bmatrix} g_{11} & 0 & 0 & \cdot & \cdot & \cdot & 0 \\ 0 & g_{22} & 0 & \cdot & \cdot & \cdot & 0 \\ 0 & 0 & g_{33} & \cdot & \cdot & \cdot & 0 \\ \cdot & \cdot & \cdot & \cdot & \cdot & \cdot & \cdot \\ \cdot & \cdot & \cdot & \cdot & \cdot & \cdot & \cdot \\ \cdot & \cdot & \cdot & \cdot & \cdot & \cdot & \cdot \\ 0 & \cdot & \cdot & \cdot & \cdot & \cdot & g_{m^*m^*} \end{bmatrix}$$

A similar bias toward foreign variables might be found for the weighting coefficients in the vector g.

To use its loss function in conjunction with its model of the world economy to calculate "optimal" settings for the home policy instruments, the home authority begins with the reduced-form equations of its model. These may be written as

(A-7a)
$$Y_t = A^h X_t^h + S_t^h,$$

where

(A-7b)
$$S_t^h = A^f X_t^f + BZ_t + LY_{t-1} + U_t$$

is the noncontrolled part of the reduced-form system. Substitution of the equations A-7a into the loss function A-14 yields

$$W_t^h = w_0^h + c'(A^h X_t^h + S_t^h) + d'X_t^h + \tfrac{1}{2}[(A^h X_t^h + S_t^h)'C(A^h X_t^h + S_t^h)] + \tfrac{1}{2}(X_t^{h'} D X_t^h).$$

After rearrangement of terms, the loss function can then be written as

(A-16)
$$W_t^h = m_{0,t} + m_t' X_t^h + \tfrac{1}{2}(X_t^{h'} M_t X_t^h),$$

where $m_{0,t}$ is a scalar; m_t is a column vector of k components; and M_t is a symmetric matrix of order $k \times k$:

(A-16a)
$$m_{0,t} = w_0^h + c'S_t^h + \tfrac{1}{2}(S_t^{h'} C S_t^h),$$

(A-16b)
$$m_t = d + A^{h'}c + A^{h'}C S_t^h,$$

(A-16c)
$$M_t = D + A^{h'}C A^h.$$

Minimization of the scalar quantity given by A-16 with respect to the vector X_t^h, setting the resulting k equations equal to zero, and solving for the optimizing vector of home instrument variables yields the result

(A-17)
$$\hat{X}_t^h = -M_t^{-1} m_t.$$

The best feasible values for the home ultimate-target variables associated with these instrument settings are obtained by substituting the values of $\hat{X}_t^h$ back into equation A-7.[10]

Multiperiod Dynamic Generalization

The following definitions are used in representing the dynamic evolution of the world economic system over a succession of time periods beginning "today" (period 1) extending to a finite horizon in the future (period T):

(A-18)
$$Y \equiv \begin{bmatrix} Y_1 \\ Y_2 \\ \cdot \\ \cdot \\ \cdot \\ Y_T \end{bmatrix}; \quad Z \equiv \begin{bmatrix} Z_1 \\ Z_2 \\ \cdot \\ \cdot \\ \cdot \\ Z_T \end{bmatrix}; \quad Y_{t-1} \equiv \begin{bmatrix} Y_{t-1,1} \\ Y_{t-1,2} \\ \cdot \\ \cdot \\ \cdot \\ Y_{t-1,T} \end{bmatrix}; \quad E \equiv \begin{bmatrix} E_1 \\ E_2 \\ \cdot \\ \cdot \\ \cdot \\ E_T \end{bmatrix};$$

10. Compare Theil, *Optimal Decision Rules for Government and Industry*, pp. 32–43. Analogous computations for "optimal" settings for the foreign instruments could be made by the policy authority of the foreign nation (employing the loss function A-15 and the foreign authority's estimates of the reduced-form equations of the world model). Note that, unless it should prove to be singular, the matrix M can be inverted even if k (the number of instruments available to the policy authority) is substantially less than n^* (the number of ultimate-target variables).

$$
X^h \equiv \begin{bmatrix} X_1^h \\ X_2^h \\ \cdot \\ \cdot \\ \cdot \\ X_T^h \end{bmatrix} ; \quad X^f \equiv \begin{bmatrix} X_1^f \\ X_2^f \\ \cdot \\ \cdot \\ \cdot \\ X_T^f \end{bmatrix} ; \quad X \equiv \begin{bmatrix} X_1 \\ \\ X_2 \\ \cdot \\ \cdot \\ \cdot \\ \\ X_T \end{bmatrix} \equiv \begin{bmatrix} X_1^h \\ X_1^f \\ X_2^h \\ X_2^f \\ \cdot \\ \cdot \\ \cdot \\ X_T^h \\ X_T^f \end{bmatrix}.
$$

Here the stacked vector Y is a complete listing of the values of each of the endogenous variables in each of the T time periods. Each subvector of Y, say Y_t, is of the order $n + m$; the stacked vector itself is of order $T(n + m)$. Note that Y and the other stacked vectors X, X^h, X^f, Z, Y_{t-1}, and E all have their elements arranged in a similar way: all the values of period 1 appear in the first subvector, all the values for period 2 appear in the second subvector, and so on up to the subvector containing the values for period T.[11]

The definitions A-18 and definitions of conforming stacked matrixes permit the structural equations of the world model for all T periods to be written as:

(A-19) $\Gamma Y + \Phi X + \Omega Z + \Lambda Y_{t-1} + E = 0.$

All four of the coefficient matrixes in A-19 are block diagonal, with each submatrix along the diagonal being equal to the corresponding single-period matrix in A-1. For example, the stacked matrix Γ of order $T(n + m) \times T(n + m)$ is simply

$$
\Gamma = \begin{bmatrix}
\Gamma & 0 & 0 & \cdot & \cdot & \cdot & 0 \\
0 & \Gamma & 0 & \cdot & \cdot & \cdot & 0 \\
0 & 0 & \Gamma & \cdot & \cdot & \cdot & 0 \\
\cdot & \cdot & \cdot & \cdot & \cdot & \cdot & \cdot \\
\cdot & \cdot & \cdot & \cdot & \cdot & \cdot & \cdot \\
\cdot & \cdot & \cdot & \cdot & \cdot & \cdot & \cdot \\
0 & 0 & 0 & \cdot & \cdot & \cdot & \Gamma
\end{bmatrix}
$$

where each submatrix on the diagonal is the $(n + m) \times (n + m)$ matrix of coefficients Γ in A-1. The submatrixes along the diagonal are all identical because it is assumed that the structural coefficients do not vary across time.[12]

The reduced-form equations of the system for all T periods can be written

(A-20) $Y = AX + BZ + LY_{t-1} + U,$

or alternatively

---

11. The stacked vector X is of order $T(k + l)$; X^h is of order Tk; X^f is of order Tl; Z is of order $T(r + s)$; Y_{t-1} and E are of order $T(n + m)$.

12. The stacked matrix Φ is of order $T(n + m) \times T(k + l)$; Ω is of order $T(n + m) \times T(r + s)$; and Λ is of order $T(n + m) \times T(n + m)$.

(A-21) $$Y = A^h X^h + A^f X^f + BZ + LY_{t-1} + U .$$

Just as the system A-19 is merely a repetition of A-1 for all T periods, so A-20 and A-21 are a restatement, time period by time period, of the single-period reduced-form equations of A-2 and A-7.[13]

This is an appropriate place to recall that the structural equations A-1 and A-19, and hence the reduced-form equations A-20 and A-21, do not explicitly allow for lagged values of the policy instruments, lagged values of the nonpolicy exogenous variables, or values of the endogenous variables lagged by more than one period. However, even if explicit allowance had been made for additional lagged effects, it would be analytically convenient at this point in the analysis to rewrite such a system of higher-order difference equations so as to convert it into a first-order system resembling A-20 or A-21.

Suppose, for example, that the structural equations had been specified to include values of the policy instruments lagged by as much as j periods, values of the nonpolicy exogenous variables lagged as much as p periods, and values of the endogenous variables lagged as much as q periods. The reduced-form equations analogous to A-20 would then have the form

(A-22)
$$Y = A_0 X + A_1 X_{t-1} + \cdots + A_j X_{t-j} + B_0 Z + B_1 Z_{t-1}$$
$$+ \cdots + B_p Z_{t-p} + L_1 Y_{t-1} + L_2 Y_{t-2} + \cdots + L_q Y_{t-q} + U .$$

But this higher-order system could be readily converted into the form of A-20 by appropriate redefinition of the variable vectors and coefficient matrixes.[14] The details of the dynamic behavior of such a system of course differ from the behavior of the simpler system without the complex lags. But none of the analytical points in this chapter is significantly altered by basing the exposition on the more dynamically complicated model.

The $n + m$ reduced-form equations that refer to the final period of the planning interval (period T) are

(A-23) $$Y_T = A^h X_T^h + A^f X_T^f + BZ_T + LY_{t-1,T} + U_T.$$

If substitution is made for $Y_{t-1,T}$, this becomes

$$Y_T = A^h X_T^h + A^f X_T^f + BZ_T + U_T$$
$$+ L(A^h X_{T-1}^h + A^f X_{T-1}^f + BZ_{T-1} + LY_{t-1,T-1} + U_{T-1}).$$

Similarly, if successive substitutions of the lagged endogenous variables are carried out, the equations A-23 finally become (with the notational convention that $L^2 = LL$, and so on):

(A-24)
$$Y_T = L^T Y_0 + U_T + LU_{T-1} + L^2 U_{T-2} + \cdots + L^{T-1} U_1$$
$$+ A^h X_T^h + LA^h X_{T-1}^h + L^2 A^h X_{T-2}^h + \cdots + L^{T-1} A^h X_1^h$$
$$+ A^f X_T^f + LA^f X_{T-1}^f + L^2 A^f X_{T-2}^f + \cdots + L^{T-1} A^f X_1^f$$
$$+ BZ_T + LBZ_{T-1} + L^2 BZ_{T-2} + \cdots + L^{T-1} BZ_1.$$

13. A, B, and L are block-diagonal stacked matrixes related to the stacked matrixes of structural coefficients (compare A-3 through A-5 above) by: $A = -\Gamma^{-1}\Phi$, $B = -\Gamma^{-1}\Omega$, and $L = -\Gamma^{-1}\Lambda$. Note also that $U = -\Gamma^{-1}E$. The stacked matrixes A^h and A^f are the block-diagonal, multiperiod analogs of the matrixes defined in A-8.

14. See Gregory C. Chow, *Analysis and Control of Dynamic Economic Systems* (Wiley, 1975), pp. 152–54.

Y_0 is the $n + m$ column vector of initial conditions—that is, the values taken on by the endogenous variables in "period 0." Note how A-24 brings out explicitly the dependence of the endogenous variables in period T on: (1) the values of the home policy instruments in each period from today (period 1) to period T, (2) the values of foreign instrument settings for all periods between today and period T, (3) the values of nonpolicy exogenous variables for all future periods up to T, (4) all the reduced-form disturbances up to period T, and (5) the initial conditions (today's past history).

If analogous expressions to A-24 are derived for the equations for each other time period, an entire $T(n + m)$ system of "final-form" equations can be written in matrix form as

(A-25) $$Y = R^h X^h + R^f X^f + QZ + L^*U + L^{**}Y_0,$$

where

(A-26) $$R^h = \begin{bmatrix} R_1^h & 0 & 0 & \cdot & \cdot & \cdot & 0 \\ R_2^h & R_1^h & 0 & \cdot & \cdot & \cdot & 0 \\ R_3^h & R_2^h & R_1^h & \cdot & \cdot & \cdot & 0 \\ \cdot & \cdot & \cdot & \cdot & & & \cdot \\ \cdot & \cdot & \cdot & & \cdot & & \cdot \\ \cdot & \cdot & \cdot & & & \cdot & \cdot \\ R_T^h & R_{T-1}^h & R_{T-2}^h & \cdot & \cdot & \cdot & R_1^h \end{bmatrix} \qquad R_j^h = L^{j-1}A^h;$$

(A-27) $$R^f = \begin{bmatrix} R_1^f & 0 & 0 & \cdot & \cdot & \cdot & 0 \\ R_2^f & R_1^f & 0 & \cdot & \cdot & \cdot & 0 \\ R_3^f & R_2^f & R_1^f & \cdot & \cdot & \cdot & 0 \\ \cdot & \cdot & \cdot & \cdot & & & \cdot \\ \cdot & \cdot & \cdot & & \cdot & & \cdot \\ \cdot & \cdot & \cdot & & & \cdot & \cdot \\ R_T^f & R_{T-1}^f & R_{T-2}^f & \cdot & \cdot & \cdot & R_1^f \end{bmatrix} \qquad R_j^f = L^{j-1}A^f;$$

(A-28) $$Q = \begin{bmatrix} Q_1 & 0 & 0 & \cdot & \cdot & \cdot & 0 \\ Q_2 & Q_1 & 0 & \cdot & \cdot & \cdot & 0 \\ Q_3 & Q_2 & Q_1 & \cdot & \cdot & \cdot & 0 \\ \cdot & \cdot & \cdot & \cdot & & & \cdot \\ \cdot & \cdot & \cdot & & \cdot & & \cdot \\ \cdot & \cdot & \cdot & & & \cdot & \cdot \\ Q_T & Q_{T-1} & Q_{T-2} & \cdot & \cdot & \cdot & Q_1 \end{bmatrix} \qquad Q_j = L^{j-1}B;$$

$$(A-29) \qquad L^* = \begin{bmatrix} I & 0 & 0 & \cdot & \cdot & \cdot & 0 \\ L & I & 0 & \cdot & \cdot & \cdot & 0 \\ L^2 & L & I & \cdot & \cdot & \cdot & 0 \\ \cdot & \cdot & \cdot & & & & \cdot \\ \cdot & & & & & & \cdot \\ \cdot & & & & & & \cdot \\ L^{T-1} & L^{T-2} & L^{T-3} & \cdot & \cdot & \cdot & I \end{bmatrix} ;$$

and

$$(A-30) \qquad L^{**}Y_0 = \begin{bmatrix} L & 0 & 0 & \cdot & \cdot & \cdot & 0 \\ 0 & L^2 & 0 & \cdot & \cdot & \cdot & 0 \\ 0 & 0 & L^3 & \cdot & \cdot & \cdot & 0 \\ \cdot & & & & & & \cdot \\ \cdot & & & & & & \cdot \\ \cdot & & & & & & \cdot \\ 0 & 0 & 0 & \cdot & \cdot & \cdot & L^T \end{bmatrix} \begin{bmatrix} Y_0 \\ Y_0 \\ Y_0 \\ \cdot \\ \cdot \\ \cdot \\ Y_0 \end{bmatrix} .$$

The final-form equations may also be expressed as

$$(A-31) \qquad Y = R^h X^h + R^f X^f + QZ + V,$$

where

$$V = L^*U + L^{**}Y_0$$

combines the effects of the stochastic error terms and the initial conditions.[15]

Multiperiod loss functions for the home and the foreign policy authorities may be specified as follows:

$$(A-32) \qquad W^h = w_0^h + c'Y + d'X^h + \tfrac{1}{2}Y'CY + \tfrac{1}{2}X^{h\prime}DX^h;$$

$$(A-33) \qquad W^f = w_0^f + g'Y + p'X^f + \tfrac{1}{2}Y'GY + \tfrac{1}{2}X^{f\prime}PX^f.$$

W^h and W^f are still scalar quantities. But Y, X^h, and X^f are the stacked column vectors defined in A-18; and c, d, g, p, C, D, G, and P are conformable stacked vectors or stacked matrixes. For example, C is of order $T(n + m) \times T(n + m)$ and D is of order $Tk \times Tk$.

A number of difficult issues must be addressed when giving concrete form to the weighting vectors and submatrixes in a multiperiod loss function. For example, should policymakers discount future losses; or should losses be weighted to be invariant with respect to time period? If the former choice is made, what is the appropriate rate of discount and how would it enter into the elements of the vectors

15. When the structural equations are linear, as assumed in the exposition here, the initial conditions do not influence the final-form coefficient matrixes R^h, R^f, and Q. That would not be the case for nonlinear structural equations.

and matrixes in the loss functions? The elements of the off-diagonal submatrixes of matrixes C, D, G, and P are weighting coefficients associated with cross-products of variables—two endogenous variables (C and G) or two instrument variables (D and P)—in two different time periods. Could these elements plausibly be assumed equal to zero, or should the loss associated with, say, rapid inflation in two successive periods be deemed to be more than twice the loss from rapid inflation in one time period only?

For the purposes of the analysis here, it is unnecessary to answer these questions and to write out multiperiod counterparts of the single-period vectors and matrixes shown above. The essential point is adequately illustrated in, for example, A-14c and A-15a: each nation's policy authority will be preoccupied with the achievement of its own national objectives.

A procedure for computing optimizing settings for a nation's policy instruments over the entire T-period planning interval closely resembles the one-period procedure outlined above. The final-form constraints of a world model, written from the perspective of the home authority, are

(A-34) $$Y = R^h X^h + S^h,$$

where

(A-35) $$S^h = R^f X^f + QZ + V.$$

Analogously with the one-period case, equations A-34 split the constraints into a "controlled" component and a residual, "noncontrolled" portion. If the equations of A-34 and A-35 are substituted into the home loss function A-32 and the terms are appropriately rearranged, the result is

(A-36) $$W^h = m_0 + m'X^h + \tfrac{1}{2}X^{h'}MX^h,$$

where m_0 is a scalar; m is a column vector of Tk components; and M is a symmetric matrix of order $Tk \times Tk$:

(A-36a) $$m_0 = w_0^h + c'S^h + \tfrac{1}{2}S^{h'}CS^h;$$

(A-36b) $$m = d + R^{h'}c + R^{h'}CS^h;$$

(A-36c) $$M = D + R^{h'}CR^h.$$

The optimizing time paths for the home instrument settings can be calculated from minimization of A-36 with respect to X^h. The outcome is a dynamic extension of the equations A-17:

(A-37) $$\hat{X}^h = -M^{-1}m.$$

An analogous procedure could be followed by the foreign authority, using the loss function A-33 and its version of the world model A-31, to obtain multiperiod, optimizing time paths $\hat{X}^f$ for the foreign instrument settings.

The computations summarized in A-36 and A-37 generate settings for the home instruments for all T periods in the future on the basis of information available at the beginning of period 1. If the home authority, period by period, actually implemented the decisions implied by A-37, the procedure would be an "open loop" policy. Another, and far preferable, approach would be to repeat the calculations of A-36 and A-37 at the beginning of period 2, taking into account actual developments in period 1 and any other new information deemed to be relevant (for example, revised judgments about some feature of the structural model); more generally, those calculations could be repeated at the beginning of every period, taking into account all the information available at the time of each decision. Such a procedure is often referred to as "open loop with feedback." Still a third approach would be to calculate a set of "feedback control equations" of the form:

$$(A\text{-}38) \qquad \hat{X}_t^h = J_t Y_{t-1,t} + j_t, \qquad t = 1,2,\ldots,T ;$$

here $Y_{t-1,t}$ would contain the most recent information about current and past values of the endogenous variables, while j_t and J_t would be, respectively, a vector and matrix of coefficients derived (for example, by dynamic programming) from a combination of the coefficients in the structural model and the national loss function.[16] Such an "optimal control" procedure would provide control *equations* for calculating the various $\hat{x}_{i,t}^h$ for each period t (using information available up through period $t - 1$).

16. See, for example, Gregory C. Chow, "Problems of Economic Policy from the Viewpoint of Optimal Control," *American Economic Review*, vol. 63 (December 1973), pp. 825–37; and *Analysis and Control of Dynamic Economic Systems*, chaps. 7–9.

APPENDIX B

Further Notes to Chapter 17: Comparison of Two-Stage and Single-Stage Strategies with Coefficient Uncertainty

FOR ITS ILLUSTRATIVE analysis of the uncertainty justification for a money strategy, chapter 17 assumes that both two-stage and single-stage policymakers use the model

$$
\begin{aligned}
Y_t &= \lambda_t M_t + u_t \\
M_t &= \eta_t H_t + v_t,
\end{aligned}
$$

(B-1)

where the coefficients λ_t and η_t and the error terms u_t and v_t are all treated as uncertain random variables. The exogenous instrument for each set of policymakers is H_t (the monetary base). The intermediate-target variable for the two-stage policymakers is M_t (the money stock). Each set of policymakers is assumed to make decisions minimizing the expected value of the loss function

$$
(B\text{-}2) \qquad L_t = (Y_t - Y_t^*)^2,
$$

where Y_t is the ultimate-target variable (income).

Combination of the two equations of B-1 gives the reduced-form equation for the ultimate-target variable:

$$
(B\text{-}3) \qquad Y_t = \lambda_t \eta_t H_t + u_t + \lambda_t v_t;
$$

with the definitions $\pi_t \equiv \lambda_t \eta_t$ and $w_t \equiv u_t + \lambda_t v_t$, B-3 may be expressed as

$$
(B\text{-}3a) \qquad Y_t = \pi_t H_t + w_t.
$$

The correct expected value of Y conditional on the instrument setting for H is

$$
(B\text{-}4) \qquad \bar{Y} = E(\pi H + w) = \bar{\pi} H + \bar{w},
$$

where a bar over a variable denotes its expected value.[1] The expected values of π and w may be expressed in terms of the underlying random variables:

$$
(B\text{-}5) \qquad \bar{\pi} = \bar{\lambda}\bar{\eta} + \sigma_{\lambda\eta},
$$

$$
(B\text{-}6) \qquad \bar{w} = \bar{u} + \bar{\lambda}\bar{v} + \sigma_{\lambda v},
$$

1. Time subscripts are henceforth omitted to simplify the notation.

518

where $\sigma_{\lambda\eta}$ is the covariance of λ and η and $\sigma_{\lambda v}$ is the covariance of λ and v. Hence B-4 may also be written as

(B-4a) $$\bar{Y} = (\bar{\lambda}\bar{\eta} + \sigma_{\lambda\eta})H + (\bar{u} + \bar{\lambda}\bar{v} + \sigma_{\lambda v}).$$

The correct variance of Y conditional on the value of H, σ_Y^2, is

(B-7) $$\sigma_Y^2 = \sigma_\pi^2 H^2 + \sigma_w^2 + 2\sigma_{\pi w}H,$$

where σ_π^2 is the variance of the composite coefficient π, σ_w^2 is the variance of the composite error term w, and $\sigma_{\pi w}$ is the covariance of π and w. If it is assumed that λ, η, u, and v are normally distributed random variables so that no higher than second-order moments of their distributions need to be considered, and if the variances of π and w and their covariance are evaluated in terms of the underlying variances and covariances, it can be shown that[2]

(B-8) $$\sigma_\pi^2 = \sigma_\lambda^2 \sigma_\eta^2 + (\sigma_{\lambda\eta})^2 + \bar{\lambda}^2 \sigma_\eta^2 + \bar{\eta}^2 \sigma_\lambda^2 + 2\bar{\lambda}\bar{\eta}\sigma_{\lambda\eta}$$

(B-9) $$\sigma_w^2 = \sigma_u^2 + \sigma_\lambda^2 \sigma_v^2 + (\sigma_{\lambda v})^2 + \bar{\lambda}^2 \sigma_v^2 + \bar{v}^2 \sigma_\lambda^2 + 2\bar{\lambda}\bar{v}\sigma_{\lambda v} + 2\bar{\lambda}\sigma_{uv} + 2\bar{v}\sigma_{\lambda u}$$

(B-10) $$\sigma_{\pi w} = \bar{\eta}\,\bar{v}\sigma_\lambda^2 + \bar{\lambda}\bar{v}\sigma_{\lambda\eta} + \bar{\lambda}\bar{\eta}\sigma_{\lambda v} + \bar{\lambda}^2 \sigma_{\eta v} + \bar{\eta}\sigma_{\lambda u} + \bar{\lambda}\sigma_{\eta u}.$$

The single-stage policymakers choose an instrument setting by using the "complete" model B-3 in conjunction with the loss function B-2 to find the value of H that minimizes expected loss. The expected value of the loss function is given by

(B-11) $$E(L) = E(Y - Y^*)^2 = (\bar{Y} - Y^*)^2 + \sigma_Y^2.$$

The "optimal" single-stage setting, $\hat{H}_{1S}$, can be calculated by substituting B-4 and B-7 into B-11, differentiating with respect to H, setting the result equal to zero, and solving for the resulting value of H:[3]

(B-12) $$\hat{H}_{1S} = \frac{\bar{\pi}(Y^* - \bar{w}) - \sigma_{\pi w}}{\bar{\pi}^2 + \sigma_\pi^2}.$$

If equations B-5 and B-6 and then B-8 through B-10 are substituted into B-12, it can be seen that the preferred single-stage setting is equivalent to

(B-12a) $$\hat{H}_{1S} = \frac{J - (2\bar{\lambda}\bar{v}\sigma_{\lambda\eta} + 2\bar{\lambda}\bar{\eta}\sigma_{\lambda v} + \bar{\lambda}\sigma_{\eta u} + \bar{u}\sigma_{\lambda\eta} + \sigma_{\lambda\eta}\sigma_{\lambda v} - Y^*\sigma_{\lambda\eta})}{K + 2(\sigma_{\lambda\eta})^2 + 4\bar{\lambda}\bar{\eta}\sigma_{\lambda\eta}},$$

where the expressions J and K are given by

2. The calculations require computation of the expected values of the product of three variables and the square of the product of two variables. For these computations, see Guy V. G. Stevens, "Two Problems in Portfolio Analysis: Conditional and Multiplicative Random Variables," *Journal of Financial and Quantitative Analysis*, vol. 6 (December 1971), pp. 1235–50; George W. Bohrnstedt and Arthur S. Goldberger, "On the Exact Covariance of Products of Random Variables," *Journal of the American Statistical Association*, vol. 64 (December 1969), pp. 1439–42.

3. See William Brainard, "Uncertainty and the Effectiveness of Policy," *American Economic Review*, vol. 57 (May 1967, *Papers and Proceedings, 1966*), pp. 413–14.

(B-13) $J = \overline{\lambda}\overline{\eta}(Y^* - \overline{u}) - \overline{\lambda}^2 \overline{\eta}\overline{v} - \overline{\lambda}^2\sigma_{\eta v} - \overline{\eta}\ \overline{v}\sigma_\lambda^2 - \overline{\eta}\sigma_{\lambda u}$

(B-14) $K = (\overline{\lambda}^2 + \sigma_\lambda^2)(\overline{\eta}^2 + \sigma_\eta^2).$

The two-stage policymakers using a money strategy split the model B-1 into a lower-stage submodel (the equation for M) and an upper-stage submodel (the equation for Y). Because the intermediate-target procedure treats the money stock as though it were exogenous in the upper-stage submodel, the two-stage policymakers use an expression for the expected value of the ultimate-target variable given by

(B-15) $\overline{Y}_{2S} = E(\lambda M + u) = \overline{\lambda}M + \overline{u}.$

For their measure of the variance of income, the two-stage policymakers use

(B-16) $(\sigma_Y^2)_{2S} = \sigma_\lambda^2 M^2 + \sigma_u^2 + 2\sigma_{\lambda u}M,$

again treating M as though it were an exogenous variable.

To calculate their target value for the money stock, M_{2S}^*, the two-stage policymakers might substitute B-15 and B-16 into B-11, differentiate with respect to the supposedly exogenous M, and derive the expression

(B-17) $M_{2S}^* = \dfrac{\overline{\lambda}(Y^* - \overline{u}) - \sigma_{\lambda u}}{\overline{\lambda}^2 + \sigma_\lambda^2}.$

The lower-stage submodel in an intermediate-target strategy is used independently of the upper-stage submodel. The expected value and variance of M are given by

(B-18) $\overline{M} = \overline{\eta}H + \overline{v}$

(B-19) $\sigma_M^2 = \sigma_\eta^2 H^2 + \sigma_v^2 + 2\sigma_{\eta v}H.$

The two-stage policymakers, making use of B-18 and B-19, could derive their lower-stage instrument setting either by choosing the value of H that would set the expected value of the money stock equal to the target value M_{2S}^* or, alternatively, by choosing the value of H that would minimize $E[(M - M_{2S}^*)^2]$. If they choose the first of these options, their instrument setting is simply

(B-20) $\hat{H}_{2S} = \dfrac{M_{2S}^* - \overline{v}}{\overline{\eta}}.$

If they choose the second option, which is more consistent with taking uncertainty into account in their decision, their instrument setting is

(B-21) $\hat{H}_{2S} = \dfrac{\overline{\eta}(M_{2S}^* - \overline{v}) - \sigma_{\eta r}}{\overline{\eta}^2 + \sigma_\eta^2}.$

Substitution of B-17 into B-21 and simplification of the resulting expression shows that the two-stage instrument setting is equivalent to

(B-22)
$$\hat{H}_{2S} = \frac{J - \sigma_\lambda^2 \sigma_{\eta v}}{K},$$

where J and K are the same expressions given above in equations B-13 and B-14.

For the special case where all four of the covariances $\sigma_{\lambda\eta}$, $\sigma_{\lambda v}$, $\sigma_{\eta u}$, and $\sigma_{\eta v}$ are equal to zero, the single-stage instrument setting in B-12a and the two-stage setting in B-22 are identical.[4] However, if one or more of those four covariances have nonzero values (in other words, whenever interdependencies exist in the uncertainties associated with the two submodels), the instrument settings differ and the two-stage strategy results in a greater expected loss than the single-stage strategy.

4. The covariance σ_{uv} and the two variances σ_u^2 and σ_v^2, although they influence the minimum expected loss that can be achieved with either policy, do not enter the expressions for the instrument settings themselves.

Supplement to Chapter 22: An Illustrative Framework for Analyzing Monetary Policy in a Small and Open Economy

THE FIRST PORTION of this appendix describes a simplified comparative-statics framework for analyzing a single nation's economy and its relationships with the rest of the world. The latter portion indicates how the comparative-statics framework must be amended to take into account some interactions of balance-sheet stocks and income-account flows that play critical roles in determining the dynamic evolution of an open economy.

This illustrative framework assumes that key variables in the world economy outside the home nation—for example, foreign real output, foreign prices, and the foreign interest rate—are not influenced by developments in the home economy. Use of the small and open paradigm with its treatment of the rest of the world as exogenous, although problematic for the reasons discussed in part 3, greatly simplifies the expositional and analytical difficulties of specifying an illustrative framework.

Comparative-Statics Relationships

The time horizon of the comparative-statics analysis here and in the corresponding sections of chapter 22 is a short run in which changes in asset stocks and in wealth are ignored.[1] For simplicity, time subscripts on the model's variables are also ignored; this omission means that the analysis ignores different speeds of response of the various aspects of macroeconomic behavior.

Home Central Bank

Assume that the home central bank has a balance sheet, expressed in home-currency units, even more simplified than that in table 20-1, namely:

Assets		Liabilities	
S^{CB}	Holdings of home-currency securities	H	Monetary base (reserve money)
		HR	Required reserves of base
πFA^{CB}	External reserve assets	HF	Net "free" reserves of base
KF	Offsetting entry for capital gains or losses on external reserve assets	NW^{CB}	Capital accounts

1. The model corresponds to the second of the three time horizons ("financial markets in the short run with the goods markets added") distinguished in Dale W. Henderson, "Modeling the Interdependence of

Currency is not included as an asset in this schematization; the reserve-money liabilities of the central bank are held only by home financial intermediaries and are designated simply as H, the monetary base. The entry KF is included on the balance sheet to isolate any capital gains or losses in the home-currency value of external reserve assets brought about by changes in the exchange rate; by definition $dKF = -(FA^{CB})d\pi$, where π is the exchange rate (home currency price of foreign currency) and FA^{CB} is the foreign-currency value of external reserve assets.[2] Define

$$\text{(C-1)} \qquad XA^{CB} = \pi FA^{CB} + KF$$

as the home-currency value of external reserves net of capital gains or losses. Assume that the capital accounts of the central bank, NW^{CB}, are exogenous and unchanged and can therefore be ignored. The balance-sheet constraint of the central bank may then be written as

$$\text{(C-2)} \qquad XA^{CB} + S^{CB} - H^s = 0,$$

where H^s is the supply of monetary base available to the home economy's financial intermediaries ("banks").

Exchange-Rate Expectations and Asset Returns

As one way of simplifying a complex matter, suppose private economic units form views about the value of the exchange rate they expect to prevail in the medium run. Denote this medium-run expected exchange rate as $\hat{\pi}$ and suppose private units expect the current exchange rate π to change according to

$$\text{(C-3)} \qquad \dot{\pi} = \psi(\pi - \hat{\pi}), \quad -1 < \psi < 0.$$

If the coefficient ψ is negative, an observed value of π below (above) $\hat{\pi}$ generates an expected depreciation (appreciation) of the home currency. A negative value of ψ is the "regressive" expectations case.[3]

Theoretical analysis of "fixed" exchange rates has typically assumed—implicitly if not explicitly—that the actual pegged value of π is also the medium-run expected value (so that $\dot{\hat{\pi}} = 0$ for the fixed-rate case).

In the discussion here, $\hat{\pi}$ is treated as exogenous—either unchanged, or altered in a way not explained in the model itself. More detailed and profound treatments of exchange-rate expectations would make $\hat{\pi}$ an endogenous magnitude dependent on, among other things, observed government policy actions.[4]

Given the assumption C-3, the return on foreign-currency-denominated securities expected by home residents is the sum of r^* and $\dot{\hat{\pi}}$, where r^* is the (exogenous) interest rate on the foreign-currency securities. Conversely, the expected return

---

National Money and Capital Markets," *American Economic Review,* vol. 67 (February 1977, *Papers and Proceedings, 1976*), pp. 190–99.

2. For example, an increase in π (a depreciation of the home currency) generates a capital gain in the home-currency value of external reserve assets and a corresponding fall in the value of KF.

3. If ψ were positive, expectations would be "extrapolative"; an observed move of the exchange rate away from the medium-run expected rate would be projected to continue further in the same direction.

4. See chapter 18. The strongest version of "rational expectations" would go even further and impose the assumptions that all decisionmaking units know the full model and hence that $\hat{\pi}$ is the expected value of the medium-run exchange rate actually generated by the model.

to foreign residents from holding home-currency-denominated securities is $r - \hat{\pi}$, where r is the interest rate on the home securities.

Home Financial Intermediaries

Assume that home-country banks issue only one type of deposit, designated M for "money," that these deposits are held exclusively by nonbanks in the home country, and that M is the economy's only asset widely accepted as a means of payment. Assume that the central bank imposes a reserve requirement, ρ, on these deposit liabilities, so that banks hold $HR = \rho M$ of required reserves of base (non-interest-earning) at the central bank. As a further simplifying device, ignore banks' loans to nonbanks and assume that the only earning assets of the banks are home-currency and foreign-currency securities. The resulting schematic balance sheet for home banks, expressed in home-currency units, is therefore:

Assets		Liabilities	
HR	Required reserves	M	Deposits ("money")
HF	Net free reserves		
S^B	Home-currency securities		
πF^B	Foreign-currency securities	NW^B	Surplus and capital accounts

Because the banks must hold required reserves at the central bank, their total of funds available for investment, Q, is only $NW^B + (1 - \rho)M$. Their investment decisions are assumed to be based on expected returns on the assets in accordance with the demand equations:[5]

(C-4a)
$$HF^d/Q = HF(\overset{-}{r}, \overset{-}{\overbrace{r^* + \hat{\pi}}}, \overset{+}{e_{HD}})$$

(C-5a)
$$S^{Bd}/Q = S^B(\overset{+}{r}, \overset{-}{\overbrace{r^* + \hat{\pi}}}, \overset{+}{e_{SD}^B})$$

(C-6a)
$$\pi F^{Bd}/Q = f^B(\overset{-}{r}, \overset{+}{\overbrace{r^* + \hat{\pi}}}, \overset{+}{e_{FD}^B})$$

(C-7)
$$Q = HF + S^B + \pi F^B = NW^B + (1 - \rho)M.$$

The symbols e_{HD}, e_{SD}^B, and e_{FD}^B denote other exogenous factors that may lead banks to change the proportions of their investable assets in the form of base, home-currency securities, and foreign-currency securities. For the system of asset demands to be internally consistent, it must always be true that $e_{HD} + e_{SD}^B + e_{FD}^B = 0$. The banks' responses to either of the expected returns must also add up to zero across the three asset-demand functions.

Although the effect of interest earnings on the size of bank investable assets is ignored (in keeping with the short-run focus of the comparative-statics analysis),

---

5. Here and in all the subsequent behavioral relationships expressed in general functional form, the signs of the partial derivatives of the function with respect to its arguments are indicated above the arguments. The superscript d denotes "demanded."

Q can be changed even in the short run in two ways. Changes in M, which are assumed to be initiated by the nonbank holders of the deposits (see below), cause Q to change in the same direction by, because of the reserve requirement, a fraction $(1 - \rho)$ of the amount of the changes in M. Second, changes in the exchange rate alter Q; if the home currency depreciates, for example, the value of Q rises from its initial level because of the increased home-currency value of the foreign-currency securities F^B. When Q changes as a result of changes in π, banks have a "wealth-effect" motive for rebalancing their asset portfolios; other things being equal, a depreciation of the home currency leads to an increased demand for home-currency securities.[6] The short-run endogeneity of Q may be represented as

(C-8)
$$Q = \bar{Q} + Q(\overset{+}{M}, \overset{+}{\pi}),$$

where $\bar{Q}$ denotes the initial (exogenously fixed) value of Q.

Substitution of C-8 and of the expression for exchange-rate expectations C-3 into C-4a through C-6a makes it explicit that (in this illustrative framework) banks' demands for assets depend endogenously on the exchange rate, the home-security interest rate, and the stock of deposit money, and exogenously on the foreign interest rate (r^*), the medium-run expected exchange rate ($\hat{\pi}$), and the initial size of the stock of investable assets held by the banks ($\bar{Q}$):

(C-4)
$$HF^d = HF(\overset{-}{r},\ \overset{+}{\pi},\ \overset{+}{M};\ \overset{-}{r^*},\ \overset{-}{\hat{\pi}},\ \overset{+}{\bar{Q}},\ \overset{+}{e_{HD}})$$

(C-5)
$$S^{Bd} = S^B(\overset{+}{r},\ \overset{+}{\pi},\ \overset{+}{M};\ \overset{-}{r^*},\ \overset{-}{\hat{\pi}},\ \overset{+}{\bar{Q}},\ \overset{+}{e_{SD}^B})$$

(C-6)
$$\pi F^{Bd} = f^B(\overset{-}{r},\ \overset{?}{\pi},\ \overset{+}{M};\ \overset{+}{r^*},\ \overset{+}{\hat{\pi}},\ \overset{+}{\bar{Q}},\ \overset{+}{e_{FD}^B}).$$

Home Nonbanks' Participation in Financial Markets

The balance sheet of home nonbanks in this illustrative framework is in principle a consolidation of the balance sheets of households and firms. It is assumed to be of the simple form (expressed in home-currency units):

	Assets	Liabilities
M	Deposits ("money")	
S^N	Home-currency securities	W^f Financial net worth
πF^N	Foreign-currency securities	
NW^B	Equity ownership of home banks	
K	Value of equity ownership in nation's physical capital stock	W^n Nonfinancial net worth ($= NW^B + K$)

6. "Wealth effects" of this type are described and analyzed in the series of joint papers by Lance Girton and Dale W. Henderson (see chapter 20, note 1) and in Peter Isard, *Exchange-Rate Determination: A Survey of Popular Views and Recent Models*, Princeton Studies in International Finance 42 (Princeton University Press, 1978).

For simplicity, nonbanks' equity ownership of the nation's capital stock and of its banks is split off from the rest of the balance sheet. Although total nonbank wealth is the sum of "financial" and "nonfinancial" net worth, only the former is taken into account in the portfolio decisions summarized here.[7]

The proportions of the three assets in the nonbanks' portfolio of financial wealth are assumed to depend on expected returns and on the nominal value of national output (Y), a proxy for the volume of transactions.[8] The demand for "money" rises and therefore the demands for both securities fall when, other things equal, Y increases:[9]

$$(\text{C-9a}) \qquad M^d/W^f = M(\overset{-}{r}, \overbrace{r^* + \hat{\pi}}^{-}, \overset{+}{\frac{Y}{W^f}}, \overset{+}{e^N_{MD}})$$

$$(\text{C-10a}) \qquad S^{Nd}/W^f = S^N(\overset{+}{r}, \overbrace{r^* + \hat{\pi}}^{-}, \overset{-}{\frac{Y}{W^f}}, \overset{+}{e^N_{SD}})$$

$$(\text{C-11a}) \qquad \pi F^{Nd}/W^f = f^N(\overset{-}{r}, \overbrace{r^* + \hat{\pi}}^{+}, \overset{-}{\frac{Y}{W^f}}, \overset{+}{e^N_{FD}})$$

$$(\text{C-12}) \qquad W^f = M + S^N + \pi F^N.$$

The exogenous "disturbances" e^N_{MD}, e^N_{SD}, and e^N_{FD} are included in the functions to allow for autonomous shifts in nonbanks' demands among the three assets in their financial portfolios.[10]

The initial asset stocks of the nonbanks are taken as exogenous and the accumulation of wealth through saving is ignored. Even though the initial home-currency level of financial wealth ($\overline{W}^f$) is given, however, its current valuation W^f can fluctuate because of the effects of exchange-rate changes on the home-currency valuation of foreign-currency assets:

$$(\text{C-13}) \qquad W^f = \overline{W}^f + W^f(\overset{+}{\pi}).$$

The nonbanks' asset-demand equations, after substitution into them of C-13 and C-3, may be written in general form as

7. It would be theoretically preferable, of course, to consider the return on physical capital and the return on bank equity as additional interest rates, to allow the market value of equity in the capital stock to diverge from its reproduction cost, and to model nonbanks' wealth-allocation decisions as a portfolio balancing of all five assets. See, for example, James Tobin, "A General Equilibrium Approach to Monetary Theory," *Journal of Money, Credit and Banking*, vol. 1 (February 1969), pp. 15–29; James Tobin and William C. Brainard, "Asset Markets and the Cost of Capital," in Bela Belassa and Richard Nelson, eds., *Economic Progress, Private Values, and Public Policy: Essays in Honor of William Fellner* (North-Holland, 1977).

8. See chapter 5 for discussion. Perceptive readers will already have noticed that the assumptions made about "money" in this illustrative framework do not adequately reflect the analysis and conclusions of part 2. A theoretically sounder framework—but one much more difficult to analyze—would assume that home nonbanks, and also home banks, hold transactions balances denominated in the foreign currency (for example, foreign-currency deposits in foreign banks).

9. It is assumed that the banks do not pay interest on their deposits so that the nominal expected return on M is zero.

10. It is implicit in the balance-sheet constraint C-12 that $e^N_{MD} + e^N_{SD} + e^N_{FD} = 0$, and that the sum of the responses across the three demands to any one of the other arguments in the functions is also zero.

(C-9)
$$M^d = M(\overset{-}{r},\ \overset{+}{\pi},\ \overset{+}{Y};\overset{-}{r^*},\ \overset{-}{\hat{\pi}},\ \overset{+}{\overline{W}^f},\ \overset{+}{e^N_{MD}})$$

(C-10)
$$S^{Nd} = S^N(\overset{+}{r},\ \overset{+}{\pi},\ \overset{-}{Y};\overset{-}{r^*},\ \overset{-}{\hat{\pi}},\ \overset{+}{\overline{W}^f},\ \overset{+}{e^N_{SD}})$$

(C-11)
$$\pi F^{Nd} = f^N(\overset{-}{r},\ \overset{?}{\pi},\ \overset{-}{Y};\overset{+}{r^*},\ \overset{+}{\hat{\pi}},\overset{+}{\overline{W}^f},\ \overset{+}{e^N_{FD}}).$$

The three variables r, π, and Y are endogenous; the other arguments of the functions are taken to be exogenous.

Foreign Participation in Home Financial Markets

Assume that foreign nonbanks do not hold home-currency money and that foreign financial intermediaries ("foreign banks") do not hold either home-currency money or home-currency base. Suppose, however, that both types of foreign economic unit do hold home-currency securities.[11]

A system of asset-demand equations for foreign nonbanks theoretically analogous to C-9 through C-11, expressed initially in units of foreign currency, can be shown to result in a demand by foreign nonbanks for home-currency securities, expressed in home-currency units as S^{FNd}, that depends positively on the home-security interest rate, r, the exchange rate, π, and the initial foreign-currency value of foreign nonbanks' wealth, $\overline{W}^*$, while it depends negatively on the foreign interest rate, r^*, the medium-run expected exchange rate $\hat{\pi}$, and the nominal value of foreign national output Y^*:

(C-14)
$$S^{FNd} = S^{FN}(\overset{+}{r},\ \overset{+}{\pi};\overset{-}{r^*},\ \overset{-}{\hat{\pi}},\ \overset{-}{Y^*},\ \overset{+}{\overline{W}^*},\ \overset{+}{e^{FN}_{SD}}).$$

The positive response of foreign nonbanks' demand for S (expressed in home-currency units) to the exchange rate is a composite of a "wealth effect" and the regressive exchange-rate expectations assumed in C-3.[12]

Define the funds available to foreign banks for investment as Q^* (in foreign-currency units). By analogy with the system of asset-demand equations for home banks, foreign banks' demand for home-currency securities, expressed in units of home currency, can be shown to be of the general form

(C-15)
$$S^{FBd} = S^{FB}(\overset{+}{r},\ \overset{+}{\pi};\overset{-}{r^*},\ \overset{-}{\hat{\pi}},\ \overset{+}{\overline{Q}^*},\ \overset{+}{M^*},\ \overset{+}{e^{FB}_{SD}}),$$

where $\overline{Q}^*$ is the initial foreign-currency level of investable asset stocks held by the foreign banks and M^* is the (exogenous) stock of foreign-currency deposit money.

11. The assumption that foreign banks and nonbanks do *not* hold means-of-payment balances denominated in the home currency is inconsistent with part 2 and can be justified, if at all, only as a way of simplifying the analysis.

12. When the home currency depreciates (π rises), the foreign-currency value of foreign wealth falls. All of the reduction in foreign wealth occurs in holdings of home-currency securities, however, so that, other things being equal, the foreign nonbanks want to shift away from foreign money and foreign-currency securities into home-currency securities. In the absence of any change in the medium-run expected exchange rate $\hat{\pi}$, moreover, the assumption C-3 says that the initial rise in π is expected to be reversed. This expected reversal (appreciation of the home currency subsequent to its initial depreciation) also leads foreign nonbanks to want to hold more home-currency securities and lesser amounts of foreign-currency-denominated assets.

Short-run Equilibrium in Home Financial Markets

Assume that home banks, given interest rates and the exchange rate, supply the amount of deposit money that home nonbanks want to hold. Then it is possible to write an "equilibrium" condition for home money supply and demand:

$$(C\text{-}16) \qquad\qquad M^s = M = M^d.$$

The total demand for home-currency monetary base is the sum of required reserves and the home banks' demand for net free reserves as given by C-4. An "equilibrium" in the demand for and supply of base thus requires:

$$(C\text{-}17) \qquad\qquad H^s = H = \rho M^s + HF^d.$$

The total supply of home-currency securities is assumed to be fixed during the short-run period analyzed in the comparative-statics model. An "equilibrium" condition for the home security market thus requires the four categories of private demands and the holdings of the home central bank to adjust to the available fixed supply $\bar{S}$:

$$(C\text{-}18) \qquad\qquad S^s = \bar{S} = S^{Nd} + S^{Bd} + S^{FNd} + S^{FBd} + S^{CB}.$$

Supply of Home-Produced Output

Imagine that the economy produces two goods: real output of a nontraded good, y_N, and real output of a tradable good, y_T. Denote the home-currency prices of the two goods as p_N and p_T.[13] Assume that the home-produced tradable good is regarded by consumers and investors in both the home and foreign nations as an imperfect substitute for a tradable good produced in the foreign nation (with exogenous foreign-currency price p^*). Thus the home country both consumes and exports the home-produced tradable good and imports the foreign-produced tradable good.

The home-currency price of the foreign-produced tradable, p_h^*, is a function of its foreign-currency price and of the exchange rate:

$$(C\text{-}22) \qquad\qquad p_h^* = \overset{+\quad +}{p_h^*(p^*, \pi)}.$$

If the home-currency price were immediately and completely adjusted to changes in the foreign-currency price and the exchange rate, it would be the product πp^*. The foreign-currency price of the home-produced tradable, p_T^f, is dependent in a similar way on the home-currency price and the exchange rate:

$$(C\text{-}23) \qquad\qquad p_T^f = \overset{+\quad -}{p_T^f(p_T, \pi)}.$$

If conventional assumptions are made about nominal wage rates being relatively inflexible in the short run, supply conditions in the two home goods markets may be represented in simplified form as a function of the three home-currency goods prices:

$$(C\text{-}24) \qquad\qquad y_N = \overset{+\quad -\quad -?\quad +}{y_N(p_N, p_T, p_h^*; e_{yN})}$$

13. Real outputs are measured in terms of money prices prevailing in some initial base period. Strictly speaking, p_N and p_T are (current-weight) price deflators whose values were unity in the initial base period.

(C-25)
$$y_T = y_T(\overset{-}{p_N}, \overset{+}{p_T}, \overset{-?}{p_h^*}; \overset{+}{e_{yT}}).$$

Increases in the own price are assumed to call forth increased output and employment at lower real wages and a constant capital stock, whereas increases in the price of the other home-produced good result, other things being equal, in lower output and employment.[14] The terms e_{yN} and e_{yT} are included to denote other exogenous factors that may influence the supply of the two goods.

National Product

Total net national product in real terms (measured in terms of the money prices of an initial base period) is:

(C-26)
$$y = y_N + y_T.$$

The nominal value of output—net national product measured in home-currency units at current prices—is given by the identity

(C-27)
$$Y = p_N y_N + p_T y_T = Py,$$

where the product deflator P, defined using current-period weights, is

(C-28)
$$P = \left(\frac{y_N}{y}\right) p_N + \left(\frac{y_T}{y}\right) p_T.$$

Fiscal Authority Receipts and Expenditures

Assume the fiscal authority taxes away a proportional amount of nominal income receipts. Nominal disposable income is then

(C-29)
$$Y_d = Y - T,$$

and nominal tax receipts of the fiscal authority, T, are given by

(C-30)
$$T = \theta Y,$$

where θ is the tax rate. Suppose the fiscal authority has real expenditures of g_N, g_T, and g_M on, respectively, the nontraded good, the home-produced tradable good, and imports. The nominal value of government expenditures, G, is therefore

(C-31)
$$G = p_N g_N + p_T g_T + p_h^* g_M.$$

With these definitions, the government's current budget surplus or deficit, Z^G, is

(C-32)
$$Z^G = T - G.$$

For simplicity, interest receipts, interest payments, and transfer payments are ignored in definitions C-26 through C-32.

If the fiscal authority pursues a discretionary-expenditure budgetary regime, the instruments of fiscal policy will be the tax rate θ and the real expenditure components

14. These supply functions assume, among other things, that (1) there is sufficient unutilized labor so that employment can be increased, and (2) there is sufficient slack in utilization of capacity so that it is physically possible to increase output with the existing capital stock. Increases in aggregate demand in the model thus raise both prices and outputs in the short run. The analysis does not try to deal with alternative views of the "Phillips curve" or the inflation process, but neither does it prejudge those issues.

g_N, g_T, and g_M; the budget surplus Z^G in that event is endogenously determined. Alternatively, if the budgetary operating regime were to make Z^G an exogenous policy instrument (for example, if it were desired to keep $Z^G = 0$), then one of the expenditure components would have to vary endogenously to keep Z^G at its preferred setting (see chapter 14).

Private Saving Behavior

The product deflator given by C-28 is not the price deflator relevant to private consumption and saving. Because home households allocate their real consumption, c, among the nontradable good, c_N, the home-produced tradable good, c_T, and expenditures on the imported tradable good produced abroad, c_M, the relevant price deflator is an index of all three prices:[15]

(C-33)
$$P_C = \left(\frac{c_N}{c}\right) p_N + \left(\frac{c_T}{c}\right) p_T + \left(\frac{c_M}{c}\right) p_h^*$$

(C-34)
$$c \equiv c_N + c_T + c_M.$$

If nominal disposable income is deflated by the consumption deflator defined in C-33,

(C-35)
$$\tilde{y}_d = \frac{Y_d}{P_C},$$

the resulting magnitude $\tilde{y}_d$ gives a measure of households' real potential ability to absorb goods and services out of their current income receipts.[16] The ratio of Y_d to the *product* deflator, P, is unaffected by the price of imports, p_h^*, and thus fails to reflect the fact that the ability of home residents to save or absorb in real terms depends not only on home output but on the relative price at which home tradable goods can be exchanged for goods purchased from the rest of the world. Given the outputs and prices of home produced goods, a rise in the price of imports lowers home residents' real potential to spend; this lowered potential should result partly in a cutback in real consumption and partly in a fall in real saving.[17]

Home households are assumed to make their saving decisions in real terms according to

(C-36)
$$s = s(\overset{+}{\tilde{y}_d}, \overset{+}{r}, \overbrace{\overset{+}{r^*} + \overset{+}{\pi}}, \overset{+}{e_s}) = s(\tilde{y}_d, r, \pi; r^*, \hat{\pi}, e_s),$$

where s is aggregate real saving and e_s represents exogenous factors determining saving behavior other than $\tilde{y}_d$ and the returns on assets.

---

15. Ex ante, the weights can be thought of as "last period's" consumption proportions and taken as exogenous. Ex post, the deflator is constructed using current-period weights.

16. Since the phrases "national product" and "national income" are typically used as synonyms, it could cause confusion to label $\tilde{y}_d$ as "real income" or "real disposable income." A cumbersome but accurate label is "real household command over goods and services resulting from current national production."

17. It can be seen from substituting C-29, C-30, and C-33 into C-35 that

(C-35a)
$$\tilde{y}_d = \frac{Y - T}{P_C} = (1 - \theta)\left(\frac{P}{P_C}\right) y.$$

The signs of the partial derivatives of $\tilde{y}_d$ with respect to the prices p_N and p_T depend on the relative weights of the home-produced goods in output and in consumption and are indeterminate until the weights are specified:

(C-35b)
$$\tilde{y}_d = \tilde{y}_d(\overset{+}{y_N}, \overset{+}{y_T}, \overset{?}{p_N}, \overset{?}{p_T}, \overset{-}{p_h^*}, \overset{-}{\theta}).$$

The magnitude of real consumption expenditures is the difference between real potential to consume and real savings:

(C-37) $$c = \tilde{y}_d - s.$$

The nominal value of savings, SV, follows from C-37, C-35, and C-33:

(C-38) $$SV = P_C s = Y_d - C,$$

where $C = P_C c$ is the value of consumption expenditures in current prices.

Home Demand for Goods

Home households are assumed to allocate their total real consumption among the three types of goods according to relative prices. Other factors influencing the allocation of consumption within the total are denoted by the exogenous disturbances e_{cN}, e_{cT}, and e_{cM}, where $e_{cN} + e_{cT} + e_{cM} = 0$:

(C-39) $$c_N/c = c_N \overset{- \;\; + \;\; + \;\; +}{(p_N, p_T, p_h^*; e_{cN})}$$

(C-40) $$c_T/c = c_T \overset{+ \;\; - \;\; + \;\; +}{(p_N, p_T, p_h^*; e_{cT})}$$

(C-41) $$c_M/c = c_M \overset{+ \;\; + \;\; - \;\; +}{(p_N, p_T, p_h^*; e_{cM})}.$$

This illustrative framework does not provide an explicit treatment of the income-account and balance-sheet decisions of firms. It merely postulates an ad hoc, short-run relationship for total net investment expenditures in real terms (i):

(C-42) $$i = i\overset{+ \;\; - \;\; +}{(y, r; e_i)}.$$

This function makes real investment depend positively on the level of aggregate real output and negatively on the home interest rate. Other factors influencing investment are impounded in the exogenous term e_i.[18]

Like consumption expenditures, investment is allocated among expenditures on the nontradable good (i_N), on the home-produced tradable good (i_T), and on imports (i_M), according to the relative prices of the three goods:

(C-43) $$i_N/i = i_N\overset{- \;\; + \;\; + \;\; +}{(p_N, p_T, p_h^*; e_{iN})}$$

(C-44) $$i_T/i = i_T\overset{+ \;\; - \;\; + \;\; +}{(p_N, p_T, p_h^*; e_{iT})}$$

(C-45) $$i_M/i = i_M\overset{+ \;\; + \;\; - \;\; +}{(p_N, p_T, p_h^*; e_{iM})}$$

(C-46) $$i \equiv i_N + i_T + i_M.$$

Exogenous factors determining the composition of investment expenditures are represented by the terms e_{iN}, e_{iT}, and $e_{iM}(e_{iN} + e_{iT} + e_{iM} = 0)$.

---

18. Less simplified models would introduce a distinction between investment in capital stock and the accumulation or decumulation of inventories; such models might also make investment depend on the foreign interest rate and on the exchange rate.

Because the home country is assumed to be small, its investors and consumers can purchase any amount of the foreign-produced tradable good at the exogenous foreign-currency price p^* without influencing that price.

Foreign Demand for Home-Produced Goods

Foreigners' demand for the home-produced tradable good in real terms, x_T, is assumed to depend on the relative foreign-currency prices of the two tradable goods, on the exogenous level of foreign real income, y^*, and on the exogenous foreign interest rate, r^*:

(C-47) $$x_T = x_T(\overset{-}{p_T^f}, \overset{+}{p^*}, \overset{+}{y^*}, \overset{-}{r^*}).$$

The foreign-currency price of home-country exports, p_T^f, is given by equation C-23.

Short-Run Equilibrium in Goods Markets

Suppose the supply of and demand for nontradable goods are brought into equilibrium, so that there is zero excess demand or supply at the then ruling prices, income, exchange rate, and interest rate:

(C-48) $$c_N + i_N + g_N - y_N = 0.$$

Suppose a similar condition prevails in the market for home-produced tradable goods:

(C-49) $$c_T + i_T + g_T + x_T - y_T = 0.$$

The expenditure side of the national income accounts and the definition of the current account in the balance of payments are implicit in the preceding goods-market relationships. For example, if equations C-48 and C-49 are added together and then consumption imports and investment imports are both added to and subtracted from the right side of the ensuing expression, the result is (all magnitudes in real terms)

(C-50) $$y_N + y_T = y = (c_N + c_T + c_M) + (i_N + i_T + i_M)$$
$$+ (g_N + g_T + g_M) + (x_T - c_M - i_M - g_M)$$
$$= c + i + g + x_T - (c_M + i_M + g_M).$$

An analogous condition holds when the variables are expressed in current prices:

(C-50a) $$Y = C + I + G + X - Im,$$

where $Im \equiv p_h^* c_M + p_h^* i_M + p_h^* g_M$ is the value of imports and $BCA \equiv X - Im$ is the nominal current-account balance in the balance of payments with the rest of the world. As equilibrium conditions, equations C-48 through C-50a embody assumptions about ex ante behavior and market clearing through price adjustment. Viewed ex post, those equations are identities.

Summary of the Comparative-Statics Relationships

The preceding description provides the components of an internally consistent comparative-statics model of a small open economy. A clearer impression of the model as a whole can be obtained if the various components are consolidated into a smaller number of key relationships.

It can be shown, for example, that the financial-sector relationships can be boiled down to three zero-excess-demand conditions in the "markets" for (1) deposit money, M, (2) the monetary base, H, and (3) home securities, S.[19] These have the general form:

excess demand for money:

$$(C\text{-}19) \qquad M(\overset{-}{r},\ \overset{+}{\pi},\ \overset{+}{Y};\ \overset{-}{r^*},\ \overset{-}{\hat{\pi}},\ \overset{+}{W^f},\ \overset{+}{e_{MD}}) - M = 0;$$

excess demand for monetary base:

$$(C\text{-}20) \qquad \rho M + HF(\overset{-}{r},\ \overset{+}{\pi},\ \overset{+}{M};\ \overset{-}{r^*},\ \overset{-}{\hat{\pi}},\ \overset{+}{\bar{Q}},\ \overset{+}{e_{HD}}) - H = 0;$$

excess demand for home securities:

$$(C\text{-}21) \qquad S^N(\overset{+}{r},\ \overset{+}{\pi},\ \overset{-}{Y};\ \overset{-}{r^*},\ \overset{-}{\hat{\pi}},\ \overset{+}{\bar{W}^f},\ \overset{+}{e\,^N_{SD}})$$

$$+\, S^B(\overset{+}{r},\ \overset{+}{\pi},\ \overset{+}{M};\ \overset{-}{r^*},\ \overset{-}{\hat{\pi}},\ \overset{+}{\bar{Q}},\ \overset{+}{e\,^B_{SD}})$$

$$+\, S^{FN}(\overset{+}{r},\ \overset{+}{\pi};\ \overset{-}{r^*},\ \overset{-}{\hat{\pi}},\ \overset{+}{Y^*},\ \overset{+}{\bar{W}^*},\ \overset{+}{e\,^{FN}_{SD}})$$

$$+\, S^{FB}(\overset{+}{r},\ \overset{+}{\pi};\ \overset{-}{r^*},\ \overset{-}{\hat{\pi}},\ \overset{+}{\bar{Q}^*},\ \overset{+}{M^*},\ \overset{+}{e\,^{FB}_{SD}})$$

$$+\, H - XA^{CB} - \bar{S} = 0.$$

It can also be shown that the real-sector relationships can be consolidated into eight equations:[20]

supply of nontradable goods:

$$(C\text{-}24a) \qquad y_N = y_N\,(\overset{+}{p_N},\ \overset{-}{p_T},\ \overset{-}{\pi};\ \overset{-}{p^*},\ \overset{+}{e_{yN}});$$

supply of home-produced tradable goods:

$$(C\text{-}25a) \qquad y_T = y_T\,(\overset{-}{p_N},\ \overset{+}{p_T},\ \overset{-}{\pi};\ \overset{-}{p^*},\ \overset{+}{e_{yT}});$$

definition of real national product:

$$(C\text{-}26) \qquad y = y_N + y_T;$$

19. The relationship C-19 is obtained by substituting C-9 into C-16; C-20 results from substitution of C-4 into C-17; C-21 represents a consolidation of C-2, C-5, C-10, C-14, and C-15 together into C-18.

20. Derivation of these relationships proceeds as follows. Substitute the functions C-22 and C-23 into the other equations for p_h^* and p_T^f. Substitute the expression for real saving in C-36 into C-37 and then substitute that expression for total consumption into the consumption-allocation equations C-39 through C-41. Next substitute C-42 into C-43 through C-45. The relation for $\bar{y}_d$ in C-51 follows from C-35b; C-52 consolidates C-30 through C-32. Finally, substitute the various ensuing equations for the components of aggregate demand into the equilibrium conditions C-48 and C-49.

definition of nominal national product:

(C-27)
$$Y = p_N y_N + p_T y_T;$$

real potential to consume:

(C-51)
$$\tilde{y}_d = \tilde{y}_d(\overset{+}{y_N}, \overset{+}{y_T}, \overset{?}{p_N}, \overset{?}{p_T}, \overset{-}{\pi}; \overset{-}{p^*}, \overset{-}{\theta});$$

government budget position:

(C-52)
$$Z^G = T(\overset{+}{Y}; \overset{+}{\theta}) - G(\overset{+}{p_N}, \overset{+}{p_T}, \overset{+}{\pi}; \overset{+}{p^*}, \overset{+}{g_N}, \overset{+}{g_T}, \overset{+}{g_M});$$

excess demand for nontradable goods:

(C-53)
$$c_N(\overset{-}{p_N}, \overset{+}{p_T}, \overset{+}{\pi}, \overset{+}{\tilde{y}_d}, \overset{-}{r}; \overset{+}{p^*}, \overset{-}{e_s}, \overset{+}{e_{cN}})$$

$$+ i_N(\overset{-}{p_N}, \overset{+}{p_T}, \overset{+}{\pi}, \overset{+}{y}, \overset{-}{r}; \overset{+}{p^*}, \overset{+}{e_i}, \overset{+}{e_{iN}})$$

$$+ g_N - y_N = 0;$$

excess demand for home-produced tradable goods:

(C-54)
$$c_T(\overset{+}{p_N}, \overset{-}{p_T}, \overset{+}{\pi}, \overset{+}{\tilde{y}_d}, \overset{-}{r}; \overset{+}{p^*}, \overset{-}{e_s}, \overset{+}{e_{cT}})$$

$$+ i_T(\overset{+}{p_N}, \overset{-}{p_T}, \overset{+}{\pi}, \overset{+}{y}, \overset{-}{r}; \overset{+}{p^*}, \overset{+}{e_i}, \overset{+}{e_{iT}})$$

$$+ x_T(\overset{-}{p_T}, \overset{+}{\pi}; \overset{+}{p^*}, \overset{+}{y^*}, \overset{-}{r^*}) + g_T - y_T = 0.$$

Taken together, the preceding relationships are a system of eleven equations in the following thirteen endogenous (or potentially endogenous) variables: y_N, p_N, y_T, p_T, y, Y, $\tilde{y}_d$, Z^G, M, π, XA^{CB}, r, and H. With still other substitutions, the comparative-statics relationships can be further consolidated into a system of five equations in the seven variables p_N, p_T, Z^G, π, XA^{CB}, r, and H.

Monetary-Policy Instruments

To complete the specification of an internally consistent framework, it is necessary to designate the domestic and external operating regimes used by the home central bank. Four variables—the interest rate, r, the monetary base, H, the exchange rate, π, and the quantity of external reserves, XA^{CB}—are potential instruments of monetary policy. The central bank may be assumed to select either r or H as its domestic instrument and either π or XA^{CB} as the external instrument. After the actual instruments have been designated, the comparative-statics relationships become a complete model (for example, a system of eleven equations determining eleven endogenous variables).

There are four possible combinations of operating regimes, and hence four different variants of the common illustrative framework (four separate "models"), as follows:

Model	Monetary-policy regimen	Endogenous financial variables
1	reserve-aggregate peg with external-reserves peg	r, π, M
2	interest-rate peg with exchange-rate peg	H, XA^{CB}, M
3	interest-rate peg with external-reserves peg	H, π, M
4	reserve-aggregate peg with exchange-rate peg	r, XA^{CB}, M

Solution of the Four Variants of the Comparative-Statics Framework

The comparative-statics conclusions summarized in chapter 22 are based on analysis of a linearized and still further simplified version of the illustrative framework described above. The main further simplification adopted was to delete the fiscal authority's receipts and expenditures from the equations (thereby suppressing fiscal policy) before solving the four models. Although I have not solved the four models in the absence of these additional simplifications, I am reasonably confident that the comparative-statics generalizations in chapter 22 are robust and not qualitatively sensitive to the simplifications.

Amending the Comparative-Statics Framework to Include Dynamic Interactions of Stocks and Flows

The framework outlined in the first portion of this appendix does not have time subscripts on its variables. It deals with a hypothetical period of time presumed to be long enough for goods prices and outputs to adjust but short enough to warrant taking the stocks of physical and financial assets as given. A more realistic analytical framework must deal explicitly with a succession of short-run time periods, date all its variables with time subscripts, and capture the interaction of variables not only within a single short-run period but across the whole succession of periods.[21]

Investment and the Capital Stock

Equations C-42 through C-46 provide a comparative-statics characterization of the flow of investment expenditures. But those relationships are so simplified they omit any mention of the services of the capital stock or of labor inputs in production functions. The short-run supplies of the output of the two home goods in equations

---

21. As in the first portion of the appendix, the purpose here is to identify the important relationships that must be incorporated in dynamic macroeconomic models, not to spell out the models themselves. Ronald McKinnon and Wallace Oates were among the first to deal analytically with some of these stock-flow interactions in stationary-state models of an open economy; see Ronald I. McKinnon and Wallace E. Oates, *The Implications of International Economic Integration for Monetary, Fiscal, and Exchange-Rate Policy*, Princeton Studies in International Finance 16 (Princeton University Press, January 1966). For references to subsequent contributions to the analysis of stationary-state and dynamic models for open economies, see Henderson, "Modeling the Interdependence of National Money and Capital Markets," and Isard, *Exchange-Rate Determination*.

C-24 and C-25 depend simply on prices; the capital stock is assumed constant. Yet the "equilibrium" of the models entails nonzero flows of net investment—in other words a *changing* capital stock.[22]

A dynamic adaptation of the comparative-statics framework would need to make ex ante investment depend not only on the current flow of production and on interest rates, as in equation C-42, but also on the stock of capital. In turn, the stock of capital would be given by an ex ante analogue of the ex post identity stating that the current-period nominal value of the stock is the sum of last period's stock (K_{t-1}), net investment (gross investment less depreciation) during the current period (I_t), and the net value of capital gains or losses if any (Vk_t):

$$(C-55) \qquad\qquad K_t \equiv K_{t-1} + I_t + Vk_t.$$

Saving and Wealth

Just as the comparative-statics framework ignored the implications of investment flows for the capital stock, the equations C-35 through C-38, representing saving and consumption behavior, ignored the interrelationship of saving and wealth.

In the schematic macroeconomy postulated here, nonbank financial wealth is allocated to home deposit money, home-currency securities, and foreign-currency securities:

$$(C-12a) \qquad\qquad W_t^f \equiv M_t + S_t^N + \pi_t F_t^N.$$

Nonfinancial net worth (equity claims) is the sum of the market value of the capital stock and equity ownership of the banks:

$$(C-56) \qquad\qquad W_t^n \equiv K_t + NW_t^B.$$

If, for simplicity, capital gains or losses on physical capital and changes in equity claims on the banks are ignored, the change in nonfinancial net worth is the flow of new (net) domestic investment:

$$(C-57) \qquad\qquad W_t^n - W_{t-1}^n \equiv K_t - K_{t-1} \equiv I_t.$$

Since the total wealth of nonbanks is the sum of financial wealth and equity claims, the ex post identity linking the stock of wealth to the flow of nominal savings (SV_t) is

$$(C-58) \qquad\qquad W_t \equiv W_t^f + W_t^n \equiv W_{t-1}^f + W_{t-1}^n + SV_t + Vf_t,$$

where Vf_t represents the total of capital gains or losses on financial wealth. Again, for simplicity, ignore capital gains or losses on financial wealth other than those associated with exchange-rate changes. The ex post change in the home-currency

---

22. This inherent contradiction can be found in much of macroeconomic theory since John Maynard Keynes, *The General Theory of Employment, Interest and Money* (Macmillan, 1936). Keynes explicitly introduced the assumption of an unchanged capital stock as a simplification valid for the short run. Careful theorists and teachers have used models employing the simplification only for the analysis of the short run. Very often, however, the limitations of the simplification have been forgotten. The longer the time horizon of an analysis, moreover, the more urgent it becomes to model the dynamic interaction of investment flows and the stock of capital. For further discussion, see James Tobin, "Deficit Spending and Crowding Out in Shorter and Longer Runs," in Harry Greenfield and others, eds., *Theory for Efficiency: Essays in Honor of Abba P. Lerner* (MIT Press, 1979).

value of foreign-currency securities can be broken down into "new investment" and "capital gains" components:

$$(\text{C-59}) \qquad \pi_t(F_t^N) - \pi_{t-1}(F_{t-1}^N) \equiv \pi_t\,(F_t^N - F_{t-1}^N) + (\pi_t - \pi_{t-1})F_{t-1}^N.$$

The combination of C-12 and C-56 through C-59 then yields an expression showing the breakdown of the nominal savings of a period into the corresponding nominal values of the new purchases of assets:

$$(\text{C-60}) \qquad SV_t \equiv (M_t - M_{t-1}) + (S_t^N - \dot{S}_{t-1}^N) + \pi_t\,(F_t^N - F_{t-1}^N) + (K_t - K_{t-1}).$$

Thus the identity for total wealth in the current period, given the preceding simplifications, can also be written as

$$(\text{C-58a}) \qquad W_t \equiv W_{t-1} + SV_t + (\pi_t - \pi_{t-1})F_{t-1}^N.$$

A dynamic model of macroeconomic behavior postulates ex ante analogues of the preceding ex post identities. Nominal planned saving for the current period must be consistent with planned purchases of financial assets and equity. Saving and consumption decisions in real terms must be taken jointly with planned changes in real wealth. Planned changes in real wealth must be equivalent to planned real savings and expected capital gains or losses.[23]

Life-cycle theories of saving and consumption suggest that the ex ante behavioral relationship for planned savings, specified earlier as equation C-36, should include real wealth as well as the interest rate and the real command over goods and services resulting from current income receipts. Hence in a dynamic model, C-36 might be respecified as

$$(\text{C-36a}) \qquad s_t = \frac{SV_t}{P_{Ct}} = s\left(\overset{+}{\frac{Y_{dt}}{P_{Ct}}}, \overset{-}{\frac{W_t}{P_{Ct}}}, \overset{+}{r_t}, \overset{+}{r_t^* + \hat{\pi}_t}; e_{st}\right).$$

Taken in conjunction with C-36a, the equation C-58a may be regarded as an ex ante identity determining the current-period nominal value of planned wealth when SV_t, π_t, and W_t are endogenous variables.

The Consolidated Budget and Balance-Sheet Constraint for the Government as a Whole

The outstanding stock of government securities was assumed constant in the short-run "equilibrium" condition, C-18 and C-21. Yet just as a nonzero flow of net

---

23. There are subtle stock-flow difficulties involved in theoretical modeling of the saving-wealth nexus. The view taken in the text is that the current period's wealth-allocation decision and the current period's saving-consumption decision have to be planned jointly, with the current period's flow of saving or dissaving adding to or diminishing the asset stocks that are priced and allocated in the current period's asset markets. This view of asset demands is sometimes referred to as "balancing at the end of the period," because households allocate a total of assets for the current period that is influenced by saving during the current period. For further discussion, see Duncan K. Foley, "On Two Specifications of Asset Equilibrium in Macroeconomic Models," *Journal of Political Economy*, vol. 83 (April 1975), pp. 303–24; Willem H. Buiter and Geoffrey Woglom, "On Two Specifications of Asset Equilibrium in Macroeconomic Models: A Note," *Journal of Political Economy*, vol. 85 (April 1977), pp. 395–402; Douglas D. Purvis, "Dynamic Models of Portfolio Behavior," and Gary Smith, "Dynamic Models of Portfolio Behavior: Comment on Purvis," *American Economic Review*, vol. 68 (June 1978), pp. 403–16; and Willem H. Buiter, "Walras' Law and All That: Budget Constraints and Balance-Sheet Constraints in Period Models and Continuous Time Models," Research Memorandum 221 (Princeton University, Econometric Research Program, December 1977).

investment changes the stock of capital, any flow imbalance in the government budget necessarily has to be financed with the retirement or new issuance of home-currency securities. Only in the very short run or only if the government budget is kept balanced over the longer run, therefore, can an analyst plausibly employ the simplification that the total stock of government securities is unchanged.

The fiscal authority's budget surplus or deficit during a period, Z_t^G, is the excess or shortfall of the flow of tax receipts (T_t) over the flow of expenditures (G_t)—see equations C-29 through C-32. The outstanding stock of government securities varies over time with the budget position:

$$(C-61) \qquad S_t = S_{t-1} - Z_t^G = S_{t-1} - (T_t - G_t).$$

Since there are five types of holders of these securities—the home central bank, home nonbanks, home banks, foreign nonbanks, and foreign banks—the identity C-61 also implies

$$(C-61a) \qquad S_t - S_{t-1} = -Z_t^G = (S_t^{CB} - S_{t-1}^{CB}) + (S_t^P - S_{t-1}^P),$$

where S_t^P is the stock of home government debt held by the four types of economic units constituting the world private sector $(S_t^P \equiv S_t^N + S_t^B + S_t^{FN} + S_t^{FB})$. The combination of the home central bank's balance-sheet constraint (see equation C-2) with equation C-61a gives the consolidated constraint for the government as a whole:

$$(C-62) \qquad T_t - G_t = Z_t^G = \Delta XA_{t.}^{CB} - \Delta H_t - \Delta S_t^P,$$

where ΔXA_t^{CB} is the change in external reserve assets, ΔH_t is the change in the stock of reserve money (monetary base), and ΔS_t^P is the change in the stock of government securities held by the world private sector. The dynamic interactions of the flows of government income-account transactions and stocks of government assets and liabilities in C-62 are the counterpart in this analytical framework of the more detailed government constraint discussed in chapters 14 and 21.[24]

As emphasized earlier, the flow expenditures and receipts associated with fiscal policy and the changes in stocks of assets brought about by debt management and monetary policy are inextricably linked. Whichever elements of C-62 may be chosen as exogenous policy instruments, the interactions of the flows and the stocks play a key role in, and therefore cannot be neglected in any longer run analysis of, the dynamic evolution of the macroeconomy.

The Saving-Wealth Nexus and the Balance of Payments

The current account in the balance of payments, BCA_t, is an integral part of the flow relationships associated with spending and saving decisions in an open economy (see equations C-48 through C-50a).

However, the current account, and indeed the entire balance of payments, is not a separate constraint beyond those already described. Nor is a current-account imbalance a flow-stock interaction that is separate from the investment-capital stock interrelationship, the saving-wealth nexus, and the interaction of the gov-

---

24. The differences between C-62 and the consolidated government constraint in chapters 14 and 21 arise because interest payments and receipts, the central bank's income-account transactions, and the foreign central bank's holdings of home-currency-denominated assets are all ignored in appendix C.

ernment budget position and the outstanding stock of government securities. The balance of payments, both ex ante and ex post, is already implicit in the budget constraints, balance-sheet constraints, and behavioral relationships of home economic units (including of course the home government).

That fact and its implications can be highlighted by combining some of the relationships already presented.[25] Consider first the current account. National product in current prices viewed from the income side of the accounts (see equations C-29 and C-38) is the sum of tax receipts, consumption expenditures, and saving:

$$(C\text{-}63) \qquad\qquad Y_t = T_t + C_t + SV_t.$$

Combining this relationship with the expenditure side of the accounts (see C-50a) yields the familiar savings-investment relationship:

$$(C\text{-}64) \qquad\qquad SV_t + Z_t^G = I_t + BCA_t.$$

That is, the current-account imbalance is the counterpart of any discrepancy between net domestic investment and the sum of saving by the home private sector and saving by the home government.

A clearer picture of the interactions of a flow current-account imbalance and the stock of wealth can be gained by substituting previous expressions for SV_t, Z_t^G, and I_t into C-64 to yield the following equation for the change in wealth:[26]

$$(C\text{-}65) \qquad\qquad \Delta W_t = \Delta K_t + \Delta S_t + BCA_t + \Delta \pi_t (F_{t-1}^N).$$

Thus changes in the stock of home private-sector wealth, measured in home-currency units, can be attributed to (1) changes in the value of the physical capital stock resulting from nonzero net domestic private investment; (2) current-period saving or dissaving by the government, which changes the outstanding stock of home-currency securities;[27] (3) an imbalance in the current account of the balance of payments; and (4) capital gains or losses resulting from changes in the exchange rate.[28]

As emphasized in chapter 22, the third of these sources of change in private-sector wealth plays a critically important role in determining the macroeconomic dynamics of an open economy. The intercountry redistribution of wealth that is the

25. On the derivation of the balance of payments from a consolidation of the budget and balance-sheet constraints of all economic units resident within a nation, see Richard Berner and others, "Modeling the International Influences on the U.S. Economy: A Multi-Country Approach," International Finance Discussion Paper 93 (Board of Governors of the Federal Reserve System, November 1976); and Guy V. G. Stevens, "Balance of Payments Equations and Exchange Rate Determination," International Finance Discussion Paper 95 (December 1976).

26. To derive C-65, substitute C-58a for SV_t, C-61a for Z_t^G, and C-57 for I_t.

27. An unbalanced government budget position changes the home private sector's wealth regardless of whether the home private sector's own holdings of government securities are changed. The exposition here ignores the issue of the degree to which home private economic units perceive government budget deficits financed by increased debt as adding to their *future* tax liabilities and hence reducing the real value of their current wealth. On this issue, see Robert J. Barro, "Are Government Bonds Net Wealth?", *Journal of Political Economy*, vol. 82 (December 1974), pp. 1095–117.

28. Equation C-65 would have included additional terms representing capital gains and losses if capital gains and losses other than those associated with exchange-rate changes had not been neglected in the earlier exposition. Strictly speaking, C-65 does not even include all the capital gains and losses associated with exchange-rate changes. Home banks incur gains or losses on their holdings of foreign-currency securities when the exchange rate changes. Since the equity in banks (NW^B) is part of the "nonfinancial" wealth of nonbanks, these gains or losses of the banks ($\Delta \pi_t F_{t-1}^B$) will also affect nonbank wealth.

counterpart of an imbalance in the current account requires portfolio rebalancing by both home and foreign wealth-owners. Those adjustments in asset portfolios are in turn the mechanism by which current-account imbalances put pressure on the exchange rate to change.

The expression developed in C-65 can be transformed further, still making use only of previously specified relationships, to derive the balance of payments as a whole:[29]

$$(C-66) \qquad BCA_t = \pi_t(\Delta F_t^N) + \pi_t(\Delta F_t^B) - \Delta S_t^{FN} - \Delta S_t^{FB} + \Delta XA_t^{CB}.$$

The current-account balance is, by definition, equal with opposite sign to the capital-account balance. The five terms on the right side of C-66 are the five types of capital flows that are the components of the capital account (private plus official). Because money holdings and direct investments in one nation by residents of another are ignored in the illustrative framework described here, the intercountry transfer of wealth that is the counterpart of a current-account imbalance must take the form of net sales or purchases of foreign-currency securities by home banks or nonbanks, net sales or purchases of home-currency securities by foreign banks or nonbanks, or changes in the external reserve assets of the home central bank.[30]

The "balance-of-payments equation" C-66, interpreted as an ex post accounting identity, holds for all possible *observed* prices, exchange rates, saving and consumption flows, and asset holdings. Interpreted as an ex ante "equilibrium condition," it does *not* hold for all possible prices, exchange rates, and values of other macroeconomic variables. Rather, it holds only for the particular values of endogenous variables that jointly satisfy all the ex ante behavioral relationships in the home economy (and, in principle, the rest of the world).[31]

Differential Speeds of Response in Macroeconomic Behavior

The comparative-statics framework is incapable of representing differential speeds of response for different aspects of macroeconomic behavior. Yet differences in the speeds at which various markets adjust, which in turn reflect differences in the speeds of the various behavioral responses of economic units, may critically influence the dynamic evolution of an open economy.

Suppose nonbank economic units make prompt adjustments in their holdings of financial assets to changes in the expected returns on those assets, whereas they sluggishly adjust their saving and consumption decisions to changes in the prices of goods. Analogously, suppose banks adjust their asset portfolios promptly, while goods producers respond more slowly in altering their production and labor-hiring decisions. Dynamic behavior with those characteristics can produce very different time paths for the economy—in particular for such variables as interest rates, the exchange rate, and external reserve assets—from those that would be observed if adjustments in asset markets and goods markets occurred equally promptly. It may

29. To derive C-66, use C-58a and C-60, and then use the first-difference forms of the central-bank balance sheet C-2 and the home bank balance sheet C-7 (with $\Delta NW^B = 0$). Capital gains and losses are not included in the capital flows as recorded in the balance of payments.

30. The changes in home private wealth must take one or another of these forms, both proximately as the current-account imbalance occurs, and over the longer run after all subsequent adjustments. The composition of the proximate and longer run changes, however, can be different.

31. See Stevens, "Balance of Payments Equations and Exchange Rate Determination."

be, for example, that "volatility" or "overshooting" in asset prices and the exchange rate—if analytical definitions are given to those concepts—can be partially explained in terms of different speeds of adjustment in the financial and real sectors of the economy.[32]

The dynamics of the various aspects of macroeconomic behavior—largely, to be sure, the "domestic" aspects—have in the last decade or two increasingly preoccupied scholars. More recently, that general concern with differential speeds of response has begun to bear modest fruit in theoretical research on open-economy models.[33] Much remains to be done, however, before these dynamics and their implications for macroeconomic policy can be clearly understood.

32. See, for example, Jürg Niehans, "Some Doubts About the Efficacy of Monetary Policy under Flexible Exchange Rates," *Journal of International Economics*, vol. 5 (August 1975), pp. 275–81; and Rudiger Dornbusch, "Expectations and Exchange-Rate Dynamics," *Journal of Political Economy*, vol. 84 (December 1976), pp. 1161–76. For a survey of the recent literature on the dynamics of exchange-rate determination, see Isard, *Exchange-Rate Determination*, pp. 26–34.

33. In addition to the references in the previous footnote, see William H. Branson, "A 'Keynesian' Approach to Worldwide Inflation," in Lawrence B. Krause and Walter S. Salant, eds., *Worldwide Inflation: Theory and Recent Experience* (Brookings Institution, 1977); William H. Branson, "Asset Markets and Relative Prices in Exchange Rate Determination," *Sozialwissenschaftliche Annalen*, Band 1 (1977), pp. 69–89; Dale W. Henderson, "The Dynamic Effects of Exchange-Market Intervention Policy: Two Extreme Views and a Synthesis," in Helmut Frisch, ed., *The Economics of Flexible Exchange Rates*, supplement to *Kredit und Kapital* (6:1980).

Selected Bibliography

Adler, Michael, and Bernard Dumas. "The Microeconomics of the Firm in an Open Economy," *American Economic Review,* vol. 67 (February 1977, *Papers and Proceedings, 1976*).

Akerlof, George A., and Ross D. Milbourne. "The Sensitivity of Monetarist Conclusions to Monetarist Assumptions: Constant Lag Versus Constant Target-Threshold Monitoring." Special Studies Paper 117. Washington, D.C.: Board of Governors of the Federal Reserve System, June 1978.

Alford, Robert R. "Paradigms of Relations Between State and Society," in Leon N. Lindberg and others, eds., *Stress and Contradiction in Modern Capitalism: Public Policy and the Theory of the State.* Lexington, Mass.: Lexington Books, 1975.

Aliber, Robert Z., ed. *The Political Economy of Monetary Reform.* London: Macmillan, 1977.

Allison, Graham T. *Essence of Decision: Explaining the Cuban Missile Crisis.* Boston: Little, Brown, 1971.

Andersen, Leonall C., and Jerry L. Jordan. "Monetary and Fiscal Actions: A Test of Their Relative Importance in Economic Stabilization," *Federal Reserve Bank of St. Louis Review,* vol. 50 (November 1968).

Andersen, Leonall C., Lawrence R. Klein, and Karl Brunner. "The State of the Monetarist Debate," *Federal Reserve Bank of St. Louis Review,* vol. 55 (September 1973).

Anderson, Robert E. "The Individual's Transactions Demand for Money: A Utility Maximization Approach," *Journal of Monetary Economics,* vol. 2 (April 1976).

Ando, Albert, and Franco Modigliani. "Some Reflections on Describing Structures of Financial Sectors," in Gary Fromm and Lawrence R. Klein, eds., *The Brookings Model: Perspective and Recent Developments.* Amsterdam: North-Holland, 1975.

———. "Impacts of Fiscal Actions on Aggregate Income and the Monetarist Controversy: Theory and Evidence," in Jerome Stein, ed., *Monetarism.* Amsterdam: North-Holland, 1976.

Ando, Albert, Franklin Fisher, and Herbert A. Simon, eds. *Essays on the Structure of Social Science Models.* Cambridge: Massachusetts Institute of Technology Press, 1963.

Ando, Albert, Richard Herring, and Richard Marston, eds. *International Aspects of Stabilization Policies.* Conference Series 12. Boston: Federal Reserve Bank of Boston, 1974.

Andrew, A. P. "What Ought to be Called Money?," *Quarterly Journal of Economics,* vol. 13 (January 1899).

Aoki, Masanao. "Noninteracting Control of Macroeconomic Variables: Implications on Policy Mix Considerations," *Journal of Econometrics,* vol. 2 (September 1974).

———. "On a Generalization of Tinbergen's Condition in the Theory of Policy to Dynamic Models," *Review of Economic Studies,* vol. 42 (April 1975).

———. *Optimal Control and System Theory in Dynamic Economic Analysis.* New York: American Elsevier, 1976.

———. "On Decentralized Stabilization Policies and Dynamic Assignment Problems," *Journal of International Economics,* vol. 6 (May 1976).

———. "A Note on the Stability of the Interaction of Monetary Policies," *Journal of International Economics,* vol. 7 (February 1977).

Aoki, Masanao, and Matthew Canzoneri. "Macroeconomic Policy in a Dynamic Two Country Model," *Annals of Economic and Social Measurement,* vol. 6 (Winter/Spring, 1978).

Argy, Victor, and Joanne Salop. "Price and Output Effects of Monetary and Fiscal Policy under Flexible Exchange Rates," *IMF Staff Papers,* vol. 26 (June 1979).

Arrow, Kenneth J. "Uncertainty and the Economics of Medical Care," *American Economic Review,* vol. 53 (December 1963).

———. "The Economics of Moral Hazard: Further Comment," *American Economic Review,* vol. 58 (June 1968).

———. "Limited Knowledge and Economic Analysis," *American Economic Review,* vol. 64 (March 1974).

Arrow, Kenneth J., and Mordecai Kurz. *Public Investment, the Rate of Return and Optimal Fiscal Policy.* Baltimore: Johns Hopkins University Press, 1970.

Athans, Michael. "Theory and Applications: Survey of Decentralized Control Methods," *Annals of Economic and Social Measurement,* vol. 4 (Spring 1975).

Bach, G. L. *Making Monetary and Fiscal Policy.* Washington, D.C.: Brookings Institution, 1971.

Baily, Martin Neil. "Stabilization Policy and Private Economic Behavior," *Brookings Papers on Economic Activity, 1:1978.*

Barro, Robert J. "Are Government Bonds Net Wealth?" *Journal of Political Economy,* vol. 82 (December 1974).

———. "Rational Expectations and the Role of Monetary Policy," *Journal of Monetary Economics,* vol. 2 (January 1976).

Barro, Robert J., and Stanley Fischer. "Recent Developments in Monetary Theory," *Journal of Monetary Economics,* vol. 2 (April 1976).

Barry, Brian. *Sociologists, Economists and Democracy.* London: Collier-Macmillan, 1970.

———. "Does Democracy Cause Inflation? A Study of the Political Ideas of Some Economists." Paper prepared for conference on the Politics and Sociology of Global Inflation. Washington, D.C.: Brookings Institution, December 1978. (Leon Lindberg and Charles Maier are editing the conference papers for publication.)

Bator, Francis M. "The Anatomy of Market Failure," *Quarterly Journal of Economics,* vol. 72 (August 1958).

Baumol, William J. "The Transactions Demand for Cash: An Inventory Theoretic Approach," *Quarterly Journal of Economics,* vol. 66 (November 1952).

Bentzel, Ragnar, and Bent Hansen. "On Recursiveness and Interdependency in Economic Models," *Review of Economic Studies,* vol. 22 (1954–55).

Bergsten, C. Fred, and Lawrence B. Krause, eds. *World Politics and International Economics.* Washington, D.C.: Brookings Institution, 1975.

Berner, Richard; Peter Clark; Ernesto Hernández-Catá; Howard Howe; Sung Kwack; and Guy Stevens. "A Multi-Country Model of the International Influences on the U.S. Economy: Preliminary Results." International Finance Discussion Paper 115. Washington, D.C.: Board of Governors of the Federal Reserve System, December 1977.

Berner, Richard; Peter Clark; Howard Howe; Sung Kwack; and Guy Stevens. "Modeling the International Influences on the U.S. Economy: A Multi-Country Approach." International Finance Discussion Paper 93. Washington, D.C.: Board of Governors of the Federal Reserve System, November 1976.

Black, Stanley W. *International Money Markets and Flexible Exchange Rates.* Princeton Studies in International Finance 32. Princeton: Princeton University Press, 1973.

———. *Floating Exchange Rates and National Economic Policy.* New Haven: Yale University Press, 1977.

Blinder, Alan S., and Robert M. Solow. "Does Fiscal Policy Matter?," *Journal of Public Economics,* vol. 2 (November 1973).

———. "Analytical Foundations of Fiscal Policy," in Blinder and others, *The Economics of Public Finance.* Washington, D.C.: Brookings Institution, 1974.

———. "Does Fiscal Policy Still Matter? A Reply," *Journal of Monetary Economics,* vol. 2 (November 1976).

Board of Governors of the Federal Reserve System. *Open Market Policies and Operating Procedures—Staff Studies.* Washington, D.C.: Board of Governors of the Federal Reserve System, 1971.

———. *Improving the Monetary Aggregates: Report of the Advisory Committee on Monetary Statistics.* Washington, D.C.: Board of Governors of the Federal Reserve System, 1976.

———. "The Implementation of Monetary Policy in 1976," *Federal Reserve Bulletin,* vol. 63 (April 1977).

———. "Monetary Policy and Open Market Operations in 1977," *Federal Reserve Bulletin,* vol. 64 (April 1978).

———. *Improving the Monetary Aggregates: Staff Papers.* Washington, D.C.: Board of Governors of the Federal Reserve System, 1978.

———. "A Proposal for Redefining the Monetary Aggregates," *Federal Reserve Bulletin,* vol. 65 (January 1979).

———. "The Redefined Monetary Aggregates," *Federal Reserve Bulletin,* vol. 66 (February 1980).

Bohrnstedt, George W., and Arthur S. Goldberger, "On the Exact Covariance of Products of Random Variables," *Journal of the American Statistical Association,* vol. 64 (December 1969).

Bosworth, Barry, and J. S. Duesenberry. "A Flow of Funds Model and its Implications," in Federal Reserve Bank of Boston, *Issues in Federal Debt Management.* Conference Series 10. Boston: Federal Reserve Bank of Boston, 1973.

Boyer, Russell S. "Optimal Foreign Exchange Market Intervention," *Journal of Political Economy,* vol. 86 (December 1978).

Brainard, William C. "Financial Intermediaries and a Theory of Monetary Control," *Yale Economic Essays,* vol. 4 (Fall 1964). (Reprinted in Donald D. Hester and James Tobin, eds., *Financial Markets and Economic Activity.* Cowles Foundation for Research in Economics Monograph 21. New York: Wiley, 1967.)

———. "Uncertainty and the Effectiveness of Policy," *American Economic Review,* vol. 57 (May 1967, *Papers and Proceedings, 1966*).

Brainard, William C., and James Tobin. "Pitfalls in Financial Model Building," *American Economic Review,* vol. 58 (May 1968, *Papers and Proceedings, 1967*).

Branson, William H. "A 'Keynesian' Approach to Worldwide Inflation," in Lawrence B. Krause and Walter S. Salant, eds., *Worldwide Inflation: Theory and Recent Experience.* Washington, D.C.: Brookings Institution, 1977.

————. "Asset Markets and Relative Prices in Exchange Rate Determination," *Sozialwissenschaftliche Annalen,* Band 1 (1977).

Brittan, Samuel. *The Economic Consequences of Democracy.* London: Temple Smith, 1977.

Brunner, Karl. "A Schema for the Supply Theory of Money," *International Economic Review,* vol. 2 (January 1961).

————. "The Role of Monetary Policy," *Federal Reserve Bank of St. Louis Review,* vol. 50 (July 1968).

————, ed. *Targets and Indicators of Monetary Policy.* San Francisco: Chandler, 1969.

————. "Money Supply Process and Monetary Policy in an Open Economy," in Michael B. Connolly and Alexander K. Swoboda, eds., *International Trade and Money: The Geneva Essays.* Toronto: University of Toronto Press, 1973.

Brunner, Karl, and Allan H. Meltzer. "The Meaning of Monetary Indicators," in George Horwich, ed., *Monetary Process and Policy: A Symposium.* Homewood, Ill.: Richard D. Irwin, 1967.

————. "Implementation Problem for Monetary Policy," *Federal Reserve Bank of St. Louis Review,* vol. 53 (March 1971).

————. "Money, Debt, and Economic Activity," *Journal of Political Economy,* vol. 80 (September/October 1972).

————. "Selection of a Monetary Aggregate for Economic Stabilization," *Federal Reserve Bank of St. Louis Review,* vol. 57 (October 1975).

————. "Aggregative Theory for a Closed Economy" and "Monetarism: The Principal Issues, Areas of Agreement, and the Work Remaining," in Jerome Stein, ed., *Monetarism.* Amsterdam: North-Holland, 1976.

Bryant, Ralph C. "Dollar Balances and the United States Balance of Payments: A Conceptual Review." Ph.D. dissertation, Yale University, 1966.

————. "Balance of Payments Adjustment: National Targets and International Inconsistency," in American Statistical Association, *Proceedings of the Business and Economic Statistics Section.* Washington, D.C.: ASA, 1968.

————. "Empirical Research on Financial Capital Flows," in Peter B. Kenen, ed., *International Trade and Finance: Frontiers for Research.* Cambridge and New York: Cambridge University Press, 1975.

Buchanan, James M., and Richard E. Wagner. *Democracy in Deficit: The Legacy of Lord Keynes.* New York: Academic Press, 1977.

Buiter, Willem H. "Optimal Foreign Exchange Market Intervention with Rational Expectations." Research Memorandum 216. Princeton: Princeton University, Econometric Research Program, November 1977. (Also in J. Martin and A. Smith, eds., *Trade and Payments Adjustment under Flexible Exchange Rates.* New York and London: Macmillan, forthcoming.)

————. "Walras' Law and All That: Budget Constraints in Period Models and Continuous Time Models." Research Memorandum 221. Princeton: Princeton University, Econometric Research Program, December 1977.

————. "The Macroeconomics of Dr. Pangloss: A Critical Survey of the New Classical Macroeconomics," *Economic Journal*, vol. 90 (March 1980).

Buiter, Willem H., and Geoffrey Woglom. "On Two Specifications of Asset Equilibrium in Macroeconomic Models: A Note," *Journal of Political Economy*, vol. 85 (April 1977).

Burger, Albert E. *The Money Supply Process*. Belmont, Calif.: Wadsworth, 1971.

Burger, Albert E., and Robert H. Rasche. "Revision of the Monetary Base," *Federal Reserve Bank of St. Louis Review*, vol. 59 (July 1977).

Burns, Arthur F. *Reflections of an Economic Policy Maker, Speeches and Congressional Statements: 1969–78*. Washington, D.C.: American Enterprise Institute for Public Policy Research, 1978.

Cagan, Philip. "Why Do We Use Money in Open Market Operations?," *Journal of Political Economy*, vol. 66 (February 1958).

————. *Determinants and Effects of Changes in the Stock of Money, 1875–1960*. Studies in Business Cycles 13. New York: National Bureau of Economic Research, 1965.

Chow, Gregory C. "How Much Could Be Gained by Optimal Stochastic Control Policies?," *Annals of Economic and Social Measurement*, vol. 1 (October 1972).

————. "Problems of Economic Policy from the Viewpoint of Optimal Control," *American Economic Review*, vol. 63 (December 1973).

————. *Analysis and Control of Dynamic Economic Systems*. New York: Wiley, 1975.

————. "Control Methods for Macroeconomic Policy Analysis," *American Economic Review*, vol. 65 (December 1975, *Papers and Proceedings, 1974*).

————. "Evaluation of Macroeconomic Policies by Stochastic Control Techniques," *International Economic Review*, vol. 10 (June 1978).

Christ, Carl F. "A Simple Macroeconomic Model with a Government Budget Restraint," *Journal of Political Economy*, vol. 76 (January/February 1968).

————. "Econometric Models of the Financial Sector," *Journal of Money, Credit and Banking*, vol. 3 (May 1971).

————. "Judging the Performance of Econometric Models of the U.S. Economy," *International Economic Review*, vol. 16 (February 1975).

Chrystal, K. Alec. "Demand for International Media of Exchange," *American Economic Review*, vol. 67 (December 1977).

Ciccolo, John H. "Is Short-run Monetary Control Feasible?," in Federal Reserve

Bank of New York, *Monetary Aggregates and Monetary Policy.* New York: Federal Reserve Bank of New York, 1974.

Claassen, Emil, and Pascal Salin, eds. *Stabilization Policies in Interdependent Economies.* Amsterdam and London: North-Holland, 1972.

——. *Recent Issues in International Monetary Economics.* Amsterdam: North-Holland, 1976.

Clower, Robert W., and Peter W. Howitt. "The Transactions Theory of the Demand for Money: A Reconsideration," *Journal of Political Economy,* vol. 86 (June 1978).

Connolly, Michael B., and Alexander K. Swoboda, eds. *International Trade and Money: The Geneva Essays.* Toronto: University of Toronto Press, 1973.

Cooper, Richard N. *The Economics of Interdependence: Economic Policy in the Atlantic Community.* New York: McGraw-Hill for the Council on Foreign Relations, 1968.

——. "Macroeconomic Policy Adjustment in Interdependent Economies," *Quarterly Journal of Economics,* vol. 83 (February 1969).

——. *Economic Mobility and National Economic Policy.* 1973 Wiksell Lectures. Stockholm: Almqvist and Wiksell, 1974.

——. "Worldwide or Regional Integration: Is There an Optimal Size of the Integrated Area?," *Economic Notes,* vol. 3 (Siena, Italy: Monte dei Paschi di Siena, 1974).

Corden, W. M. *Inflation, Exchange Rates and the World Economy.* Chicago: University of Chicago Press, 1977.

Craine, Roger, and Arthur Havenner. "A Stochastic Optimal Control Technique for Models with Estimated Coefficients," *Econometrica,* vol. 45 (May 1977).

——. "The Optimal Monetary Instrument: An Empirical Assessment." Special Studies Paper 100. Washington, D.C.: Board of Governors of the Federal Reserve System, July 1977.

——. "Optimal Monetary Policy under Uncertainty," Special Studies Paper 101. Washington, D.C.: Board of Governors of the Federal Reserve System, July 1977.

——. "Coefficient Uncertainty and Policy Aggressiveness: An Empirical Assessment." Special Studies Paper 105. Washington, D.C.: Board of Governors of the Federal Reserve System, February 1978.

Craine, Roger, Arthur Havenner, and James Berry. "Fixed Rules vs. Activism in the Conduct of Monetary Policy," *American Economic Review,* vol. 68 (December 1978).

Craine, Roger, Arthur Havenner, and Peter Tinsley. "Optimal Macroeconomic Control Policies," *Annals of Economic and Social Measurement,* vol. 5 (Spring 1976).

Crotty, James R. "Specification Error in Macro-econometric Models: The Influence of Policy Goals," *American Economic Review,* vol. 63 (December 1973).

Cruz, J. B., Jr. "Survey of Nash and Stackelberg Equilibrium Strategies in Dynamic Games," *Annals of Economic Social Measurement,* vol. 4 (Spring 1975).

Dam, Kenneth W. *The GATT: Law and International Economic Organization.* Chicago: University of Chicago Press, 1970.

Daniel, Betty C. "Analysis of Stabilization Policies in Open Economies Under Conditions of Inflation and Inflationary Expectations." Ph.D. dissertation, University of North Carolina, 1976.

Davis, Richard G. "Implementing Open Market Policy with Monetary Aggregate Objectives," in Federal Reserve Bank of New York, *Monetary Aggregates and Monetary Policy.* New York: Federal Reserve Bank of New York, 1974.

de Graaff, J. V. *Theoretical Welfare Economics.* London and New York: Cambridge University Press, 1957.

De Grauwe, Paul. "The Interaction of Monetary Policies in a Group of European Countries," *Journal of International Economics,* vol. 5 (August 1975).

————. *Monetary Interdependence and International Monetary Reform.* Lexington, Mass.: Lexington Books, 1976.

de Leeuw, Frank. "A Model of Financial Behavior," in James S. Duesenberry and others, eds., *The Brookings Quarterly Econometric Model of the United States.* Chicago: Rand McNally, 1965; Amsterdam: North-Holland, 1965.

————. "A Condensed Model of Financial Behavior," in James S. Duesenberry and others, eds., *The Brookings Model: Some Further Results.* Chicago, 1969.

DeRosa, Paul, and Gary H. Stern. "Monetary Control and the Federal Funds Rate," *Journal of Monetary Economics,* vol. 3 (April 1977).

de Vries, Margaret. *The International Monetary Fund, 1966–1971: The System Under Stress.* 2 vols. Washington, D.C.: International Monetary Fund, 1977.

Dornbusch, Rudiger. "Capital Mobility, Flexible Exchange Rates and Macroeconomic Equilibrium," in Emil Claassen and Pascal Salin, eds., *Recent Issues in International Monetary Economics.* Amsterdam: North-Holland, 1976.

————. "The Theory of Flexible Exchange Rates and Macroeconomic Policy," *Scandinavian Journal of Economics,* vol. 78 (1976).

————. "Expectations and Exchange-Rate Dynamics," *Journal of Political Economy,* vol. 84 (December 1976).

Dornbusch, Rudiger, and Paul Krugman. "Flexible Exchange Rates in the Short Run," *Brookings Papers on Economic Activity, 3:1976.*

Downs, Anthony. *An Economic Theory of Democracy.* New York: Harper and Row, 1957.

————. *Inside Bureaucracy.* Boston: Little, Brown, 1967.

Dunning, John H., ed. *Economic Analysis and the Multinational Enterprise.* London: Allen and Unwin, 1974.

Einzig, Paul, and Brian S. Quinn. *The Euro Dollar System: Practice and Theory of International Interest Rates.* 6th ed. New York: St. Martins Press, 1977.

Enzler, Jared, Lewis Johnson, and John Paulus. "Some Problems of Money Demand," *Brookings Papers on Economic Activity, 1:1976.*

Fair, Ray C. "On Modeling the Economic Linkages among Countries," in Rudiger Dornbusch and Jacob A. Frenkel, eds., *International Economic Policy: Theory and Evidence.* Baltimore: Johns Hopkins University Press, 1979.

Fair, Ray C., and Dwight M. Jaffee. "Methods of Estimation for Markets in Disequilibrium," *Econometrica,* vol. 40 (May 1972).

Fand, David I. "Some Issues in Monetary Economics," *Federal Reserve Bank of St. Louis Review,* vol. 52 (January 1970).

Farr, Helen T.; Lance Girton; Henry S. Terrell; and Thomas H. Turner. "Foreign Demand Deposits at Commercial Banks in the United States," in Board of Governors of the Federal Reserve System, *Improving the Monetary Aggregates: Staff Papers.* Washington, D.C.: Board of Governors of the Federal Reserve System, 1978.

Farr, Helen T., Richard D. Porter, and Eleanor M. Pruitt. "Demand Deposit Ownership Survey," in Board of Governors of the Federal Reserve System, *Improving the Monetary Aggregates: Staff Papers.* Washington, D.C.: Board of Governors of the Federal Reserve System, 1978.

Fase, M. M. G., and J. B. Kune. "The Demand for Money in Thirteen European and Non-European Countries," *Kredit und Kapital* (3:1975).

Federal Reserve Bank of Boston. *Controlling Monetary Aggregates.* Conference Series 1. Boston: Federal Reserve Bank of Boston, 1969.

―――. *Controlling Monetary Aggregates II: The Implementation.* Conference Series 9. Boston: Federal Reserve Bank of Boston, 1973.

―――. *Managed Exchange-Rate Flexibility: The Recent Experience.* Conference Series 20. Boston: Federal Reserve Bank of Boston, 1978.

Federal Reserve Bank of New York. *Monetary Aggregates and Monetary Policy.* New York: Federal Reserve Bank of New York, 1974.

Feige, Edgar L., and Douglas K. Pearce. "The Substitutability of Money and Near-Monies: A Survey of the Time-Series Evidence," *Journal of Economic Literature,* vol. 15 (June 1977).

Fellner, William. *Towards a Reconstruction of Macroeconomics: Problems of Theory and Policy.* Washington, D.C.: American Enterprise Institute for Public Policy Research, 1976.

Fischer, Stanley. "Long-term Contracts, Rational Expectations, and the Optimal Money Supply Rule," *Journal of Political Economy,* vol. 85 (February 1977).

————, ed. *Rational Expectations and Economic Policy.* Chicago: University of Chicago Press, 1980.

Fisher, Franklin M. "On the Independent Use of Two or More Sets of Policy Variables," *Journal of Political Economy,* vol. 75 (February 1967).

Fisher, Franklin M., and Albert Ando. "Two Theorems on *Ceteris Paribus* in the Analysis of Dynamic Systems," *American Political Science Review,* vol. 56 (March 1962).

Fleming, J. Marcus. "Domestic Financial Policies Under Fixed and Floating Exchange Rates," *IMF Staff Papers,* vol. 9 (November 1962).

————. "Targets and Instruments," *IMF Staff Papers,* vol. 15 (November 1968).

————. "The SDR: Some Problems and Possibilities," *IMF Staff Papers,* vol. 18 (March 1971).

Foley, Duncan. "On Two Specifications of Asset Equilibrium in Macroeconomic Models," *Journal of Political Economy,* vol. 82 (April 1975).

Fox, Karl A., Jati K. Sengupta, and Erik Thorbecke. *The Theory of Quantitative Economic Policy with Applications to Economic Growth, Stabilization and Planning.* 2d ed. Amsterdam: North-Holland, 1973.

Freedman, Charles. "Micro Theory of International Financial Intermediation," *American Economic Review,* vol. 67 (February 1977, *Papers and Proceedings, 1976).*

————. "A Model of the Eurodollar Market," *Journal of Monetary Economics,* vol. 3 (April 1977).

Freeman, George. "Recent Innovations in the Bank of Canada's Approach to Monetary Policy." Paper prepared for conference on International Financial Relations. Geneva, Switzerland: Graduate Institute of International Studies, December 1976.

Frenkel, Jacob A. "Adjustment Mechanisms and the Monetary Approach to the Balance of Payments: A Doctrinal Perspective," in Emil Claassen and Pascal Salin, eds., *Recent Issues in International Monetary Economics.* Amsterdam: North-Holland, 1976.

Frenkel, Jacob A., and Kenneth W. Clements. "Exchange Rates in the 1920's: A Monetary Approach." Working Paper 290. New York: National Bureau of Economic Research, October 1978.

Frenkel, Jacob A., and Harry G. Johnson, eds. *The Monetary Approach to the Balance of Payments.* Toronto and Buffalo: University of Toronto Press, 1976.

Frenkel, Jacob A., and Richard M. Levich. "Covered Interest Arbitrage: Unexploited Profits?" *Journal of Political Economy,* vol. 83 (April 1975).

Friedman, Benjamin M. *Economic Stabilization Policy: Methods in Optimization.* Amsterdam and Oxford: North-Holland, 1975; New York: American Elsevier, 1975.

————. "Targets, Instruments, and Indicators of Monetary Policy," *Journal of Monetary Economics,* vol. 1 (October 1975).

————. "Financial Flow Variables and the Short-Run Determination of Long-Term Interest Rates," *Journal of Political Economy,* vol. 85 (August 1977).

————. "The Inefficiency of Short-Run Monetary Targets for Monetary Policy," *Brookings Papers on Economic Activity, 2:1977.*

————. "Crowding Out or Crowding In? Economic Consequences of Financing Government Deficits," *Brookings Papers on Economic Activity, 3:1978.*

————. "Optimal Expectations and the Extreme Information Assumptions of Rational Expectations Macromodels," *Journal of Monetary Economics,* vol. 5 (January 1979).

Friedman, Benjamin M., and Kenneth C. Froewiss. "Bank Behavior in the Brunner-Meltzer Model," *Journal of Monetary Economics,* vol. 3 (April 1977).

Friedman, James. *Oligopoly and the Theory of Games.* Amsterdam: North-Holland, 1977.

————. "Cournot, Bowley, Stackelberg and Fellner, and the Evolution of the Reaction Function," in Bela Belassa and Richard Nelson, eds., *Economic Progress, Private Values, and Public Policy: Essays in Honor of William Fellner.* Amsterdam: North-Holland, 1977.

Friedman, Milton. "The Case for Flexible Exchange Rates," in Friedman, *Essays in Positive Economics.* Chicago and London: University of Chicago Press, 1953.

————. "The Effects of a Full-Employment Policy on Economic Stability: A Formal Analysis," in Friedman, *Essays in Positive Economics.* Chicago and London: University of Chicago Press, 1953.

————. "The Quantity Theory of Money: A Restatement," in Friedman, ed., *Studies in the Quantity Theory of Money.* Chicago and London: University of Chicago Press, 1956. (Reprinted in Friedman, *The Optimum Quantity of Money and Other Essays.* Hawthorne, N.Y.: Aldine, 1969.)

————. *A Program for Monetary Stability.* New York: Fordham University Press, 1959.

————. "Should There Be an Independent Monetary Authority?" in Leland Yeager, ed., *In Search of a Monetary Constitution.* Cambridge: Harvard University Press, 1962.

————. "A Theoretical Framework for Monetary Analysis," *Journal of Political Economy,* vol. 78 (March/April 1970).

————. "Comment on Tobin," *Quarterly Journal of Economics,* vol. 84 (May 1970).

Friedman, Milton, and Anna Jacobson Schwartz. *A Monetary History of the United States, 1867–1960.* Studies in Business Cycles 12. Princeton: Princeton University ... s for the National Bureau of Economic Research, 1963.

————. *Monetary Statistics of the United States: Estimates, Sources, Methods.* Studies in Business Cycles 20. New York: National Bureau of Economic Research, 1970.

Frohlich, Norman, Joe A. Oppenheimer, and Oran R. Young. *Political Leadership and Collective Goods.* Princeton: Princeton University Press, 1971.

Fromm, Gary, and Lawrence R. Klein. "The NBER/NSF Model Comparison Seminar: An Analysis of Results," *Annals of Economic and Social Measurement,* vol. 5 (Winter 1976).

Frost, Peter A. "Short-Run Fluctuations in the Money Multiplier and Monetary Control," *Journal of Money, Credit and Banking,* vol. 9 (February 1977).

Garbade, Kenneth D. *Discretionary Control of Aggregate Economic Activity.* Lexington, Mass.: Lexington Books, 1975.

Gilbert, J. C. "The Demand for Money: The Development of an Economic Concept," *Journal of Political Economy,* vol. 61 (April 1953).

Girton, Lance, and Dale W. Henderson. "A Two-Country Model of Financial Capital Movements as Stock Adjustments with Emphasis on the Effects of Central Bank Policy." International Finance Discussion Paper 24. Washington, D.C.: Board of Governors of the Federal Reserve System, March 1973.

————. "Financial Capital Movements and Central Bank Behavior in a Two Country, Short-Run Portfolio Balance Model," *Journal of Monetary Economics,* vol. 2 (January 1976).

————. "Critical Determinants of the Effectiveness of Monetary Policy in the Open Economy," in *Bank Credit, Money and Inflation in Open Economies,* supplement to *Kredit und Kapital* (3:1977).

————. "Central Bank Operations in Foreign and Domestic Assets under Fixed and Flexible Exchange Rates," in Peter B. Clark, Dennis E. Logue, and Richard J. Sweeney, eds., *The Effects of Exchange Rate Adjustments.* Washington, D.C.: Government Printing Office, 1977.

Girton, Lance, and Don Roper. "A Monetary Model of Exchange Market Pressure Applied to the Post-War Canadian Experience," *American Economic Review,* vol. 67 (September 1977).

Goldberger, A. S., A. L. Nagar, and H. S. Odeh. "The Covariance Matrices of Reduced-Form Coefficients and of Forecasts for a Structural Econometric Model," *Econometrica,* vol. 29 (October 1961).

Goldfeld, Stephen M. "The Demand for Money Revisited," *Brookings Papers on Economic Activity,* 3:1973.

————. "The Case of the Missing Money," *Brookings Papers on Economic Activity,* 3:1976.

Goldfeld, Stephen M., and Alan S. Blinder. "Some Implications of Endoge Stabilization Policy," *Brookings Papers on Economic Activity, 3:1972.*

Goodhart, C. A. E. *Money, Information and Uncertainty.* London and Basingstoke: Macmillan, 1975.

Grassman, Sven. *Exchange Reserves and the Financial Structure of Foreign Trade.* Lexington, Mass.: Lexington Books, 1973.

———. "A Fundamental Symmetry in International Payment Patterns," *Journal of International Economics,* vol. 3 (May 1973).

———. "Currency Distribution and Forward Cover in Foreign Trade: Sweden Revisited, 1973," *Journal of International Economics,* vol. 6 (May 1976).

Gurley, John G., and Edward S. Shaw. *Money in a Theory of Finance.* Washington, D.C.: Brookings Institution, 1960.

Halm, George N., ed. *Approaches to Greater Flexibility in Exchange Rates: The Burgenstock Papers.* Princeton: Princeton University Press, 1970.

Halperin, Morton H., with Priscilla Clapp and Arnold Kanter. *Bureaucratic Politics and Foreign Policy.* Washington, D.C.: Brookings Institution, 1974.

Hamada, Koichi. "Alternative Exchange Rate Systems and the Interdependence of Monetary Policies," in Robert Z. Aliber, ed., *National Monetary Policies and the International Financial System.* Chicago: University of Chicago Press, 1974.

———. "A Strategic Analysis of Monetary Interdependence," *Journal of Political Economy,* vol. 84 (August 1976).

———. "On the Political Economy of Monetary Integration: A Public Economics Approach," in Robert Z. Aliber, ed., *The Political Economy of Monetary Reform.* New York: Macmillan, 1977.

———. "Macroeconomic Strategy and Coordination under Alternative Exchange Rates," in Rudiger Dornbusch and Jacob A. Frenkel, eds., *International Economic Policy: Theory and Evidence.* Baltimore: Johns Hopkins University Press, 1979.

Hamburger, Michael J. "Behavior of the Money Stock: Is There a Puzzle?" *Journal of Monetary Economics,* vol. 3 (July 1977).

Hansen, Bent. "On the Effects of Fiscal and Monetary Policy: A Taxonomic Discussion," *American Economic Review,* vol. 58 (September 1973).

Helliwell, John F. "Trade, Capital Flows, and Migration as Channels for International Transmission of Stabilization Policies," in Federal Reserve Bank of Boston, *International Aspects of Stabilization Policies.* Conference Series 12. Boston: Federal Reserve Bank of Boston, 1974.

———. "Adjustment Under Fixed and Flexible Exchange Rates," in Peter B. Kenen, ed., *International Trade and Finance: Frontiers for Research.* Cambridge, Eng., and New York: Cambridge University Press, 1975.

Helliwell, John F., and Robert McRae. "The Interdependence of Monetary, Debt, and Fiscal Policies in an International Setting," in Robert Z. Aliber, ed., *The Political Economy of Monetary Reform.* London: Macmillan, 1977.

Hendershott, Patric H. *A Flow-of-Funds Financial Model: Estimation and Application to Financial Policies and Reform.* Lexington, Mass: Lexington Books, 1977.

Henderson, Dale W. "Modeling the Interdependence of National Money and Capital Markets," *American Economic Review,* vol. 67 (February 1977, *Papers and Proceedings, 1976*).

―――. "Financial Policies in Open Economies," *American Economic Review,* vol. 69 (May 1979, *Papers and Proceedings, 1978*).

―――. "The Dynamic Effects of Exchange Market Intervention Policy: Two Extreme Views and a Synthesis," in *The Economics of Flexible Exchange Rates,* supplement to *Kredit und Kapital* (6:1980).

Hernández-Catá, Ernesto; Howard Howe; Sung Kwack; Guy Stevens; Richard Berner; and Peter Clark. "Monetary Policy under Alternative Exchange-Rate Regimes: Simulations with a Multi-Country Model," in Federal Reserve Bank of Boston, *Managed Exchange-Rate Flexibility: The Recent Experience.* Conference Series 20. Boston: Federal Reserve Bank of Boston, 1978.

Hester, Donald D., and James L. Pierce. *Bank Management and Portfolio Behavior.* Cowles Foundation for Research in Economics Monograph 25. New Haven: Yale University Press, 1975.

Hewson, John, and Eisuke Sakakibara. *The Eurocurrency Markets and Their Implications.* Lexington, Mass.: Lexington Books, 1975.

Hicks, John R. "A Suggestion for Simplifying the Theory of Money," *Economica,* vol. 2 (1935). Reprinted in American Economic Association, *Readings in Monetary Theory.* Philadelphia: Blakiston, 1951.

Hirsch, Fred. "SDRs and the Working of the Gold Exchange Standard," *IMF Staff Papers,* vol. 18 (July 1971).

―――. *Social Limits to Growth.* Cambridge: Harvard University Press, 1976.

―――. "The Bagehot Problem," *Manchester School,* vol. 45 (September 1977).

―――. "The Ideological Underlay of Inflation," in Fred Hirsch and John H. Goldthorpe, eds., *The Political Economy of Inflation.* London: Martin Robertson, 1978.

Hodgman, Donald R. *National Monetary Policies and International Monetary Cooperation.* Boston: Little, Brown, 1974.

Holbik, Karel, ed. *Monetary Policy in Twelve Industrial Countries.* Boston: Federal Reserve Bank of Boston, 1973.

Holmes, Alan R., and others. "The Strategy of Monetary Control," *Federal Reserve Bulletin,* vol. 62 (May 1976).

Holmes, Alan R., Paul Meek, and Rudolf Thunberg. "Open Market Operations in the Early 1970's: Excerpts from Reports Prepared in 1971, 1972, and 1973," in

Federal Reserve Bank of New York, *Monetary Aggregates and Monetary Policy*. New York: Federal Reserve Bank of New York, 1974.

Horsefield, J. Keith, and Margaret de Vries. *The International Monetary Fund, 1945-1965: Twenty Years of International Monetary Cooperation*. 3 vols. Washington, D.C.: International Monetary Fund, 1969.

Horwich, George, ed. *Monetary Process and Policy: A Symposium*. Homewood, Ill.: Richard D. Irwin, 1967.

Howe, Howard; Ernesto Hernández-Catá; Guy Stevens; Richard Berner; Peter Clark; and Sung Y. Kwack. "Assessing International Interdependence with a Multi-Country Model." International Finance Discussion Paper 138. Washington, D.C.: Board of Governors of the Federal Reserve System, April 1979.

Infante, Ettore F., and Jerome L. Stein. "Does Fiscal Policy Matter?" *Journal of Monetary Economics,* vol. 2 (November 1976).

International Monetary Fund. *International Reserves: Needs and Availability*. Washington, D.C.: IMF, 1970.

————. *International Monetary Reform: Documents of the Committee of Twenty*. Washington, D.C.: IMF, 1974.

————. *The Monetary Approach to the Balance of Payments*. Washington, D.C.: IMF, 1977.

Isard, Peter. *Exchange-Rate Determination: A Survey of Popular Views and Recent Models*. Princeton Studies in International Finance 42. Princeton: Princeton University Press, 1978.

————. "Expected and Unexpected Changes in Exchange Rates: The Roles of Relative Price Levels, Balance-of-Payments Factors, Interest Rates and Risk." International Finance Discussion Paper 156. Washington, D.C.: Board of Governors of the Federal Reserve System, April 1980.

Janssen, J. M. L., L. F. Pau, and A. Straszak, eds. *Models and Decision Making in National Economies*. Proceedings of the Second International Conference on Dynamic Modelling and Control of National Economies, Vienna, 1977. Amsterdam: North-Holland, 1979.

Johnson, Harry G. "The Case for Flexible Exchange Rates, 1969," in George N. Halm, ed., *Approaches to Greater Flexibility in Exchange Rates: The Burgenstock Papers*. Princeton: Princeton University Press, 1970.

Johnson, Harry G., and Alexander K. Swoboda, eds. *The Economics of Common Currencies*. London: Allen and Unwin, 1973.

Kahn, Alfred E. "The Tyranny of Small Decisions: Market Failures, Imperfections, and the Limits of Economics," *Kyklos,* vol. 19 (1966).

Kalchbrenner, John H., and Peter A. Tinsley. "On the Use of Optimal Control in the Design of Monetary Policy." Special Studies Paper 76. Washington, D.C.: Board of Governors of the Federal Reserve System, July 1975.

————. "On the Use of Feedback Control in the Design of Aggregate Monetary Policy," *American Economic Review,* vol. 66 (May 1976, *Papers and Proceedings, 1975*).

Kalchbrenner, John H., and Peter A. Tinsley, with James Berry and Bonnie Garrett. "On Filtering Auxiliary Information in Short-Run Monetary Policy," in Karl Brunner and Allan H. Meltzer, eds., *Optimal Policies, Control Theory and Technology Exports.* Carnegie-Rochester Conference Series 7. Amsterdam: North-Holland, 1977.

Kareken, John H. "Commercial Banks and the Supply of Money: A Market-Determined Demand Deposit Rate," *Federal Reserve Bulletin,* vol. 53 (October 1967).

————. "The Optimum Monetary Instrument Variable," *Journal of Money, Credit and Banking,* vol. 2 (August 1970).

Kareken, John H., and others. "Determining the Optimum Monetary Instrument Variable," in Board of Governors of the Federal Reserve System, *Open Market Policies and Operating Procedures: Staff Studies.* Washington, D.C.: Board of Governors of the Federal Reserve System, July 1971.

Kareken, John H., Thomas Muench, and Neil Wallace. "Optimal Open Market Strategy: The Use of Information Variables," *American Economic Review,* vol. 63 (March 1973).

Kemp, Murray C. *The Pure Theory of International Trade.* Englewood Cliffs, N.J.: Prentice-Hall, 1964.

Kendrick, David. "Applications of Control Theory to Macroeconomics," *Annals of Economic and Social Measurement,* vol. 5 (1976).

Kenen, Peter B. "The Theory of Optimum Currency Areas: An Eclectic View," in Robert A. Mundell and Alexander K. Swoboda, eds., *Monetary Problems of the International Economy.* Chicago: University of Chicago Press, 1969.

————, ed. *International Trade and Finance: Frontiers for Research.* Cambridge, Eng., and New York: Cambridge University Press, 1975.

————. *Capital Mobility and Financial Integration: A Survey.* Princeton Studies in International Finance 39. Princeton: Princeton University Press, 1976.

Keohane, Robert O., and Joseph S. Nye, Jr. *Transnational Relations and World Politics.* Cambridge: Harvard University Press, 1972.

————. *Power and Interdependence: World Politics in Transition.* Boston: Little, Brown, 1977.

Keynes, John Maynard. *The General Theory of Employment, Interest and Money.* London: Macmillan, 1936.

Kindleberger, Charles P. "Government and International Trade." Princeton Essays in International Finance 129. Princeton: Princeton University Press, 1978.

————. "Dominance and Leadership in the International Economy: Exploitation, Public Goods and Free Rides," in Centre National de la Recherche Scientifique, *Hommage à François Perroux*. Grenoble: University Press of Grenoble, 1978.

Klein, Lawrence R., and Edwin Burmeister, eds. *Econometric Model Performance: Comparative Simulation Studies of the U.S. Economy*. Philadelphia: University of Pennsylvania Press, 1976.

Kouri, Pentti. "The Exchange Rate and the Balance of Payments in the Short Run and in the Long Run: A Monetary Approach," *Scandinavian Journal of Economics*, vol. 78 (1976).

Kouri, Pentti, and Jorge Braga de Macedo. "Exchange Rates and the International Adjustment Process," *Brookings Papers on Economic Activity, 1:1978*.

Krause, Lawrence B., and Walter S. Salant, eds. *European Monetary Unification and Its Meaning for the United States*. Washington, D.C.: Brookings Institution, 1973.

————, eds. *Worldwide Inflation: Theory and Recent Experience*. Washington, D.C: Brookings Institution, 1977.

Kubarych, Roger M. *Foreign Exchange Markets in the United States*. New York: Federal Reserve Bank of New York, 1978.

Kuhn, Thomas S. *The Structure of Scientific Revolutions*. 2d ed. Chicago: University of Chicago Press, 1970.

Kuznets, Simon. *Modern Economic Growth: Rate, Structure, and Spread*. Studies in Comparative Economics 7. New Haven: Yale University Press, 1966.

————. "Quantitative Aspects of the Economic Growth of Nations; X. Level and Structure of Foreign Trade: Long-Term Trends," *Economic Development and Cultural Change*, vol. 15 (January 1967).

Kydland, Finn E. "Noncooperative and Dominant Player Solutions in Discrete Dynamic Games," *International Economic Review*, vol. 16 (June 1975).

————. "Decentralized Stabilization Policies: Optimization and the Assignment Problem," *Annals of Economic and Social Measurement*, vol. 5 (Spring 1976).

Kydland, Finn E., and Edward C. Prescott. "Rules Rather Than Discretion: The Inconsistency of Optimal Plans," *Journal of Political Economy*, vol. 85 (June 1977).

Laidler, David E. W. *The Demand for Money: Theories and Evidence*. Scranton: International Textbook, 1969.

Laursen, Svend, and Lloyd A. Metzler. "Flexible Exchange Rates and the Theory of Employment," *Review of Economics and Statistics*, vol. 32 (November 1950).

LeRoy, Stephen F. "Efficient Use of Current Information in Short-Run Monetary Control." Special Studies Paper 66. Washington, D.C.: Board of Governors of the Federal Reserve System, September 1975.

LeRoy, Stephen, F., and David E. Lindsey. "Determining the Monetary Instrument: A Diagrammatic Exposition," *American Economic Review,* vol. 68 (December 1978).

LeRoy, Stephen F., and Roger N. Waud. "Observability, Measurement Error, and the Optimal Use of Information for Monetary Policy. Special Studies Paper 72. Washington, D.C.: Board of Governors of the Federal Reserve System, December 1975.

Levin, Jay H. "Decentralization vs. Coordination of Monetary Policies Between the United States and the Rest of the World Under Flexible Exchange Rates." Wayne Economic Papers 4. Wayne State University, Department of Economics, January 1977.

Lieberman, Charles. "The Transactions Demand for Money and Technological Change," *Review of Economics and Statistics,* vol. 59 (August 1977).

Lindbeck, Assar. "Endogenous Politicians and the Theory of Economic Policy." Seminar Paper 35. Stockholm: Institute for International Economic Studies, October 1973.

―――. "Stabilization Policy in Open Economies with Endogenous Politicians," *American Economic Review,* vol. 66 (May 1976, *Papers and Proceedings, 1975*).

Lucas, Robert E., Jr. "Econometric Policy Evaluation: A Critique," in Karl Brunner and Allan H. Meltzer, eds., *The Phillips Curve and Labor Markets.* Carnegie-Rochester Conference Series 1. Amsterdam: North-Holland, 1976.

―――. "Rules, Discretion, and the Role of the Economic Adviser," in Stanley Fischer, ed., *Rational Expectations and Economic Policy.* Chicago: University of Chicago Press, 1980.

Luce, R. Duncan, and Howard Raiffa. *Games and Decisions: Introduction and Critical Survey.* New York: Wiley, 1957.

McCallum, Bennett T. "Price Level Adjustments and the Rational Expectations Approach to Macroeconomic Stabilization Policy," *Journal of Money, Credit and Banking,* vol. 10 (November 1978).

McCallum, Bennett T., and William G. Dewald, eds., papers, conference on Rational Expectations, American Enterprise Institute, January 1980, supplement to *Journal of Money, Credit and Banking* (in press).

Machlup, Fritz. *A History of Thought on Economic Integration.* New York: Columbia University Press, 1977.

McKinnon, Ronald I. "Optimum Currency Areas," *American Economic Review,* vol. 53 (September 1963).

―――. *Private and Official International Money: The Case for the Dollar.* Princeton Essays in International Finance 74. Princeton: Princeton University Press, 1969.

―――. *The Eurocurrency Market.* Princeton Essays in International Finance 125. Princeton: Princeton University Press, 1977.

McKinnon, Ronald I., and Wallace E. Oates. *The Implications of International Economic Integration for Monetary Fiscal and Exchange-Rate Policy.* Princeton Studies in International Finance 16. Princeton: Princeton University Press, 1966.

March, James G., and Herbert A. Simon, with Harold Guetzkow. *Organizations.* New York: Wiley, 1958; London: Chapman and Hall, 1958.

Mathieson, Donald J. "The Impact of Monetary and Fiscal Policy Under Flexible Exchange Rates and Alternative Expectations Structures," *IMF Staff Papers,* vol. 24 (November 1977).

Mayer, Helmut W. "The BIS Concept of the Eurocurrency Market," *Euromoney,* vol. 7 (May 1976).

————. "The BIS Statistics of International Banking: Coverage, Netting-out Methods, Problems of Interpretation." Paper prepared for the 1979 conference of the International Association for Research in Income and Wealth.

————. *Credit and Liquidity Creation in the International Banking Sector,* Economic Papers 1. Basle, Switzerland: Bank for International Settlements, November 1979.

Mayer, Thomas. "The Structure and Operation of the Federal Reserve System: Some Needed Reforms," in U.S. Congress, House of Representatives, Committee on Banking, Currency and Housing, *Financial Institutions and the Nation's Economy.* Washington, D.C.: Government Printing Office, 1976.

————. *The Structure of Monetarism.* New York: Norton, 1978.

Meade, James E. *The Balance of Payments.* Vol. 1: *The Theory of International Economic Policy.* London: Oxford University Press, 1951.

Miller, Merton H., and Daniel Orr. "A Model of the Demand for Money by Firms," *Quarterly Journal of Economics,* vol. 80 (August 1966).

————. "The Demand for Money by Firms: Extensions of Analytic Results," *Journal of Finance,* vol. 23 (December 1968).

Mints, Lloyd W. *A History of Banking Theory in Great Britain and the United States.* Chicago: University of Chicago Press, 1945.

Modigliani, Franco, Robert Rasche, and J. Philip Cooper. "Central Bank Policy, the Money Supply and the Short Term Rate of Interest," *Journal of Money, Credit and Banking,* vol. 2 (May 1970).

Morgenstern, Oskar. "Thirteen Critical Points in Contemporary Economic Theory: An Interpretation," *Journal of Economic Literature,* vol. 10 (December 1972).

Mosley, Paul. "Towards a 'Satisficing' Theory of Economic Policy," *Economic Journal,* vol. 86 (March 1976).

Muellbauer, John, and Richard Portes. "Macroeconomic Models with Quantity Rationing," *Economic Journal,* vol. 88 (December 1978).

Muench, Thomas, and Neil Wallace. "On Stabilization Policy: Goals and Models," *American Economic Review,* vol. 64 (May 1974, *Papers and Proceedings, 1973*).

Mundell, Robert. *International Economics*. New York: Macmillan, 1968.

Mundell, Robert A., and Alexander K. Swoboda, eds. *Monetary Problems of the International Economy*. Chicago and London: University of Chicago Press, 1969.

Mussa, Michael. "A Monetary Approach to Balance-of-Payments Analysis," *Journal of Money, Credit and Banking*, vol. 6 (August 1974).

―――. "The Exchange Rate, The Balance of Payments and Monetary and Fiscal Policy Under a Regime of Controlled Floating," *Scandinavian Journal of Economics*, vol. 78 (1976).

―――. "Macroeconomic Interdependence and the Exchange Rate Regime," in Rudiger Dornbusch and Jacob A. Frenkel, eds., *International Economic Policy: Theory and Evidence*. Baltimore: Johns Hopkins University Press, 1979.

―――. "Empirical Regularities in the Behavior of Exchange Rates and Theories of the Foreign Exchange Market," in Karl Brunner and Allan H. Meltzer, eds., *Policies for Employment, Prices, and Exchange Rates*. Carnegie-Rochester Conference Series 11. Amsterdam: North-Holland, 1979.

Neary, J. Peter, and Joseph E. Stiglitz. "Towards a Reconstruction of Keynesian Economics: Expectations and Constrained Equilibria." Working Paper 376. New York: National Bureau of Economic Research, August 1979.

Niehans, Jürg. "Monetary and Fiscal Policies in Open Economies Under Fixed Exchange Rates: An Optimizing Approach," *Journal of Political Economy*, vol. 76 (July/August 1968).

―――. "Some Doubts About the Efficacy of Monetary Policy Under Flexible Exchange Rates," *Journal of International Economics*, vol. 5 (August 1975).

―――. *The Theory of Money*. Baltimore and London: Johns Hopkins University Press, 1978.

Niehans, Jürg, and John Hewson. "The Eurodollar Market and Monetary Theory," *Journal of Money, Credit and Banking*, vol. 8 (February 1976).

Nyberg, Lars, and Staffan Viotti. "Controllability and the Theory of Economic Policy: A Critical View," *Journal of Public Economics*, vol. 9 (1978).

Okun, Arthur M. *The Political Economy of Prosperity*. Washington, D.C.: Brookings Institution, 1970.

―――. "Fiscal-Monetary Activism: Some Analytical Issues," *Brookings Papers on Economic Activity*, 1:1972.

―――. *Prices and Quantities: A Macroeconomic Analysis*. Washington, D.C.: Brookings Institution, forthcoming.

―――. "Rational-Expectations with Misperceptions and a Theory of the Business Cycle," in Bennett T. McCallum and William G. Dewald, eds., papers, conference on Rational Expectations, American Enterprise Institute, January 1980, supplement to *Journal of Money, Credit and Banking* (in press).

Olson, Mancur. "The Principle of 'Fiscal Equivalence': The Division of Responsibilities Among Different Levels of Government," *American Economic Review,* vol. 59 (May 1969, *Papers and Proceedings, 1968*).

———. *The Logic of Collective Action: Public Goods and the Theory of Groups.* 2d ed. Cambridge: Harvard University Press, 1971.

Olson, Mancur, and Richard Zeckhauser. "An Economic Theory of Alliances," *Review of Economics and Statistics,* vol. 48 (August 1966).

Organization for Economic Cooperation and Development. *Monetary Policy in Japan.* Monetary Studies Series. Paris: OECD, 1972.

———. *Monetary Policy in Italy.* Monetary Studies Series. Paris: OECD, 1973.

———. *Monetary Policy in the United States.* Monetary Studies Series. Paris: OECD, 1974.

———. *Monetary Policy in Germany.* Monetary Studies Series. Paris: OECD, 1974.

———. *Monetary Policy in France.* Monetary Studies Series. Paris: OECD, 1974.

———. *The Role of Monetary Policy in Demand Management: The Experience of Six Major Countries.* Monetary Studies Series. Paris: OECD, 1975.

———. *Monetary Targets and Inflation Control.* Monetary Studies Series. Paris: OECD, 1979.

Parkin, Michael, Ian Richards, and George Zis. "The Determination and Control of the World Money Supply Under Fixed Exchange Rates, 1961–71," *Manchester School of Economics and Social Studies,* no. 3 (September 1975).

Patinkin, Don. *Money, Interest, and Prices: An Integration of Monetary and Value Theory.* 2d ed. New York: Harper and Row, 1965.

Pau, Louis F. "Research on Optimal Control Adapted to Macro- and Microeconomics: A Survey," *Journal of Economic Dynamics and Control,* vol. 1 (August 1979).

Phelps, Edmund S., and John B. Taylor. "Stabilizing Powers of Monetary Policy Under Rational Expectations," *Journal of Political Economy,* vol. 85 (February 1977).

Pierce, James. "The Myth of Congressional Oversight of Monetary Policy," *Journal of Monetary Economics,* vol. 4 (April 1978).

Pierce, James L., and Thomas D. Thomson. "Some Issues in Controlling the Stock of Money," in Federal Reserve Bank of Boston, *Controlling Monetary Aggregates II: The Implementation.* Boston: Federal Reserve Bank of Boston, 1973.

Pindyck, Robert S. "The Cost of Conflicting Objectives in Policy Formulation," *Annals of Economic and Social Measurement,* vol. 5 (Spring 1976).

Poole, William. "Optimal Choice of Monetary Policy Instruments in a Simple Stochastic Macro Model," *Quarterly Journal of Economics,* vol. 84 (May 1970).

————. "Rulers-of-Thumb for Guiding Monetary Policy," in Board of Governors of the Federal Reserve System, *Open Market Policies and Operating Procedures—Staff Studies*. Washington, D.C.: Board of Governors of the Federal Reserve System, 1971.

————. "Interpreting the Fed's Monetary Targets," *Brookings Papers on Economic Activity, 1:1976*.

Poole, William, and Charles Lieberman. "Improving Monetary Control," *Brookings Papers on Economic Activity, 2:1972*.

Porter, Richard C. "A Model of Bank Portfolio Selection," *Yale Economic Essays*, vol. 1 (Fall 1961). (Reprinted in Donald D. Hester and James Tobin, eds., *Financial Markets and Economic Activity*. Cowles Foundation for Research in Economics Monograph 21. New York: Wiley, 1967.)

Prescott, Edward C. "The Multi-Period Control Problem Under Uncertainty," *Econometrica*, vol. 40 (November 1972).

————. "Should Control Theory Be Used for Economic Stabilization?" in Karl Brunner and Allan H. Meltzer, eds., *Optimal Policies, Control Theory and Technology Exports*. Carnegie-Rochester Conference Series 7. Amsterdam: North-Holland, 1977.

Purvis, Douglas D. "Dynamic Models of Portfolio Behavior, *American Economic Review*, vol. 68 (June 1978).

Roberts, Steven M. "Congressional Oversight of Monetary Policy," *Journal of Monetary Economics*, vol. 4 (August 1978).

Roberts, Steven M., and Marvin S. Margolis. "Control of the Money Stock with a Reserve Aggregate," *Journal of Money, Credit and Banking*, vol. 8 (November 1976).

Roper, Don. "Macroeconomic Policies and the Distribution of the World Money Supply," *Quarterly Journal of Economics*, vol. 85 (February 1971).

————. "The Role of the Demand for Money versus Neutrality in Monetarist Thought," September 1975, unpublished manuscript. Earlier version, "Two Ingredients of Monetarism in an International Setting," *Intermountain Economic Review*, vol. 6 (Spring 1975).

Sachs, Jeffrey D. "Wages, Flexible Exchange Rates, and Macroeconomic Policy," *Quarterly Journal of Economics*, vol. 94 (June 1980).

Salant, Stephen W. "Exhaustible Resources and Industrial Structure: A Nash-Cournot Approach to the World Oil Market," *Journal of Political Economy*, vol. 84 (October 1976).

Salant, Walter S. "International Transmission of Inflation" and "A Supranational Approach to the Analysis of Worldwide Inflation," in Lawrence B. Krause and Walter S. Salant, eds., *Worldwide Inflation: Theory and Recent Experience*. Washington, D.C.: Brookings Institution, 1977.

Sandell, Nils R., Jr.; Pravin Varaiya; Michael Athans; and Michael G. Safonov. "Survey of Decentralized Control Methods for Large Scale Systems," *IEEE Transactions on Automatic Control,* vol. AC-23 (April 1978).

Sargent, Thomas J., and Neil Wallace. " 'Rational' Expectations, the Optimal Monetary Instrument and the Optimal Money Supply Rule," *Journal of Political Economy,* vol. 83 (April 1975).

―――. "Rational Expectations and the Theory of Economic Policy," *Journal of Monetary Economics,* vol. 2 (April 1976).

Schelling, Thomas C. *The Strategy of Conflict.* Oxford: Oxford University Press, Galaxy Books, 1963.

―――. "On the Ecology of Micromotives," in Robin Marris, ed., *The Corporate Society.* New York: Macmillan, 1974.

Scitovsky, Tibor. *Money and the Balance of Payments.* Chicago: Rand McNally, 1969.

Sen, Amartya K. *Collective Choice and Social Welfare.* London: Oliver and Boyd, 1970.

―――. *On Economic Inequality.* London: Oxford University Press, 1973.

Shafer, Jeffrey R. "The Macroeconomic Behavior of a Large Open Economy with a Floating Exchange Rate." Ph. D. dissertation, Yale University, 1976.

Shubik, Martin. *Strategy and Market Structure: Competition, Oligopoly and the Theory of Games.* New York: Wiley, 1959.

―――. "Game Theory Models and Methods in Political Economy," in Kenneth Arrow and Michael D. Intriligator, eds., *Handbook of Mathematical Economics.* Amsterdam: North-Holland, 1980.

Shupp, Franklin R. "Uncertainty and Optimal Stabilization Policy," *Journal of Public Economics,* vol. 6 (October 1976).

Silber, William L. *Portfolio Behavior of Financial Institutions: An Empirical Study with Implications for Monetary Policy, Interest-Rate Determination, and Financial Model Building.* New York: Holt, Rinehart, and Winston, 1970.

Simon, Herbert A. "Theories of Decision-Making in Economics and Behavioral Science," *American Economic Review,* vol. 49 (June 1959).

Simon, Herbert A., and Albert Ando. "Aggregation of Variables in Dynamic Systems," in Albert Ando, Franklin Fisher, and Herbert A. Simon, eds., *Essays on the Structure of Social Science Models.* Cambridge: Massachusetts Institute of Technology Press, 1963.

Smith, Gary. "Dynamic Models of Portfolio Behavior: Comment on Purvis," *American Economic Review,* vol. 68 (June 1978).

Solomon, Robert. *The International Monetary System, 1945-1976: An Insider's View.* New York: Harper and Row, 1977.

Solomon, Robert, with Anne Gault. "The Economic Interdependence of Nations: An Agenda for Research." Report prepared for National Science Foundation. Washington, D.C.: Brookings Institution, 1977.

Stein, Jerome L. "The Optimum Foreign Exchange Market," *American Economic Review*, vol. 53 (June 1963).

————, ed. *Monetarism*. Amsterdam: North-Holland, 1976.

Steinbruner, John D. *The Cybernetic Theory of Decision: New Dimensions of Political Analysis*. Princeton: Princeton University Press, 1974.

Stevens, Guy V. G. "Two Problems in Portfolio Analysis: Conditional and Multiplicative Random Variables," *Journal of Financial and Quantitative Analysis*, vol. 6 (December 1971).

————. "Balance of Payments Equations and Exchange Rate Determination." International Finance Discussion Paper 95. Washington, D.C.: Board of Governors of the Federal Reserve System, December 1976.

Sumner, M. T. "The Operation of Monetary Targets," in Karl Brunner and Allan H. Meltzer, eds., *Monetary Institutions and the Policy Process*. Carnegie-Rochester Conference Series 13. Amsterdam: North-Holland, forthcoming.

Swamy, P. A. V. B., and P. A. Tinsley. "Linear Prediction and Estimation Methods for Regression Models with Stationary Stochastic Coefficients." Special Studies Paper 78. Washington, D.C.: Board of Governors of the Federal Reserve System, 1976. (Also in *Journal of Econometrics*, in press.)

Swoboda, Alexander K. *The Euro-Dollar Market: An Interpretation*. Princeton Essays in International Finance 64. Princeton: Princeton University Press, 1968.

Taylor, John B. "Monetary Policy During a Transition to Rational Expectations," *Journal of Political Economy*, vol. 83 (October 1975).

————. "Control Theory and Economic Stabilization: A Comment" in Karl Brunner and Allan H. Meltzer, eds., *Optimal Policies, Control Theory and Technology Exports*. Carnegie-Rochester Conference Series 7. Amsterdam: North-Holland, 1977.

————. "Estimation and Control of a Macroeconomic Model with Rational Expectations," *Econometrica*, vol. 47 (September 1979).

Theil, Henri. *Linear Aggregation of Economic Relations*. Amsterdam: North-Holland, 1954.

————. *Economic Forecasts and Policy*. 2d rev. ed. Amsterdam: North-Holland, 1961.

————. "Linear Decision Rules for Macrodynamic Policy Problems," in Bert G. Hickman, ed., *Quantitative Planning of Economic Policy*. Washington, D.C.: Brookings Institution, 1965.

Theil, Henri, with P. J. M. van den Bogaard. *Optimal Decision Rules for Government and Industry.* Amsterdam: North-Holland, 1964; Chicago: Rand McNally, 1964.

Thomson, Thomas D., James L. Pierce, and Robert T. Parry. "A Monthly Money Market Model," *Journal of Money, Credit and Banking,* vol. 7 (November 1975).

Tinbergen, Jan. *Economic Policy: Principles and Design.* Amsterdam: North-Holland, 1956.

————. *On the Theory of Economic Policy.* 2d ed. Amsterdam: North-Holland, 1963. (1st ed., 1952.)

Tinsley, Peter A. "On Proximate Exploitation of Intermediate Information in Macroeconomic Forecasting." Special Studies Paper 59. Washington, D.C.: Board of Governors of the Federal Reserve System (April 1975).

Tinsley, Peter A., and Bonnie Garrett, with M. E. Friar. "The Measurement of Money Demand." Special Studies Paper 133. Washington, D.C.: Board of Governors of the Federal Reserve System, October 1978.

————. "An Exposé of Disguised Deposits," in Supplement to *Journal of Econometrics* (in press).

Tobin, James. "The Interest-Elasticity of Transactions Demand for Cash," *Review of Economics and Statistics,* vol. 38 (August 1956).

————. "Money, Capital, and Other Stores of Value," *American Economic Review,* vol. 51 (May 1961).

————. "The Monetary Interpretation of History," *American Economic Review,* vol. 55 (June 1965).

————. "A General Equilibrium Approach to Monetary Theory," *Journal of Money, Credit and Banking,* vol. 1 (February 1969).

————. "Money and Income: Post Hoc Ergo Propter Hoc?" *Quarterly Journal of Economics,* vol. 84 (May 1970).

————. *Essays in Economics.* 2 vols. Amsterdam: North-Holland, 1971, 1975.

————. "Deficit Spending and Crowding Out in Shorter and Longer Runs," in Harry Greenfield and others, eds., *Theory for Efficiency: Essays in Honor of Abba P. Lerner.* Cambridge: Massachusetts Institute of Technology Press, 1979.

————. "Discussion," in Bennett T. McCallum and William G. Dewald, eds., papers, conference on Rational Expectations, American Enterprise Institute, January 1980, supplement to *Journal of Money, Credit and Banking* (in press).

Tobin, James, and William C. Brainard. "Asset Markets and the Cost of Capital," in Bela Belassa and Richard Nelson, eds., *Economic Progress, Private Values, and Public Policy: Essays in Honor of William Fellner.* Amsterdam: North-Holland, 1977.

Tobin, James, and Willem Buiter. "Long-Run Effects of Fiscal and Monetary Policy on Aggregate Demand," in Jerome Stein, ed., *Monetarism*. Amsterdam: North-Holland, 1976.

Tower, Edward, and Thomas D. Willet. *The Theory of Optimum Currency Areas and Exchange-Rate Flexibility*. Special Papers in International Economics 11. Princeton: Princeton University Press, 1976.

Trezise, Philip H., ed. *The European Monetary System: Its Promise and Prospects*. Washington, D.C.: Brookings Institution, 1979.

Triffin, Robert. *Europe and the Money Muddle*. New Haven: Yale University Press, 1957.

―――. *Gold and the Dollar Crisis*. New Haven: Yale University Press, 1960.

Tucker, Donald P. "Macroeconomic Models and the Demand for Money Under Market Disequilibrium," *Journal of Money, Credit and Banking*, vol. 3 (February 1971).

Turnovsky, Stephen J. "Optimal Choice of Monetary Instrument in a Linear Economic Model with Stochastic Coefficients," *Journal of Money, Credit and Banking*, vol. 7 (February 1975).

―――. "The Dynamics of Fiscal Policy in an Open Economy," *Journal of International Economics*, vol. 6 (May 1976).

van Ypersele de Strihou, Jacques. "Sharing the Defense Burden Among Western Allies," *Yale Economic Essays*, vol. 8 (Spring 1968).

Vaubel, Roland. "International Shifts in the Demand for Money, Their Effects on Exchange Rates and Price Levels, and Their Implications for the Preannouncement of Monetary Expansion," *Weltwirtschaftliches Archiv*, Band 116 (1980).

Vernon, Raymond. *Sovereignty at Bay: The Multinational Spread of U.S. Enterprises*. New York and London: Basic Books, 1971.

Viner, Jacob. *Studies in the Theory of International Trade*. New York: Harper, 1937.

von Neumann, John, and Oskar Morgenstern. *Theory of Games and Economic Behavior*. 5th ed. Princeton: Princeton University Press, 1953.

Wallich, Henry. "From Multiplier to Quantity Theory," in Bela Belassa and Richard Nelson, eds., *Economic Progress, Private Values, and Public Policy: Essays in Honor of William Fellner*. Amsterdam: North-Holland, 1977.

Waud, Roger N. "Proximate Targets and Monetary Policy," *Economic Journal*, vol. 83 (March 1973).

Whitman, Marina von N. "Global Monetarism and the Monetary Approach to the Balance of Payments," *Brookings Papers on Economic Activity, 3:1975*.

Wilbratte, Barry J. "Some Essential Differences in the Demand for Money by Households and by Firms," *Journal of Finance*, vol. 30 (September 1975).

Fair, Ray C., 63n
Fand, David I., 76n
Farr, Helen T., 57n, 128n
Fase, M. M. G., 54n
Feige, Edgar L., 54n
Fellner, William, 256n, 260, 310, 312n, 479n
Fischer, Stanley, 53n, 54n, 57n, 63n, 88n, 310n, 311n
Fisher, Franklin M., 157n, 507n
Fleming, J. Marcus, 164n, 424, 425, 476n
Foley, Duncan K., 383n, 537n
Fox, Karl A., 15n
Fratianni, M., 186n, 356n, 458n
Freedman, Charles, 93n, 101n, 383n
Freeman, George, 6n
Frenkel, Jacob A., 85n, 129, 377n, 467n
Friedman, Benjamin M., 15n, 46n, 57n, 60n, 156n, 171n, 255n, 278n, 311n, 342n, 509n
Friedman, James W., 465n, 466n
Friedman, Milton, 16n, 41n, 43n, 48n, 55, 56n, 58, 71n, 73, 74, 125–27, 251, 254, 261n, 324n, 350, 432n
Frisch, Helmut, 406n, 541n
Froewiss, Kenneth C., 60n
Frohlich, Norman, 480n
Fromm, Gary, 55n, 175n
Frost, Peter A., 60n

Garbade, Kenneth D., 170n, 252n, 346–47
Garrett, Bonnie, 54n, 57n, 73n
Gault, Anne, 4n
Gelting, Jorgen, 143n
Gilbert, J. C., 41n
Girton, Lance, 128n, 186n, 356n, 359n, 362n, 374n, 458n, 525n
Goldberger, Arthur S., 179n, 180n, 519n
Goldfeld, Stephen M., 53n, 54n, 57n, 73n, 308n
Gold, Joseph, 470n
Goldthorpe, John H., 321n, 418n
Goodhart, C. A. E., 57n, 58n, 59n
Grassman, Sven, 84n
Greenfield, Harry, 536n
Gurley, John G., 62n, 359n

Haberler, Gottfried, 399n, 479n
Hadley, G., 506n
Halm, George N., 436n
Halperin, Morton H., 317n
Hamada, Koichi, 466, 467, 468n, 470n, 476n
Hamberger, Michael J., 73n
Hansen, Bent, 228n, 230n, 267n
Havenner, Arthur, 296n, 297n, 301n, 342n, 347
Heller, H. Robert, 372n
Helliwell, John F., 435n

Hendershott, Patric H., 60, 62n
Henderson, Dale W., 186n, 356n, 359n, 362n, 374n, 383n, 394n, 406n, 424n, 458n, 465n, 522n, 525n, 535n, 541n
Herring, Richard, 143n, 151n
Hester, Donald D., 60
Hewson, John, 101n, 383n
Hickman, Bert G., 15n
Hicks, John R., 41n, 46
Hildreth, Clifford G., 127n
Hirsch, Fred, 321n, 418n, 468n, 476n
Hodgman, Donald R., 61n
Holbik, Karel, 61n
Holmes, Alan R., 6n
Horsefield, J. Keith, 471n
Horst, Thomas O., 92n
Horwich, George, 254n
Howe, Howard, 181n
Howitt, Peter W., 54n
Hume, David, 377n

Imlah, Albert, 4n
Infante, Ettore F., 262n
Intriligator, Michael D., 465n
Isard, Peter, 355n, 383n, 525n

Jaffee, Dwight M., 63n
Janssen, J. M. L., 194n
Johnson, Harry G., 129, 324n, 377n, 436
Johnson, Lewis, 73n
Johnston, J., 155n
Jordan, Jerry L., 247n

Kahn, Alfred E., 468n
Kalchbrenner, John H., 15n, 252n, 289n
Kanter, Arnold, 317n
Kareken, John H., 60, 170n, 216n, 278n, 337n, 450n
Kemp, Murray C., 434n, 476n
Kendrick, David, 194n
Kenen, Peter B., 189n, 355n, 399n, 435n, 438n
Keohane, Robert O., 4n, 140n, 159n
Keynes, John Maynard, 46, 183n, 536n
Kindleberger, Charles P., 470n
Klein, Lawrence R., 55n, 68n, 175n, 260n, 261n
Kouri, Pentti, 406n
Krause, Lawrence B., 4n, 143n, 144n, 181n, 441n, 541n
Krugman, Paul, 431n
Kubarych, Roger M., 85n, 359n
Kuhn, Thomas S., 16n, 137n, 142n, 144n, 206n
Kune, J. B., 54n
Kurz, Mordecai, 194n
Kuznets, Simon, 4n
Kydland, Finn E., 309, 310, 316n, 467n

Laidler, David E. W., 53n, 55n, 57n, 73n
Laursen, Svend, 399n
Leavis, F. R., 206
LeRoy, Stephen F., 216n, 278n, 289n, 290n, 337n, 342n, 343n
Levich, Richard M., 85n
Levin, Jay H., 466
Lieberman, Charles, 70n, 76n, 342n
Lindbeck, Assar, 148n
Lindberg, Leon N., 316n, 321n, 388n
Lindsey, David E., 337n, 342n
Logue, Dennis E., 356n, 383n
Lucas, Robert E., Jr., 17n, 308n, 310
Luce, R. Duncan, 465n

McCallum, Bennett T., 310n, 311n
McClam, Warren D., 6n
McKean, Roland N., 305n
McKinnon, Ronald I., 87n, 101n, 150n, 411n, 424n, 535n
Maier, Charles, 321n, 388n
March, James G., 16n, 317n
Margolis, Marvin S., 76n
Marston, Richard, 143n, 151n
Martin, J., 394n
Mathieson, Donald J., 429n
Mauskopf, Eileen, 73n
Mayer, Helmut W., 101n
Mayer, Thomas, 48n, 320n, 322n
Meek, Paul, 6n
Meiselman, David, 261n
Meltzer, Allan H., 17n, 60, 228n, 252n, 254n, 260n, 261n, 289n, 309n
Metzler, Lloyd A., 399n
Milbourne, Ross D., 54n
Miller, Merton H., 54n
Mill, John Stuart, 388n
Modigliani, Franco, 55n, 60, 127n, 262n
Morgenstern, Oskar, 464, 465n
Mosley, Paul, 164n
Muellbauer, John, 57n, 63n
Muench, Thomas, 17n, 278n, 450n
Mundell, Robert A., 151n, 189n, 399n, 424, 425, 435n, 467n
Mussa, Michael, 129n

Nagar, A. L., 179n, 180n
Neary, J. Peter, 311n
Nelson, Richard, 217n, 330n, 341n, 466n, 525n
Niehans, Jürg, 43n, 54n, 57n, 58n, 88n, 164n, 466, 467, 476n, 541n
Nordhaus, William D., 257n
Nyberg, Lars, 194n
Nye, Joseph S., 4n, 140n, 159n

Oates, Wallace E., 150n, 424n, 535n
Odeh, H. S., 179n

Okun, Arthur M., 54n, 63n, 116n, 127n, 185n, 311n, 327n, 349n
Olson, Mancur, Jr., 148n, 469–70, 472n, 473n, 478, 479n, 480n
Oppenheimer, Joe A., 480n
Orr, Daniel, 54n

Palm, Franz, 175n
Parkin, Michael, 140n
Parry, Robert T., 60n
Patinkin, Don, 43n
Pau, Louis F., 194n
Paulus, John, 73n
Pearce, Douglas K., 54n
Phelps, Edmund S., 311n
Pierce, James L., 60, 76n, 333n
Pindyck, Robert S., 316n, 467n
Poole, William, 46, 76n, 333n, 337–38, 342n, 344n
Porter, Richard C., 60n
Porter, Richard D., 57n, 73n
Portes, Richard, 57n, 63n
Prescott, Edward C., 296n, 309, 310
Promisel, Larry J., 21n
Pruitt, Eleanor M., 57n
Purvis, Douglas D., 383n, 537n

Quandt, Richard E., 466n
Quinn, Brian S., 101n

Raiffa, Howard, 465n
Rasche, Robert H., 60n
Richards, Ian, 140n
Roberts, Steven M., 76n, 333n
Robson, J. M., 388n
Roper, Don E., 73, 151n, 466

Sahay, S. N., 180n
Sakakibara, Eisuke, 101n, 383n
Salant, Walter S., 4n, 143n, 144n, 181n, 441n, 466n, 476n, 541n
Salin, Pascal, 151n, 377n
Samuelson, Lee, 478n
Samuelson, Paul A., 261n
Sandell, Nils R., Jr., 193n, 316n, 467n
Sargent, Thomas J., 17n, 308n, 310n
Schelling, Thomas C., 465n, 468n
Schwartz, Anna Jacobson, 41n, 43n, 48n, 58, 73, 125–27, 254n
Scitovsky, Tibor, 41n
Sen, Amartya K., 13n, 200n
Sengupta, Jati K., 15n
Shafer, Jeffrey R., 181n, 236n
Shaw, Edward S., 62n, 359n
Shell, Karl, 55n
Shubik, Martin, 465n
Shupp, Franklin R., 296n, 301n
Silber, William L., 62n

Simon, Herbert A., 16n, 317n, 507n
Simpson, Thomas D., 73n
Smith, A., 394n
Smith, Adam, 4n
Smith, Gary, 63n, 383n, 537n
Smith, Warren L., 324n
Solomon, Robert, 4n, 370n, 441n, 456n
Solow, Robert M., 73n, 224n, 228n, 262n,
    263n, 308n
Steinbruner, John D., 144n, 317n
Stein, Herbert, 479n
Stein, Jerome L., 48n, 224n, 262n, 394n
Stern, Gary H., 76n
Stevens, Guy V. G., 92n, 519n, 539n
Stiglitz, Joseph E., 311n
Straszak, A., 194n
Swamy, P. A. V. B., 168n
Sweeney, Richard J., 356n, 383n
Swoboda, Alexander K., 87n, 101n, 151n,
    189n, 399n, 424n

Tavernier, Karel, 186n, 356n, 458n
Taylor, John B., 309n, 311n
Teigen, Ronald L., 324n
Terrell, Henry S., 128n
Theil, Henri, 15, 95n, 151, 164, 170n, 171n,
    175n, 178n, 509n, 511n
Thomson, Thomas D., 60, 76n
Thorbecke, Erik, 15n
Thorn, Richard S., 46n
Thunberg, Rudolf, 6n
Tinbergen, Jan, 15, 149n, 151, 172n, 173n
Tinsley, Peter A., 15n, 54n, 57n, 73n, 168n,
    170n, 252n, 278n, 283n, 289n
Tobin, James, 41n, 46n, 54n, 55n, 57n, 87n,
    88n, 91n, 217n, 228n, 254n, 261n, 262n,
    311n, 342n, 343n, 525n, 536n

Tower, Edward, 394n
Trezise, Philip H., 441n
Triffin, Robert, 441n, 476n
Tucker, Donald P., 57n
Tufte, Edward R., 257n
Turner, Thomas H., 128n
Turnovsky, Stephen J., 296n, 311n, 429n

van den Bogaard, P. J. M., 15n, 164n, 170n,
    171n, 173n, 509n
van Ypersele de Strihou, Jacques M., 470n
Vernon, Raymond, 92n, 160n
Viner, Jacob, 4n, 377n
Viotti, Staffan, 194n
von Neumann, John, 464, 465n

Wagner, Richard E., 257n
Wallace, Neil, 17n, 170n, 278n, 308n, 310n,
    450n
Wallich, Henry C., 101n, 261n, 330n, 341n
Waud, Roger N., 46n, 278n, 289n, 290n
Weintraub, Robert, 333n
Whitman, Marina von N., 129n, 144n
Wilbratte, Barry J., 57n
Willett, Thomas D., 394n
Williamson, John L., 456n
Woglom, Geoffrey, 383n, 537n
Woolley, John T., 319n

Yeager, Leland B., 324n
Young, Oran R., 480n
Young, Richard M., 296n

Zeckhauser, Richard, 469n
Zellner, Arnold, 175n
Zis, George, 140n

Subject Index

Actual instruments. *See* Policy instruments
Asian Development Bank, 476n
Assets
  Eurocurrency, 18, 22, 99–102
  External reserve (of central bank),
    356–59, 368, 372–73, 381–82, 393,
    412–16, 454–56
  Macroeconomic sector demands for,
    94–99, 109–10, 113–14
  Microeconomic demand functions for,
    53–57, 88–94
  Schematic classification for closed
    economy, 50–53, 210, 222
  Schematic classification for open
    economy, 89, 93, 97–99, 356–59
  Substitutability, 102–03, 160, 178–79,
    185, 375, 395–98, 451–52, 523–27
  Unit-of-account attributes of, 43n
  See also Interest rates; Liquid assets
Autonomy of national economic policy
  Controllability and, 149–50, 191–99,
    487–88
  Defined, 174–76
  Exchange-rate variability and, 423–32
  Interdependence and, 135, 149–50,
    177–87, 487–88
  Policy multipliers and, 174–75, 181–87,
    423–32

Balance of payments
  Capital-account transactions, 83n
  Currency denomination of international
    transactions and, 84
  Current-account, 83n; dynamics of
    wealth transfer through, 405–06,
    428–30, 538–40
  Defined, 83n
  Equilibrium, 448
  Monetary approach to, 129–31, 355, 377n
Balance sheet
  Central bank, 50–52, 210–14, 356–59, 522
  Commercial bank, 52, 93, 94–95, 524,
    527
  Fiscal authority, 50, 220–22, 356–59,
    379–82

Nonbank, 52, 89, 525, 527
Bank credit as intermediate target of
  monetary policy, 124–25, 450n
Bank of England, 6, 251n
Bank reserves
  Ability of central bank to control
    precisely, 213–16
  Definitions of different reserve
    aggregates, 51, 211
  As potential and actual instrument of
    monetary policy, 210–14, 365–67
  Reserve-aggregate operating regimes,
    215–16, 232–33, 343–47, 372–73
Banks, commercial
  Closed economy, 50–52, 57–63
  Open economy, 92–95, 99–102, 524–27
  See also Bank reserves; Money supply
    process
Bretton Woods system, 8, 370–72, 411, 418,
  471n, 475n
Budget statements and constraints
  Central bank, 210, 212–13, 356–59,
    522–23
  Fiscal authority, 222–25, 356–59, 379–82,
    529–30
  Foreign government, 459–60
  See also Consolidated government
    budget constraint

Canada
  Money stock, 21–23
  Use of money strategy, 6
Capital flows, portfolio-balance approach
  to, 355
Capital gains and losses
  Associated with exchange-rate changes,
    525–26, 536
  Treatment in budget constraints, 212n,
    536–37
  Wealth and, 404
Capital stock, 404–05, 535–36
Central American Common Market, 477
Central bank
  Balance sheet and budget statement,
    50–52, 210–14, 356–59, 522; deposit

liability to foreign central bank, 359;
external-reserve assets, 358; interest
earnings, 359; reserve liabilities to
commercial banks, 51, 211; volume
of currency in circulation, 211
Coordination of policies with fiscal
authority, 242–43, 326–30
Discount rate, 13, 210n
Exchange-market intervention, 356–65,
373–78
External reserve assets, 356–59, 368,
372–73, 381–82, 393, 412–16, 454–56
As monetary authority, 11
Open market operations, 210, 226, 227,
362–64, 383
Policy objectives, 5, 12–13, 238–39,
318–19, 330–33, 488
Policy operating regimes, 210–220,
232–33, 240, 343, 365–73, 385–86,
411–416. See also Instrument choice
Political independence, 242–43;
arguments for and against, 318–21;
and monetary-policy rules, 321–25
See also Monetary policy; National
economic policy
Certainty-equivalent instrument
manipulation. See Fine tuning
Closed economy, 3
Coefficient uncertainty. See Uncertainty
Collective action. See Public goods
Comparative statics analysis
Choice between fixed and flexible
exchange rates in, 410–11
Dynamic aspects ignored in, 342–47,
404–16, 428–32, 535–41
Illustrative framework for small and open
economy, 522–35
Instrument choice for closed economy,
337–42
Instrument choice for open economy,
393–404, 423–27
Consolidated government budget constraint
Closed economy, 228–31
Open economy, 381–85
World, 459–63
Consumption, life-cycle theory of, 537
Controllability of national economy
In absence of international constraints,
419–23
Defined, 173, 193–95
Discretionary external operating regimes
and, 430–32
Exchange-rate variability and, 426–27
Interdependence and, 191–99, 423–32,
473, 487–88, 499–500
National welfare and, 205–06
And supranational constraints, 417–19
See also Interdependence

Controllability, technical definition in
control theory, 193–95
Control of national money stock. See
Money stock as intermediate target;
Money supply process
Control theory (optimal control), 15,
165–70, 191–95, 252n, 282–84, 344–47,
508–17. See also Theory of economic
policy
Cooperation among nations
Cooperative games defined, 465
Explanations for noncooperative
behavior, 468–70
Noncooperative games defined, 465
Rationales for, 463–68, 470–81
Coordination of nations' macroeconomic
policies, 477–81, 500
Cournot-Nash solutions, of games, 312–13,
465–68
Currency (notes and coin)
Demand for, 56–57, 59
Issuance of, 57–63, 77, 211–14
See also Money
Currency denomination
Invoicing versus settlement, 83n
Of means of payment for international
transactions, 83–88
Cybernetic theories of decisionmaking, 16,
317

Data availability. See Information flow
Debt. See Government debt
Debtor-creditor relationships, international,
97–99, 114–16
Demand for money. See Money demand
Deposits
Acceptability as means of payment,
53–54, 83–88
Demand and time, 52–53
Eurocurrency, 18, 99–102
See also Money
Descriptive concepts and definitions of
money. See Money
Deutsche Bundesbank, 6, 251n
Discount rate, as monetary-policy
instrument, 13, 45, 209–10
Discretion
Defined, 249–50
In policy actions: arguments against,
294–95; and central-bank
independence, 322–24; pegging rules
versus, 234–36; self-imposed limits
on, 309–13
Rules versus, 249–50, 294–95, 310,
496–97
See also Instrument variation; Rules
Discretionary exchange-rate regime. See

External monetary policy, operating regimes

Discretionary external-reserves regime. *See* External monetary policy, operating regimes

Discretionary instrument adaptation
  Description, 243–44, 247–48
  Capacity for coping with uncertainty, 297–305, 344–51, 442–44, 491–92, 496–97, 518–21
  Distinguished from fine tuning, 348–51, 444, 496–97
  Efficiency in use of information, 278–94, 303–05, 442–44, 491
  For external monetary policy, 412–16, 495–96
  Role of monetary aggregates in, 449–51
  See also Strategy choice

Discretionary interest-rate regime. *See* Domestic monetary policy, operating regimes

Discretionary reserve-aggregate regime. *See* Domestic monetary policy, operating regimes

Disequilibrium macroeconomics, 57, 62–63

Disturbance multipliers, 187–90

Domestic monetary policy
  Comparative-statics analysis of instrument choice, 337–42
  Instrument choice versus instrument variation, 342–47, 493–95
  Operating regimes, 209–20, 232–33, 240, 342–43
  Potential instruments, 45, 209–14
  Symbiosis between external monetary policy and, 377–78
  See also Monetary policy; National economic policy; Strategy choice

Economic integration. *See* World economic integration

Economic interdependence. *See* Interdependence

Economic openness. *See* Interdependence

Economic policy. *See* National economic policy

Economic structure, 14–15. *See also* Macroeconomic models; World economic structure

Economic welfare. *See* Loss function; Welfare

Effectiveness of policy instruments. *See* Policy multipliers

Endogenous variables, 14, 63–68, 136, 152–53, 210–14, 306–09, 342–43, 411–16

Eurocurrency assets and liabilities, 18, 99–102

European Economic Community, 477, 480n

European Monetary System, 370n

Exchange-rate peg. *See* External monetary policy, operating regimes

Exchange rates
  Asset-market approach to, 355
  Crawling peg for, 371
  Current-account imbalance and, 405–06, 445
  Expectations of future, 90–92, 102–03, 400n, 408, 523–24
  Fixed, 103, 377, 387–91, 393–401, 410–11, 415–16
  Flexible, 9, 103, 387–91, 410–11, 415–16, 468n; and independence of monetary policy, 420; insulating properties of, 434; and interdependence, 432, 463–64
  Management of, in discretionary monetary policy, 412–16
  Variability: and ability to attain ultimate objectives, 419, 423–27; and disintegration of world economy, 419, 438–41, 500; and economic integration, 439; and freedom for policy to focus on domestic economy, 419, 436–38; greater, 387–91; and insulation of national economy, 417, 419, 420–23; and monetary-policy independence, 417–18; regimens, 388–91, 393–404, 420–23; supranational constraints on, 369–72, 391, 417–18; and viability of national policy regimens, 419, 420–23
  See also External monetary policy; National economic policy; Foreign exchange market

Exogenous variables, 14, 136n, 154–55, 210–14, 306–09, 342–43

Expectations
  Of exchange-rate changes, 90–92, 102–03, 400n, 408, 523–24
  Of government policy actions, 17, 242n, 255–56, 306–14, 330–33, 451–52, 492
  Of returns on assets, 53n, 90–92
  See also Rational expectations

External monetary policy
  Comparative-statics analysis of external pegging regimes, 391–404, 410–11, 423–27
  Exchange-market intervention, 356–65, 373–78
  External regimes compared in a dynamic context, 404–10, 411–16, 428–32
  Instrument choice versus instrument variation, 411–16, 430–32, 493–96
  Interactions with domestic monetary policy, 362–65, 373–78, 445–49
  Operating regimes, 365–73, 412–13;

Summary of reasons for rejecting, 303–05, 488–93
See also Intermediate-target strategy; Strategy choice
Money supply process
Aggregate supply functions, open economy, 94–96, 108–22
Basic elements, 58
Central bank control over money stock (controllability proposition), 47, 69, 70–71, 74–76, 108–25, 263–64, 313–14, 446–49
Disaggregated structural approaches, 60–62
Microeconomic behavior of financial intermediaries, 58, 92–94
Multiplier approaches, 58–60
Stability of, 74–76, 108–22, 123–31
Multipliers. *See* Disturbance multipliers; Policy multipliers

National economic policy
Alternative policy regimens for, 231–34, 379–86, 445–46
Basic hypotheses about interdependence and, 135–36, 177, 197; evaluation of, 177–81; implications for welfare, 203–06; refinements of, 181–84; significance of, 184–87
Controllability of national economy, 135, 171, 191–93; in closed economy, 149–50, 202; defined, 193–95; determinants of, 159–61, 191–99; increased interdependence and, 195–99; policy multipliers and, 176
De facto control over, 4–5, 149–50, 176, 487
Defined, 11–12
De jure sovereignty over, 4–5, 149–50, 487
Holistic unity of, 228–37, 377–78, 379–86, 445–46, 488
Myopic perspective of, 369, 376, 391, 418, 453–64, 499
Performance of national policymakers, 200–03
Simple analytics of policy problem, 163–64, 507–08
Successfulness of policy, 172–73, 200–06
Tension between economic and political structure and, 148–49
See also Fiscal policy; Monetary policy
Nearly closed paradigm. *See* Interdependence, paradigms for modeling
Nonbanks, 50

Asset demand-and-supply behavior, 53–57, 83–92, 94–95, 108, 525–27
Balance sheet, 52, 89, 525, 527
Eurocurrency assets of, 101–02
Foreign, 94–95
In foreign-exchange market, 84n
Nonpolicy disturbances
Cross-national transmission of, 147–48, 159, 187–90, 395–410, 432–41, 453–64
Defined, 15, 154–55
Normative economics, 16. *See also* Money, prescriptive concept and definition

Observed empirical regularity hypothesis, 43, 49
Oligopoly theory, applied to interdependence, 150
Open economy, 3, 83, 156–61
Openness. *See* Interdependence
Operating regimes. *See* Domestic monetary policy; External monetary policy; Fiscal policy
Outside reserve assets, 357–59, 454–56, 460–63, 475–77, 481

Pareto optimality, 466–68, 469
Pegging rules. *See* Instrument variation; Policy instruments
Performance of policymakers. *See* National economic policy
Policy actions
Activist behavior, 348
Defined, 13, 209, 231
Discretion in, 234–36, 294–95, 309–13, 322–24
Effectiveness, 171–74
Nonindependence of different nations' actions, 453–70
Nonindependence of monetary and fiscal actions, 228–37, 379–86
Private-sector decisionmaking and, 306–09, 451–52
Policy authority (policymakers), 11
Abstraction of reality, 12, 315–18
Loss function of, 12–13, 164–69, 241–43, 508–11
See also National economic policy; Policy instruments
Policy instruments, 13–14
Actual versus potential, 13, 63, 210–14, 365–69
Boundary constraints on and costs of variation in, 165, 173–74, 185–86, 365, 454–64, 508–10
Effectiveness, 171–74, 201n

Endogenous and exogenous variables,
    210–14, 342–43, 411–16
Fiscal, 221–25, 232–33
Monetary, 13, 44–46; domestic, 210–14,
    232–33; external, 365–73, 412–15
Pegging rules, 342–47, 411–16, 493–96
Precision of control over, 14, 46, 209–10,
    213–14, 224, 337–38, 367–68, 420–23
World, 475–77
See also Instrument choice; Instrument
    variation
Policy loss function. See Loss function
Policymaking models. See Macroeconomic
    models; Model choice
Policy multipliers
Autonomy and, 174–76, 181–87, 424, 431
Defined, 171–74
Home versus foreign, 174–76
Instrument effectiveness distinguished
    from overall successfulness of
    policy, 172–73, 200–06
Types of national, 174
Uncertainty about, 174, 183–86, 196, 242,
    259–63, 295–303, 348–51, 442–44,
    518–21
Policy regimen, defined, 230–33, 385–86,
    412–13. See also Fiscal policy;
    Monetary policy; Strategy choice
Politics
Insulating central bank from, 256–57,
    318–21
In monetary policy decisionmaking,
    315–18
Money strategy choice and, 256–57,
    325–26
Positive economics, 16. See also Money,
    descriptive concepts and definitions
Potential instruments. See Policy
    instruments
Prescriptive concept and definition of
    money. See Money
Price level
Expectation of inflation and, 255
In money-demand function, 53, 69
Money stock to predict, 126
As ultimate-target variable, 70
Public goods, 468–73, 475–77, 480–81

Rational expectations
Basic hypothesis, 311
Continuing research on, 309–11
Implications for economic policy, 17,
    255–56, 306–14, 330–33, 451–52, 497
Insufficient rationale for money rule,
    313–14
Strong form, 311
Recursive models. See Macroeconomic
    models

Reduced-form equations. See
    Macroeconomic models
Reliability proposition. See Money
    demand; Money stock as intermediate
    target
Reserve-aggregate peg. See Domestic
    monetary policy, operating regimes
Reserve assets, external. See Central bank;
    External monetary policy; Outside
    reserve assets
Reserve-requirement ratio, 13, 45, 61, 65n,
    209–10, 396n, 399n, 524–25
Reserves (commercial bank). See Bank
    reserves
Rules
Defined, 249–50
Discretion versus, 249–50, 294–95, 310,
    496–97
And independence of central bank,
    321–25
Instrument versus intermediate-target,
    313–14, 330–31
Insulation, arguments for, 319–26
Rational expectations, arguments for,
    311–21
See also Discretion; Instrument variation

Saving
By foreign residents, 400–02, 410
By home residents, 398–400, 410
Interdependence of wealth and, 404–05
Life-cycle theory of, 537
SDRs. See Special drawing rights
Securities
Central-bank portfolio, 214n, 359, 375
Outstanding stock of government, 537–38
Shift from home-currency to foreign-
    currency, 396–97
Shift to home money from home, 395–96
Single-stage strategy. See Discretionary
    instrument adaptation; Strategy choice
Small and open paradigm. See
    Interdependence, paradigms for
    modeling
Social welfare function. See Loss function
Special drawing rights (SDRs), 475n
Central bank: holdings, 358; sale of, 360
International Monetary Fund and, 481
As outside reserve asset, 475–77
Stackelberg solutions of games, 312–13,
    465–68
Stochastic error terms, 155, 169–70, 190,
    279, 282–84, 298, 338–42, 394, 505, 518
Stock-flow interactions, 355, 404–10, 424,
    428–32, 534–41
Strategy choice
Alternative strategies identified, 240–41,
    243–52

Defined, 238–41
Distinguished from model choice, 238–43, 259, 264
Economics of strategy choice, summary conclusions, 303–05
Evaluation of alternative strategies, 241–43, 252–53
Instrument choice less important than instrument variation, 342–43, 411–16, 493–94
Periodicity of decisionmaking, 243–46
Policy problem prior to strategy choice, 238–40
Political aspects, 306–33
Putative justifications for money strategy, 253–57
Single-stage strategies defined, 240–41, 243–45, 247–48
Tactics versus strategy distinction, 240n
Two-stage (intermediate-target) strategies defined, 240–41, 245–46, 248–49
And uncertainty, 253–54, 259–63, 295–303, 348–51, 442–44, 518–21
Use of new information in revising decisions, 246–49, 278–94
See also Discretionary instrument adaptation; Instrument choice; Instrument variation; Intermediate-target strategy
Structural models. See Macroeconomic models
Structure. See Economic structure; World economic structure
Substitutability, asset, 102–03, 160, 178–79, 185, 375, 395–98, 451–52, 523–27
Successfulness of policy
Defined, 201
Distinguished from instrument effectiveness, 172–73
And national welfare, 199–206
And performance of policymakers, 200–03
Supply of money. See Money supply process; Money stock, definitions
Supranational institutions, 8, 145, 365, 369–72, 391, 417–19, 470–77, 480–81. See also International monetary system
Supranational paradigm. See Interdependence, paradigms for modeling
Supranational traffic regulations, 8, 470–75
Surrogate targets. See Intermediate-target strategy; Money stock as intermediate target

Targets. See Intermediate-target strategy; Loss function; Ultimate targets

Tax rates, 222–23
Tax revenues, 222–23
Theory of economic policy
Basic concepts and definitions, 11–15
Cybernetic critique of, 16, 317
Discretionary adaptation versus fine tuning, 348–51
Failure to deal with political-sociological considerations, 12, 206, 315–33, 497
Multiperiod dynamic, 165–67, 174–75, 278–84, 511–17
Optimal control theory, 15, 165–70, 191–95, 252n, 282–84, 344–47, 508–17
Optimizing determination of target values, 164–65, 508–11
Rational expectations challenge to, 16–17, 306–14, 451–52, 497
Simple analytics, 15–16, 163–64, 507–08
And uncertainty, 167–70, 173–74, 179–80, 183–87, 189–90, 259–63, 295–303, 348–51, 442–44, 518–21
See also Discretionary instrument adaptation; Loss function; Model choice; National economic policy; Strategy choice
Transaction costs, 54, 85n, 87
Transactions school, money demand, 54, 55, 70, 83–94, 110–11, 114
Transfer payments, control of, 220
Two-stage strategy. See Intermediate-target strategy; Strategy choice

Ultimate targets, 12
Variables compared with intermediate variables, 6, 14; explanation, 12–13, 44–45, 238–39; flow of information for, 239, 288–91, 305; link between money and, 69–70, 72–74, 108–25; policymaking focus on, 485–86
See also Loss function; Theory of economic policy
Uncertainty
Coefficient uncertainty, 174, 242, 295–303, 348–51, 442–44, 518–21
As justification for money strategy, 253–55, 297–303, 518–21
Model choice and, 295–97
Pervasive element in policy decisions, 167–70, 242, 259–63, 295–97, 348–51, 442–44
Policy multipliers and, 174, 179–80, 183–87, 297–303, 348–50, 518–21
Unit of account, money as, 43
United Kingdom
Money stock, 32–33
Use of money strategy, 6, 251

Utility school, money demand, 55, 56, 70, 91, 111n, 114n

Velocity of money. *See* Money

Wages, 66, 255–56
Welfare
    Interdependence and national, 199–200, 203–06
    Social, 12–13
    See also Loss function
West Virginia, as example in money-stock analysis, 18–19, 140–41
World Bank, 471n, 475n, 481
World economic integration
    Attempts at, 441n

Defined, 438
And exchange-rate variability, 439–41
World economic structure
    Characteristics of, 159–61
    Debtor-creditor relationships in, 97–98
    Dynamic evolution of, 165–67, 511–17
    Governmental budget constraint for world as a whole, 459–63
    Models for, 152–56
    Openness, 156–57, 159
    And political structure, 148–49
    Reduced-form representation of, 161–63, 505–07

Yale portfolio-balance tradition, 55